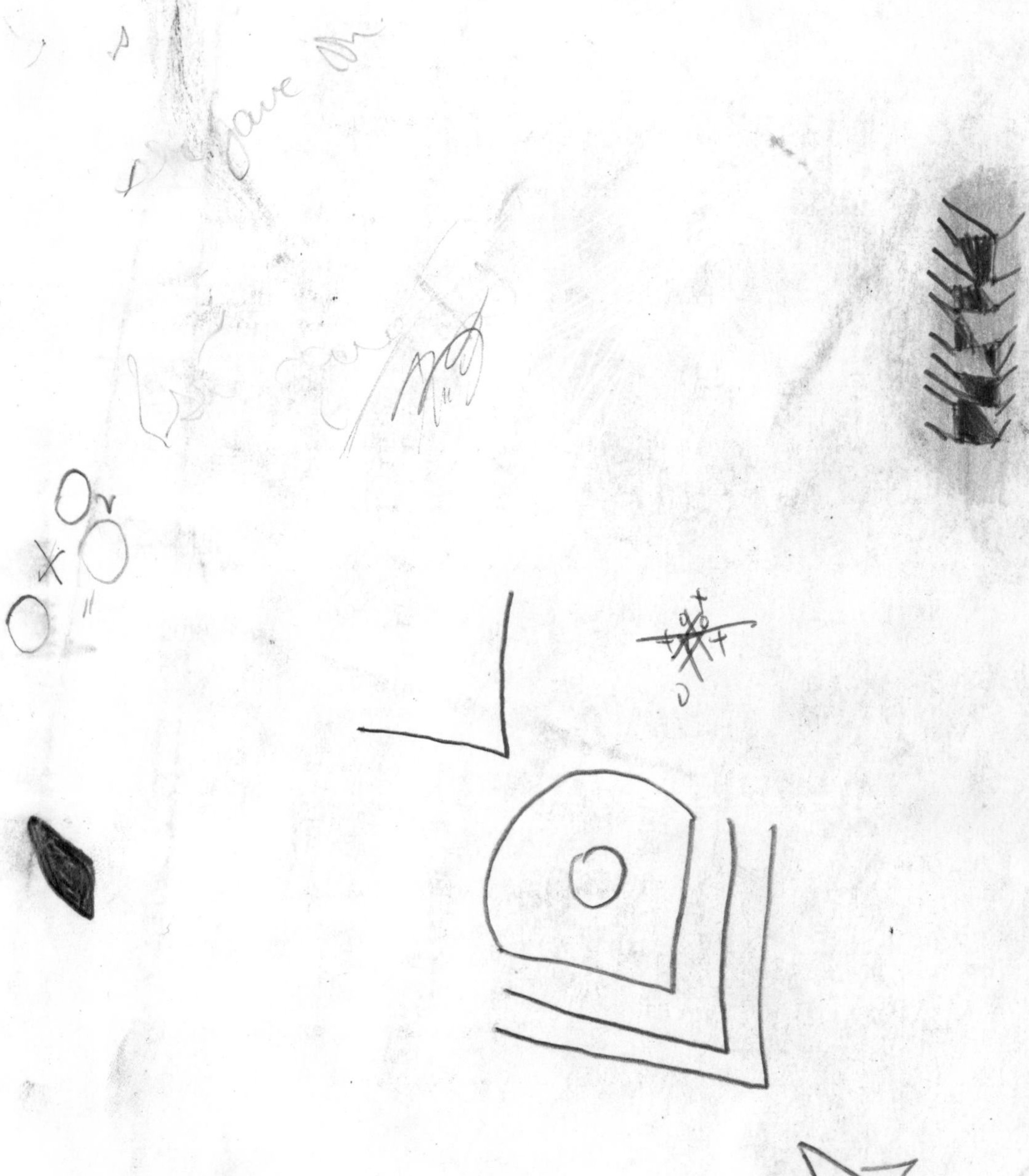

English Writing and Language Skills

Fourth Course

Critical Readers and Contributors

The authors and the publisher wish to thank the following people, who helped to evaluate and to prepare materials for this series:

Charles L. Allen, Baltimore Public Schools, Baltimore, Maryland
Kiyoko B. Bernard, Huntington Beach High School, Huntington Beach, California
Sally Borengasser, Rogers, Arkansas
Deborah Bull, New York City, New York
Joan Colby, Chicago, Illinois
Phyllis Goldenberg, North Miami Beach, Florida
Beverly Graves, Worthington High School, Worthington, Ohio
Pamela Hannon, Kirk Middle School, Cleveland, Ohio
Carol Kuykendall, Houston Public Schools, Houston, Texas
Wayne Larkin, Roosevelt Junior High School, Blaine, Minnesota
Nancy MacKnight, University of Maine, Orono, Maine
Catherine McCough, Huntington Beach Union School District, California
Lawrence Milne, Ocean View High School, Long Beach, California
Al Muller, East Carolina University, Greenville, North Carolina
Dorothy Muller, East Carolina University, Greenville, North Carolina
John Nixon, Santa Ana Junior College, Santa Ana, California
Jesse Perry, San Diego City Schools, California
Christine Rice, Huntington Beach Union School District, Huntington Beach, California
Jo Ann Seiple, University of North Carolina at Wilmington, Wilmington, North Carolina
Joan Yesner, Brookline, Massachusetts
Seymour Yesner, Brookline Education Center, Massachusetts

Classroom Testing

The authors and the publisher also wish to thank the following teachers, who participated in the classroom testing of materials from this series:

David Foote, Evanston High School East, Evanston, Illinois
Theresa Hall, Nokomis Junior High School, Minneapolis, Minnesota
Carrie E. Hampton, Sumter High School, Sumter, South Carolina
Pamela Hannon, Proviso High School East, Maywood, Illinois
Wayne Larkin, Roosevelt Junior High School, Blaine, Minnesota
Grady Locklear, Sumter High School, Sumter, South Carolina
William Montgomery, Hillcrest High School, Jamaica, New York
Josephine H. Price, Sumter High School, Sumter, South Carolina
Barbara Stilp, North High School, Minneapolis, Minnesota
Joseph Thomas, Weymouth North High School, East Weymouth, Massachusetts
Travis Weldon, Sumter High School, Sumter, South Carolina

Teachers of the Huntington Beach Union High School Writing Program:

Cassandra C. Allsop
Eric V. Emery
Michael Frym
Barbara Goldfein
Joanne Haukland
Don Hohl
Sandra Johnson
Carol Kasser
Patricia Kelly
Stephanie Martone
Lawrence Milne
Richard H. Morley
John S. Nixon
Catherine G. McCough
Kathleen C. Redman
Christine Rice
Michael D. Sloan
S. Oliver Smith
Glenda Watson
Dorothy Augustine, District Consultant in Writing

English Writing and Language Skills

Fourth Course

W. Ross Winterowd

Patricia Y. Murray

HARCOURT BRACE JOVANOVICH, PUBLISHERS

Orlando New York Chicago San Diego Atlanta Dallas

The Series:

English Writing and Language Skills, First Course
English Writing and Language Skills, Second Course
English Writing and Language Skills, Third Course
English Writing and Language Skills, Fourth Course
English Writing and Language Skills, Fifth Course
English Writing and Language Skills, Complete Course

A test booklet and teacher's manual are available for each title.

W. ROSS WINTEROWD is the Bruce R. McElderry Professor of English at the University of Southern California. Since 1975, Dr. Winterowd has traveled widely as a writing consultant for numerous schools in North America.

PATRICIA Y. MURRAY is director of the writing program and the writing laboratory at the University of Michigan—Flint. Dr. Murray taught junior and senior high school English in the Los Angeles city schools. She is also a consultant in curriculum development and teacher training.

Design: Michael Rogondino

Photo Credits 11, Magnum; Burk Uzzle; 14, Stock, Boston: Frederick Bodin; 17, Black Star: Ivan Massar; 18, Archive: Charles Harbutt; 32, Leonard Kaplan; 35, Jeroboam, Inc.: © Cheryl Traendly; 37, New York State Historical Association, Cooperstown; 121, Monkmeyer: David Strickler; 179, Archive: Charles Harbutt; 182, Stock, Boston: Owen Franken; 238, HBJ Photo, reprinted by permission from *Life: Its Forms and Changes,* Second Edition by Paul Brandwein et al. (1972); 301, Monkmeyer: David Conklin; 350, Photo Researchers, Inc.: © Bruce Roberts; 419, Archive: Bill Burke; 434, Gregg Gaar Collection; 435, © Gregg Gaar; 523, Stock, Boston: Jerry Berndt.

Part- and Chapter-Opener Photographs by Lee Youngblood

Illustrations by Pat Rogondino

Printed in the United States of America

ISBN 0-15-311553-X

Contents

7 Mechanics

8 Speaking/Listening

PART 1 Writing

1 Personal Writing

The Purpose of Personal Writing

Writing that is about the writer's thoughts and feelings is called *personal writing.*

The purpose of personal writing is to share something of yourself with your readers: your thoughts and feelings, your observations and experiences. Personal writing may take many forms, including the diary, journal, personal letter, autobiography, and personal essay. The skills necessary for personal writing include the ability to observe yourself and the physical world carefully and to record these observations in an interesting way. Other essential skills are the ability to organize and develop your thoughts. Each of these skills is also basic to many other kinds of writing.

In this chapter you will read about and practice two forms of personal writing: the journal and the autobiography.

The Language of Personal Writing

Every person who talks has a *speaking voice* made up of such features as the words he or she uses, the way these words are pronounced, and the way they are arranged in sentences. Depending on the situation, a person's speaking voice may change. In conversation with good friends, for example, speakers tend to use simpler words and shorter sentences than they might on more formal occasions.

When you write, you have a *writing voice.* Your writing voice is largely determined by the words you choose and by the way you use them. One sign of a good writer is the ability to change writing voices according to the situation. When you write a letter to a friend, you want a writing voice that sounds natural and friendly, but when you write a science report, you want a writing voice that sounds authoritative.

Personal writing calls for a natural writing voice.

Personal writing should sound almost as though you are talking with your reader. One way to ensure such a voice is to write about yourself in the first person, using such words as *I*, *my*, and *me*. These first-person words let you make the simple, direct statements that are often a part of your personal speaking voice. A sentence such as *The writer thinks his (or her) first ambition was to be a circus clown* sounds more natural when written as *I think my first ambition was to be a circus clown*.

Another way to promote a natural speaking voice is to use words that are a natural part of your vocabulary. This does not mean, however, limiting your writing vocabulary to short, simple words. If a longer word says precisely what you want to say, then use that word, but do not use longer words just to sound more important. Government park signs may ask you to "extinguish" campfires, but your personal writing will sound more natural when you write that you "put out" your campfire. In personal writing would you "terminate your employment" or "quit your job"?

An important part of the language of personal writing is choosing *specific* words—words that help readers understand exactly what you feel and think and what you observe and experience. Used properly, specific words help re-create the feeling, thought, observation, or experience. *Sensory* words—words about sights, sounds, tastes, smells, and textures—are specific, as are words of dialogue, proper nouns, and figures or numbers.

Reading Personal Writing

Emancipation Day, January 1, 1863, was the day slavery officially ended in the United States. At Camp Saxton, South Carolina, a young woman named Charlotte Forten watched the ceremony marking the occasion. Having lived in the North, Charlotte Forten was never a slave herself, but the ceremony had a special meaning for her, and her excitement comes through in her writing. As you read the following passage in which Charlotte Forten describes her experiences on Emancipation Day, look for ways she achieves a natural writing voice. What specific sensory words does she use to help the reader share her experiences?

Following this selection is a For Thought and Discussion activity.

New-Year's Day, Emancipation Day, was a glorious one to us. General Saxton and Colonel Higginson had invited us to visit the camp of the First Regiment of South Carolina Volunteers on that day, "the greatest day in the nation's history." We enjoyed perfectly the exciting scene on board the steamboat *Flora*. There was an eager, wondering crowd of the freed people, in their holiday attire, with the gayest of headkerchiefs, the whitest of aprons, and the happiest of faces. The band was playing, the flags were streaming, and everybody was talking merrily and feeling happy. The sun shone brightly, and the very waves seemed to partake of the universal gayety, for they danced and sparkled more joyously than ever before. Long before we reached Camp Saxton, we could see the beautiful grove and the ruins of the old fort near it.

Some companies of the First Regiment were drawn up in line under the trees near the landing, ready to receive us. They were a fine, soldierly looking set of men, and their brilliant dress made a splendid appearance among the trees. It was my good fortune to find an old friend among the officers. He took us over the camp and showed us all the arrangements. Everything looked clean and comfortable; much neater, we were told, than in most of the white camps.

An officer told us that he had never seen a regiment in which the men were so honest. "In many other camps," said he, "the Colonel and the rest of us would find it necessary to place a guard before our tents. We never do it here. Our tents are left entirely unguarded, but nothing has ever been touched." We were glad to know that. It is a remarkable fact, when we consider that the men of this regiment have all their lives been slaves; for we all know that Slavery does not tend to make men honest.

For Thought and Discussion

Even though the preceding passage was written over one hundred years ago, it sounds modern because Charlotte Forten writes with a natural voice. She writes in the first person, makes short and direct statements, and uses specific details. Look back over the passage and find at least three examples of each of the following items.

1. Sentences where Charlotte Forten writes about herself and her companions in first person

   Example

   We enjoyed perfectly the exciting scene on board the steamboat Flora.

2. Sentences that are short and direct statements

   Example

   New-Year's Day, Emancipation Day, was a glorious one to us.

3. Sentences that have specific details

   Example

   There was an eager, wondering crowd of the freed people, in their holiday attire, with the gayest of headkerchiefs, the whitest of aprons, and the happiest of faces. [Details of sight]

Writing Practice 1

Use the Preparing to Write section that follows to help you with ideas for this assignment.

Select an important event in your life, such as winning an award, starting your first part-time job, or learning to swim. Then write an account of this event so that readers can share it with you. As you write, concentrate on developing a natural voice for personal writing by writing about yourself in first person, by making appropriate simple and direct statements, and by using specific details.

Preparing to Write

Before beginning any writing assignment, you may ask yourself the following questions.

1. What is the purpose of this writing assignment?
2. Who is the audience?
3. How can information be gathered about the topic?

The purpose of Writing Practice 1 is to give you practice in using a natural writing voice. If you need help doing this, review the section The Language of Personal Writing, which begins on page 2.

The *audience* for an assignment refers to the people who will read your writing. As you work through the writing chapters of this textbook, you will read how important it is to write for a particular audience. For your first assignment your audience is probably your teacher and classmates. Keep this audience in mind as you write your paper.

When you write about yourself, you are writing about a topic you know better than anyone else. Even so, you may need a system for gathering information about your topic. A simple system to use is the *who? what? when? where? why? how?* system (also called the *5Whow? system*) that reporters use.

To use the *5Whow?* system, ask yourself pertinent questions such as the following ones.

1. Who was involved in the event?
2. What happened?
3. When did the event happen?
4. Where did it happen?
5. Why did it happen?
6. How did it happen?

Answer these questions completely, using specific details and taking notes as you answer. When you finish, your notes might look something like the following ones.

Event: Taking My Drivers Test

1. Who was involved in the event?
   The license examiner, Officer Susan Williams
   Looked like every picture I have ever seen of a Marine drill sergeant
   Seemed to be about eight feet tall, but was probably about five feet
   Wore dark sunglasses that covered half her face
   Never smiled
2. What happened?
   Smooth ride to highway for road test
   Made proper stop at every stop sign and stoplight
   Turned around to come back to patrol office
   Car ran out of gas
   Examiner told me to get my car filled with gas and come back next week.
3. When did it happen?
   On a bright spring morning in April
   On my sixteenth birthday
4. Where did it happen?
   In the parking lot of the highway patrol office and on the nearby highway

The patrol office looked like the old castle on the mountain in the Dracula movie I saw last night.

5. Why did it happen?
I took the test to get my drivers license. The car ran out of gas because my brother had used the car the night before, and I forgot to check the gauge.
6. How did it happen?
Just as I was ready to turn the car around and return to the patrol office, I felt the car begin to lurch forward. The engine sputtered slightly, and the car lurched a few more feet, then completely died.

Notice that the preceding notes include specific details about when and where the event happened; they also tell what the day and place were like.

Another important question to ask yourself is what you felt and thought during the event. Writing about your thoughts and feelings helps readers to share the event with you, as you can tell from the following description of the writer's thoughts and feelings when the car ran out of gas.

> *"The test is over!" I thought. "Nothing can stop me now." I leaned back confidently in my seat, turning to glance at the examiner sitting beside me. Just at that moment I felt the car begin to lurch forward. The engine sputtered slightly, and the car moved forward a few more feet and then completely died. I knew the worst had happened. The car was out of gas!*

Keeping a Journal

A *journal* is a series of personal writing pieces called *entries.*

The content of entries varies, depending on the reason for keeping the journal. By law, a ship's captain must keep a journal, called a *log,* in which is recorded such information as the ship's position, the type of cargo it carries, weather conditions, and circumstances surrounding illnesses, injuries, and deaths on board. Writers often keep journals, and they do so for several reasons: to record and comment on personal experiences, to practice writing, and to collect a source of ideas for other kinds of writing. As a writer you should consider keeping a journal for these same reasons.

In this chapter you will write several entries for a *public journal.* (A *public journal* is written for an audience and does not include thoughts, feelings, or experiences the writer does not want to share. These topics can best be written about in a private journal or diary kept at home.) You will also practice using the personal writing voice that is used by anyone who keeps a journal.

Reading Journal Writing

Selma Lagerlöf, of Sweden, was the first woman to win the Nobel Prize for Literature. In 1873, during a visit with her aunt and uncle in Stockholm, she kept a journal as a record of her experiences and observations. As you read the following entries from that journal, look for characteristics of a natural writing voice.[1]

Following this selection is a For Thought and Discussion activity.

A *winch* is a crank with a handle for turning.

Monday, 24 February. *In the parlour.*

Cousin Allan has a toy that I never tire of looking at. It is a small, inexpensive toy; in fact, it is only a stick of wood about the length of my hand. But the remarkable thing about it is that it can fly.

At one end of the stick is a small wheel with eight tiny wings made of stiff paper. At the other end is a little "winch" of steel wire, and between the wheel and the winch runs an elastic band.

When Allan wants the stick to fly he turns the winch round and round until the rubber band is stretched to its utmost. He twists the winch until it can't turn, and puts the toy down. The rubber band begins to lose its tautness, thereby setting the paper wheel in motion. It turns very fast and, after two or three revolutions, it shoots upward, drawing the stick along. If the band has been drawn tight enough, the stick goes up all the way to the ceiling, flying back and forth up there, knocking against the plaster, as if it would bore its way out to the open.

The stick is green, and the wings on the wheel are red and white. When the little machine flies round the room, it looks exactly as if it were a witch flying on a broomstick.

Yesterday afternoon, as I sat studying my lesson, Allan wound up his toy and let it fly. I shut my grammar and followed it with my eyes. As the toy rose toward the ceiling it flashed upon me that one ought to be able to make a real flying machine—one that could be used by man, with the little flying stick as a pattern.

At first I thought that this was just nonsense; but now I'm beginning to wonder if it wouldn't be a good idea. It would be a great pleasure for us human beings to be able to travel by air. But I don't believe the big gas-filled balloons have any future. They are forever bursting, and even if they do not burst they move with the wind and are carried hither and thither, no one knows where.

But if one had a large enough wheel with steady wings and a connecting rod, like the wheel on a spindle, at which one could sit and work with the feet to make the wheel revolve, I think that would be a good flying machine.

Thursday, February 27.

When my machine is ready I'm going to fly to Stockholm. How the Stockholmers will stare and how they will wonder what kind of bird that is! Centralplan will be black with people gazing, spellbound, at the sky. And when Aunt Georgina, sitting at the bedroom window sewing, sees all the people, she calls to Uncle Oriel and Ulla to come and look out.

And when the airship comes near, it flies back and forth a couple of times over Centralplan that the people may behold it; then, to the amazement of everyone, it descends in the yard of Klara Strandgata Number 7.

I wonder what Uncle Oriel will say then.

But I shall tell him, at once, that it was here at Number 7, with Aunt and Uncle, that I caught the idea for the great invention, and because of that I have made my first journey by air to their home.

---

[1]From *The Diary of Selma Lagerlöf*, translated by Velma Swanton Howard. Reprinted by permission of Doubleday & Company, Inc.

For Thought and Discussion

Selma Lagerlöf's journal entries are about a simple experience she had with her cousin's toy. The experience was important to her, however, because it made her think. The writer's choice of specific words helps communicate this experience to her readers. She writes, for example, that the toy is "a stick of wood about the length of my hand." What are at least five other instances in which the writer uses specific words to communicate her experience?

Writing Practice 2

For this assignment think about a simple experience you have had that made you think. For example, perhaps you once watched a harried clerk ring up a large order of groceries while two small children occupied themselves with opening packages. As you watched, you thought about a computerized order-at-home system for buying groceries. Use specific words to describe your experience in a journal entry.

Writing Descriptions

A description is a word picture that helps the reader form a mental image of the subject.

The ability to write good descriptions is important in journal writing for two reasons. First, the purpose of writing a public journal is to share something of yourself with your readers, and one way to do this is to write descriptions of people, places, and events in your life. Second, descriptions can help re-create important moments in your life, or you may want to use the details you have recorded for other kinds of writing.

Descriptions may include either *factual* or *personal details.*

Factual detail is used in objective description that does not include the writer's thoughts and feelings. For example, think of a person you know and forget for a moment how you feel about him or her. Then look for factual details about the person that almost anyone would agree on, such as the following ones.

1. She is about five feet, six inches tall.
2. She weighs 120 pounds.
3. She has brown eyes and brown hair.
4. She is wearing blue jeans and a yellow sweater.
5. She is carrying four books.

An important part of factual detail is *accuracy.* Factual details can be checked in reference books or through observation, and careful writers make certain their details are accurate.

Personal detail is shaped by the writer's thoughts and feelings and is used to describe the subject as it appears to the writer. Often the writer selects details that help convey a main, or central, impression he or she has about the subject. For example, the following short passage is from a letter written by Laura Ingalls Wilder while on a train in Nevada. What is her central impression about the Great Salt Lake? What details help to convey this central impression?[1]

> I crossed Great Salt Lake in the moonlight last night and it was the most beautiful sight I've seen yet. Miles and miles of it on each side of the train, the track so narrow that it could not be seen from the window. It looked as though the train was running on the water. I undressed and lay in my berth and watched it, the moonlight making a path of silver across the water and the farther shore so dim and indistinct and melting away into the desert as though there was no end to the lake.

Laura Ingalls Wilder's central impression was that the Great Salt Lake was "the most beautiful sight I've seen yet." The details about the train running on water, the moonlight, and the shore "melting away" help support the impression.

Reading Journal Writing

Kodoku: Sailing Alone Across the Pacific is the journal of a young Japanese man named Kenichi Horie, who crossed the Pacific Ocean alone in a small sailboat. The Japanese word *kodoku* means roughly "solitude," and in his journal Kenichi Horie describes the experience of being alone on the vast ocean. As you read the following entry describing the writer's experience during a storm, look for examples of both factual and personal details.[2]

Sailing on the *port tack* means "sailing to the left of the wind's direction."

Starboard is the right side. The *portside* is the left side.

> 14th day out: May 25th, Friday
>
> *5:00 a.m. Wind has dropped a good deal. Take in the "sea anchor." Winds from the north. Sail her on the port tack, course ENE. High seas, little wind. I don't like it. The storm is up and we're still afloat. But this is just the beginning. What's it going to be like in the long days ahead? My confidence is shaken.*
>
> *The whole boat is a soaking mess. Gear all over the place. Things stored starboard are now portside. Looks as though a wizard had been through, making things jump into opposite places. Too tired to do much about it, though.*
>
> The way the gear in the cabin got mixed up was fantastic. It was almost unbelievable. The stuff in the port shelf went right across the cabin and landed in the starboard shelf. The port shelf was full of things from the starboard one. And I was sure it wasn't *me* that was mixed up. I had carefully fixed places for each item I had carried, and each had its proper place. The medical supplies went on the starboard shelf towards the bow. Books belonged to the port shelf on the side near the cabin entrance. But after the storm everything was completely jumbled.

---

[1]Specified excerpt (p. 20) from *West From Home: Letters of Laura Ingalls Wilder, San Francisco 1915* edited by Roger Lea MacBride. Copyright © 1974 by Roger Lea MacBride.

[2]From *Kodoku: Sailing Alone Across the Pacific* by Kenichi Horie, translated by Takuichi Ito and Kaoru Ogimi. Copyright by Charles E. Tuttle Company, Inc. Reprinted by permission of the publisher, Tokyo, Japan.

The shelves are fixed on the cabin walls just above the berths. If anything dropped from either of the shelves, it would land on the berths or on the cabin floor. It would be impossible for it to crawl back on the shelf it dropped from, much less the *opposite* shelf. The only way anything could land on the opposite shelf would be for it to *fly!* But, how? Wings? What wings? Well, then, magic. That's all it could be—magic.

The motion must have been so violent during the storm that everything inside the cabin was sent off in a mad whirlwind of a high trapeze. The most acrobatic was the stuff in the toolbox. I had fixed it by the steps at the companionway. It was a fairly deep box with a simple lid on its top. The only way anything could get out of that box was straight up. But that's just what all my tools must have done, because they all ended up in the fo'c'sle!

The *companionway* is the stairway.

Fo'c'sle, short for *forecastle*, is the forward part of the upper deck.

During the storm I was too busy trying to hold myself down. I had no time to worry about the mad circus that was going on in the cabin. But when I think about it now, it must have been those curling, breaking seas that had done it. Those crests were terribly steep. Most even had an overhang as they came crashing down. As the *Mermaid* was lying to her stern anchor, she would climb, stern first, these steep walls of sea. She would almost flip over ends-on as she came up to the crest. But then her "sea anchor" would yank her stern down into the valley of the next sea as the first one went roaring past.

For Thought and Discussion

As a record of an ocean voyage, Kenichi Horie's journal has many factual details, including such information as the number of days at sea, the date, and the time of the journal entry. The entry also has personal details, such as the writer's comment that the cabin "Looks as though a wizard had been through . . ." What other examples of factual and personal details do you find in the selection?

Use the Preparing to Write section below to help gather information for these assignments.

Writing Practice 3

After studying the photograph on page 11, write a journal entry describing what you see in it, using only factual details.

Writing Practice 4

Use both factual and personal details to write a journal entry describing what you see in the photograph on page 11.

Preparing to Write

As you study the photograph, think about your central impression of what you see. Next select details from the photograph that support your central impression. For example, if you feel there is a sense of sadness about the scene, supporting details might include seemingly sad expressions on the faces of the young girls and the rundown appearance of the house in the background. The fact that there are girls in the photograph is a factual detail, but your feeling or thought about them is a personal detail.

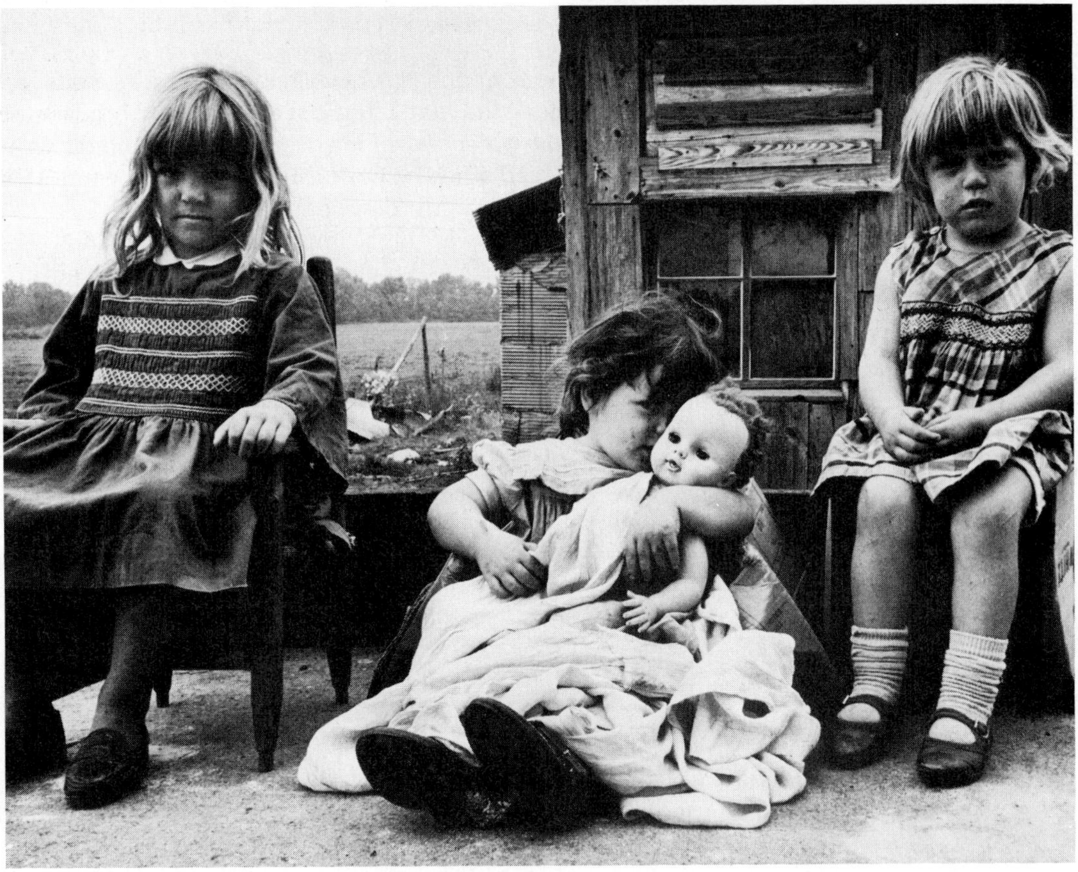

Describing with Sensory Details

To re-create an experience with words, writers often use *sensory details*, details of *sight*, *sound*, *taste*, *smell* and *touch*. In the following excerpt from his book *The Names*, N. Scott Momaday uses sensory details to describe his home.[1]

> I see: There is moonlight on the Southern Plains. I see the black trees in the north, where the river runs and my father has set out poles on the bank. When he goes before daylight with the lantern to take them up there will be catfishes on the lines, their heads flat and green and shining, and their wide mouths grinning under their whiskers. There is a whole silence on the earth—only here and there are surfaces made of sound, frogs purring at the water's edge, a rooster crowing across the distance, the river running and lapping. And the plain rolls like water in the low light; the light is like chalk on the ripples

---

[1]From *The Names* by N. Scott Momaday. Copyright © 1976 by N. Scott Momaday. Reprinted by permission of Harper & Row, Publishers, Inc.

of the land; the slow, warm wind seems to ruffle the soft light, to stir it up like dust. Oklahoma shines like the moon.

N. Scott Momaday's description has details about sights, sounds, and touch. Details of sight include the "flat and green and shining" heads on the catfish. "Frogs purring at the water's edge" is a detail of sound, and the writer uses a detail of texture (touch) when he writes about the warm wind. What other sensory details do you find in the description?

Good writers are especially aware of the importance of observation. They can remember sights, sounds, tastes, smells, and textures of their environment and are also able to recall memories of their thoughts and feelings about the experiences. One way to train yourself to be observant is to concentrate on each sense separately. Think first about what you see. Imagine for a moment that everything around you is frozen in space and carefully study details of shapes and colors in your environment. Then allow movement to begin and study the movements. How exactly do people move? What objects move in your environment? (A moving object might be a clock's hands.) How do the objects move?

Next concentrate on hearing individual sounds. If you cannot distinguish one sound from another, close your eyes as you listen. In the modern world there is seldom anything approaching total silence; a place that appears silent probably has many sounds. At 4 A.M. on a deserted city street, the rain hits the top of garbage cans, and a prowling cat pushes aside loose rubble in its search for prey. In the distance a muted siren wails.

You can sometimes have the experience of tasting something even though you may not be eating or drinking at the time. Some observers say, for example, that fear has a taste; others taste the salt in the air at the seashore. Be alert for tastes such as these. In a situation where you are not tasting something, imagine what you would like to be eating or drinking and how the food or drink would taste.

As you concentrate on smells, try to identify the source of the odor. Ask yourself whether the smell is pleasant or unpleasant and try to decide why it has that effect on you. Perhaps the smell is pleasant because it reminds you of a food you enjoy, or perhaps it is unpleasant because it reminds you of a bad experience.

Textures are things in your environment that you can physically feel. Textures most often noticed are the ones most extreme—very rough textures (such as sandpaper) or very soft textures (such as a kitten's fur). In your environment you are constantly being touched—by the air flowing over you, by the grass flickering against you as you walk, by rain and snow. Learn to be alert to these textures that may not be so obvious.

Your thoughts and feelings about sensory experiences are also important.

Does your experience make you think anything in particular? How does it make you feel? Human emotions are complex and may range from extremes, such as grief or rage, to less powerful emotions, such as boredom or a sense of calmness. Writing about these inner experiences helps re-create your world for readers.

Writing Practice 5

For this assignment take pen and paper to a nearby place, perhaps a crowded place, such as a shopping center or a city street, or a quieter place, such as a bench in the park. Divide your paper into five columns, giving each column one of these labels: SIGHTS, SOUNDS, SMELLS, TASTES, and TEXTURES. As you sit, concentrate on observing details about the place with each of your senses and write your observations under the appropriate headings. When you have finished, write down your thoughts and feelings about the place.

Example

Place: Empty lot of old service station

SIGHTS	*SOUNDS*	*SMELLS*
Tail fins of deserted old car from an earlier generation	*Whine of diesel truck on nearby highway*	*Faint oily smell*
TASTES	*TEXTURES*	
In my mind I taste the salted peanuts I always bought at service stations while on family trips.	*Flicker of ant crawling across bare feet*	

Writing Practice 6

Imagine yourself a part of the photograph on page 14 and think about what you see, hear, smell, taste, and touch. Write a journal entry describing the scene as though you were actually in it, using sensory details to help re-create the scene for your readers.

Describing People and Places

The purpose of describing people and places is to re-create them for readers.

You can begin to re-create people with words by describing their physical appearance, but the inner person is also important. Notice how Nora Ephron, in the following selection from *Crazy Salad*, describes both the physical characteristics and personality of Bernice Gera, the first woman to become an official baseball umpire.[1]

> Bernice Gera lives in a three-room walk-up apartment in Queens. In it there is a candle shaped like a softball, an ashtray shaped like a mitt, a lighter shaped like a bat, a crocheted toaster cover shaped like a doll wearing a baseball cap, an arrangement of dried flowers containing a baseball, powder puffs, and a small statue of Mickey Mouse holding a bat. On the wall is a very large color photograph of Mrs. Gera in uniform holding a face mask, and a few feet away

[1]From "Bernice Gera, First Lady Umpire" in *Crazy Salad: Some Things About Women* by Nora Ephron. Copyright © 1975 by Nora Ephron. Reprinted by permission of Alfred A. Knopf, Inc.

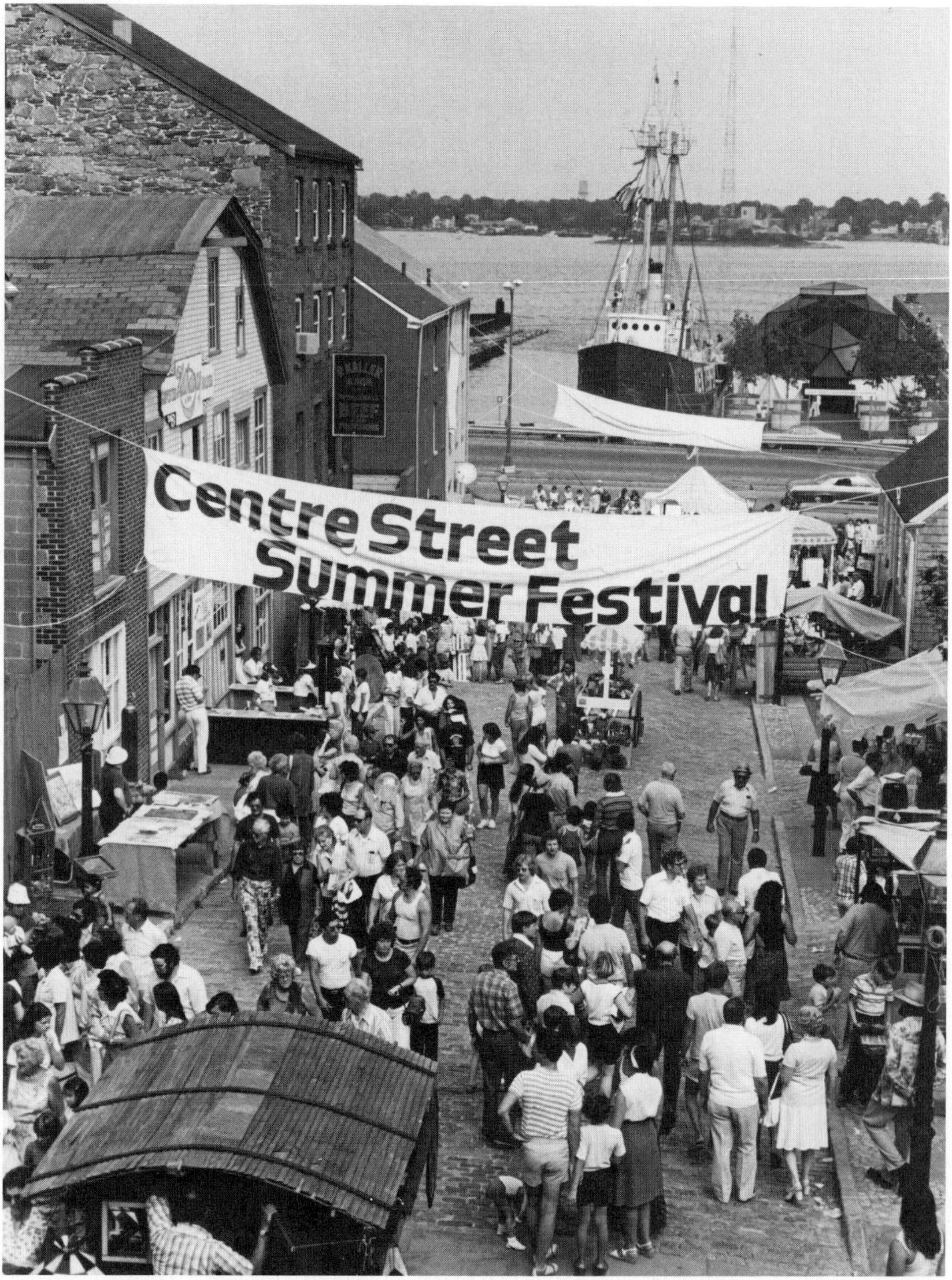
Centre Street
Summer Festival

hangs a poem that reads: "Dear God, Last night I did pray/That You would let me in the game today. /And if the guys yell and scream, /Please, God, tell them You're the captain of the team." All the available shelf space is crammed with trophies and plaques; there must be 40 or 50 of them, some for bowling (she averages 165) but most for baseball, for her career on a women's softball team in Detroit, and for her charity batting exhibitions against people like Roger Maris and Sid Gordon. "I can hit the long ball," she says, and she can, some 350 feet. There is also a framed clipping of an old Ripley's "Believe It Or Not," a syndicated feature that has come a long way since the days when it printed items that were remotely unbelievable. "Believe It Or Not," it reads, "a New York City housewife has won 300 large dolls for needy youngsters living at the children's shelter of the Queensboro Society for the Prevention of Cruelty to Children by her skill at throwing a baseball at amusement parks."

Mrs. Gera is a short, slightly chunky woman who wears white socks and loafers; her short blondish-brown hair is curled and lacquered. Around her neck is a gold charm decorated with a bat, mitt, and pearl baseball which she designed and had made up by a local jeweler. Her voice is flat and unanimated, unless, of course, she is talking about baseball: She can describe, exultantly, one of the happiest days of her life, when she had a tooth extracted and was able to stay home from work to see the Pirates win the World Series in 1960. Bernice Gera is, more than anything, a fan, an unabashed, adoring fan, and her obsession with baseball dates back to her childhood, when she played with her older brothers on a sandlot in the Pennsylvania mining town where she was raised. "I have loved, eaten, and lived baseball since I was eight years old," she says. "Put yourself in my shoes. Say you loved baseball. If you love horses, you can be a jockey. If you love golf or swimming, look at Babe Didrikson and Gertrude Ederle. These are great people and they had an ability. I had it with baseball. What could I do? I couldn't play. So you write letters, begging for a job, any job, and you keep this up for years and years. There had to be a way for me. So I decided to take up a trade. I decided to take up umpiring."

To re-create Bernice Gera for readers, Nora Ephron provides details about the umpire's physical appearance, the way she dresses, how she sounds when describing a baseball experience, and how she sounds when not talking about baseball. Putting Bernice Gera into the familiar setting of her apartment and then describing that setting tells readers even more about her. Finally the actual words of the first woman umpire tell readers that this is not a person who gives up easily.

When describing people, you can simply tell readers about the person, as Nora Ephron does when she writes "Mrs. Gera is a short, slightly chunky woman who wears white socks and loafers." Another way to describe people is to show readers how a person behaves and then let them draw their own conclusions. Nora Ephron does not tell readers that Bernice Gera is a baseball fanatic; she lets the words of the sports fan speak for themselves.

Specific, sensory details are important in describing places.

Sensory details help readers share the sights, sounds, tastes, odors, and textures of the places you describe. In the following short essay, "Freedom to Breathe," Aleksander Solzhenitsyn, the exiled Russian writer, describes an experience he had while standing in a small garden. What are the sensory details he uses to re-create this experience?

> A shower fell in the night and now dark clouds drift across the sky, occasionally sprinkling a fine film of rain.
>
> I stand under an apple tree in blossom and I breathe. Not only the apple tree but the grass round it glistens with moisture; words cannot describe the sweet fragrance that pervades the air. I inhale as deeply as I can, and the aroma invades my whole being; I breathe with my eyes open, I breathe with my eyes closed—I cannot say which gives me the greater pleasure.
>
> This, I believe, is the single most precious freedom that prison takes away from us: the freedom to breathe freely, as I now can. No food on earth, no wine, not even a woman's kiss is sweeter to me than this air steeped in the fragrance of flowers, of moisture and freshness.
>
> No matter that this is only a tiny garden, hemmed in by five-story houses like cages in a zoo. I cease to hear the motorcycles backfiring, radios whining, the burble of loudspeakers. As long as there is fresh air to breathe under an apple tree after a shower, we may survive a little longer.[1]

Details such as "dark clouds drift across the sky" help readers visualize the setting of Aleksander Solzhenitsyn's experience. From details such as "motorcycles backfiring," readers can hear the sounds that surround the writer. What details of smell and taste does the writer use?

People may be an important part of a place. A writer could not re-create a truck stop for readers without a description of the men and women who sit hunched on stools over greasy cups of coffee, trading jokes and information about roads and weather conditions. In some cases the place itself may seem changed by the people who are there. An empty football stadium seems a much different place from one filled with jostling, screaming fans. A shopping center during a busy season is different from a shopping center at other times of the year.

Sometimes, writers wish to establish a particular mood, or feeling, in their descriptions. The mood of Aleksander Solzhenitsyn's description, for example, is solemnity and thoughtfulness. By selecting only details that help to establish this mood, the writer maintains it throughout the description.

Writing Practice 7

Use the Preparing to Write section on page 18 to help you with ideas for these assignments.

Examine the people in the photograph on page 17 first for details of physical appearance and then decide about the inner characteristics of the people. Write a journal entry describing both the physical and inner qualities of one of the people.

Writing Practice 8

For this assignment select an important person in your life or use yourself as the subject. Then write a journal entry describing your subject as completely as possible.

---

[1]From "Freedom to Breathe" in *Stories and Prose Poems* by Alexander Solzhenitsyn, translated by Michael Glenny.

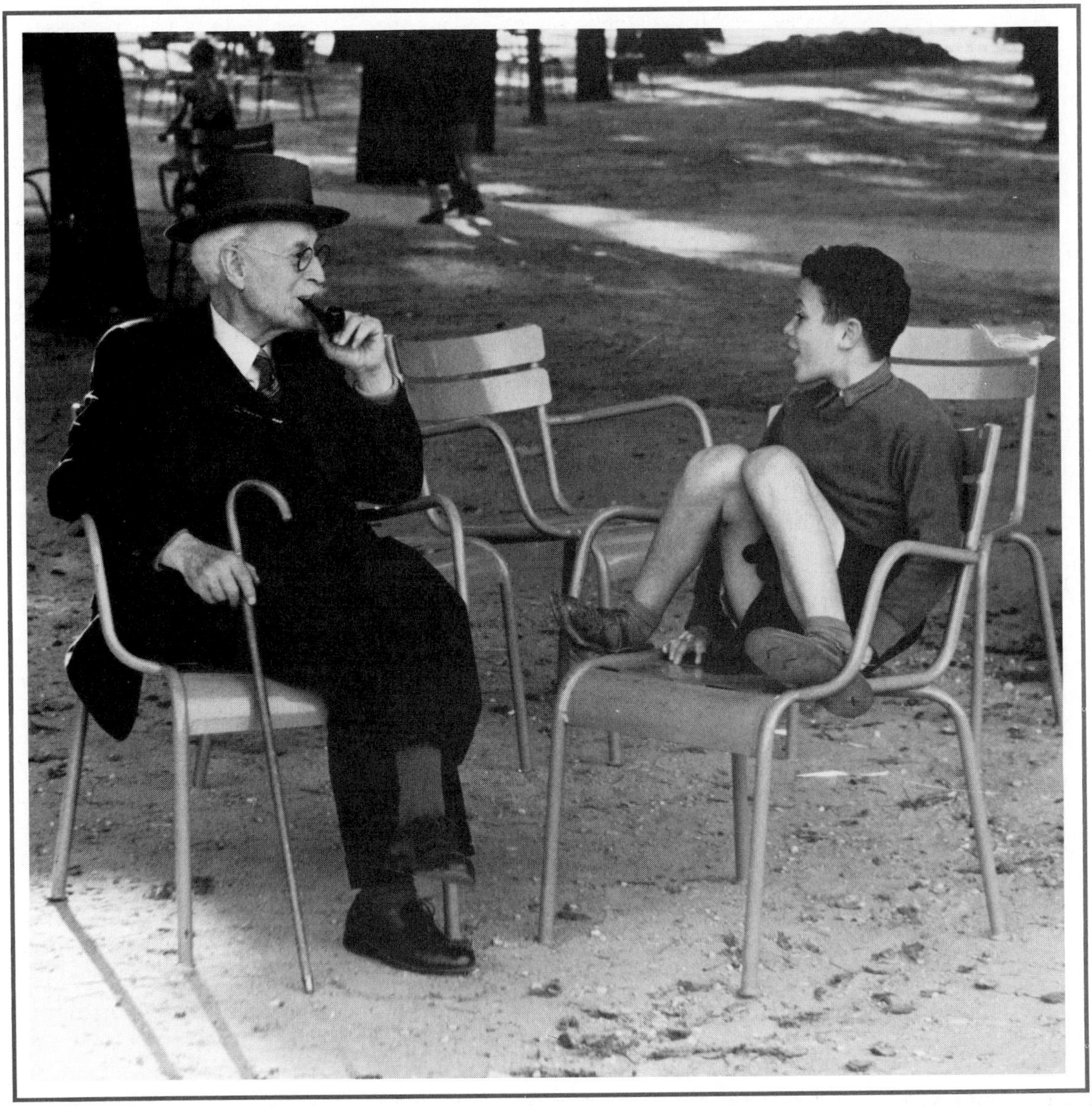

Writing Practice 9

Read the Preparing to Write section that follows before you begin these assignments.

Imagine yourself a part of the photograph on page 18 and think about the sights, sounds, smells, tastes, and textures you experience. Write a journal entry describing the place and the people there as though you were a part of the scene, using sensory details to help readers share your experiences.

Writing Practice 10

For this assignment select an important place in your life. Think about the people who are a part of the place and why they are important. Using sensory details, describe the place and people in a journal entry.

Preparing to Write

Asking questions such as the following ones can help you gather information for descriptions of people and places. As you ask yourself the appropriate questions, make notes of specific details to use in your writing.

QUESTIONS ABOUT PEOPLE

1. What is the person's physical appearance? (Shape of facial features, color of eyes and hair, hairstyle, shape of face, markings on face such as freckles, body build, posture, height)
2. How does the person dress?
3. How does he or she walk and talk?
4. Does he or she have any unusual mannerisms or gestures?
5. Does he or she have an outstanding behavior characteristic, such as biting the lower lip or shaking the head?
6. What are the inner qualities of the person?
7. How does he or she behave when angry? When happy?
8. What places does the person enjoy most? What do these places reveal about him or her?
9. In what ways is this person different from other people?
10. How has the person changed with time?

QUESTIONS ABOUT PLACES

1. What is this place? What is its purpose?
2. What sights are likely to be seen there?
3. What sounds are likely to be experienced there?
4. What are common smells associated with the place?
5. What tastes are a part of the place?
6. What textures do people experience there?
7. What people are a part of this place? How do they help to make the place what it is?
8. How is this place similar to other places in the same category? (For example, if the place is a race track, how is it like other race tracks?)
9. How is this place different from other places in the same category?
10. How has the place changed over time?

Before you begin writing, decide about the purpose of your description and then select the details that will help you achieve this purpose. If, for example, you want to describe the courage of a friend with a severe physical disability, you might use more details about the person's inner qualities and behavioral characteristics than about his or her physical appearance.

Writing for Readers: The Follow-Up

When you write only for yourself, your writing does not have to please or make sense to anyone else, nor do you have to be especially concerned with "correctness." Writing a public journal, however, means writing for readers. The public journals that you have read in this chapter usually have been revised and proofread before publication. This means that the writer and the writer's editors have made changes in the original writing to make it clearer and more interesting.

Revising means "making changes in the content of the writing itself." *Proofreading* means "checking the writing for errors in spelling, grammar, and mechanics."

You have probably been revising your writing for some time without being aware of it. You do this when you write a sentence, decide it does not "sound" quite right, and then rewrite it before continuing. Every piece of public writing needs a final revision, however, a revision that comes after the writer has finished an entire draft. The ideal way to do a final revision is to put the piece of writing away for a day or two and then come back to it with a fresh eye.

As you read back over your paper, you may want to add or delete words or sentences, rearrange parts, or make substitutions. The changes you make when revising should depend on your original purpose for writing. The purpose of writing a public journal is to share something of yourself—your ideas and impressions—with readers. Reflecting your flow of ideas and impressions, journal writing should sound natural, as if you were talking. With this purpose in mind, use the following checklist to revise journal entries.

Checklist for Revising Journal Entries

1. The journal entry has a natural writing voice. Journal writers write in first person, use words that are a natural part of their vocabularies, and make simple and direct statements when appropriate.
2. Journal entries have specific words that help readers understand the writer's thoughts, feelings, observations, and experiences.
3. The writer keeps readers in mind by writing on subjects of interest to them.
4. Details of factual description are accurate.
5. Details of personal description reflect how the writer thinks and feels about his or her subject.
6. Sensory details help readers see, hear, taste, smell, and feel what the writer describes.
7. Descriptions of people include details about both the inner and outer person.
8. Details are chosen to establish the mood the writer wishes to communicate.

When you have completed your revision, check your writing for errors in grammar and mechanics by using the following checklist. (Since you will be using it often, you might want to copy it into your notebook.) Check your writing carefully against each item on the list. If you can make corrections neatly on your finished draft, do so; if not, copy your paper over.

Following the Checklist for Proofreading is a section titled For Extra Help. Page numbers in this box refer you to sections in the textbook that will give you help with specific problems.

Remember that proofreading is the final stage in the process of writing.

Checklist for Proofreading

1. The paper is carefully written or typed and is not marred by smears, messy smudges, or crossed-out words.
2. Sentence structure is accurate. There are no fragments or run-on sentences. Punctuation is used correctly to link compound sentences.
3. Singular verbs are used with singular subjects, and plural verbs are used with plural subjects.
4. All pronouns have clear antecedents. Plural pronouns are used to refer to plural nouns, and singular pronouns are used with singular nouns.
5. Pronouns are the correct subject or object form.
6. Singular pronouns such as *either*, *each*, *anybody*, *everybody*, or *nobody* are used with singular verbs.

7. The writer uses verb tenses consistently and accurately.
8. The writer avoids unnecessary shifts in pronouns, such as *I* to *you*, or *they* to *you*.
9. Confusing verbs such as *lie/lay*, *sit/set*, *leave/let* are used correctly.
10. The endings *s*, *'s*, *-ing*, or *-ed* are used correctly with nouns and verbs.
11. Capitalization is used correctly at the beginning of sentences and with proper nouns and adjectives.
12. Each word is spelled correctly.
13. Punctuation is used correctly throughout the writing.
14. Contractions such as *they're*, *it's*, or *you're* are not confused with possessive pronouns.
15. Confusing words such as *farther/further*, *fewer/less* or sound-alikes such as *desert/dessert*, *since/sense* are used and spelled correctly.
16. Dialogue is punctuated and capitalized correctly.
17. Slang is used only when appropriate.

For Extra Help

Sentence Structure	Pages 482–505
Subject–Verb Agreement	Pages 398–408
Pronoun Reference	Pages 365–369
Pronoun Form	Pages 369–377
Indefinite Pronoun Agreement	Pages 366–368
Consistent Verb Tense	Pages 412–414
Unnecessary Shift in Pronouns	Pages 377–378
Confusing Verbs	Pages 408–411
Noun Plurals and Possessives	Pages 335–345
Capitalization	Pages 603–616
Spelling	Pages 554–570
Punctuation	Pages 571–602
Contractions	Page 595
Confusing Words	Pages 555–564
Spelling Rules	Pages 564–569
Punctuating Dialogue	Pages 599–600

Writing Practice 11

From the journal entries you have made in this chapter, select one for revision. Using the Checklist for Revising Journal Entries on page 20, revise the entry as you would for publication. When you have finished, use the Checklist for Proofreading to check your entry for errors.

Ideas for Journals

The following suggestions for journal entries will help you with ideas for keeping a journal of your own.

1. If you live in the city, keep an urban journal in which you write about people, places, and experiences that are an important part of city life. If you live in the country or a small town, keep a country or a small town journal.
2. Keep a seasonal journal in which you write about people, places, and experiences that are an important part of summer, winter, spring, or fall.
3. Write a series of journal entries that catalogue and describe a trip you have taken or would like to take.
4. Write one or more entries about current events, describing an event and your reactions to it.
5. Write about a moment when you felt particularly good or bad. Try to capture the moment in words and try to explain why it affected you the way it did.
6. Write a journal entry with unusual ideas about a common subject, such as a garbage can, a fog, or worms.
7. Write an entry describing the person you were five years ago.
8. Write an entry describing your favorite place five years ago.
9. Write an entry describing the person you would like to be ten years from now.
10. Write an entry telling about a story or poem that made you think or feel.

Writing an Autobiographical Narrative

An *autobiographical narrative* is a story about the writer told from his or her point of view.

The purpose of writing an autobiographical narrative is to share an interesting or unusual episode in your life with readers. The episode does not have to be of great significance to be interesting, but it should be one that was important to you, perhaps one that taught you something about yourself or about someone else, or one that changed you in some way. As a writer your job is to show readers how the episode affected you and why it was important in your life.

An autobiographical narrative is a story, and as such it has characters and setting, but the emphasis is usually on the action. Descriptions of character and setting are usually brief, limited to details that help readers understand the action and its effect on you. For example, suppose you write a narrative about how you conquered your fear and killed a dangerous snake in your backyard. Because it is important for readers to understand your fear of snakes, you describe this part of your behavior, perhaps telling how you acquired the fear and about some earlier experiences with reptiles. To establish the setting, you would not describe your entire backyard, but a description of the tangled weeds and underbrush hiding the snake would be appropriate.

Thoughts and feelings are important details that help build an autobiographical narrative.

Unless readers know your reactions to events, they cannot share the experience with you. One way to reveal thoughts and feelings in a narrative is to state them directly. You may say, for example, "I have never been more afraid in my life." Another way is to show behaviors that reveal your thoughts and feelings. A sentence such as "My hands were icy, and I could barely feel myself breathing" shows your physical reactions to an emotion.

Conflict and *suspense* are important elements in an autobiographical narrative.

Conflict is a struggle either within a person or between one person and some other person or force. Conflict within a person, or *inner conflict*, is the struggle people have within themselves when making a difficult decision or regretting a wrong action. *Outer conflicts*, conflicts between people or between a person and some outside force, are such conflicts as an argument between friends, a fight to save victims from a burning building, or a campaign by a disabled person to end society's discrimination.

Suspense, which keeps readers involved by making them wonder what will happen next, is often the result of conflict. Suspense may also be created if the writer describes a setting so that readers know something will happen there, or if a character description makes readers wonder what the character will do next.

Events in a narrative are usually arranged *chronologically* in the order in which they actually happened. Following chronological order, an autobiographical narrative about running away from home at age six might begin with the writer's making preparations for running away. The experience of leaving home and becoming lost might follow, and the narrative might end with the writer's returning home. Writers sometimes scramble the order, perhaps beginning with the final event and then relating the first ones, to capture the reader's interest early.

Reading Autobiographical Narrative

The following excerpt is from the autobiography of Dwight David Eisenhower, who was the thirty-fourth President of the United States, serving two terms between 1953 and 1961. As you read the selection, notice how President Eisenhower describes an incident that might have seemed small to others but that was important to him. Also, look for the elements of autobiographical narrative you read about in the previous section.[1]

> My earliest memory involves an incident that occurred two or three months before my fifth birthday. I took a long trip to a strange and far-off place—Topeka—for a tough and prolonged war.

---

[1] From "Sauce for the Gander" from *At Ease* by Dwight D. Eisenhower. Reprinted by permission of Doubleday & Company, Inc. and Robert Hale, Ltd.

Following this selection is a For Thought and Discussion activity.

My mother's sister, Aunt Minnie, was visiting us. We lived in a little cottage on Second Street in Abilene. It was decided that I would return with her to Topeka where a considerable number of Mother's relatives lived.

It was a day trip and during the course of the morning the heat of the railroad car and the monotony of the noise made me very sleepy. "Does this train have a sleeping car?" I asked her, using a scrap of worldly knowledge I had presumably picked up while listening to a family conversation. "It's not really necessary to go to a sleeping car," my aunt replied. "Just lie down on the seat and I'll make sure you have a good nap." I did and she was right.

After leaving the train, we next had to take a long ride by horse and buggy to my relatives' farm out beyond the northern outskirts of Topeka. I can remember looking down through the floorboards, watching the ground rush past and the horses' feet, which seemed to slide. When we arrived, life became even more confusing. It was peculiar to be surrounded by so many strangers. It seemed to me that there were dozens or hundreds of people—all grownups—in the house. Even though they were, somehow, my family, I felt lonesome and lost among them.

I began to wander around outside. In the rear of the house was an old-fashioned well, very deep, with a wooden bucket and a long rope threaded through a pulley. My uncle Luther found me, fascinated by the well, and he offered a long story about what would happen to me if I fell in. He spoke in such horrible terms that I soon lost any ambition to look over the fearful edge into the abyss below. Looking around for less dreadful diversion, I noticed a pair of barnyard geese. The male resented my intrusion from our first meeting and each time thereafter he would push along toward me aggressively and with hideous hissing noises so threatening my security that five-year-old courage could not stand the strain. I would race for the back door of the house, burst into the kitchen, and tell any available elder about this awful old gander.

Ignominiously means "shamefully."

Thus the war began. In the early parts of the campaign, I lost a skirmish every half hour and invariably had to flee ignominiously and weeping from the battlefield. Without support, and lacking arms of any kind, it was only by recourse to distressing retreat after retreat to the kitchen that I kept myself from disaster.

My enemy was that bad-tempered and aggressive gander. I was a little boy, not yet five years old, who was intensely curious about the new environment into which he was thrust and determined to explore its every corner. But the gander constantly balked me. He obviously looked upon me as a helpless and harmless nuisance. He had no intention of permitting anyone to penetrate his domain. Always hopeful that he would finally abandon his threatened attacks on my person, I'd try again and again, always with the same result.

An *adversary* is an enemy.

Uncle Luther decided that something had to be done. He took a worn-out broom and cut off all the straw except for a short hard knob which he probably left so that in my zeal, if I developed any, I might not hurt my odd adversary. With the weapon all set, he took me out into the yard. He showed me how I was to swing and then announced that I was on my own.

The gander remained aggressive in his actions, and I was not at all sure that my uncle was very smart. More frightened at the moment of his possible scolding than I was of aggression, I took what was meant to be a firm, but was really a trembling, stand the next time the fowl came close. Then I let out a yell and rushed toward him, swinging the club as fast as I could. He turned and I gave him a satisfying smack right in the fanny. He let out a most satisfactory squawk and ran off. This was my signal to chase him, which I did.

Belligerent means "quarrelsome."

From then on, he would continue his belligerent noises whenever he saw me (and the stick). He kept his distance and I was the proud boss of the back yard. I never make the mistake of being caught without the weapon. This all turned out to be a rather good lesson for me because I quickly learned never to negotiate with an adversary except from a position of strength.

For Thought and Discussion

1. The third and fourth paragraphs of the preceding excerpt tell about President Eisenhower's trip from Abilene to Topeka, Kansas, to visit relatives. When he writes about "the heat of the railroad car and the monotony of the noise," he uses specific details to describe the experience. What are other descriptive details he uses in the two paragraphs?
2. Thoughts and feelings are important details in an autobiographical narrative. In the fourth paragraph President Eisenhower says that he felt "lonesome and lost." At what other times in the narrative does the writer reveal thoughts and feelings?
3. This narrative involves both an inner and outer conflict. What are they?
4. The narrative begins with President Eisenhower reflecting on an episode from his childhood. He relates the series of events in this episode in chronological order. In your own words relate this sequence of events.
5. Many autobiographies involve writers' looking back as adults on earlier parts of their lives. In looking back on an experience, you often see it a different way than when you were involved in it at the time. How do you think President Eisenhower's looking back on his childhood experience affected the way he remembered the event?

Writing Practice 12

Use the Preparing to Write section that follows to help you with this assignment.

Write an autobiographical narrative about an event in your life that was important to you.

Preparing to Write

If you have written in your journal about an important event in your life, you have a good source of details for your narrative. Another way to gather information is to ask yourself questions about the incident, such as the following ones.

1. Who was involved?
   Once you have named the people involved in the incident, ask yourself questions that will help you accumulate details about them. What are their physical characteristics? How did their personalities or characters affect what happened? Since your autobiographical narrative is always about you, ask these questions about yourself also.
2. What happened?
   Go back over the action of the incident you are writing about as carefully as you can, remembering as many details as possible. If you are writing

about an event that happened in your childhood, use your family members as resources for ideas.

3. Where did the event happen?
   Once you have thought of specific places, try to write down details that will help readers visualize them. Ask yourself how the place affected the action. If a certain part of the place had a direct effect on what happened, this is the part you want to describe in your narrative.
4. When did the event happen?
   What was the specific time of the event?
   Were you a different person then than you are today?
   Did that difference have anything to do with the action?
5. Why did the event happen?
   Were you in some way responsible for the incident, as President Eisenhower's childhood curiosity was responsible for the episode with the gander?
6. How did the event affect the people involved?
   What were your thoughts and feelings while the event was taking place? What effect did it have on you? Did the event change your point of view, your feelings, or your life in some way?

Revising Your Autobiographical Narrative

The purpose of writing an autobiographical narrative is to share an interesting or unusual episode in your life with readers. The following checklist will help you decide whether or not you have achieved your purpose. Use it by evaluating your narrative in terms of each item. If your writing seems weak in any area, revise it to correct the weakness. When you have finished your revision, check your writing for errors by using the Checklist for Proofreading on pages 20–21.

Checklist for Revising Autobiographical Narrative

1. The emphasis in the narrative is on the action.
2. The details of character and setting help readers understand the action.
3. The narrative involves a clear conflict of some kind.
4. Important details of thought and feeling are included.
5. The narrative includes suspense that keeps readers involved.
6. The events in the narrative are arranged in the order they happened. If the order is changed, there is a reason for doing so.
7. The narrative is written in a natural voice.

2 Discovering Subject Matter

Creativity and Writing

Creativity is the ability to think in an original way.

Creative individuals depend on both conscious and unconscious thought for their ideas. *Conscious thought* is deliberate; when you sit down and list writing topics, you are using conscious thought. *Unconscious thought* often occurs at unexpected moments when you are not deliberately thinking about a problem and may result in a flash of inspiration. Albert Einstein, for example, said that some of his best ideas occurred to him while he was shaving in the morning.

In this chapter you will read about ways to stimulate both conscious and unconscious thought as a way of helping you to discover subject matter for writing.

Brainstorming

Brainstorming is a system that uses both conscious and unconscious thought to gather ideas for writing.

A *brainstorm* is a sudden idea. *Brainstorming* means "producing as many ideas as you can without stopping to judge them." In brainstorming, you focus your thoughts on one subject, letting as many ideas as possible come into your mind about it.

Brainstorming can be done alone or with a group. If you brainstorm alone, sit in a quiet place with plenty of blank paper and a pen or pencil. To focus your thoughts write your subject in large letters on a sheet of paper. Then let your thoughts roam freely over the subject, writing down ideas in words, phrases, or even complete sentences as they come to you.

During brainstorming, do not stop to decide which ideas are good and which ones are silly. Accept *all* ideas; your mind should be free to play creatively during brainstorming. You can sift through your ideas later and select the most useful ones.

The following ideas are the result of one writer's brainstorming about the subject *The car of the future:*

THE CAR OF THE FUTURE

Smaller than cars today
May hold only one person
Lighter
Aluminum
Styrofoam
Fuel crisis
Fuel efficient
Gasohol
Alcohol
Water
Solar energy
Electric battery
Perfectly safe car
Recharging stations will spring up all over country.
Electric cars will be used for short-distance driving.
Can fly like a helicopter
James Bond
Goes in water also
Supersonic
Moves on tracks
Shaped like bullet
Silver bullet
Rubber bumpers
Rubber everything

This writer's thoughts wandered over all aspects of the subject—from the type of engine, to the design of the car, to safety features. A student writing on this subject might dismiss some ideas—building a car of styrofoam or powering a car with water—as impractical. The purpose of brainstorming, however, is to accumulate creative ideas, and this student has gathered many.

Brainstorming in a group gives you the advantage of obtaining other people's thoughts, as well as your own.

Other people's thoughts may also stimulate your own thinking, helping you come up with new ideas. To brainstorm in a group, select one person—a recorder—to announce the topic and to write down ideas as group members think of them. If your group gets stuck, have the recorder read over the list of ideas. The entire process should not take more than fifteen minutes.

Writers who brainstorm often discover they know more about a subject than they thought. They may also discover parts of the subject they need to learn more about. The writer brainstorming the car of the future, for example, might decide to find out more about alternate fuels for tomorrow's cars. Also, brainstorming may suggest a way of limiting the subject by revealing the area in which most of the writer's knowledge lies.

Writing Practice 1

Either alone or in a group, select one of the following subjects or make up one of your own. Write the subject in large letters on a sheet of paper. (In a group ask one member to serve as recorder.) Then brainstorm your subject for fifteen minutes or so, gathering as many ideas as possible without stopping to evaluate them.

1. Unusual ways of earning money
2. Ideas for inexpensive birthday gifts
3. Reducing traffic accidents
4. The ideal vacation
5. New ideas for conserving energy
6. New courses for high schools
7. Space travel in the year 2500
8. Dress in the year 2500
9. Making good grades
10. Increasing attendance at school-sponsored events, such as basketball games and dances

---

Clustering Ideas

The purpose of the *clustering system* is to encourage a flow of ideas and to group ideas as they come.

To *cluster* ideas begin by writing down and circling a word or phrase that names the subject. Next let your mind wander freely over the subject, writing down new ideas around the circled word or phrase. One writer's cluster for the subject *Spring* might look like the following diagram.

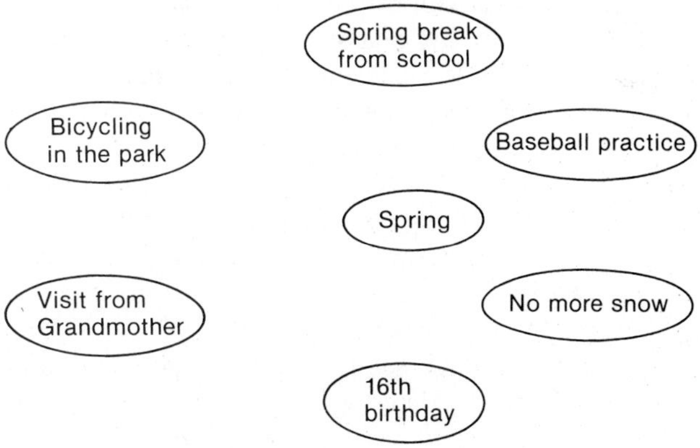

As the next diagram shows, one word or phrase may lead to another. Keep adding ideas, circling each word and drawing a line to the next idea to see the connections your mind is making:

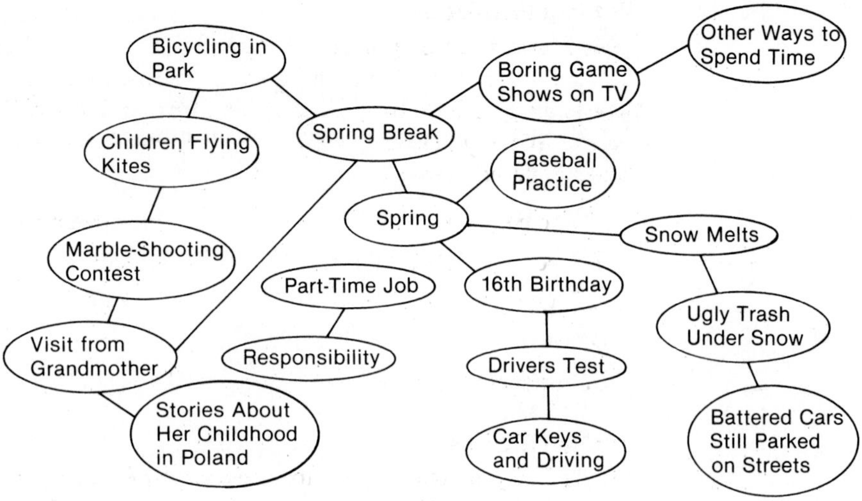

This writer now has the beginnings of several subjects for writing, such as the following ones:

1. A grandmother's childhood in Poland
2. Spring in the park
3. Using leisure time
4. Cleaning up city neighborhoods
5. Becoming sixteen

Writing Practice 2

Read the following short poem about television. Write the title in large letters on a sheet of paper. Then, alone or in a group with a recorder, brainstorm about the poem for about fifteen minutes. Write down any idea or feeling about the poem that comes to you or anything any word in the poem suggests to you. Do not stop to think whether or not your responses are "correct."

The Forecast[1]

Perhaps our age has driven us indoors.
We sprawl in the semi-darkness, dreaming sometimes
Of a vague world spinning in the wind.
But we have snapped our locks, pulled down our shades,
Taken all precautions. We shall not be disturbed.
If the earth shakes, it will be on a screen;
And if the prairie wind spills down our streets
And covers us with leaves, the weatherman will tell us.

—*Dan Jaffe*

---

[1]"The Forecast" by Dan Jaffe. Copyright © 1964 by Dan Jaffe. Reprinted by permission of the author.

Writing Practice 3

Select one word or phrase for clustering from the following list or make up a list of your own. Write the word or phrase on a sheet of paper, clustering ideas around it as they come to you. Use circles and lines to show relationships. When you finish, make a list of possible subjects for writing based on the clustered ideas.

1. icicle
2. science fiction movies
3. work
4. up
5. shopping centers
6. adventure
7. 1980s
8. heroic
9. around
10. they

Writing Practice 4

Write down on a sheet of paper a word or phrase the photograph on page 32 suggests to you. Cluster ideas around the word or phrase as they come to you, using circles and lines to show relationships. When you finish, make a list of possible writing subjects based on the clustered ideas.

Writing from Different Points of View

An important part of creativity is looking at a subject from different points of view.[1]

In the early 1800s the French army used a system of raised dots to communicate urgent messages at night. When Louis Braille saw the system, he looked at it from a different point of view, saw that the raised dots could be more than a method for night reading, and adapted them for the blind. Because of Louis Braille's creativity, millions of sightless people have benefited from the Braille system of printing and writing.

In the following sections you will learn to look at a subject from three different points of view. The first point of view "freezes" the subject in time; the second shows how the subject moves in time and space; and the third shows how the subject is made up of many parts and how all of these parts working together fit into a much larger background. These viewpoints can be written as three questions:

1. What is it? (What are the features or characteristics of the subject?)
2. How does the subject change or vary?
3. What are its relationships? (How do its parts work together? How is it related to a larger background?)

What Is It?

When you ask *What is it?* you ask about the appearance and definition of your subject—whether it is an object, a person, an idea, or a concept. For

---

[1]This section is based on ideas in *Rhetoric: Discovery and Change* by Richard E. Young, Alton L. Becker, and Kenneth E. Pike (New York: Harcourt Brace Jovanovich, 1971).

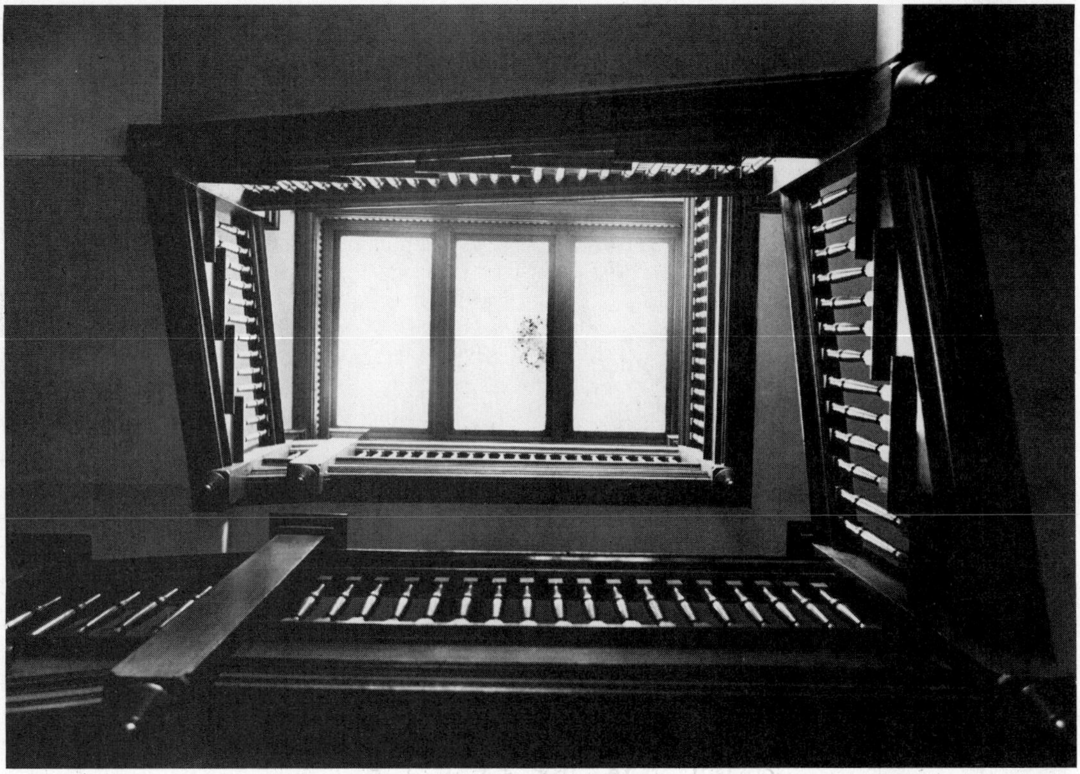

example, if you were to describe a bicycle, you would look at it as an object in itself, noting physical details, such as size, shape, color, design, and accessories. In a sense you would "freeze" the bicycle in time and space, describing it with words in the same way a photographer might show it in a close-up or "stop action" shot.

Comparing your object with similar objects will also point out its distinct features.

For example, how does this bicycle compare to other bicycles? Perhaps it is larger or smaller, in better or worse condition, has more or fewer gears, and so on. Showing how your subject is like or different from others paints an even sharper, clearer picture of it.

When your subject is an idea or a concept, such as the American system of democratic government, the first step is to define the subject. According to most dictionaries, the word *democracy* means "a government ruled by the people." The second step is to compare American democracy with similar forms of government. The British system of government, also a democracy, is like the American system in that both include representatives, elected by the people, who make the laws. The two governments also have differences: the head of the American government is the President, an elected official; the head of the British government is a king or queen, who inherits the throne.

Writing Practice 5

Write a paragraph describing in detail a familiar object or one you can observe at a "close-up" view. Before you begin, you might ask yourself the following questions about your subject.

1. What color is it?
2. What size is it?
3. What shape is it?
4. How much does it weigh?
5. How is it designed?
6. What details mark its surface?
7. Where is it located?
8. How does it compare with others like it?

Writing Practice 6

Choose one of the following ideas or concepts and write a paragraph describing it in detail. Since your subject is not a physical object, you cannot describe it by size, weight, or other physical details; instead, ask yourself questions such as the following ones.

1. How can it be defined? (You can check a dictionary to find out.)
2. How is it like similar words?
3. How is it different from similar words?
4. Where and when might you use this term?

IDEAS AND CONCEPTS

Honesty	Photosynthesis
Forgiveness	School
Good manners	Jazz
Entertainment	Champion
Work	

How Does It Change or Vary?

When you ask *How does it change or vary?* you consider how the subject or its parts change over time. Over a period of time, for example, a bicycle exposed to weather and hard use will show signs of wear and damage. The finish chips and peels and must be redone, or the leather seat begins to fray, or perhaps the front wheel is dented in an accident. How much can it change before it is no longer a bicycle?

You can also examine the way an idea or a concept changes over time. In describing how the American system of democratic government has changed since the Constitution was first written, you would note such changes as an increase in the size of the House of Representatives and the fact that women have been given the right to vote.

You can also ask how an abstract subject can vary without losing its identity. If the United States were to make the Presidency a hereditary office, would the government still be a democracy? If only people owning property worth $100,000 or more were allowed to vote, or if senators and representatives were elected for life, would the United States still have a democratic form of government?

Writing Practice 7

Choosing one of the following subjects or one of your own, write a paragraph describing how the subject changes over time and how much it can vary without losing its identity. Before you begin, ask yourself questions such as the following ones about your subject.

1. How has the subject changed over time?
2. Is the change caused by outside forces, such as weather, animals, or people?
3. How can the subject vary without losing its identity?

SUBJECTS

Your science or history textbook	Popular music
Men's or women's hairstyles	A shoe
The Olympic games	Horror movies

What Are Its Relationships?

When you ask *What are its relationships?* you consider how the parts of a subject are related to each other and how the subject itself is related to other subjects. For example, you can describe a bicycle by noting how the wheels, gears, and spokes work together to make the bicycle move. To understand the American system of democratic government, it is important to know how its parts—the Presidency, the Congress, and the Supreme Court—work together.

The whole subject also fits into a larger background and relates to other subjects. Perhaps your old bicycle is just one object you have discarded and left in the corner of the garage with roller skates, junior high school yearbooks, pictures of once favorite movie stars, and stuffed animals. All these objects may be part of a childhood you are leaving behind.

The American democratic government, a political system, is related to a national economic system that allows people to make, sell, and buy goods; a religious system that provides for spiritual needs; and an educational system that prepares students for adult life. In what way do these systems work together?

Writing Practice 8

After choosing a subject from the following list or making up one of your own, write a paragraph describing how the parts of the subject work together

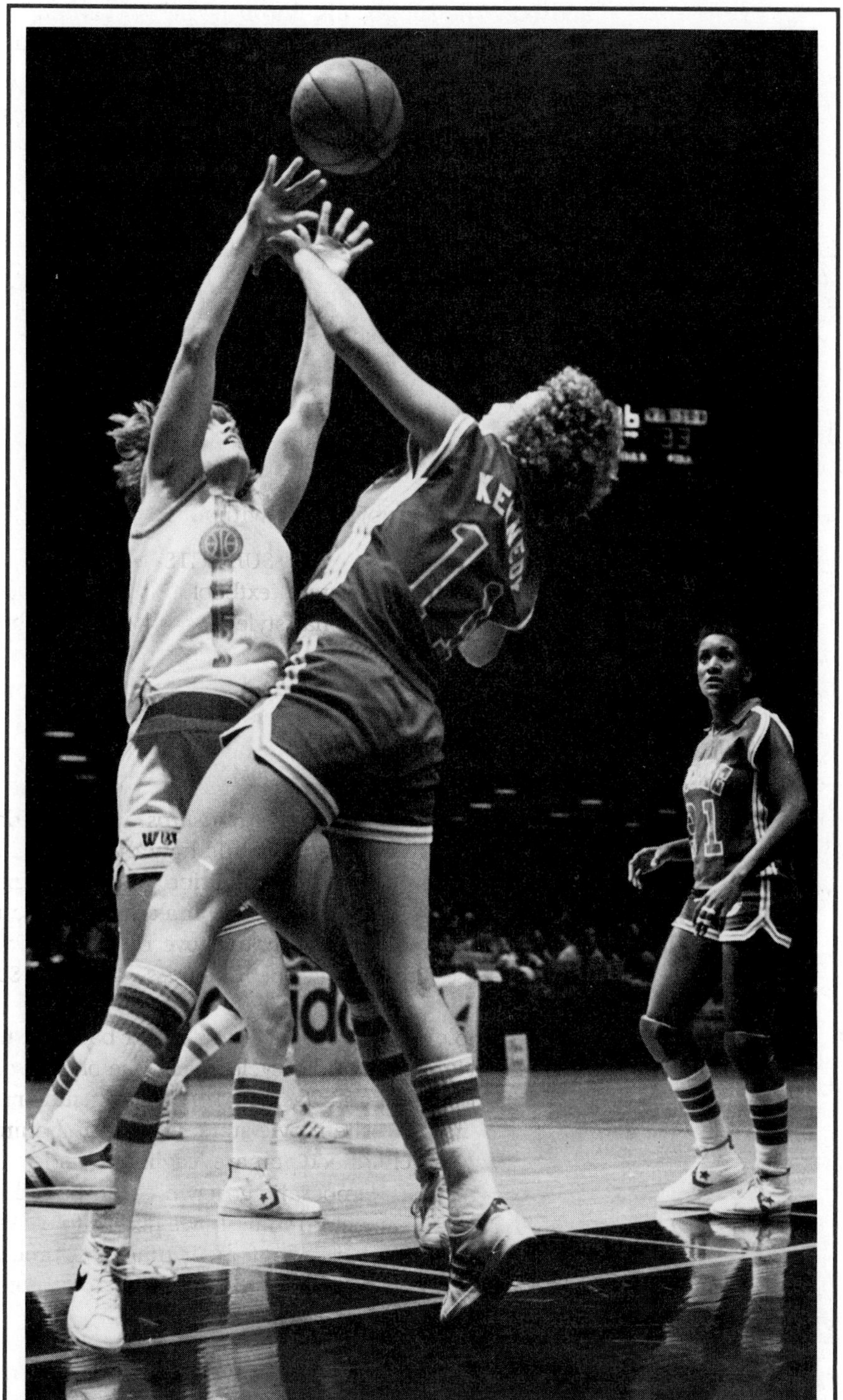

and how the subject fits into a larger background of subjects. Before you begin, ask yourself questions such as the following ones.

1. What are the parts of the subject?
2. How do these parts work together?
3. Of what larger system is the subject a part?
4. How do other systems work with the subject?

SUBJECTS

Telephone
Television
Ballpoint pen
Alarm clock
School student council

Writing Practice 9

Use one of the following viewpoints to describe in a paragraph what you see in the photograph on page 35.

1. The subject itself
   (Describe an individual player as she appears now.)
2. How the subject changes over time
   (Describe the player moments before the picture was taken, as the picture was taken, and moments after the picture was taken.)
3. The relationships of the subject
   (Describe how the subject relates to the ball, the other players, and the crowd.)

Writing Practice 10

Use each of the following viewpoints to write a complete description of an old car in a junkyard or in a parking lot.

1. The subject itself
   (Describe one of the cars as it appears now.)
2. How the subject changes over time
   (Describe the car as it must have looked when it was new and tell how it changed over the years.)
3. The relationships of the subject
   (Describe the junkyard as you think it would look and tell how the car fits into the junkyard.)

A New Set of Questions

In this and the following sections, you will learn a new set of questions for gathering information, called the *Pentad.* (The Pentad was devised by an important American thinker named Kenneth Burke.) The Pentad questions

look like the basic *who? what? where? when? why?* and *how?* questions, but there are important differences. The five questions can be phrased in the following way.

1. What was done? (What was the action? What happened?)
2. Who did it? (Who committed the act or caused the action to happen?)
3. How was it done? (By what means or with what instrument was it done?)
4. Where and when was it done? (What was the time and the place?)
5. Why was it done? (What was the purpose of the act?)

The five Pentad questions can lead to other questions that help you think about your subject. The following questions are examples of ones you might ask to explore Edward Hicks' painting, "The Peaceable Kingdom," which is reproduced on this page. As you read, ask the questions to yourself and jot down the answers on a sheet of paper.

1. The Action: What is happening?

First the painting itself is an action because the artist painted it. However, the painting itself portrays several actions. Ask the following questions about what you see happening in "The Peaceable Kingdom."

a. What is happening? What activities do you see? What are the figures in the background doing? What are the children doing? What are the animals doing?

b. Look at the postures of the figures in the painting. Do they tell you anything about the people or animals involved?

c. Notice the variety of kinds of animals in the painting. Would you expect to find these animals together in such a peaceful setting?

d. Does there appear to be any connection between the figures of the men in the background and the figures of the children and animals in the foreground?

2. The Actors: Who causes the action or is in the action?

a. The first person who caused the action, the painting itself, is the artist who painted it. Can you guess anything about the artist from the painting itself? Since you know the artist's name (Edward Hicks), you can find out more about him in your library.

b. Who are the figures in the painting? Can you tell from their dress or belongings what kind of people they are?

c. Can you identify each of the animals represented in the painting? Do they look realistic? If you think they do not, how would you describe them?

3. The Scene: Where and when is the action taking place?

a. From details of dress, where do you think this scene takes place?

b. Look closely at the details of trees, river bank, and vegetation. In what part of the world would you expect to find a similar scene? From a realistic viewpoint would you ordinarily find lions, leopards, and tigers in such a setting?

c. What shades of light and dark do you see? What time of day might it be? What time of year? What century?

4. The Means: How is the action done?

a. To answer the question *How is the action done?* you need to think again of the painting itself as the action. What instruments has the painter used to make this painting?

b. What contrasts has the painter used to shade the painting? What has he emphasized? Is the emphasis on people, animals, scenery, or the relationships among them?

c. If the scene is not a realistic one, how has the painter drawn figures and background? What effect on the viewer does this way of depicting life have?

d. What sense of texture is in the painting? What suggestion of emotion is there? Can you imagine sounds that might be part of the scene?

e. There is another way to look at how the action is done in this painting. Imagine what has happened before this scene took place and ask yourself this question: How has the peaceful gathering of animals and children come about? How has the peaceful gathering of the traders come about?

5. The Reason: Why is this action done?

a. First consider the painter's reasons for painting this work. Why do you think he painted "The Peaceable Kingdom"? Is he presenting a beautiful scene with pleasant figures and a happy feeling? Why would an artist want to do that? Might there be other reasons for painting this work? What might they be?

b. Perhaps the painter is making a statement about a subject of importance to him and to viewers. Can you say what that statement might be?

c. Of what significance is the title of the painting? Does the title suggest something about the painter's purpose?

d. Why do you think young children were chosen by the painter to include in the grouping of animals? Is there a relationship between young children and the peaceful attitude of the animals?

e. What comment does the painting make by combining a scene between traders and a scene of children among animals?

f. What is the mood of this painting? What feeling do you get from it? Is it a mood or feeling you think was intended by the artist?

Writing Practice 11

From the notes you made while asking yourself the questions about "The Peaceable Kingdom," write a short description of the painting. Include appropriate ideas and details you thought of during the questioning process.

Asking Questions About the Action

The first questions in the Pentad are about the *action.*

An *action* is any physical or mental thing that has happened or is happening. An event, such as climbing a mountain, is an action. Stories, poems, plays, songs, television shows, movies, paintings, and buildings are also actions because they are the result of someone's mental and physical action. A thought is a mental action. The thought, for example, that high school graduation requirements should be changed or that the television show *Star Trek* makes a serious comment on human nature involves the mental action of putting together ideas and reasons.

The following questions can be asked about the action.

1. What is it?
2. What happened?
3. What is happening?
4. What will happen?
5. What could happen?

Even though the answer may seem obvious, always ask yourself Question 1. Question 2 is for actions in the past. If you write about an event from your childhood, for example, you would ask yourself *What happened?* For present actions ask yourself Question 3. Questions 4 and 5 are about future actions or the results of actions. Asking yourself all these questions will show how an action has changed over time.

One writer gathered the following notes by applying the *action* questions to the thought *The television show* Star Trek *is more than an adventure show; it also makes serious comments about human nature.*

1. What is it?

   Star Trek is a long-running, science fiction television show that began in the late 1960s. Reruns of the show can still be seen on many television stations.

2. What happened?

   Since its beginning, the creators of *Star Trek* were determined to present more than a simple adventure show. From its first episode *Star Trek* has explored human nature as humans explored the stars.

3. What is happening?

   Star Trek is seen today in syndicated reruns on many independent stations. The show is still so popular that many viewers have seen every episode several times and yet continue to watch faithfully.

4. What will happen?

   Old episodes of *Star Trek* will probably continue to be shown because of its popularity.

5. What could happen?

   It is possible, but unlikely, that the surviving members of the original cast would reunite to film new episodes. In such an event the show would probably continue its longstanding tradition of treating serious themes.

Asking Questions About Actors

The second set of questions in the Pentad is about the *actors*, the people or things involved in the action or responsible for the action.

The following questions can be asked for complete information about the actors.

1. Who or what is responsible for the action?
2. Who are the people involved in the action?
3. What are the actors like?

Applying the *actor* questions to the *Star Trek* subject led to the following information.

1. Who are the people responsible for the action?

   Gene Rodenberry, a Hollywood scriptwriter, created the show. He had the idea for years, but many people told him it would never work.

2. Who are the people involved in the action?

   The three main characters on the show are Captain James T. Kirk, the commander of the *Enterprise;* Dr. Leonard McCoy, the chief medical officer; and Commander Spock, the first officer. The entire crew of the *Enterprise,* 430 people, are also involved. One fourth of the crew are women, with duties ranging from engineers to security guards.

3. What are the actors like?

   Dr. Leonard McCoy is an emotional person; he approaches problems from a human angle. Mr. Spock, the son of a Vulcan father and a human mother, uses only logic to make his decisions. (Long ago the Vulcans eliminated emotions and learned to operate solely on logic and reason.) Captain Kirk, who is responsible for final decisions, is a highly intelligent, balanced person, using both reason and emotion to carry out his responsibilities.

Writing Practice 12

Select one of the following physical or mental actions or make up one of your own. Then ask the *action* and *actors* questions that apply to your topic and write them on a sheet of paper. Beneath each question write out an answer.

1. My grandparent (or other person) has been an important influence on my life.
2. ________ , a game show on television, is ridiculous.
3. The courage of ________ , a person with a serious disability, is an inspiration to everyone.
4. This (object, place, or event) has been important in my life.
5. My first memories of school are good (or bad) ones.
6. My community needs strict rules about animals kept as pets.
7. Martin Luther King, Jr., made a great contribution to the fight against prejudice.
8. My first part-time job is one I will never forget.
9. A favorite book helps me forget my problems for a while.
10. A person doesn't have to be an athlete to be a champion.

Asking Questions About Scene

The third part of the Pentad asks questions about *scene,* or the time and place where the action occurs.

Scene questions, such as the following ones, ask for descriptive details that help re-create the scene.

1. Where is the action happening?
2. Where did the action happen?
3. Where will the action happen?
4. What is the place like?

5. When did the action happen?
6. What is the historical background of the time?

Applying the *scene* questions to the *Star Trek* subject produces the following information.

1. Where is the action happening?
   Most of the *Star Trek* action takes place on the starship *Enterprise* or on alien planets where the *Enterprise* lands.
2. What is the place like?
   The *Enterprise* is a large, saucer-shaped spaceship with two large engineering pods containing technical equipment. On the ship are spacious crew quarters, a sick bay, and even a large garden room. Most of the planets the *Enterprise* visits are "Class M" planets, where humans can survive without special equipment. The planet Vulcan, the home of Mr. Spock, is a hot, dusty planet with a thin atmosphere. The ears of Mr. Spock and other Vulcans are cupped to capture the sound waves in that thin air.
3. When did the action happen?
   The time of *Star Trek* is not explicitly stated, but it probably happens about A.D. 2300.
4. What is the historical background of the time?
   At this time the problems of the earth have been solved. The earth has not been destroyed by a nuclear war or suffocated with pollution. Many planets coexist in peace and have joined together to form the "Limited Federation of Planets."

Asking Questions About Means

The fourth question in the Pentad, *How is the action done?* is applied even when the actors are not human.

The *means* question can be applied to the subject *The television show* Star Trek *makes serious comments about human nature* to gather the following information.

1. What methods are used to make these serious comments?
   The three main characters are used to show that people need both logic and emotion. Mr. Spock operates on logic and Dr. McCoy on emotion. The success of Captain Kirk, when he uses both logic and emotion, shows that humans should base actions on both logic and emotion.
2. The plots are also used to comment on human nature.
   One particular show involved a rocklike creature that was destroying everything in its path and interfering with mining operations on an alien planet. Captain Kirk's mission was to find the creature, destroy it, and restore the mining operations. During his investigation, however, Kirk found that the mines were destroying the creature's eggs and, therefore, the creature's ability to produce offspring. This show pointed out how important it is for leaders to gain knowledge before they act.

Asking Questions About Purpose

The last question in the Pentad, about reason, asks *Why is this action done?*

Not all actions have a reason. Accidentally knocking over a chair is an action, but you may not have done it for a reason. Only when the actors do something for a purpose is there a reason. The following information can be gathered when the reason question is applied to the subject *The television show* Star Trek *makes serious comments about human nature.*

1. What is the purpose of these serious comments? Why are they made?

   I think the creator and the writers of *Star Trek* make these statements to show the potential of human beings. Working together and using both reason and emotion, human beings can solve problems and make the world a better place for everyone.

Writing Practice 13

For this assignment use the topic you selected for Writing Practice 12 or select a new one. Ask yourself the *scene*, *means*, and *purpose* questions that apply to your topic. Then write the questions and your answers to them on a sheet of paper.

3 The Paragraph

Paragraph Writing

A paragraph can fulfill several functions. In dialogue (written conversation) a new paragraph indicates a change of speaker. In an essay, special paragraphs may serve as introductions or conclusions, while long pieces of writing often contain brief paragraphs, or transitions, that help the reader move from one idea to another. In exposition (writing that explains a topic), an important kind of paragraph is a group of related sentences that focuses on a central idea or thought. In this chapter you will learn to write such paragraphs.

The Topic-Restriction-Illustration-Pattern

The *TRI (Topic-Restriction-Illustration) pattern* is the framework for many paragraphs. The first two parts of the pattern (*Topic* and *Restriction*) identify the central idea of the paragraph. *Illustration*, the third part of the pattern, further develops the central idea with examples, reasons, comparisons, or other specific statements.

The *topic sentence* of a paragraph introduces the central idea or *topic* that the rest of the paragraph develops. Since the topic sentence covers everything that will be discussed in its paragraph, it will be more general than the other sentences. Assume that a writer chooses the subject *Women's rights.* A single paragraph cannot develop every idea about women's rights, so the writer must limit the subject to a topic: *Women's rights in ancient Greece*, for instance. This one clear, central idea can now be stated in a topic sentence:

In ancient Greece women did not have the same rights as men.

The writer's next step is to *restrict* the topic so that it can be developed in a single paragraph:

> Greek women were barred from participating in certain religious ceremonies and from taking part in important festivals.

Once the topic is restricted, the writer can add *illustrations,*—specific statements that support, explain, or expand the main idea more clearly and completely through facts, examples, reasons, comparisons and contrasts, or other methods of development.

Topic:	In ancient Greece women did not have the same rights as men.
Restriction:	Greek women were barred from participating in certain religious ceremonies and from taking part in important festivals.
Illustration:	For example, women were not allowed even as spectators at the famous Olympiad, the festival known today as the Olympics.
Illustration:	Instead, women began a festival of their own called the Herea.
Illustration:	This was also an international amateur sports competition but with fewer events and much less public acclaim.

The finished paragraph—a topic sentence, a restriction sentence, and three sentences illustrating the restricted topic—would have the following form.

> In ancient Greece women did not have the same rights as men. Greek women were barred from participating in certain religious ceremonies and from taking part in important festivals. For example, women were not allowed even as spectators at the famous Olympiad, the festival known today as the Olympics. Instead, women began a festival of their own called the Herea. This was also an international amateur sports competition but with fewer events and much less public acclaim.

Writing Practice 1

Use the Preparing to Write section that follows to help you with ideas for this paragraph.

On a sheet of paper, develop each of the following paragraphs by supplying the missing elements. In some of the paragraphs, you are given the topic and restriction sentences; in others you must supply the restriction. In each paragraph write appropriate illustration sentences. For the fifth paragraph you are asked to use your own topic.

1.	Topic:	Music is often called "the universal language."
	Restriction:	One kind of music that appeals to a large number of people is country and western.
	Illustration:	
	Illustration:	
2.	Topic:	Volunteer youth organizations provide essential services to hospitals and their patients.
	Restriction:	
	Illustration:	
	Illustration:	

3. Topic: Sports can be dangerous.
Restriction:
Illustration:
Illustration:
Illustration:

4. Topic: Exciting movies make good entertainment.
Restriction:
Illustration:
Illustration:
Illustration:

5. Topic:
Restriction:
Illustration:
Illustration:
Illustration:

Preparing to Write

Brainstorming, one of the methods discussed in the chapter "Discovering Subject Matter" on pages 27–29, can be used to find ideas for paragraphs. Suppose, for example, that you want to write a paragraph based on the restriction *Some sports can be dangerous.* Write that statement on a sheet of paper and quickly list any and all ideas relating to it that come to your mind. Perhaps you will recall the time your favorite player was injured or the day you accidentally broke a window playing sandlot baseball. Also, consider sports that are not usually dangerous, such as croquet or badminton, imagining how they could have dangerous results. Put down everything that comes into your mind without making judgments about the quality of the ideas. When you have finished, look over your work to find appropriate ideas for your paragraph.

Writing Practice 2

Using one of the topic-restriction-illustration patterns you wrote for Writing Practice 1, write a complete paragraph. Include more illustration sentences if they are needed and add any words necessary to make your paragraph easy to follow.

Combining the Topic and Restriction Sentences

One important way to vary the topic-restriction-illustration pattern is to combine the topic and restriction parts into one sentence. When you combine these parts, you limit your topic in the first sentence. To develop your paragraph you need only add illustration sentences.

The topic-restriction sentence is demonstrated in the following paragraph about the *commedia dell' arte*, a type of Italian comedy that enjoyed great popularity from the sixteenth through the eighteenth century. The topic and restriction are stated in the first sentence: "Of all the *commedia dell' arte's* contributions to the theatre, perhaps the greatest is its legacy of stock characters." Here the general topic is *the contributions of the* commedia dell' arte; the restriction is *the specific contribution of stock characters*. The remaining sentences are illustrations of the topic-restriction sentence:

> Of all the *commedia dell' arte's* contributions to the theatre, perhaps the greatest is its legacy of stock characters. It created *Arlecchino*, the acrobatic clown or harlequin whose job it was to keep the crowd laughing. He wore a black mask, motley clothes, and carried a wooden sword, forerunner of the slapstick. It created the stock character of the sophisticated rogue—a coward at heart—who would do anything for money. *Brighella* was his original name in the *commedia*. Then there was the rich, complacent merchant, always miserly and mean, who spent his time counting money and guarding his beautiful young wife or daughter. He was called *Pantalone*. The list continues with caricatures of the pompous, learned doctor (known as *Il Dottore*), the boastful but easily cowed professional soldier (*Il Capitano*), and the gossipy old woman (*La Ruffiana*) who takes pleasure in trying to keep the lovers apart. As for the lovers, he was the handsome *Inamorato* and she the exquisite *Inamorata*, eternally in love and destined for one another, a destiny often thwarted but always eventually fulfilled in the turnings and comic upheavals of each *commedia dell' arte* plot.

Writing Practice 3

Each of the following items is a combination topic-restriction sentence. Select two of these. On a separate sheet of paper, write out three or four illustration sentences for each combined topic-restriction sentence.

1. The sidewalks were full of people on the first warm day in spring.
2. Despite all our efforts the car simply would not start.
3. Training for athletic competition is a long and painstaking job.
4. Everyone had a reason for not finishing the assignment.
5. The telephone has easily been one of modern science's most important contributions to improve our lives.

Varying the Basic Paragraph Patterns

Using variations of the TRI (Topic-Restriction-Illustration) pattern gives the writer more options and greater flexibility. In the following paragraph, for example, the topic is introduced in the first sentence and restricted in the second sentence.

> Today meteorologists provide day-by-day information about the approach of harsh winter weather. [TOPIC] A hundred years ago, however, rural families depended on folk superstitions to predict the winter's severity. [RESTRICTION]

For example, heavy coats on spring buds were thought to be an omen of a harsh winter. [ILLUSTRATION] Tough, thick skins on the apples harvested in early autumn were another sign that the winter would be severe. [ILLUSTRATION] The paper nests of white-faced hornets were also closely observed, for nests placed unusually high suggested deep snow. [ILLUSTRATION] Cutting into the Thanksgiving turkey was exciting not only for the hungry children gathered at the table, but also for their parents, who believed a dark breastbone in the turkey meant long winter storms. [ILLUSTRATION] Unusually thick feathers on that same turkey would have been noted during butchering as another indication of rough weather ahead. [ILLUSTRATION] On the other hand, an extra-wide brown band on a woolly bear caterpillar was a sign of a mild winter. [ILLUSTRATION]

The TRI pattern can also be varied by reversing the order, placing the illustrations at the beginning of the paragraph and the restriction at the end. Notice how the TRI pattern is reversed in the following paragraph.

A hundred years ago cutting into the Thanksgiving turkey was exciting not only for the hungry children gathered at the table, but also for their parents, who believed a dark breastbone in the turkey meant long winter storms. [ILLUSTRATION] Unusually thick feathers on that same turkey would have been noted during butchering as another indication of rough weather ahead. [ILLUSTRATION] Heavy coats on spring buds and tough, thick skins on the apples harvested in early autumn were thought to be omens of a severe winter. [ILLUSTRATION] On the other hand, an extra-wide brown band on a woolly bear caterpillar was a sign of a mild winter. [ILLUSTRATION] Even the paper nests of white-faced hornets were closely observed, for nests placed unusually high suggested deep snow. [ILLUSTRATION] Today meteorologists provide day-by-day information about the approach of harsh winter weather. [TOPIC] A hundred years ago, however, rural families depended on folk superstitions to predict the winter's severity. [RESTRICTION]

In the next paragraph (another variation of the TRI pattern), the topic and restriction appear in the middle of the paragraph.

A hundred years ago cutting into the Thanksgiving turkey was exciting not only for the hungry children gathered at the table, but also for their parents, who believed a dark breastbone in the turkey meant long winter storms. [ILLUSTRATION] Unusually thick feathers on that same turkey would have been noted during butchering as another indication of rough weather ahead. [ILLUSTRATION] Today meteorologists provide day-by-day information about the approach of harsh winter weather. [TOPIC] A hundred years ago, however, rural families depended on folk superstitions to predict the winter's severity. [RESTRICTION] For example, heavy coats on spring buds were thought to be an omen of a harsh winter. [ILLUSTRATION] Tough, thick skins on the apples harvested in early autumn were another sign that the winter would be severe. [ILLUSTRATION] On the other hand, an extra-wide brown band on a woolly bear caterpillar was a sign of a mild winter. [ILLUSTRATION] Even the paper nests of white-faced hornets were closely observed, for nests placed unusually high suggested deep snow. [ILLUSTRATION]

Writing Practice 4

Use the Checklist for Revising Paragraphs on pages 49–50 to revise this assignment.

Use the following topic, restriction, and illustrations to write two paragraphs. In the first paragraph vary the basic TRI pattern by beginning with illustrations and ending with the restricted topic. For the second paragraph write a topic sentence, follow it with the restriction, and add the illustrations. You may have to change words or add *for example*, *also*, *another*, or similar words to connect the statements in your paragraph.

Topic:	People have not always dressed sensibly.
Restriction:	The history of fashion shows that people have often worn clothing that was not only uncomfortable but also harmful.
Illustration:	A knight's armor in the fourteenth century was so heavy and unwieldy that he could not stand up without help, making him an easy target once off his horse.
Illustration:	During the nineteenth century it was popular for women to wear whalebone corsets so tight that breathing was difficult.
Illustration:	Both men and women in different eras have favored shoes with exaggerated toes or heels that made walking awkward and even dangerous.

For Your Journal

What folk superstitions are common in your family or the area where you live? Is spilling salt bad luck, for example? Does anyone you know predict the weather or the change of seasons by looking at signs of nature? In your journal write about superstitions and what they mean or describe someone you know who takes superstitions seriously. You might want to formulate a class list of superstitions or use the library to find information about how certain superstitions originated.

Revising and Proofreading Paragraphs

When writers *revise* their writing, they reexamine it—adding, taking out, or changing words and sentences until they are satisfied that the writing is their best work. Use the following checklist as a guide for revising your paragraphs. As you do, look closely at the structure of your paragraph. The paragraph should have a clear central idea appearing either in the restriction or the topic-restriction sentence. Each illustration sentence should develop the central idea. If a sentence does not present new information that relates to the central idea, rewrite it or take it out.

After revising your paragraph, *proofread* it carefully. When you proofread, you reread your writing, correcting errors in spelling, punctuation, and grammar. The checklist on pages 20–21 is a good guide for proofreading.

Checklist for Revising Paragraphs

On page 50 is a complete checklist for revising paragraphs. Your teacher may ask you now to concentrate only on those items you have studied. As you work through this chapter, refer back to this checklist for help in revising and check your writing against those points you have covered in your study.

1. The paragraph has a clear central idea.
2. The central idea is sufficiently restricted to be developed in a paragraph.
3. The central idea is adequately developed with specific illustration sentences.
4. Each illustration sentence relates clearly to the central idea and presents new information.
5. The writer uses some method of organization to arrange the sentences in a clear way.
6. Transition words, pronouns, paraphrase, and repetition are used to improve the paragraph coherence.
7. The writer uses an appropriate method of development: descriptive detail, facts and statistics, examples, reasons, comparison, or a combination of methods.
8. The concluding sentence restates the central idea in a new and interesting way.

Question-Answer Paragraphs

A second paragraph pattern you will find useful begins by asking a question and then suggesting an answer. Sometimes, the question will appear in the same paragraph with its answer. At other times, especially when the answer is a long one covering several paragraphs, the question or questions come in a separate paragraph. The following two-paragraph question-answer from Simone de Beauvoir's *All Said and Done* shows how this pattern works.

> I love travelling as much as ever I did. In 1962 I had lost my appetite for it, but the taste has come back to me. During these last ten years I have visited and revisited a great many places. What have these explorations brought me?
>
> In the first place they form an integral part of a much wider project that still means a great deal to me—the project of knowing. To be sure, seeing is not enough: one can pass through towns and countryside without understanding anything about either. I need conversation and reading to give me a clear notion of a country, but they alone cannot provide me with the equivalent of the flesh-and-blood presence of things. When I walk about the streets, mingling with the crowd, a town and its inhabitants begin to exist for me with a fullness that words cannot possibly convey. And then I am far more interested in places that have a connection with my actual life than in those that I have called to mind only by means of words.

Integral means "essential."

To the question "What have these explorations brought me?" the writer begins to answer by telling what, "In the first place," visiting and revisiting towns and countryside mean to her.

The question-answer pattern often presents a *problem* in question form, followed by several sentences that offer the *solution* to the problem. Notice in the following example that the paragraph begins with introductory sentences that explain the situation. Then the question "What was causing this drop in water pressure?" is asked, followed by an explanation that gives the solution to the problem.

Statement of the Problem

In the late 1940s city water department engineers in a large American city noticed that water pressure began to drop suddenly at regular thirty-minute intervals during the evening hours. Never having experienced this situation before, the engineers were puzzled as to its cause.

Question

Solution and Answer

What was causing the drop in water pressure? In order to answer this question, the department made an intensive investigation to find the reasons behind the problem. By questioning a large number of people in the city, investigators found that about every thirty minutes between 7 and 10 o'clock in the evening, many faucets were being turned on and toilets flushed. From these facts the water department reasoned that television, at that time a new form of evening entertainment, was the cause of the phenomenon. Viewers were leaving their sets during station breaks and program changes—about every half hour—to use their kitchens and bathrooms. Of course, not everyone had television sets, nor did all those who had them leave as programs changed. But enough television viewers did, so as to account for the problem.

Writing Practice 5

Use the Preparing to Write section that follows to help you with ideas for this assignment.

Choose a subject from the following suggestions or use one of your own. Then phrase the subject as a question and write a short paragraph that uses the question-answer pattern. Your question may present a problem, if you wish. If it does, be sure your answer gives a solution to the problem.

1. Explaining a game such as hockey to a student from another country
2. Training an animal
3. Providing care for the elderly or for preschool children
4. Communicating with hearing impaired or visually impaired persons
5. Maintaining a bicycle, motorcycle, or car

Preparing to Write

Before you begin writing your question-answer paragraph, turn the topic you chose into a question that you can answer. Then jot down several facts, reasons, or illustration you can use in the answer to the question.

Example

TOPIC	QUESTION	ANSWER
Money for vacation	*What is the best way for me to make enough money for summer vacation?*	*Get a part-time job at the local market.* *Do neighborhood chores.* *Tutor summer school students.* *Make and sell artificial flowers.*

Unity in the Paragraph

An effective paragraph has *unity*—that is, the sentences combine to produce a single, complete unit of thought.

A paragraph is unified when it states only one central idea that is developed by all other statements in the paragraph. The following paragraph from Donald Sandner's *Navaho Symbols of Healing* is unified because it has one central idea. What is it?[1]

> The position of women in Navaho culture is important in several ways. For one thing, they own most of the property. For another, lineage is reckoned through the mother: a Navaho *belongs* to his mother's clan, and is said to be merely "born for" his father's. Furthermore, the women have a strong and decisive voice in family affairs and are responsible for much of the work, including crop raising, care of the animals, weaving (a major source of income), and household chores.

This paragraph is unified because it presents information about one central idea: "The position of women in Navaho culture is important in several ways." All the other sentences relate to the central idea, providing more information about it.

You can test the unity of a paragraph by checking the relationship between each sentence and the central idea. Be certain that each statement relates to the restriction of the topic. The following paragraph, for example, lacks unity because the writer has included sentences that do not relate to its restricted topic: "The origin of most sports is a mystery." Notice how the two underlined sentences distract the reader from the central idea.

> The origin of most sports is a mystery. We do know that some sports had their beginnings in the necessities of survival: hunting, fishing, and swimming—all were at one time skills people needed to live. <u>I myself enjoy fishing very much, but I don't believe in killing larger animals.</u> Other sports originated with the nobility. Court tennis, falconry, and archery (although the latter certainly had its roots in necessary skills) were at one time enjoyed only by members of the royal family and by the nobility. On the other hand, games such as football and boxing originated with the masses. <u>Football may look wild and uncontrolled, but much skill goes into planning and executing the maneuvers.</u> Nonetheless, we do not know if these sports developed gradually, or if one person was instrumental in inventing them. One exception is basketball, which we know was invented by James Naismith of Springfield, Massachusetts, in 1891. The other great inventors of games, if there are any, remain anonymous.

Even when the central idea appears at the end or in the middle of a paragraph, all the sentences illustrating that idea should relate to it. In the next example, from Rachel Carson's *Silent Spring*, the writer introduces the topic (dependence of animal life on water, soil, and plants) in the first sentence but does not restrict it until the middle of the paragraph: "Our attitude

---

[1]From *Navaho Symbols of Healing* by Donald Sandner. Reprinted by permission of Harcourt Brace Jovanovich, Inc.

toward plants is a singularly narrow one." As you read, think how the sentences before and after the central idea relate to it.[1]

> Water, soil, and the earth's green mantle of plants make up the world that supports the animal life of the earth. Although modern man seldom remembers the fact, he could not exist without the plants that harness the sun's energy and manufacture the basic foodstuffs he depends upon for life. Our attitude toward plants is a singularly narrow one. If we see any immediate utility in a plant we foster it. If for any reason we find its presence undesirable or merely a matter of indifference, we may condemn it to destruction forthwith. Besides the various plants that are poisonous to man or his livestock, or crowd out food plants, many are marked for destruction merely because, according to our narrow view, they happen to be in the wrong place at the wrong time. Many others are destroyed merely because they happen to be associates of the unwanted plants.

Writing Practice 6

Use the Checklist for Revising Paragraphs on pages 49–50 to revise this assignment.

Write both a topic sentence and then a restriction sentence or a combined topic-restriction sentence for one of the following broad subjects. Then write a paragraph that illustrates your topic. Remember that the topic and restriction sentences or the topic-restriction sentence may appear at the beginning, middle, or end of your paragraph.

1. Being the eldest (middle/youngest/only) child
2. Finding a job
3. Inventing a much-needed product
4. The ideal school
5. The major problems of teenagers today

The Concluding Sentence

You can improve the unity of some paragraphs by adding a *final*, or *concluding, sentence* that restates the central idea in a new and interesting way or that sums up the information presented.

The following paragraph about the role of air power in World War I develops the central idea in the first sentence. As you read, notice how the writer restates this idea at the end of the paragraph.[2]

Reconnaissance means "exploratory journey."

> With the passage of time, legends have arisen over the accomplishments of some of the World War I aces, but most historians agree that the role played by air power during this struggle was more romantic than decisive. The most important missions the airplane carried out were reconnaissance and artillery fire control. And when the war bogged down into static front-line trench warfare and increasingly effective camouflage techniques evolved, aerial recon-

---

[1]From "Earth's Green Mantle" in *Silent Spring* by Rachel Carson. Copyright © 1962 by Rachel Carson. Reprinted by permission of Houghton Mifflin Company, Laurence Pollinger Limited, and the Estate of the late Rachel Carson. Published in Great Britain by Hamish Hamilton Ltd.

[2]From *The National Air and Space Museum* by C. D. B. Bryan. Copyright © 1979 by the Smithsonian Institution, published by Harry N. Abrams, Inc. Reprinted by permission of the publisher.

> naissance became less and less significant. No airplane or Zeppelin sank or even seriously disabled any major naval vessel. No war industry was halted by strategic bombing. No major battle's outcome was decided by either control of the air or lack of its control. And so, even though vast technical progress was made in aviation development during World War I, what one celebrates are the men and not so much the machines.

The central idea of the paragraph is that although World War I flying aces became legendary, the role of the airplane during the war was not significant. Notice how the concluding sentence returns to that idea: "And so, even though vast technical progress was made in aviation development during World War I, what one celebrates are the men and not so much the machines." This final sentence accomplishes two things: (1) it gives more information about the topic, telling readers that during World War I technical progress was made in aviation; and (2) it restates the central idea in a new and interesting way.

In the following paragraph from Ralph Waldo Emerson's essay "Self-Reliance" (1841), the final sentence summarizes a main idea in seven simple and memorable words. As you read the excerpt, notice how Emerson's use of language differs from the way we speak and write today. How, for example, does Emerson use the word *man* in the expression ". . . if you would be a man, . . ."? What is he referring to when he mentions "aged ladies"?

> A foolish consistency is the hobgoblin of little minds, adored by little statesmen and philosophers and divines. With consistency a great soul has simply nothing to do. He may as well concern himself with his shadow on the wall. Out upon your guarded lips! Sew them up with packthread, do. Else, if you would be a man, speak what you think today in words as hard as cannon balls, and tomorrow speak what tomorrow thinks in hard words again, though it contradict every thing you said today. Ah, then, exclaim the aged ladies, you shall be sure to be misunderstood. Misunderstood! It is a right fool's word. Is it so bad to be misunderstood? Pythagoras was misunderstood, and Socrates, and Jesus, and Luther, and Copernicus, and Galileo, and Newton, and every pure and wise spirit that ever took flesh. To be great is to be misunderstood.

Writing Practice 7

Use the Checklist for Revising Paragraphs on pages 49–50 to revise this assignment.

After selecting one of the following subjects or a subject of your own, write both a topic and restriction sentence or a topic-restriction sentence on a sheet of paper. Then write a paragraph based on your sentence, paying close attention to paragraph unity and ending with an effective concluding sentence.

1. Why conflict sometimes occurs between parents and teenagers
2. How the "inner you" differs from the image others have of you
3. A memory about a person who is special to you
4. The advantages (or disadvantages) of a part-time job
5. Why you like a particular sport or hobby

Coherence in Paragraphs

In *coherent paragraphs* (paragraphs that make sense and are easy to follow), the illustration sentences are organized in a clear way.

In a paragraph that describes a person, place, or thing, writers may organize the illustration sentences by their location in space *(spatial organization).* In a paragraph about an event or a series of actions, writers often use *chronological order,* discussing what happened first, what followed, and what happened last. In a paragraph illustrated with reasons, writers often arrange the reasons from least important to most important, using *order of importance.*

In the following paragraph Arthur M. Schlesinger, Jr., uses *chronological order* to describe the unhappy progression of events during the Great Depression.[1]

> Across the country the dismal process was beginning, ushering in a new life for millions of Americans. In the twenties wage earners in general found ample employment, satisfaction in life, hope for the future. Now came the slowdown—only three days of work a week, then perhaps two, then the layoff. And then the search for a new job—at first vigorous and hopeful; then sober; then desperate; the long lines before the employment offices, the eyes straining for words of hope on the chalked boards, the unending walk from one plant to the next, the all-night wait to be first for possible work in the morning. And the inexorable news, brusque impersonality concealing fear: "No help wanted here" . . . "We don't need anybody" . . . "Move along, Mac, move along."

Inexorable means "unalterable."

In the following paragraph from "A Scottish Childhood" by Christian Miller, notice how the writer uses a *spatial order* based on the physical relationships between items to give readers a clear picture of the towers and chimneys on a Scottish castle. What relationship exists between the enclosed area and the nail-studded door? Between the rooftop and the iron railings?[2]

> The top of the tower was flat. It was divided into two parts. Where the stairs ended, a trapdoor led to the higher part, an enclosed area a few yards square, carrying only the flagstaff. At one side, a heavy, nail-studded door opened onto a lead-covered rooftop, surrounded by iron railings. Here were the chimneys of the central tower—the big one, which plunged straight down to the dining room, and the smaller ones leading to the library, schoolroom, and other rooms in the tower. Here, too, were the mystery chimneys, from fireplaces in rooms that nobody could find. We tied a bell on the end of a rope and lowered it down these chimneys. Yard after yard of rope vanished over the edge of the chimney pot. One of us jerked the end while others ran round the rooms below, listening for the sound of the bell; it rang, muffled, in the thickness of a wall.

A *flagstaff* is a flagpole.

---

[1]From *The Crisis of the Old Order 1919–1933* by Arthur M. Schlesinger, Jr. Copyright © 1957 by Arthur M. Schlesinger. Reprinted by permission of Houghton Mifflin Company.

[2]From "A Scottish Childhood" by Christian Miller. Copyright © 1979 by Christian Miller. Reprinted by permission of Wallace & Sheil Agency, Inc., and Anthony Sheil Associated Ltd. Published in Great Britain under the title "A Childhood in Scotland."

> What was there? We listened from every angle in the passages and nearby rooms, and measured the walls. Yes, there was space for a room. But where was the door? Where were the windows? We searched the outside walls, but two hundred years previously a tax had been imposed on windows, and many had been bricked up; some of these bricked-up windows were painted on the outside to look as if they were still in use, and some were not. We never found the hidden rooms.

The door is "at one side" of the enclosed area; the rooftop "is surrounded by" iron railings. Notice how these words give the reader a clear understanding of where the objects are located in space. What other words show the relationship between objects?

In an expository paragraph developed with reasons or examples, the illustration sentences are often arranged in *order of importance.* In the following paragraph from Arthur C. Clarke's *Report on Planet Three,* notice how the sentence order progresses from least to most important. What idea does the author consider most important?[1]

Transmutation means "the change of one thing into another."

> Ours is the century in which all of man's ancient dreams—and not a few of his nightmares—appear to be coming true. The conquest of the air, the transmutation of matter, journeys to the Moon, even the elixir of life—one by one the marvelous visions of the past are becoming reality. And among them, the one most fraught with promise and peril is the machine that can think.

Use the Checklist for Revising Paragraphs on pages 49–50 to revise this assignment.

Writing Practice 8

Each of the following sentences states a central idea that can be developed into a paragraph. Choose one statement to write about in a paragraph and develop sentences to illustrate it. You may want to restrict the central idea further in a restriction sentence. Use whatever order is indicated to arrange your sentences. If you prefer, think of your own central idea and organize your sentences with one of the three methods discussed in the preceding section.

A. Use *chronological order* with the following central ideas.

1. The summer passed so slowly I felt suspended in time.
2. From the minute I woke up I knew the day was going to be a lost cause.
3. The place had changed dramatically over the last years.

B. Use *spatial order* with the following central ideas.

1. My room may look like a disaster area, but I can find everything I need there blindfolded.
2. As I opened the door to the alien spacecraft, I noticed a panel of blinking red lights.
3. On my first day of high school, just finding the way from one class to another was confusing.

C. Use *order of importance* with the following central ideas.

1. There are three things I value most in another person.

2. Most of the time I'm easy to get along with, but a few things drive me crazy.
3. I know just what I want from a good (book/movie/other entertainment or sport).

Transition Words

You can also increase the coherence of paragraphs by using *transition words*—words or phrases that help the reader move smoothly from one sentence to another and that make the relationships between sentences clear.

The following are some common transitions and their uses.

TRANSITIONS	USES
For example, for instance	*To introduce illustrations*
And, also, in addition, besides, another, moreover, furthermore	*To add details, facts, examples*
But, nevertheless, on the other hand, however, on the contrary, yet, still, despite, similarly, in the same way	*To show comparison*
First, second, third, next, then, later, meanwhile, eventually, finally	*To show chronological order*
At the top, above, below, behind, near, far away, on the right, on the left, about	*To show spatial order*
Least, most, least important, more importantly, most important	*To show order of importance*
So, for this reason, thus, in conclusion, therefore, finally	*To make a conclusion*

Notice how the underlined transitions in the following paragraph, adapted from Jacques Cousteau's *The Ocean World,* improve coherence by showing the relationship between ideas. (How does *For example* relate the second sentence to the beginning sentence?)[1]

A *sonic device* is a machine that can send sound signals (through water).

> Several marine laboratories are studying the shark-dolphin relationship with the hope of making the dolphin's behavior useful to man. For example, experiments with lemon sharks and bottle-nosed dolphins show that if given the choice, sharks will avoid dolphins. Therefore, the researchers have been training dolphins to be used for shark control. For instance, one dolphin has been taught to ward off sharks in captivity on a command from a sonic device. The dolphin, on cue, will chase and hit the shark. Soon the scientists will conduct these experiments in the open sea, with the hope of employing dolphins to defend divers from sharks. Someday such trained dolphins may help ocean-

---

[1]Slightly adapted from *The Ocean World* by Jacques Cousteau. Reprinted by permission of Harry N. Abrams, Inc., Publisher.

auts by acting as watchdogs around undersea habitats. In addition, they may police coastal beaches, warding off sharks and protecting swimmers.

Other Ways to Increase Coherence

Pronouns, *paraphrases*, and *repetition* also contribute to coherence.

Pronouns are effective in linking sentences and ideas in a paragraph because they refer to nouns mentioned earlier. In the following example the pronoun *he* refers back to *Muhammad Ali* and helps link the two sentences.

> *Muhammad Ali* came in third in the People's Almanac Poll listing the fifteen greatest male athletes from 1900 to 1977. *He* is ranked behind Jim Thorpe and Babe Ruth.

When you *paraphrase* words, you restate them in a different way without changing the meaning. Paraphrasing adds variety to your writing and also helps the reader move smoothly from idea to idea. In the following example the words *difficult journey* are a paraphrase of *trip*.

> The *trip* progressed westward across rivers, steep canyons, and barely defined trails. The *difficult journey* demanded courage and stamina.

Repeating the same word over and over can make writing dull; however, careful *repetition* of a key word or phrase often helps the reader move smoothly from sentence to sentence. In the following paragraph from Nora Ephron's *Scribble, Scribble*, notice how repetition of the key word *Double-Crostic* (a difficult crossword puzzle) gives the paragraph coherence.[1]

> It is one of the great surprises of my adult life that I am not particularly good at doing the Double-Crostic. When I was growing up, I thought that being able to do the Double-Crostic was an adult attribute, not unlike buying hard-cover books, and that eventually I would grow into it. My mother, who was indirectly responsible for this misapprehension, was a whiz at Double-Crostics and taught me how to do them. In those days, the Double-Crostic was available through three sources: every week in the *Saturday Review*, every other week in the *New York Times Magazine* and twice a year in a Simon and Schuster anthology containing fifty or so new puzzles. The first two puzzles in each anthology were geared to beginners—to idiots, to be more precise—and I could usually solve one of them in about a month, using an atlas, a dictionary, a thesaurus, a Bartlett's and an occasional tip from my mother, who would never have been caught dead using any source material at all. There are many things I will never forgive my mother for, but heading the list is the fact that she did the Double-Crostic in ink. [underscores added]

The following three paragraphs are taken from an essay on waste disposal in New York City titled "Garbage." Notice how the writer uses all four methods (transition devices, pronouns, paraphrase, and repetition) to give the passage coherence.

---

[1]From "Double-Crostics" in *Scribble, Scribble: Notes on the Media* by Nora Ephron. Copyright © 1975 by Nora Ephron. Reprinted by permission of Alfred A. Knopf, Inc.

1. Transition showing order in time
2. Pronoun referring to *barges*
3. Pronoun referring to *landfill sites*
4. Repetition
5. Pronoun referring to *Fresh Kills*
6. Paraphrase of *Fresh Kills*
7. Transition showing spatial order
8. Transition showing spatial order
9. Repetition
10. Pronoun referring to *Fresh Kills*
11. Pronoun referring to *gulls*
12. Pronoun referring to *garbage*
13. Pronoun referring to *garbage*
14. Repetition
15. Paraphrase of *Fresh Kills*
16. Paraphrase of *Fresh Kills*
17. Repetition
18. Transition showing connection of ideas
19. Repetition
20. Paraphrase of *Fresh Kills*

After (1) the garbage has been burned, the cooled residue is dumped onto barges, which (2) are towed off by tugboats to one of five landfill sites around the city. The largest of these (3) is the 3,000-acre Fresh Kills site on Staten Island.

Fresh Kills (4), which (5) daily receives about 11,000 tons of garbage, is a strange place. Much of this former swampland (6) resembles the ash heaps of *The Great Gatsby*. Vast, forlorn, endless. A vision of death. In the foreground (7), a discarded funeral wreath. A doll with outstretched arms. A man's black sock. A nylon stocking. And, beyond (8), refrigerators, toilets, bathtubs, stoves.

Yet Fresh Kills (9) is also—in places and in its (10) own way—unexpectedly beautiful. Thousands of gulls wheel in the air. Banking sharply, they (11) dip down one by one to settle in for a good feast. In areas where the garbage is fresh, there is an overpowering stench, but where it (12) is older, its (13) blanket of earth is covered with grass, bushes, shrubs, trees. Summertime in Fresh Kills (14) is a time of flowers and birdsong. A volunteer vegetable garden flourishes in the landfill (15). Here, in the world's largest compost heap (16), the seeds and sprouts of kitchen scraps thrive. Come fall, offices all around New York's City Hall are decorated with gourds and pumpkins harvested at Fresh Kills (17). In the fall, too (18), quail and pheasants scurry through Fresh Kills' (19) underbrush, creating a problem for the Department of Sanitation: Hunters try to poach on this municipal game preserve (20).[1]

Writing Practice 9

Write a well-developed paragraph about one of the following topics or about a topic of your choice. Use the techniques you have learned (transitions, pronouns, paraphrase, and repetition) to make your paragraph coherent. Your teacher may ask you to underline the words or phrases that add coherence.

---

[1]From "Garbage" by Katie Kelley. Copyright © 1979 by *Saturday Review*. All rights reserved. Reprinted with permission.

1. My best friend and I couldn't be more alike or more different. (Suggestion: Use pronouns and the words *but, nevertheless, on the other hand, for example, despite, similarly,* and *in the same way.*)
2. When I became lost, the first thing I did was retrace my steps. (Suggestion: Use *first, second, third, next, then, later, meanwhile, eventually,* and *finally.*)
3. Across the field we saw a strange scene taking place. (Suggestion: Use pronouns and the words *at the top, above, below, behind, near,* and *far away.*)
4. Every morning I got up early and went down to the sea. (Suggestion: Use repetition of *sea* as a key word.)
5. For the first time in my life, I knew what fear really meant. (Suggestion: paraphrase *fear.*)

Paragraph Development by Descriptive Details

The illustration sentences in a paragraph develop the central idea by providing additional detailed information about it. When a paragraph is not developed effectively, readers may misunderstand or reject the writer's central idea.

One method of developing a paragraph is to use descriptive details.

Writers often use specific, descriptive details to create images of people, scenes, and events. These are often sensory details that describe the look, sound, feel, taste, or smell of something. The following paragraph from Bruce Chatwin's *In Patagonia* is about a writer who has been walking for two days and is hoping that a truck will pick him up. What specific details are used to describe the road? The sound of the guanaco?[1]

A *guanaco* is a wild animal related to the llama and the camel.

> Walked all day and the next day. The road straight, grey, dusty, and trafficless. The wind relentless, heading you off. Sometimes you heard a truck, you knew for certain it was a truck, but it was the wind. Or the noise of gears changing down, but that also was the wind. Sometimes the wind sounded like an unloaded truck banging over a bridge. Even if a truck had come up behind you wouldn't have heard it. And even if you'd been downwind, the wind would have drowned the engine. The one noise you did hear was a guanaco. A noise like a baby trying to cry and sneeze at once. You saw him a hundred yards off, a single male, bigger and more graceful than a llama, with his orange coat and white upstanding tail. Guanacos are shy animals, you were told, but this one was mad for you. And when you could walk no more and laid out your sleeping bag, he was there gurgling and snivelling and keeping the same distance. In the morning he was right up close, but the shock of you getting out of your skin

[1]From *In Patagonia* by Bruce Chatwin. Copyright © 1977 by Bruce Chatwin. Reprinted by permission of Summit Books, a Simon & Schuster division of Gulf & Western Corporation, and Deborah Rogers Ltd., Literary Agency. Published in Great Britain by Jonathan Cape Ltd.

A *galleon* is an ancient sailing ship.

was too much for him. That was the end of a friendship and you watched him bounding away over a thorn bush like a galleon in a following sea.

For Your Journal

Perhaps the paragraph from *In Patagonia* reminds you of a time when you were alone and in a strange place. In your journal write your impressions of that place. What sounds did you hear? Try to recall other details, such as sights, smells, tastes, or the way things felt. If you were alone in an attic, for example, perhaps you remember the feel of dust on the tops of old boxes or chairs. Including descriptive details helps readers share your experience.

Writing Practice 10

Use the Preparing to Write section that follows to help you with ideas for this assignment.

Write a paragraph about one of the following topic or topic-restriction sentences or make up one of your own. Develop your topic with at least four sentences that include good descriptive details.

1. The day before the holiday the department store was jammed with shoppers struggling to get to the counters.
2. I could feel a storm building in the air.
3. No modern supermarket can surpass the fun of shopping in an old-fashioned general store.
4. The old car stood on cinder blocks in the front yard.
5. Magazines and newspapers often picture a "better world" that will supposedly be created if readers buy certain products.

Preparing to Write

One way to find ideas for writing assignments is to draw on your own experience. For example, suppose that you chose the following central idea for your paragraph: "The day before the holiday the department store was jammed with shoppers struggling to get to the counters." If you have had a similar experience of being in a crowded place, recall how it felt to push your way through the crowd. Ask yourself what sights, sounds, tastes, and smells you would find in a crowded department store during a holiday. Perhaps you will think of shiny decorations or displays of merchandise. Then use the *who? what? where? when? why?* and *how?* questions to give your readers a clear, specific picture of the merchandise display. *What* smells came from the perfume counter? *How* were the hats and gloves arranged? *Whom* did you see? *How* did these people act?

You can combine the details you gather into descriptive sentences: "The counters were covered with bottles of perfume and tiny jewelry boxes. Shoppers rummaging through trays of woolly hats and gloves had thrown one salesperson into confusion. By the children's counter I heard shrieks of laughter as one little boy propelled a wind-up monkey down the aisle." Remember to ask yourself questions about *all* your senses.

Revising and Proofreading

Use the Checklist for Revising Paragraphs on pages 49–50 as a guide to revising your paragraph. When you have completed your revision, check your writing for grammar and mechanics by using the Checklist for Proofreading on pages 20–21.

Paragraph Development by Facts and Statistics

Many expository paragraphs can be developed most effectively with *facts* and *statistics* that support the central idea.

A *fact* is information that has been or can be proved true. For example, the statement "Bats are the only flying mammals" is a fact science has proved. A *statistic* is a fact containing a number: "There are *1,000* living species of bats."

As you read the following paragraph from Barbara Ward's essay "Triage," identify the facts and statistics the writer uses to develop her point about the world supply of food.[1]

> In the last ten years, at least one-third of the increased world demand for food has come from North Americans, Europeans and Russians eating steadily more high-protein food. Grain is fed to animals and poultry, and eaten as steak and eggs. In real energy terms, this is about five times more wasteful than eating grain itself. The result is an average American diet of nearly 2,000 pounds of grain a year—and epidemics of cardiac trouble—and 400 pounds for the average Indian.

The first sentence gives a statistic: one-third of the increased demand for food worldwide in the last ten years has come from North Americans, Europeans, and Russians. What other facts does the paragraph present to show the problems with the food supply? What statistics does it give about these facts?

When you develop a paragraph with facts and statistics, use enough information to make your point but avoid using facts and statistics that are not related to your central idea. Using the *who? what? when? where? why?* and *how?* questions will help you decide what information you need to develop the paragraph's central idea.

Writing Practice 11

Use the Checklist for Revising Paragraphs on pages 49–50 as a guide to revising this assignment.

Select one of the following sentences to use as a topic or topic-restriction sentence for a paragraph developed with facts and statistics or write a similar sentence of your own. Using a dictionary, encyclopedia, or other reference work, make a list of at least four facts or statistics by asking yourself the *who? what? when? where? why?* and *how?* questions. Once you have collected your information, write a paragraph adequately developing your central idea.

---

[1]From "Triage" by Barbara Ward. Copyright © 1976 by the New York Times Company. Reprinted by permission.

1. Yearly contracts for sports superstars total in the millions of dollars.
2. Many animals have highly developed ways of communicating.
3. Smoking is dangerous.
4. Martial arts for young people are increasingly popular.
5. Preparing for a long hiking (sailing/cross-country skiing) trip can be expensive.

Paragraph Development by Examples

An *example* is a specific case that illustrates a general idea or statement.

Examples can make a writer's meaning clear by answering the question "What do you mean by that?" Key words or phrases such as *for example, for instance, that is,* and *for this reason* are often used to introduce a specific example. In the following paragraph, what examples does the writer use to prove that the ancient Chinese depended on intuition and experience to warn them of earthquakes?

> Today professional quake-watchers in China use modern scientific methods and equipment such as "tiltmeters" and "creepmeters" that trace and record the shifting movement of the earth's crust. However, before such advanced technology was available, the Chinese depended more upon intuition, keen observance of nature, and experience to predict earthquakes. For instance, rural Chinese who lived in areas where earthquakes were likely to occur claimed to know something was wrong because their animals acted strangely before an earthquake. Horses reared, cows would not enter their pens, fish and frogs leaped out of their ponds, snakes came out of their holes, and even pandas in the zoo acted differently. People noticed changes in the level and smell of well water as well as the eerie noises in suddenly swelling ground. These signs were clues to the people of the past that helped them predict and prepare for an earthquake.

Writing Practice 12

The Checklist for Revising Paragraphs is on pages 49–50.

Select one topic or topic-restriction sentence from the following list or write one of your own. On a separate sheet of paper, list three or four examples that could be used to develop the central idea in your sentence. Finally write a paragraph, using your topic or topic-restriction sentence and examples.

1. It is hard for me to lose my temper.
2. Some cartoon characters are so popular they are practically national celebrities.
3. Nearly everything costs more these days.
4. Several books (songs/films/people) have influenced my life.
5. A single room in a house can be furnished and decorated in many ways.

Paragraph Development by Reasons

Reasons explain an idea or opinion by answering the question *why?*

The following paragraph from Henry David Thoreau's *Walden* is developed with reasons that support the central idea: The writer prefers not to eat meat or fish. As you read, identify the reasons the author uses.

> I have found repeatedly, of late years, that I cannot fish without falling a little in self-respect. I have tried it again and again. I have skill at it, and, like many of my fellows, a certain instinct for it, which revives from time to time, but always when I have done I feel that it would have been better if I had not fished. I think that I do not mistake . . . . Having been my own butcher and scullion and cook, as well as the gentleman for whom the dishes were served up, I can speak from an unusually complete experience. The practical objection to animal food in my case was its uncleanness; and besides, when I had caught and cleaned and cooked and eaten my fish, they seemed not to have fed me essentially. It was insignificant and unnecessary, and cost more than it came to. A little bread or a few potatoes would have done as well, with less trouble and filth. Like many of my contemporaries, I had rarely for many years used animal food, or tea, or coffee, etc.; not so much because of any ill effects which I had traced to them, as because they were not agreeable to my imagination. The repugnance to animal food is not the effect of experience, but is an instinct. It appeared more beautiful to live low and fare hard in many respects; and though I never did so, I went far enough to please my imagination. I believe that every man who has ever been earnest to preserve his higher or poetic faculties in the best condition has been particularly inclined to abstain from animal food, and from much food of any kind. It is a significant fact, stated by entomologists—I find it in Kirby and Spence—that "some insects in their perfect state, though furnished with organs of feeding, make no use of them"; and they lay it down as "a general rule, that almost all insects in this state eat much less than in that of larvae. The voracious caterpillar when transformed into a butterfly . . . and the gluttonous maggot when become a fly" content themselves with a drop or two of honey or some other sweet liquid. The abdomen under the wings of the butterfly still represents the larva. . . . The gross feeder is a man in the larva state; and there are whole nations in that condition, nations without fancy or imagination, whose vast abdomens betray them.

Writing Practice 13

The Checklist for Revising Paragraphs is on pages 49–50.

The following list suggests topics for paragraphs you can develop with reasons. On a separate sheet of paper, write three or four reasons in support of the topic you select or in support of a similar topic of your own. Then use these reasons to write a paragraph on your topic.

1. Why I do (or do not) believe large cars should be banned
2. Why I do (or do not) believe we should elect a woman President of the United States
3. Why I do (or do not) believe in UFO's
4. Why all public facilities should (or should not) provide for the safety and convenience of disabled people
5. Why I do (or do not) enjoy being alone

Paragraph Development by Comparison and Contrast

When you develop a paragraph by comparison and contrast, you point out similarities and differences between people or places, ideas, opinions, points of view, and so on.

In using the comparison-and-contrast method, it is important to compare similar features of *both* items. For example, if you are comparing two books and discuss the exciting characters in one, you should also discuss the characters in the other. Listing the ways the two items to be compared are alike and different will ensure that you discuss the same features in both items. For example, the following lists are based on the differences between the human brain and the electronic computer.

THE HUMAN BRAIN	THE "ELECTRONIC BRAIN"
1. Composed of trillions of nerve cells	1. Composed of 10 million electrical components
2. Can be used to create, exercise initiative, deduct, reach conclusions, doubt, reason logically	2. Can only be used to compute
3. Can solve a problem with no further instruction	3. Must be programmed — told all the steps in advance — to solve a problem
4. Spends the time in actual computation	4. Spends time locating steps and information stored in its memory bank

Writers use either the *block method* or the *point-by-point method* to arrange the sentences in a comparison-and-contrast paragraph.

In the *block method* all the sentences about one item are grouped together in one block. For example, a writer using the *block method* to discuss the differences between the computer and the human brain might discuss the computer first, mentioning that it is composed of 10 million electrical components, that it can only compute, that it must be programmed, and that it uses time in locating information in its memory bank. Then the writer would move on to discuss all the features of the human brain together in a second block. On the other hand, *point-by-point comparison and contrast* involves moving back and forth between the two items, discussing how both items compare in terms of one point before moving to a second point. In the following paragraph from Gene Stanford's *Steps to Better English*, the writer uses the point-by-point method to discuss the differences between the human brain and the computer.[1]

> An electronic computer, while able to perform certain mathematical calculations more quickly than man's brain, does not have the brain's complex structure. While a human brain consists of trillions upon trillions of nerve cells, a so-called "electronic brain" contains only about 10 million electronic com-

---

[1]From *Steps to Better English* by Gene Stanford, "Aspects of English" Series. Copyright © 1972 by Holt, Rinehart and Winston, Publishers. Reprinted by permission of the publishers.

> ponents. A human has the ability to create, to exercise initiative, to deduct, to reach conclusions, to doubt, to reason logically. A computer can only compute; it can multiply, divide, add, subtract, and perhaps extract roots. Also it must be carefully "programmed" in order to arrive at an answer; that is, it must be told in advance all the steps necessary to perform a particular operation. A man, however, can be given a problem and go on to solve it with no further instruction. Most of the time taken up by a computer for problem solving is in locating the appropriate steps and intermediate values stored in its massive memory banks. The human brain, on the other hand, uses most of its time in actual computations. In short, a human brain is vastly more complex and versatile than that of a computer and therefore far superior.

After stating the restricted topic in the first sentence, the writer deals first with the human brain, then the "electronic brain," then the human brain, followed by the computer, and so on throughout the entire paragraph. A concluding sentence continues the pattern by stating that the human brain is superior to the computer.

In the following paragraph from Robert Palmer's *Street Songs*, the writer remembers a time during the 1950s when he belonged to a teen group called the Tweeds. Does the writer use the *point-by-point* or *block method* to compare the Tweeds and another popular group, the Greasers?[1]

> Our world was divided into Tweeds and Greasers, both wanting to be "tough" and irresistible. The Tweeds were would-be Ivy Leaguers who bought Hollywood's Tab Hunter–Robert Wagner hard-sell—white bucks, khaki pants, button-down shirt, red-striped tie. We were shiny, formal, and eager. We trusted our facade to work for us as successfully as it had worked for our film heroes. They wore make-up; we had Clearasil. We wanted to be perfect. The Greasers swallowed James Dean and Marlon Brando whole. They were big on silence and scruffiness. They were losers in life, and, what's more, they didn't care; they gloried in it. That's why they were dangerous—they had nothing to lose. With their leather jackets, DA's, T-shirts with cigarette packs rolled in the turned-up sleeves, they wanted to be left alone. We wanted to be accepted.

A *facade* is an imposing appearance usually concealing something inferior.

DA's are hairstyles combed straight back from the forehead and sides.

After identifying the two groups, this writer uses the block method to compare them. First he discusses the Tweeds—their clothing, the movie stars they liked, and their desire to be perfect. Then he discusses the Greasers—the stars they admired, their lack of ambition, and their clothing.

Writing Practice 14

For help with revising this assignment, refer to the section Revising and Proofreading Paragraphs on page 49.

On a separate sheet of paper, write a topic or topic-restriction sentence for one of the following subjects or choose a similar subject of your own. Then list three or four ways in which the two items are alike or different. Then write a paragraph about your topic, using either the block method or the point-by-point method. You may emphasize similarities, differences, or both.

1. Growing up today—Growing up in my parents' day

---

[1]From the "Introduction" by John Lahr to *Baby, That was Rock and Roll* by Robert Palmer. Copyright © 1978 by John Lahr. Reprinted by permission of John Lahr and Georges Borchardt, Inc.

2. Animal behavior—Human behavior
3. Living in a small town (or rural area)—Living in a large city
4. Working at school subjects—Working at a part-time job
5. Air travel today—Air travel in the twenty-first century

For Your Journal

How do you think the teenagers of the 1980s will be remembered? The writer of the paragraph on page 66 uses the details *white bucks*, *leather jackets*, and film idols *Tab Hunter* and *Marlon Brando* to describe the teens of the fifties. In your journal write about the appearance, fads, heroes, and goals of your generation. Remember to use specific details that will help your readers picture today's teen generation.

Development by a Combination of Methods

Many paragraphs, especially longer ones, are often developed with more than one method.

The following paragraph about the history of denim, from Hazel Todhunter's book *Make It in Denim*, combines data with descriptive details and reasons.[1]

> Denim is the fashion phenomenon of recent years, but it has a long history. Two hundred years ago the clipper ships sailing to trade with the Americas used sails made of a fabric developed in Nîmes, France. [fact and statistic] Because the colonies grew the cotton for the fabric and had a growing textile industry, it was not long before the fabric itself was being produced in the New World. [reasons] The material was strong, durable, cheap, and white. Settlers going west took it with them, they even covered their wagons with it. [descriptive details] They used it for overalls and dungarees, but since the color was not very practical they dyed it blue, using a dye extracted from an indigenous plant—indigo. [facts] In California, men were trying to make fortunes digging gold out of the hills. Another enterprising young man, Levi Strauss, made waist overalls for them. [fact] At first they were made of sailcloth, but later from *Tissus de Nîme*, now called denim. [fact] [brackets added]

Indigenous means "native to that region."

The first sentence of the preceding paragraph states the central idea: "Denim is the fashion phenomenon of recent years, but it has a long history." To develop this idea the writer traces the beginning of denim fabric, gives reasons for its production in America, explains how it came to be used for clothing, and presents descriptive details of its use by the early settlers. What data does the writer include about the history of denim?

[1]From *Make It in Denim* by Hazel Todhunter. Copyright © 1977 by Hazel Todhunter. Reprinted by permission of Taplinger Publishing Company, Inc., and B. T. Batsford Ltd. London.

The Checklist for Revising Paragraphs is on pages 49–50.

Writing Practice 15

Use one of the following subjects or think of your own subject to write about in a paragraph developed with a combination of methods. Write a clear topic or topic-restriction sentence for your paragraph and use *descriptive details* and *examples* or any other two methods of development.

1. The experience of trying to repair something
2. An experience of succeeding at something
3. An experience with a friend or relative
4. An experience of being in charge of something
5. An experience of working for a goal

4 Expository Writing

The Purpose of Exposition

The purpose of *expository writing*, or *exposition*, is to explain factual information.

In high school and college, two important kinds of expository writing are the expository composition, or essay, and the essay examination. In the following sections you will study and practice the steps involved in developing the expository essay: finding and focusing a subject, gathering and recording information, organizing the information, and writing and revising the essay. You will also learn to organize and to write the kinds of items you are most likely to find on essay examinations.

Planning the Expository Essay

The first step in writing an expository essay is the same as that for other kinds of writing—finding a subject. When your teacher assigns a subject, part of your work has been done for you. When you are not assigned a subject, the best way to find one is to take time to think over your own experiences.

As you think of subjects based on your experiences, keep in mind that expository writing deals with information and explanations. It would not be appropriate, for example, to base an expository essay on the first day at your new job, since that would be narrative writing. You could, however, write an explanation of the steps in training for your job or an explanation or definition of your job. You might also find ideas for writing in your journal or from subjects you have studied in school or read about on your own.

Writing Practice 1

Using your own experience and your journal as a source of ideas, make a list of five subjects on which you could base an expository essay. Remember that the purpose of exposition is to present information.

Examples

a. Surviving freshman year
b. How not to catch a fish
c. New computer games

Focusing Your Subject

Focusing your subject means limiting it or narrowing it to the specific topic of your essay.

The purpose of limiting your subject is to produce a topic that you can write about interestingly and well in one paper. If your subject is too large, the information you present to the reader will be too general or vague to be interesting. Assume, for example, that you want to write about space exploration, a subject that could include earth-orbiting satellites, the space race between the U.S.S.R. and the United States, moon landings, space probes of other planets (such as Venus, Mars, and Saturn), and the data produced by *Skylab.* The range of this subject is so great that to write about it properly you would have to turn your composition into a book.

You can narrow the subject of space exploration to a specific topic by focusing on one of its parts, perhaps the space race or data produced by *Skylab.* Depending on the length of your composition, you may want to limit the boundaries of your topic even further. For example, you could write about one particular part of the space race, such as the first accomplishments of *Sputnik 1* in 1957 and *Explorer 1* in 1958. You could also write about practical uses of the data about earth produced by *Skylab,* such as information about crops, mineral deposits, and global pollution.

The following are other examples of limiting a general subject to a topic for an expository essay.

Subject: Communication in the animal world
Topic: How bees communicate by "dancing"

The preceding topic limits or narrows the *general* subject of animal communication to the *particular* kind of communication that bees express with their dances.

Subject: Popular music
Topic: How rock-and-roll originated

This preceding topic limits the *general* subject of popular music to one *particular* kind of music, rock-and-roll. It further limits the subject to the *origins* of rock-and-roll.

Subject: Musical instruments
Topic: How to play the *khora*

This topic limits the *general* subject of popular music to one *particular* kind of instrument for making popular music, the *khora* of Africa.

Writing Practice 2

The ten subjects that follow are too general and need to be limited for use in an expository essay. On a separate sheet of paper, write a limited topic for each subject.

Example

a. The Sierra Club

a. How the Sierra Club helps protect the environment in Yosemite Park

1. Consumer problems
2. Fads
3. Minority rights
4. Natural resources
5. Rock stars
6. The Olympics
7. Pollution
8. Student government
9. Dolphins
10. Science fiction

Gathering Information for the Expository Essay

For more information on the points-of-view method, see pages 31–36.

Gathering information is an important step because the information you present about a topic forms the basis of the entire essay. In addition to using your journal as a source of details, you can also use any of the methods in the chapter "Discovering Subject Matter." The example in this section shows how to find ideas about a topic by using the *points-of-view* method.

With the points-of-view method, you look at a topic from three different perspectives to discover information about it. The first point of view examines the features and characteristics of the topic; the second studies how the topic changes or varies; and the third looks at how the individual parts fit together and how the topic fits into a larger background. For example, imagine that you are interested in the general subject of unusual methods of travel and have narrowed this subject to the topic of ballooning. By using the points-of-view method, you can examine the topic in three different ways to gain a range of information about it.

Ballooning: What is it?

The first point of view examines the features and characteristics of a topic, asking the question "What is it?" When you look at ballooning from this point of view, you pose the following sorts of questions.

What is a balloon?
What do balloons used for travel look like?

What materials are used to make them?
What air or gasses make balloons rise?

What is ballooning?
What is the purpose of ballooning?
How do balloonists control their balloons?
How is ballooning like similar means of travel?
What makes ballooning different from travel by similar means, such as airships?

This first point of view, in effect, freezes your topic in time: you look at it as you would a photograph of an object to learn about its features.

Writing Practice 3

Choose one of the following suggestions as a topic to explore by the "What is it?" point of view or use a similar topic of your choice. On a separate sheet of paper, write out a list of questions to help you examine the features and characteristics of the topic. Then write answers to your questions.

1. Scuba diving
2. Germs
3. Ragtime
4. Pony express
5. Pyramids

Ballooning: How has it changed?

The second point of view examines a topic to learn how it changes over a period of time, asking the question "How has it changed or varied?" When you consider ballooning from this point of view, you ask the following sorts of questions.

How have balloons changed?
Are balloons made of different materials now from when they were invented in 1783?
How has the shape of balloons changed since 1783?
Has the use for balloons changed since they were invented?

How has ballooning changed?
Have people's attitudes toward ballooning changed over time?
Has ballooning changed since the first balloonist crossed the English Channel in 1785?

By investigating the topic from this second point of view, you learn about changes in the appearance, construction, use, and popularity of balloons and ballooning. This point of view observes your topic as a process of change: you learn about the variations that time or a change of place bring to your topic.

Writing Practice 4

Select one of the following topics to explore by the "How has it changed?" point of view or use a similar topic of your choice. On a separate sheet of paper, write out a list of questions you would ask to learn about the changes and variations in your topic over time. When you have finished, write the answers to your questions.

1. Hockey
2. Blue jeans
3. Manners
4. Automobiles
5. Movies

Ballooning: What are its relationships?

The third point of view examines how the parts of a topic relate to one another and how the topic itself relates to a larger background, asking the question "What are its relationships?" When you consider ballooning from this point of view, you ask questions such as the following ones.

How does a balloon work?
What is each necessary part in a balloon?
How does each part in a balloon work to make the balloon function properly?

How does ballooning fit into other categories?
How does ballooning relate to other sports and hobbies?
How does ballooning relate to other attempts people have made to fly?
How does ballooning relate to other unusual interests you might have?
How does ballooning relate to other inventions with practical applications?

By investigating ballooning from this third point of view, you look at the topic as if you were examining it under a microscope; you learn what its parts are and how they function together. Then you look at the topic from a broader perspective so that you learn what larger categories it fits into and how it relates to them.

Writing Practice 5

Select one of the following topics to explore by the "What are its relationships?" point of view or write a similar topic of your choice. On a separate sheet of paper, write a list of questions you would ask to learn about the parts of the topic and how they work together and about how the topic fits into larger relationships or categories. When you have finished, write out the answers to your questions.

1. A particular comic strip
2. Ghosts
3. Student government
4. Submarines
5. Saber-toothed tigers

Recording Information for the Expository Essay

As you explore your topic, you will find many ideas about it. You will probably remember the most relevant ideas, but other thoughts, impressions, and details will most likely be forgotten unless you record them as they occur to you.

Note-taking is the simplest and most efficient way to record your ideas.

When writers jot down their thoughts without a system, they may find themselves writing on the backs of envelopes or on bits of scratch paper. You will save time in the long run if you record each idea separately on note cards or on a separate slip of paper. For example, assume that you have chosen the topic of the women's liberation movement. The first note you write might look like the following one.

> <u>Attitudes about women's liberation</u>
>
> I have a different attitude about women's liberation than my sister because she is ten years older and things have changed a good deal since she was my age.

Write down your notes in whatever way is most helpful to you, always putting a heading on each note for easy reference later. Sometimes, your notes will be words or phrases:

1. My talks with Mother about her childhood
2. The issue of using *Ms.* instead of *Miss* or *Mrs.*
3. The Equal Rights Amendment

Sometimes, your notes will be complete sentences:

1. Why does my sister feel she was treated differently because she was a girl?
2. The equal-work-for-equal-pay issue is the most widely supported women's lib demand.
3. Some television shows still show women in stereotyped roles.

Sometimes, your notes will be paragraphs:

I think things are changing because of the women's liberation movement. When my grandmother was in school, everybody expected her to get married right away. Her father told her she could go to college if she wanted but that it was a waste of money. When my mother was in school, she did well in math but wasn't encouraged to be a mathematician because it was "a man's field." In my class, though, I know three girls who want to be engineers, and their families are very proud.

Writing Practice 6

Using a topic you have already selected or a new one, apply the points-of-view system, brainstorming, clustering, or any other technique to gather information. As you do, make notes on 3 × 5 note cards or on similar-sized slips of paper. Save these notes to use in a later assignment.

Organizing Your Notes

One of the easiest ways to organize your notes is to separate them into stacks, making each idea a separate group and putting all the notes about one idea together. The following notes were collected for an expository essay titled "A Teenager Looks at the Women's Liberation Movement." The notes appear in the order in which they were written and have not yet been organized. As you read through them, try to find some general ideas you could use to group these notes together.

1. What is women's liberation? Does it mean the same thing now as when the movement began?
2. The history of the women's movement goes back to the nineteenth century when the suffragettes concentrated on getting the vote.
3. Talked with mother about her friends—they were all married before they were twenty.
4. Mother said she was brought up to believe that a woman's place was in the home.
5. Women on television and in movies not true to life
6. The percentage of women in top-level jobs in this country is still low. Other countries, especially in Scandinavia, have higher rates of employed women in executive positions.
7. When mother was little, she wasn't allowed to play with boys because they were "too rough."
8. Organizations for women—what do they do?
9. Even though I'm strong, my brother is always the one who is asked to carry in the groceries or move the chairs around.
10. I know girls who ask boys for dates, but it's still mostly the other way around. When Mother was my age, she didn't know any girls who asked boys out.

11. My parents have always encouraged me to do whatever I was really interested in, such as going to college or getting a job or studying the subjects I wanted.
12. Talked about women's liberation with my friend Jim. He said, "Liberation from what?"
13. My parents have a traditional life. Dad works outside the house, and mother works at home taking care of us and keeping house.
14. Girls' intramural sports are very popular today. My teachers say that when they were in school no one paid much attention to girls' sports.
15. Women artists
16. Reading about "role models." A *role model* is someone to look up to and try to follow. In work situations boys have more role models than girls because there are more men in the professions than women. I think this is true. For instance, our next-door neighbor is an electrician, and the fathers of two of my friends are electricians. I don't know any women electricians.
17. My grandfather's attitude compared with my father's attitude about women
18. When my English teacher was growing up, her brothers didn't have to help with the dishes because it was "women's work."
19. I've never been told, "You can't do that because you're a girl."
20. Statistics on the percentage of women who go on to college

Some of the preceding notes are general, and some are specific. Each note deals with the same topic, but you would not try to incorporate all the notes into one composition. When you take notes, however, do not try to decide beforehand what you will use in your paper. Put down whatever thoughts, questions, or impressions come to you and later determine which ones you will use.

Writing Practice 7

Many of the thoughts and ideas expressed in the sample notes on pages 75–76 relate to one another. For example, Notes 7 and 18 both have to do with traditional attitudes about women. Read through the notes to find at least three other general categories into which the notes can be grouped. Write these categories on a sheet of paper and then list beneath these headings the notes that fit into these categories.

Making an Informal Outline

An *informal outline* is a plan for writing.

Begin making an informal outline by separating your notes into stacks according to categories, so that when you finish you will have perhaps four or five groups of notes with related information.

The stacks of notes will suggest the form of your outline. (You can arrange your notes until the order makes sense to you.) As you organize your thoughts, you will probably find that some of your notes will have to be discarded and that new ideas will occur to you as you go along. Always feel free to add more ideas or to delete any information that does not contribute to the main idea of your composition.

The following informal outline is developed from the sample notes on pages 75–76. As you read, notice that each separate section represents a group of ideas.

A Teenager Looks at Women's Liberation

- The Women's Liberation Movement
  - Definition
  - History
  - Issues
    - Issues about attitudes
    - Issues about jobs
- Mother's life before women's lib
  - Traditional attitudes of her family
    - Attitudes about college
    - Attitudes about "a woman's place"
  - Traditional attitudes of society
    - Attitudes about dating
    - Attitudes about "a woman's place"
- My life after women's lib
  - Traditional attitudes
    - Stereotyping on radio and TV
    - Lack of women in top-level jobs
  - Changing attitudes
    - Encouragement of parents
    - More women in college

For information about preparing a formal outline, see pages 106–108.

Notice that in the preceding informal outline numbers are not used to designate headings; instead, divisions and subdivisions are shown by indentions and spacing. (The *formal outline*, which is most often used in preparing research papers, does have a definite numbering system of numerals and letters.) The preceding sample outline shows one way to plan an expository essay, but using the same notes you could organize the composition in other ways that would be equally effective. There are no strict rules for making an informal outline. Its purpose is simply to give you a guide for writing a clear, well-organized composition.

Writing Practice 8

Using notes you have gathered for an expository essay or new ones you develop for this assignment, write an informal outline. Discard any notes that do not fit into your plan for the composition.

Writing the Thesis Statement

A *thesis statement* is a sentence that clearly states the thesis, or topic, of the composition.

Writing a thesis statement helps you to focus the main point of your essay and helps the reader understand exactly what will be covered in your paper. For example, imagine that you have decided to write a composition on the subject of black holes and have narrowed the subject to the topic *Formation of a black hole.* To develop a thesis statement decide on the main idea you want to express about the topic. One possible thesis statement might be "Although scientists are not certain about the exact nature of black holes, they do agree about how black holes are formed." This thesis statement tells the reader that the composition will explain how black holes are formed.

Another way to narrow the subject of black holes is to define them. A possible thesis statement for a composition defining black holes is, "When some stars die, the force of gravity causes them to collapse inward; a star that keeps on collapsing is called a *black hole.*" This thesis statement gives a brief definition and indicates that the purpose of the composition is to make a thorough definition of black holes.

Writing Practice 9

For this assignment use a topic you have already developed or a new one you develop from the following list of general subjects. Then write a thesis statement that expresses the main idea you will explain in your composition.

Example

a. *Subject: Movies*
Topic: Irritating behavior of movie audiences
Thesis statement: Three kinds of behavior among movie audiences are particularly annoying: loud whispering and talking, constant moving up and down aisles, and finding seats before previous showing has ended.

1. Caves
2. Democracy
3. Parade floats
4. Disco (or other music)
5. Car repair
6. Free agency in baseball (or other sports terminology)
7. Microscopes
8. Saturdays
9. Magic (astrology/ESP)
10. Cooking

Writing the Expository Essay

The basic form of an expository essay consists of the introduction, the body, and the conclusion.

The *introduction* identifies the topic and gives some information about it to interest the reader. The *body*, usually several paragraphs long, develops the topic stated in the introduction. The *conclusion* gives a brief summary of the main ideas, reemphasizes an important point, or restates the topic.

Writing the Introduction

The *introduction* is usually the first paragraph of a composition. The purpose of the introductory paragraph is to present the basic idea that will be discussed and to interest the reader.

You may choose to begin your introductory paragraph with the thesis statement itself, or you may begin with a general remark leading into the thesis statement. The important rule for beginning writers to remember is to include the thesis statement somewhere in the first paragraph. The following introductory paragraph begins with interesting information and ends with the thesis statement.[1]

> Long after the American West had been comparatively citified, a large part of western Canada, known as the North Peace Country, remained a wilderness. The Peace River, which gives the region its name, flows from the Canadian Rockies to the Arctic Sea, through some of the wildest canyons and most fertile farmland in North America. In both its history and its terrain, the North Peace is a microcosm of the Canadian West.

From the thesis statement the reader can tell that the essay will deal with the history and terrain of the North Peace as it relates to the Canadian West. In the sample expository compositions on pages 81 and 87, you will find two more examples of introductory paragraphs.

Writing Practice 10

Write an introductory paragraph incorporating a thesis statement you have already written or one you write for this assignment. You may begin the paragraph with the thesis statement or lead into it using other information. Underline your thesis statement when you have finished.

Writing the Body

The *body* of the essay is the main part of the paper.

The purpose of the body is to develop the topic stated in the introduction

[1]From "History at Peace" by Carol Easton in *Westways*, June 1976. Copyright © 1976 by the Automobile Club of Southern California. Reprinted by permission of *Westways*.

by presenting information and illustrations about it. The body paragraphs should follow a logical organization, should include a sufficient number of illustrations, and should be unified.

For a review of methods of organization, see pages 55–57.

Logical organization is an ordering of thoughts and ideas that makes sense. If the paper explains the steps in a process, the arrangement of ideas will probably follow the order in which the steps are done. For a paper explaining reasons, the reasons might be arranged in the order of their importance, with the most important being saved for last. There are also other ways to organize information in an expository essay, but the important point is that readers can easily follow the progression of ideas.

For a review of using examples to develop your writing, see page 63.

Sufficient illustrations are necessary to develop the topic of your paper. Illustrations include details, examples, facts and figures, and reasons that support and explain the thesis. Specific illustrations make your paper interesting as well as informative.

For a review of methods to achieve unity, see pages 52–54.

A *unified composition* is one in which each idea presented relates to the thesis statement. Each paragraph develops a different aspect of the thesis statement, but all of the paragraphs deal with the same basic idea.

Writing the Conclusion

The purpose of the *conclusion* is to bring the reader back to the main idea of the paper by restating it in a new way.

A good conclusion also gives the reader a sense of completion, of having come to the end of a discussion or argument. Writers use different techniques in writing conclusions. Some refer back to the thesis statement and briefly summarize the main points of the paper. Some conclude with an interesting quotation or statistic about the topic, and some end on a personal note or statement of opinion. You may use any of these methods of writing a conclusion, but remember that the conclusion is not the place to add new ideas; all the significant ideas about your subject belong in the body.

The following conclusion is taken from Kent Dannen's essay about the life and work of the famous conservationist Enos Mills. Notice that the paragraph makes a general statement about Enos Mills' accomplishment and that it ends with a personal statement about ecological preservation.[1]

> Enos Mills was proud of the work that he had done to preserve the wild beauty of the Rockies for later generations of Americans. He believed when he died that protection in national parks assured the immortality of wild beauty, that wild gardens forever would be sources of inspiration. But we know now that our gardens will inspire us forever only if those who love them continue to defend the wilderness with the single-minded devotion shown by Enos Mills, father of Rocky Mountain National Park.

---

[1]From "Rocky Mountain Man" by Kent Dannen in *Westways*, August 1976. Copyright © 1976 by the Automobile Club of Southern California. Reprinted by permission of *Westways*.

Writing Practice 11

For this assignment use the introduction for an expository composition that you wrote for Writing Practice 10 or write a new one. Then write the body of the composition, developing the thesis statement that you presented in the introductory paragraph.

Reading an Expository Essay

In the following essay, "The Spider and the Wasp," Alexander Petrunkevitch explains how a certain species of wasp uses the tarantula spider as a source of food for its young. After you have finished reading, you should be able to identify the introduction, body, and conclusion of the essay, as well as the thesis statement.[1]

The Spider and the Wasp

[1] To hold its own in the struggle for existence, every species of animal must have a regular source of food, and if it happens to live on other animals, its survival may be very delicately balanced. The hunter cannot exist without the hunted; if the latter should perish from the earth, the former would, too. When the hunted also prey on some of the hunters, the matter may become complicated.

[2] This is nowhere better illustrated than in the insect world. Think of the complexity of a situation such as the following: There is a certain wasp, *Pimpla inquisitor,* whose larvae feed on the larvae of the tussock moth. *Pimpla* larvae in turn serve as food for the larvae of a second wasp, and the latter in their turn nourish still a third wasp. What subtle balance between fertility and mortality must exist in the case of each of these four species to prevent the extinction of all of them! An excess of mortality over fertility in a single member of the group would ultimately wipe out all four.

[3] This is not a unique case. The two great orders of insects, Hymenoptera and Diptera, are full of such examples of interrelationship. And the spiders (which are not insects but members of a separate order of arthropods) also are killers and victims of insects.

In this context *carnivorous* means "insect-eating."

[4] The picture is complicated by the fact that those species which are carnivorous in the larval stage have to be provided with animal food by a vegetarian mother. The survival of the young depends on the mother's correct choice of a food which she does not eat herself.

Progeny means "descendants."

[5] In the feeding and safeguarding of their progeny the insects and spiders exhibit some interesting analogies to reasoning and some crass examples of blind instinct. The case I propose to describe here is that of the tarantula spiders and their arch-enemy, the digger wasps of the genus Pepsis. It is a classic example of what looks like intelligence pitted against instinct—a strange situation in which the victim, though fully able to defend itself, submits unwittingly to its destruction.

[6] Most tarantulas live in the Tropics, but several species occur in the temperate zone and a few are common in the southern U.S. Some varieties are

[1] "The Spider and the Wasp" by Alexander Petrunkevitch from *Scientific American,* August 1952.

Formidable means "causing fear or dread."

large and have powerful fangs with which they can inflict a deep wound. These formidable looking spiders do not, however, attack man; you can hold one in your hand, if you are gentle, without being bitten. Their bite is dangerous only to insects and small mammals such as mice; for a man it is no worse than a hornet's sting.

[7] Tarantulas customarily live in deep cylindrical burrows, from which they emerge at dusk and into which they retire at dawn. Mature males wander about after dark in search of females and occasionally stray into houses. After mating, the male dies in a few weeks, but a female lives much longer and can mate several years in succession. In a Paris museum is a tropical specimen which is said to have been living in captivity for 25 years.

[8] A fertilized female tarantula lays from 200 to 400 eggs at a time; thus it is possible for a single tarantula to produce several thousand young. She takes no care of them beyond weaving a cocoon of silk to enclose the eggs. After they hatch, the young walk away, find convenient places in which to dig their burrows and spend the rest of their lives in solitude. Tarantulas feed mostly on insects and millepedes. Once their appetite is appeased, they digest the food for several days before eating again. Their sight is poor, being limited to sensing a change in the intensity of light and to the perception of moving objects. They apparently have little or no sense of hearing, for a hungry tarantula will pay no attention to a loudly chirping cricket placed in its cage unless the insect happens to touch one of its legs.

Riffling means "rippling."

[9] But all spiders, and especially hairy ones, have an extremely delicate sense of touch. Laboratory experiments prove that tarantulas can distinguish three types of touch: pressure against the body wall, stroking of the body hair and riffling of certain very fine hairs on the legs called trichobothria. Pressure against the body, by a finger or the end of a pencil, causes the tarantula to move off slowly for a short distance. The touch excites no defensive response unless the approach is from above where the spider can see the motion, in which case it rises on its hind legs, lifts its front legs, opens its fangs and holds this threatening posture as long as the object continues to move. When the motion stops, the spider drops back to the ground, remains quiet for a few seconds and then moves slowly away.

[10] The entire body of a tarantula, especially its legs, is thickly clothed with hair. Some of it is short and woolly, some long and stiff. Touching this body hair produces one of two distinct reactions. When the spider is hungry, it responds with an immediate and swift attack. At the touch of a cricket's antennae the tarantula seizes the insect so swiftly that a motion picture taken at the rate of 64 frames per second shows only the result and not the process of capture. But when the spider is not hungry, the stimulation of its hairs merely causes it to shake the touched limb. An insect can walk under its hairy belly unharmed.

[11] The trichobothria, very fine hairs growing from disklike membranes on the legs, were once thought to be the spider's hearing organs, but we now know that they have nothing to do with sound. They are sensitive only to air movement. A light breeze makes them vibrate slowly without disturbing the common hair. When one blows gently on the trichobothria, the tarantula reacts with a quick jerk of its four front legs. If the front and hind legs are stimulated at the same time, the spider makes a sudden jump. This reaction is quite independent of the state of its appetite.

Tactile means "related to the sense of touch."

[12] These three tactile responses—to pressure on the body wall, to moving of the common hair and to flexing of the trichobothria—are so different from one another that there is no possibility of confusing them. They serve the tarantula adequately for most of its needs and enable it to avoid most annoyances and dangers. But they fail the spider completely when it meets its deadly enemy, the digger wasp Pepsis.

[13] These solitary wasps are beautiful and formidable creatures. Most species are either a deep shiny blue all over, or deep blue with rusty wings. The largest have a wing span of about four inches. They live on nectar. When excited, they give off a pungent odor—a warning that they are ready to attack. The sting is much worse than that of a bee or common wasp, and the pain and swelling last longer. In the adult stage the wasp lives only a few months. The female produces but a few eggs, one at a time at intervals of two or three days. For each egg the mother must provide one adult tarantula, alive but paralyzed. The tarantula must be of the correct species to nourish the larva. The mother wasp attaches the egg to the paralyzed spider's abdomen. Upon hatching from the egg, the larva is many hundreds of times smaller than its living but helpless victim. It eats no other food and drinks no water. By the time it has finished its single gargantuan meal and become ready for wasphood, nothing remains of the tarantula but its indigestible chitinous skeleton.

Gargantuan means "enormous."

[14] The mother wasp goes tarantula-hunting when the egg in her ovary is almost ready to be laid. Flying low over the ground late on a sunny afternoon, the wasp looks for its victim or for the mouth of a tarantula burrow, a round hole edged by a bit of silk. The sex of the spider makes no difference, but the mother is highly discriminating as to species. Each species of Pepsis requires a certain species of tarantula, and the wasp will not attack the wrong species. In a cage with a tarantula which is not its normal prey the wasp avoids the spider, and is usually killed by it in the night.

[15] Yet when a wasp finds the correct species, it is the other way about. To identify the species the wasp apparently must explore the spider with her antennae. The tarantula shows an amazing tolerance to this exploration. The wasp crawls under it and walks over it without evoking any hostile response. The molestation is so great and so persistent that the tarantula often rises on all eight legs, as if it were on stilts. It may stand this way for several minutes. Meanwhile the wasp, having satisfied itself that the victim is of the right species, moves off a few inches to dig the spider's grave. Working vigorously with legs and jaws, it excavates a hole 8 to 10 inches deep with a diameter slightly larger than the spider's girth. Now and again the wasp pops out of the hole to make sure that the spider is still there.

[16] When the grave is finished, the wasp returns to the tarantula to complete her ghastly enterprise. First she feels it all over once more with her antennae. Then her behavior becomes more aggressive. She bends her abdomen, protruding her sting, and searches for the soft membrane at the point where the spider's leg joins its body—the only spot where she can penetrate the horny skeleton. From time to time, as the exasperated spider slowly shifts ground, the wasp turns on her back and slides along with the aid of her wings, trying to get under the tarantula for a shot at the vital spot. During all this maneuvering, which can last for several minutes, the tarantula makes no move to save itself. Finally the wasp corners it against some obstruction and grasps one of its legs in her powerful jaws. Now at last the harassed spider tries a desperate but vain

defense. The two contestants roll over and over on the ground. It is a terrifying sight and the outcome is always the same. The wasp finally manages to thrust her sting into the soft spot and holds it there for a few seconds while she pumps in the poison. Almost immediately the tarantula falls paralyzed on its back. Its legs stop twitching; its heart stops beating. Yet it is not dead, as is shown by the fact that if taken from the wasp it can be restored to some sensitivity by being kept in a moist chamber for several months.

[17] After paralyzing the tarantula, the wasp cleans herself by dragging her body along the ground and rubbing her feet, sucks the drop of blood oozing from the wound in the spider's abdomen, then grabs a leg of the flabby, helpless animal in her jaws and drags it down to the bottom of the grave. She stays there for many minutes, sometimes for several hours, and what she does all that time in the dark we do not know. Eventually she lays her egg and attaches it to the side of the spider's abdomen with a sticky secretion. Then she emerges, fills the grave with soil carried bit by bit in her jaws, and finally tramples the ground all around to hide any trace of the grave from prowlers. Then she flies away, leaving her descendant safely started in life.

[18] In all this the behavior of the wasp evidently is qualitatively different from that of the spider. The wasp acts like an intelligent animal. This is not to say that instinct plays no part or that she reasons as man does. But her actions are to the point; they are not automatic and can be modified to fit the situation. We do not know for certain how she identifies the tarantula—probably it is by some olfactory or chemo-tactile sense—but she does it purposefully and does not blindly tackle a wrong species.

Olfactory means "of the sense of smell."

[19] On the other hand, the tarantula's behavior shows only confusion. Evidently the wasp's pawing gives it no pleasure, for it tries to move away. That the wasp is not simulating sexual stimulation is certain, because male and female tarantulas react in the same way to its advances. That the spider is not anesthetized by some odorless secretion is easily shown by blowing lightly at the tarantula and making it jump suddenly. What, then, makes the tarantula behave as stupidly as it does?

[20] No clear, simple answer is available. Possibly the stimulation by the wasp's antennae is masked by a heavier pressure on the spider's body, so that it reacts as when prodded by a pencil. But the explanation may be much more complex. Initiative in attack is not in the nature of tarantulas; most species fight only when cornered so that escape is impossible. Their inherited patterns of behavior apparently prompt them to avoid problems rather than attack them. For example, spiders always weave their webs in three dimensions, and when a spider finds that there is insufficient space to attach certain threads in the third dimension, it leaves the place and seeks another, instead of finishing the web in a single plane. This urge to escape seems to arise under all circumstances, in all phases of life and to take the place of reasoning. For a spider to change the pattern of its web is as impossible as for an inexperienced man to build a bridge across a chasm obstructing his way.

[21] In a way the instinctive urge to escape is not only easier but more efficient than reasoning. The tarantula does exactly what is most efficient in all cases except in an encounter with a ruthless and determined attacker dependent for the existence of her own species on killing as many tarantulas as she can lay eggs. Perhaps in this case the spider follows its usual pattern of trying to escape, instead of seizing and killing the wasp, because it is not aware of its danger.

In any case, the survival of the tarantula species as a whole is protected by the fact that the spider is much more fertile than the wasp.

For Thought and Discussion

1. The general subject of Alexander Petrunkevitch's essay is *Animal species that use other animal species as sources of food.* What is the topic?
2. The thesis statement of this essay is not given until the fifth paragraph. What sentence or sentences contain the thesis statement?
3. In the introduction (paragraphs 1–5), the writer gives several examples of animals (mostly insects) that feed upon each other. What else does Alexander Petrunkevitch accomplish in this introduction? Why do you think this essay has such a long introduction?
4. The body of the essay (paragraphs 6–17) is divided into two parts. In the first part (paragraphs 6–12), the writer explains information about the tarantula that helps readers understand its behavior. What does Alexander Petrunkevitch explain in the second part of the body?
5. In the long conclusion (paragraphs 18–21), the writer attempts to explain why the tarantula behaves as it does. What explanation does he give for the tarantula's allowing the wasp to overpower it?

Writing Practice 12

Write the first draft of an expository essay. As you do, follow the steps discussed in this chapter: (*a*) limit your subject to a specific topic suitable for a short essay, (*b*) gather information by using one or more suitable methods, (*c*) take notes on your information, (*d*) organize your notes, (*e*) prepare an informal outline, and (*f*) write the composition. (If you have followed these steps throughout the chapter, your teacher may allow you to use material you have already prepared.)

When you have completed the first draft of your essay, revise and proofread it according to the directions in the following section.

Revising an Expository Essay

If possible, set your paper aside for a few days so that you will approach your revision with a fresh and more critical eye. Then use the following checklist as a guide to revising your essay. (Your teacher may also have suggestions for revision.)

Checklist for Revising an Expository Essay

1. The topic is suitably narrow.
2. The introduction contains a thesis statement that clearly states the topic of the essay.

3. The introduction presents the basic ideas to be discussed in the essay.
4. The introduction helps to interest the reader in the ideas to follow.
5. Each paragraph in the body presents new information about the topic.
6. The information in the essay is organized in some logical way.
7. The essay includes sufficient illustrations about the topic.
8. The essay is unified.
9. The conclusion returns to the main idea of the essay, which is restated in some way.
10. The title of the essay gives clear and specific information about its content.

When you have completed your revision, rewrite your paper. Then check it for errors in grammar and mechanics by using the proofreading checklist on pages 20–21.

Writing a Title

The *title* of an expository essay should give clear and specific information about its content. The purpose of a title is to tell the reader what the essay is about. When titles are too general, the reader does not know what to expect. For example, on page 87 is an essay titled "How to Tame a Hawk." From the title you can tell that the essay is probably about taming hawks. A more general title, such as "Hawks," would not convey the content of the essay as clearly. Instead, readers might expect to read about the habits of hawks or the history of hawks.

Thinking of your thesis statement may help you decide on a proper title for your essay. Many writers wait to compose their title until they have finished the essay; others like to have a working title as they go along. You may choose either way, but remember to make your title a kind of brief preview of the content of your paper.

The Process Analysis Essay

A *process analysis essay* explains the steps in a process: how to cook a meal, throw a curve ball, or solve a math problem.

An expository composition that explains a process tells the reader clearly and completely how to do or understand something. It presents information in an orderly way, taking the reader step by step through the process itself. For clarity a process essay normally is organized according to the steps in the process, telling the first step first, then the second step, then the third step, and so on.

The following expository composition explains a specialized process: how to tame a hawk. As you read through the essay, adapted from Jack Samson's *Falconry Today*, follow the notes in the left-hand margin. These notes explain how each paragraph presents information about the process of taming a hawk.

How to Tame a Hawk[1]

The introduction defines *falconry* and gives background information. The last sentence is the thesis statement.

Falconry—hunting with hawks—is one of the few surviving sports that date to the earliest days of recorded human history. Today the popularity of falconry in the United States is growing, especially among young people who are drawn by the nostalgic value as well as by the simple thrill of the sport. Falconry, however, is a sport that requires much preparation and patience. In fact, one of the most difficult and important lessons a beginner has to learn is how to tame the hawk.

This paragraph tells what equipment is needed and where the hawk is kept.

The first equipment a novice falconer needs is a set of jesses. (*Jesses* are strips of light but very tough leather that always remain on the hawk's legs.) Leather jesses should be fastened to the legs as soon as possible after capture. A leash or length of leather should then be fastened to the jesses, and finally the end of the leash is fastened to a perch in a dark room. The hawk is kept in a darkened room until it has calmed down and realized that it is not being attacked or hurt.

The second paragraph of the body gives ways to calm the hawk and get it used to a human.

Whatever the kind of hawk—an eyas hawk (raised from the nest), passager (immature hawk), or haggard (adult)—the beginner will have the same basic problem at first: to calm down the hawk and get it used to its new owner and environment. The initial weeks of captivity are the most important. Falconers in olden days slept beside the cages, keeping a candle or a lantern lit most of the time, and stroking and quietly talking to the birds. A gentle voice, slow movement, and constant encouragement from the falconer are vital in these early stages if the hawk is to accept and tolerate its new partner.

This paragraph explains the significance of the hawk's eating and tells how the hawk should be fed.

The newly acquired hawk must be induced to take food. It may not do this for several days, but even the hawk that has undergone severe trauma during capture will eventually succumb to the temptation of fresh meat. The hawk's first food in captivity is the beginning of its accepting a human, although each hawk has its own timetable in arriving at this compromise. The hawk should eat all its meals from the hand of the falconer at this stage, since it must come to associate food with the human. The falconer should try to get the hawk to eat voluntarily. Force-feeding a hawk may provide the nourishment to keep it alive but does nothing to establish a compatible relationship between bird and owner.

This paragraph gives information about how long it takes to tame a hawk.

There is no rule about how long it will take for a captured hawk to gentle down and stop frantically resisting the owner's attempts to approach it slowly or to hold it on a gloved fist. Some hawks can be gentled in days, but others may take months. Also, there is no hard-and-fast formula for the number of hours a day or night a falconer must spend with a hawk to gentle it. The time in the "mew"—the darkened room to which a falconer brings a new hawk—varies with the wildness of each bird and with the degree of trauma experienced in its capture.

The conclusion explains the purpose behind the process of taming a hawk and tells what qualities experienced falconers think most important for taming a hawk properly.

The gentling of hunting hawks is simply aimed at setting up some form of communication between human and bird. Until the hawk stops fearing the falconer, no training to hunt can begin. It is a long time from the moment of capture—when the hawk, screaming in rage and defiance, falls on its back with wings spread, beak open, and talons straining to sink into a hand—to when a hawk will perch on a gloved hand within inches of a falconer's face, accept food from the human's hand, and allow its feathers to be stroked. Experienced

[1] Adapted from *Falconry Today* by Jack Samson. (Walck, 1976). Reprinted by permission of the author.

falconers know that eventually the moment will come, but it takes patience and persistence. Learn how to wait, they tell the young falconers. That is one of the most valuable secrets to the ancient art of falconry.

For Your Journal

After reading "How to Tame a Hawk," perhaps you will recall an experience you have had with an animal, perhaps training a dog or horse, learning how to milk a cow, or encountering an animal in its natural surroundings. As a journal entry, write your memory of that experience. Include sensory details of the creature's appearance—perhaps the texture of its coat or its color, as well as sounds the animal made and smells you associate with it. Also, write of your own thoughts and feelings about the experience.

Writing Practice 13

Use the Preparing to Write section that follows to help you with ideas for this assignment.

Using one of the following subjects or one of your choice, write an expository composition that explains a process. As you do, follow the steps you have read about in planning and writing a composition: (a) narrow the subject to a topic that can be covered in detail, (b) gather information about the topic, (c) take notes, (d) make an informal outline based on your notes, (e) write the thesis statement, and (f) write the composition, using the informal outline as a guide. The guidelines for writing a good expository composition on pages 85–86 will help you.

1. How to do a household chore more efficiently
2. How to study for a test
3. How to cook your favorite dish
4. How you choose your clothing
5. How to prepare for a backpacking expedition or other outing
6. How to get elected (class president, secretary, treasurer)
7. How an appliance, such as a blender, works

Preparing to Write

An expository essay that explains a process is basically a "how to" paper. Your purpose is to give information about how to do or understand something. As you consider potential subjects, be certain they fit into this "how to" category.

A "how to" essay is best written from experience. Even if you read a great deal about a subject, you will find it difficult to explain a process you have never gone through yourself. One way to begin finding a subject is to allow time to think about your own areas of interest and experience. You may have a talent or hobby, such as painting, roller-skating, swimming, or playing a musical instrument. Perhaps you are fascinated by science fiction, jazz, comic books, poetry, or organic gardening. All these areas are potential subjects for a "how to" paper.

As you think of your own areas of interest and experience, write them down on a piece of scratch paper. Then look at each subject and try to decide how you would narrow it down to a "how to" topic. For example, if the area you enjoy most is painting, you could think of the processes that are a part of painting. Perhaps you could write a composition about how to paint a still life or how to work with watercolors. If you cannot find a simple process to explain in your first area of interest, go to the next area on your list.

Give yourself sufficient time to think about each area. Some ideas will probably come to you immediately; others, however, take time. Do not be discouraged if you cannot think of a topic right away. Also, it is important to remember that your area of interest or experience does not have to be unusual. Having a unique topic does not necessarily make a paper interesting. How you approach the topic and what you have to say about it are more important.

Improving Coherence in the Expository Essay

Coherent writing is writing in which the logical relationships between ideas are apparent.

Writers can improve the coherence of their expository essays in several ways. The simplest approach is to use *transitional devices*—words and phrases such as *first, second, then, now,* and *also.* Other methods are the use of *pronouns* to refer to nouns or other pronouns; *paraphrase,* the restating of words and phrases; and *repetition,* the repeating of key words and phrases. In the following paragraphs from "How to Tame a Hawk," the transitions, which are underlined, are explained.[1]

Repetition: *falconry* is repeated three times in the introduction. Paraphrase: *the sport* means "falconry."

Falconry—hunting with hawks—is one of the few surviving sports that date to the earliest days of recorded human history. Today the popularity of falconry in the United States is growing, especially among young people who are drawn by the nostalgic value as well as by the simple thrill of the sport. Falconry, however, is a sport that requires much preparation and patience. In fact, one of the most difficult and important lessons a beginner has to learn is how to tame the hawk.

Transitional device: *first* tells order of process; paraphrase: *novice falconer* means "the beginner." Use of pronoun: *it* refers to the hawk.

The first equipment a novice falconer needs is a set of jesses. (*Jesses* are strips of light but very tough leather that always remain on the hawk's legs.) Leather jesses should be fastened to the legs as soon as possible after capture. A leash or length of leather should then be fastened to the jesses, and finally the end of the leash is fastened to a perch in a dark room. The hawk is kept in a darkened room until it has calmed down and realized that it is not being attacked or hurt.

Writing Practice 14

Divide a sheet of paper into four columns with the following headings: *Transition Words, Pronouns, Paraphrases,* and *Repetition.* Then read over your

[1]Adapted from *Falconry Today* by Jack Samson. (Walck, 1976.) Reprinted by permission of the author.

process analysis paper to find examples of each kind of transition and copy these words and phrases into the proper columns on your paper. When you have finished, look over your list to determine whether or not you have given your reader enough help with coherence. If not, concentrate on increasing the emphasis on coherence as you revise your paper.

Revising a Process Analysis Essay

Revise your process analysis essay in two ways. First revise as you write, rereading and rethinking your sentences as you work. Look back at each sentence and paragraph to be certain that your ideas follow in an order that makes sense and that you are saying exactly what you mean. Second revise after finishing your first draft. The first draft, or copy, of a composition is sometimes called a *rough draft*. When you revise, you smooth out passages and then rewrite your paper as a final draft.

For a review of revision, see pages 85–86.

The best way to revise a rough draft is to wait at least a day after finishing it. This distance will give you a new perspective on your composition, and you are more likely to find the places that are unclear or difficult to follow. Reading your composition as if you knew nothing about the subject will also help you to improve the clarity of your writing.

Use the following checklist to revise your process analysis paper, checking it carefully against each of the points. (Your teacher may wish to read your paper first or may give you additional instructions about revision.) Make your changes on your rough draft and then recopy your paper before turning it in. As a final step, proofread your paper using the Checklist for Proofreading on pages 20–21.

Use the Checklist for Proofreading on pages 20–21 to check your writing for features that do not conform to ESE.

Checklist for Revising a Process Analysis Essay

1. The topic is sufficiently limited for the length of the paper.
2. The purpose of the paper is clearly identified in a thesis statement.
3. The introductory paragraph includes the thesis statement and presents interesting background information about the topic.
4. Each paragraph of the body develops the thesis statement.
5. Each step in the process is clearly and fully explained.
6. The composition has a logical organization.
7. The composition includes sufficient illustrations about the topic.
8. The composition makes use of transitions to improve coherence.
9. The conclusion refers back to the main idea of the composition by restating it in a new way.
10. The composition has a title that previews the content of the paper.

Writing Examination Essays

Much of what you have already learned about writing expository essays will help you to write good examination essays. Both types of essays require working with a limited topic, developing a thesis statement, and supporting your main idea with illustrations such as examples, quotations, facts, and figures. Successful essay examination writing, however, also depends on your ability to understand each direction exactly, to write directly and thoroughly, and to budget your time properly.

Types of Essay Examinations

Items on essay examinations generally fall into three categories: comparison, trace, and explain. Determining each item's type will help you to organize your ideas.

The purpose of *comparison items* is to test your understanding of the relationship between two aspects of a subject: how they are alike and how they are different from one another.

Comparison items often are given when you are studying two or more historical periods, works of literature, systems, processes, or people. For example, suppose your class has been studying systems of government around the world. A possible question for an essay exam might be "What are the similarities and differences between the U.S. Congress and the British Parliament?" The words *similarities and differences* are cue words that will help you recognize the comparison type of essay. In the following sample items other frequently used cue words are *italicized.*

> Tell how the wet tropics and the dry tropics are *alike and different.*
>
> What are the *similarities and differences* between Shakespeare's lovers in the two plays you have read?
>
> What characteristics do animal communication and human language have *in common?*

The purpose of *trace items* is to test your understanding of the interrelating parts of your subject or to test your understanding of how your subject works as a process.

Trace items often occur when you are studying the steps in a process, a series of events and their outcome, or how something is assembled. If your class has studied, for example, the process of digestion, or the events leading up to the French Revolution, or the procedure for putting together an automobile engine, you might expect to be tested on this information with a trace item.

Some trace items can be identified by the word *trace* itself, as in "*Trace* the important events of 1789 leading up to the French Revolution." Other important cue words for trace items are *italicized* in the following examples.

List and discuss the *steps* in the human digestive process.

Review the major *steps* in assembling a car engine.

Outline what happens during photosynthesis.

Enumerate and discuss the accomplishments made during the reign of Julius Caesar.

The purpose of *explain items* is to test your ability to analyze a subject. Explain items often are given when you have been studying causes, results, definitions, or interpretations. In an explain item you are instructed to give information to explain the reason or cause of your subject, the results of your subject, the definition of a relevant word or phrase, or interpretations of the meaning of your subject.

The most frequently used words in explain items are *explain* and *discuss*. Other similar words that you can look for are *describe, tell, analyze, interpret, criticize,* and *define*. In the following examples of explain items, the cue words are *italicized.*

Describe the effects of PCB on the drinking water supply in the United States.

Discuss the major dangers to human health caused by smoking.

Analyze the importance of the blockades used during the Civil War.

Define the word *metaphor* and give an *interpretation* of the central metaphor in the following poem.

Writing Practice 15

The following sample essay directions fall into the categories of comparison, trace, or explain items. Number a sheet of paper 1–15 and write out the correct category after each direction or question number.

Example

a. Compare the major scientific predictions of Leonardo da Vinci with those of H. G. Wells.

a. comparison

1. Outline the process involved in the formation of a volcano.
2. Enumerate the steps taken in compiling a dictionary.
3. In what ways are bee and ant colonies like human social structures? In what ways are they different?
4. Describe the role of the Supreme Court in the government of the United States.
5. What is hyperventilation and how does it affect the body?
6. Discuss the importance of the "Underground Railroad" during the Civil War.
7. Review the reasons that Verdi's first opera caused a riot.
8. How are soccer and football alike?
9. Trace the development and formation of the State of Israel.

10. Tell what characteristics the writing styles of William Faulkner and Ken Kesey have in common.
11. Explain the term *plutocracy* and give two examples of it from your reading.
12. Discuss three groups that tried to form utopian societies.
13. Analyze the role of the adrenal glands in the human body.
14. Liken and contrast the contributions of two scientists you have studied in this class.
15. List and discuss the steps by which members of the electoral college are elected in this state.

Planning Your Writing Time

One of the biggest problems students face in taking exams is budgeting time. Some, for example, spend too much time writing everything they know about one or two questions and find they cannot finish the examination. Organizing your writing will help you avoid such problems.

First, allow time to preview the entire examination. Read through all the directions and items before you begin writing, so that you know the kinds of items on the exam and which ones you can answer readily. It is best to write the answers to items you are sure of first to get full credit for what you know and leave the more difficult questions until later. For a one-hour exam you should allow five minutes for previewing the items.

Second, budget time for each question. To ensure enough time to finish the exam, make a rough estimate of the amount of time you can spend on each item. If your examination is an hour long and you need to answer three items, budget five minutes for previewing, five minutes at the end for reviewing your answers, and a little over fifteen minutes for each item. If your teacher assigns point values for each item, take the points into consideration when budgeting your time. For example, if the first two items are worth twenty-five points and the final item is worth fifty points, you will know that you should budget twice as much time for writing the final item as for the first two.

Writing down the exact time you should begin answering each item helps you keep track of your total time for the examination and sets a schedule for completing the work. If you find yourself falling behind schedule, you may want to leave an item and go on to the next one in order to finish. If you do not finish an item, leave sufficient blank space between it and the next one, so that you can go back during the reviewing period to complete it.

Third, allow time to review and check your answers. Always leave a short amount of time at the end of the exam to reread your answers, checking to be certain that you have answered each item thoroughly and that you have made no errors in grammar, punctuation, or spelling. Often you will be writing quickly, and it is easy to leave out words or make other careless mistakes. For a one-hour exam allow about five minutes for this checking procedure.

Reading Directions

Be sure to read all directions carefully and completely before you begin writing an essay.

Directions for each item often contain important cue words that tell you how to organize your answer. In the following sample examination directions the notes in the left-hand margin explain the specific items of the exam.

1. Fact about playwrights
2. Cue word
3. Direction and cue
4. Content and organization
5. Direction
6. Direction

> Unlike the novelist, the [1] writer of a play seldom uses a narrator's voice to talk directly to the audience in order to guide their responses to characters and actions. [2] *Select* a play you have read this year and [3] *write an essay* explaining how the playwright guides the audience's emotions to the central characters and action. You might consider such [4] techniques by the playwright as using similar or contrasting characters, the effect of setting on the audience, and the characters' responses to each other. [5] *Give examples* from the play you select. [6] *Do not give* a plot summary.

The preceding examination has four separate instructions: (1) select a play you have read this year, (2) write an essay of explanation, (3) give examples from the play, and (4) do not give a plot summary of the play. You must understand each of these instructions in order to write a good essay in response.

Examination items also indicate the range of information you can cover in your essay. Careful reading will tell you how to limit each answer. For example, the preceding examination limits the scope of your essay to one play that you have read during the year. You may not discuss more than one play, and you may not discuss a play you read two years ago. Because careful reading of directions is so important, never skim over them to save time. Read them thoroughly. If your teacher permits, underline the cue words and the specific instructions for easy reference.

Writing Practice 16

Each of the following examinations contains several instructions. Read each item thoroughly. On a separate sheet of paper, list the separate directions in each. Also, identify any cue words you find.

Example

a. From your readings on Mayan civilization, choose one aspect of Mayan culture that interests you and write an essay telling why you feel it was important. Write at least three paragraphs on this subject. Do not make a list of accomplishments of the civilization.

a. *Choose one aspect of Mayan culture that interests you.* (direction)
Write an essay of explanation. (direction)
Telling why (cue words)
Write at least three paragraphs. (direction)
Do not make a list of accomplishments. (direction)

1. In many countries farmers have successfully used crop rotation to help the quality of the land. From your readings in this class, select two examples of successful crop rotation and write an essay analyzing why they were successful. Include information explaining why each particular crop was chosen to rotate with the other.
2. Democracy, government by the people, originated in ancient Greece and flourished in the city-state of Athens. There are many differences, however, between Athenian democracy and Western democracy as it is practiced today. Write an essay comparing Athenian democracy and Western democracy. Be sure to include the making of laws and the voting system in your points of comparison.

Organizing Your Essay Examination

Organizing your thoughts before you begin to write is essential for essay examinations.

As a first step you may want to jot down key words or phrases that occur to you as you read each examination item during the previewing period. You can write your ideas in the margins of the examination sheet or on a piece of scratch paper, if one is allowed. These ideas will serve as an idea bank to help you get started on the answer.

Second write a very brief outline for each question if time allows. You do not want to waste valuable writing time making a complete outline, but a rough idea of what point to begin with, what examples to use, and what sequence to write in will help make your answer complete and coherent.

Third write the most important information in the opening sentences or opening paragraph, if it is a longer essay. An essay exam answer is different from an essay you write over an extended period of time. Essay answers should get directly to the point, answer the item in clear and concise language, and be brief but complete.

Unless your directions instruct otherwise, you do not need to write an introduction to your essay. You may focus attention on the topic by repeating a word or phrase from the exam directions in your opening statement or by referring directly to the topic by name. For example, read the following sample essay item.

> List three important changes in the game of baseball since 1950. Explain the effects of each change.

Notice how, in the following first sentence of a response, the writer repeats a key phrase in the item and introduces the information sought.

> Since 1950 baseball has doubled the number of its teams, gone to a more lively ball to increase distance, and admitted the unionization of baseball players.

Getting directly to the point in an exam essay serves two purposes. First if for some reason you are unable to finish the essay, you have at least indicated that you know part of the answer. Second giving the three changes makes a kind of outline for the essay: you can discuss the changes in the order that you have first given them.

After you have made your main point in the opening sentence, follow it up by developing your ideas and supporting them with illustrations, such as details, examples, quotations, facts, and figures.

The following sample essay answer shows how to focus on the most important information first and then discuss it in detail. As you read, follow the notes in the margin.

First sentence makes main point; second sentence explains feudal system.

Instructions: Identify and explain the social structure of Europe during the Middle Ages.

> The feudal system was the social structure of Europe during the Middle Ages. The system has been described as a pyramid, with a broad base of peasants at the bottom, several levels of nobility in the middle, and the king at the top. In a feudal society all members had certain rights and duties connected with those rights. The king, to begin with, was lord of the entire realm and owned all the land. His duties included protecting all of those who served his kingdom. Since he couldn't rule everywhere at once, the king divided his realm into parcels of land called *fiefdoms*, each controlled by a vassal in chief. Vassals were nobles who were tenants of the king. In return for their land, they owed the king a share of their crops, taxes, military service, and above all, their loyalty. The chiefs of the fiefdoms in turn divided their lands and responsibilities among lesser noblemen, down to the lowest knights in the hierarchy. The knights parceled out the actual farming to the peasants who were bound to the land. Being bound meant that the peasants could not leave the land to find a better place; their duty was to their lord. It was their right, though, to have the protection of their lord, who was responsible for them. Because of the duties and privileges of each group, the feudal system was a strong, interlaced social structure.

Example of king's rights and duties

Definition of *fiefdom*
Definition of *vassal*
Example of vassals' rights and duties

Definition of *bound*

Example of peasants' rights and duties
Concluding statement

Writing Practice 17

On a separate sheet of paper, write two opening sentences for one or more of the following essay examinations. Include the main information you would use for the essay in the opening sentence and try to repeat some of the phrases from the item.

1. Many of the changes in the sport of football over the last thirty years have been highly controversial. Select two of these changes and write an essay explaining their effect on the game.
2. Television's effect on reading and studying habits among young people is a much-debated subject. Using your personal experience or the experiences of your friends, write an essay analyzing television's impact. Make clear whether or not you believe the effect has been positive or negative.

3. A stereotyped view of men is that they are always supposed to be strong, silent types who do not express much emotion and who are more concerned with action than thought. Draw on your knowledge of characters in fiction, movies, on television, or in history and write an essay about one man who does not fall into this stereotype. List and explain the important characteristics of his that do not fit the stereotyped model.
4. "Honesty is the best policy" is a saying people like to repeat. Is the saying always true? Write an essay giving your opinion about the value of being completely honest in every situation.
5. Mark Twain once said, "Everyone complains about the weather, but no one does anything about it." The same is often true, unfortunately, of the future. Many people are concerned about what the future will bring but are uncertain of what to do about it. Write an essay comparing how you feel about the future with how your parents (or one of your friends/siblings/teachers) feel about the future. Write not only about your personal future but also about the future in general of this country and of this planet.

Writing the Comparison-and-Contrast Essay

In a comparison-and-contrast examination you will find at least two items to liken and contrast: two people, events, attitudes, and so on. To write an effective response you should define or identify both items in your essay. For example, if you are comparing common law with Napoleonic law, you should define both of your terms at the beginning of the essay. If the terms cannot be defined in a simple sentence, give examples and details to describe them. In a comparison of wet tropics and dry tropics, for instance, you would give a brief definition of each and then describe the characteristics of temperature, degree of moisture, location, and vegetation of each.

For a review of developing comparison paragraphs, see pages 65–67.

Next it is important to decide on the points of comparison. Ask yourself how the items are alike and how they are different. Decide before you begin writing whether you will use a point-by-point comparison or a block comparison in your essay. As you reread your essay at the end of the exam, use the following checklist.

The Comparison-and-Contrast Essay

1. The terms are defined clearly and completely.
2. The terms are adequately described with examples and details.
3. The items are compared to show likenesses.
4. The items are contrasted to show differences.
5. Illustrations (such as details, examples, facts, and figures) are used to support the essay.
6. The essay stays within the limits of the directions.
7. The essay is legible and has no errors in grammar, punctuation, or spelling.

8. The question is answered completely; the instructions are followed carefully.

Writing the Trace Essay

In responding to a trace item, you should first be sure of its scope. For example, if the directions cover only the time period of the Boxer Rebellion in China, do not write about the years before or after this period. To go outside the boundaries set by the exam detracts from your concentration on your response and in some cases can result in a wrong answer.

Next be certain to define any terms that are important to your essay. Sometimes, the instructions specify a definition; however, if you are using a key term or an unusual term, you should define it even if you are not instructed to do so. Do not waste time defining commonly accepted terms unless the definition is in some way relevant to your essay. For example, in writing about the electoral college, you would not need to make a complete definition of the word *democracy*. You would need to define it, however, if you were writing about the origin of the Democratic party.

For more information about using chronological order in writing, see pages 55–56.

Finally trace examinations usually ask you to follow a sequence of some kind. As you think through your response or write your brief outline, be certain that you keep the steps or the chain of events in their proper order.

As you reread your essay at the end of the exam, use the following checklist.

The Trace Essay

1. The response stays within the scope of the instructions.
2. The terms are defined clearly and completely.
3. The ideas are presented in a proper sequence.
4. Illustration (such as examples, details, facts, and figures) is used to support the essay.
5. The essay is legible and has no errors of grammar, punctuation, or spelling.
6. The questions are answered completely; the directions are followed exactly.

Writing the Explain Essay

Since there is a wide range of explain instructions, first be certain that you spot the cue word in the exam so that you follow the instructions exactly. If you are asked to define a term and give an example, do just that. Do not compare it with another term or explain its history. Staying focused on the exact directions is essential to writing a good essay answer.

Some explain items may be long and complex, requiring careful reading and interpretation on your part. The instructions may direct you to do several things in your response. Allow yourself enough time to organize your thoughts so that you cover all parts of the directions. The following is an example of a complex explain item.

> Several kinds of "escape" literature have become extremely popular in the twentieth century. Discuss one type of escape literature that is currently popular, name at least one writer who does that kind of writing, and describe briefly his or her work. Finally account briefly for the popularity of escape literature in the twentieth century.

This item directs you to do four things:

1. *Discuss one type of escape literature that is currently popular.*
   Name one type of escape literature, describe it, and explain what it is like.
2. *Name at least one writer who does that kind of writing.*
   When *at least* appears in a question, you know that you are not required to give more than one example. If there is time to write about more than one, you can do so, or you can add another example at the end of the examination during the review time.
3. *Describe briefly his or her work.*
   The cue word *describe* tells you to give characteristic details and examples of the writer's work. *Briefly* tells you to summarize the most important points and not try to write everything you know about the subject.
4. *Account briefly for the popularity of escape literature in the twentieth century.*
   This statement asks you to make a judgment and to give reasons why the literature is popular. Base your response not only on your personal opinion but also on reasons discussed in class and on reasons from the reading you have done on the subject.

In beginning the explain essay, you should define or identify any key terms. For the preceding exam you should include a brief definition of escape literature in your opening statement.

As you reread your answer at the end of the exam, use the following checklist.

The Explain Essay

1. All the key terms are defined or identified.
2. The instructions are thoroughly followed in the order given.
3. The response is supported with sufficient illustrations to make the point clear.
4. The essay stays within the limits of the directions.
5. The essay is legible and has no errors of grammar, punctuation, or spelling.

Writing Practice 18

Using the essay items listed in Writing Practice 17 or a question your teacher assigns, write a response. As you do, follow these steps: (a) preview the exam, (b) make notes about the questions and instructions, (c) budget your time, (d) write a brief outline or list of important points for each instruction, (e) keep to a schedule in writing your responses, (f) include the most important information in the first sentences of the essay, and (g) allow reviewing time after you have responded to each instruction.

5 Research Writing

Writing a Research Paper

Whatever your career plans, whether you plan to work as a scientist, a teacher, a plant supervisor, or an owner of your own business, your job will probably require you to locate and evaluate information, organize ideas or tasks, and communicate effectively with others. Because the research paper requires all these skills, you may be asked to write this kind of paper in high school and college classes as preparation for your future.

The *research*, or *term*, *paper* is a long, formal essay presenting specific information drawn from several sources.

Writing a research paper involves the same skills used in writing an expository essay but also requires using library resources and identifying those sources in footnotes and a bibliography. For some research papers you simply bring together the existing information on the topic in an organized way. Others require you to answer a specific question or draw conclusions.

Preparing a research paper requires thorough planning and careful work. In this chapter you will learn how to follow each step in the research process: choosing and limiting a topic, finding and evaluating sources of information, taking notes, making an outline, writing a rough draft and footnotes, and preparing the final draft with a bibliography. Your research paper will be easier to write and more effective if you follow the procedure outlined in this chapter.

Choosing and Limiting a Topic

Once you have decided on an interesting subject, limit it to a topic that is neither too general nor too specific. Your topic should be broad enough to include interesting information and narrow enough so that you can discuss it in depth. If your teacher suggests a certain length for the assignment, that suggestion will also influence how you narrow the topic.

One way to decide whether or not your topic is adequately limited is to check your library's resources. If you find whole books written on your topic, it is probably too general; on the other hand, if you find very little information on the topic, it may be too limited. If your topic covers many years (the history of American film, for example) or many categories or groups (religions of the world), it is probably too general for a research paper.

Suppose you are interested in almost everything connected with motion pictures. You probably already realize that the history of motion pictures or even a history of motion pictures before World War II is too broad a topic. Since you know the earliest motion pictures were silent, you decide to focus on that time period. However, an hour in the library convinces you that this topic is still too general. After looking at the books and articles that most interest you, you decide to focus on a particular event—the change from silent movies to sound.

Writing Practice 1

Divide a sheet of paper into two columns with the headings *Subjects* and *Limited Topics.* Use the brainstorming technique described on pages 27–29 to discover general subjects that interest you and list them in the first column. (You may also want to look at the list of subjects on pages 113–114.) In the second column write five good topics for a short research paper that you have developed from the subjects in the first column.

Writing Practice 2

Using the card catalogue in your library and the *Readers' Guide to Periodical Literature,* find two or more books and two or more articles with information about your research topic or about a topic you choose for this assignment. On a separate sheet of paper, write the titles of the books and articles, the name and dates of the magazines where the articles appear, and the names of the authors. If you cannot locate enough sources, think about how the topic can be broadened.

Getting an Overview

When you have decided on your topic, the next step is to get an overview, or general idea, of what is involved in that topic. If you have decided to discuss the transition from silent movies to sound, for example, you could check the entries under *sound* and *motion pictures* in several encyclopedias for an overview. You could also look through books with general information about movie history. *Subject* cards in the card catalogue, the *Readers' Guide,* and encyclopedias are also good places to find background information on your topic.

Developing Basic Questions

Methods for gathering information are discussed in the chapter "Discovering Subject Matter."

After you read enough background information to have a general understanding of your topic, you can then list the basic questions you will try to answer in your paper. This list will help later as you decide what information to put on your note cards. (Using the *who? what? where? when? why? how?* system is one way to gather ideas for questions.) Once you have listed the questions your paper will answer, arranging them as an informal preliminary outline is helpful. After developing this outline, you may discover new areas that your questions do not cover, or you may find that your topic involves too many questions and must be limited even further.

A preliminary outline of basic questions for a research paper on the advent of sound movies might look like the following one.

Why were the earliest movies silent?
Why did it take so long for the first sound motion pictures to appear?
What problems did inventors face in adding sound to moving pictures?
How and when were these problems solved?
Who solved them?
When did the first sound motion picture appear?
Where was the first sound motion picture produced?
How did the silent film industry react to the sound motion picture?
How did sound affect the film industry?

Writing Practice 3

After reading to gain background information, prepare a list of basic questions about your research paper topic or a topic you select for this assignment. The *who? what? where? when? why? how?* system described in the above paragraph or another system for gathering information will help you develop ideas for questions. Finally organize your list of questions as an informal outline.

Gathering Information

The next step in the research process is to gather information for your paper from books and magazines, personal interviews, pamphlets, and other resources. The library chapter on pages 198–219 will tell you how to locate and use library resources.

The Bibliography Card

Because readers often want to know what books, articles, and pamphlets were used in a writer's research, the writer attaches a list of these sources, called a *bibliography*, at the end of the research paper. As you gather information, note the title, author, place and date of publication, and other necessary information on a *bibliography card*. Having such cards will make it much easier for you to prepare the final bibliography.

The order in which title, author, and publishing information are presented in a bibliography card, and later in a bibliography, and the marks of punctuation that separate these items follow a standard form. The form used by most writers and researchers is the one found in the *MLA Handbook*, published by the Modern Language Association. Although the MLA form is used in this chapter, your teacher may ask you to use one of the many other acceptable forms.

The following bibliography card shows the form for a book; magazines, newspapers, pamphlets, and personal interviews have a slightly different form.

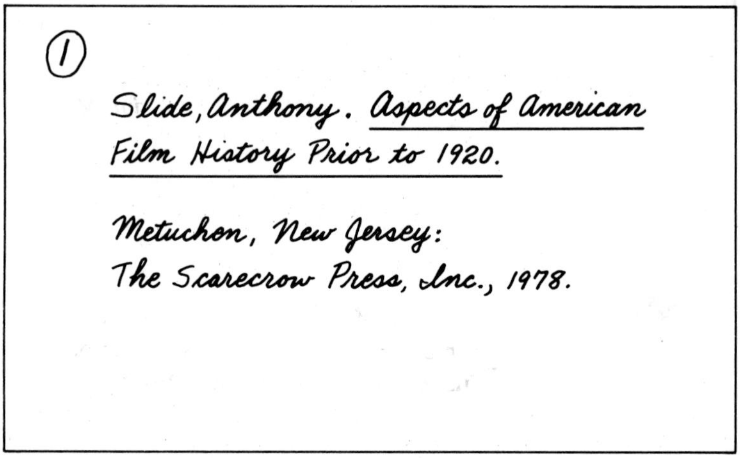
1

Slide, Anthony. Aspects of American Film History Prior to 1920.

Metuchen, New Jersey:
The Scarecrow Press, Inc., 1978.

The circled number in the upper-left corner of the preceding sample bibliography card identifies Anthony Slide's book as source Number *1.* Numbering each source will save time later when you take notes from that source.

The following list, composed of fictitious authors and titles, shows the format for other kinds of bibliography entries. Notice that the punctuation marks separating items of information have been enlarged to help you become familiar with their use in a bibliography entry.

Note that punctuation in bibliography differs from the punctuation in footnotes (pages 110–111).

BOOK BY ONE AUTHOR

Fleece, Jason. *Searching for Gold*. Rome: Myth Press, 1978.

BOOK BY MORE THAN ONE AUTHOR

Bow, Mary, and John Arrow. *Straight Shooting*. Lansing: University Press, 1983.

ESSAY WITHIN A COLLECTION OF PIECES BY DIFFERENT AUTHORS

Windward, Lee. "Sailing the Open Seas." In *Sailor Beware*. Ed. Travis Seek and Lindsay Find. New York: Mainsail Books, 1984.

EDITION OF A WORK OF LITERATURE

Austere, Jane. *Gone with the Times*. Ed. Pamela Perfect. London: Lowe Classics, 1933.

ARTICLE IN AN ENCYCLOPEDIA OR OTHER REFERENCE WORK

Line, Sally. "Eels." *Encyclopedia Animalia*. 1982 ed.

ARTICLE FROM A MONTHLY MAGAZINE

Manly, Strouther. "Fowl Flight." *Wings*. May 1980, pp. 43–50.

ARTICLE FROM A NEWSPAPER (NO AUTHOR GIVEN)

"Ninety Per Cent Voter Turnout." *Athens Gazetteer*, 5 Nov. 1980, p. 37.

REVIEW OF A FILM, BOOK, OR PLAY

Knight, Daly. Rev. of *Afternoon of a Morning Person*, by Woolsey Wakely. *Search*, 12 Jan. 1982, p. 53.

INTERVIEW

Midas, David. Investment Broker. Personal Interview, Worldwide Investment Analysis. 9 Mar. 1980.

RADIO OR TELEVISION PROGRAM

"Moving Monsters." *Movietime Matinee*, CBS, 23 Jan. 1979.

PAMPHLET

U.S. Cong. House. *Report on Air Disasters*, by J. R. Daedalus. Washington, D.C.: GPO, 1979.

Writing Practice 4

Prepare a bibliography card for each source you will use in your research paper or select a topic for this assignment and prepare five bibliography cards, using sources from your library.

Taking Notes

The next step in the research process is to take notes from the sources you have located. This step will be easier if you keep your list of basic questions in mind. When a piece of specific information relates to your list of questions, record that information on a note card but avoid taking notes on unrelated information. For example, you may discover intriguing facts about the first movies produced in color, but if your topic is limited to the advent of sound movies, you will not need this information. Skim a book's table of contents and use the index at the back of the book to locate sections or pages related to your topic.

Putting your notes on note cards will make the task of organizing them later much easier. If you take notes on cards, limiting each card to information about one item or idea, you can arrange these cards later to fit the organization of your outline.

Before you begin to take notes on a card, place the circled bibliography card number for that source in the upper-right corner of the card. For example, if *Birth of the Talkies* is source Number 2, every note card with information from this source should have the circled Number 2 in the upper-right corner. Putting this source number on the card saves work; you will not have to list the title of the source on each note card. Under the source number place the page number(s) from which your note is taken. You may also want to put a topic heading in the upper-right corner of the card.

It is important to take notes carefully. Usually you will summarize or record information in your own words. You may want to write your notes in phrases or use abbreviations and symbols (& for *and*, for example) but be certain your notes are complete enough to understand later. Sometimes, you will want to record an author's exact words because they are important or especially well-chosen. Do this sparingly, however, remembering to quote exactly and to put quotation marks around the author's words. Plagiarism, using another's words as your own, is an unfair and illegal practice. If you take notes in your own words and mark quotations, you can avoid this word and idea theft.

Notice the location of the source number, page number, and topic heading on the following sample note card.

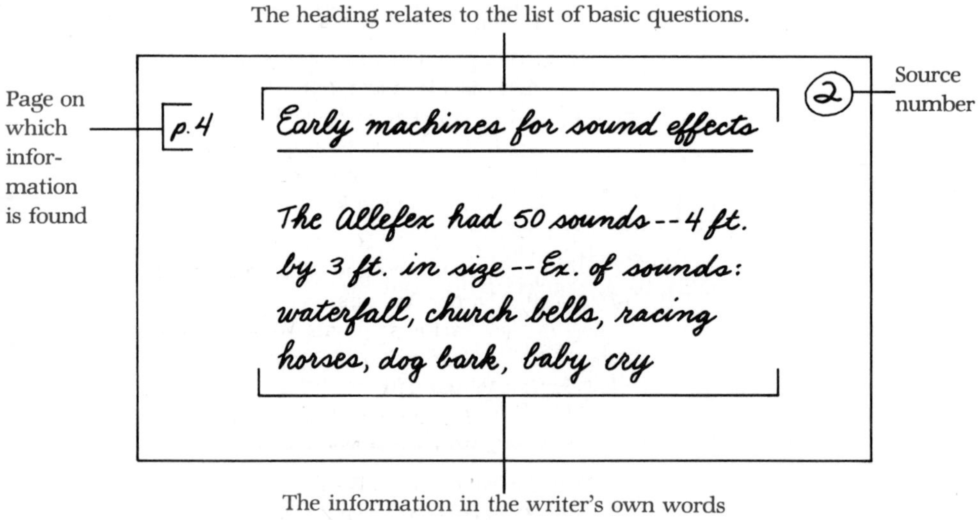
The heading relates to the list of basic questions.
Page on which information is found
p.4
Early machines for sound effects
2
Source number
The Allefex had 50 sounds--4 ft. by 3 ft. in size--Ex. of sounds: waterfall, church bells, racing horses, dog bark, baby cry
The information in the writer's own words

After taking notes on all your sources, sort the cards into stacks that correspond to your list of questions. Do you have enough information to answer each question adequately? Have you located new information that will require changing some of your basic questions or have you discovered new questions? This is the time to look up any further information you need.

Writing Practice 5

Using your research paper topic or another topic you select for this assignment, write note cards on the information you find in at least four sources.

The Formal Outline

Once you have reviewed your note cards and sorted them into stacks that correspond to your basic questions, you can prepare a *formal outline*. Because a research paper involves organizing many small pieces of information clearly

Steps in preparing an informal outline are discussed on pages 76–77.

and logically, an outline that lists the points to be discussed in the best order is almost essential. The formal outline uses Roman numerals (*I, II, III*), capital letters (*A, B, C*), and Arabic numbers (*1, 2, 3*) to show the order, relationship, and relative importance of the ideas in the paper.

The headings in a formal outline share a similar pattern. An outline in which all the headings are stated as complete sentences is a *sentence outline;* one in which only words and phrases are used as headings is called a *topic outline.* These two forms should not be mixed in the same outline. Decide beforehand whether you will use a sentence outline or topic outline.

The following topic outline is for a research paper on the transition from silent to sound movies.

I. Sound with early silents
    A. Background music
    B. Special sound effects
    C. Singers and actors

II. Attempts to link film and sound
    A. Edison's Kinetophone
        1. Problem with synchronization
        2. Problem with amplification
    B. The sound-on-film process
    C. De Forest's work

III. The Reaction of Hollywood
    A. Resistance of most film companies
    B. Warner Brothers
        1. Partnership with Western Electric
        2. Production of *Don Juan*
    C. William Fox
        1. Purchase of Case-Spondable system
        2. Movietone News Service

IV. Arrival of the "talkies"
    A. Success of *The Jazz Singer*
    B. Problems to surmount
        1. Technicians and equipment
        2. Stationary microphones
        3. Voices of silent film stars

V. Importance of silent films today

Notice in the preceding sample outline that there are always two or more divisions under a heading (see Roman numerals I–III) or none at all (see Roman numeral V). The divisions (or subheadings) show how a broad point is subdivided into smaller parts; when a point cannot be divided into two or more parts, there is no reason for a subheading.

Following is the first part of the outline in sentence form.

I. The early silent films were accompanied with sound.
    A. Organs and pianos were used in the background.
    B. Stagehands created special effects.
    C. Singers performed songs, and actors spoke dialogue.

Writing Practice 6

Using the information you have gathered on note cards for your paper or new information you gather for this assignment, write either a formal sentence or a topic outline for a research paper on the topic.

The Rough Draft

The next step is to write a rough, or first, draft of the research paper, using your formal outline and note cards. The term *rough* indicates that this draft will not be a perfect, final product; most writers focus on putting their ideas into clear, well-organized sentences and paragraphs at this stage. Later, in the final draft, they concentrate more closely on spelling, punctuation, and grammar.

Writing your rough draft will be easier if you organize your note cards to correspond with your outline. Since a research paper is a longer essay, remember the paragraph- and essay-writing skills you have studied or review this information. You may find that some of your notes do not fit the final organization of your paper or that you need more details to develop your topic. (Do not be afraid to omit or add information to improve the quality of your paper.)

Two important parts of writing a rough draft are incorporating the quoted material you plan to use and adding footnotes.

Using Quotations

If you plan to use an author's exact words in your research paper, you will need to know the procedures for placing quotations. Long quotations, usually more than three lines of poetry or five lines of prose, are separated from the body of the paper. A short statement followed by a colon usually introduces the long quotation, and the quotation is then indented five spaces from the left-hand margin. (The first line of the quotation is indented another five.) If you write your paper in longhand, be certain that your reader can tell you are quoting directly by making the indention obvious and by introducing the quotation. Because this special form indicates that the passage is a quotation, the quotation marks at the beginning and end of the passage are omitted.

The following example, part of the paper "Sound Comes to the Movies," shows how to introduce and indent a long quotation.

> Meanwhile, other scientists were experimenting with a different method of linking sound with film: the sound-on-film process, in which electrical currents are used to capture the sound directly on photographic film. Frederic Thrasher, author of *Okay for Sound,* provides the following explanation of the process:
>
> > When the sound is reproduced, a photoelectric cell is used to convert the variations in the light beam as it passes through the "sound track" of the moving film, into electrical currents which in turn are changed into sound at the loudspeakers.[4]

Short quotations of fewer than three lines are not indented; quotation marks at the beginning and end of such passages indicate that the words are a quotation. A short quotation should fit smoothly into the sentence or paragraph to which it is added, as the following examples show.

> The death of the young bride is foreshadowed in Act II of *Medea* when her attendants talk of "frightening irrational things"[5] and the face of nature "flawed with omens."[6]

> Millions identified with such silent stars as Charlie Chaplin, "the bum who wanted above all else to attain human dignity,"[1] and Mary Pickford, "America's sweetheart."

In the preceding examples the words enclosed in quotation marks are quoted exactly; however, they fit grammatically into the rest of the sentence.

Adding Footnotes

Footnotes—notes placed at the bottom, or foot, of the paper—tell readers where they can locate important information or exact quotations used in the paper. (Your teacher may prefer that you use *endnotes*, placed at the end of the paper.) Any material you have quoted exactly must be footnoted to give the author credit. Rare, unusual facts or ideas developed by a particular author are also footnoted, since these are the products of that author's research or original thinking. However, when several sources mention the same facts or ideas, the information is considered general knowledge and does not require a footnote.

As they write their rough drafts, many students find it helpful to put the footnote immediately after the material to which it refers. Later, the footnotes can be moved to the bottom of the page or assembled at the end of the paper.

The model on pages 114–119 shows how footnotes appear in a finished research paper. As you examine that model, notice the following important points about footnotes.

1. They are numbered consecutively (*1, 2, 3*).
2. They appear at the bottom of the page on which a source is used or on a separate page at the end of the paper.
3. The slightly raised numbers (by half a line) in the paper identify material that is footnoted and tell the reader which footnote to see for information about that source.
4. Four lines of space separate the last line of text and the first footnote.
5. The first line of the footnote is indented five spaces.
6. One space separates the raised footnote number and the first word of the footnote itself.
7. Information within the footnote is single-spaced; footnotes are separated by a double space.
8. An abbreviated form is used for the second and all later footnotes referring to a source already footnoted.

The following sample footnotes show the MLA form for various sources; your teacher may ask you to use this form or another accepted footnote form. Notice that the order and punctuation used in footnotes differs from that used in a bibliography. The punctuation marks have been emphasized to help you become familiar with their use in footnotes.

BOOK BY ONE AUTHOR

[1] Jason Fleece, *Searching for Gold* (Rome: Myth Press 1978), p. 2.

BOOK BY MORE THAN ONE AUTHOR

[2] Mary Bow and John Arrow, *Straight Shooting* (Lansing: University Press, 1983), pp. 24–25.

ESSAY WITHIN A COLLECTION OF PIECES BY DIFFERENT AUTHORS

[3] Lee Windward, "Sailing the Open Seas" in *Sailor Beware*, eds. Travis Seek and Lindsay Find (New York: Mainsail Books, 1984), p. 10.

EDITION OF A WORK OF LITERATURE

[4] Jane Austere, *Gone with the Times*, ed. Pamela Perfect (London: Lowe Classics, 1933), p. 111.

ARTICLE IN AN ENCYCLOPEDIA OR OTHER REFERENCE WORK

[5] Sally Line, "Eels," *Encyclopedia Animalia*, 1982 ed.

ARTICLE FROM A MONTHLY MAGAZINE

[6] Strouther Manly, "Fowl Flight," *Wings*, May 1980, p. 43.

ARTICLE FROM A DAILY NEWSPAPER (NO AUTHOR GIVEN)

[7] "Ninety Per Cent Voter Turnout," *Athens Gazetteer*, 5 Nov. 1980, Sec. 1, p. 37, col. 1.

REVIEW OF A FILM, BOOK, OR PLAY

[8] Daly Knight, rev. of *Afternoon of a Morning Person*, by Woolsey Wakely, *Search*, 12 Jan. 1982, p. 53.

INTERVIEW

[10] Personal interview with David Midas, Investment Broker, World Wide Investment Analysis, 9 Mar. 1980.

RADIO OR TELEVISION PROGRAM

[11] "Moving Monsters," *Movietime Matinee*, CBS, 23 Jan. 1979.

PAMPHLET

[9] U.S. Cong., House, *Report on Air Disasters*, by J. R. Daedalus (Washington, D.C.: GPO, 1979), p. 2.

Since your first footnote for a source provides complete information, the second and all later references to that same source use an abbreviated form.

Usually this abbreviated form includes only the author's last name and the page number for the information you are footnoting. If you use two books by the same author, add a shortened form of the book's title after the author's last name. The following segment from a footnote page shows how this abbreviated form is used.

[1] Arthur Knight, *The Liveliest Art* (New York: The New American Library, 1957), p. 144.

[2] Knight, p. 106.

[3] Frank Manchel, *When Pictures Began to Move* (Englewood Cliffs, N.J.: Prentice-Hall, Inc., 1969), p. 48.

[4] Frank Manchel, *When Movies Began to Speak* (Englewood Cliffs, N.J.: Prentice-Hall, Inc., 1969), p. 48.

[5] Manchel, *When Pictures*, p. 7.

Writing Practice 7

Using your note cards and formal outline, write the rough draft of your research paper. You may want to read the model research paper on pages 114–119 before you begin. Add footnotes to your paper wherever they are needed and be certain to insert quotations correctly.

The Bibliography

After you have completed a rough draft of the research paper, write the final bibliography, using the bibliography cards you prepared earlier. The final bibliography includes only those sources you actually used. Before beginning, be certain that the information on your bibliography cards is accurate, complete, and in the correct order. Then arrange your cards alphabetically by the author's last name. If no author is listed for a source, alphabetize it by the first major word in the title. Taking the information directly from your cards, write the bibliography on a separate sheet of paper. If an entry requires more than one line, indent the second and all other lines five spaces. If you use two sources written by the same author, do not rewrite the author's name in the second listing; instead, use a long dash in place of the name for all other sources by that author. The following example shows the listings for two books by Frank Manchel.

Manchel, Frank. *When Movies Began to Speak*. Englewood Cliffs, N.J.: Prentice-Hall, Inc., 1969.

———. *When Pictures Began to Move*. Englewood Cliffs, N.J.: Prentice-Hall, Inc., 1969.

Before beginning your bibliography, look closely at the sample bibliography on page 119. Notice that only the listings for magazine and newspaper articles indicate the page numbers on which the article can be found; no page numbers are listed for books.

The bibliography form in this section conforms to the MLA style. Your teacher may prefer that you use one of the many other widely accepted styles.

The Final Draft

Before you begin the final draft of your research paper, revise your rough draft carefully. Check that you have covered all the important points about your topic and have arranged information in the best possible order. Read the rough draft thoroughly and take out any details that do not relate to your topic or contribute to your paper as a whole.

The following is a rough draft of a paragraph in the research paper "Sound Comes to the Movies" on pages 114–119. As you read, notice the deletions and corrections the writer has made. The notes in the left-hand margin explain the changes.

Too wordy

Unnecessary information

Unnecessary repetition

The success of *The Jazz Singer* saved Warner Brothers and convinced the other major movie producers to investigate and invest in sound movie systems~~.~~, ~~However, there were still~~ but many problems ~~to surmount. Since Warner Brothers owned the rights to Vitaphone, the other companies had to choose from a variety of sound-on-disc or sound-on-film systems~~ remained. Finding capable technicians and installing sound equipment in studios were the least of ~~these problems~~ them. Noisy cameras had to be placed in special soundproof booths, called "ice boxes," from which more than one cameraman was pulled just in time to prevent suffocation. For a# while the concept of the moving camera disappeared. Movement on the screen became slow and artificial; actors were weighted down with concealed microphones or forced to stand awkwardly in front of microphones hidden in flowerpots or behind large objects. Many silent film stars had to be trained to use their voices, and despite the voice coaches who were rushed to Hollywood, more than one star failed to make the transition.

In revising the preceding paragraph, the writer decided to take out one piece of information. Even though this information relates to the topic, it detracts from the paragraph as a whole by breaking up the flow of ideas. While it is difficult to take out details you have carefully researched, in revision it is important to think of the general organization of ideas and delete any information that does not contribute to the paper as a whole.

As you write the final draft, place your footnotes at the bottom of the page or assemble them on a separate sheet of paper as endnotes, if your teacher prefers. If you included footnotes as you wrote the rough draft, you will already have the right amount of space left at the bottom of the page. If you did not, allow two lines at the bottom of the page for each footnote. See pages 110–111 for an example of footnotes in a final draft.

Before turning in your final draft, proofread it carefully, correcting errors in spelling, punctuation, and grammar. Check your footnotes and bibliography thoroughly to be certain you have not made careless errors in form.

Writing Practice 8

Using the Checklist for Revising the Research Report that follows and any suggestions your teacher may have, revise your rough draft and write a final version of your research report. Remember that revision is not a patchwork process. In your final draft, readers should not be able to tell where you have made changes. As a final step, proofread your paper, using the proofreading checklist on pages 20–21.

Checklist for Revising the Research Report

As a further aid, use the checklist for revising expository compositions on pages 85–86.

1. The subject is limited to a topic that can be developed in a research paper.
2. The topic is adequately developed with factual information from outside sources.
3. Each item of information in the final paper explains or develops the topic in some way.
4. Important theories, unusual or specific facts, and quotations are footnoted.
5. Information in footnotes is ordered correctly, and footnotes follow a standard form, such as MLA.
6. Information in the bibliography is ordered correctly according to a standard form.
7. If quotations are used, they are placed correctly in the paper.

Subjects for Short Research Reports

You can use the following general subjects as ideas for research reports. Remember to limit the subject you choose to a suitable topic.

1. Invention of the motorcycle
2. History of gothic romance fiction

3. Cave paintings
4. Investigation of the Loch Ness Monster
5. Invention of computers
6. Strip mining and the environment
7. The disappearance of the dinosaur
8. The space shuttle
9. History of a railroad in your area
10. The legends about vampires
11. History of weather forecasting
12. Extinct animal species
13. Investigation of the Yeti (Abominable Snowman)
14. The growth of the cosmetics industry in the U.S.
15. Theories about Stonehenge
16. Inventions that failed
17. The Great Pyramid of Giza
18. The role of the samurai in Japanese culture
19. The Aztec calendar
20. Early horror films

Reading a Research Report

Skip four lines between title and text.

Indent five spaces.

Double-space throughout.

Sound Comes to the Movies

"Silent" movies, popular from the early 1900s to about 1930, were never really silent. Audiences usually enjoyed background music, often provided by a theater organ or ragtime piano, as they watched the action on the screen. At appropriate times the sounds of thunder, waterfalls, or stampeding horses were created from the orchestra pit by hidden stagehands, who rattled, scraped, and banged all sorts of objects together. Sometimes, singers performed a song written especially for the movie, or actors toured with the film to speak portions of the dialogue. None of these sounds, however, came from the film itself; for this reason, the films were called "silents."

The idea of talking movies was an old one. In 1877, Thomas Edison showed

Skip three lines between text and long quotation.

Indent long quote five spaces from left-hand margin.

Skip three lines between long quotation and text.

his new talking machine, the phonograph, to a group of reporters. One was so impressed that he made the following predictions in the *Scientific American:*

> It is already possible by ingenious optical contrivances to throw stereoscopic photographs of people on the screen in full view of the audience. Add the talking phonograph to counterfeit their voices, and it would be difficult to carry the illusion of real presence much further.[1]

This "illusion of real presence" was to be the goal of scientists and inventors for the next fifty years. Before actors on the screen would actually speak to the audience, however, a way to link film and sound had to be found. In 1895, Thomas Edison made one of the first attempts to do so with a machine called a "Kinetophone." The Kinetophone connected Edison's phonograph with another machine that projected film for one person—a kind of peep show. However, this experiment did not result in sound's coming to the movies for two reasons. In the first place, Edison was unable to synchronize, or match, the film with the sound. Also, he failed to develop a means to amplify, or increase, the sound, so that it could be heard by a larger audience. Discouraged, Edison abandoned his Kinetophone project in 1913.[2]

Raise footnote number by half a line.

Meanwhile, other scientists were experimenting with a different method of linking sound with film: the sound-on-film process, in which electrical currents are used to capture the sound directly on photographic film. Frederick Thrasher, author of *Okay for Sound*, provides the following explanation of the process:

Skip four lines between text and footnote.

Number footnotes consecutively.

[1] Harry M. Geldud, *The Birth of the Talkies* (Indiana: Indiana University Press, 1975), p. 9.

[2] Frank Manchel, *When Movies Began to Speak* (Englewood Cliffs, N.J.: Prentice-Hall, Inc., 1969), pp. 2–3.

> When the sound is reproduced, a photoelectric cell is used to convert the variations in the light beam as it passes through the "sound track" of the moving film, into electrical currents which in turn are changed into sound at the loudspeakers.[3]

Although inventors would continue to experiment with separate sound and film devices, the sound-on-film process proved more successful. Because the sound was captured directly on the film, the process eliminated one major obstacle to talking motion pictures—that of synchronization.

The other great obstacle—that of amplifying sound—was surmounted by an inventor named Lee De Forest in 1907. Often called "the father of radio," De Forest invented an amplifier tube that allowed sound to be made sufficiently loud for a large audience. De Forest also worked from 1912 to 1922 to perfect the sound-on-film process and in 1921 exhibited a movie of himself talking. Although he went on to film stage musicals and even introduced the first sound newsreel in 1924, he was unable to gain the attention of the major film companies.[4]

Incorporate short quotations into text.

By 1924, silent films were enjoying wide success as millions of movie-goers the world over enjoyed films with such popular silent stars as Charlie Chaplin, "the bum who wanted above all else to attain human dignity,"[5] and Mary Pickford, "America's Sweetheart." The major film companies, riding the wave of success, had invested heavily in stockpiles of new equipment and large inventories for production of silent films. These men, many of whom had made

[3] Frederic Thrasher, ed. *Okay for Sound* (New York: Duell, Sloan, and Pearce, 1946), p. 7.

Use shortened form after the work is first cited.

[4] Geldud, pp. 98–99.

[5] Frank Manchel, *When Pictures Began to Move* (Englewood Cliffs, N.J.: Prentice-Hall, Inc., 1969), p. 39.

huge fortunes in the silent film industry, were unwilling to risk it all on an experiment that had not even developed a completely reliable technology. Thus, most of the major film producers remained unimpressed with the technological marvel of the sound-on-film process.

One film company, however, was far from successful. In 1925, Warner Brothers, on the verge of bankruptcy, formed a partnership with Western Electric, which now owned the rights to De Forest's amplifier tube. This partnership gave Warner Brothers the right to use a sound-on-film process called "Vitaphone" and thus to produce sound movies.[6] Using this system, the company produced their first sound film, *Don Juan*, which was first shown at Broadway's Warner Theater on August 6, 1926. In the history of film, however, *Don Juan* is not considered the first "talkie" because its sound consisted only of music, nor did it attract much interest or much of an audience. The era of the "talkie" had not yet arrived.[7]

Meanwhile, another important technological advance had been made that was to help bring sound to films. Working from an idea of De Forest's, Theodore W. Case and Earl I. Spondable developed an attachment that allowed sound films to be shown on silent projectors, thus eliminating the need for heavy investment in new equipment. The movie mogul William Fox purchased the Case-Spondable sound-on-film process and used it in the development of Movietone News Service. From their beginning in January of 1927, the Movietone Newsreels were enormously popular. Audiences were amazed to see and hear

Use a shortened form of the title for authors with two or more books.

[6] Manchel, *When Movies*, pp. 5–7.

[7] Alexander Walker, *The Shattered Silents: How the Talkies Came to Stay* (New York: William Morrow and Company, 1979), p. 26.

celebrities such as Charles Lindbergh, who was filmed taking off on his famous trans-Atlantic flight. Sound had come to newsreels, but not yet to the movies.[8]

Undeterred by the mild reception of *Don Juan*, Sam Warner had gone on in 1926 to make a sound film called *The Jazz Singer*, based on the popular Broadway musical about a son who wanted to become a jazz singer against his father's wishes. The film was a huge success for three reasons: the appeal of the show's star, Al Jolson; the three songs sung by Jolson; and nine words of dialogue spoken by Jolson. These nine words—"You ain't heard nothin' yet, folks. Listen to this!"—marked the end of the silent film era.[9]

The success of *The Jazz Singer* saved Warner Brothers and convinced other major movie producers to investigate and invest in sound movie systems, but many problems remained. Finding capable technicians and installing sound equipment in studios were the least of them. Noisy cameras had to be placed in special soundproof booths called "ice boxes," from which more than one cameraman was pulled just in time to prevent suffocation.[10] For a while, the concept of the moving camera disappeared. Movement on the screen became slow and artificial; actors were weighted down with concealed microphones or forced to stand awkwardly in front of microphones hidden in flowerpots or behind large objects. Many silent film stars had to be trained to use their voices, and despite the voice coaches rushed to Hollywood, more than one film star failed to make the transition.

New technological developments gradually improved both the sound quality of films and the mobility of cameras, and by 1931, film companies had

[8] Manchel, *When Movies*, p. 7.
[9] Manchel, *When Movies*, p. 10.
[10] Manchel, *When Movies*, p. 13.

moved to the sound-on-film process used in the industry today.[11] Although the great era of silent films ended over fifty years ago, the artistry of the first silent stars, the directors, and camera operators continues to influence each new generation of filmmakers. And for the millions of fans all over the world who continue to watch their favorite "silents" at movie revival houses and on late-night television, the Golden Age of the silent film has never really ended.

[11]Bernard Fredericks, "Sound Recording," in *Hollywood Speaks! An Oral History*, ed. Mike Steen (New York: G. P. Putnam's Sons, 1974), pp. 319–325.

Skip four lines between heading and first entry.

Bibliography

Begin at left margin.

Indent five spaces.

Long dash indicates same author as previous entry.

Fielding, Raymond, ed. *A Technological History of Motion Pictures and Television.* Berkeley: University of California Press, 1967.

Galliazzo, Tony. "Sound in the Movies: A Capsule History from Edison's Cylinder to Multiple-Track 70mm Stereo." *Modern Photography.* January 1971, pp. 48ff.

Geldud, Harry M. *The Birth of the Talkies.* Indiana: Indiana University Press, 1975.

MacGowan, Kenneth. *Behind the Screen.* New York: Dell Publishing Company, 1965.

Manchel, Frank. *When Movies Began to Speak.* Englewood Cliffs, N.J.: Prentice-Hall, Inc., 1969.

———. *When Pictures Began to Move.* Englewood Cliffs, N.J.: Prentice-Hall, Inc., 1969.

Stanley, Robert H. *The Celluloid Empire: A History of the American Movie Industry.* New York: Hastings House Publishers, 1978.

Steen, Mike, ed. *Hollywood Speaks! An Oral History.* New York: G. P. Putnam's Sons, 1974.

Thrasher, Frederic, ed. *Okay for Sound.* New York: Duell, Sloan, and Pearce, 1946.

Walker, Alexander. *The Shattered Silents: How the Talkies Came to Stay.* New York: William Morrow and Company, 1979.

Wright, Basil. *The Long View.* New York: Alfred A. Knopf, 1974.

6 Persuasive Writing

Writing to Persuade

Persuasive writing is writing that tries to convince readers to think, believe, or act a certain way.

When you write persuasively, your goal is to convince readers to accept the ideas or action that you support. In this chapter you will study how words work to affect a reader's emotions and reasoning. You will also read about the importance of knowing your audience. Finally you will learn methods of arguing from emotion and from logical reasoning, both to improve your own persuasive writing and to help you evaluate the many kinds of persuasive writing you encounter daily.

The Appeal to Emotion

Some persuasive writing appeals to your emotions. People who have a product to sell or a cause to advance often appeal to your emotions to persuade you to buy, believe, or act. For example, the advertisement on page 121 makes such an appeal: the advertisers want you to have a warm feeling for the people on the bicycles so that you will trust the company that makes them. In addition, the ad attempts to sell you on the idea that the riders are having fun and that if you buy one of their bicycles you will have fun, too.

The photograph on the next page is part of an advertisement for bicycles. Do you think the ad would convince you to buy one of the company's bicycles? What features are most convincing?

Descriptive words are often used to appeal to your emotions. Soft drink commercials, for example, use words such as *refreshing taste* or *tart and tingling*. (They do not use words to describe the health hazards of soft drinks.)

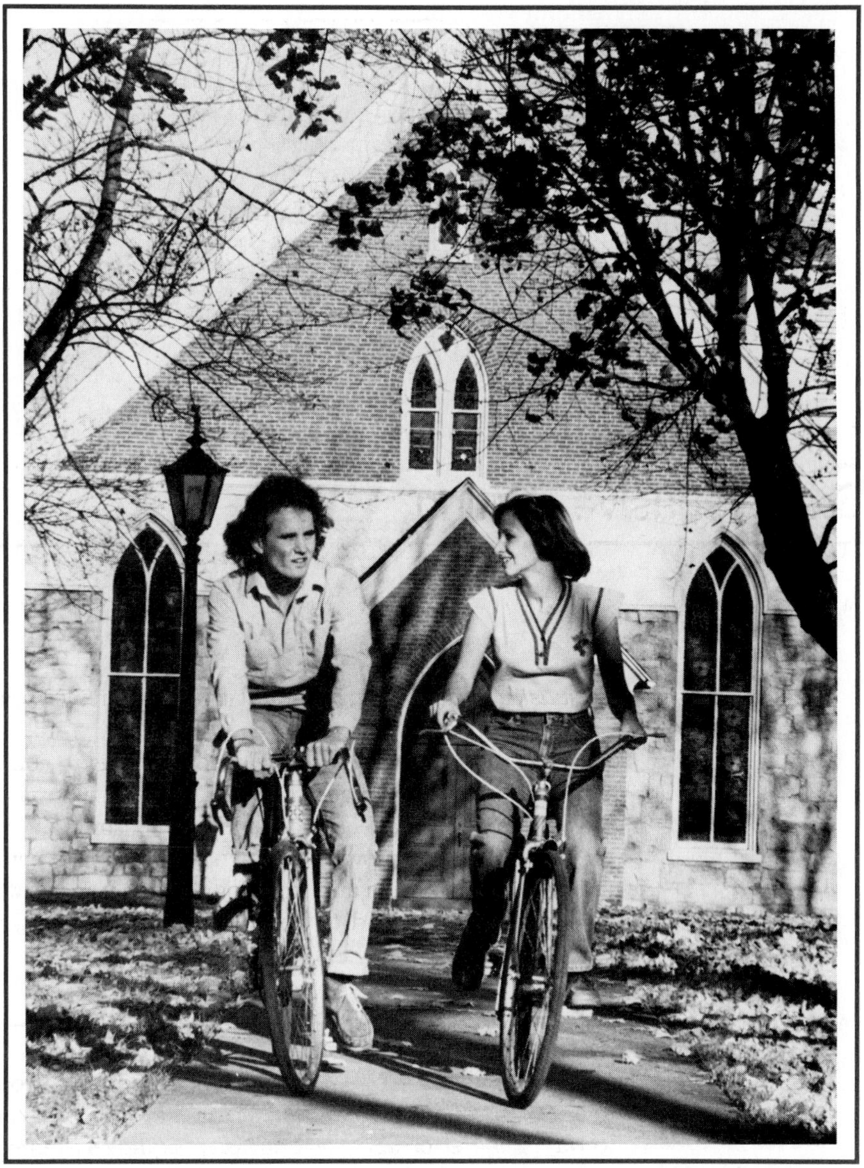

Think of an advertisement for your favorite food. What descriptive words does the ad use to persuade you to buy the product?

An appeal to your emotions is not necessarily dishonest. Ads for sending money to help needy children may appeal to your sense of decency, and public service ads that ask you to lower your thermostat may appeal to your sense of duty. What is important is to recognize when appeals are based on emotion, so that you can decide whether or not you want to be influenced.

Writing Practice 1

Imagine that you are an ad writer for a nationwide magazine. You have a new account, Fly-Way Vacation Airlines, and you want to impress them with your first ad. You have written the following basic format, but now you must complete a final draft. On a separate sheet of paper, write out the ad, filling in the words you would choose from the group in parentheses. You may substitute words of your own if you can think of improvements. Be prepared to discuss your choices in class.

> (Fly, Jet, Slip) away to (sunny, warm, torrid) Jamaica! (Sandy, Shining, Beautiful) beaches, jungle waterfalls, (sweet, friendly, welcoming) smiles, sailing in the (inviting, brilliant, glowing) sunshine, dancing in the (romantic, fantastic, wonderful) moonlight—all this (awaits, is in store for, we promise) you in (friendly, beautiful, exciting) Jamaica. The new (inexpensive, low-cost, cheap) air fares put a Jamaican holiday within your (reach, budget, financial range). We have vacations for singles, (newlyweds, honeymooners, just-marrieds), families, (sportsmen, sports lovers, sports nuts), everyone—at the (top, most elegant, finest) resort in Jamaica. Contact your travel agent, or send in this (handy, convenient, easy-to-mail) coupon. (Act Now! Do It Today! Don't Delay!)

Writing Practice 2

The following words are frequently found in magazine advertisements. Choose several words from this list and write a short advertisement for a product of your choice, either a real one or one you invent. Remember that your purpose is to make the product so appealing that your readers will want to buy it.

clean	eye-catching	marvelous	safe	sun-filled
comfortable	fresh	mellow	sharp	super
convenient	fun-filled	quality	shimmering	time-saving
cool	incomparable	refreshing	smooth	tingling
crackling	inexpensive	rich	special	warm
crisp	magical	robust	strong	winning

Advertising Techniques

Some of the techniques used in advertising are also used in other types of persuasive writing and can be identified by name.

1. *Card Stacking*

This approach involves using only the evidence that will prove one side of an argument. The arguer "stacks the cards" heavily on one side and ignores the other, making it seem that there is only one possible conclusion. For example, if you were to write an editorial attacking student apathy about local politics but neglect to say that the student political volunteer rate had increased dramatically during the previous year, you could be accused of "card stacking."

2. *Name Calling*

People respond emotionally to labels, or names, a writer gives to individuals, groups, ideologies, or ideas. For example, if you write, "He's just a dropout," some people will have a strong negative reaction to the term *dropout* without waiting for specific information about the individual. In politics the label *radical* provokes extreme reactions. Labeling is usually a deceptive technique because it puts attention on a generality and avoids the particular person or issue.

3. *Glittering Generalities*

Statements using words and phrases that sound impressive—*freedom, honor, peace, duty*, and so on—in a general way are called *glittering generalities*. They have appeal, a glittering surface, but little or no substance. For example, a campaign statement such as, "We all enjoy the highest standard of living of any other nation in the world," is designed to give the voter a good feeling rather than to convey truthful information. That good feeling will help readers accept the idea behind the statement, which may be that they should vote for this particular candidate, who is patriotic because he or she has faith in the economy.

4. *Transfer*

Transfer is a common approach used by persuasive writers when they want the positive quality of a famous person to transfer to a product or cause. When you see an advertisement that shows a film star or sports figure using a product, the advertisers want your good feelings about the famous person to transfer to the product and to a good feeling about yourself if you buy the product.

The reverse of this approach is called *guilt by association*. If a product is associated with someone who produces a negative impression, you will not want to identify with him or her. For example, you may have noticed ads against smoking that feature very unattractive people. The message is that if you smoke, you will be identified in a negative way with the people in the ad.

5. *Testimonial*

A *testimonial* is a direct endorsement of a product, person, or cause. A famous person may lend his or her name for the advertisement and may also speak directly in the ad. A well-known politician may endorse a young politician for office, through a testimonial praising the young politician. When a sports star appears in an ad telling you to eat the brand of cereal he or she eats, this is another kind of testimonial. This approach is very similar to the transfer technique.

6. *Plain Folks*

The *plain folks* approach attempts to make you feel comfortable with the people in the advertisement because they are "plain folks" just like you. Television ads showing housewives doing the laundry, husbands helping to clean out sinks, or an office worker talking about a headache remedy use the plain folks approach. The potential buyer is supposed to think, "Those people are just like me and my family, and if they use that product I should, too."

7. *Bandwagon*

"Everybody's doing it" is the motto of the *bandwagon* approach. It suggests that a product is good or a cause is right because it has wide support, and the appeal is for you to *jump on the bandwagon*, an expression meaning "to join the crowd." This approach tries to make you feel that if you buy the "right" brand of tennis shoes or vote for the right candidate, you will be accepted as an insider, not set apart from the crowd.

Writing Practice 3

Look through several magazines or newspapers and select an ad that demonstrates one or more of the persuasive approaches discussed in the previous section. On a separate sheet of paper, write out the approach or approaches that the ad uses to be effective. (You will find that many ads use a combination of approaches.)

The Appeal to Reason

Persuasion through logical reasoning is called *argumentation.* In the next sections you will learn the techniques of sound reasoning, both to use in your own writing and to recognize in the arguments you hear and read.

When you use sound reasoning, you do not resort to any of the persuasive techniques such as card stacking or glittering generalities. Instead, your argument is both *truthful* and *valid.*

The word *truthful* you already know. The word *valid* has a special definition when it refers to reasoning: in a valid argument one idea proceeds logically from another. To understand the difference between truthful and valid, consider a statement that is obviously not truthful: "Pigs can fly." The following three statements are an attempt to prove that pigs can fly.

First Statement: *All winged things can fly.*

In formal argumentation the first statement is a general statement, called the *first*, or *major*, *premise.*

Second Statement: *All pigs have wings.*

The second statement talks about a subset of the first statement (in this case "pigs" are a subset of "all winged things") and is called the *second*, or *minor*, *premise.*

Third Statement: *Therefore, pigs can fly.*

The third statement is a conclusion that proceeds logically from the first two statements. In a logical argument when the first two statements are accepted, then the conclusion must be accepted as well. This is what is meant by a *valid argument.*

Even though the argument about pigs is valid, it is obviously not true. The first premise, that all winged things can fly, can easily be disproved; many winged things (such as ostriches, for example) cannot fly. The second premise, that all pigs have wings, is contradicted by experience.

A good argument is both valid and truthful, as the following example demonstrates.

First Premise: *All United States senators are United States citizens.*

By definition a United States senator must be a citizen to hold office; you can check on this information in an encyclopedia or a history book.

Second Premise: *Margaret Chase Smith was a United States senator.*

Notice that the preceding premise relates to the first: "Margaret Chase Smith" is a subset of the larger class of senators in general. You can check on the truthfulness of this statement in a reference book.

Conclusion: *Therefore, Margaret Chase Smith was a United States citizen.*

Since both the first and second statements are true, you can draw the *valid* and *truthful* conclusion that Margaret Chase Smith was a United States citizen.

In everyday talking and writing, arguments are usually not formally stated with a major and minor premise. However, these premises are often included in the arguments without being stated. When you pay attention to the premises of an argument—what the speaker or writer *assumes* to be true—you can better judge the reasoning of the argument.

Often you will find that arguments are not logical for two reasons: first the arguer jumps to a quick conclusion without giving enough evidence to support the conclusion; and second the arguer does not give the right kind of evidence to justify the conclusion of the argument. The writing practice that follows will help you to examine the importance of providing the right kind of evidence for your arguments.

Writing Practice 4

As you read through each of the following statements, think about the kind and amount of evidence you would need to prove each one. Select the five statements that most interest you. On a separate sheet of paper, list the resources you would need to prove the statements. If you cannot prove the statement, write why you cannot.

1. More people are injured each year in accidents in the home than in industrial or auto accidents.

2. Last year the grades in the sophomore history class were two *A*'s, seven *B*'s, fifteen *C*'s, and four *D*'s. This year they were one *A*, four *B*'s, eighteen *C*'s, and six *D*'s. Sophomore history students are getting worse every year.
3. Racial prejudice is more common among teenagers and adults than it is among children from the ages of 1 to 10.
4. Young people today (men and women) are stronger and more physically capable than young people of past generations.
5. Don't believe everything you read in newspapers. At least half of it is untrue.
6. Typewritten papers get higher grades than handwritten ones.
7. The two most important causes of fatal automobile accidents are speeding and drinking.
8. Answering *true* for all of the questions on a true-false test should give you a score of at least 50. I used that system on a test recently and scored 60.
9. Everyone who became ill had eaten the shrimp salad at the picnic, but not everyone who ate shrimp salad there became ill, so it couldn't have been the shrimp salad that caused the food poisoning.
10. Few people spend time reading good books because most people spend their free time watching television.

Recognizing False Reasoning

False reasoning consists of *logical fallacies*, errors in reasoning. As a reader, you need to be aware of these logical fallacies so as not to be fooled into drawing a wrong conclusion. As a writer, you should be aware of these common errors in order to avoid them yourself.

1. *Begging the Question*

In logic the question is the issue being argued. When someone makes a statement that assumes the truth without proving it, that person's argument *begs the question*. This fallacy is also called *arguing in a circle*. For example, consider the following statement.

> Sheila is a terrible liar. I know that because she lies all the time.

The writer claims that the conclusion is true simply by stating that it is: Sheila is a liar because she lies. Begging the question avoids the real issue of an argument by assuming the conclusion to be true without offering proof.

2. *Ignoring the Question*

Ignoring the question means "losing sight of the main issue," as in the following example.

> Jim should have been given the Most Valuable Player Award after the baseball season. He worked hard all season to improve his batting average, was well-liked by the team, and was often praised by the coach. Yes, Jim was cheated out of a well-deserved award.

Jim's friend is ignoring the main issue: What did Jim do as a baseball player to merit the award? The preceding argument offers evidence of Jim's popularity and hard work but no proof that he was the best player on the team.

3. Ad Hominem *Argument*

Ad hominem is a Latin phrase meaning, literally, "to the man." An ad hominem argument diverts the audience's attention from the question by making a personal attack on an individual. It is often an appeal to prejudice. You may find the ad hominem argument in political writing, as in the following example.

> What can you expect from candidate Gomez? Her political cronies are from the ultraliberal wing of the party that wants to lead us into a welfare state. She has been self-employed all her life and doesn't know how to work within an organization. Furthermore, how can you trust the mother of a ten-year-old child who doesn't want to stay at home and be a good parent?

Nothing in this argument speaks to the issue of candidate Gomez's qualifications for the job. Instead, it makes an emotional appeal based on loaded words *(welfare state)* and prejudicial assumptions about self-employed workers and mothers.

4. *Oversimplification*

Sometimes, an arguer will make a conclusion about a problem without fully taking into consideration the causes behind it. By hurrying to solve the problem, the speaker or writer assumes that it has a single cause or preceding event, as in the following example.

> Ever since Mr. Janos became high school principal, student test scores have improved. Mr. Janos must be responsible for the improvement.

Any cause-and-effect argument such as the preceding one must be able to stand up under close examination. The following questions reveal that the argument oversimplifies the issue.

a. Is the single event assumed to be sufficient cause, or are there other causes that have not been considered?

In the preceding argument the single assumed cause is Mr. Janos' becoming principal. What other causes could be at work? For example, were the test scores of incoming freshmen improving anyway? Were test scores nationally improving? Were there any other staff changes at the high school?

b. Do the other causes more adequately explain the effect?

It seems unlikely that one person could affect the test scores of an entire school. It is more likely that one or more of the other causes suggested influenced the scores.

c. Is the conclusion based on the right cause or causes, and is the conclusion truthful and valid?

In the argument about Mr. Janos, the conclusion is based on an oversimplified cause, so it is neither truthful nor valid.

5. *Either-Or Argument*

Another kind of oversimplification is the *either-or argument*, which draws extreme conclusions and ignores the possibility of variations in between. For example, "Either you deliberately forgot to bring your homework to class as a gesture of defiance, or you think you can get everyone's sympathy by acting absent-mindedly." This kind of oversimplification allows only two conclusions, and both are probably wrong. Many arguments are unsuitable to either-or conclusions. With issues of behavior, ethics, morality, and religion, for example, absolute statements of right or wrong are usually impossible.

6. *False Comparison*

Comparing one thing to another is an effective way of making a subject clear to an audience. A false comparison, however, can lead to a false conclusion. Sometimes, persuasive writers will insert a false conclusion to mislead their audience. Occasionally the false comparison is an unintentional oversimplification, as in the following example.

> A common saying in Presidential election years is, "Don't switch horses in midstream." This saying suggests that conventional wisdom advises against bringing in a new President after four years.

The comparison is obviously false. A President after four years in office is not "midstream" at all but is at the end of a period of time designated by the Constitution.

Writing Practice 5

Look through ads or articles for examples of false reasoning or listen for arguments that use false reasoning. Magazine articles, newspaper editorials, talk shows, and conversations are all good sources to explore. On a separate sheet of paper, write a paragraph explaining one example of false reasoning that you find. State the argument and show why it is badly reasoned. Be prepared to discuss what sort of evidence or what other changes would be needed to improve the argument.

Writing Practice 6

The following sentences are conclusions to be supported by reasons in an argument. Select a conclusion you support. On a sheet of paper, write three or more valid and truthful reasons to support each conclusion. If you need to, use reference books or other material to find supporting evidence.

Before you write, think carefully about whether or not your reasons could be supported with sufficient evidence.

1. My school's system of elections does (or does not) ensure that the best candidates for student offices will win.
2. The grading system in this school is (or is not) fair to the majority of students.
3. Today's movies do (or do not) provide teenagers with good models of human behavior.
4. The legal age limit for all drivers should (or should not) be lowered to age fourteen.
5. Security is (or is not) more important than happiness.

Reading a Persuasive Essay

Writers of persuasive essays, articles, and editorials want to convince their readers to believe as they do and perhaps to act in a certain way. In the essay that follows, Marya Mannes wants to convince her readers that cheating, lying, bribing, and other forms of corruption are partly due to society's unwillingness to draw a definite line between right and wrong. As you read this essay, try to determine the kinds of arguments the writer uses to persuade readers to accept her point of view. Does she appeal mostly to emotion or to reason? What evidence does she present to support her ideas?[1]

Following this selection is a For Thought and Discussion activity.

The Thin Grey Line

[1] "Aw, they all do it," growled the cabdriver. He was talking about cops who took payoffs for winking at double parking, but his cynicism could as well have been directed at any of a dozen other instances of corruption, big-time and small-time. Moreover, the disgust in his voice was overlaid by an unspoken "So what?": the implication that since this was the way things were, there was nothing anybody could do.

[2] Like millions of his fellow Americans, the cabdriver was probably a decent human being who had never stolen anything, broken any law or willfully injured another; somewhere, a knowledge of what was probably right had kept him from committing what was clearly wrong. But that knowledge had not kept a thin grey line that separates the two conditions from being daily greyer and thinner—to the point that it was hardly noticeable.

[3] On one side of this line are They: the bribers, the cheaters, the chiselers, the swindlers, the extortioners. On the other side are We—both partners and victims. They and We are now so perilously close that the only mark distinguishing us is that They get caught and We don't.

[4] The same citizen who voices his outrage at police corruption will slip

---

[1] "The Thin Grey Line" by Marya Mannes. Copyright © 1963 by Marya Mannes. Reprinted by permission of Harold Ober Associates Inc.

the traffic cop on his block a handsome Christmas present in the belief that his car, nestled under a "No Parking" sign, will not be ticketed. The son of that nice woman next door has a habit of stealing cash from her purse because his allowance is smaller than his buddies'. Your son's friend admitted cheating at exams because "everybody does it."

[5] Bit by bit, the resistance to and immunity against wrong that a healthy social body builds up by law and ethics and the dictation of conscience have broken down. And instead of the fighting indignation of a people outraged by those who prey on them, we have the admission of impotence: "They all do it."

[6] Now, failure to uphold the law is no less corrupt than violation of the law. And the continuing shame of this country now is the growing number of Americans who fail to uphold and assist enforcement of the law, simply—and ignominiously—out of fear. Fear of "involvement," fear of reprisal, fear of "trouble." A man is beaten by hoodlums in plain daylight and in view of bystanders. These people not only fail to help the victim, but, like the hoodlums, flee before the police can question them. A city official knows of a colleague's bribe but does not report it. A pedestrian watches a car hit a woman but leaves the scene, to avoid giving testimony. It happens every day. And if the police get cynical at this irresponsibility, they are hardly to blame. Morale is a matter of giving support and having faith in one another; where both are lacking, "law" has become a worthless word.

[7] How did we get this way? What started this blurring of what was once a thick black line between the lawful and the lawless? What makes a "regular guy," a decent fellow, accept a bribe? What makes a nice kid from a middle-class family take money for doing something he must know is not only illegal but wrong?

[8] When you look into the background of an erring "kid" you will often find a comfortable home and a mother who will tell you, with tears in her eyes, that she "gave him everything." She probably did, to his everlasting damage. Fearing her son's disapproval, the indulgent mother denies him nothing except responsibility. Instead of growing up, he grows to believe that the world owes him everything.

[9] The nice kid's father crosses the thin grey line himself in a dozen ways, day in and day out. He pads his expenses on his income-tax returns as a matter of course. As a landlord, he pays the local inspectors of the city housing authority to overlook violations in the houses he rents. When his son flunked his driving test, he gave him ten dollars to slip the inspector on his second test. "They all do it," he said.

[10] The nice kid is brought up with boys and girls who have no heroes except people not much older than themselves who have made the Big Time, usually in show business or in sports. Publicity and money are the halos of their stars, who range from pop singers who can't sing to ballplayers who can't read: from teen-age starlets who can't act to television performers who can't think. They may be excited by the exploits of spacemen, but the work's too tough and dangerous.

[11] The nice kids have no heroes because they don't believe in heroes. Heroes are suckers and squares. To be a hero you have to stand out, to excel, to take risks, and above all, not only choose between right and wrong, but defend the right and fight the wrong. This means responsibility—and who needs it?

[12] Today, no one has to take any responsibility. The psychiatrists, the sociologists, the novelists, the playwrights have gone a long way to help promote irresponsibility. Nobody really is to blame for what he does. It's Society. It's Environment. It's a Broken Home. It's an Underprivileged Area. But it's hardly ever You.

[13] Now we find a truckload of excuses to absolve the individual from responsibility for his actions. A fellow commits a crime because he's basically insecure, because he hated his stepmother at nine, or because his sister needs an operation. A policeman loots a store because his salary is too low. A city official accepts a payoff because it's offered to him. Members of minority groups, racial or otherwise, commit crimes because they can't get a job, or are unacceptable to the people living around them. The words "right" and "wrong" are foreign to these people.

[14] But honesty is the best policy. Says who? Anyone willing to get laughed at. But the laugh is no laughing matter. It concerns the health and future of a nation. It involves the two-dollar illegal bettor as well as the corporation price-fixer, the college-examination cheater and the payroll padding Congressman, the expense-account chiseler, the seller of pornography and his schoolboy reader, the bribed judge and the stealing delinquent. All these people may represent a minority. But when, as it appears now, the majority excuse themselves from responsibility by accepting corruption as natural to society ("They all do it"), this society is bordering on total confusion. If the line between right and wrong is finally erased, there is no defense against the power of evil.

[15] Before this happens—and it is by no means far away—it might be well for the schools of the nation to substitute for the much-argued issue of prayer a daily lesson in ethics, law, and responsibility to society that would strengthen the conscience as exercise strengthens muscles. And it would be even better if parents were forced to attend it. For corruption is not something you read about in the papers and leave to courts. We are all involved.

For Thought and Discussion

1. In "The Thin Grey Line" Marya Mannes writes for a general audience. Do you think the argument she presents relates to the experience of most people? How?
2. What is the main point the writer makes in this essay? Does she support her argument with sufficient evidence or reasons? What are they?
3. Does this essay make any emotional appeals to the reader? If so, cite examples of emotional language used.
4. Does the author use any of the persuasive techniques you have studied? If so, where does she use them?
5. Does this essay commit any logical fallacies that you have studied? If so, what are they?
6. In paragraphs 12–14, Marya Mannes argues that "Today, no one has to take any responsibility." Is this a valid argument? Why or why not?
7. Do you agree with the solution the author suggests for the problem? Be prepared to discuss why you do or do not feel that her solution is convincing.

Planning a Persuasive Essay

The *persuasive essay* is an essay that makes an argument. It can argue for or against an issue; it can make an appeal to emotion, to reason, or to both; it can use the persuasive and logical approaches you read about earlier in this chapter. Before beginning a persuasive essay, you want to know three things: (1) the point of view you will take, (2) the nature of your audience, and (3) the method of your argument and the evidence you will use.

Knowing Your Point of View

To be persuasive you must first know your subject thoroughly. You must be able to cite reasons and give evidence in support of your argument. When you already have definite opinions about a subject, review them carefully to be certain they can be supported by logical argument. When you need to write about a subject you do not know well, explore the issues thoroughly before deciding on a point of view.

You may want to begin by talking with friends and family about the subject. Seeing different sides to the issue can help clarify your own point of view. Next research your subject to find as much reliable information about it as possible. You will want to see resources and perhaps consult an authority on the subject. Another way to gather information is to interview people or take an informal poll to get a perspective or a general opinion about your subject.

Finally it always helps to be generally informed about current local, national, and global events. Being aware of important issues will give you a background of information that will help when you form your own opinions. Newspapers, books, magazines, and news programs are sources you can consult daily.

Knowing Your Audience

Advertisers know that in order to write successful advertisements, they must understand the nature of their audience: its age range, interests, and buying power. Television ads, for example, are scheduled to appeal to a particular viewing audience. Products such as golf balls or running shoes that would interest sports fans appear during weekend sports programs; new toys are advertised during the morning children's programs.

The better that writers know the audience they write for in a persuasive essay, the better they are able to make arguments geared to convince that audience. The writer of the following letter is a high school senior involved in community efforts to develop a forest area as a public park. He addresses this letter to an adult friend, but similar letters will be sent to members of community clubs, service organizations, churches, and synagogues. As you read the letter, decide how effectively it will appeal to an adult audience.

Following this letter is a For Thought and Discussion activity.

2330 Glenmary Drive
Harristown, KY 42501
April 29, 1984

Dear Ms. Wong,

Would you like to enjoy a pine-scented, shady picnic area, a tree-lined nature trail, and a scenic view overlooking forests and fishing streams? These benefits, and more, can be yours when Harristown's Forest Park is developed and opened for everyone to enjoy.

At present the park is reserved for use by a limited number of clubs. However, an additional 1,500 acres, developed for recreational use, would give the park two public picnic areas, a nature trail for hikers, a horseback-riding trail, and a scenic drive. In the future an outdoor theater and a lakeside campsite will put summertime entertainment and relaxation just a short drive from town.

The Harristown Forest Park Action Committee invites you to a benefit carnival next Saturday, May 5, at the county fairgrounds, from 9 A.M. to 11 P.M. There will be rides, a giant barbecue, games, and amusements for everyone. Proceeds from the carnival will go toward the development of Forest Park.

We hope you agree that planned development of our nearby natural resources is a good way to provide recreation for all ages. Join us at the carnival and visit the Forest Park Action Committee booth to find out more about our plans. We need your help to make Forest Park a place all of us can enjoy.

Sincerely,

Jim Stuvic

Jim Stuvic

For Thought and Discussion

1. Does Jim's letter use language that will make his readers sympathetic toward the committee's efforts to develop Forest Park? What sentences do you think are most effective?
2. What does Jim's letter ask the reader to do specifically?
3. Do you think Jim's opening question is an effective way to begin an appeal? Why or why not?
4. Jim's letter does not directly state that the reader should contribute to the development of Forest Park, but it does suggest reasons that Ms. Wong and others might want to do so. What are those reasons?

5. If you were a member of Jim's committee and could rewrite his letter to make it more effective, what changes would you make?

Writing Practice 7

Jim's audience for the Forest Park letter consists of adults who could be expected to take an interest in the project and to contribute time and money toward making it a success. If Jim were to write to a different audience (perhaps his friends and other high school students, for example), he would rephrase parts of the letter in order to appeal to that special audience.

Rewrite Jim's letter for one of the following specific audiences. Keep the main idea of the letter and use the same information but change the language to suit the audience you select. Feel free to add any facts or ideas that would increase the persuasiveness of the letter.

1. High school students
2. Retired people
3. Friends interested in hiking and camping
4. City officials, such as the mayor
5. Residents of the community

Writing Practice 8

Write an announcement that could be read over your school's public address system or published in the school paper. Your purpose is to persuade your listeners to adopt a course of action. Choose one of the following situations or make up one of your own as the basis for your announcement. Remember to support your argument with reasons why your audience should do as you ask.

1. A controversial speaker is coming to lecture students about a proposed local law that would place a 9 P.M. curfew on everyone under eighteen years of age. You want as many students as possible to attend in order to show their response.
2. School officials have canceled a midwinter music festival because the last two festivals were poorly attended. You announce a weekend rally to show that students want a festival this year and will plan ways to make it a success. You want a big turnout at the rally.
3. Vandalism has destroyed parts of your campus. You feel that your classmates can do more to keep the campus clean and safe. Suggest ways students can prevent vandalism and give them reasons for caring about their campus.
4. Select a controversial issue from a book, a newspaper, or magazine. It can be a local, state, national, or even global problem. State your views on the issue and convince your audience to write letters to their (local or national) elected representatives in support of your position.

5. A schoolwide election will be held to decide whether or not friendly visitors from another galaxy should be allowed to observe a typical day in your school. State your views on the subject and convince your audience to vote the way you suggest.

Organizing Your Ideas: The Thesis Statement

A *thesis statement* of an essay resembles the topic sentence of a paragraph: it states the main idea to be treated.

In a persuasive essay the thesis statement tells the subject of the argument and the writer's point of view on the subject. Thesis statements such as the following ones make the writer's opinion clear.

> High school students should have complete freedom in making decisions about which courses to take.
>
> The United States should keep its commitment to develop alternate sources of energy by putting more money into researching solar power.
>
> More courses on marriage and families should be offered in high school so that every graduate will understand the responsibilities of married life.

A good thesis statement gives an opinion that can be supported with sound reasoning and evidence. Value judgments—statements putting a higher value on one thing over another—are not suitable as thesis statements because they are not arguable. For example, the opinion "Table tennis is more fun than bumper pool" is a value judgment, not a statement that can be argued logically. Any opinion based solely on taste is also unsuitable for a thesis statement. For example, "Art history is my favorite subject" may be a true statement, but it is not one that can be changed by an appeal to logic. When you write a thesis statement, remember to express an opinion that you can support with logical argument and evidence.

One way to develop a thesis statement is to ask yourself questions about the subject, as the following examples demonstrate.

SUBJECTS	QUESTIONS
School vandalism	What can students do to prevent vandalism on campus? What are the principal causes of vandalism at this school? Who is responsible?
Junk food ads on radio and television	Should junk food advertising be banned on radio and television? Does the government have an obligation to prevent the advertising of unhealthy foods?
Teenage unemployment	What are the causes of teenage unemployment in the community? What can be done to improve the situation?

Asking questions can help you focus your interest in the subject. If, for example, you have chosen to write about school vandalism, think about why vandalism is a problem. You may decide that the problem is student apathy and concentrate on reasons and ways for students to become involved in the prevention of vandalism. On the other hand, you may decide that the real problem is the motives of the vandals themselves and focus on what can be done to help them.

So far you have defined the problem and asked questions to help establish your point of view. Since the thesis statement in a persuasive essay tells your point of view and often your conclusion about an issue, it is a good idea to research your subject thoroughly before formulating the thesis statement. You want to be certain of your ideas and opinions before planning an essay around them.

After investigating the subject and assembling information about it, you are ready to compose your thesis statement. The following thesis statements based on the subject of vandalism give two examples of different conclusions.

1. Vandalism has grown into a major problem because of student apathy. Students should know that damage to valuable equipment affects all school activities and should volunteer to help in the new School Watch program and the Speakers' Bureau.
2. The real cause of vandalism is the lack of work opportunities for teenagers locally. Students should join the Committee on Youth Employment to help seek solutions to the problem.

Each thesis statement does the following: (a) it sets forth the main subject of the essay "Vandalism"; (b) it expresses the writer's point of view on the major cause of the problem, which is student apathy in the first statement and lack of employment opportunities in the second; and (c) it asks its audience to act, by helping with a School Watch program and a Speakers' Bureau in the first and by joining the Committee on Youth Employment in the second.

Writing Practice 9

Choose one of the following topics or write one of your own. Then use the steps you have read about to arrive at a thesis statement: (a) write questions about the topics, (b) investigate the topic, and (c) write a thesis statement to use for an essay on the topic. Remember that in a persuasive essay the thesis statement appeals to the audience *to do* or *believe* something. For this practice assume that your audience consists of your teacher and classmates.

1. Should physical education be a required subject in high school?
2. Should people report shoplifters if they observe them in action?
3. Should boxing be outlawed as too violent?
4. Should the United States require draft registration in peacetime?
5. Should women be drafted?

6. Should knowledge of a foreign language be a high school graduation requirement?
7. Should there be a nationwide legal drinking age of twenty-one?
8. Should the United States send funds to help victims of floods, earthquakes, and other natural disasters in countries with anti-American policies?
9. Should a college education be free for all high school graduates?
10. Should the government devote more of its budget to space exploration?

Organizing Your Ideas: The Topic Outline

The persuasive essay, like other essays, follows a general pattern of organization. The *introductory paragraph*, sometimes called the *thesis paragraph*, introduces the main idea and usually contains the thesis statement. The *body*, usually several paragraphs long, explains the main idea and presents reasons and evidence in support of the writer's opinion. The *conclusion* summarizes the points of the paper or restates the thesis for emphasis in a new way.

Informal outlines are discussed on pages 76–77.

Preparing an informal outline, such as the following one, will help you to organize your ideas and plan your arguments.

Vandalism
- "Don't care" attitude of students
- Ways of cutting it down
  - School Watch program
  - Speakers

Damage caused by vandalism
- Broken office machines and typewriters
  - Business classes canceled
  - School work not completed
- Damage to sports equipment
  - Fewer sports activities
  - Gym closed weekends

Solutions to vandalism
- School Watch program
  - Student volunteers for campus patrol
  - Hall guards for coordinators
- Speakers' Bureau
- School referendum on problem
- Volunteers for visiting parent and civic groups

Student Involvement
- Students as source of problem
- Students as solution

Writing the Persuasive Essay

Writing the Introductory Paragraph

In a good persuasive essay the opening paragraph establishes the topic in a way that will immediately interest the reader. The introductory paragraph often includes a thesis statement that clearly and directly sets forth the main point of the essay.

In "The Thin Grey Line" by Marya Mannes on pages 129–131, the writer does not include a thesis statement in the opening paragraph. Experienced writers often vary the standard practice of including the thesis statement in the introduction by leading up to the statement with examples or evidence. In "The Thin Grey Line" the thesis statement does not appear fully expressed until paragraph 5: "Bit by bit, the resistance to and immunity against wrong that a healthy social body builds up by law and ethics and the dictation of conscience have broken down."

Less-experienced writers usually take the direct approach of including the thesis statement in the introductory paragraph, where it presents the main idea of the essay and establishes the writer's opinion about it. The following example demonstrates how to include the thesis statement in the introductory paragraph.

> "Class canceled due to lack of equipment." "Sorry, no open gym this weekend." Are these the kinds of signs you expect to see at Jefferson High? If you think it cannot happen here, then you should know about the recent wave of vandalism on campus. If you do not know about the problem, you are part of the problem: student apathy and indifference is allowing the vandalism to go unchecked. Perhaps it has not affected you personally. Your locker has not been smashed, or your gym class equipment has not been stolen, but it is just a matter of time. The administration is doing what it can to improve the condition, but students can take steps to help, too. Join the new School Watch system designed to keep the entire campus safe, or join the Speakers' Bureau to discuss the issue and increase everyone's awareness of the problem.

Writing Practice 10

Using a thesis statement you have already developed in this chapter or making up a new one, write an introductory paragraph for a persuasive essay. In your paragraph include a thesis statement that clearly and directly sets forth the main idea of the essay.

Writing the Body of the Essay

When you write a persuasive essay, it is important to keep in mind the audience for which you are writing and the purpose of your essay.

The audience for a persuasive essay helps determine what points you will make and how you will make them. For example, the essay on vandalism would be written differently for an audience consisting of students, of readers of the local newspaper or a national magazine, or of members of a parent-teacher association.

The purpose in writing a persuasive essay is to convince your audience to accept your point of view. Decide before you begin writing whether your purpose is to change your audience's mind or to call them to action. You can achieve your purpose with appeals to emotion or appeals to reason, but most persuasive writers use a combination of the two. Persuasion by emotional appeal only is very difficult to maintain throughout an essay, and an appeal to reason by itself is usually not as effective as an appeal to logic combined with appeals to emotion.

For example, in "The Thin Grey Line" Marya Mannes argues logically about the effect of public indifference on public morality. She supports her argument with examples of dishonest behavior from real-life situations and includes a wide range of experiences to support her claim that the problem is a dangerous one for all members of society. In paragraph 6 she argues that "failure to uphold the law is no less corrupt than violation of the law." What examples does she give of this failure? Look through the essay for other examples of logical argument.

Marya Mannes combines logical argument with an appeal to her readers' emotions to make her essay more persuasive. She uses emotional language to make readers feel the extreme nature of the problem: "And instead of the fighting indignation of a people outraged by those who prey on them, we have the admission of impotence: 'They all do it.' " Words like *indignation* and *outraged* invite the audience to feel indignant and outraged as well. What are the other emotionally laden words in her sentence? Look through the essay for other examples of emotional language or other kinds of emotional appeal.

In a persuasive essay the appeals to logic and emotion are directed toward the same purpose: to persuade the audience. As you write a persuasive essay, keep your purpose in mind; this will prevent you from straying from the main point of the paper. The whole purpose of "The Thin Grey Line" is to convince the reader that he or she has a moral responsibility to draw a line between right and wrong for the good of the society. Marya Mannes does not stray from the subject by going into an explanation of laws affecting moral behavior or even by examining the causes of the present problem in depth. She concentrates on the problem itself. One way to keep your purpose in mind is to have your thesis statement in front of you as you write; this will help focus your attention.

Methods of developing paragraphs are discussed in Chapter 3, "The Paragraph."

Writing Practice 11

Using a thesis paragraph you have already written or one you write for this assignment, write the body of a persuasive essay. Begin by writing down three major points you will cover. Then develop these points into three separate paragraphs supported with examples and details. Try to include both an appeal to emotion and an appeal to reason in your paragraphs.

Writing the Conclusion

The *conclusion* of a persuasive essay often summarizes the arguments of the essay and for emphasis restates the thesis in a slightly different way. A summary of arguments helps the reader see how each point adds up to a valid conclusion. Restating the thesis helps to bring the argument full circle by demonstrating that the ideas expressed in the introduction have been treated fully.

Persuasive essays can also end by making a call to action. For example, the essay on vandalism could end by urging students to join the School Watch and Speakers' Bureau. Persuasive essays can also conclude with a prediction about what will happen if the audience does not support the writer's point of view. The vandalism essay, for example, could end with a bleak description of a school closed down because of damages. Still another way to conclude a persuasive paper is to offer solutions to the problem. Any of these types of endings can be combined with an appeal to action, as it could in the vandalism paper calling for student participation in preventing the problem. Finally persuasive papers often conclude with an emotional statement about the subject. For example, the vandalism essay could end with an emotional appeal about the need for students to band together, emphasizing school loyalty and pride. Reread the conclusion to "The Thin Grey Line" and decide what method Marya Mannes uses to end her persuasive essay.

Writing Practice 12

Write a conclusion for your persuasive essay. Use one of the methods you read about in the preceding section or a combination of methods.

Writing Practice 13

Look back at the persuasive essay and outline the argument. That is, write a sentence stating the main idea that you are trying to persuade your audience to adopt. Then outline the major points that you give in your essay as reasons or evidence. Looking at this outline summary of your argument, do you find it convincing?

Writing Practice 14

Use the following checklist to revise your persuasive essay after it is completed. (Your teacher may want to read your essay first before you begin the revision.) Check your essay carefully against each item and then rewrite it to incorporate any changes you need to make or that your teacher asks you to make.

Checklist for Revising a Persuasive Essay

1. The thesis statement is an arguable one, not a value judgment or a matter of personal taste.
2. The thesis statement is clear and direct. It gives the topic of the essay and expresses a point of view.

3. The essay is directed to a specific audience and uses language suitable for that audience.
4. The argument of the essay uses sound reasoning.
5. The essay presents sufficient evidence to support the conclusion.
6. The essay avoids false reasoning.
7. The essay is unified. Each paragraph helps develop the thesis statement.
8. The essay is coherent. The reader can move easily from one idea to the next.
9. The argument of the essay focuses on one important point.
10. The language of the essay is persuasive.

7 Business Writing

Form for a Business Letter

Social letters vary a good deal in appearance, but when you write a business letter, you should follow a definite form.

Begin by choosing good quality plain white paper. Business letters should be written on standard-sized stationery—either 8½ × 11 inches or 5½ × 8½ inches. Typewritten letters are preferable because they are easier to read, but if you do not have access to a typewriter or do not type well, write in ink in your most legible handwriting. To keep your handwriting in even lines, try putting a sheet of heavily lined paper under your page so that you can see the lines as you write.

The appearance of your letter is important because it tells the receiver something about you. A good business letter should be neat with few—if any—corrections. It should contain no mistakes in spelling, grammar, or punctuation, and it should follow the business letter form exactly.

The first page of a business letter should be framed in white by the margins around the letter. In order to decide where to begin writing, you will have to judge the length of your letter. The top and bottom margins should be equal; the left- and right-hand margins should also be about equal. Whether you are typing or writing, the left-hand margin should be kept as straight as possible.

Do not write or type on the back of the first sheet of a business letter. If your letter takes up more than a single sheet, begin a second page with the name of the person to whom you are writing, the page number 2, and the date as the heading. (See page 161 for an example of the heading on a second page.) Leave about an inch from the top of the second sheet to the one-line heading and four lines of space below the heading. If your letter does require a second page, it should contain at least three lines of the body of the letter.

The correct form for a business letter is shown in the following example.

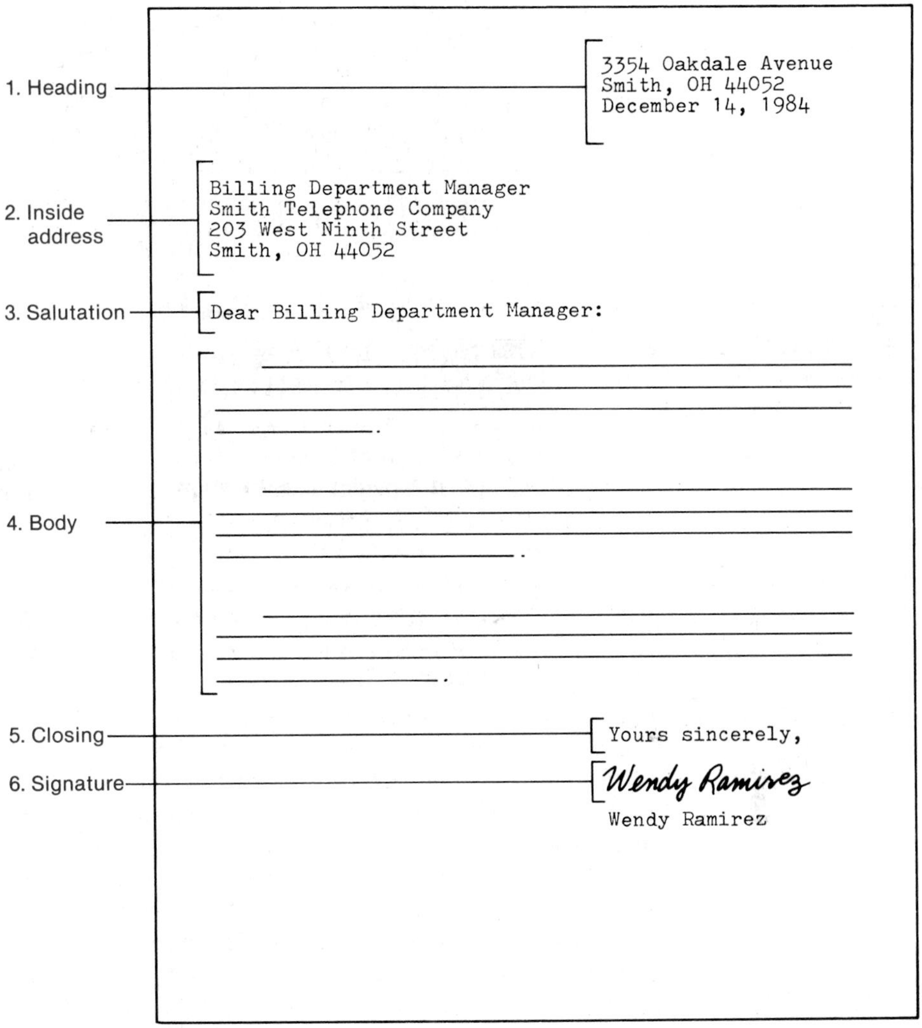

1. *Heading*

The three-line heading goes in the upper right-hand part of the first page. The first line contains your street address or rural route and apartment number, if there is one. The second line contains your city, state, and ZIP code number. The date on which the letter is written goes on the third line. Notice that the only commas in the heading occur between the city and the state on the second line and between the day of the month and the year on the third line. There is no comma between the state and the ZIP code or at the end of the lines of the heading. If your street address contains an apartment number, a comma goes between the name of the street and the apartment number.

12712 Speedway Overlook Road, Apartment 5

2. *Inside Address*

The inside address gives the name of the person or company to whom you are writing, the street address, the city, state, and ZIP code. If you are writing to a particular person, you can include a short title to go on the first line along with the name.

Ms. Glenda Ferris, Manager

However, if the title is a long one, it should be written on a separate line.

Mr. Wayne Chong
Manager of Customer Service Relations

The inside address begins four lines below the heading and is even with the left-hand margin.

If you do not know the name of the person who will be handling your letter, you may address it to a title (such as *Director of Advertising* or *Personnel Director*) or to a department (such as *Admissions Office* or *Complaint Department*). It is always a good idea to specify the department in the company to which you are writing.

3. *Salutation*

Skip two lines of space below the inside address and then write the salutation, the word *Dear* followed by the name of the receiver. In a business letter the salutation is always followed by a colon.

Dear Ms. Olofski: Dear Mr. Williamson:

When you do not know the name of the person to whom you are writing, you may use "Dear Sir or Madam" as your salutation, or you may use the title of the person or department.

Dear Black Magic Soil Sales Department:
Dear Box Office Manager:
Dear Credit Department Manager:

4. *Body*

Skip two lines of space after the salutation and begin the body of your letter. A business letter should be single-spaced with a line of space between paragraphs. If you use the semiblock style, as in the example on page 143, each paragraph will be indented a few spaces. In the block style, however, each paragraph begins at the left-hand margin. (See pages 145–147 for more information about block and semiblock styles.)

As in any kind of writing, you should begin a new paragraph when you change the subject of your writing. Many business letters, such as an order letter, contain only a single paragraph; others may contain several paragraphs or even more than one page.

5. *Closing*

Skip two lines of space after the body and write your closing. The left-hand margin of the closing should be aligned with the left-hand margin of the heading. The following examples show appropriate closings for a business letter.

Yours truly,	Very truly yours,
Sincerely yours,	Sincerely,

Notice that the closing is always followed by a comma. When you write a closing of more than one word, only the first word is capitalized.

6. *Signature*

Your signature should always be written in ink, neatly and legibly, below the closing. If you type your letter, skip four lines of space and type your name. Then sign your name in ink in the space between the closing and your typewritten name.

Semiblock, Block, and Full Block Style

You may choose from three basic business letter forms when it comes to deciding whether or not to indent your paragraphs and how to align the parts of the business letter. Any of these styles is acceptable for handwritten or typed business letters.

1. *Semiblock Form*

The model letter on page 143 and all of the sample letters in this chapter are written in the semiblock form. Each paragraph of the letter's body is indented either five or ten spaces. The heading, closing, and signature are aligned somewhat to the right of the center of the paper. All the other parts of the business letter (the inside address, the salutation, and the body) begin at the left-hand margin.

2. *Block Form*

The block form differs from the semiblock form in only one respect: paragraphs in the body of the letter are not indented. Every paragraph begins at the left-hand margin.

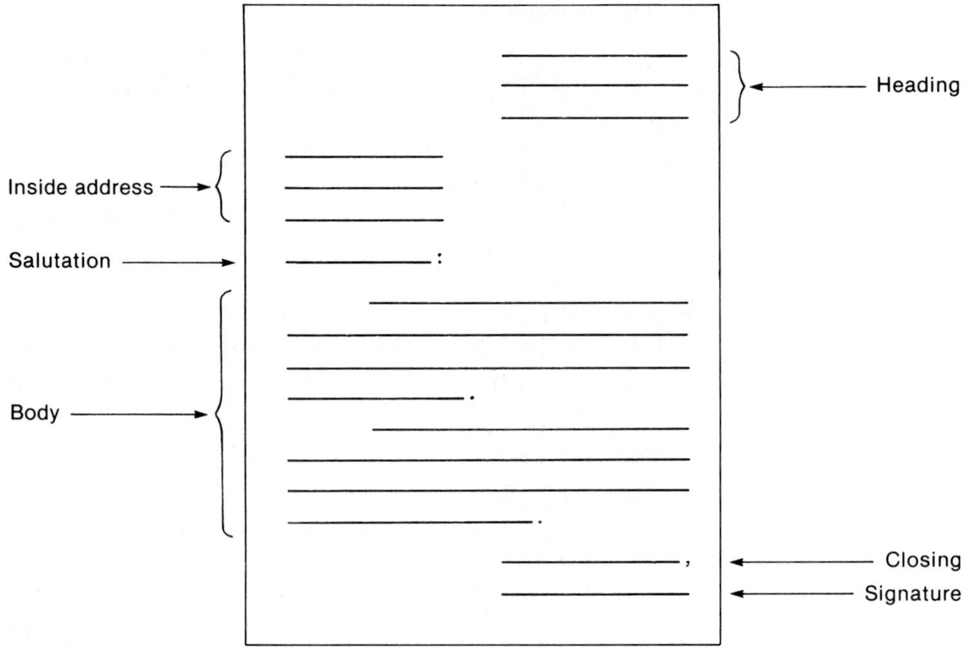

(semiblock form)

The only difference between block and semiblock forms is that paragraphs are indented in the semiblock form.

(block form)

(full block form)

3. *Full Block Form*

In the full block style every part of the business letter begins at the left-hand margin. The paragraphs in the body of the letter are not indented. Many people think that the full block form looks unbalanced because everything begins at the left, but this form does save some time for the typist because there are no indentions.

A diagram of the three business letter forms is shown on page 146.

Writing Practice 1

On a sheet of paper, set up forms for two of the following business letters. Draw lines to indicate the body of the letter and write all of the other parts according to the information provided. Use today's date or a future date in the heading of your letter.

1. Seymour Marzulli, who lives at 556 Bloomfield Avenue, Apartment 2, in Camden, New Jersey 08109, is writing to the Service Manager of Eastern Auto Car Parts, 101 South Essex Avenue in Orange, New Jersey 07050.
2. Mrs. Gail P. Bunch, who lives at 1240 Filmore Street, San Francisco, California 94115, is writing to the subscription department of *Sports Illustrated Magazine*, 541 N. Fairbanks Court, Chicago, Illinois 60611.
3. David B. Saltzman lives at 272 Noviembre Drive in El Paso, Texas 79935. He is writing Jim McNeil, Order Department Manager, at McNeil Brothers Nurseries, Inc., 603 Bowman Drive, Dansville, New York 14437.
4. Ms. Noreen Clematis lives at 4700 North Prospect Road in Peoria, Illinois 61614. She is writing to the Admissions Department at the University of Colorado, Boulder, Colorado 80309.
5. Roger Carpathia, who lives at 14968 S.E. Caruthers Court in Portland, Oregon 97233, is writing to the librarian at the Multnomah County Medical Society, 2188 S.W. Park Avenue, Portland, Oregon 97201.

Folding the Letter

There are two acceptable ways to fold a business letter, depending on the size of the stationery and the size of the envelope.

1. If you are using a long envelope for a letter on 8½ × 11 inch paper or a short envelope for a letter on 5½ × 8½ inch stationery, fold your letter into thirds as follows:
   a. Fold the bottom third of the paper one third of the way to the top and make a crease.
   b. Fold the top third of the paper down and make a second crease. Your letter will now be folded in thirds.
   c. Insert the letter into the envelope with the open end at the top.

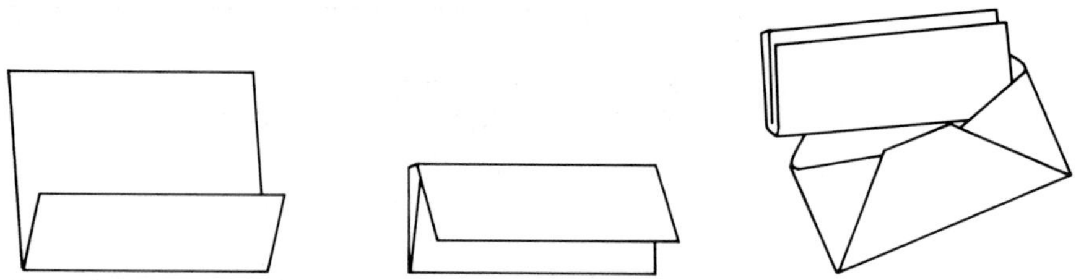

2. If your envelope is too small for the letter to fit when folded in thirds, fold your letter as follows:
   a. Fold the letter in half, bringing the bottom half up. Make a crease.
   b. Fold the right third of the letter toward the left side and make a crease.
   c. Fold the left third of the letter over the right third and make a crease.
   d. Insert the letter into the envelope with the open end at the top.

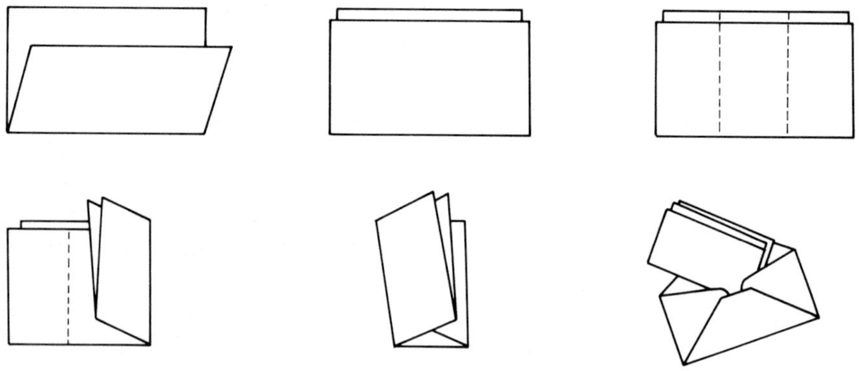

Addressing the Envelope

Like your stationery, the envelope in which you mail a business letter should be plain white and standard sized. The name and address of the person or company you are writing to should be typed or written exactly as it appears on the inside address of the letter. Begin writing the address slightly below and to the left of the envelope's center. Your name and address belong in the upper left-hand corner as the return address.

See page 149 for a list of state abbreviations accepted by the post office. Always be certain to include a ZIP code in your return address and in the address of the receiver, since letters without ZIP codes may be delayed. If you do not know the ZIP code of the person to whom you are writing, look it up in the ZIP code directory found in every post office and most libraries.

```
Kathie Bartholomew
3068 South Linden Road, Apt. 608
Flint, MI 48507


                    Greenway Distributors
                    Card Services Division
                    5832 Dangerfield Road
                    Hillside, IL 60162
```

Abbreviations The United States Post Office has approved the following two-letter abbreviations for states, possessions of the United States, and Canadian provinces to be used with ZIP codes.

Alabama	AL	Missouri	MO	Wisconsin	WI
Alaska	AK	Montana	MT	Wyoming	WY
Arizona	AZ	Nebraska	NE	Canal Zone	CZ
Arkansas	AR	Nevada	NV	District of Columbia	DC
California	CA	New Hampshire	NH	Guam	GU
Colorado	CO	New Jersey	NJ	Puerto Rico	PR
Connecticut	CT	New Mexico	NM	Virgin Islands	VI
Delaware	DE	New York	NY	Alberta	AB
Florida	FL	North Carolina	NC	British Columbia	BC
Georgia	GA	North Dakota	ND	Manitoba	MB
Hawaii	HI	Ohio	OH	New Brunswick	NB
Idaho	ID	Oklahoma	OK	Newfoundland	NF
Illinois	IL	Oregon	OR	Northwest Territories	NT
Indiana	IN	Pennsylvania	PA	Nova Scotia	NS
Iowa	IA	Rhode Island	RI	Ontario	ON
Kansas	KS	South Carolina	SC	Prince Edward Island	PE
Kentucky	KY	South Dakota	SD	Quebec	PQ
Louisiana	LA	Tennessee	TN	Saskatchewan	SK
Maine	ME	Texas	TX	Yukon Territory	YT
Maryland	MD	Utah	UT	Labrador	LB
Massachusetts	MA	Vermont	VT		
Michigan	MI	Virginia	VA		
Minnesota	MN	Washington	WA		
Mississippi	MS	West Virginia	WV		

Writing Practice 2

On a sheet of paper, draw outlines for four envelopes. Address all of the following envelopes, using your name and home address for the return address.

1. You are writing to Mr. Perry Milefski, president of Interstate Motor Freight Lines, 500 Trade Center, Montgomery, Alabama 36108.
2. You are writing to the order department of Magic Mountain Photo Supply Company, 728 Warm Springs Road, Ketchum, Idaho 83340.
3. You are writing to the Personnel Department, Ben Franklin Bank, North Main Office, 1068 Westminster Street, Providence, Rhode Island 02909.
4. You are writing to Dr. Chu Ming, Director, Community Health Services, Inc., 2590 N. Germantown Road, Memphis, Tennessee 38134.

Content of a Business Letter

A letter may be written in exactly the right form yet may be an absolute failure. What you say and how you say it are even more important than the form of the letter.

Before you begin to write, it is a good idea to think about what you want to say. Ask yourself the following three questions.

1. What do you want the reader to do? (What is the purpose of your letter?)
2. What must the reader know in order to do this? (What information must be included in your letter?)
3. How can you get the reader to do this? (What is the most effective way of wording what you want to say?)

If you spend just a few minutes thinking about the answers to these questions, the content of your business letter is practically guaranteed to be effective.

Be complete. Include all of the information your reader needs to know.

People who read business letters usually process many letters a day. They must be able to read and react to a letter quickly. Business letters should never leave the reader with unanswered questions. If essential information is left out of the letter, the reader will have to take the time to write a letter asking for that information, and long delays will result.

Consider the business letter on page 151. What is wrong with this letter? The person who tries to process it will have the following unanswered questions.

1. What is the writer's account number?
2. What is the name of the record the writer is being billed for?
3. What is the price of the record?
4. When and how was the record returned to the company?
5. Was the record insured when it was mailed? Does the writer have a receipt for it?

164 E. 82nd Street, Apt. 8C
New York, NY 10028
April 10, 1984

Credit Collections, Inc.
169 W. 34th Street
New York, NY 10001

Dear Credit Department Manager:

You have been billing me for a record I returned to Silverdust Record and Tape Club. It was defective, and I have no intention of paying for a defective record that I no longer have. Please stop sending me bills and credit my account.

Yours truly,

Loren McAffee

Loren McAffee

Writing Practice 3

Rewrite the model letter to the Credit Department Manager of Credit Collections, Inc. Provide all of the missing information, making up any details that you need. You may want to write more than one paragraph in your letter.

Use the Checklist for Proofreading Business Letters on page 163 to check your letter for errors.

Be clear and concise. Say everything that you need to say as clearly and as briefly as you can.

A business letter is no place to show off your new vocabulary of difficult words, nor is it appropriate to be chatty. A good way to develop a clear, concise writing style is to write as if you were speaking to the person—including only the essential details. Be careful to avoid old-fashioned phrases and clichés in your writing:

Waiting to hear from you, I remain Yours truly,

What is wrong with the following business letter?

9 Tricorne Road
Lexington, MA 02173
July 30, 1984

Order Department
Plainview Chronograph, Inc.
708 Fischer Avenue
Chicago, IL 60648

Dear Order Department:

On May 15, 1984, I ordered a calculator chronograph wristwatch (model 132-D) and enclosed a check for $69.95. You have cashed the check, but the wristwatch has never arrived. What happened?

The watch was supposed to be a graduation present for my older brother Jim. My two sisters and I saved our money for months and washed cars to earn the $69.95 for the watch.

Whenever the mail comes, all of us rush to the mailbox to see if the watch has arrived, but so far we've been disappointed every time.

If for some reason my order cannot be filled, then I think I want my money back or else maybe I want to order another watch. Which do you think would be quicker? Awaiting your reply, I am

Yours truly,

Lee Ann Zambie

Lee Ann Zambie

The writer of the preceding letter rambles on and on about who the watch was for and how she and her sisters earned the money to buy the watch. This information is of no interest to the person who is trying to process the letter. The writer is also unclear about what she wants the reader to do—process the order, refund the money, or send a different watch. If she wants a different watch, she has neglected to include the model number and price.

Writing Practice 4

Rewrite the letter to the Order Department at Plainview Chronograph, Inc., providing the reader with all the necessary information. (In a real-life letter you might want to enclose a photostat of both sides of a canceled check as

A Checklist for Proofreading Business Letters is on page 163.

proof that the company has received the money for an item you had not received.) If you decide to order a different watch, make up the model number and price.

Be courteous. The tone of a business letter should be pleasant.

Business writing is, by definition, unemotional. The language is neutral, and feelings—except for thanks and appreciation—are best left unexpressed. It is the information in a business letter that counts, not the feelings.

Even if you are extremely angry at a mistake that a company has made, being sarcastic or offensive is improper. The person who reads and processes your letter is almost certainly not the person who caused your problem, so your anger would be totally misdirected.

Letter of Request

By following the guidelines for form and content already given in this chapter, you can write an effective business letter to cover any situation. You will benefit, however, from additional practice with the five common types of business letters discussed in this and the following sections.

In a *letter of request,* you are asking for something—information, a catalogue, maps, or an appointment. Occasionally you will write a letter asking someone in the business world to do a special favor. For example, you might write to ask a psychologist to visit your psychology class to discuss the kinds of help available in your community to students with emotional problems, or you might write to the director of a local film company, asking to arrange for a class visit.

A letter of request should be especially courteous. If you are asking for information, it is always a good idea to include a stamped, self-addressed envelope with your request.

If you are thinking about going to college, you will be writing several letters of request for college catalogues and for interview appointments. Look at the example letter of request on page 154 written to the Director of Admissions at a college.

Writing Practice 5

Write one of the following letters of request.

A Checklist for Proofreading Business Letters is on page 163.

1. Write a letter to the Sierra Club, 530 Bush Avenue, San Francisco, California 94108. Ask for information about student membership rates and about local activities in your area. Ask also for a list of current environmental legislation that the club is endorsing.
2. Write a letter to the Metropolitan Museum of Art, Box 255, Gracie Station, New York, New York 10028. Ask for their current catalogue of books, stationery, reproductions, and gifts sold at the museum's gift shop.

4608 Alpine Avenue
Cincinnati, OH 45242
November 18, 1984

Director of Admissions
University of Chicago
5801 S. Ellis Avenue
Chicago, IL 60637

Dear Director of Admissions:

I am a senior in high school and will graduate next June. I am interested in pursuing a career in physics, and my science teacher has told me that the University of Chicago has an exceptional physics department.

Will you please send me your current catalogue for the College as well as any additional information you may have about courses of study in the physical sciences and in mathematics?

Thank you very much.

Yours sincerely,

Emma Jane Catlip

Emma Jane Catlip

3. Write a letter to the Personnel Director at Highspeed Airlines Employment Office, Hartsfield Atlanta International Airport, Atlanta, Georgia 30366. Ask for information about requirements for becoming a flight attendant.
4. Write a letter to the Consumer Information Center, Department 38, Pueblo, Colorado 81009. Ask for the catalogue of free and low-cost pamphlets published by the Government Printing Office.

Order Letter

In an *order letter,* you are requesting that a company send you merchandise. You should describe the merchandise completely and exactly. Write the size, model number, color, and any special features of the merchandise you are ordering. You might also mention when and where you saw the merchandise advertised.

Be sure to state in the letter how you are paying for the order. Usually either a check or a money order is enclosed with an order letter. Never send cash through the mail; it may be lost, and you have no proof that you sent it. A sample order letter is shown below.

Writing Practice 6

Write one of the following order letters.

A Checklist for Proofreading Business Letters is on page 163.

1. Order twenty-four color wallet photos to be made from a photograph or negative that you are enclosing with your letter. Write to the Order Department, Terra Cotta Studios, P.O. Box 987, Long Island City, New York 11101. You are enclosing $1.95 for the photos plus $.75 to cover postage and handling for a total of $2.70.

6798 Beaumont Woods Place
Honolulu, HI 96822
April 8, 1984

Save the Seals
A Nonprofit Corporation
P.O. Box 10987
Los Angeles, CA 90048

Dear Save the Seals Order Department:

Please send me one small-sized adult T-shirt with a blue seal hand-screened on white 100 per cent cotton. The lettering on the T-shirt says, "Save the Seals." I saw the T-shirt advertised in the spring issue of the National Audubon Society's magazine.

I am enclosing a check for $7.50 for the T-shirt and for postage and handling.

Thank you very much.

Yours truly,

Lin Tang

Lin Tang

2. Enclose $12.50 for resoling your Long-Wear running shoes, which you are mailing separately via parcel post. Describe the shoes exactly so that when they arrive, they will be easily identified as yours. Write to Pat and Mike's Olympic Resoling, Inc., 5800 Lacy Road, Madison, Wisconsin 53711.
3. Send $4.95 for a copy of *Wilderness Log Cabins*, a book of instructions on how to build twenty-five different designs of log cabins. Write to Walden Wilderness Homes, Rural Route 90, Lake of the Forest, Kansas 66012.
4. Write to Native American Crafts Company at 1069 West Via Del Condito, Phoenix, Arizona 85039. Enclose $14.95 for a pair of soft glove-tanned natural color leather moccasins, size 7, fringed style with a hard sole.

Letter of Adjustment

The purpose of a *letter of adjustment* is to convince a company or an individual to replace damaged merchandise, refund money, or correct an error in billing. You must present all the information that is needed in order to correct the mistake. State the problem and then present the evidence as clearly and logically as possible. It may help to describe the problem step by step, in chronological order. Remember, however, not to include unnecessary details. Be clear and concise.

After you have described the problem, tell the company or individual what it is you want done. Do you want new merchandise, or do you want a refund? Do you want your account credited? If you are not sure of the best method of making the adjustment, say so.

A letter of adjustment should always be courteous in tone. Assume that the company is reliable and that you are going to receive the adjustment you are asking for. If you do not hear from the company within several weeks, you should send a follow-up letter, citing the date of your first letter and restating the problem. A sample letter of adjustment is on page 157.

Writing Practice 7

Write one of the following letters of adjustment, using your name and address and the current date. Make up any details that you need in order to write an effective letter.

A Checklist for Proofreading Business Letters is on page 163.

1. You bought a pair of terry-cloth shorts for $8.95 from Sportswear, Inc., 2086 Tupello Road, Baton Rouge, Louisiana 70808. The first time that you washed the shorts, they shrank so badly that they no longer fit. Tell how you are returning the shorts and what you want the company to do.
2. Your local telephone company has charged you for a long-distance call to Mexico City, Mexico, that you did not make. Enclose a copy of the bill and state the amount of the call and when it was made. You wish the company to credit your account.

5908 S. Crestwood Avenue
Richmond, VA 23226
February 10, 1984

Customer Service Department
Bellview Stationery Supplies, Inc.
1090 Eastwood Avenue
Franklinton, NC 27525

Dear Customer Service Department:

On December 18 I ordered 500 white gummed labels with my name and address. I mailed you a check for $4.25 to pay for the labels ($3.50) and the postage and handling charge ($.75).

I am attaching a sample of the labels, which arrived yesterday. Please note that the address is incorrect. It should be 5908, not 6908.

Please send me a new order of address labels with the correct name and address as shown below:

Kathleen Hovland
5908 S. Crestwood Avenue
Richmond, VA 23226

If you wish me to return the incorrect labels, please let me know and I will be glad to do so. Thank you for your help.

Very truly yours,

Kathleen Hovland

Kathleen Hovland

3. You ordered a natural color twin-size quilt-top kit for $23.95 from the Homecrafts Company, P.O. Box 4290, Hicksville, New York 11804. When the package arrived, it was smashed and torn, and you found that the kit's contents were badly soiled. Tell how you are returning the kit and what you want the company to do.
4. You tried a new brand of dry cat food for your cat. The package says that satisfaction is guaranteed or your money will be refunded. Your cat refuses to taste the cat food, let alone eat it. Write to YumYums, Inc., 1008 Twinlakes Boulevard, Kankakee, Illinois 60901. Enclose the box top of YumYums and ask for a refund.

Letter of Appreciation

There will be occasions when you want to write a letter thanking someone for special efforts on your behalf or for his or her work in general. A *letter of appreciation* is the business letter counterpart of a thank-you note. Since people in business and public life often receive critical letters and complaints, a letter of praise or thanks for work well done is always appreciated.

When writing a letter of appreciation, be sure to identify yourself, usually at the beginning of the letter. Then explain why you are writing the letter, expressing your thanks briefly and courteously. A sample letter of appreciation is shown below. How well do you think the writer has carried out the guidelines for a letter of appreciation?

289 Tanglewood Drive
Biloxi, MS 39531
March 19, 1984

The Honorable Jean D'Angelo
House Office Building
Washington, D.C. 20013

Dear Ms. D'Angelo:

I am an eleventh grader at Norland High School in Biloxi, Mississippi. My government class has been studying legislation that is currently in the House of Representatives and the Senate that directly affects funding for special high school science programs. I am assigned to study and discuss the bill (HR-108) that you introduced into the House in February.

Everyone in my class agrees that this is a very good bill and one that will help school systems provide additional resources for students who are interested in the sciences. We have asked our parents to write letters expressing their support of the bill to their representatives in Congress.

We hope that your legislation passes. Thank you for your good work.

Yours truly,

Jason Rothstein

Jason Rothstein

Writing Practice 8

Write a letter of appreciation to someone you think is doing a good job. The following are some suggestions.

A Checklist for Proofreading Business Letters is on page 163.

1. A teacher or an official in your school
2. An elected official in your city or county
3. Your senator or representative in Congress
4. A community leader
5. A business group that has sponsored an athletic team

Letter of Application

Suppose that you hear about a job from a friend or relative or see a job advertised in the newspaper. Take the time to plan and write a perfect letter of application. Your letter will have to impress the employer enough so that he or she will want to see you for an interview. A *letter of application* should give the impression that the writer is neat and responsible, as well as qualified for the job. When many letters are received for a single job, those that are messy or contain errors in spelling and grammar are quickly discarded.

A letter of application should contain the following information.

a. *When and how you heard about the job.* Identify the job for which you are applying and tell when and how you heard about it.

b. *Personal data.* Include your age, year in school, grade average, health, and any other information that might be relevant to the job.

c. *Your qualifications.* List previous experience, special training, interest in the field, and long-range career plans. You may not have had any direct experience in the kind of job for which you are applying. If so, try to think of experiences you have had that are in some way related to the job. (See, for example, the sample letter that follows.) Also, be sure to include personal characteristics such as reliability and a willingness to work hard.

d. *Your references.* Give the names and addresses of two or three adults who can attest to your character and ability. References should never be relatives. Any adult who knows you well, such as a teacher, neighbor, member of the clergy, or former employer, may serve as a reference. Before giving a person's name as a reference, however, ask that person for permission.

e. *Request for an interview.* Ask for an interview, at the employer's convenience, and be sure to tell when and where you can be reached by telephone to make an appointment.

Before you begin writing your letter of application, write a first draft in pencil. Revise the letter to make it sound as good as you can. Proofread the final letter carefully for errors in spelling, punctuation, and grammar. Then write the final letter neatly in ink or on a typewriter. If you are not satisfied that your letter of application looks perfect, rewrite it until you are satisfied. A sample letter of application is on pages 160–161.

1204 Churchill Road
Lyndhurst, Ohio 44124
March 30, 1984

Ms. Jane Ferrara
Director, Department of Parks and Recreation
Lyndhurst City Hall
17908 Mayfield Boulevard
Lyndhurst, Ohio 44124

Dear Ms. Ferrara:

I am writing to apply for the position of assistant recreation instructor at one of the city parks during the summer months. I have learned from an article in today's Herald that the city will be hiring six high school students to work as assistant recreation instructors this summer. Please consider me as an applicant.

I am a junior at East Hills High School. During the past three years my grade point average has been 3.3, or B+. I am preparing for college and am interested in majoring in physical education. For the past six years I have been a member of various track-and-field teams. I have been the assistant manager of a Little League team sponsored by the Optimists' Club for the past two years.

Last summer I worked as an assistant counselor at Park Day Camp with a boys' group of nine- and ten-year-olds. Mrs. Katie Oppenheim, director of the camp, can tell you about my reliability and ability to work with young people.

Ever since I can remember, I have been interested in athletics. I consider myself proficient in track-and-field events, soccer, baseball, football, and tennis. I also hold an American Red Cross Lifesaving Certificate.

The following persons can tell you more about my character and qualifications for the job.

Mrs. Katie Oppenheim, Director of Park Day Camp
2610 Fenwick Road, University Heights, Ohio

Writing Practice 9

A Checklist for Proofreading Business Letters is on page 163.

Think about the kind of summer job you would like to have. Use the classified pages of your telephone directory to find the name of a company that might have this kind of a job and write a letter of application. Be sure to include all of the information listed on page 159. Proofread your letter carefully, following the correct form for business letters.

Writing a Personal Résumé

Instead of writing a long letter of application, you may choose to outline your background and experience in a personal résumé. A sample résumé is shown on page 162. Notice that the résumé is written in outline form, which makes it easy to read and gives it a neat and businesslike appearance. Remember

Ms. Jane Ferrara 2 March 30, 1984

Mr. Philip Wenszlaw, Physical Education Instructor and Coach, East Hills High School, 1411 Eastwood Road, Mayfield Heights, Ohio

Mrs. Annemarie Cantwell, Principal of East Hills High School, 1411 Eastwood Road, Mayfield Heights, Ohio

At your convenience, I would be glad to come to City Hall for an interview. You can reach me at home after school and in the evenings. My telephone number is 394-1689.

Yours sincerely,

Louis Novallo

Louis Novallo

that the purpose of the résumé is to interest your employer in you. You do not have to include every bit of information about your life and should, in fact, only include information that would have a direct bearing on whether or not you are qualified for the job. Usually you can use the same résumé to apply for several jobs.

A personal résumé usually includes the following kinds of information: personal, education, skills, work experience, and references.

The letter of application that accompanies your résumé will be a brief covering letter. Do not repeat information given in the résumé; instead, begin your letter by identifying the job for which you are applying and by telling how you heard about the job. Then state that you are enclosing a résumé of your qualifications and references. Close your covering letter with a request for an interview.

Theresa A. Nardoia

Address:	14410 Peerless Place Newark, New Jersey 07114
Telephone:	498-6220
Personal:	Born September 19, 1969 in Newark, New Jersey Marital status: Single Health: Excellent Height: 5'4" Weight: 110 Social Security Number: 073-92-2068
Education:	Junior, Salazzaro High School, college preparatory course 3.0 grade point average (B)
Extracurricular activities:	
	Vice president, Key Club, a service organization Captain, girls' basketball team Member, student council
Skills:	Can type 65 words per minute Can operate microfilm and duplicating machines Can speak Spanish fluently
Work experience:	
	Central Newark Community Center, Newark, NJ -- Volunteer office work and help interview Spanish-speaking clients on Saturdays from 1983 to date
	Ryan Community School, Newark, NJ -- Assisted instructor in summer programs for teaching English skills to Spanish-speaking students, summer 1983
References:	Dr. Orin Lorenzo, Pastor, Newark United Methodist Church, Newark, New Jersey Dr. Natalie Crohn, Director, Central Newark Community Center, Newark, New Jersey Ms. Julia Wolk, Instructor, Ryan Community School, Newark, New Jersey

Writing Practice 10

Choose a summer job that interests you and write a personal résumé that you might send to a prospective employer.

Proofreading a Business Letter

Before you mail a business letter, proofread it carefully to be certain that it is complete, follows standard form, and is free from errors. Use the following checklist as a guide in proofreading your business letter.

Checklist for Proofreading Business Letters

FORM AND APPEARANCE

1. The letter is neatly written in ink or typed with no smudges or obvious corrections.
2. The letter is centered on the page with each part having the correct amount of spacing above and below.
3. The left-hand margins are exactly even. The left-hand margin of the heading aligns with the left-hand margin of the closing. The left-hand margin of the inside address aligns with the left-hand margin of the salutation.
4. The right-hand margin of the body of the letter is fairly even.
5. Your signature is legible and written in ink.

PUNCTUATION

1. In the heading and inside address, a comma comes between the city and state. There should be no comma between the state and ZIP code.
2. A comma comes between the day of the month and the year in the heading.
3. A colon follows the salutation.
4. A comma follows the closing.

CAPITALIZATION

1. Capitalize the names of streets, cities, and states in the heading and inside address.
2. Capitalize the month in the heading.
3. Capitalize the title of the person to whom you are writing and the names of the department and company listed in the inside address.
4. Capitalize the word *Dear* and all nouns in the salutation.
5. Capitalize only the first word of the closing.

Filling Out Forms

Businesses and government offices use forms to obtain and store information. Since you will be filling out such forms for the rest of your life, the following sections will give you some instruction and practice on how to do so accurately and efficiently.

The following guidelines apply to all types of forms—short or long, simple or complicated.

1. Always use blue or black ink or a typewriter. Never use a pencil.
2. Print—do not write—the information requested in the form. Be certain that any numbers that you write are clear and legible.

3. Read the directions carefully and completely before beginning to fill out the form. Often directions come at the beginning of the form, but occasionally they are written at the end. A complicated form, such as an income tax return, may have an accompanying booklet of instructions. These instructions give detailed explanations and definitions of terms.
4. Read the fine print carefully.
5. Most forms require a signature at the end of the form. Sign your name as you usually write it.

Social Security Application

A *Social Security number* is an identification number you will use in filling out job applications, license applications, voter registration forms, and nearly every other form in your life. In order to get your number, you must fill out a Social Security application like the one shown on page 165.

Look first at the way the form is organized to see what parts you will fill out. The form asks for information in numerical order but notice that the numbers are not all in the usual top-to-bottom order. In filling out the form, follow the numbers carefully.

As you should before filling out any form, read the Social Security application through completely to find out what information is called for. If you do not know some of the information, you must find it so you can respond correctly. Now read each line carefully and fill it out by printing in black or blue ink or by typing. Print in the space between the horizontal lines that correspond to the number at the left.

	First Name	Middle	Last Name
1. Print Full Name you will use in work or business	Helen	A.	Kulik

For Numbers 8, 9, and 10 of the form, you will place a check mark (√) or an *X* in the proper box. If you check *Yes* in Number 10, you must also print the state in which you applied for a Social Security number, the date you applied, and the Social Security number, if you know it.

The area in the upper-right corner and the space at the bottom of the application are reserved for Social Security personnel to mark. Remember, do not write in any area that does not specifically tell you to do so.

Read Number 14 carefully because it tells you of your responsibilities in signing the application. Then *sign* your name in the space provided. Your signature is a way of identifying yourself, so you should decide whether to sign the full name you were given at birth, a middle initial, two initials, or another form of your name. Notice that Numbers 1 and 2 ask for your name two different ways. In Number 1 print the name you use as your legal signature on Number 14. In Number 2 print the name that appears on your birth certificate. For some people the names will be exactly the same, but for most people the names will be slightly different.

Read the instructions on the back of the application for Numbers 1, 3, 5, 10, 11, and 14.

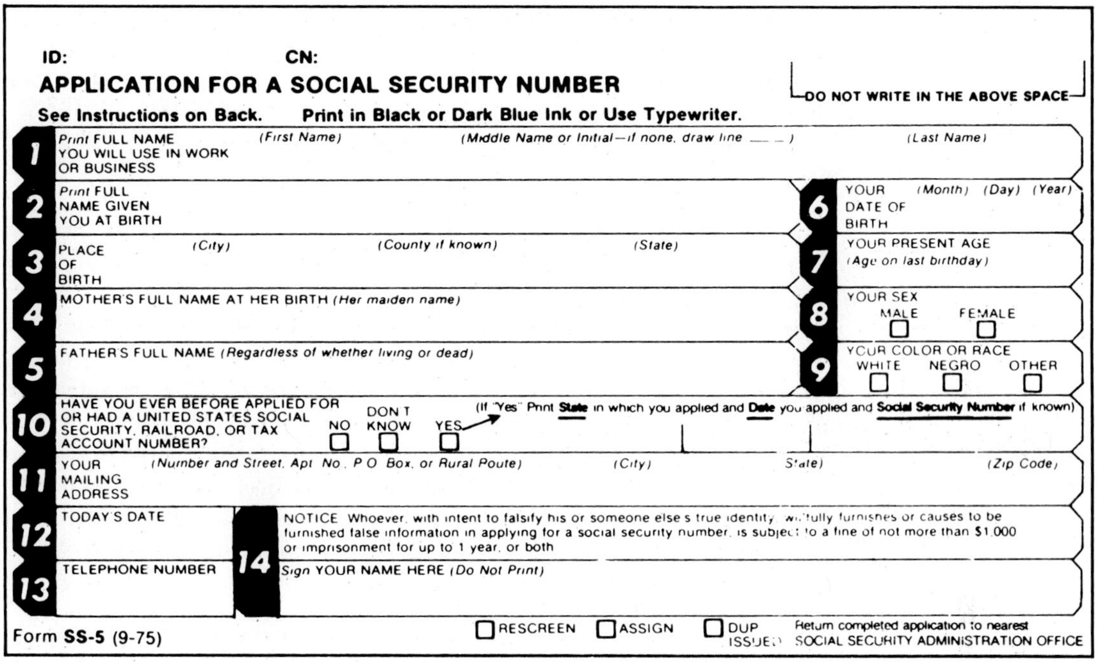

ID: CN:

APPLICATION FOR A SOCIAL SECURITY NUMBER

DO NOT WRITE IN THE ABOVE SPACE

See Instructions on Back. Print in Black or Dark Blue Ink or Use Typewriter.

1 Print FULL NAME YOU WILL USE IN WORK OR BUSINESS (First Name) (Middle Name or Initial—if none, draw line — —) (Last Name)

2 Print FULL NAME GIVEN YOU AT BIRTH

6 YOUR DATE OF BIRTH (Month) (Day) (Year)

3 PLACE OF BIRTH (City) (County if known) (State)

7 YOUR PRESENT AGE (Age on last birthday)

4 MOTHER'S FULL NAME AT HER BIRTH (Her maiden name)

8 YOUR SEX MALE ☐ FEMALE ☐

5 FATHER'S FULL NAME (Regardless of whether living or dead)

9 YOUR COLOR OR RACE WHITE ☐ NEGRO ☐ OTHER ☐

10 HAVE YOU EVER BEFORE APPLIED FOR OR HAD A UNITED STATES SOCIAL SECURITY, RAILROAD, OR TAX ACCOUNT NUMBER? NO ☐ DON'T KNOW ☐ YES ☐ (If "Yes" Print **State** in which you applied and **Date** you applied and **Social Security Number** if known)

11 YOUR MAILING ADDRESS (Number and Street, Apt No., P O Box, or Rural Route) (City) (State) (Zip Code)

12 TODAY'S DATE

14 NOTICE Whoever, with intent to falsify his or someone else's true identity, willfully furnishes or causes to be furnished false information in applying for a social security number, is subject to a fine of not more than $1,000 or imprisonment for up to 1 year, or both

13 TELEPHONE NUMBER

Sign YOUR NAME HERE (Do Not Print)

Form SS-5 (9-75) ☐ RESCREEN ☐ ASSIGN ☐ DUP ISSUED Return completed application to nearest SOCIAL SECURITY ADMINISTRATION OFFICE

1. HELEN A. KULIK

2. HELEN ANNETTE KULIK

Writing Practice 11

On a separate sheet of paper, fill in the information called for on the Social Security application as if you were applying for your own Social Security number. Make your responses correspond exactly to the numbers of each item.

Drivers License Examination Application Form

To get your drivers license you will have to take and pass a written examination and a driving test. Before you can apply for a license in most areas, you will have to pass an approved driver education course if you are under eighteen years of age. In addition, you will need the approval of your parent, legal guardian, or other responsible adult who will sign your application. Before you begin the application procedure, get a copy of your state drivers information booklet and study the rules and procedures you will need to know in order to pass the tests. In the booklet you will find directions on how to apply for a license, what identification you will need, information about the kind of questions you will be asked, and special instructions if you want a license to drive a vehicle other than an automobile.

Before you fill out the application form, look at how it is organized. Then read the instructions completely and carefully. On the sample form on this page, you will notice that the gray shaded areas are reserved for the department issuing your license to record information about your test results, restrictions on your license and identification. Do not write in any space except where instructed. As in filling out all forms, print legibly in ink or type in the information. Where you are to sign your name *(Signature of Applicant)*, write your name as you normally do. It should be the same name you use on other legal forms, such as the Social Security application, bank checks, and contracts.

On the Applicant's Declaration Sheet (on page 166), the top line is for a current drivers license number. If you are applying for a license for the first time, you will not have any number to put in that space. In the next item you will check *Operator* because you want a license to operate a motor vehicle. However, you might also want to operate a moped, so you would also check that box. People who need a chauffeur's license for business purposes or who need a license for legal identification will check one of the other boxes. If you want a license to operate a motorcycle, check to see if there is a special application form for that examination.

APPLICANT'S DECLARATION SHEET

DE-36 (3/80)

MICHIGAN DRIVER LICENSE NUMBER

APPLICATION DESIRED
☐ OPERATOR
☐ CHAUFFEUR
☐ MOPED
☐ PERSONAL I.D.

(FOR DEPARTMENT USE ONLY)

LICENSE EXP. YEAR:	LICENSE TYPE:	DATE ISSUED:
COUNTY CODE:	APPLICATION NUMBER:	
ENDORSEMENTS:	PREVIOUS LIC. (STATE-NO. EXP. YEAR)	

(FIRST NAME) (MIDDLE NAME) (LAST NAME)

(CURRENT RESIDENCE ADDRESS) (APT. OR LOT NO.) (COUNTY)

(CITY OR TOWN) Michigan (ZIP CODE)

EYE COLOR | ___ ft. ___ in. HEIGHT | WEIGHT | SEX | MONTH DAY YEAR DATE OF BIRTH

CORRECTIVE LENSES REQUIRED? (check one) YES ☐ NO ☐

OTHER RESTRICTIONS:

DRIVER ED. CERTIFICATE AND T.I.P. INFORMATION

DRIVER ED. CERTIFICATE NUMBER: | ISSUING SCHOOL CODE:

BIRTH CERTIFICATE NUMBER: | STATE & COUNTY ______

VALIDATE DRIVER ED. CERTIFICATE? ☐

ISSUED T.I.P. ☐

HOME PHONE:

PLEASE ANSWER THE FOLLOWING QUESTIONS BY CHECKING YES OR NO

1. Do you have a physical disability or handicap? (Do not include glasses) Yes ☐ No ☐
2. Have you ever been subject to a recurrent or uncontrolled loss of consciousness? Yes ☐ No ☐
3. Is your driving privilege currently suspended, revoked or denied? Yes ☐ No ☐
4. Will you need a classified endorsement? Yes ☐ No ☐
5. Will you be operating a motorcycle on public streets and highways? Yes ☐ No ☐

ROAD SIGN TEST		DATE ___/___	PASS ☐	FAIL ☐
		DATE ___/___	PASS ☐	FAIL ☐
WRITTEN TEST	#	DATE ___/___	PASS ☐	FAIL ☐
	#	DATE ___/___	PASS ☐	FAIL ☐
	#	DATE ___/___	PASS ☐	FAIL ☐

(SIGNATURE OF APPLICANT) (DATE)

REMARKS:

FEE DUE:

THE PERSON DESCRIBED IS AUTHORIZED TO OPERATE A MOTOR VEHICLE WHEN ACCOMPANIED BY AN EXAMINER CERTIFIED BY THE MICHIGAN DEPARTMENT OF STATE

INITIAL OF EXAMINER

On the sample form you would print above the line that asks for some kind of information:

JILL	ANN	McINTYRE
NAME First	Middle	Last

Follow the directions for filling in information exactly and give all the information requested. For example, if you do not know the county or township you live in, find out that information before you submit your application.

Be sure to sign your legal name where it is indicated. Also, put the date of your signature in the appropriate place.

Writing Practice 12

Since you may not live in the state where the sample form is used, try to get the form used in your state and fill it in accurately. If you cannot get your state's form, make a copy of the application for a drivers license examination on page 166 and fill in the information called for.

8 Imaginative Writing

Elements of Fiction and Drama

Short stories, novels, and plays are constructed from several basic elements: *characters*, *setting*, and *plot* are the most common. When you read stories and plays, you want to know who is involved (characters), when and where the story takes place (setting), and what happens to the characters (plot). Almost all imaginative fiction has at least these three elements, though much of it has even more.

Creating Characters

Playwrights do not provide audiences with descriptive details and explanations about the characters seen on stage. Instead, the dialogue—the words the characters speak—must reveal motivations for their actions and their reactions to each other. In the following selection from *An Enemy of the People* by Henrik Ibsen, Dr. Stockmann, Medical Officer of the Municipal Baths, reveals his discovery that the town's public baths, known for their beneficial effects, are contaminated. As you read, imagine what Dr. Stockmann is like, based on his dialogue and the way he talks.[1]

HOVSTAD. What are you driving at, Doctor?

DR. S. [*standing still by the table*]. Isn't it the universal opinion that our town is a healthy spot?

HOVSTAD. Certainly.

---

[1]From *An Enemy of the People* by Henrik Ibsen (Dryden Press Edition, 1947). Courtesy of Holt, Rinehart and Winston, Publishers.

DR. S. Quite an unusually healthy spot, in fact—a place that deserves to be recommended in the warmest possible manner either for invalids or for people who are well—

MRS. S. Yes, but my dear Thomas—

DR. S. And we have been recommending it and praising it—I have written and written, both in the "Messenger" and in pamphlets—

HOVSTAD. Well, what then?

DR. S. And the Baths—we have called them the "main artery of the town's life-blood," the "nerve-centre of our town," and the devil knows what else—

BILLING. "The town's pulsating heart" was the expression I once used on an important occasion—

DR. S. Quite so. Well, do you know what they really are, these great, splendid, much praised Baths, that have cost so much money—do you know what they are?

HOVSTAD. No, what are they?

MRS. S. Yes, what are they?

DR. S. The whole place is a pesthouse!

PETRA. The Baths, father?

MRS. S. [*at the same time*]. Our Baths!

HOVSTAD. But, Doctor—

BILLING. Absolutely incredible!

DR. S. The whole Bath establishment is a whited, poisoned sepulchre, I tell you—the gravest possible danger to the public health! All the nastiness up at Mölledal, all that stinking filth, is infecting the water in the conduit-pipes leading to the reservoir; and the same cursed, filthy poison oozes out on the shore too—

HORSTER. Where the bathing-place is?

DR. S. Just there.

HOVSTAD. How do you come to be so certain of all this, Doctor?

DR. S. I have investigated the matter most conscientiously. For a long time past I have suspected something of the kind. Last year we had some very strange cases of illness among the visitors—typhoid cases, and cases of gastric fever—

MRS. S. Yes, that is quite true.

DR. S. At the time, we supposed the visitors had been infected before they came; but later on, in the winter, I began to have a different opinion; and so I set myself to examine the water, as well as I could.

MRS. S. Then that is what you have been so busy with?

DR. S. Indeed I have been busy, Katherine. But here I had none of the necessary scientific apparatus; so I sent samples, both of the drinking-water and of the sea-water, up to the University, to have an accurate analysis made by a chemist.

HOVSTAD. And have you got that?

DR. S. [*showing him the letter*]. Here it is! It proves the presence of decomposing organic matter in the water—it is full of infusoria. The water is absolutely dangerous to use, either internally or externally.

MRS. S. What a mercy you discovered it in time.

DR. S. You may well say so.

HOVSTAD. And what do you propose to do now, Doctor?

DR. S. To see the matter put right—naturally.

HOVSTAD. Can that be done?

DR. S. It must be done. Otherwise the Baths will be absolutely useless and wasted. But we need not anticipate that; I have a very clear idea what we shall have to do.

MRS. S. But why have you kept this all so secret, dear?

DR. S. Do you suppose I was going to run about the town gossiping about it, before I had absolute proof? No, thank you. I am not such a fool.

PETRA. Still, you might have told us—

DR. S. Not a living soul. But to-morrow you may run round to the old Badger—

MRS. S. Oh, Thomas! Thomas!

DR. S. Well, to your grandfather, then. The old boy will have something to be astonished at! I know he thinks I am cracked—and there are lots of other people think so too, I have noticed. But now these good folks shall see—they shall just see—! [*Walks about, rubbing his hands.*] There will be a nice upset in the town, Katherine; you can't imagine what it will be. All the conduit-pipes will have to be relaid.

HOVSTAD [*getting up*]. All the conduit-pipes—?

DR. S. Yes, of course. The intake is too low down; it will have to be lifted to a position much higher up.

PETRA. Then you were right after all.

DR. S. Ah, you remember, Petra—I wrote opposing the plans before the work was begun. But at that time no one would listen to me. Well, I am going to let them have it, now! Of course I have prepared a report for the Baths Committee; I have had it ready for a week, and was only waiting for this to come. [*Shows the letter.*] Now it shall go off at once. [*Goes into his room and comes back with some papers.*] Look at that! Four closely written sheets!—and the letter shall go with them. Give me a bit of paper, Katherine—something to wrap them up in. That will do! Now give it to—to—[*stamps his foot*]—what the deuce is her name?—give it to the maid, and tell her to take it at once to the Mayor.

It is clear from his dialogue that Dr. Stockmann is disturbed by his discovery: "The whole Bath establishment is a whited, poisoned sepulchre, I tell you—the gravest possible danger to the public health!" It is also apparent that he plans to take action:

HOVSTAD. And what do you propose to do now, Doctor?

DR. S. To see the matter put right—naturally.

HOVSTAD. Can that be done?

DR. S. It must be done. Otherwise the Baths will be absolutely useless and wasted. . . .

Based on the excerpt from the play, how do Billing, Petra, Hovstad, and Mrs. Stockmann react to Dr. Stockmann's announcement? Do you think they will be sympathetic to his plans to clean up the public baths? Is there any indication in the dialogue that Dr. Stockmann may be opposed in his efforts?

Novelists and short story writers can describe characters directly, as well as indirectly through dialogue. As you read the following opening paragraphs from Doris Lessing's "Through the Tunnel," look for details that help you visualize and understand the young boy and his mother.[1]

> Going to the shore on the first morning of the holiday, the young English boy stopped at a turning of the path and looked down at a wild and rocky bay, and then over to the crowded beach he knew so well from other years. His mother walked on in front of him, carrying a bright striped bag in one hand. Her other arm, swinging loose, was very white in the sun.
>
> The boy watched that white, naked arm, and turned his eyes, which had a frown behind them, toward the bay and back again to his mother. When she felt he was not with her, she swung around.
>
> "Oh, there you are, Jerry!" she said. She looked impatient, then smiled. "Why, darling, would you rather not come with me? Would you rather—" she frowned, conscientiously worrying over what amusements he might secretly be longing for which she had been too busy to imagine.
>
> He was very familiar with that anxious, apologetic smile. Contrition sent him running after her. And yet, as he ran, he looked back over his shoulder at the wild bay; and all morning, as he played on the safe beach, he was thinking of it.
>
> Next morning, when it was time for the routine of swimming and sunbathing, his mother said, "Are you tired of the usual beach, Jerry? Would you like to go somewhere else?"
>
> "Oh, no!" he said quickly, smiling at her out of that unfailing impulse of contrition—a sort of chivalry. Yet, walking down the path with her, he blurted out, "I'd like to go and have a look at those rocks down there."

The mother in "Through the Tunnel" looks "impatient" as she walks in front of her son, "carrying a bright striped bag in one hand." The writer says that the mother frowns, "conscientiously worrying over what amusements he might secretly be longing for. . . ." With these words the writer lets readers know that the mother is anxious about her son. What other descriptive details let you see the mother and her son and reveal the relationship between them?

Writing Practice 1

Assume that you are preparing to write a short story or play. Before you begin, be certain you have your main character clearly in mind. Then write a paragraph describing this person. Tell what the character looks like, but more important, what he or she is like inside. The following questions will help you create your character:

1. What is the physical appearance of your character? If you were to meet him or her on the street, what would you notice first? For example, does he or she have curly red hair, an awkward slope to the shoulders, unusual height?
2. If your character were to walk into your house, how would your parents

---

[1]From *The Habit of Loving* by Doris Lessing (T. Y. Crowell). Copyright © 1957 by Doris Lessing. Reprinted by permission of Harper & Row, Publishers, Inc., and Curtis Brown Ltd., London, on behalf of Doris Lessing.

or friends react? Would he or she be a friend of yours, an enemy, or someone you would not even notice?

3. What is your character's dream or goal? Is he or she an ambitious person who always needs to win or is the character someone who lets others lead? Does your character know what he or she wants in life?
4. Imagine that your character has come home after a long day and stands for a moment looking in the mirror. What goes through his or her mind? Is the character pleased or displeased with the image in the mirror?

Creating a Setting

A play or story always takes place someplace at some time. In a play the setting is created partly by the author's *stage directions*, partly by the action, and partly by the dialogue. On stage the setting is made clear by the furniture, costumes, painted backgrounds, music, and lighting. A printed program may also establish the setting by telling you that Act I takes place in the Forest of Arden or that Scene 2 takes place the next afternoon.

You can see how a writer creates setting through stage directions in the following excerpt from George Bernard Shaw's *Pygmalion.* What details describe the time and place? What characters are a part of the setting?[1]

Act One

> London at 11:15 P.M. Torrents of heavy summer rain. Cab whistles blowing frantically in all directions. Pedestrians running for shelter into the portico of St. Paul's church (not Wren's cathedral but Inigo Jones's church in Covent Garden vegetable market), among them a lady and her daughter in evening dress. All are peering out gloomily at the rain, except one man with his back turned to the rest, wholly preoccupied with a notebook in which he is writing.
>
> The church clock strikes the first quarter.

Novelists and short story writers can tell you where and when the story takes place through descriptive details as well as through the plot and characters. The setting may be realistic, resembling places that actually exist or might exist, or the setting may be highly unrealistic, as it might appear in the mind of one or more characters. For example, in the following passage from Katherine Anne Porter's *Pale Horse, Pale Rider*, a hospital corridor is exaggerated in its dimensions, and hospital attendants appear dreamlike to a girl who is desperately ill.[2]

> Miss Tanner appeared beside her, handed her an unsealed envelope, took it back, unfolded the note and gave it to her.

---

[1]From "Pygmalion" by Bernard Shaw in *Collected Plays With Their Prefaces: Definitive Edition in Seven Volumes.* Reprinted by permission of The Society of Authors on behalf of the Bernard Shaw Estate.

[2]From *Pale Horse, Pale Rider* by Katherine Anne Porter. Copyright 1937, 1965 by Katherine Anne Porter. Reprinted by permission of Harcourt Brace Jovanovich, Inc. and Jonathan Cape Ltd.

"I can't see it," said Miranda, after a pained search of the page full of hasty scratches in black ink.

"Here, I'll read it," said Miss Tanner. "It says, 'They came and took you while I was away and now they will not let me see you. Maybe tomorrow they will, with my love, Adam,' " read Miss Tanner in a firm dry voice, pronouncing the words distinctly. "Now, do you see?" she asked soothingly.

Miranda, hearing the words one by one, forgot them one by one. "Oh, read it again, what does it say?" she called out over the silence that pressed upon her, reaching towards the dancing words that just escaped as she almost touched them. "That will do," said Dr. Hildesheim, calmly authoritarian. "Where is that bed?"

"There is no bed yet," said Miss Tanner, as if she said, We are short of oranges. Dr. Hildesheim said, "Well, we'll manage something," and Miss Tanner drew the narrow trestle with bright crossed metal supports and small rubbery wheels into a deep jut of the corridor, out of the way of the swift white figures darting about, whirling and skimming like water flies all in silence. The white walls rose sheer as cliffs, a dozen frosted moons followed each other in perfect self-possession down a white lane and dropped mutely one by one into a snowy abyss.

What is this whiteness and silence but the absence of pain? Miranda lay lifting the nap of her white blanket softly between eased fingers, watching a dance of tall deliberate shadows moving behind a wide screen of sheets spread upon a frame. It was there, near her, on her side of the wall where she could see it clearly and enjoy it, and it was so beautiful she had no curiosity as to its meaning. Two dark figures nodded, bent, curtsied to each other, retreated and bowed again, lifted long arms and spread great hands against the white shadow of the screen; then with a single round movement, the sheets were folded back, disclosing two speechless men in white, standing, and another speechless man in white, lying on the bare springs of a white iron bed. The man on the springs was swathed smoothly from head to foot in white, with folded bands across the face, and a large stiff bow like merry rabbit ears dangled at the crown of his head.

What details from the preceding selection establish the *real* place of the action? What details show that the time and place seem fantastic and unreal to the sick patient, Miranda?

Writing Practice 2

Assume that you are going to write a story or play and that you want to describe a setting for it. Before you begin, make a list of the sights and sounds, tastes and smells that someone would notice while walking through the setting you choose. Then make another list of the reactions you would have to that setting if you were a character in the story or play. Finally write a paragraph telling about this scene, using as many details as possible. Use the following questions to help you plan your setting.

1. What is the season, the time of day, and the time of year when your scene begins?

2. What is the first thing you notice about the scene? For example, is it deserted or full of people? Is the area beautiful, ordinary, or ugly? What makes it that way?
3. What sounds do you associate with the scene? If it is peaceful, do you hear the sounds of people? Animals? If it is noisy, do you hear the grinding of machines or the shouts of children playing in the street?
4. What tastes or smells would a person notice in this scene?
5. Imagine that you are in the middle of the scene and then look straight ahead and ask yourself what you see. Look to the right and left and notice what you see there. Turn around and notice how the scene changes. Now focus on something small in your scene, perhaps small enough to fit in your hand. What does it look like?

Creating a Plot

A *plot* is a plan or outline of action for a play or story.

In most stories conflict is an important part of plot. Conflict may take place inside a character. For example, a character may have an inner battle about what to do in a certain situation. Even more frequently, however, conflict takes place between two or more characters. The conflict in a story, and what the characters decide to do about it, is often the central point of the story.

Conflict may also involve the circumstances in which characters find themselves. In the novel *Walkabout* by James Vance Marshall, two American children survive a plane crash in the Australian Outback, a desolate desert region far from any towns or settlements. They attempt to walk to Adelaide, the city in which their uncle lives, but grow hungry and tired from lack of food and water and from walking in the hot sun. Suddenly a native boy appears. Although they cannot understand each other's language, the American children and the bush boy, as he is called, make friends. The native boy knows they need to be led to safety, but he also believes that the American girl has seen the image of death in his eyes and that he will certainly die. In the following chapter the bush boy has started to leave Mary and Peter, the stranded children who need him in order to survive. As you read, notice how their dependence on the native boy and his near desertion intensify the problem of survival.[1]

> The children watched him. The girl was pale and breathing quickly. The boy was whimpering; shocked, frightened, caught up in a cross fire of emotions he couldn't begin to understand. But one fact did penetrate the haze of his bewilderment. The bush boy, for the second time since their meeting him, was deserting them. Their lifeline, once again, was drifting away.

---

[1]From *Walkabout* by James Vance Marshall. Copyright © 1959 by James Vance Marshall. Revised edition copyright © 1971 by William Morrow and Company, Inc. Reprinted by permission of William Morrow and Company, Inc., and Clerkenwell House. Published in Great Britain by Michael Joseph Ltd.

Suddenly and violently, he flung off his sister's hand and rushed stumbling into the desert.

"Come back!" His voice was frightened. "Come back. Come back."

The bush boy walked on, unheeding, apparently unhearing, like a sleepwalker. But Peter wouldn't be denied. Blindly he launched himself at the bush boy's legs, clutching him round the knees.

"You're not to go," he panted.

And he hung on, like a leech.

The bush boy was jerked to a halt, was shaken out of his trance. He put his hands on the white boy's shoulders, pushing him gently away. But Peter wouldn't release his grip.

"You're not going." He repeated it over and over again. "Not going. Not going. Not going."

The bush boy squatted down, so that his face was close to the little one's, so that the little one could look into his eyes and see the terrible thing that was there. With their faces less than eighteen inches apart the two boys stared into each other's eyes.

But to the bush boy's astonishment, the little one didn't draw back; gave no exclamation of terror; seemed to see nothing wrong. He got to his feet. Puzzled. For a moment hope came surging back. Perhaps the lubra had been mistaken; perhaps the Spirit of Death had been only passing through him, resting awhile as he passed from one tribe to another; perhaps he had left him now.

A *lubra* is a female adolescent.

He retraced his steps, back toward the girl.

But as soon as he neared her, hope drained away. For at his approach the lubra again shrank back; in her eyes all the former terror came welling up.

The bush boy knew then that he was going to die. Not perhaps today, nor tomorrow, nor even the next day. But soon. Before the coming of the rains and the smoking of spirits out of the tribal caves. This knowledge numbed his mind, but didn't paralyze it. He was still able to think of other things. Of the queer strangers, for example—the lubra and the little one—of what would happen to them. When he died, they would die too. That was certain, for they were such helpless creatures. So there'd be not one victim for the Spirit of Death but three. Unless he could somehow save them?

It seemed, on the face of it, an impossible undertaking. With a stem of yacca he traced a pattern in the sand: circle after circle, symbolic rings of protection against Wulgaru, the Spirit of Death. And at last, in a moment of sudden inspiration, he saw what had to be done. He must lead the strangers to safety, to the final goal of his walkabout, the valley-of-waters-under-the-earth. And they must waste no time. For who knew how much time they would have.

A *yacca* is a kind of evergreen tree.

He gathered up the *worwora* and smoothed out the ash of the fire.

"Kurura," he said, and struck out across the desert.

The little one followed him at once. But the lubra didn't move. He thought for a long time that she had decided to stay by the billabongs, but in the end she too started to follow, keeping a long way behind.

A *billabong* is a blind channel leading out from a river.

Writing Practice 3

The following suggestions are for conflicts within one character, between two characters, and between characters and their situation. Choose one from this list and use it as the basis for the plot of your own story. Then write the opening paragraph of the story in which you establish for readers the nature of the conflict. If you prefer, create your own conflict.

1. The characters are a scientist from earth and a creature from Venus, also a scientist. They have been assigned to work together on a space probe in a far galaxy; they will be isolated for two years as they do their exploration. The problem is that all Venusians are mind readers, so the creature always knows what the earth scientist is thinking. At first this amuses the human, but he or she quickly grows to resent it, feeling that his or her privacy is being invaded.
2. The characters are an elderly couple. They have lived in their home at the edge of town for over forty years. Now the city has purchased land next to their property to build a large manufacturing plant, and it needs to buy their land as well. The conflict arises when the city planners find that the elderly couple refuse to sell or move.
3. A West Point cadet (male or female) observes his or her best friend cheating on an exam. The school's honor code requires that a witness report such an incident or face the possibility of expulsion along with the cheater. The conflict arises from the decision the character has to make.

Creating Dialogue

A *dialogue* is a conversation between two or more characters.

Short stories, novels, and plays all make use of dialogue between and among characters as a means of telling the story.

Dialogue lets the reader or audience hear what the characters have to say about themselves and others. As a reader or viewer, you notice not only what they say but also how they say it, what kind of mood they are in, and how they react to other characters. For example, listen to the characters in the following dialogue from Mary Lavin's short story, "One Summer." Vera, a young woman, has just brought her dying father home from the hospital with a live-in nurse. Vera and her father have always been quite close; she has recently rejected a proposal of marriage because she cannot bear to leave him alone. What do you learn about Vera and her father from this dialogue?[1]

> When Vera went in to her father, he looked up, "Oh, is it you!" he said, obviously disappointed.
>
> "Yes, it's me," she said flatly. "Are you comfortable, Father? Will I fix your pillows?"
>
> "No!" Impatiently, he put out his hand. "Leave them! She'll do them. She has a knack."
>
> "Well, I should hope so! It's part of her training. I don't think we should leave everythiing to her, all the same," she said. "Is there nothing you'd like *me* to do?"

---

[1]From "One Summer" by Mary Lavin in *The New Yorker*, September 11, 1965. Copyright © 1965 by The New Yorker Magazine, Inc. Reprinted by permission.

He was lying back, looking up at the ceiling, but he glanced around the room. "You could get her a chair," he said. He frowned at the hard bentwood chair beside his bed. "She ought to have a big armchair. Where did you put her, anyway?"

"Up beside Lily," she said dully.

"Isn't it dark up there under the roof?" He didn't actually frown, but she could see he was dissatisfied. And then he said something outrageous. "Why didn't you give her your room?"

"I gave her the room Lily had got ready for her," she said tartly, but under his stare she weakened. "It would have been an awful job to move out all my things."

"You'd have time to do it now while she's downstairs," he said, so casual it was almost sly.

But from below at that moment came the sound of laughter. "I think it would be a great mistake to move her away from Lily," she said. "They seem to be getting on famously."

"She'd be nearer to me if she was in your room."

Even this short piece of dialogue tells you something about the two characters. Vera is hurt by her father's obvious preference for the nurse's attentions. She asks, "Is there nothing you'd like *me* to do?" and you can imagine the aggrieved tone of voice she uses. Her father is oblivious to Vera's emotions and considers only how to make the nurse more comfortable, even requesting that Vera give up her own room. When Vera does not refuse her father directly but makes excuses instead, you learn even more about the type of relationship they have.

Dialogue is essential to a play, for it is through dialogue alone that the audience knows who the characters are and what the plot is about. Before creating your own dialogue, look back at the selection from *An Enemy of the People* on pages 168–170 and notice how the spoken words of the characters reveal their personalities and motivations.

Writing Practice 4

Write a brief dialogue between two characters of your choice. The purpose of the dialogue is to introduce your readers to the characters and to show them in conflict. The conflict can be an inner conflict of one character that is revealed in the dialogue, or it may be a conflict between the two characters. If you like, write about characters you have already created for an assignment in this chapter.

Rules for punctuating dialogue are discussed on pages 599–600.

Writing Practice 5

Using the elements of character, setting, plot, and conflict, write a short story or play. If you wish, incorporate one of the paragraphs describing character, setting, or plot that you wrote for an earlier writing practice. Your story or play can be realistic, or it can be a story or play of fantasy or science fiction. If you write a short story, include dialogue between characters. If you write a short play, indicate who speaks the lines by placing the speaker's name first, followed by a colon (:) and then the dialogue. You may include notes

Use the Preparing to Write section that follows to help you with ideas for this assignment.

in parentheses ( ) to show how the words are to be said or what the speaker is doing:

> Karen: (Looks at Mary, sighs, moves back toward desk and stands there a moment) Well, there doesn't seem to be any other way with you; you'll have to be punished.

The photographs on pages 179–180 may be helpful as inspirations for your story or short play. Look at each photograph, deciding what the people are doing and what kind of people they are. Then try to imagine what kind of conflict might be involved in their relationship. Use any of these ideas as the basis for your story or play.

Preparing to Write

Some playwrights like to work out ideas for scenes by giving suggestions to actors and watching them improvise dialogue. Whether you are writing dialogue for a short story or a scene in a play, you might try the following to help you create dialogue between characters. First you will need to divide into groups of three or four. One person should be the "playwright," the one who records the dialogue; the others are actors. Brainstorm together to generate some basic ideas for a brief dialogue based on one of the following situations or, if you prefer, a situation of your own.

1. Two (or three) men or women argue about who was the most popular forty years ago when they were in high school together.
2. The year is A.D. 3000. Two (or three) creatures are watching a sports match and find they disagree about the scoring.
3. Two men or women are planning an important party. They are quite snobbish and want to invite only the "right" people. As they plan, they realize that their ideas of which people are "right" are very different.
4. The scene is a classroom. The teacher announces to the class that he or she is an alien and that the entire school is about to be transported to another planet for observation.

Before you begin working on the dialogue, ask yourself three questions:

> Where is the scene taking place?
> What is your character like (what sort of person are you)?
> What do you feel about the other characters in the scene?

For example, in the first suggested situation you could build a scene around two men who have been friends for life but who realize that each has a completely different version of what they were like in high school. Another possibility is to build a scene around two people meeting at a high school reunion after many years who remember that they never really liked each other in school. At first they are friendly and warm, then cool, then angry.

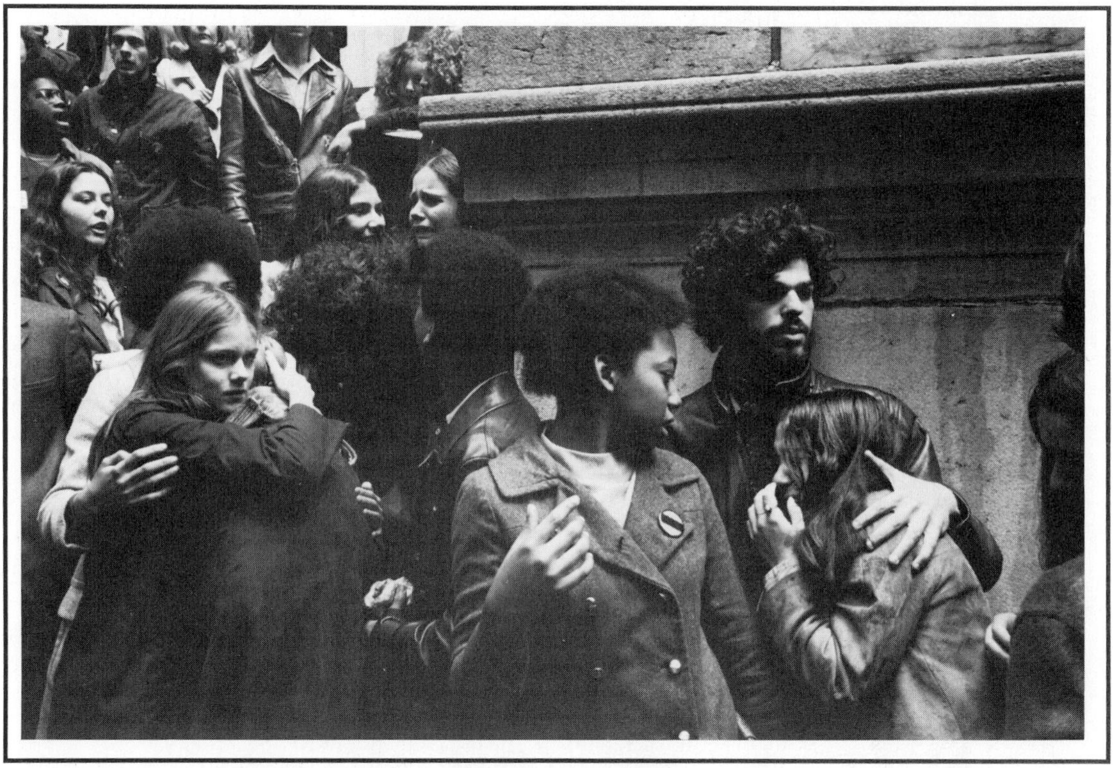

Elements of Poetry

From its beginnings poetry has been closely associated with music. The earliest known poems were meant to be sung or chanted rather than spoken. In the nineteenth century the word *song* could mean either "a poem" or "words set to music." The lyrics to popular songs today use the elements traditionally associated with poetry: rhyme, meter, and verse patterns.

Formal poetry is poetry that follows a standard form.

Formal poetry uses a pattern of repeating sounds called *rhyme* and *alliteration*, a pattern of repeating rhythm called *meter*, and a pattern of repeating lines called *stanzas*. Just as in a song, when a beautiful tune increases your enjoyment of the words to the lyrics, so in poetry the musical effects of repeating sounds and rhythms increase your enjoyment of the poem.

Rhyme in Poetry

Words that rhyme share the same sounds. In rhyming poems the rhyming words come at the end of each line. In most formal poetry the rhyming words rhyme exactly.

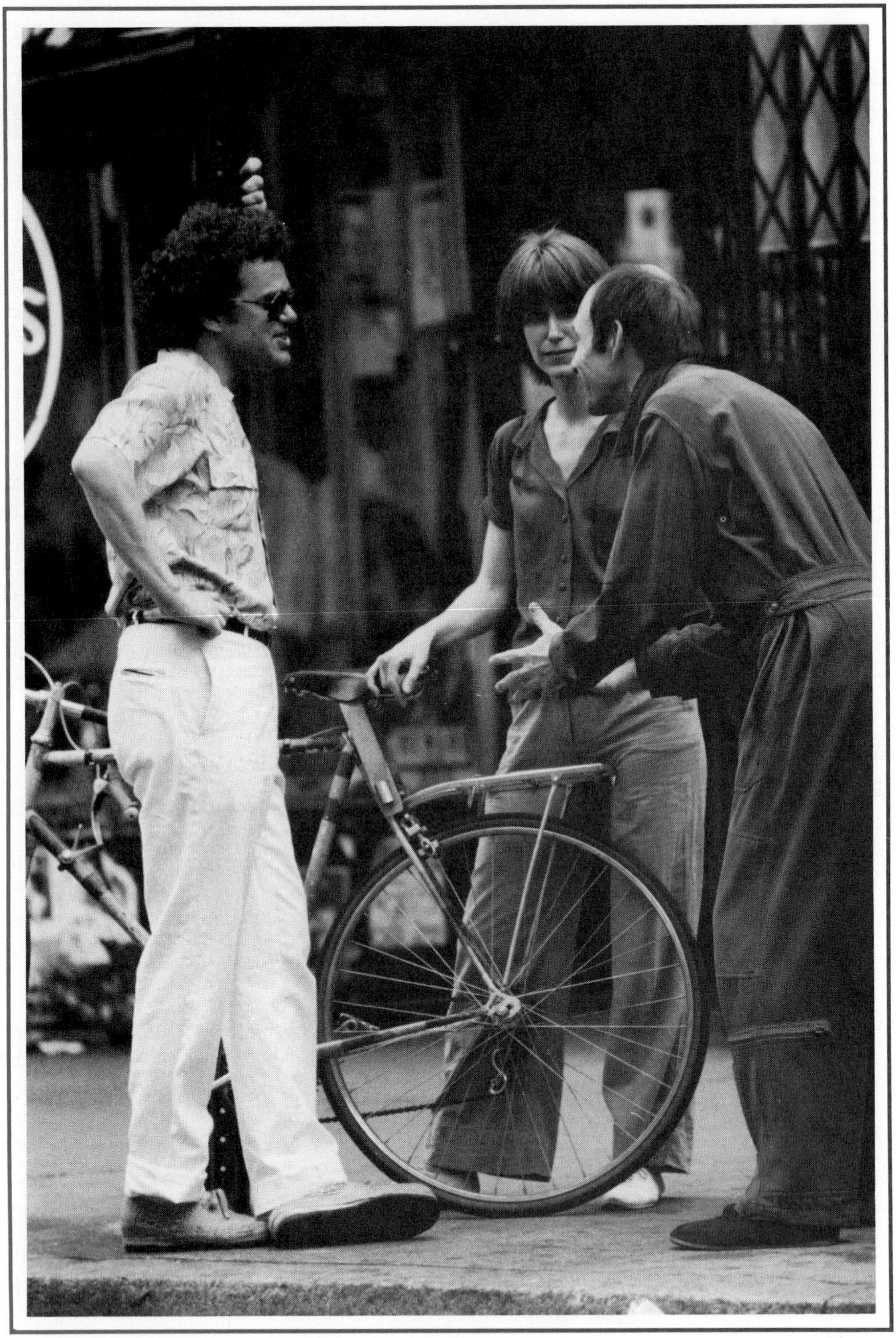

To Know the Dark[1]

To go in the dark with a light is to know the light.
To know the dark, go dark. Go without sight,
and find that the dark, too, blooms and sings,
and is traveled by dark feet and dark wings.

—*Wendell Berry*

Exact rhyme (also called *full*, or *perfect, rhyme)* means the repetition of almost identical sounds. Sometimes, only the first letter in the words differs, as in Wendell Berry's rhyming words *light/sight* and *sings/wings.* When words sound similar but not almost identical, the effect is called *near rhyme.* (This is also known as *half,* or *slant, rhyme.)* In near rhyme, words may share repeating vowel sounds (such as *m**oo**n/bl**oo**m, J**u**ne)* or repeating consonant sounds (*so**ng**/cla**ng**/ri**ng***). These different types of near rhyme have terms of their own.

Another kind of sound effect in poetry is the *repetition* of exact words. How many times does the poet repeat the word *dark* in "To Know the Dark"? What other words are repeated exactly?

Assonance is the repetition of vowel sounds to create a rhyme: *show/stone, us/sun, field/knees. Consonance* is the repetition of consonant sounds to create a rhyme: *tongue/sang, book/thick, waste/mast.*

Another musical effect poets use is called *alliteration.* Words alliterate when they *begin* with the same sound. Alliteration can be used to emphasize the meaning of the words, as in the following stanza from "The Waking" by Theodore Roethke:[2]

I **w**ake to **s**leep, and take my **w**aking **s**low.
I **f**eel my **f**ate in what I cannot **f**ear.
I learn by **g**oing where I have to **g**o.

—*Theodore Roethke* [boldface added]

The following poem by Lucille Clifton uses alliteration as its primary musical effect. Identify each pair of alliterating words as you read the poem and be prepared to discuss how the use of alliteration helps the meaning of the poem.

---

[1] "To Know the Dark" from *Farming: A Hand Book* by Wendell Berry. Copyright © 1970 by Wendell Berry. Reprinted by permission of Harcourt Brace Jovanovich, Inc.

[2] From "The Waking" copyright 1953 by Theodore Roethke from the book *The Collected Poems of Theodore Roethke* by Theodore Roethke. Reprinted by permission of Doubleday & Company, Inc. and Faber and Faber Ltd.

let there be new flowering[1]

let there be new flowering
in the fields let the fields
turn mellow for the men
let the men keep tender
through the time let the time
be wrested from the war
let the war be won
let love be
at the end

—*Lucille Clifton*

Writing Practice 6

Write a poem of at least four lines that uses the musical effects of rhyming words and alliteration. You may use exact rhyme, assonance and consonance, or a mixture of these. Do not use the same rhyming word in each of the four lines, however. Either rhyme the first two lines, and the third and fourth lines, or rhyme the first and third lines, and the second and last lines.

Preparing to Write

Many poems are based on a strong memory of a person, a place, or an experience. Try to recall such a memory that you feel deeply about and use that memory to begin your poem. Do not begin by simply thinking of pairs of rhyming words, however. Rhyme and other musical effects are there to help the sense and the strength or beauty of the poem; the rhyme alone is not the poem.

When you have thought of a memory, begin by writing down words you associate with it. Use words that bring back the sights, sounds, tastes, and smells of the experience. For example, suppose that you remember being with your grandfather in his house when you were a child. You might write down some of the following words.

> leather-bound books, eyeglasses, old mirrors, unshaven, large hands, white hair, smell of dried flowers, fruit in a bowl by his chair

Next try to remember what is most important about your memory. What is the first sight that comes into your mind as you remember? Do you see things or persons or actions? Remember the feelings you had about your grandfather then. Perhaps this memory is special to you because it is one of the last memories you have of your grandfather. As you think, write down the words as they come to you.

Perhaps you recall your grandfather standing by a window, staring thoughtfully at the winter scene. You remember this clearly because it was the winter your grandfather died, and you write the following words.

---

[1] "let there be new flowering" from *An Ordinary Woman* by Lucille Clifton. Copyright © 1974 by Lucille Clifton. Reprinted by permission of Random House, Inc.

My grandfather stares through the window
In the winter of his last year.

The words *window* and *winter* alliterate. Now you need to think of a rhyming word for *window.* Look back at your word list to see if there is something you can use. Perhaps you were very little then and remember looking up at your grandfather's figure against the window, so you might write the following line.

I am seven, I play in his shadow.

Now that you have a rhyming word for *window,* you next need a final line for the poem. This last line has special importance, for you want it to tell the most significant thing about your memory. Perhaps you remember that the sunlight was shining on your grandfather's white hair, making it appear like a halo around his head:

Sunlight halos his white hair.

Now you have a rhyming word to go with *year* and a complete poem that tells readers about the strong feeling you had for your grandfather:

My grandfather stares through the window
In the winter of his last year.
I am seven, I play in his shadow.
Sunlight halos his white hair.

When you have finished your poem, think of a title for it.

Meter in Poetry

Meter means "rhythmic pattern of sound."

The meter of a poem is like the rhythm of a piece of music. You can determine the meter of a poem by listening to the pattern of stressed and unstressed syllables. *Stressed* means "accented," or "spoken more loudly." In most words over one syllable, you can easily hear which syllable is stressed, or accented:

POetry oHIo caNOE

When you say these words aloud, you pronounce the syllable in capital letters louder than the other syllables. Another way of writing stress marks is to use an accent (′).

The speech that people use in their everyday lives is rhythmic. For example, if you say, "I just got home from school," you are using a rhythmic speech pattern:

I jú́st got hóme from schóol.

The difference between your everyday speech rhythms and the rhythms of poetry is consistency. In your usual speech you do not intentionally speak in regular rhythms, but when poets choose to write using regular meter, each line of the poem follows that meter with only minor variations. As with rhyme, poets try to choose a meter that helps enhance the meaning of the poem.

In the following poem by Naomi Replansky, the rhythm is that of a child's skipping rope song. In this meter there are four stresses to each line. (The first two stanzas are marked.) Read the poem aloud and listen to the stresses in each line until you hear four.

An Inheritance[1]

Fíve dollars, fóur dollars, thrée dollars, twó,
Óne, and nóne, and whát do we dó?

Thís is the wórry that néver got sáid,
But rán so óften in my móther's héad

And showed so plain in my father's frown
That to us kids it drifted down.

It drifted down like soot, like snow,
In the dream-tossed Bronx, in the long ago.

I shook it off with a shake of my head,
I bounced my ball, I ate warm bread,

I skated down the steepest hill.
But I must have listened, against my will:

When the wind blows wrong, I can hear it today.
Then my mother's worry stops all play

And, as if in its rightful place,
My father's frown divides my face.

—*Naomi Replansky* [stress marks added]

This regular, singsong meter is appropriate to the poem. Naomi Replansky is writing about a childhood experience of realizing how much her parents were worried about money. Even though this is a serious subject, the poet is thinking about how this worry was passed on to her from childhood, so the childhood skipping rope rhythms fit the subject of the poem.

Regular meter can produce many different effects, depending on the kind of rhythm used in the poem. In the following poem by Robert Frost, the mood is very different from "An Inheritance." Read the poem aloud and listen for five stresses in each line. (The first stanza is marked for you.) Also, listen for the mood of the poem. What feeling is the poet telling you about?

---

[1]"An Inheritance" by Naomi Replansky. First printed in *A Geography of Poets*, Edward Field, Bantam, 1979. Reprinted by permission of Naomi Replansky.

Acquainted with the Night[1]

I have been one acquainted with the night.
I have walked out in rain—and back in rain.
I have outwalked the further city light.

I have looked down the saddest city lane.
I have passed by the watchman on his beat
And dropped my eyes, unwilling to explain.

I have stood still and stopped the sound of feet
When far away an interrupted cry
Came over houses from another street,

But not to call me back or say good-bye;
And further still at an unearthly height,
One luminary clock against the sky

Proclaimed the time was neither wrong nor right
I have been one acquainted with the night.

—*Robert Frost* [stress marks added]

The meter in this poem is regular, but it does not produce a singsong effect. Rather it is a steady rhythm, like the rhythm of someone walking. The speaker in this poem is telling you what it means to be "one acquainted with the night." It is a lonely experience, and the meter of the poem helps you feel it, through a steady, walking rhythm. What lines in the poem most help you understand the experience?

Writing Practice 7

Write a short poem using a regular meter in each line. It will probably be helpful to reread Naomi Replansky's poem on page 184, which uses four stresses to the line, and Robert Frost's poem, which uses five stresses to the line. The following ideas can be used as suggestions for your poem.

1. In "An Inheritance" Naomi Replansky writes about inheriting her parents' worry and her father's frown that went with the worry. Write a poem about a quality (not an object or anything material) that you have inherited from your parents or grandparents. For example, think of some way in which you are like one of your parents or grandparents. Are you independent, shy, stubborn, curious, or carefree? Like Naomi Replansky

---

[1]"Acquainted with the Night" from *The Poetry of Robert Frost* edited by Edward Connery Lathem.

you may want to begin your poem by saying how this quality was passed down to you and how you feel about it.

2. "Acquainted with the Night" tells about someone who feels isolated, apart from others. Robert Frost associates this feeling with walking by himself at night. Write a poem about feeling isolated or alone. Before you begin, think about what you do when you feel alone. Do you go to a special place? Do you go out walking? What do you notice around you when you are feeling alone? Is the aloneness a sad feeling, a frightening feeling, or a satisfying feeling? In your poem tell the reader your feelings and observations.

Free Verse, or Nonformal Poetry

Over the last century poets writing in English have been exploring ways of making poems without using all the formal elements of rhyme and regular meter and stanzas. This experimentation has spread so that most poets today are writing what is called *free verse*, or *nonformal poetry.*

Poets today, like poets of all centuries and languages, are fascinated by the possibilities of words: how words sound and mean and fit and flow together. Rather than using words according to formal patterns, however, many contemporary poets are writing poems that try to convey insights and experiences in new ways.

One way poets create new effects is by using everyday language and speech rhythms in their poems. Listen to the ordinary speech rhythms in the following poem by Robert Hayden.

Those Winter Sundays[1]

Sundays too my father got up early
and put his clothes on in the blueblack cold,
then with cracked hands that ached
from labor in the weekday weather made
banked fires blaze. No one ever thanked him.

I'd wake and hear the cold splintering, breaking.
When the rooms were warm, he'd call,
and slowly I would rise and dress,
fearing the chronic angers of that house,

Chronic means "constant."

[1]"Those Winter Sundays" from *Angle of Ascent: New and Selected Poems*, by Robert Hayden.

Speaking indifferently to him,
who had driven out the cold
and polished my good shoes as well.
What did I know, what did I know
of love's austere and lonely offices?

—*Robert Hayden*

Offices here means "acts performed for someone."

Read the poem aloud or listen to someone else read it aloud. You will hear that this poem has its own sense of music and rhythm, even though it does not use formal rhyme or meter. For example, the first line in the poem sounds like someone talking; it has an everyday speech rhythm. What other lines in the poem also sound like ordinary speech?

Mixed in with the casual speech rhythms are lines that give the poem a musical effect. To create this effect the poet uses assonance, consonance and alliteration, as in the following lines from "Those Winter Sundays."

. . . cracked hands that ached	Assonance:	*cracked/hands*
from labor in the weekday weather made	Consonance:	*cracked/ached*
banked fires blaze.	Assonance:	*ached/labor/made*
	Alliteration:	*weekday/weather*

What other examples of assonance, consonance, and alliteration do you find in the preceding poem?

Another important way that Robert Hayden's poem presents its experience is through imagery. An *image* is a vivid sensory detail, a description that helps you see, hear, feel, taste, or smell. The images that the poet Robert Hayden uses make the picture of his father come alive. For example, the poet begins by telling you that his father got up early, in the "blueblack cold." The word *blueblack* helps you to imagine the scene: cold enough to turn a person's fingers blue, so dark and early that it was still black outside. What other images in the poem help you picture the scene and the situation?

Writing Practice 8

Write a nonformal poem (one that does not use regular rhyme or rhythm), paying special attention to sensory details to help your subject come alive for the reader. Write at least five lines. Since the poem in the preceding section dealt with an experience involving another person, you may want to base your own poem on a shared experience, perhaps with a family member or a friend. The following list of suggestions may be of help.

1. Watching your father or mother make breakfast
2. Helping someone train for a sport

3. Taking care of a younger sister or brother
4. Walking to school with a friend
5. Having an argument with a friend or family member
6. Going out on Saturday night
7. Waiting for your mother or father to get home when you were little
8. Trying to get your older sister or brother to pay attention to you
9. Talking on the telephone and losing track of time
10. Eating with family or friends at a holiday time
11. Feeling sick and having someone take care of you
12. Working hard with a family member on a difficult job
13. Waking up in the middle of the night
14. Remembering something pleasant that happened long ago
15. Celebrating a birthday

Line Breaks in Nonformal Poetry

When poets do not count out stresses for each line or end each line with a rhyming word, how do they decide where to break off a line of poetry? The answer is that each poet has his or her own rules about line breaks. The length of the line depends on the subject of the poem and how the poet is writing about it. For example, if you were writing a poem about sights you glimpsed from a moving car, you might write in very short lines:

> Proud mother duck
> parades with ducklings attached.
> Two women patiently
> flick reed poles
> into brown water—waiting.
> Lean, long-legged,
> the running man
> wearing earphones
> tunes out the world.

In general, short lines give poems a compressed, staccato effect, like rapid phrases of music. What other subjects can you think of that would be appropriate for short lines of poetry?

Long lines of poetry tend to give a flowing, melodic effect. The following section of a poem by Diane Wakoski uses long lines to create the effect of someone so enthusiastic about the subject that she goes on and on, flooding the reader with images.

An *ode* is a poem of praise.

[from] **Ode to a Lebanese Crock of Olives**[1]

for Walter's Aunt Libby's diligence
in making olives

As some women love jewels
and drape themselves with ropes of pearls, stud their ears
with diamonds, band themselves with heavy gold,
have emeralds on their fingers or
opals on white bosoms,
I live with the still life
of grapes whose skins frost over with the sugar forming
 inside,
hard apples, and delicate pears;
cheeses,
from the sharp fontina, to icy bleu,
the aromatic chevres, boursault, boursin, a litany of
thick bread, dark wines,
pasta with garlic,
soups full of potato and onion;
and butter and cream,
like the skins of beautiful women, are on my sideboard.

—*Diane Wakoski*

The preceding poem uses long lines to convey an overflow of praise for its subject. What other subjects would fit into long lines of poetry?

The following poem by Carl Rákosi uses a different effect. Instead of varying the length of the lines, the poet separates some words from the others.

As you read this poem aloud, pause before you read the words that have been set off.

Assiduous means "diligent."

[from] **The Experiment with a Rat**[2]

Every time I nudge that spring
                    a bell rings
and a man walks out of a cage
assiduous and sharp like one of us
and brings me cheese.
            How did he fall
                        into my power?

—*Carl Rákosi*

---

[1]From "Ode to a Lebanese Crock of Olives" in *Waiting for the King of Spain* by Diane Wakoski, Black Sparrow Press, 1976. Reprinted by permission of the author.

[2]"The Experiment with a Rat" by Carl Rákosi from *ERE-Voice*, New Directions, 1971. Reprinted by permission of Carl Rákosi.

Setting words apart focuses attention on them, making them stand out on the page. It also helps create a sense of rhythm. For example, suppose the last thought of the preceding poem had been written in the following manner.

How did he fall into my power?

You would read the preceding line all together, in one breath. However, the question is written on two lines in the original poem.

How did he fall
                into my power?

You read the question with a brief pause after the word *fall*. Line breaks are one important way the poet has of showing how a poem should be read.

Writing Practice 9

Write a nonformal poem, paying close attention to line length and line breaks. Use one of the following suggestions to get started or write the poem on a subject of your choice. As you write, remember to use specific sense details to help the reader experience your poem.

1. Think of a subject appropriate to short lines: an action such as a race, an event such as an eclipse, or an experience such as watching lightning. Write a poem on the subject, using short lines.
2. Think of a subject appropriate to long lines: an action such as waves hitting a beach, an event such as a snowfall, or an experience such as drifting off to sleep or dreaming. Write a poem on the subject, using long lines to convey your meaning.
3. You may decide to write a poem that has both long lines and short lines. An action that involves a series of continuous motions and stops, such as riding a bicycle, swimming, mowing a lawn, or washing a car, might be appropriate to a mixture of long and short lines. Try writing your poem first, and then read the poem aloud as you look for the best places to break the lines. You may try several different versions until you find the one that best conveys your meaning.

Figurative Language

An important way poems communicate is through figurative language.

The two most widely used types of figurative language are *simile* and *metaphor*.

Simile and metaphor are special types of comparisons. When people make comparisons in everyday life, they usually compare things that are similar: "This house looks just like the one I grew up in." When poets use simile and metaphor, they make comparisons between things that are not apparently similar but that have hidden similarities. For example, find the comparisons in the following lines from the poem "My Teeth."

[from] **My Teeth**[1]

The up-front ones are marvelous,
tiny dancers braving the wind,
shapely and disciplined.

—Ed Ochester

While there is no apparent similarity between teeth and dancers, the poet makes you think of ways in which they are alike. He calls them both "shapely and disciplined." In what other ways are your teeth like dancers?

Similes

A *simile* is a comparison stated with *like, as,* or *than* and sometimes with verbs such as *seems* or *appears.*

The comparison must be between two different types of items. For example, the comparison "Central High seems just like my old school" is not a simile for the reason that two *similar* types are being compared.

The following simile is from the poem "Tulips" by Sylvia Plath, a poem about being in the hospital.[2]

They have propped my head between the pillow and the sheet-cuff
Like an eye between two white lids that will not shut.

—Sylvia Plath

The poet uses a simile to make two connections. The pillow and sheet-cuff seem to her like eyelids, and her head seems like the eye between the eyelids.

As you read the final two stanzas from "Tulips," identify as many similes as you can. The poet is speaking about the bright red tulips in her hospital room.

Before they came the air was calm enough,
Coming and going, breath by breath, without any fuss.
Then the tulips filled it up like a loud noise.
Now the air snags and eddies round them the way a river
Snags and eddies round a sunken rust-red engine.
They concentrate my attention, that was happy
Playing and resting without committing itself.

---

[1]From "My Teeth" in *Dancing on the Edges of Knives* by Ed Ochester. Copyright 1973 by Ed Ochester. Reprinted by permission of the author and the University of Missouri Press.

[2]From "Tulips" in *Ariel* by Sylvia Plath. Copyright © 1962 by Ted Hughes. Published in Great Britain by Faber & Faber Limited, London. Reprinted by permission of Harper & Row, Publishers, Inc. and Olwyn Hughes, Literary Agent.

The walls, also, seem to be warming themselves.
The tulips should be behind bars like dangerous animals;
They are opening like the mouth of some great African cat,
And I am aware of my heart: it opens and closes
Its bowl of red blooms out of sheer love of me.
The water I taste is warm and salt, like the sea,
And comes from a country far away as health.

—*Sylvia Plath*

The kind of simile a poet chooses depends on the whole poem. For example, in "Tulips" Sylvia Plath writes that the tulips fill up the air in her room "like a loud noise." Since she is in a hospital, where everything should be quiet, the effect of a loud noise is shocking. The simile says that the tulips are not beautiful to her, but are something shocking.

Writing Practice 10

Write a short poem in which you use similes to make a comparison between two different types of items. You might like to write a poem that is a list of similes about one subject. For example, a humorous poem could begin: "You are as beautiful as . . ." and then continue with a list of similes. Things can be beautiful in different ways, so you might write:

You are as beautiful as a new pair
    of patent leather boots,
as beautiful as a field of wet hay,
as beautiful as French toast,
as beautiful as algebra . . .

If you prefer, you may write about another quality instead of beauty:

You're as funny as . . .
The evening is as sad as . . .
The icicle is as delicate as . . .

You may, instead, write about any other quality that interests you. Decide before you begin writing if you want a humorous effect, a beautiful effect, a melancholy effect, or some other effect.

Metaphors

Like a simile a *metaphor* makes a connection between two different types of items. Unlike a simile a metaphor does not use any linking words, such as *like*, *as*, *seems*, or *appears*.

A metaphor tells you, in effect, that two unlike items are the same in some special way. Poets use metaphor to help their readers discover connections and correspondences between things.

In the following poem Robert Bly uses metaphor to express two important connections that he notices. Try to identify them as you read.

Taking the Hands[1]

Taking the hands of someone you love,
You see they are delicate cages . . .
Tiny birds are singing
In the secluded prairies
And in the deep valleys of the hand.

—*Robert Bly*

The poet compares the hands "of someone you love" with "delicate cages," such as those that hold singing birds. If this were a simile, it would read, "You see they are *like* delicate cages." Since it is a metaphor, there is no connecting word. In this way metaphors are more concise than similes and sometimes have a more intense effect on the reader.

Robert Bly also compares the hand to a landscape of prairies and deep valleys. The first metaphor in the poem is stated directly: "You see they are delicate cages." The second metaphor is called an *implied metaphor* because the connection between the two items is implied rather than stated directly. The phrase "the deep valleys of the hand" tells you that the poet is likening the hand to a landscape with deep valleys.

Metaphor shows the reader how to see the world in a new way by making connections that are unusual and interesting. Another reason poets use metaphor is to express their thoughts in compressed language. For example, in the following lines from "London 1802" by William Wordsworth, the poet uses compressed language to express abstract ideas.

A *fen* is a low, marshy area covered with water.

Milton! thou shouldst be living at this hour:
England hath need of thee: she is a fen
Of stagnant waters: altar, sword, and pen,
Fireside, the heroic wealth of hall and bower,
Have forfeited their ancient English dower
Of inward happiness. . . .

What does the poet refer to with the words "altar, sword, and pen,/ Fireside, the heroic wealth of hall and bower, . . ."? Each refers to a whole segment of the English population. Can you name each of the groups identified in this compressed language? What other metaphor do you find in these lines?

Many poems commonly use a combination of simile and metaphor to convey their ideas, feelings, and impressions. The following poem by J. P. White describes a river flooding a town. As you read, notice how the poet uses figurative language to help share the experience of the flood.

---

[1]"Taking the Hands" from *Silence in the Snowy Fields* by Robert Bly, Wesleyan University Press, 1962.

Flood[1]

Our town slept as the river rose.

The black belly of sky
under which it dreamed
was swollen with tons of rain.

All night it rained,
a troop of men driven back to the roof's edge.
Lightning tangled over the water.

Wind snapped off the arms of our one oak.
Dogs shrunk into doorways weeping with cold.
I remember watching my sisters crouch beneath a candle
inside the crammed darkness of our swimming house.

Fed by such a fierce thickening of rain,
our red sleek river jammed in the night,
spilling its banks, lashing every house
with its matted tail of mud & water.

There are those that will tell you
it sounded like the rumbling echo
of a train lost in a tunnel.

But I will ask you to imagine
a thin black horse
standing in a field
grinding its oats.

—*J. P White*

The first example of figurative language in the preceding poem is the metaphor, "black belly of sky." The poet also uses an implied metaphor in the lines, "lashing every house/with its matted tail of mud & water," which compare the river to an animal lashing its tail. Where in the poem do you learn what animal it is? Identify the simile and the last metaphor of the poem.

The images in "Flood" are all realistic. The poem describes a natural disaster, using words that help the reader see, hear, and feel the experience. Many poets use figurative language for an effect that is the opposite of realistic. They want the reader to react to a thought or an image that is in some way strange or mysterious. The following poem by Bill Knott uses first a metaphor and then a simile to express the poet's feelings about the nature of poetry.

---

[1]"Flood" from *In Pursuit of Wings* by J. P. White. Reprinted by permission of Panache Books.

Poem to Poetry[1]

for Jennifer Kidney

Poetry,
you are an electric,
a magic, field—like the space
between a sleepwalker's outheld arms . . .

—*Bill Knott*

How are the images in the preceding poem unlike the images from "Flood"? What does "Poem to Poetry" tell you about Bill Knott's idea of poetry?

When a poet uses metaphor to compare an object, an animal, or a concept to a human being, that metaphor is called *personification.* Personification gives human qualities, thoughts, or actions to nonhuman subjects.

Some poets personify objects by letting them speak as if they were human, as in the following lines from the poem "Mirror" by Sylvia Plath.[2]

I am silver and exact. I have no preconceptions.
Whatever I see I swallow immediately
Just as it is, unmisted by love or dislike.

—*Sylvia Plath*

In the preceding lines the mirror speaks and describes itself with human qualities.

Poets also use personification as an extended metaphor, carrying the comparison throughout the poem. The following poem by Emily Dickinson continues the comparison of a mountain with a human through both stanzas.

The Mountain

Omnifold means "all-encompassing."

The mountain sat upon the plain
In his eternal chair,
His observation omnifold,
His inquest everywhere.

The seasons prayed around his knees,
Like children round a sire:
Grandfather of the days is he,
Of dawn the ancestor.

—*Emily Dickinson*

---

[1] "Poem to Poetry" from *The Naomi Poems* by Bill Knott. Copyright © 1968 by Bill Knott. Reprinted by permission of Follett Publishing Company.

[2] From "Mirror" in *Crossing the Water* by Sylvia Plath. Copyright © 1963 by Ted Hughes. Originally appeared in *The New Yorker.* Published in Great Britain by Faber & Faber Limited, London. Reprinted by permission of Harper & Row, Publishers, Inc. and Olwyn Hughes, Literary Agent.

In showing the mountain as a person, Emily Dickinson describes it as sitting in an "eternal chair," observing its surroundings. What other phrases indicate personification in the poem? How are the seasons personified?

Writing Practice 11

Write a poem based on a metaphor (begin or end your poem with the metaphor), using additional images and similes if you wish. Some of the following suggestions may be helpful in writing your poem.

1. Reread the Robert Bly poem on page 193 for an example of a simple love poem. You might base your own poem on hands as well, or on the eyes of someone you love, or the voice of someone you love. Think of what the person's eyes, voice, or hands remind you of most. Perhaps the hands themselves remind you of birds; perhaps they remind you of a sound, like a whisper. Use the comparison you think of as the metaphor for your poem.
2. Reread the poem "Flood" on page 194. Perhaps you also have been through an exciting or frightening experience. Using your experience as the main idea of your poem, describe your experience using similes or metaphors. Include as many vivid sense images as you can.
3. Reread the poem "Poem to Poetry" on page 195. This poem has a mysterious feel to it. You can write your own mysterious "Poem to Poetry" or a mysterious poem to anything else: "Poem to Outer Space," "Poem to the Law of Gravity," "Poem to Spaghetti," or "Poem to Sleep." Use the form of Bill Knott's poem as an example of how to structure your own poem. For example, you can begin as he does, using your own subject: "Dunk shots/you are. . . ," or "Car engines/you are. . . ," or "Geometry/ you are. . ." for whatever subject you choose. Then continue the poem with a metaphor and a simile as your descriptions.
4. Reread the poem "The Mountain" on page 195. To create a poem using personification, think of an animal or object (such as a crocodile, a butterfly, a window or a streetlight, the rain or the night). Then imagine how it might be like a human being. Is it a young or an old person? Try to think of it in a human action of some kind, speaking or thinking, dreaming or feeling a strong emotion. Think of how it would be clothed or how it would act. Use some of your comparisons as the basis of your poem.

PART

2 Resources for Writing

9 The Library

Library Resources

Library resources can be divided into two main categories: materials and people. Materials include the traditional hardcover library books, magazines, newspapers, and more recently, such acquisitions as paperbacks, records, films and filmstrips, and special equipment called *microfilm* and *microfiche readers* for reading materials that have been reduced and stored on film.

The most important library resources, however, are the librarians, for it is they who are responsible for selecting materials and for organizing them so that they can be efficiently and easily used. In this chapter you will learn the methods used by most librarians to organize materials. As you work in your school's library, however, you may find that you have special needs or problems. If so, a professionally trained librarian or library aides are there to help you.

The Arrangement of Books

The most important division of library books is between fiction and nonfiction.

Usually housed in separate areas of the library, books of fiction and nonfiction are also arranged on the shelves in different ways.

Events and people in *fiction* are from the writer's imagination; *nonfiction* is about real-life people and events.

1. *Fiction*

Books of fiction are arranged alphabetically, first by the last name of the author, and then by his or her first name. Books by the same author are arranged alphabetically by the first major word in the title. (The pronoun *I* is considered a major word, but the articles *a*, *and*, and *the* are not.) For example, Anne Tyler's books *Morgan's Passing*, *The Tin Can Tree*, *If Morning*

Ever Comes, and *A Slipping Down Life* are arranged on the shelves in the following order: *If Morning Ever Comes*, *Morgan's Passing*, *A Slipping Down Life*, and *The Tin Can Tree*. In some libraries science fiction and mysteries are separated from the rest of the fiction.

Library Exercise 1

On a sheet of paper numbered 1–10, arrange the following works of fiction in the order they are found on library shelves.

1. *Song of Solomon* by Toni Morrison
2. *Sula* by Toni Morrison
3. *Innocent Blood* by P. D. James
4. *Tinker, Tailor, Soldier, Spy* by John Le Carré
5. *The Spy Who Came In from the Cold* by John Le Carré
6. *Smiley's People* by John Le Carré
7. *The Dead Zone* by Stephen King
8. *A State of Siege* by Janet Frame
9. *The Edge of the Alphabet* by Janet Frame
10. *Owls Do Cry* by Janet Frame

2. *Nonfiction*

In most school libraries books of nonfiction are arranged according to a system developed by Melvil Dewey, an American librarian. Under this system all nonfiction is classified under ten general subject areas and assigned a range of numbers as follows:

000–099 General Works	Includes encyclopedias, periodicals, book lists, and other reference books.
100–199 Philosophy	Includes the fields of psychology, conduct, and personality.
200–299 Religion	Includes the Bible and other religious texts; theology books and mythology.
300–399 Social Sciences	Includes economics, education, etiquette, fairy tales, folklore, legends, government, and law.
400–499 Language	Includes grammars and dictionaries of different languages, including English.
500–599 Science	Includes animals, astronomy, biology, botany, chemistry, geology, general science, mathematics, anthropology, and physics.
600–699 Technology	Includes agriculture, aviation, business, engineering, health, home economics, manual training, and television.
700–799 The Arts	Includes movies, painting, sculpture, photography, recreation, and sports.
800–899 Literature	Includes poetry, drama, essays, criticism, and history of literature.
900–999 History	Includes geography, travel, history, and collective biography.

The Dewey Decimal Number

Every nonfiction book is assigned a number, called its *Dewey decimal number,* that appears on the spine of the book.

For example, *Under the Sign of Saturn,* a book about art by Susan Sontag, falls into the *700–799* classification range for "The Arts" and the *700* range for books with general information about art. Depending on the size of the library, a book may have several decimals in its classification number, so that *Under the Sign of Saturn* might bear the number *700.9* or *700.904,* but it will always have the *700* number.

In additional to its Dewey decimal number, a nonfiction book is also identified with the first or first two letters of the author's last name and a special number (which together are called the *author number*) and the first letter of the first major word in the book's title. These letters and numbers make up the book's *call number,* a unique number assigned to no other book in the library. The following illustration of the call number for Susan Sontag's *Under the Sign of Saturn* shows how the call number appears on the book's spine.

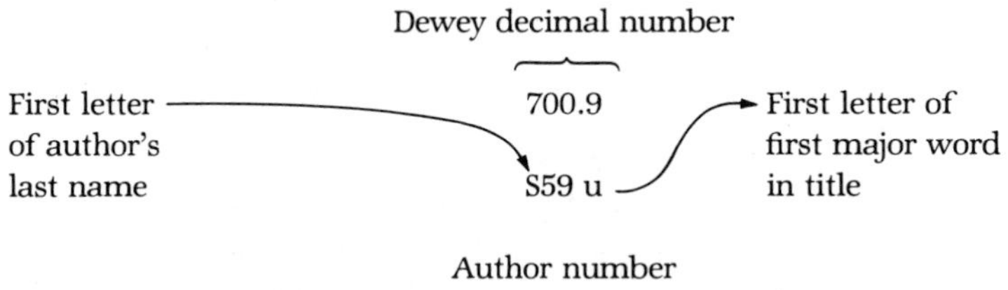

Shelves in the nonfiction area are usually labeled with Dewey decimal numbers: *700–723.81,* for example. To find a particular book locate the shelves with the appropriate range of books. For Susan Sontag's book you would begin your search with the *700* books. Move along the shelf until you find books numbered *700.9.* If you find books numbered *701,* you know you have gone too far. The next step is to locate the *700.9* books with the letter *S* beneath the Dewey decimal number. If there are several books with the letter *S* for this particular Dewey decimal number, look next for the number and then for the final letter that indicates the first major word in the title of that book.

Library Exercise 2

On a sheet of paper numbered 1–10, write the subject area and the range of numbers assigned by the Dewey decimal system to each of the following nonfiction books.

Example

a. *The American Heritage Dictionary of the English Language*

a. Language 400–499

1. *The New Black Poetry*
2. *A History of Latin America*

3. *The Complete Book of Cat Care*
4. *Fielder's Choice: An Anthology of Baseball Fiction*
5. *The Murder Book: An Illustrated History of the Detective Story*
6. *The Great Potato Cookbook*
7. *U.S. Energy Policy*
8. *Jim Fixx's Second Book of Running*
9. *Photography*
10. *Italian Folklore*

Library Exercise 3

On a sheet of paper, list the following call numbers in the order they would be arranged on library shelves.

1. 802.14
B23k
2. 801.34
S24m
3. 800.17
C13p
4. 800.67
C42m
5. 800.13
A17z
6. 800.24
A19m
7. 804.11
B18k
8. 800.09
A15b
9. 801.343
S241
10. 801.23
T23m

Biography and Autobiography

A *biography* is an account of a person's life, written by another; an *autobiography* is a writer's own account of his or her life.

In most libraries *biographies* and *autobiographies* are shelved separately from other works of nonfiction and are labeled with either the letter *B* or the number *921* and beneath that the first letter of the subject's last name: $\genfrac{}{}{0pt}{}{B}{W}$ or $\genfrac{}{}{0pt}{}{921}{W}$ for a biography of Richard Wright, for example. *Collective biographies,* which contain the biographies of two or more people, are usually labeled with the number *921* and the first letter of the author's or editor's last name: $\genfrac{}{}{0pt}{}{921}{S}$

Using the Card Catalogue

The *card catalogue* is a large cabinet with a series of drawers arranged alphabetically according to labels on the drawers: for example *A–Boc, Bod–Cau, Ma–Me,* and so on. Inside, most nonfiction books have at least three cards: *author, title,* and *subject. Author cards,* which are filed alphabetically by the author's or editor's last name, are useful when you want to find books by a particular writer. If you know the title of the work, looking for the *title card*, which is filed alphabetically by the first major word in the title, is the most direct approach. Especially useful for researchers are the *subject cards*. These cards are filed alphabetically by general subject headings, and there is at least one subject card for every nonfiction book in the library. A book on dieting, for example, might appear on subject cards headed *Nutrition*, *Dieting*, and *Weight Reduction*.

By using the card catalogue, you can quickly determine whether or not your library has the information you need on a given subject. The author, title, and subject cards all give basically the same information about a book: the call number, author, title, publisher and place of publication, and date of copyright. In addition, the cards may also contain information about illustrations and occasionally a summary of the book's contents.

Two other important cards in the card catalogue are the *cross-reference cards* "See" and "See also." The "See" card is used to refer users to a different heading. For example, a library might file all books on dieting under the heading "Weight control," but library users are likely to check under "Dieting" first, so the "See" card refers them to the proper heading. The "See also" card is an indication that more information about a subject can be found under a different heading.

Library Exercise 4

For this assignment select one of the subjects in the following list or use one of your choice. Looking under at least two different headings in your school's card catalogue, determine whether or not your library has any books on the subject. If there are books listed in the card catalogue, write down authors, titles, and call numbers for at least two of them.

SUBJECTS	HEADINGS
Extinction of whales	Whales, Wildlife preservation, Mammals
The Aztec culture	Aztecs, South American Indians
The uses of holography	Holography, Lasers
Witchcraft in Salem	Witchcraft, Salem
The lost continent of Atlantis	Atlantis, Continents

Library Exercise 5

Using your school library's card catalogue, determine whether or not the library has books by any of the following authors. If you find author cards for any of the writers, copy down at least one title for each author and that particular book's call number.

1. Sylvia Porter
2. William Manchester
3. Ann Landers
4. Joyce Brothers
5. Jim Fixx
6. Pauline Kael
7. Leo Rosten
8. Susan Sontag
9. Will Durant
10. Carl Sagan

The Library of Congress System

The *Library of Congress system*, a newer method for classifying books, divides knowledge into categories designated by letters of the alphabet:

A General Works
B Philosophy
C History
D General History
E–F History—American
G Geography, Anthropology, Recreation
H Social Sciences
J Political Science
K Law
L Education
M Music
N Fine Arts
P Language and Literature
Q Science
R Medicine
S Agriculture
T Technology
U Military Science
V Naval Science
Z Library Science

Categories are further subdivided with a system of letters and numbers, as they are in the Dewey decimal system. Unlike the older system, however, the Library of Congress classification system is used with both fiction and nonfiction. If your school library uses the Library of Congress system, ask a librarian or teacher for help in learning the divisions.

The Parts of a Book

Sometimes, locating a book is only the first step. If you want to know whether or not a particular book will be helpful to you in your research, you must also be able to evaluate the book to determine its usefulness. Knowing the parts of a book will help you to do this.

1. *The Frontispiece (frun′-tis-pēs′)*

The *frontispiece* is an illustration that faces or immediately precedes the title page. Not every book has one.

2. *The Title Page*

The *title page* contains the complete title of the book, the name of the author(s) or editor(s), the name of the publishing company, and the place of publication.

3. *The Copyright Page*

The *copyright page* is usually the other side of the title page. A *copyright* is a legal right granted to an author or a publisher to publish, sell, and distribute a work for the life of the author plus an additional fifty years. In addition, if the book is substantially updated or changed, the copyright can be renewed then. The date and holder of the copyright will be printed on the copyright page. If the copyright has been renewed, that information will also be printed there.

Information about copyright is important for two reasons. First it tells you that the work is legally owned by a person or company and that you have the right to use it only under certain restricted conditions. Second it tells you whether or not the information inside is current. For some subjects updated information is important; a book with a latest copyright of 1950 obviously would not be a source of current information.

4. *Preface, Foreword, and Introduction*

The *preface, foreword,* and *introduction* of a book, most often written by the author or by an expert in the field, usually contain general comments about the content, organization, and scope of the book. By skimming these sections, you can sometimes determine whether or not the material you need will be discussed in greater depth in the book.

5. *The Table of Contents*

In nonfiction books the *table of contents* usually shows the major divisions and subdivisions of the book. By scanning the contents, you can not only determine whether your subject is covered in that particular book but also the extent to which it is treated.

6. *The Glossary*

Usually appearing at the end of the book, *the glossary* is a minidictionary defining special terms used in the text.

7. *The Bibliography*

A *bibliography* is an alphabetical listing of sources the author or editor found helpful in preparing the book or of closely related sources. Usually found in the back of a book, the bibliography is sometimes divided into sections by subject headings. For example, the bibliography of Joseph P. Lash's book *Helen and Teacher*, a biography of Helen Keller and her teacher Anne Sullivan Macy, contains the following headings: *Books by Helen Keller, Books Relating to Helen Keller, Magazines and Other Materials Relating to Helen Keller.*

8. *The Index*

The *index* is an alphabetical listing of topics covered in the book, with page numbers. The index is more detailed than the table of contents, since the index generally covers every topic discussed in the book, regardless of the thoroughness of the coverage. To determine whether or not a book contains the information you need, look first for a general heading. If the heading is subdivided, continue looking until you find the appropriate subheading. For example, the following index entry is from Joseph Lash's *Helen and Teacher*. All the subheads in the entry are about Samuel Langhorne Clemens, better known as Mark Twain. Information about the friendship between Helen Keller (*HK*) and Clemens is on pages 193–194, 304–306, 357–362, 380–381, and on page 439.

> Clemens, Samuel Langhorne (Mark Twain): Bacon-Shakespeare controversy and, 360–62; on HK-ASM relationship, 289–90, 450; HK education fund and, 209–10; HK friendship with, 193–94, 304–6, 357–62, 380–81, 439; *Innocents Abroad*, 260; *Is Shakespeare Dead?*, 362; pessimism, 307; on plagiarism, 146–48, 290, 343

Library Exercise 6

Using this textbook as your source, answer the following questions.

1. Does this book have a frontispiece?
2. Who are the authors of this textbook?
3. What is the publishing company? The place of publication?
4. What is the date of copyright for this book?
5. On what page of the textbook will you find a poem by Dan Jaffe?
6. On what page does the table of contents begin?
7. How many chapters does this book contain?
8. What is the title of the chapter that discusses gathering information for writing?
9. According to the index, on what pages is *brainstorming* discussed?

Using the Readers' Guide to Periodical Literature

The *Readers' Guide to Periodical Literature*, often called the *Readers' Guide*, is an author and subject index to periodicals of general interest published in the United States.

Published twice a month except for February, July, and August when it is published once a month, the *Readers' Guide* consists of subject and author entries to periodicals arranged alphabetically. (Once a year the *Readers' Guide* is published as a hardcover volume covering the months of March–February.) A separate section in the back of the *Guide* lists book reviews, arranged alphabetically by the last name of the authors reviewed. The periodicals covered by the guide are indexed in its front, where you will also find an explanation of the abbreviations used in the *Guide.* Most libraries have the *Readers' Guide,* but they may not always have the magazines you need. Your librarian may have posted a list of the magazines and dates to be found in your library.

The sample column from the *Readers' Guide* on pages 207–208 of this textbook shows how to read the entries. Suppose you want to find some information about spaniels. Since the guide is arranged alphabetically, the logical place to look would be under the subject heading "Spaniels." You could also look under the subject "Dogs," but in general the more specifically you can limit your subject, the sooner you will find the information you need. Using the sample on page 208, you find under the heading "Spaniels" one entry: "Are Britts in Trouble?" This article about the Brittany spaniel by D. M. Duffy was published in the March 1980 issue of *Outdoor Life.* The illustrated article can be found on page 164 and following pages. You may have already consulted books and other reference materials and discovered that D. M. Duffy is an authority on spaniels. With this knowledge you could also look up the name Duffy, D. M. in the *Readers' Guide.*

Two headings you will see frequently in the *Readers' Guide* are "See" and "See also." The "See" entries tell you that the subject you want is listed a different way and that you should look under another heading. The "See also" heading tells you that you will find additional information about your subject under another heading.

Library Exercise 7

Using the sample *Readers' Guide* column reprinted on pages 207–208 of this textbook, find the answers to the following questions and write them on a sheet of paper.

1. What magazine contains a recent article about traveling in Spain?
2. Clarence Spangle is a businessman. What article was written about him?
3. Under what additional heading would you find information about tracking space vehicles?
4. Where would you find an article on shuttle engine testing in the space program?
5. Who wrote an article about the actress Sissy Spacek?
6. What article would give you information about the Spanish government?
7. Who wrote the article about Spain's naval history titled "Sailing by the Stars"?
8. How many "See also" references are there under the subject heading "Spain"?

9. What is the title of the one article listed about Japan's role in developing propulsion systems for space vehicles?
10. Under what heading would you look to find an article about Spanish artists?

SPACE vehicles—*Continued*

Propulsion systems

Ariane. il Space World Q-2-194:13-26 F '80
Ariane launcher in Kourou test. il Aviation W 112:65 Ja 28 '80
Comets in a storm: tight money for space [battle for funds over Solar Electric Propulsion System in Halley's comet/Tempel 2 flight] il Sci News 117:101-2 F 16 '80
Experimental solar array wing [Solar Electric Propulsion array wing] il Space World P-10-192:8-11 D '79
Japan pushes space launcher development. il Aviation W 112:51 Ja 28 '80
Lunar goal required huge booster [Apollo] D. Dooling. Space World Q-1-193:26-7 Ja '80
Monsters of Huntsville [test firing of Saturn rocket boosters at George C. Marshall Space Flight Center; reprint from June 1962 issue] P. O'Neil. Fortune 101:188 F 11 '80
Problem of propellant slumping delayed shuttle solid stacking. Aviation W 112:71 Ja 21 '80
Solar sailing. T. Morgan. il Astronomy 8:24-8 Ja '80

Specifications

U.S. launch vehicles: Int'l. launch vehicles [tables] Aviation W 112:108-9 Mr 3 '80

Testing

Shuttle engine test milestones nearing. C. Covault. il Aviation W 112:39-41 Mr 10 '80

Specifications

Leading U.S. & international spacecraft [tables] Aviation W 112:106-7 Mr 3 '80

Secondary subject heading — **Testing**

Key shuttle power-on tests approach. C. Covault. il Aviation W 112:39-41 Ap 7 '80

Tracking

"See also" reference — *See also* Artificial satellites—Tracking

SPACE warfare. See Space flight—Military use

Subject heading — **SPACEK, Sissy**

Kicking free of her ankle socks. A. Johnston. il pors Macleans 93:55-6 Mr 10 '80

SPACELAB missions (proposed) See Space stations—Spacelab missions (proposed)

"See" reference — **SPACEMEN.** See Astronauts

SPAIN

See also
Art and state—Spain
Astronomical observatories—Spain
Barcelona, Spain
Basque Provinces
Cultural property. Protection of—Spain
Freedom of the press—Spain
Santiago, Spain

Cultural relations

United States

"See" reference — *See* United States—Cultural relations—Spain

Description and travel

Travel/Spain. J. H. Silverman. Art News 79:56-7 Mr '80

"See also" reference
Title of article
Name and issue of magazine
Subject heading
Information about article
Volume and page numbers

Diplomatic and Consular Service

Guatemala

See also
Guatemalan seizure of Spanish embassy, 1980

History

Spanish American War, 1898

See United States—History—Spanish American War, 1898

History, Naval

Sailing by the stars [sixteenth and seventeenth century Spanish literature] J. M. Goicoechea. il Americas 32:3-8 Mr '80

Industries

See also

Airlines—Spain

Politics and government

Lost momentum. il Time 115:40 Mr 24 '80
Spain's struggling democracy. R. Alan. il World Press R 27:23-4 + Ja '80

SPANGLE, Clarence W.
New boss at Memorex. K. K. Wiegner. por Forbes 125:165 F 18 '80

SPANIARDS
See also
Basques

SPANIELS
Are britts in trouble? [Brittany spaniel] D. M. Duffy. il Outdoor Life 165:164 + Mr '80

SPANISH AMERICAN War. 1898. See United States—History—Spanish American War. 1898.

SPANISH Americans in the United States. See Latin Americans in the United States

SPANISH artists. See Artists. Spanish

SPANISH conquistadors in Peru. See Peru—History

Reference Books

Reference books, books containing specialized knowledge, are usually kept in special sections of the library and marked on the spine with *R*.

Most reference books cannot be checked out; instead, they are reserved for everyone's use. In large libraries a *reference librarian* is often available for users who need special help with reference materials.

The Dictionary

The reference book you probably use most often is the dictionary. The sample dictionary page on page 209 of this textbook is from *Webster's New World Dictionary*. The key that follows the sample page provides a review of the basic information contained in most dictionaries.

2 **nerv·ous** (nʉr′vəs) *adj.* [ME. *neruous* < L. *nervosus*] **1.** orig., strong; sinewy **2.** vigorous in expression; animated **3.** of the nerves **4.** made up of or containing nerves **5.** characterized by or having a disordered state of the nerves **6.** characterized by or showing emotional tension, rest-
3 lessness, agitation, etc. **7.** fearful; apprehensive —**nerv′ous·ly** *adv.* —**nerv′ous·ness, ner·vos′i·ty** (-väs′ə tē) *n.*

☆**nervous breakdown** a psychotic or neurotic disorder that impairs the ability to function normally: a popular, nontechnical term

☆**nervous Nellie** [orig. used of high-strung racehorses: in reference to *old Nell*, jocular name for a nag] [Slang] a timid person who is easily upset and is hesitant to act

nervous system all the nerve cells and nervous tissues in an organism, including, in the vertebrates, the brain, spinal cord, ganglia, nerves, and nerve centers: it coordinates and controls responses to stimuli and conditions behavior and consciousness

4 **ner·vure** (nʉr′vyoor) *n.* [Fr.: see NERVE & -URE] *Zool. same as* VEIN (*n.* 2)

5 **nerv·y** (nʉr′vē) *adj.* **nerv′i·er, nerv′i·est** **1.** [Rare] strong; vigorous; sinewy **2.** [Brit.] nervous; excitable; jittery
6 **3.** full of courage; bold ☆**4.** [Colloq.] rudely bold; brazen; impudent —**nerv′i·ly** *adv.* —**nerv′i·ness** *n.*

7 **n.e.s.** not elsewhere specified

nes·ci·ent (nesh′ənt, -ē ənt) *adj.* [L. *nesciens*, prp. of *nescire*, to be ignorant of: see NICE] **1.** lacking knowledge; ignorant **2.** *same as* AGNOSTIC —**nes′ci·ence** *n.*

8 **ness** (nes) *n.* [ME. *nesse* < OE. *næs* & ON. *nes*, akin to OE. *nosu*, NOSE] a promontory; headland: now chiefly in place names [*Inverness*]

-ness (nis, nəs) [ME. *-nesse* < OE. *-nes(s)*, akin to G. *-niss*, Goth. *-nassus* (for *-assus*, with *n-* < end of the base of weak verbs ending in *-atjan*)] *a n.-forming suffix meaning* state, quality, or instance of being [*greatness, sadness, togetherness*]

Nes·sel·rode (nes′'l rōd′) *n.* [after ff.] a mixture of preserved fruits, chopped nuts, etc., used in ice cream, puddings, pies, or the like

Nes·sel·rode (nes′'l rōd′; *Russ.* nyes′sil rô′dye), Count **Karl Robert** 1780–1862; Russ. statesman & diplomat

nest (nest) *n.* [ME. < OE., akin to G. *nest* < IE. ***nizdos** < base ***ni-**, down + ***sed-**, to sit, whence L. *nidus*, W. *nyth*] **1.** the structure made or the place chosen by birds for laying their eggs and sheltering their young **2.** the place used by turtles, hornets, fish, etc. for spawning or breeding **3.** a cozy or snug place to live or rest; retreat **4.** *a)* a resort, haunt, or den: used esp. in an unfavorable sense *b)* the people who frequent such a place [*a nest of criminals*] **5.** a brood, swarm, or colony of birds, insects, etc. **6.** a set or series of similar things, each fitting within the one next larger —*vi.* **1.** to build or live in or as in a nest **2.** to fit one into another **3.** to hunt for birds' nests: usually in the present participle —*vt.* **1.** to make a nest for **2.** to place or settle in or as in a nest **3.** to fit (an object) closely within another —**nest′a·ble** *adj.* —**nest′er** *n.*

‡**n'est-ce pas?** (nes pä′) [Fr., lit., is it not?] isn't that so?

nest egg **1.** an artificial or real egg left in a nest to induce a hen to lay more eggs there **2.** money, etc. put aside as a reserve or to establish a fund

nes·tle (nes′'l) *vi.* **-tled, -tling** [ME. *nestlen* < OE. *nestlian*: see NEST & -LE] **1.** orig., to nest **2.** to settle down comfortably and snugly **3.** to draw or press close for comfort or in affection **4.** to lie sheltered or partly hidden, as a house among trees —*vt.* **1.** to rest or press (a baby, one's head, etc.) in a snug, affectionate manner **2.** to settle or house as in a nest; shelter —**nes′tler** *n.*

nest·ling (nest′liŋ, nes′-) *n.* [ME. (akin to G. *nestling*): see NEST & -LING[1]] **1.** a young bird not yet ready to leave the nest **2.** a young child

Nes·tor (nes′tər) [L. < Gr. *Nestōr*] **1.** a masculine name **2.** *Gr. Myth.* a wise old counselor who fought with the Greeks at Troy —*n.* [*also* **n-**] any wise old man

Nes·to·ri·an·ism (nes tôr′ē ən iz′m) *n.* the doctrine attributed to Nestorius (patriarch of Constantinople, 428–431 A.D.) that the divine and the human existed as two distinct natures in Jesus: declared heretical in 431 —**Nes·to′ri·an** *n., adj.*

9a **net**[1] (net) *n.* [ME. < OE. *nett*, akin to G. *netz* (Goth. *nati*) < IE. base ***ned-**, to twist together, whence L. *nodus*, a knot] **1.** a fabric made from string, cord, etc., loosely knotted or woven in an openwork pattern and used to trap or snare birds, fish, etc. **2.** anything that catches or entraps; trap; snare **3.** any of various devices made of meshed fabric, used to hold, protect, or mark off something [*a hairnet, tennis net*] **4.** a fine, meshed lacelike cloth, used to make curtains, trim garments, etc. **5.** *same as* NETWORK (sense 2) **6.** *Tennis, Badminton*, etc. a ball or shuttlecock that hits the net, whether or not it goes over: in full, **net ball** —*vt.* **net′ted, net′ting** **1.** to make into net or a net **2.** to make with net **3.** to trap or snare with or as with a net **4.** to protect, shelter, or enclose with or as with a net **5.** *Tennis*, etc. to drive (the ball) into the net —*vi.* to make nets or network —*adj.* **1.** of or like net **2.** caught in a net; netted —**net′like′** *adj.*

net[2] (net) *adj.* [ME., trim, clean < Fr.: see NEAT[1]] **1.** remaining after certain deductions or allowances have been made, as for expenses, weight of containers or waste materials, nonessential considerations, etc. **2.** after all considerations; final [*net loss*] —*n.* a net amount, profit, weight, price, result, etc. —*vt.* **net′ted, net′ting** to get or bring in as a net; clear as profit, etc. 9b

Neth. Netherlands

neth·er (neth′ər) *adj.* [ME. *nethere* < OE. *neothera*, akin to G. *nieder* < IE. base ***ni-**, down (cf. NEST) + compar. suffix] **1.** lying, or thought of as lying, below the earth's surface [*the nether world*] **2.** lower or under [*the nether tip of a crescent*] 10

Neth·er·lands (neth′ər ləndz) **1.** country in W Europe, on the North Sea: 12,978 sq. mi.; pop. 12,597,000; cap. Amsterdam; seat of govt. The Hague **2.** kingdom consisting of the independent states of the Netherlands & Netherlands Antilles Du. name, NEDERLAND —**Neth′er·land′er** (-lan′dər, -lən dər) *n.*

Netherlands Antilles islands in the West Indies, constituting a part of the kingdom of the Netherlands & comprising two of the Leeward Islands & part of another & three islands off the coast of Venezuela: 394 sq. mi.; pop. 210,000; cap. Willemstad

Netherlands (East) Indies former island possessions of the Netherlands, in the East Indies: now part of Indonesia

Netherlands Guiana *former name of* SURINAM

Netherlands New Guinea *former name of* WEST IRIAN

neth·er·most (neth′ər mōst′) *adj.* [ME. *nethermest*: see NETHER & -MOST] lowest; farthest down

neth·er·ward (-wərd) *adv.* in a downward course, or direction: also **neth′er·wards**

nether world *Theol. & Myth.* the world of the dead or of punishment after death; hell

Né·thou (nā to͞o′), **Pic de** (pēk də) *Fr. name of* Pico de ANETO

net national product a country's total output of goods and services during a specified period of time, valued at current market prices and after allowance for replacement of capital goods 11

ne·tsu·ke (net′soo kā′, -kē′; net′ skē′) *n.* [Jap.] an ornamental button or figure of ivory, wood, etc., once used to attach a purse or other article to a kimono sash

Net·tie, Net·ty (net′ē) a feminine name: see ANTOINETTE, HENRIETTA, JEANNETTE

net·ting (net′iŋ) *n.* **1.** the act or process of making nets **2.** the action or right of fishing with nets **3.** netted material

netting knot *same as* SHEET BEND: see KNOT, illus.

net·tle (net′'l) *n.* [ME. *netle* < OE. *netele*, akin to G. *nessel* < IE. base ***ned-**, to twist together, whence NET[1]: from the use of such plants as a source of spinning fiber] **1.** any of a genus (*Urtica*) of annual and perennial weeds of the nettle family with stinging hairs **2.** any of various other stinging or spiny plants —*adj.* designating a family (Urticaceae) of chiefly tropical plants usually covered with stinging hairs, including the ramie and the nettle —*vt.* **-tled, -tling** **1.** to sting with or as with nettles **2.** to irritate; annoy; vex —*SYN.* see IRRITATE —**net′tler** *n.* 12

nettle rash *same as* URTICARIA

net·tle·some (-səm) *adj.* that nettles or irritates

net ton *same as* SHORT TON

net-winged (-wiŋd′) *adj.* having a network of veins in the wings: said of insects

net·work (net′wʉrk′) *n.* [NET[1] + WORK] **1.** any arrangement or fabric of parallel wires, threads, etc. crossed at regular intervals by others fastened to them so as to leave open spaces; netting; mesh **2.** a thing resembling this in some way; specif., *a)* a system of roads, canals, veins, etc. that connect with or cross one another *b) Radio & TV* a chain of transmitting stations controlled and operated as a unit *c)* a group, system, etc. of interconnected or cooperating individuals **3.** the making of nets or netted fabric —*adj.* broadcast over all or most of the stations of a network

Neu·châ·tel (nö shä tel′) **1.** canton of W Switzerland, on the Fr. border: 308 sq. mi.; pop. 157,000 **2.** its capital, on the Lake of Neuchâtel: pop. 51,000 **3. Lake of**, lake in W Switzerland: 84 sq. mi.

Neu·en·burg (noi′ən boorkh′) *Ger. name of* NEUCHÂTEL

Neuf·châ·tel (cheese) (no͞o′shə tel′, nyo͞o′-; *Fr.* nö shä tel′) [Fr., after *Neufchâtel*, town in N France] a soft, white cheese prepared from whole milk or skim milk and eaten fresh or cured 13

Neuil·ly-sur-Seine (nö yē sür sen′) city in NC France: suburb of Paris: pop. 73,000

neuk (nyo͞ok) *n.* [Scot.] a nook; corner

neume, neum (nyo͞om, no͞om) *n.* [Fr. < ML. *neuma*, prob. ult. < Syriac *ne'mo*, a sound, tone, song, altered in form and sense by association with Gr. *neuma*, a sign & *pneuma*, a breath] any of a set of signs used in medieval church music before the invention of an exact music notation and placed over words in order to aid the memory by indicating direction of melody, manner of performance, etc. —**neu·mat′ic** *adj.*

neur- *same as* NEURO-: used before a vowel

Library Exercise 8

Using the sample dictionary page reprinted on page 209 of this textbook, find answers to the following questions. Write your answers on a sheet of paper numbered 1–10.

Synonyms are words with nearly the same meanings.

1. What is one example of a compound word or phrase given as an entry?
2. What is the synonym given for *nettle?*
3. What is a Scottish word for *corner?*
4. What is the pronunciation information given for the word *netsuke?*
5. What are the guide words on the sample page?
6. Which entry word has the most meanings listed after it?
7. How is the word *nescient* divided into syllables?
8. What is the new name of Netherlands Guiana?
9. What two words are spelled the same but are given as separate entries and have different meanings?
10. What is the adjective form of *nest?*

Review of Dictionary Information

1. Guide words are printed at the top of the page to show the first and last word on that page.
2. Word entries are printed in **boldface** type in alphabetical order.
3. Other forms of the word are also given. These forms may include plurals, principal parts of verbs, and comparative forms of adjectives and adverbs.
4. Syllables are indicated in word entries with a raised dot between syllables. These syllable markers show where words may be divided at the end of a line of writing.
5. Pronunciation is shown with diacritical marks and simplified spellings. These follow the word entry and are in parentheses.
6. Usage markers show whether or not the word is used in formal English. Meanings of abbreviations for usage labels can usually be found in the front of the dictionary.
7. The part of speech is shown by an abbreviation. The meanings of part-of-speech abbreviations are also listed in the front of the dictionary.
8. Word origins are shown in brackets after the part-of-speech abbreviation. Look in the front of the dictionary for help in reading the history of a word.
9. A new word entry is given for each word. When one entry has exactly the same spelling as the one that follows it, the two are distinguished by raised numbers.
10. Definitions of the words are numbered with Arabic numbers, with the oldest meanings having the lowest numbers. When a word has many definitions, the definitions are grouped according to the part of speech.

11. Phrases and compound words appear as entries.
12. Synonyms (words that mean nearly the same) often appear after definitions. *See* means "see the dictionary entry for the word."
13. Information about people, places, and events is often given.
14. A pronunciation key is often found at the bottom of every other page. A more complete key can be found in the front of the dictionary.

Special Dictionaries

Unabridged dictionaries are larger and more extensive versions of the standard dictionary found in most classrooms. In addition to the information found in standard abridged dictionaries, unabridged dictionaries give more extensive information on word histories, usage, foreign words and phrases commonly used in English, new words, and idiomatic expressions. These helpful reference books also explain in greater detail distinctions between words with similar meanings. In addition, they often contain tables and charts on such subjects as constellations, crusades, glacial epochs, radio frequencies, and standard time throughout the world.

Use an unabridged dictionary when you want to find complete information about a word or when you need specialized information. A comparison of the following two entries for the word *fate*, one from an abridged dictionary[1] and the other from an unabridged dictionary,[2] shows how the two kinds of dictionaries differ.

fate (fāt) ***n.*** [ME. < L. *fatum*, prophetic declaration, oracle < neut. pp. of *fari*, to speak: see FAME] **1.** the power or agency supposed to determine the outcome of events before they occur; destiny **2.** *a*) something inevitable, supposedly determined by this power *b*) what happens or has happened to a person or entity; lot; fortune **3.** final outcome **4.** death; destruction; doom —***vt.*** **fat′ed, fat′ing** to destine: now usually in the passive —**the Fates** *Gr. & Rom. Myth.* the three goddesses who control human destiny and life: see CLOTHO, LACHESIS, and ATROPOS

[1]**fate** \'fāt, *usu* -ād·+V\ *n* -s [ME, fr. L or MF; MF *fate*, fr. L *fatum* prophetic declaration, oracle, what is ordained by the gods, destiny, fate, fr. neut. of *fatus*, past part. of *fari* to speak — more at BAN] **1 a :** the principle or determining cause or will by which things in general are supposed to come to be as they are or events to happen as they do **b :** foreordination by which either the universe as a whole or particular happenings are predetermined; *specif* **:** necessity as inherent in the nature of things to which the gods as well as men are subject ⟨∼ in Greek tragedy becomes the order of nature in modern thought —A.N.Whitehead⟩ — compare DETERMINISM **2 a :** whatever is destined or inevitably decreed esp. for a person **:** an appointed lot ⟨her ∼ was to remain a spinster⟩ **b :** RUIN, DISASTER; *esp* **:** DEATH ⟨the villain met his ∼ at the hands of the hero⟩ **c :** ultimate lot or disposition **:** final outcome **:** END ⟨the congress decided the bill's ∼ by a single vote⟩ ⟨the explorer's party left no trace of the ∼ that overcame them⟩ ⟨the importance of an individual thinker . . . depends upon the ∼ of his ideas in the mind of his successors —A.N.Whitehead⟩ **d :** the circumstances that befall something ⟨all human beings live as members of organized groups and have their ∼ inextricably bound up with that of the group to which they belong —Ralph Linton⟩ **3 :** one of the goddesses of fate or destiny esp. of classical times·supposed to determine the course of human life — usu. used in pl. and then sometimes cap. ⟨waiting there, standing like a ∼ in the center of the carpet, a gaunt, gray, somber woman —G.W.Brace⟩ ⟨my great-aunts, formidable ∼*s* who sat in judgment on all the events of their time —Hugh Dickinson⟩ ⟨the ∼*s* . . . have smiled with an astonishing kindness on his wanderings in the jungle —*Geog. Jour.*⟩

---

[1]From *Webster's New World Dictionary*, Second College Edition. Copyright © 1980 by Simon & Schuster, a division of Gulf & Western Corporation. Reprinted by permission.

[2]From *Webster's Third New International Dictionary*. © 1976 by G. & C. Merriam Co., Publishers of the Merriam-Webster Dictionaries. Reprinted by permission of the publishers.

The first entry is from the abridged version of *Webster's New World Dictionary.* The second entry, from the unabridged *Webster's Third New International Dictionary*, gives more thorough explanations of word meanings and illustrates the explanations with quotations from different authors to show the word in context.

Since unabridged dictionaries are so large, libraries usually display them on a table or dictionary stand for easy use. The unabridged dictionaries your library is most likely to have are the *Webster's Third New International Dictionary*, the *Random House Dictionary of the English Language: Unabridged Edition*, and *Funk and Wagnalls New Standard Dictionary of the English Language.*

Dictionaries of synonyms are also available in the reference area of the library. A dictionary of synonyms can help you improve your vocabulary and make your writing more precise and interesting. When using this aid, however, remember that synonyms do not have exactly the same meaning. The word *doom*, for example, is listed as a synonym for *fate.* The words *doom* and *fate* share the meaning of "destiny," but *doom* is always negative, while *fate* can have positive or negative overtones. When you find a synonym, always read its definition thoroughly to be certain it is exactly the word you want.

Three commonly used dictionaries of synonyms are *Roget's Thesaurus of English Words and Phrases, Funk and Wagnalls Standard Handbook of Synonyms and Antonyms*, and *Webster's Dictionary of Synonyms.* The Funk and Wagnalls dictionary organizes its words alphabetically with detailed descriptions of the variations in meaning for each synonym. Webster's is also organized alphabetically and has antonyms in parentheses after the synonyms for each word. *Roget's Thesaurus*, however, is organized differently. In this widely used resource, words are arranged by ideas rather than in alphabetical order. Words are first grouped into large classes of ideas (such as *sensation)*, then into smaller categories (such as *sensation in general, touch*, and *taste).* Each of these categories consists of smaller numbered categories, as on page 213.

The words in **boldface** type can also be found under their own headings in the index.

To find a synonym in the thesaurus, use the index to locate the number of the category in which the word is grouped. The entries on the bottom of page 213 are given for the word *touch.* (Notice that the first twelve entries are for *touch* as a noun; the last eleven entries are for *touch* as a verb.) What is the category number that refers to the noun *touch* as one of the senses?

The noun *touch* as it is related to *feel* has the category number 425. At the top of page 213, you will see this category from the *Roget's Thesaurus.* Notice how the category is further subdivided.

Roget's Thesaurus is a valuable tool because it contains more than a quarter of a million synonyms. However, since no definition of these synonyms is included, always use the thesaurus to refresh your memory about words whose meanings you already know or use it in conjunction with a dictionary.

425. TOUCH

.1 NOUNS **touch,** thigmo–; sense of touch, tactile sense, cutaneous sense; taction, contact 200.5; **feel,** feeling; hand-mindedness; light touch, lambency, whisper, breath, kiss, caress; lick, lap; brush, graze, glance; stroke, rub; tap, flick 283.6; finger tip caress, tentative poke.
.2 **touching, feeling, fingering, palpation, handling,** manipulation; petting, caressing, stroking, rubbing, frottage, friction 350; pressure 283.2.
.3 touchableness, **tangibility, palpability,** tactility.
.4 **feeler,** tactile organ, tactor, tactile cell; tactile process, tactile corpuscle, **antenna**; tactile hair, vibrissa; cat whisker; barbel, barbule; palp, palpus.
.5 **finger, digit,** digiti–, dactyl(o)–; forefinger, index finger, index; ring finger, annulary; middle finger, medius, dactylion; little finger, pinkie [informal], minimus; thumb, pollex.
.6 VERBS **touch, feel,** feel of, palpate; **finger,** pass *or* run the fingers over, feel with the fingertips, thumb; **handle,** palm, paw; **manipulate,** wield, ply; twiddle; poke at, prod 283.11; tap, **flick** 283.15; come in contact 200.10.
.7 **touch lightly,** touch upon; kiss, **brush,** sweep, graze, brush by, glance, scrape, skim.
.8 **stroke, pet, caress,** fondle; **nuzzle,** nose, rub noses; feel up [slang]; rub, rub against, massage, knead 350.6.
.9 **lick, lap,** tongue, mouth.
.10 ADJS **tactile,** tactual; hand-minded.
.11 touchable, **palpable, tangible,** tactile.
.12 lightly touching, lambent, playing lightly over, barely touching.

This excerpt is from the index to *Roget's Thesaurus.*

touch
n. admixture 44.7
communication 554.1
contact 200.5
feel 425
implication 546.2
knack 733.6
motif 901.7
music 462.31
sense 422.5
signal 568.15
small amount 35.4
tap 283.6
v. affect 855.16
beg 774.15
borrow 821.3
contact 200.10
equal 30.5
excite pity 944.5
feel 425.6
relate to 9.5
sense 422.8
signal 568.22
tap 283.15

Library Exercise 9

Select five words from the following list and find each in *Roget's Thesaurus* or another dictionary of synonyms. On a separate sheet of paper, write out five synonyms listed for each word. Indicate when the synonyms are not used in Edited Standard English by writing out *coll.* (colloquial), or *slang*, or whatever other term the dictionary uses.

1. vicious	11. disagreement
2. hardy	12. constant
3. somber	13. bashful
4. ruffle	14. alienation
5. pounce	15. abandon
6. oppressive	16. confused
7. joy	17. fantasy
8. ideal	18. infinite
9. frantic	19. nonconformity
10. exception	20. presentiment

Encyclopedias

An *encyclopedia* is a collection of articles on a wide variety of subjects, arranged alphabetically.

Encyclopedias vary in size from thirty volumes to one volume. The multivolume sets usually have a separate volume, called an *index,* that refers the user to volumes and pages where subjects are covered. The subject of *holography,* for example, might be treated in articles headed "Holography," "Lasers," and "Dr. Denis Gabor" (credited as the inventor of holography). Only by checking the index could you be certain that you have found all the information the encyclopedia contains on your subject. Another important volume that is part of many encyclopedias is the yearbook. Published annually, the yearbook is a way of keeping information current that might otherwise become dated very quickly.

The four general encyclopedias most often found in school libraries are *Collier's Encyclopedia* (twenty-four volumes), *Encyclopaedia Britannica* (thirty volumes), *Encyclopedia International* (twenty volumes), and *World Book Encyclopedia* (twenty-two volumes). The best known one- and two-volume encyclopedias are the *Columbia Encyclopedia,* the *Columbia-Viking Concise Encyclopedia,* and the *Lincoln Library of Essential Information* (two volumes).

The *Encyclopaedia Britannica* has a relatively new approach to locating information. The first eleven volumes amount to an index with entries arranged in alphabetical order. By first looking up an article in this *Micropaedia,* the user can learn not only the various places where the subject is treated in greater depth but also basic reference data about the subject. The remaining nineteen volumes, called the *Macropaedia*, contain more detailed articles about many subjects.

Limited in their treatments of most subjects, encyclopedias can best be used as springboards to further research. By giving an overview of the subject, encyclopedias can help users identify questions to answer and particular areas to explore. Also, references at the end of many encyclopedia articles often refer users to books with more specialized information.

Library Exercise 10

Using the index of an encyclopedia in your school library, look up one of the following subjects or another one of your choice. Then write down the volume and page numbers of at least two encyclopedia articles about the subject. Finally read one of the articles and write a brief summary of it in your own words.

1. Comets
2. Etruscan civilization
3. Hypnosis
4. Impressionism
5. The invention of plastic
6. Madame Curie
7. The Ukraine
8. Air traffic control
9. Katherine Anne Porter
10. Spelunking

Almanacs and Atlases

An *almanac* is an annually published book of facts and figures on a wide range of subjects.

Consult an almanac when you need to find up-to-date information on current events, sports, politics, industry, arts and entertainment, and many other areas. Almanacs contain historical facts and figures. An almanac can tell you the date of the Russian Revolution, current census figures, the amount of the Gross National Product, and the names of winners of the Nobel Prize. Commonly used almanacs include the *World Almanac and Book of Facts*, the *Information Please Almanac*, and *The Official Associated Press Almanac.*

Another popular almanac, *The People's Almanac*, prints specialized information with an unusual slant. In it you will find a reprint of the world's first-known photograph, a brief history of popular inventions (such as the fork and the rubber band), and lists of everything from eleven strange post-cards to the twenty-five most-written-about people of all time.

An *atlas* is a book of maps.

Standard atlases contain geographical maps of all the countries in the world, as well as special maps and charts indicating a range of information from topography, climate, population, and industry to sea currents. Some of the most commonly used atlases are the *Hammond Contemporary World Atlas*, *Goode's World Atlas*, the *Rand McNally New Cosmopolitan World Atlas*, and *The Encyclopaedia Britannica Atlas.*

Usually the reference section also contains *historical atlases*, books of maps from various periods in history. These atlases show changing boundaries of countries, the growth of empires and the flow of languages and cultures, as well as replicas of early maps. The *Historical Atlas of the United States*, Shepherd's *Historical Atlas*, Heyden's *Atlas of the Classical World*, and the *Rand McNally Atlas of World History* are all popular historical atlases that your school library may have.

Library Exercise 11

Select at least five of the following twenty questions and use an almanac or atlas to find the answers. Write your answers on a separate sheet of paper and indicate the source where you found them.

1. What is the name of the current poet laureate of England?
2. How many islands compose the state of Hawaii?
3. Who is the current president of Greece?
4. What are the first- and second-largest natural lakes in the world?
5. Which coast of Australia is the most mountainous?
6. What was the site of the 1896 Olympic games?
7. What is the name of the part of the English Channel that is closest to France?
8. What languages are spoken in South Africa?
9. What is the second-largest country in South America?
10. Who was the first woman lawyer in the United States?
11. What four European countries are islands?
12. What is the number of nuclear power plants in the United States?
13. What is the form of government in Ireland?
14. Which country in the world has the greatest population density?
15. What type of vegetation is prevalent in Florida?
16. Who was the winner of the last perfectly pitched game of baseball?
17. What is the distance between Portland, Oregon, and Miami, Florida?
18. What is the height of the tallest mountain in Europe?
19. To which country does the Isle of Man belong?
20. What are the largest (by population) two cities in the world?

Biographical Reference Books

Biographical reference books are sources for information about famous people. These works usually contain more extensive information than encyclopedia entries.

Webster's Biographical Dictionary presents short biographies of famous people, in one volume. *Who's Who* is an annually published British work giving current information on famous living people, primarily English. *Who's*

Who in America, revised every two years, is a similar publication about famous living Americans. In addition, there are specialized Who's Who publications such as *Who's Who in American Law, Who's Who in Hollywood,* and so on. *Current Biography* deals with prominent people in the news. Published monthly, the pamphlets are bound together in book form at the end of the year with a cumulative index for easy reference.

Another generally used biographical reference is *The New Century Cyclopedia of Names.* This three-volume work contains brief biographies, plus information on a variety of proper names: mythical and literary characters, places, and events. In addition, most arts and professions have specialized biographies for their field. To find information about writers, for example, you could consult *The Writers Directory, Twentieth Century Authors,* or *British Authors of the 19th Century,* to name a few.

Library Exercise 12

Select two of the following names and look them up in one or more biographical reference books. On a separate sheet of paper, write a brief paragraph on the information you find about each person and include the source you used for each.

1. Nancy Gomez (golfer)
2. Kahlil Gibran (poet and artist)
3. Twyla Tharp (dancer)
4. Louise Nevelson (artist)
5. Claudio Arrau (pianist)
6. Jay Silverheels (actor)
7. Walter Lippmann (journalist)
8. Bessie Smith (American singer)
9. Oriana Fallaci (Italian journalist)
10. Barbara Tuchman (writer)

Literature Reference Books

Literature reference books give information on sources of quotations and on authors and their works.

Probably the most well-known literature reference work is Bartlett's *Familiar Quotations.* This work is useful when you need to know the author of a quotation or the exact quote itself. Assume, for example, that you want to know who first said or wrote the expression "All or nothing." To find this information look in the index, where every quotation is listed alphabetically by its first major word and also by each important word. "All or nothing," then, is listed both under *all* and *nothing.* You would find that Henrik Ibsen is the author of this quotation and that it is from his play *Brand.*

If, on the other hand, you wanted to look for several of Ibsen's quotations, you would look in the author index, which comes before the index of quotations. The authors in Bartlett's are listed chronologically (with Ibsen, for example, coming before Gertrude Stein). For this reason it is often faster to use the author index.

Another reference work for quotations, Stevenson's *Home Book of Quotations*, organizes its information by subject rather than by author or first line. This is a helpful book for finding quotations on special subjects to use in your writing.

An *encyclopedia of world literature* is a useful way to find information about the history of literature, a particular writer, a genre of literature (*story, poem, play*), or a literary term (*alliteration, tragedy, symbol*). One of the best-known reference works of this type is *Cassell's Encyclopedia of World Literature.*

Cassell's Encyclopedia of World Literature is divided into three parts. Part I, titled "General Subjects," contains historical information about the literature of many different countries and regions and information on general literary topics. The latter category includes articles on genres of literature, such as the novel, short story, poem, and play; articles on movements and areas of literature, such as Classicism, Romanticism, and Mythology; and articles on general topics, such as censorship and copyright laws. Part II of the work is a collection of biographies of writers who died before August 1, 1914. Part III contains biographies of later writers.

The *Short Story Index* is useful for finding a specific story, a story by a certain author, or stories on a given subject. The main part of the *Index*, the *Index to Short Stories*, contains three types of entries arranged in alphabetical order: *author, title*, and *subject.*

The *author entry* is the most complete, containing the author and title of the story, and the author (or editor) of the title of the collection where the short story can be found, as the following sample entry shows.

Cheever, John
  The season of divorce
    Holmes, P. C. and Lehman, A. J. eds.
      The Challenge of Conflict

The preceding entry is for the author John Cheever. His short story "The Season of Divorce" can be found in a collection of stories titled *The Challenge of Conflict.* P. C. Holmes and A. J. Lehman are the editors of the collection.

If the story has been published in a magazine, then the title and date of the periodical are given, as the following sample shows.

Gardner, John
  Trumpeter
    Esquire 86: 114–16 D'76

John Gardner's story "Trumpeter" can be found in the December 1976 issue of *Esquire* magazine (Volume 86) on pages 114 through 116. The title and subject entries list only the author and title of the short story. For more information refer to the author entry.

Granger's Index to Poetry is useful when you want to find where a particular poem has been anthologized. The main entry in *Granger's Index to Poetry* is the title and first-line entry. Titles and first lines are arranged in alphabetical order by the first major word in the title or first line. When the first line of a poem is listed, the title is printed immediately after it. This entry gives information about collections or periodicals where the poem has been published.

Library Exercise 13

For each of the following fifteen questions, write the source you would consult to find the answer: Bartlett's *Familiar Quotations*, Stevenson's *Home Book of Quotations*, *Cassell's Encyclopedia of World Literature*, the *Short Story Index*, or *Granger's Index to Poetry*. Write your answers on a separate sheet of paper numbered 1–15.

1. Where would you find information on the life of the poet Gwendolyn Brooks?
2. Where would you find the name of an anthology that contains the poem "Ariel" by Sylvia Plath?
3. Where would you find the titles of short stories about adolescence?
4. Where would you find the name of the author of the short story "The Jilting of Granny Weatherall"?
5. Where would you find an explanation of the term *metaphor?*
6. Where would you find the last words of the writer Gertrude Stein?
7. Where would you find copyright information?
8. Where would you find the source of the phrase, "The salt of the earth"?
9. Where would you find the title of a poem about winter?
10. Where would you find the title of a short story by Kawabata?
11. Where would you find out about the literary activities of Ezra Pound?
12. Where would you find a saying of Confucius?
13. Where would you find a poem with the first line, "When you are old and gray and full of sleep"?
14. Where would you find an explanation of the Romantic Movement?
15. Where would you find a line from Shakespeare with the words *winter* and *discontent?*

10 Developing Vocabulary Skills

Expanding Your Vocabulary

The best way to increase your vocabulary is to read many kinds of writing. As you encounter words over and over again in new situations, they become a part of your vocabulary. However, you can expand your vocabulary more easily if you know some ways to understand the new words you meet. In this chapter you will learn how clues to the meanings of words can be found in surrounding words, phrases, and sentences, and you will analyze the parts of words that carry meaning. Also, you will study how the meanings of words can vary according to their use and how different words can express different meanings for the same idea.

Words in Context

The other words and sentences that surround a word are its *context.*

Context clues are hints about meaning supplied by surrounding words, phrases, and sentences. These include *experience clues, definition* or *paraphrase clues, example clues,* and *clues of comparison and contrast.*

1. *Experience Clues*

Experience with a situation can help you guess the meaning of a word. In the sentence "Sue's mother called Sue's excuse for coming home late a *prevarication,*" you may not be certain of the meaning of *prevarication,* but you may know what could happen in Sue's situation, and you can guess the word has something to do with a *lie.* The following sentences give other examples of experience clues.

> After a *cursory* examination of the envelope, Norton tore it open and read the statement of the bill.

(People often go quickly to the contents of an envelope without reading the envelope.)

> I had been sitting in the sun for an hour, and the *incessant* buzzing of the flies was getting on my nerves.

(Your own experience with flies should remind you of the annoying way flies buzz around without stopping.)

2. *Definition or Paraphrase Clues*

Often a writer explains a word for you by defining it or by restating or paraphrasing it. The definition, or paraphrase, may follow the word and be set off by commas, or the definition or paraphrase may come later in the sentence or even in another sentence.

Definition or paraphrase clues are often found in science or social studies textbooks. Notice how the words *nucleic acid* and *nucleotides* are defined in the following excerpt from *Biological Science: An Inquiry Into Life.*[1]

> Only recently have biologists come to understand the importance of *nucleic* (new·KLAY·ik) *acids* and *nucleotides* (NEW·kle·o·tides) in the life of cells and organisms. Like proteins, nucleic acids are long chains of simpler units. But the units are not amino acids, as in proteins. They are nucleotides. Each nucleotide molecule is built from rings of carbon and nitrogen. Each molecule also contains atoms of hydrogen, oxygen, nitrogen, and phosphorus. Each nucleic acid is built from only four kinds of nucleotides. As in proteins, the order of the units in the chain is very important.

In the following excerpt from *Men and Nations: A World History,* the word *karma* is explained by the rest of the sentence, which provides its own definition for the concept of karma.

> Buddha accepted the Hindu doctrine of karma, that the progress of the soul depends on the life a person leads, and that good is rewarded and evil punished.

3. *Example Clues*

Sometimes, the meaning of a word is indicated by examples. For instance, in the sentence "Some acronyms, such as *radar (radio detecting and ranging*), are a part of everyday language," the meaning of *acronym* is suggested by the example word *radar,* which is formed from the first letters of a series of words. Words like *for example, for instance, such as, like,* and *other* often indicate example clues.

---

[1]From page 70 in *Biological Science: An Inquiry Into Life,* Fourth Edition by Hickman et al. Published by Harcourt Brace Jovanovich, Inc., 1980. Reprinted by permission of the Biological Sciences Curriculum Study (BSCS).

> Although it looks like a lizard, the newt is an *amphibian* like the frog.

(Frogs live both in and out of water, while lizards are associated with dry environments, so the meaning of *amphibian* is hinted by the example of a frog.)

> There was a spirit of *camaraderie* among the construction workers. For example, during lunch two workers shared their sandwiches with a co-worker who had forgotten her lunch. By the fence four of them were singing a popular song and passing around a thermos of coffee.

(The actions described in the preceding excerpt are friendly, so *camaraderie* must mean "friendship.")

4. *Comparison-and-Contrast Clues*

In comparison-and-contrast clues a word's meaning may be made clearer by contrasting or likening it to a more familiar word or group of words. Clues that show a similarity in meaning between one word and others are often introduced by *and, another, like,* and *as.* Clues that offer a contrast to a word often are introduced by words such as *but, however, instead, although, though, on the other hand,* and *still.*

> Jon's *petulant* voice rose above the noise of the vacuum cleaner and reminded his father of the whine of a puppy that feels ignored.

(The word *petulant* is compared directly with a puppy's whine.)

> Robin *quelled* his fear of the dark woods and fell asleep, but Jamie let his fears loose and could not sleep.

(Jamie did not control his fears; this action is contrasted with Robin who *quelled*, or controlled, his fears.)

Vocabulary Exercise 1

In each of the following sentences, the meaning of the *italicized* word is suggested by context clues. On a sheet of paper, write what you think is the meaning of the word and write the clue on which you base your guess. Check the meaning by looking the word up in a dictionary.

1. In some situations it may be wiser to seem *docile* than to reveal a negative feeling.
2. Stamp collecting may be a *lucrative* hobby for some but a waste of money for others.
3. The *turgid* river was a hazard to the troops, who were unprepared for rough waters.
4. The *nomenclature*, or system of naming, now used in botany is in part the work of Linnaeus.
5. "You'll need a bigger belt for your *girth!*" the new salesman said. Then he blushed when he realized he might have embarrassed the customer.

6. For Priscilla rock collecting was an *avocation*, but it took more of her time than her actual job in the museum.
7. When she broke the hair dryer, Rosaria tried to *mollify* her sister by buying her a new brush.
8. The lion was *satiated;* it had eaten almost the entire zebra.
9. Kiyo examined the *callus* between her thumb and finger. She wished she could exchange her chore of sweeping the steps for another one!
10. "Julio is a *braggart*," Delia told Anna. "No matter what you do, he's done it better or faster or neater."

Connotation and Denotation

When you look up an unfamiliar word in the dictionary, you are looking for its *denotative*, or dictionary, *meaning*. For example, the dictionary meaning for *scrawny* is "lean" or "thin." *Lean* and *thin* are synonyms (words that have the same general meaning) for *scrawny*.

However, words also have *connotative meanings*, meanings that include the feelings people associate with a word. Denotative and connotative meanings of words often differ. The dictionary, for example, assigns the same denotation to *lean* and *scrawny*, but a "*scrawny* yellow cat" may give you a different image than a "*lean* yellow cat." Although *lean* and *scrawny* are synonyms, the word *lean* is usually associated with a pleasant, attractive appearance while *scrawny* is often associated with something unpleasant.

Besides *pleasant* or *unpleasant* connotations, words can have *formal* or *informal* connotations, *modern* or *historical* connotations. For example, although the dictionary defines a *fiddle* as a *violin*, the first word is associated with an informal, usually rural setting, while the second word is associated with a more formal setting. Today you may refer to a room in your house as a *living room*, but a hundred years ago you might have called it the *parlor*. Words that lack a strong association with a feeling, that lack a formal or an informal situation, or that lack a specific period of time have a *neutral connotation*.

Using a word correctly or making the appropriate choice from several synonyms involves understanding the word's connotation as well as its denotation. For example, speakers and writers addressing the general public would probably use words with formal or neutral connotations. In a private conversation with close friends, the same individuals might be more likely to use slang or other words with informal connotations.

Understanding the context in which a word will be used will help you decide which of two or three synonyms would be most appropriate. For example, since the following sentence discusses the appearance of a famous musician at Carnegie Hall, *violin* is a better choice than *fiddle*.

> She held her *violin* at her side as she acknowledged the applause of the audience at Carnegie Hall.

Vocabulary Exercise 2

Each of the following passages contains a word or phrase whose connotation is inappropriate for the context. On a separate sheet of paper, write out each sentence, substituting a more appropriate synonym for the inappropriate word.

Example

a. With great finesse the butler started hacking the turkey with a large silver knife.

a. With great finesse the butler started carving the turkey with a large silver knife.

1. My friend Phil has a new plaid waistcoat.
2. The slaughter of John F. Kennedy placed the responsibilities of the Presidency on the shoulders of Lyndon Baines Johnson.
3. Looking sternly at the defendant, the judge ordered him sent to the slammer for a period of no less than five years.
4. A dignified, fat old gentleman walked contentedly through Central Park.
5. "When's the omnibus leaving for the wrestling match?" Jim yelled to his friends.
6. Watch out! That guy ahead of you is driving like a bedlamite.
7. The museum contains several fine examples of barbaric American paintings.
8. The League of Women Voters, who sponsored the local book exchange last Saturday, raked in several thousand dollars that will be donated to the library fund.
9. This report from the manager of the sales department recommends that the company hire some pushy sales personnel.
10. I admire your brother so much; his pigheadedness about going to the university has certainly been rewarded.

Word Structure

Word structure, the way parts are combined to form a word, can provide a key to the meaning of unfamiliar words.

For example, the words in the following list are called *derivative* because they are formed, or derived, from shorter words. Although you may not know the meaning of all the derivatives, you should be able to identify a familiar word within the longer word. What are these "hidden" words?

collector	immortal
difference	irregularity
existence	misspell
fearsome	unfearful
illegal	unthinkable

The words *collect, differ, exist, fear, legal, mortal, regular, spell,* and *think* in the preceding list are called *roots* because they are the base, or root, to which groups of letters called *affixes* are added to form new derivatives. For example, the affixes *un-* and *-ful* were added to the root *fear* to create the new word *unfearful.* The affix *-some* added to the same root creates the word *fearsome.* The other affixes in the preceding list are *mis-, il-, im-, -or, -ence, ir-, -ity,* and *-able.*

The following list also contains derivatives that are made from roots and affixes. Remove the affixes and decide how these roots differ from those in the first list.

conclude	transfer
presume	venerable
revolve	width

When you removed the affixes *trans-, -th, pre-, con-, re-,* and *-able,* you probably discovered that the roots were not words. Not all roots are complete words. Roots that can appear with affixes *(untruth, truthful)* and stand alone *(truth)* are called *free forms. Bound forms,* on the other hand, are roots that are not words without affixes (*presume* and *conclude* but not *sume* or *clude).*

Many English roots and affixes are borrowed from Latin or Greek words and keep the same meaning they had in the original language. If you learn the meanings of common Latin and Greek roots and affixes, then you will be able to determine the meaning of unfamiliar derivatives formed from these parts. For instance, knowing that the Greek root *graph* means "to write" will help you understand derivatives such as *telegraph, mimeograph,* and *graphology.* Understanding that the Latin affix *ante-* means "before" makes it easier to define derivatives such as *antebellum* or *anteroom.*

Affixes are divided into two groups. Affixes that precede, or come before, a root are called *prefixes;* affixes that follow the root are called *suffixes.*

Vocabulary Exercise 3

On a separate sheet of paper, write the dictionary definition for each of the prefixes and suffixes in the following list. Then combine various prefixes, suffixes, and roots until you have created ten new words (derivatives) that are listed in the dictionary. Write out each derivative and its dictionary meaning.

Example

	PREFIXES	ROOTS, MEANING	SUFFIXES
a.	mono-	-gamy- (marriage)	-ous

a. mono-: one

-ous: having, characterized by

monogamy: the practice of being married to only one person at a time

monogamous: a person or group of people characterized by monogamy

PREFIXES	ROOTS, MEANING	SUFFIXES
ad-	-tech- (skill)	-able
dis-	-junct- (join)	-(n)ical
ex-	-port- (carry, way of carrying)	-er
in-	-cogn- (know)	-ure
pre-	-dic-, -dict- (say, speak)	-less
sub-	-fer- (carry)	-ment
trans-	-pon-, -pos- (place, put)	-or
un-	-spec- (look)	-ive
re-	-tract- (draw, pull)	-ion, -tion,
de-	-scribe-, -script- (write)	-ation, -ition

Prefixes The short affixes added to the front of a word are called *prefixes.*

The following list shows some of the most common prefixes in the English language and their most often used meanings.

PREFIX	MEANING	EXAMPLE
anti-	against	anticlimax
be-	around, about, by	bewitch
bi-	two	bifocal
cata-	down, away, thoroughly	cataclysm
circum-	around	circumlocution
de-	away, from, off	derail
dis-	not	disenchant
eu-	good	eulogize
ex-	former	ex-governor
extra-	beyond	extraneous
hemi-	half	hemisphere
hyper-	excessive, over	hyperventilate
il-	not	illegible
im-	not	impossible
in-	not, into, within	indecorous
inter-	between	intercede
intro-, intra-	within	introspection
non-	not	nonporous
post-	after	post-mortem
pre-	before	prefabricate
pro-	forward, favoring	prognosis
re-	back, backward, again	revile
super-	over, above, extra	superfine
trans-	across, beyond	transport
ultra-	beyond, excessively	ultraviolet

Vocabulary Exercise 4

Write out the following sentences on a separate sheet of paper, supplying the appropriate words from the following list. Underline the prefix in each word you use from the list.

antibiotic	disavowed	inactive	prolong
anticipate	disintegrate	paraphrase	reactivated
biannual	illogical	posthumous	uninspired

Example

a. The club scheduled their ______ meetings for July and November.
a. The club scheduled their biannual meetings for July and November.

1. The essay question called for a ______ of the author's main ideas.
2. Jorge thought studying so much made him ______ , so he joined the swimming team.
3. The mayor angrily ______ any knowledge of the budget scandal.
4. Although they selected beautiful pieces, the orchestra's playing was ______ .
5. One blast from the ray gun caused the whole spaceship to ______ .
6. The doctor tried a new ______ to bring down the sick child's fever.
7. Not wanting to ______ the students' anxiety, the teacher passed back the tests.
8. The candidate's argument was so ______ that no one could make sense of it.
9. In storage for many years, the ship was ______ and took its place once again in the fleet.
10. The committee made a ______ award to the famous painter whose premature death had saddened everyone.

Suffixes

Affixes that follow the root are called *suffixes.*

You are already familiar with how suffixes are used grammatically to show number and tense. For example, you know that adding the suffix *-ed* to the verb *paint (painted)* shows that the action occurred in the past. You also know that the *-s* or *-es* suffix is used to form plurals: *(girl, girls).* However, suffixes are also used to create new derivatives or to change the part of speech to which a word belongs. For instance, when the suffix *-er* is added to the verb *photograph,* the noun *photographer,* meaning "one who photographs," is formed. When the suffix *-ology* is added to the root *-graph-*, meaning "to write," the derivative *graphology,* meaning "the study of handwriting," is created. If the root *bio* means "life," what does the derivative *biology* mean?

The following list shows some of the suffixes used most frequently in the English language and the meanings they usually carry. Since these endings often determine the part of speech for words, the suffixes are classified by the part of speech they form.

NOUN-FORMING SUFFIXES	MEANING	EXAMPLE
-age	process, state, rank	lineage
-ance	the condition of, act of	dominance
-ation	action, state of	demonstration
-dom	state, rank, condition	serfdom
-hood	state, rank, condition	parenthood
-ism	act, manner, doctrine	barbarism
-ist	doer, believer	monopolist
-ment	means, result, action	bedevilment
-ness	quality, state	pretentiousness
-tude	quality, state, result	fortitude

ADJECTIVE-FORMING SUFFIXES	MEANING	EXAMPLE
-able	able to	sociable
-en	made of	ashen
-ful	having qualities of	purposeful
-ish	suggesting	fiendish
-less	lacking	graceless
-like	like, similar	lifelike
-some	apt to, showing	loathsome
-ward	in the direction of	windward

VERB-FORMING SUFFIXES	MEANING	EXAMPLE
-ate	become, form, treat	designate
-en	cause to be	enlighten
-esce	become, continue	coalesce
-fy	make, cause to have	amplify
-ize	make, cause to be	dramatize

Vocabulary Exercise 5

Each of the following words combines a root and a suffix. On a separate sheet of paper, write out the definition of each word, including the meaning of the suffix. Underline the suffix in each word.

Example

a. Freedom

a. Freedom: the state or condition of being free

1.	Suffrage	11.	Leaden
2.	Forbearance	12.	Winsome
3.	Industrialization	13.	Dreadful
4.	Christendom	14.	Brackish
5.	Statehood	15.	Codify
6.	Activism	16.	Catholicism
7.	Rightist	17.	Deify
8.	Wonderment	18.	Guileless
9.	Righteous	19.	Putrefy
10.	Marketable	20.	Potentate

Mastery Exercise A

In the following passages from *Last Flight*, Amelia Earhart describes some of her experiences as an early aviator and world traveler. On a separate sheet of paper, write a definition for each underlined word, using context clues or word structure to help you. Briefly explain how the clues or structure led to your definition. Finally check your definitions with those in the dictionary.[1]

Example

a. After midnight the moon set and I was alone with the stars. I have often said that the lure of flying is the lure of beauty, and I need no other flight to convince me that the reason flyers fly, whether they know it or not, is the esthetic appeal of flying.

a. esthetic: *appreciating beauty*

The "lure of flying is the lure of beauty," so esthetic *must have something to do with appreciating beauty.*

1. In addition to enjoying its beauty, that dawn over the Pacific was disconcerting. For the sun made its appearance well to the right of the course I was following. It seemed to me I should be flying much more in its direction than I was. For a brief moment I wondered if all night long I had been headed for Alaska! I checked my charts and I checked my compass and everything seemed to be as it should—so I could only conclude that the sun was wrong and I was right!

2. Here are verbatim extracts from my log book as they were penciled in it that night over the Pacific:
"Clipper ship 2 photographs.
1:15 rainbow
1:30 ship
Ice in carb. Rt engine in and out.
Leaned too much. Then rainbow.

[1]From *Last Flight* by Amelia Earhart. Copyright 1937 by George Palmer Putnam; copyright 1965 by Mrs. George Palmer Putnam. Reprinted by permission of Harcourt Brace Jovanovich, Inc.

Many a stay-at-home girl would welcome practical training in what to do when the doorbell fails to function, the plumbing clogs, the gas-range leaks, the fuse blows out, the windmill pump goes haywire, and the thousand-and-one other mechanical indispositions that can occur
3. about the house, often easily enough fixed if one has rudimentary knowledge how to fix them.

4. At a concert given in my honor I admired the cowboy regalia worn by the musicians. Forthwith, to my embarrassment (and pleasure!) I found that Secretary of State Portes Gil had ordained that I should have such a one for myself. This outfit is as traditional as the pink coat of the British huntsman or the kilts of the Highlander. Mine, as delivered some
5. days later, is a formal creation of blue and silver, topped by a picturesque sombrero, heavy with corresponding trimmings.

From a pilot's standpoint that was an interesting journey. The start
6. made before midnight was lit by a generous moon which gilded the hills gloriously, but by the time I had reached the arid stretches of the Gulf of California there crept up a white haze which made it difficult to tell what was water and what was sand ahead. Only when I could catch a glimpse of the moonlight on the water or see the black shadows of crinkled sand directly below, could I tell which was which. Even the mechanical difficulties which beset the early hours of the flight—chiefly an engine which overheated because of a faulty propeller setting—could
7. not mar the rare loveliness of the night and of the far-flung countryside which slumbered beneath.

I circled the ship several times, wanting the Captain to be sure to notice
8. me. Then I lined myself up with the wake of the vessel, which I could see for more than a mile behind it, and found that the course I had
9. been flying coincided exactly with the track made by the ship, which was a very good check on direction. I could not talk directly with the steamer, so I radioed San Francisco asking for its position and within fifteen minutes received word that I was then three hundred miles off the coast of California, exactly on my course.

Being fairly sure they could understand little of what I said, I became slightly careless with words. I commented on the scenery, which wasn't
10. much, and made other remarks. After flying over this monotonous fog—you have no idea how wearying it can be—for one hour, for two hours, for three hours, I remember saying into my little hand microphone: "I am getting tired of this fog." My message was picked up "I'm getting tired." So a nurse and physician were dispatched to the airport
11. at Oakland to revive the exhausted flyer when and if she arrived. Of course I wasn't tired at all.

12. Just about then an insect, or possibly some infinitesimal speck of dirt, lodged in my eye. In addition to being extremely painful, that minute
13. accident played havoc with my sight. So, with the maps, such as they were, blurred even to my "good eye," which at once went on strike in

sympathy with its ailing mate, and having the feeling of being lost anyway, I decided to set down and ask the way.

We had picked mid-March as about the best time for the flight from the standpoint of weather—so far as one could expect consistent "bests" on such a long route. Setting back the date three months would see seasons relentlessly progress. In some places progress would be with benefit to pilots, in others the reverse. Here rains began, there they
14. abated, here winds were favorable, there monsoons and choking dust-storms were due. So we set to studying again the weather maps of the
15. world and consulting with meteorologists who know the habits of fogs and rains and temperatures around the long equator. [Underscores added.]

Mastery Exercise B

Each of the following sentences has an underlined word formed with affixes. Number a separate sheet of paper 1–10 and write out the definition of each word, indicating the meaning of its affix or affixes.

Example

a. Since Hannah has been put in charge of the committee, her attitude has been insufferable.

a. Insufferable: in (not) plus the root suffer (to tolerate) plus able (capable of being); not to be tolerated, unbearable.

1. The drama coach gave a pep talk to mobilize the cast's energies before the performance.
2. The seaward breezes cast a chill over the tiny fishing village.
3. As an accountant he was valued for his thoroughness and his exactitude.
4. During the French Revolution many innocent people were remorselessly executed.
5. The codefendant in the case was not called on to testify.
6. One of the country's demands was a unilateral withdrawal of troops from the disputed area.
7. The Victorian heroine suffered from unrequited love for chapter after chapter.
8. Some drugs used in Canada and Great Britain are unobtainable in this country because of the strict standards of the Food and Drug Administration.
9. After it rained during his entire vacation, Kim's disillusionment with Seattle was complete.
10. The problems involved in tax reform are difficult but not insurmountable.

Using a Word List

Mastering some new words each week is a good way to increase your vocabulary and strengthen your reading and writing skills. If you study ten words from the following vocabulary list each week of the school year, you will have added over 360 words to your vocabulary.

Although some of the words in the list may be familiar, look up each word in the dictionary. Often words have more than one meaning, and listing all the dictionary definitions in your notebook will ensure that you understand the various ways a specific word can be used. Check the pronunciation of the word and repeat it aloud several times. Under the dictionary definition list several synonyms for the word and write one or two sentences that include the word in an appropriate context. Finally analyze the word's structure, locating any prefixes, suffixes, and roots that form the word. Many dictionaries also contain information at the end of the entry about derivatives. For example, the entry for *fortify*, a verb, might also show the words *fortifiable*, an adjective, and *fortifier*, a noun. Noticing these derivatives will help you add even more words to your vocabulary.

You can easily test your knowledge at the end of the week by writing each new word in a sentence. After learning new words, try to use them as often as you can in your writing and speaking. It is also a good idea to review the words you have already learned each time that you study another group of ten. Your review may be as simple as looking back at the words you have studied before and saying their meanings to yourself.

Vocabulary List

abacus	barker	besiege	catapult
abduction	barnacle	besmear	cataract
abhor	barrage	bestir	cavalcade
abracadabra	barrow	bestrew	centrifuge
abridgement	base	bestride	char
absurdity	basenji	bewail	charisma
acclamation	beau	biangular	chasm
accursed	beck	bibliography	chattel
Achilles' heel	becloud	biceps	chemotherapy
acme	beeline	biform	citadel
acoustic	befits	bisect	classical
affirmative	beggarly	botanical	daub
agape	beholden	brochure	decentralize
agenda	behoove	buoyancy	demoralize
albino	bejewel	cagey	denationalize
amplify	belladonna	calisthenics	deportation
annihilation	belle	canny	deservedly
anthology	belligerent	capitalist	devise
arterial	bemoan	carnivorous	diligence
atrocity	beret	cascade	discretion

diversity
documentary
dominion
dormant
drone
dupe
dynasty
earmark
eaves
eloquence

elude
elusive
emphatically
empower
endurable
enliven
entwine
eradicate
escapade
espionage

essence
ethnic
eviction
exploit
exuberant
facilities
facsimile
factoring
fallacy
fend

fermentation
fervent
feudalism
fiend
finagle
fiscal
fixative
fjord
flagrant
flippant

foolery
fountainhead
frenzied
froth
funnel
fusion
futurity
gadabout
gallows
gangling

gastric
gelatine
generalize
genial
ghetto
glaciation
gladiators
gnarled
gory
gouge

grouse
guild
gulch
guru
haggle
harass
hautiness
heartfelt
henchman
highbrow

hilt
homage
horrendous
hostilities
hover
humanism
humanitarian
huskiness
illiterate
impracticable

inconvenient
indicator
indorse
induction
inferiority
infirmity
influential
initiation
inset
insomniac

interdependence
intrigue
ionize
irksome
jigger
jimmy
jive
joust
jubilation
judiciary

jurisdiction
jurist
kangaroo court
keen
khaki
kibitzer
kleptomaniac
knack
knoll
koala

laggard
larceny
larynx
lattice
lavish
leery
legitimate
linguist
loon
lore

lozenge
lustrous
luxurious
magistrate
malcontent
marital
milestone
minimize
mitosis
modification

monitor
monsoon
multilateral
mutilation
mystify
nationalism
negotiate
neuter
nicety
nil

ninny
nonchalant
nonpartisan
notation
nothingness
nuclear fission
null and void
nutriment
oaf
obligation

obtuse
octagonal
omen
onrush
onyx
opal
operatic
opinionated
oppressors
optics

oratory
organic
ornery
orthodox
ostracize
overproduction
pacify
palette
pallet
paprika

par
paramount
parasite
parch
parentage
parley
parliamentary
partition
passable
paternity

pearly
pedigree
pellet
perennial
perforated
petrified
pharmaceutical
philharmonic
philosophical
phosphorus

pious
poised
populous
predetermined
quadrangle
quaver
queasy
quest
quibble
quietude

quota
quotient
radius
rasp
receptacle
recognition
refinement
renegade
revival
rigamarole

rogue
roly poly
roundabout
rout
rustle
scandalize
sequential
shale
sheik
shoddy

simplicity
siphon
smug
snorkel
solder
sovereign
tactful
tapestry
teamster
tentative

theological
tier
titan
trestle
trousseau
turbulent
turmoil
twinge
tyrannous
unabridged

unapproachable
unbiased
uncorrupted
undeniable
undiminished
undistinguished
undoubtedly
upheaval
uproot
upstanding

valor
vanity
vastly
vault
vegetative
veneer
veranda
verifiable
vim
vivid

vocalize
vulgarism
wallflower
wallow
well-being
welterweight
wheeze
whim
wiretapping
wispy

woeful
wrathful
yachting
yearling
yeoman
yoke
zeal
zest
zoological
zoologist

PART

3 Reading

11 Reading Science Materials

Categories of Materials

Most books and articles about science fall into two categories. Some, written for an audience without extensive scientific training and background, are called *popular books* and *articles.* Gordon Rathay Taylor's *The Biological Time Bomb,* which explores some of the possible dangers in current biological research, or Maya Pine's *The Brain Changers: Scientists and the New Mind Control,* about the benefits and possible dangers in modern brain research, are examples of popular science books. Articles on science that appear in *Newsweek* and *Time* are also part of this category.

On the other hand, *textbooks* and *factual scientific articles,* which make up the second category, are written for readers who want to develop a more formal knowledge of science. You do not read your science textbook for a general idea or for entertainment but to learn about scientific processes, concepts and their relationships, scientific data, and vocabulary.

Knowing the kind of scientific material you are reading is important to decide *how* you will read. In this chapter you will learn more effective ways to read in the field of science.

Varying Reading Rates

The keys to more effective reading are (a) identifying your purpose before you begin reading and (b) selecting the rate of reading most effective for your purpose.

Four basic types, or rates, of reading are *light reading, scanning, skimming,* and *close reading.* In the next sections of this chapter, you will learn how to use each of these techniques to read science materials quickly, efficiently, and effectively.

Light Reading

Light reading is the relaxed method you use when you read for pleasure.

You might use this rate to read popular works on science when you do not have to remember specific details unless they particularly interest you.

Scanning

Scanning is the fastest type of reading.

In fact, scanning really is not reading at all but is looking over written material very quickly to locate a specific piece of information. For example, you use scanning when you check a telephone directory for a friend's number or when you look in the index of a book to locate the page on which a topic is discussed. Scanning saves time, provided you know what facts or details you are looking for.

Assume that you want to find the atomic weight of oxygen from the Atomic Diagrams and Data chart that appears on page 238.

Although there is much information in the chart, scanning the headings at the top of the chart shows that the information is listed under nine columns: *Element*, *Symbol*, *Atomic number*, *Diagram*, *Protons*, *Neutrons*, *Electrons*, *Mass number*, and *Atomic weight*. The hard and long method to answer the question "What is the atomic weight of oxygen?" would be to start searching all of the columns until you locate the information. An easier, more efficient method is to scan the *Element* column until you find *oxygen* and then look to the right for the information under the *Atomic weight* column. If you followed these instructions, you found that the atomic weight of oxygen is 16. You did not bother with other information about the element oxygen or other elements listed. Instead, you used scanning to locate only what you needed to know.

Scanning is also helpful in surveying new material to be read. You can scan to determine the headings of the chapter or selection, to find vocabulary words that are identified in *italicized* or **boldface** type, or to see if any experiments are suggested.

Activity 1

Scan the chart Atomic Diagrams and Data on page 238 and write the answers to the following questions on a separate sheet of paper.

1. What is the symbol for hydrogen?
2. What is the symbol for oxygen?
3. What is the symbol for magnesium?
4. What is the mass number of nitrogen?
5. What is the mass number of sodium?
6. How many neutrons does oxygen have?
7. How many protons does carbon have?
8. What is the mass number of carbon?

9. What is the mass number of chlorine?
10. What is the atomic weight of chlorine?

Skimming

Another type of reading, *skimming*, is even more helpful in becoming acquainted with new materials.

When you skim, you read quickly to get a general idea of content. You do not read to find out *all* there is to know about the life cycle of amphibians, for example. You want only general information, a sense of what the material is about. When you are doing research, you can skim books or articles to find

Atomic Diagrams and Data

Element	Symbol	Atomic number	Diagram	Protons	Neutrons	Electrons	Mass number	Atomic weight
Hydrogen	H	1		1	0	1	1	1
Carbon	C	6	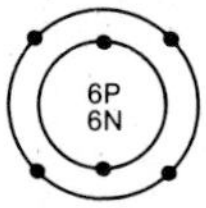	6	6	6	12	12
Nitrogen	N	7	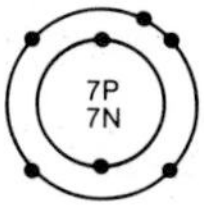	7	7	7	14	14
Oxygen	O	8	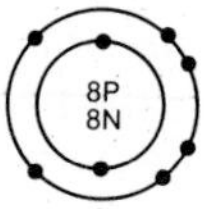	8	8	8	16	16
Sodium	Na	11	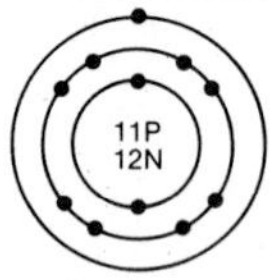	11	12	11	23	23
Magnesium	Mg	12	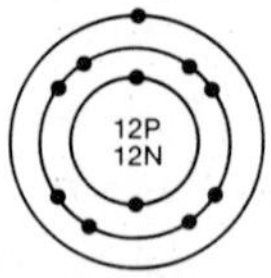	12	12	12	24	24
Chlorine	Cl	17	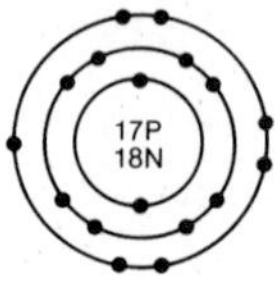	17	18	17	35	35.5

out if they discuss your topic. You can also use skimming to preview reading assignments in textbooks.

Activity 2

Practice skimming for a general idea of the following descriptions of books about science from *Books for You.* Try to discover the general idea of each book. Look for important ideas rather than reading each word. Then on a separate sheet of paper, write the letter of the statement that best describes the general idea of each book.[1]

Example

Dineley, David. **Earth's Voyage through Time** (© 1973). Knopf 1974.

A detailed survey of the planet on which we live, beginning with its birth 4.5 million years ago. This book considers many questions that have long puzzled scientists about the origin of earth and the changes it is constantly undergoing.

a. This book attempts to prove the earth is 4.5 million years old.
b. This book attempts to explain what will happen to the earth's animal population in the future.
c. This book attempts to look at questions about the origins of the earth.

(The answer is *c.*)

1. Evans, Howard Ensign. **Life on a Little Known Planet** (© 1968). Dell 1972.

   The little known planet is earth, but the life is the world of insects and their marvelous mechanisms for adaptation and survival.

   a. This book examines life on earth from an alien's point of view.
   b. This book is about insect control.
   c. This book is about how insects live, survive, and adapt.

2. Halacy, D. S., Jr. **The Weather Changers.** Har-Row 1968.

   Everybody talks about the weather, but this book shows what some people have been doing about it. Halacy describes efforts to induce rain, suppress hail and lightning, disperse fog, and modify hurricanes, as well as changes caused by air pollution.

   a. This book is about attempts to control the weather.
   b. This book is about hurricanes.
   c. This book is about rainmaking.

3. Hawkins, Gerald S. **Splendor in the Sky.** Har-Row 1969.

   A history of astronomy: how the Egyptians, Greeks, and Romans viewed the heavens; what discoveries of Copernicus, Kepler, and Newton

---

[1]From *Books for You*, Kenneth Donelson, Editor. Copyright © 1976 by the National Council of Teachers of English. Reprinted by permission of the publisher and the editor.

brought to our understanding of stars and planets; and what currently is of major interest to astronomers.

a. This book is about the famous astronomers Copernicus, Kepler, and Newton.
b. This book is about contemporary astronomers and their interests.
c. This book is a history of astronomy.

4. Jastrow, Robert. **Red Giants and White Dwarfs** (© 1969). NAL 1971.

The director of the Goddard Institute for Space Studies describes the nature of the universe, from the smallest subatomic particles to the grandest of galactic structures, pointing out along the way earth's place in this scheme.

a. This book is about the Goddard Institute of Space Studies.
b. This book describes the structure of the universe.
c. This book describes the earth.

5. Russell, Helen Ross. **Earth, the Great Recycler.** Nelson 1973.

Spaceship Earth is composed of a series of delicately balanced systems: water, energy, food, and the earth itself, which together comprise the ecosphere, the narrow band on the planet that supports life.

a. This book is about a manmade spaceship named *the Earth.*
b. This book compares earth with other planets.
c. This book is about the life support systems on earth.

Understanding Study Aids

Using skimming to preview a reading assignment in a textbook is often easy because textbook writers provide their readers with many *study aids.*

One of the first things you should do when you begin to work with an unfamiliar textbook is to identify the types of study aids used. These are often described in the introduction or in a special section on using the textbook. If the study aids are not explained, you can use your skimming and scanning skills to identify them and note how they are used. Understanding the study aids discussed in this section will help you learn more efficiently and more effectively.

1. *Headings*

Headings are generally used to identify the subject of a chapter or sections of a chapter. Headings may appear in ALL CAPITAL LETTERS, in **boldface type,** in different sizes of type, in colors, or in *italicized type.* Textbooks often use a combination of types of headings to show the relationships among the materials. Very often, in fact, you can understand the outline of a chapter by looking at the headings (major heading for main topics, subheadings for subtopics, and even smaller headings for supporting topics). You may want to outline a chapter from one of your textbooks by listing the headings. Noting the information on the different headings will help you identify the major concepts in a reading assignment.

2. *Marginal notes*

Marginal notes (notes printed in the margin to the left or the right of the page's main text) frequently identify important concepts, important vocabulary words with or without their definitions, or key questions to think about as you read the material *(purpose questions)*. It is a good idea to skim these notes as you preview the chapter. When you read the chapter carefully, you may or may not need to refer to them again.

3. *Footnotes*

Footnotes may appear at the bottom of the page or at the end of the chapter. Numbers or special marks printed immediately after a word in the text (*word*[1], *word*[2], *word*[+], or *word**) indicate there is a footnote about that material. A footnote provides one of the following: (a) additional information, (b) the source for information printed in the text, or (c) lists of sources that can be used to gain more information about a topic. Skimming footnotes as you survey the chapter will tell you how much attention you will need to give the footnotes later. For example, if the footnotes add information that will help you understand the ideas and concepts in the text, you will want to study them carefully in your close reading of the chapter. However, if the footnotes give sources of information or suggestions for further reading, you can glance over them quickly and come back after you have read the chapter.

4. *Visual aids*

Visual aids (charts, graphs, tables, illustrations, and photographs) help readers see something explained in the text or present information in a helpful form. For example, the chart on atomic weights on page 238 allows readers to locate information about the weight and structure of chemical elements quickly. It is a good idea to include the visual aids in your initial survey of the chapter because they give you a good idea of what you will be reading about and help you visualize some of the concepts or instruments you will study.

5. *Vocabulary Aids*

Vocabulary aids in textbooks identify and sometimes define important words. These important words may be printed in **boldface type**, or in *italics* or may be underlined or printed in color. Sometimes, important names of people, places, or difficult technical words are followed by a phonetic spelling that explains how the letters in the word should be pronounced.

> *metabolism* (me·tab′ə·lizm) or *nucleic* (no͞o·klē′·ik) *acid.*

Important key words may also be defined in footnotes or in the margins, or the definition may follow the word in the text: "In this chapter all members of the *subphylum Vertebrata* (fishes, amphibians, reptiles, birds, and mammals) will be discussed."

Understanding and using the study aids in your science book will make your reading easier and more effective. Unfortunately most unskilled readers do not take advantage of study aids. Notice the wealth of information provided by the study aids in the following material from the textbook *Life: Its Forms and Changes.*

Activity 3

Using the sample pages from *Life: Its Forms and Changes,* write out your answers to the following questions in complete sentences on a sheet of notebook paper.

1. What is the subject heading on Sample page 162?

162

Subject heading (all capitals)

2. ORGANIC COMPOUNDS IN PROTOPLASM

Now let's look at some of the organic compounds more closely. Let's try to understand how protoplasm is able to make some of these compounds.

We will begin with a simple investigation into an organic compound with which you are familiar—albumen, a protein. Albumen is fairly easy to get if you can get the white of an egg. You may have already used it to make a model of protoplasm.

Suppose you were to take the white of an egg and place a bit of it in boiling water. It becomes solid. You know this solid as the white of an egg.

This simple investigation is of the utmost importance. It teaches us the effect of heat on some substances in protoplasm. Can you change the egg white back as it was before you placed it in the boiling water? No, you cannot. Can a baby chicken hatch from a fertilized egg that has been boiled? No, it cannot. Boiling somehow kills protoplasm.

The point to remember, then, is that the activities of protoplasm take place at a temperature lower than boiling—lower than most chemical reactions in a laboratory. For instance, your body is maintained at a temperature of 98.6°F (37°C).*

Parenthetical expression containing additional information

Footnote indicator

How is it that cells (that is, the protoplasm of cells) carry out their activities at temperatures lower than the temperatures in the test tube of the chemist?

You may already be familiar with enzymes. However, if you are not, try this investigation for yourself. ■

Symbol referring to suggested activity (experiment)

Protoplasm, then, is able to carry on its life activities because of one kind of organic substance, *enzymes.* You have already studied one type of enzyme, the digestive enzyme diastase. Recall that you also studied the digestive function of saliva (which has a kind of starch-splitting enzyme in it). But the enzymes in protoplasm do a wide variety of things, as you will see. Some enzymes *synthesize* (build up) many complex organic compounds, while other enzymes break them down.

Italicized word and definition

Enzymes are necessary in the synthesis of the important organic compounds found in protoplasm—the familiar compounds we mentioned before: carbohydrates, fats, proteins, and nucleic acids.

Let's examine the class of organic compounds known as carbohydrates.

Carbohydrates — Subheading

Suppose you took some potato starch, corn starch, and a piece of bread and added a drop of a very weak iodine solution to each. Each would turn a blue-black color. This is a well-known test for starches. You are already familiar with the test for sugar that uses Benedict's solution.

Sugars, starches, and woody materials, such as cellulose, are some of the common carbohydrates.

As you may know, there are a number of different sugars. The kind of sugar you eat at the table is called *sucrose.* Most sugar that we buy is sucrose and much of it comes from sugar cane plants. In fact, we often call it cane sugar. Sugar beets produce sucrose, too, and quite a bit of sugar sold in stores is beet sugar. You might find it interesting to read the labels of sugar sacks at a grocery store to discover whether the sugar is cane sugar or beet sugar. The chances are that you will find both kinds for sale. There is really no difference between cane sugar and beet sugar. Both are pure sucrose.

Footnote — * 212°F (or 100°C) is the boiling point of water.

2. Using the subject heading and subheading on page 162, answer the following question: Are carbohydrates organic compounds?
3. What three important vocabulary words appear on Sample page 162?
4. How is your attention called to these words?
5. Is the footnote reference on page 162 a number or a symbol?
6. What information is given in the footnote?
7. What is the title given to the activity (experiment) suggested on page 163?

163

■ AN APPRENTICE INVESTIGATION into the Action of Enzymes

Take six test tubes and place in each one about 1 teaspoon of a 1 percent starch solution. Into two of the tubes add about ½ teaspoon of saliva. Into two others, add a pinch of ***diastase*** (dī′ə·stāz), an enzyme that breaks down starch. Leave the last two test tubes with only the starch solution.❶

Phonetic spelling

Place all the tubes in warm (not hot) water for about five minutes. Then add to each tube about ½ teaspoon of Benedict's solution. Now place all the tubes in a beaker of hot water.❷ You can keep the water hot by placing the beaker on an electric hot plate, but do not boil it. Why? What results do you find?❸

Reference to visual aid

As you have seen, the tubes containing diastase and saliva became green to orange-red. This color change shows that sugar is present. Benedict's solution, as you may know, is changed from blue to green or orange-red in the presence of sugar. Hence the diastase and the saliva both changed the starch to sugar. Saliva contains an enzyme that acts much like diastase. Why are the other two tubes still blue?

An Investigation On Your Own

The enzyme ***urease*** (yo͝or′ē·āz) functions to break up urea, a waste substance produced by cells, into ammonia and carbon dioxide. You can test for the presence of ammonia by using the indicator phenolphthalein (fē′nōl·thāl′ēn). Three or four drops of a 1 percent solution of phenolphthalein in alcohol turn a solution containing ammonia a pink color.

Determine first how fast urease acts. Can you slow down the action of urease?

Be certain to include a careful control experiment in your design of experimental procedure. How will you measure the slowing action of the enzyme?

❶

❷

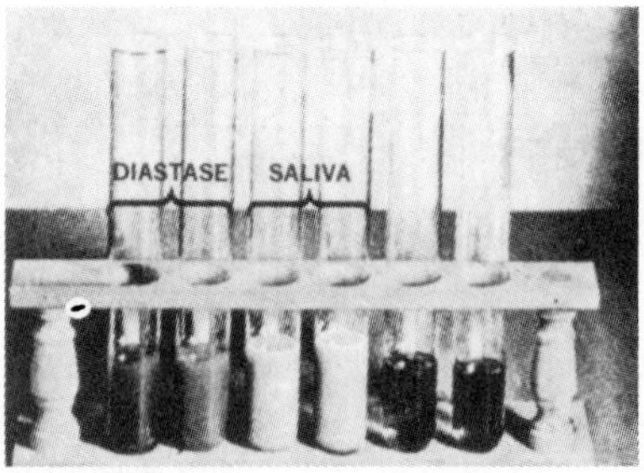

❸

8. The phonetic spellings for three words are given on Sample page 163. What are the words?
9. What do the circled numbers on Sample page 163 refer you to?
10. Using the information in the text and in the footnote, answer the following question: Is your body temperature above or below the boiling point of water? Indicate the number of degrees above or below.

Activity 4
Choose one chapter in your science textbook and identify five kinds of study aids used in that chapter. On a sheet of paper, list each kind of study aid and write an example of it. Your teacher may ask you to read and explain your list in class.

Close Reading

The purpose of *close*, or *study*, *reading* is to remember and understand major ideas, details, and the relationships between the two.

Close reading of science materials requires precision in (a) following directions; (b) identifying details or characteristics, such as size, shape, number, color, function, location, body parts, and structure; (c) comparing and contrasting characteristics, structures, or concepts; (d) identifying and understanding causes and effects; and (e) seeing relationships and their significance in order to draw conclusions from given data.

Close reading involves giving careful attention to individual sentences, to main ideas, and to the relationships between the individual sentences in a passage and main idea. Understanding the methods by which the writer organizes information and the patterns of writing he or she uses will make close reading easier. In the following sections you will study commonly used methods of organization and patterns of writing.

Identifying Inductive and Deductive Organization

Scientific writing is organized either *deductively* or *inductively*.

Writing organized *deductively* begins with the main idea and supports it with evidence or data. In the following passage, organized deductively, the reader locates the main idea at the beginning and then reads on to see what evidence or data is used to support that idea. Notice how the details in the passage from the textbook *Biology* support the main idea: "It is his brain that gives man his unique place in the animal kingdom."[1]

> It is his brain that gives man his unique place in the animal kingdom. Basically, man's brain possesses the essentials of any brain, but some of the essential parts are developed to a higher degree. In man the brain is made up of a large number of nerve cells—more than 15 billion. Each nerve cell carries

[1]From *Biology* by Smallwood and Green. Copyright © 1968 by the Silver Burdett Company. Reprinted by permission of the publisher.

> information of only a simple type. Mixing, or associative, areas must be provided, where incoming information can converge and be assorted. The human brain has large areas that are used for this purpose. Finally, there is a constant feedback from every new incident to every incident that has been before, and vice versa.

If the main idea appears at the end of the passage or does not appear at all and must be interpreted, the passage is organized *inductively*. When the main idea is unstated, you have to infer or decide for yourself what the main idea is. You identify the details being related about the topic and then interpret the relationship between them to determine the main idea.

The following passage from the textbook *Biological Science: An Inquiry Into Life* is organized inductively; therefore, the reader must work toward the main idea that is not stated until the end of the paragraph.[1]

> The chromosomes are in pairs; genes are in pairs. The chromosome pairs separate during meiosis; the gene pairs separate during meiosis. The chromosome pairs are formed again at fertilization; the gene pairs are formed again at fertilization. These parallels in behavior are too remarkable to be merely a coincidence. At least so thought a young graduate student, Walter S. Sutton, in 1902. He proposed the hypothesis that the genes are parts of chromosomes.

If a passage is organized inductively, you must collect the data, even if you are not certain why, until you get to the main idea. In other words, you have to remember details and sometimes concepts, until you find out how they fit together.

Some writers use the inductive pattern extensively, while other writers rely on the deductive pattern. In most scientific materials, however, you will find both patterns, and you will read more successfully if you identify the patterns and know how to deal with them.

Activity 5

Read each of the following passages. On a sheet of paper, identify each passage as having *deductive* or *inductive* organization. To complete this activity successfully you must first identify the main idea in each paragraph.[2]

1. Scientists now believe the process of photosynthesis occurs in two main steps. One of these steps can occur in the dark, and thus is known as the **dark reaction** and the other, called the **light reaction,** can occur *only* in the light. It was believed not long ago that the dark reaction could occur only in the dark, but it is now known that this reaction also occurs in the light.

   (From *Life: Its Forms and Changes*)

---

[1]From page 648 in *Biological Science: An Inquiry Into Life*, Third Edition by John A. Moore et al. Published by Harcourt Brace Jovanovich, Inc., 1973. Reprinted by permission of the Biological Sciences Curriculum Study (BSCS).

[2]From *Life: Its Forms and Changes*, Second Edition by Paul F. Brandwein et al. Copyright © 1972 by Harcourt Brace Jovanovich, Inc. Reprinted by permission of the publisher.

2. What happens when sugar or salt dissolves in water? Each of these white solids disappears, but if you taste the solution you know the sugar or salt is still present. If you have ever let salt water in a pan "boil away," you know that the salt remains behind on the bottom of the pan. Or if you have ever left a sugar solution, for example, a glass of iced tea containing a great deal of sugar, exposed to the air, you may have observed that the water evaporates and leaves the solid behind.

   If you had determined the amount of salt or sugar you added to the water, and determined it again after the water evaporated, what would you have found? (Why not try this at home?) The amount of salt or sugar left after evaporation is the same as the amount you started with. Dissolving and evaporating neither creates nor destroys matter; the Law of Conservation of Mass is confirmed once again.[1]

   (From *Energy: Its Forms and Changes*)

3. Stems of plants conduct materials from leaves to roots, and vice versa. Two kinds of materials are transported. One is water plus dissolved mineral salts, taken in by the roots. The other is sugars, formed in leaves and other photosynthetic cells. Usually the water and salts are transported in an upward direction from the roots, through the stem, and into the leaves. In the summer the soluble sugars pass in the opposite direction. Early in the spring, however, food that has been stored in the roots and stem begins to move upward. In the case of sugar maples, we say, "The sap is rising," and start to tap the trees to make maple sugar.[2]

   (From *Biological Science: An Inquiry Into Life*)

4. *When matter undergoes chemical change, the total amount of matter remains unchanged.* As we have examined the quantities of matter, the weights (or masses) of elements and compounds involved in chemical reactions, we have developed further this basic concept of chemical change, sometimes called the Law of Conservation of Matter. Within the limits of the chemist's ability to measure weights of reacting substances, this holds true for all chemical changes: There is no loss or gain of weight during any chemical reaction. In the reaction that takes place between hydrogen and oxygen to form water, for example, the sum of the equation weights of the reactants is equal to the equation weight of the product.[3]

   (From *Matter: Its Forms and Changes*)

---

[1]From *Energy: Its Forms and Changes* by Paul F. Brandwein et al. Reprinted by permission of Harcourt Brace Jovanovich, Inc.

[2]From page 369 in *Biological Science: An Inquiry Into Life,* Third Edition by John A. Moore et al. Published by Harcourt Brace Jovanovich, Inc., 1973. Reprinted by permission of the Biological Sciences Curriculum Study (BSCS).

[3]From *Matter: Its Forms and Changes,* Second Edition by Paul F. Brandwein et al. Copyright © 1972 by Harcourt Brace Jovanovich, Inc. Reprinted by permission of the publisher.

5. When you dipped a pencil in water, it was wet when you removed it. Some of the water molecules *adhere* to the molecules of the wood. Pour some water into a narrow test tube. Look closely at the points where the water touches the glass. There is an attractive force between water molecules and the molecules of the glass. This attraction causes the surface of the water in a jar or tube to curve upward where it meets the glass. If the tube is thin enough, the water actually rises in the tube. This is called **capillary action.** The word *capillary* means "hairlike" and refers to the thinness of the tube. Capillary action does not occur only in tubes. It occurs whenever two surfaces to which water molecules adhere are close enough together.[1]

(From *Energy: Its Forms and Changes*)

Patterns of Writing

The major patterns used in scientific writing are *comparison and contrast, cause and effect, sequential order,* and *explanation and description.* Often more than one pattern will be used in a chapter or passage. Identifying the pattern the writer uses and knowing how to read material using each pattern will make close study of science textbooks easier.

The *comparison-and-contrast pattern* concentrates on the similarities and differences between two objects or processes.

In *comparison and contrast* the reader must identify the items being compared and determine the points, or characteristics, used in making the comparison. Finally the reader must identify and keep straight the similarities and differences of each item. Writers often use *structure words* such as *but, however,* and *on the other hand* to contrast items. Structure words such as *like, and, also,* and *similarly* are used to point out similarities.

The *cause-and-effect pattern* shows how one or more causes lead to, or result in, a specific effect.

If a passage is organized *deductively,* however, the effect may be stated at the beginning (as the main idea) and be followed by the causes. In cause-and-effect passages the reader should concentrate on understanding the relationship between cause and effect. Sometimes, the reader may be expected to hypothesize—that is, use the given data in a passage to draw a conclusion about a cause or an effect that is not stated in the text. Cause-and-effect passages often contain structure words such as *consequently, as a result, because,* or *in consequence.*

Sequential order presents a series of steps or events in the order they occur or should be carried out.

An experiment, for example, is usually presented in sequential order. In this pattern the reader should concentrate on identifying each step and on understanding how the steps follow one another. Structure words such as

---

[1]From *Energy: Its Forms and Changes* by Paul F. Brandwein et al. Reprinted by permission of Harcourt Brace Jovanovich, Inc.

first, second, next, before, after, and *finally* are common in passages of sequential order.

Explanation and description, the last pattern of writing, incorporates sentences that combine the other patterns.

Reading explanation and description involves identifying the topic (what is being explained or described), the kind of details, and the relationships between the details and the main idea. Such passages may explain why, when, or how something happens, what something looks like, how it functions, or what it is made up of.

Understanding Scientific Vocabulary

One of the characteristics of scientific writing is the use of specialized, technical *scientific vocabulary* or terminology. Understanding the scientific vocabulary you encounter in your close reading of an assignment is important. If you skip terms, phrases, or names that have special meanings or that refer to scientific processes, you may not understand the passage at all or you may misinterpret the main idea.

Remember that important words are often defined in footnotes or marginal notes. More and more textbooks are including definitions in context and using color-coding and *italicizing* to highlight vocabulary words. In your close reading of scientific materials, remember what you know about using a word's structure and its context to get meaning. When you skim a chapter, notice what words are identified as important and become familiar with them so that you will understand them more fully when you study the chapter. Finally keep a small dictionary beside you and look up unfamiliar words as you read.

Activity 6

All of the following passages are from the textbook *Life: Its Forms and Changes.* Use the close-reading skills you have studied as you read each selection. On a sheet of notebook paper, write answers to the questions after each selection.[1]

Examples

Water is important to all living organisms, since it is the solvent that dissolves the many substances that living protoplasm needs.

a. What is important to all living organisms?
a. Water is important to all living organisms.
[*This statement should also lead you to ask* how or why *water is important.*]

b. What function or purpose does it serve?
b. Water functions as a solvent, dissolving the substances taken in by protoplasm.

---

[1]From *Life: Its Forms and Changes,* Second Edition by Paul F. Brandwein et al. Copyright © 1972 by Harcourt Brace Jovanovich, Inc. Reprinted by permission of the publisher.

c. What structure or key word tells you that the reason for water's importance is given?

c. The word since *answers the question* why? *and indicates that a reason will follow.*

1. As you shall see, many of the substances needed for life could not be used by the cell if they were not dissolved in water.

   a. The pronoun *they* in the sentence refers to what?
   b. What is a requirement for many substances to be used by a cell?
   c. According to the sentence, are you beginning or ending a discussion of the topic?

2. Recall that digestive enzymes secreted by cells break down food substances so that they are fit for absorption by the body.

   a. What word tells you that the material has been discussed before?
   b. What secretes digestive enzymes?
   c. What function or purpose do these digestive enzymes serve?

3. Proteins differ in function as much as they do in composition and structure.

   a. In what three ways do protein molecules differ?

4. Because of the water loss, the plants quickly wilt and probably will die.

   a. What is the effect of water loss on the plants?
   b. What structure word tells you that the sentence is a cause-and-effect sentence?
   c. Rewrite the sentence putting the cause after the effect.

5. All living membranes seem to be able to regulate their permeability **(pûr′mē·ə·bil′ə·tē)** to some extent. By permeability we mean the quality of membranes that allows substances to diffuse through them.

   a. What characteristic do all living membranes appear or seem to have in common.
   b. What does the word *regulate* mean?
   c. Can all living membranes regulate their permeability completely?
   d. What is the definition of *permeability?*

6. As you can see, then, bacteria can cause disease or illness in two ways: they produce poisonous or toxic waste materials, and they actually digest and destroy living tissues.

   a. What is the topic of the sentence (the thing being discussed)?
   b. What effect(s) can bacteria have according to the sentence?
   c. What are the two ways that bacteria cause disease or illness?

7. There is another characteristic, other than jointed legs, that distinguishes the arthropods from other invertebrates. All arthropods have a kind of skeleton, but it is an outside skeleton, or exoskeleton. An arthropod's exoskeleton forms a tough, jointed suit of armor.

   a. What is the topic being discussed?

b. What are two characteristics of arthropods that make them different from other invertebrates?
c. Where is the arthropod's skeleton?
d. Are arthropods invertebrates? What word told you this?

8. Many mushrooms are good to eat, *but some are deadly*. One mushroom, the Amanita **(am'ə·nī'tə)**, looks very much like an edible mushroom, but its poison is almost certain to cause death if it is eaten. There is no known remedy for its poison. *Never pick mushrooms and eat them.* Buy them in the grocery store.
   a. Are all mushrooms good to eat?
   b. What structure word in the first sentence tells you that two things are being contrasted?
   c. What is the name of a mushroom you should not eat?
   d. What does *edible* mean?
   e. What is the effect of eating Amanita?
   f. Is there a remedy?
   g. Is it a good idea to pick mushrooms and eat them?

9. Suppose there were no decay-producing bacteria or fungi. What would be the result?
   a. What characteristic of bacteria or fungi does the sentence discuss?
   b. The two sentences ask you to hypothesize from what you have read. Have they given you a cause and asked you to hypothesize an effect, or have they given you an effect and asked you to hypothesize a cause?

10. Although penicillin and most other antibiotics are made from molds, some are made from bacteria. *Streptomycin* and *chloromycetin* are both obtained from bacteria.
   a. What is penicillin made from?
   b. Are all antibiotics made from molds?
   c. What are streptomycin and chloromycetin?
   d. What do streptomycin and chloromycetin come from?

11. Below 800 feet in the ocean there is generally no variation at all in the temperature in winter and summer. In the shallow tidal pools, however, the water temperature varies greatly because of contact with the air above it. How well do you think a fish accustomed to living 800 feet below the surface would do if you forced it to live in a tidal pool? Why? (Ignore pressure differences in answering this question.)
   a. What is the difference between ocean water at 800 feet and ocean water in shallow tidal pools?
   b. What comparison-and-contrast word was used in the second sentence to indicate the contrast?

c. What causes the temperature of the shallow water to vary?
d. What cause-and-effect word was used to indicate the relationship?
e. The last sentence asks you to hypothesize a result or an effect—what would happen to the fish? What is the cause or circumstance that would lead to this result?

12. You may thus recognize a species of maple by its characteristic leaves. Of course, each tree has other specific characteristics: buds, bark, and types of branching, among others.

a. What kind of tree is identified in the sentences?
b. What characteristic can be used to tell the different species of maple apart?
c. Leaves are used to study trees. What are three other characteristics that are studied?

13. Fats, like carbohydrates, are made of atoms of carbon, hydrogen, and oxygen. However, the atoms are arranged differently.

a. What two things are being compared?
b. How are they alike?
c. How are they different?
d. What comparison word is used? What contrast word is used?

14. Mitotic division of chromosomes always results in daughter cells with chromosomes identical in both number and kind to each other and to the parent cell.

a. What kind of division of chromosomes is being discussed?
b. How do the original, or parent, cell and the resulting daughter cells (new cells) compare?
c. In what two ways are the chromosomes of parent and daughter cell alike?

15. There are twenty-six letters in our alphabet. By arranging these letters in different ways, we form all the thousands upon thousands of different words by which we communicate with each other. Change one letter in the word *house* and you get something totally different: *mouse.* By changing the order of letters, you change *pin* to *nip; last* to *salt* to *slat,* and so on with many other words. The numbers of ideas and thoughts that can be developed simply by changing the number, order, and position of twenty-six letters is really amazing.

It is even more amazing that all of the thousands upon thousands of proteins, each greatly different from the others, are made up of only twenty-four or so **amino (ə·mēn′nō) acids** that can be compared to the letters of our alphabet. These amino acids are the building blocks from which proteins are made, just as the letters of our alphabet are the building blocks from which all words are made.

a. What point does the first paragraph make about the letters of our alphabet?
b. What in the second paragraph is compared to the letters of our alphabet?
c. How many amino acids are there?
d. What do various amino acids combine to form?
e. How many proteins are there?
f. The writer used an example of something you know about to describe something you are just learning about. Why is this a helpful technique?

PART

4 Sentence Combining

12 Joining Sentences

Achieving Sentence Variety

As you read the following paragraph, think about how you might make changes to improve it.

> The custodian pushed his mop down the hall. The hall was dirty. The hall had been neglected for months. The custodian was working nights. The custodian was paying for his daughter's schooling. He wanted his daughter to have a bright future. The mop moved slowly. It moved carefully. It covered every crack in the floor. It left a gleaming trail behind.

Although there are no errors in the paragraph, the writing seems immature. Each sentence is isolated from the others; there is no flow from one sentence into the next.

If you were to rewrite the paragraph by combining some of the sentences, you might produce the following paragraph.

> The custodian pushed his mop down the dirty hall, which had been neglected for months. He was working nights to pay for his daughter's schooling, because he wanted her to have a bright future. Slowly, carefully, the mop moved, covering every crack in the floor, leaving a gleaming trail behind.

Joining sentences or parts of sentences together shows how ideas relate to each other, gives the paragraph a smoothness and fluency it did not have originally, and makes the paragraph more interesting for readers.

In this chapter and the following one, you will learn ways to write more-interesting sentences, using a method called *sentence combining.* In the sentence-combining exercises you will use a model, or pattern, to combine two or more sentences. You will also complete some "free" exercises that allow you to use your own patterns and combinations. If you are unfamiliar with any of the grammatical terms used in this chapter, refer to the definitions in the "Using Grammar" part of this book.

Joining Sentences with Sentences

Several words in the English language may be used to make effective connections between sentences. The first group of *connectors* joins two statements of equal importance by indicating a relationship between the two:

and connects two similar ideas
but connects opposing ideas
for provides a reason
nor indicates a negative
or indicates a choice
so shows a cause and its effect
yet connects opposing ideas

Note: The grammatical term for these connectors is *coordinating conjunctions.*

The following models show how connectors are used to combine two sentences into one. The word in parentheses, called a *signal*, indicates which connector to use. Unless the two combined sentences are very brief and closely related, a comma precedes the connector.

Sentences:	Maria repaired the broken fence. I washed the grimy storm windows. (AND)
Combined:	Maria repaired the broken fence**,** *and* I washed the grimy storm windows.
Sentences:	Jennifer didn't boast when she succeeded. She didn't cry when she failed. (NOR)
Combined:	Jennifer didn't boast when she succeeded**,** *nor* did she cry when she failed.

Notice that *nor* follows the same pattern as other connectors but causes a change in word order. In addition, the word *not* (in the form of the contraction *n't*) is removed from the second sentence because *nor* already indicates a negative.

Exercise 1

The following sentences can be combined with one of the sentence connectors in the previous section. In the first five sentences you are given a signal in the form of a connecting word in parentheses; for the last five sentences choose the connector you think makes the most sense. Study the examples first and then write out each newly combined sentence on a sheet of paper.

Examples

a. The teens have organized a campaign to save the big oak.
It is the oldest tree in La Salle County. (FOR)

a. The teens have organized a campaign to save the big oak, for it is the oldest tree in La Salle County.

b. Anna didn't want to go biking Sunday.
She didn't want to stay home. (NOR)

b. Anna didn't want to go biking Sunday, nor did she want to stay home.

1. Do you want to go out Saturday evening?
Do you already have plans? (OR)

2. Ryan was injured in yesterday's soccer tournament.
He will be unable to attend tonight's rehearsal. (SO)

3. Mrs. Romero was confined to a wheelchair for six months.
She never missed a day of work. (YET)

4. A month ago Anita stopped eating rich desserts.
She has lost six pounds. (AND)

5. Dad always helps with the housework.
My mother is working full time. (FOR)

A list of connectors is on page 255.

6. Saturday's picnic was canceled because of the heavy rain.
We have rescheduled it for next Sunday afternoon.

7. Mrs. Alvarez works at the lumberyard.
On Saturday she serves as a volunteer at the art center.

8. My brother loves to cook.
I would rather help with yardwork.

9. I had to leave early for an appointment.
I missed the lecture on African art.

10. My great-aunt grows all her own vegetables.
She freezes half of what she raises.

Connecting Closely Related Sentences

When two sentences of equal importance are also closely related in thought, they can be combined with a semicolon. The signal (**;**) indicates that two related sentences can be combined in this way.

Sentences:	Monday we visited your cousin in the country. Tuesday we went to a folk concert in Adams Park. (;)
Combined:	Monday we visited your cousin in the country**;** Tuesday we went to a folk concert in Adams Park.
Sentences:	Anita has already finished writing her science report. She plans to type it tonight after school. (;)
Combined:	Anita has already finished writing her science report**;** she plans to type it tonight after school.

Exercise 2

Combine each of the following sets of sentences into a single sentence. Since the sentences lack signals, decide whether to use a connector and a comma, or a semicolon. (Some sentences can be combined in more than one way.) Study the example before you write your new sentences out on a sheet of notebook paper.

Example

a. Mr. Ortiz leaves for the hospital at 5 every morning.
He doesn't mind getting up that early.

a. Mr. Ortiz leaves for the hospital at 5 every morning, but he doesn't mind getting up that early.

or

Mr. Ortiz leaves for the hospital at 5 every morning; he doesn't mind getting up that early.

1. Granville I. Hicks was an electrical genius.
He applied for over thirty-five different patents.
2. Carlotta saves almost all the money she earns at the gas station.
She plans to study at the university next year.
3. Leon doesn't like his new red sweater.
He doesn't like the red plaid tie that matches it.
4. My grandmother can't afford calling us very often.
She writes my brother and me a long letter every week.
5. Our new neighbors are very friendly.
My little brother is still too shy to speak to them.
6. Mr. Chang is a salesman for a furniture company.
Mrs. Chang is a dental hygienist.
7. My sister and her husband have a four-year-old daughter.
They plan to adopt another child within the next four months.
8. Please lend me that novel you were reading.
I'll return it within a week.
9. Commuting to the university involves a two-hour trip.
Juanita has learned to study on the bus.
10. Very few people could attend the meeting on Thursday.
It was rescheduled for a week from Monday.

Using Paired Connectors

Paired connectors can also be used to make a connection between two sentences of equal importance. *Either* ... *or* indicates a choice between alternatives. *Not only* ... *but also* indicates an additional idea in the second sentence. When sentences are combined with paired connectors, a comma precedes the second connector.

Sentences:	Clean your room now. Set aside time on Saturday morning to clean it. (EITHER . . . OR)
Combined:	*Either* clean your room now, *or* set aside time on Saturday morning to clean it.
Sentences:	My grandmother refinished her dining room chairs. She caned the seats on the chairs. (NOT ONLY . . . BUT ALSO)

Combined: *Not only* did my grandmother refinish her dining room chairs, *but* she *also* caned the seats on the chairs.

Note: The grammatical term for these paired connectors is *correlative conjunctions.*

Sometimes, you will want to change the word order of sentences when you combine them with paired connectors. For example, in the preceding example, *refinished* was changed to *did refinish.* Word order in sentences combined with *either . . . or* may also change slightly.

Sentences: You can write your report in longhand.
You can double-space your typing. (EITHER . . . OR)

Combined: You can *either* write your report in longhand, *or* you can doublespace your typing.

Exercise 3

After studying the example, combine the following sets of sentences, using paired connectors. Write each newly combined sentence on a sheet of paper. (Remember to insert a comma before the second connector.)

Example

a. We must learn to use less of our energy resources.
We must explore safe, new energy sources. (NOT ONLY . . . BUT ALSO)

a. Not only must we learn to use less of our energy resources, but we must also explore safe, new energy sources.

1. This class teaches us to create new ideas.
It teaches us how to express our ideas effectively. (NOT ONLY . . . BUT ALSO)
2. Sam should turn down that noisy stereo.
He should save his money for a set of earphones. (EITHER . . . OR)
3. Keeping your school free from litter does promote an attractive environment.
It saves the school a great deal of money. (NOT ONLY . . . BUT ALSO)
4. We toured the city fire department.
We watched a demonstration of rescue techniques by city fire fighters. (NOT ONLY . . . BUT ALSO)
5. You can study cardiopulmonary resuscitation in health class.
You can take a one-day course about it from the Red Cross. (EITHER . . . OR)

Using Adverb Connectors

Some *adverbs* can also be used to connect sentences of equal importance. Adverb connectors such as those in the following list indicate special kinds of relationships between two sentences. When an adverb connector is used, a semicolon separates the connected sentences, and a comma follows the adverb connector.

however *instead* *nevertheless* *on the other hand*	connect opposites
consequently *hence* *therefore* *thus*	suggest a conclusion is being made
besides *furthermore* *in addition* *moreover*	signal that an additional point is being made
indeed *in fact*	give emphasis to the writer's ideas

Sentences: Many Americans are working hard to conserve energy.
Our country still faces a critical shortage of energy resources. (NEVERTHELESS)

Combined: Many Americans are working hard to conserve energy**;** *nevertheless***,** our country still faces a critical shortage of energy resources.

Sentences: Langston Hughes is noted both for his poetry and his fiction.
His book *Not Without Laughter* is an outstanding novel about a teenage boy. (IN FACT)

Combined: Langston Hughes is noted both for his poetry and his fiction**;** *in fact***,** his book *Not Without Laughter* is an outstanding novel about a teenage boy.

Exercise 4

Use an adverb connector to write a combined sentence from each of the following pairs of sentences. When a signal is not given, choose the connecting adverb that makes the most sense. Study the examples carefully before you begin, noticing the punctuation before and after the connecting adverb.

Examples

a. The banks were closed.
Tanya couldn't deposit her check. (THEREFORE)
a. The banks were closed; therefore, Tanya couldn't deposit her check.

b. If you want to borrow the car to go to the library, you may.
Be sure to drive safely and watch the icy roads. (HOWEVER)
b. If you want to borrow the car to go to the library, you may; however, be sure to drive safely and watch the icy roads.

1. Kim wrote the best essay in the class.
She was awarded a certificate of achievement. (CONSEQUENTLY)

2. Ms. Espinosa did not think her client was well enough to testify.
   The evidence was clearly in their favor without his testimony. (BESIDES)
3. Carl was severely reprimanded for his misbehavior.
   All privileges and freedoms were taken away from him for a month. (IN FACT)
4. I left home early this morning.
   I was caught in traffic and missed my appointment. (HOWEVER)
5. Michael likes to read and write short stories.
   He enjoys teaching others to write. (FURTHERMORE)
6. Kim's father is concerned about energy conservation.
   He bought a car that averages thirty-five miles per gallon of gas.
7. Your idea sounds fabulous to me.
   Others may not be so enthusiastic.
8. Joey Montez has a hearing impairment.
   He is one of the top students in the class.
9. The school officials wanted to schedule homeroom in the morning hours.
   They decided on the afternoon.
10. A smoke detector is an essential safety device in the home.
    Having some type of burglar alarm is also a good idea.

Connecting Sentences of Unequal Importance

To combine a major statement with one of lesser importance, connecting words called *subordinators* may be used. Subordinators such as those in the following list link a lesser statement to a major statement by indicating the relationship between the two.

after	before	whenever
although	even though	where
as if	just as	wherever
as long as	just when	whether
as soon as	since	while
as though	so that	unless
because	when	until

Note: The grammatical term for the subordinators is *subordinating conjunctions.*

Subordinate clauses are discussed on pages 524–540.

When a subordinator is placed in front of a statement, the resulting string of words cannot stand alone as a separate sentence; it becomes dependent on the major statement. For example, when the subordinator *because* is added to the statement *She was a star athlete,* a new structure called a *subordinate clause* is created. This clause cannot stand alone but is dependent on another sentence:

Sentences:	Several scholarships were available to Elena. She was a star athlete. (BECAUSE)
Combined:	Several scholarships were available to Elena *because* she was a star athlete.

Subordinate clauses do not always follow the sentence to which they are attached. In the following example the subordinate clause (a subordinator and statement) appears at the beginning of a combined sentence. A subordinate clause at the beginning of a sentence is usually separated from the rest of the sentence by a comma. A subordinate clause at the end of a sentence usually does not require a comma.

Sentences:	You scrape the old paint off the porch railing. (IF) The new paint will be less likely to chip.
Combined:	*If* you scrape the old paint off the porch railing**,** the new paint will be less likely to chip.
Sentences:	Daniel vacuumed the living room this morning. He left for the basketball game. (BEFORE)
Combined:	Daniel vacuumed the living room this morning *before* he left for the basketball game.

Exercise 5

On a sheet of paper, combine the following pairs of sentences by using subordinators. In the examples the signals appear at the end of the sentence that you are to make into the subordinate clause. When you combine the sentences, however, place the subordinator at the beginning of the clause. When no signal is given, choose the subordinator you think works best. (The sentences without signals can be written in more than one way.)

Examples

a. Jason walked into the room. (AS SOON AS)
Everyone shouted "Happy birthday!"

a. As soon as Jason walked into the room, everyone shouted "Happy birthday!"

b. The survivors huddled together in the center of the lifeboat.
They feared a shark attack.

b. The survivors huddled together in the center of the lifeboat because they feared a shark attack.

or

Because they feared a shark attack, the survivors huddled together in the center of the lifeboat.

1. The night guards heard a suspicious noise. (WHEN)
They checked the grounds for intruders.
2. This mystery won't be solved.
Detective Columbo arrives. (UNTIL)
3. You will be sure to receive a good grade in this class.
You do your best work. (IF)

A list of subordinators is on page 260.

4. Plants grow best in fresh air outdoors. (EVEN THOUGH)
   Many can be grown quite successfully indoors if given good care.
5. I am afraid of heights. (ALTHOUGH)
   I will climb the ladder to fix the swag lamp.
6. Maria Santos is the best candidate for the office.
   She will probably win the election.
7. Michelle tells an unexpected joke.
   The class breaks out in laughter.
8. Mr. Ramirez typed the letter and left it for Ms. Parkins' approval.
   He left the office.
9. Max was a mere six years old.
   He first learned to ice-skate.
10. Ms. Conkle tutored her child every other evening.
    His reading would improve.

Review Exercise A

This exercise is a paragraph practice, covering the combining signals you have studied. Follow the signals and combine the sentences in the order in which they appear. Study the examples before you begin and then write out your sentences as a paragraph.

Examples

a. Lucy Terry was kidnaped from Africa.
   She was still a young child. (WHEN)

a. Lucy Terry was kidnaped from Africa when she was still a young child.

b. She was sold into slavery. (AFTER)
   She spent the rest of her youth in Deerfield, Massachusetts.

b. After she was sold into slavery, she spent the rest of her youth in Deerfield, Massachusetts.

c. In 1746 the town was attacked.
   Many settlers were killed. (AND)

c. In 1746 the town was attacked, and many settlers were killed.

d. Lucy Terry wrote a poem describing the attack.
   It was the first American poem written by a black woman. (IN FACT)

d. Lucy Terry wrote a poem describing the attack; in fact, it was the first American poem written by a black woman.

e. Lucy Terry did write poetry.
   She created short stories. (NOT ONLY . . . BUT ALSO)

e. Not only did Lucy Terry write poetry, but she also created short stories.

f. The stories sometimes saddened the other slaves.
The tales described the painful journey to America. (BECAUSE)
The Africans were captured. (AFTER)

f. The stories sometimes saddened the other slaves because the tales described the painful journey to America after the Africans were captured.

PARAGRAPH FORM

Lucy Terry was kidnaped from Africa when she was still a young child. After she was sold into slavery, she spent the rest of her youth in Deerfield, Massachusetts. In 1746 the town was attacked, and many settlers were killed. Lucy Terry wrote a poem describing the attack; in fact, it was the first American poem written by a black woman. Not only did Lucy Terry write poetry, but she also created short stories. The stories sometimes saddened the other slaves because the tales described the painful journey to America after the Africans were captured.

1. Abijah Prince married Lucy Terry in 1756.
He bought her freedom from slavery. (MOREOVER)
2. Abijah had been a slave.
He was freed. (BUT)
His owner died. (WHEN)
3. Lucy and Abijah settled in Vermont.
He received land from a settler there. (AFTER)
4. Later, a man claimed part of the Princes' farm as his property.
Lucy was forced to defend her right to the land in court. (CONSEQUENTLY)
5. Lucy appealed the case to the Vermont Supreme Court.
She had lost the case in her hometown. (EVEN THOUGH)
It was tried there. (WHEN)
6. Lucy Prince won her case before the Vermont Supreme Court.
The judge said she was one of the best lawyers in Vermont. (IN FACT)
7. Mrs. Prince was a vigorous woman.
She often crossed the Green Mountains on horseback. (INDEED)
She was over seventy years old. (ALTHOUGH)
8. She made this journey from Vermont to Massachusetts across the mountains.
She could visit her friends in the town where she was raised. (SO THAT)
9. Mrs. Prince lived.
She was ninety-one years old. (UNTIL)
10. Her life in America started painfully.
She accomplished many things. (NEVERTHELESS)
She will be remembered for her determination. (AND)

Review Exercise B

The following sets of sentences contain no signals. Using a variety of the different connectors you have learned, combine each set into one sentence. (There may be several ways to make the combinations.) On a sheet of paper, write out your new sentences as a paragraph.

1. Native Americans killed many buffalo.
   Members of the tribe used almost every part of the buffalo for some valuable purpose.
2. The meat of the buffalo was eaten fresh.
   It was cut into strips and dried in the sun to be eaten later.
3. Some of the meat was pounded.
   It could be mixed with dried berries to make a concentrated food called pemmican.

HINT: Try a (SO THAT) connection here.

4. The skin of the buffalo was tanned.
   The tanned hides were made into moccasins, leggings, shirts, and other articles of clothing.
5. Some buffalo skins were not tanned.
   The long hair left on the hides made warm robes and blankets for winter.
6. The hides were practical.
   They were works of art.
   Members of the tribe painted picture calendars on them.
7. An important occurrence was chosen for each year.
   It was depicted in a drawing on the inside of the robe.
8. Even small parts such as hooves and horns were not discarded.
   The hooves were boiled into glue.
   The horns were fashioned into spoons.
9. Sled runners could be made from the ribs.
   The sinew around the bones made an excellent bowstring.
10. Nothing was wasted.
    Even the buffalo's tail was used—as a flyswatter.

Writing Exercise A

Native Americans recorded a memorable event from each year of their lives by painting the event inside a buffalo robe. Suppose you were to create a picture-calendar of your life. Think about the pictures you would draw to represent the past two years. Perhaps you would draw yourself as an excited, wide-eyed freshman entering a new high school or show yourself on a lake learning to water-ski. Write about the two events you would choose for your calendar, painting a vivid word picture of them for your reader.

As you write, remember to use some of the sentence-combining skills you have learned.

13 Inserting Sentences

Inserting Modifiers

Inserting *modifiers* from one sentence into another sentence allows a writer to produce interesting, economical writing. (When one word describes another word, it *modifies* that word and is called a *modifier.*) The modifier *interesting* in the following example has been inserted into the first sentence, called the *base sentence.*

Base Sentence:	The lecture included a slide presentation and music.
Insert:	The lecture was interesting.
Combined:	The *interesting* lecture included a slide presentation and music.

Since *interesting* modifies (or describes) the same lecture mentioned in the base sentence, the modifier can be inserted without altering the writer's meaning. The new sentence, consequently, is a more interesting and more economical version of the original sentences.

Any number of modifiers can be inserted into the base sentence, as the following example shows.

Base Sentence:	The person has an attitude.
Insert:	The person is successful.
	The attitude is positive. (,)
	The attitude is refreshing.
Combined:	The *successful* person has a *refreshing, positive* attitude.
or	
	The *successful* person has a *positive, refreshing* attitude.

Successful modifies *person; positive* and *refreshing* both describe *attitude.* (Notice that the modifiers *positive* and *refreshing* can be interchanged.)

The signals you will use in this lesson indicate the correct punctuation for sentences that have modifiers. The signal (,) means a comma should be placed *before* the modifier when it is inserted into the base sentence. The signal (AND) means that this word should be included *before* the modifier. Use a comma plus *and* before the modifier when you see the signal (,AND).

Exercise 1

Combine the following sets of sentences by inserting modifiers. Consider the first sentence the base sentence and use the signals in parentheses. Study the examples carefully; then write out each combined sentence on a sheet of notebook paper.

Examples

a. The boy ran into the house to escape the rain.
The boy was sneezing.
The boy was sniffling. (,)
The house was warm.
The rain was cold.
The rain was wet. (,)

a. The sneezing, sniffling boy ran into the warm house to escape the cold, wet rain.

b. The police lieutenant awoke refreshed from her nap.
The lieutenant was overworked.
The nap was short.
The nap was well-deserved. (,)

b. The overworked police lieutenant awoke refreshed from her short, well-deserved nap.

1. Their money was hidden in the garage above a beam.
The garage was detached.
The beam was wooden.

2. Celia installed a stereo and a radio in her car.
The radio was AM-FM.
Her car was sporty.
Her car was new. (,)

3. Mrs. Cohen searched in the drawers of her desk to find the bill.
The drawers were messy.
The drawers were disorganized. (,)
Her desk was a roll-top.
The bill was for the telephone.

4. The coyote howled with a cry in the distance.
The coyote was solitary.
The coyote was young. (,)
The cry was strange.
The cry was mournful. (AND)
The distance was dark.

5. The guitar was ready for the concert at the park.
The guitar was tuned.
The guitar was repaired. (AND)
The guitar was electric.
It was an outdoor concert.
It was a municipal park.

6. When the tiger disappeared from the cage, the audience applauded the magician's trick.
The tiger was frightening.
The cage was locked.
The cage was iron.
The audience was amazed.
The magician was young.
The trick was incredible.

7. Sitting in the car, Sergio watched the rain on the windows and shook his head, wondering why he hadn't replaced the battery.
The car was stranded.
The rain was heavy.
The rain was beating. (,)
The battery was old.
The battery was run-down. (,)

8. The child gazed out the window, watching the people in the street.
She was bored.
She was restless. (AND)
The window was open.
The people were busy.
The street was crowded.
The street was noisy. (,)

9. The surfer caught the wave, her body riding with the force of the ocean.
The surfer was alert.
The surfer was eager. (,)
The wave was thrilling.
Her body was graceful.
The force was tremendous.

10. The man made a wish on the object, aware of the danger but hoping for the best.
The man was anxious.
The man was greedy. (,)
The object was mysterious.
The object was small. (,)
The danger was possible.

Inserting Phrases as Modifiers

A *phrase modifier*, a string of words (with no subject and no verb) that acts as an adjective or adverb, provides more specific information and can also be inserted into a base sentence.

As the following examples show, the phrases are attached as closely as possible to the word or words they modify in the base sentence. In these examples underlining acts as a new signal to show you which words to insert into the base sentence.

Base Sentence: The crowd enjoyed the refreshments that were served.
Insert: The refreshments were <u>in the lobby</u>.
The refreshments were enjoyed <u>during intermission</u>.
Combined: The crowd enjoyed the refreshments that were served *in the lobby during intermission.*

Base Sentence: Mrs. Ortega jogged and then left.
Insert: She jogged <u>early in the morning</u>.
She jogged <u>on the quiet streets</u>.
She left <u>quite punctually</u>
She left <u>at 8</u>.
She left <u>for work</u>.
Combined: Mrs. Ortega jogged *early in the morning on the quiet streets* and then left *quite punctually at 8 for work.*

or

Early in the morning on the quiet streets, Mrs. Ortega jogged and then left *quite punctually at 8 for work.*

but not

Quite punctually, Mrs. Ortega jogged *early in the morning on the quiet streets* and then left *for work at 8.*

As the preceding example illustrates, phrase modifiers can be inserted at different places in the base sentence as long as they are still clearly attached to the words they modify. *Quite punctually* cannot be moved to the beginning of the sentence because this phrase tells when Mrs. Ortega left for work, not when she jogged.

Phrase modifiers often begin with prepositions—words such as these:

above	at	between	near	to
across	before	beyond	on	toward
after	behind	by	over	under
against	below	down	past	underneath
along	beneath	during	through	until
among	beside	in	throughout	up

Exercise 2

In the first five sentences insert the underlined phrases into the base sentence (the first sentence in each set). The last five sentences have no underlining clues. For these sentences decide what phrases can be added to the base sentence, using all the information that is given. Study the following examples; then write each combined sentence on a sheet of paper. Remember that some phrases may be inserted at different places for variety.

Long introductory phrases are often followed by a comma when they precede the subject of the sentence.

Examples

a. The athlete ran swiftly.
He ran at the sound of the gun.
He ran toward the finish line.
He was in the Number 10 jersey.

a. The athlete in the Number 10 jersey ran swiftly toward the finish line at the sound of the gun.

or

At the sound of the gun, the athlete in the Number 10 jersey ran swiftly toward the finish line.

b. You could clearly see a figure jogging.
The figure was on the top of the distant bluff.
The jogging was alongside a dog.
It was a dog with pointed ears.

b. You could clearly see a figure on top of the distant bluff, jogging alongside a dog with pointed ears.

1. He posted the announcement.
The announcement was of the high school play.
He posted it on the bulletin board.
He posted it above the testing schedule.

2. Jesse agreed to run.
His agreement was against his better judgment.
The running was for student council.
The running would be against the most popular girl.
The girl was in the class.

3. He stood, singing.
He was singing very noisily.
He was in the shower.
He was under the beating water.

4. The teen dashed after the little girl who was unaware.
The teen dashed without regard for his own welfare.
The teen dashed into the street.
She was unaware of the approaching truck.
The truck was behind her.

5. Juan and Rosa were opposites, but they admired each other.
They were opposites in tastes.
They were opposites in upbringing. (,)
They were opposites in values. (,AND)
They admired in secret.
They admired from a distance.

6. She sat watching the players kicking the ball and wondered.
   She was without the slightest desire to participate.
   The players were in their striped shirts and solid shorts.
   They were kicking the ball down the muddy field.
   She wondered at their serious obsession.
   The obsession was with the game.
7. He grew tired of waiting.
   He grew tired toward the end of the day.
   He was waiting for her call.
   He was like a lonely mutt.
   The mutt was without a master.
8. Eric and Coleen practice their skating routines.
   They practice for weeks.
   They practice before every competition.
   They practice with great care.
   They practice in the rink.
   The rink is near their hometowns.
9. Chichén Itzá is the site.
   The site is of ancient pyramids, an observatory, and a ballpark that were built.
   They were built by the Mayans.
   They were built over 2,000 years ago.
   They were built in the Yucatán Peninsula of Mexico.
10. Mr. Jones counted his money while his eyes feasted.
    He counted it after each workday.
    He counted it into stacks.
    The stacks were of coins.
    The stacks were across the table.
    The feast was on the gold and silver.
    The gold and silver were before him.

Inserting Participial Phrases

You can also add information to a sentence by inserting phrases that begin with a present or past participle verb form.

Base Sentence:	Ann Petry gradually devoted more and more of her time to creative writing.
Insert:	Ann Petry was trained as a pharmacist.
Combined:	*Trained as a pharmacist,* Ann Petry gradually devoted more and more of her time to creative writing.

For a more detailed discussion of participial phrases, see pages 508–509.

Some verbs must be changed to the *-ing* form when they are inserted as descriptive phrases. In the following example the signal (ING) indicates that a change in the verb is necessary.

Base Sentence: The elderly man contributed his time and money to the local clean-up campaign.
Insert: He remembered how lovely the neighborhood had been. (ING)
Combined: *Remembering how lovely the neighborhood had been*, the elderly man contributed his time and money to the local clean-up campaign.

As the next few examples show, participial phrases may be inserted at the beginning, in the middle, or at the end of the base sentence. However, to avoid confusing or illogical statements, the phrase must always be clearly attached to the word or words it describes.

Base Sentence: The small puppy crouched by its owner.
Insert: The puppy was frightened by the thunder.
Combined: The small puppy, *frightened by the thunder*, crouched by its owner.

or

Frightened by the thunder, the small puppy crouched by its owner.

but not

The small puppy crouched by its owner, *frightened by the thunder.*

A comma usually follows these phrases when they are inserted at the beginning of a sentence. A phrase appearing in the middle or at the end of the sentence is set off with a comma or paired commas only if it provides additional information that *is not essential* to the sentence's meaning. A phrase that provides information *essential* to the sentence's meaning is not set off with commas when it appears in the middle or at the end of the sentence.

Notice how commas are used in the following examples.

Base Sentence: Dogs are often struck by cars.
Insert: Dogs are allowed to run loose in the street.
Combined: Dogs *allowed to run loose in the street* are often struck by cars.
[No commas are used because the phrase provides essential information about which dogs are struck by cars.]

Base Sentence: My grandfather and I enjoyed cooking the elaborate dinner.
Insert: We swapped recipes. (ING)
We corrected one another constantly. (AND + ING)
Combined: My grandfather and I**,** *swapping recipes and correcting one another constantly***,** enjoyed cooking the elaborate dinner.
[Commas set off the phrase because it is not essential.]

In the preceding example notice that two participial phrases connected by *and* are inserted into the base sentence.

Exercise 3

After studying the examples, combine the following sets of sentences by inserting the underlined participial phrases into the base sentences (the first sentence in each set). Be sure to insert the phrases in the places that make the most sense, using commas where necessary. Many phrases can be attached to the beginning of sentences for variety. Write out each combined sentence on a sheet of paper.

Examples

a. Mrs. Garcia has built a small greenhouse beside her garage.
Mrs. Garcia has used her retirement productively. (ING)

a. Using her retirement productively, Mrs. Garcia has built a small greenhouse beside her garage.

b. Locusts swarmed in the fields.
They were creating chaos.
They were causing fear among the peasants. (,)

b. Creating chaos, locusts swarmed in the fields, causing fear among the peasants.

1. Su Ling continued to work out every day.
She was encouraged by her coach.
2. Ms. Garrison gave us all a warm hug.
She was delighted by the surprise going-away party.
She was saddened at the thought of leaving. (BUT)
3. George gave Harry the signal.
He turned out the lights. (ING)
4. Marsha stood at the edge of the diving board.
She positioned herself carefully. (ING)
She waited for the sound of the gun. (ING)
5. Quickly, he threw the blanket on the fire.
He stamped his feet. (ING)
All the flames were out. (UNTIL)
6. The freeway continued for miles.
It wound through the mountains. (ING)
It ended by a picturesque lake. (ING)
7. Anita has no manners.
She always chews with her mouth open. (ING)
She never cares about her appearance. (ING)
8. The lion leapt with all of its strength.
It spotted the zebra. (ING)
9. George Washington Carver discovered nearly 300 uses for the peanut.
He experimented almost daily. (ING)
10. Carver left his owner after the Civil War in order to gain an education.
He was once kidnaped by slave catchers.
He was recovered by his owner. (AND)

Exercise 4

On a sheet of paper, write each of the following sets of sentences as one combined sentence, using participial phrases. The ten sets of sentences contain no signals. In some cases the base sentence will be the first sentence in the set, but you may choose the second or third sentence in other sets as the base. You may need to change a verb to the *-ing* form in order to insert a phrase.

Examples

a. Bert tuned his guitar.
He strummed a few chords.

a. Tuning his guitar, Bert strummed a few chords.

or

Strumming a few chords, Bert tuned his guitar.

b. The old miner patted the horse on its back.
He watched the horizon cautiously.
He was waiting for something to happen.

b. Patting the horse on its back, the old miner watched the horizon cautiously, waiting for something to happen.

or

Watching the horizon cautiously, the old miner patted the horse on its back, waiting for something to happen.

1. The girls skated down the hill.
They were gaining speed.
They were enjoying the exciting feeling.
2. The dancer performed an intricate tap routine under a spotlight.
He was dressed in a black tie and tails.
The spotlight was surrounded by darkness.
3. The outlaw stared at the approaching sheriff.
The outlaw was nervously tapping his holstered gun.
He was wondering if this would be his last shoot-out.
4. Doreen chased the petty thief.
She ran like an experienced athlete.
She yelled for help.
5. His sister had been given up for dead many years ago.
She was discovered.
She was living in Toledo.
She was married to a doctor.
6. The two students argued heatedly about politics.
They created a disturbance in the hall.
7. Sonia carried her son to safety.
She was frightened by the force that was shaking the structure around her.
She protected the child from the falling plaster.

8. The small girls skipped along.
   They avoided the cracks in the pavement.
   They sang a song that they had learned in school.
9. Mark read through the chapter.
   He underlined the major concepts.
   He took notes on important dates and events.
10. The white rabbit nibbled Alice's lettuce.
    The rabbit hopped around the garden.
    The rabbit wrinkled its nose with delight.

Review Exercise A

Combine each of the following sets of sentences by following the signals. On a separate sheet of paper, write the combined sentences in the order they appear so that they form a paragraph. Study the examples before you begin.

Examples

a. The director sewed together pieces of fabric.
   The director was finishing costumes.
   They were for the school play.
   The director is talented.
   The director is young. (,)
   The fabric is dark.
   The fabric is gaudy. (,)

a. Finishing costumes for the school play, the talented, young director sewed together pieces of dark, gaudy fabric.

b. He hummed quietly.
   He was turning the seams.
   The seams were on the colorful garments.
   He did this with expertise.

b. He hummed quietly, turning the seams on the colorful garments with expertise.

c. Actors tried on their costumes.
   They were all around him.
   They were enthusiastic.
   They were amateur actors.
   They were laughing.
   They laughed with excitement.

c. All around him, enthusiastic amateur actors tried on their costumes, laughing with excitement.

d. The director ignored the clamor.
   He was totally absorbed.
   The absorption was with his work.
   The work was last minute.
   It was the clamor of the students.
   It was excited clamor.

d. The director, totally absorbed with his last-minute work, ignored the excited clamor of the students.

PARAGRAPH FORM

Finishing costumes for the school play, the talented, young director sewed together pieces of dark, gaudy fabric. He hummed quietly, turning the seams on the colorful garments with expertise. All around him, enthusiastic amateur actors tried on their costumes, laughing with excitement. The director, totally absorbed with his last-minute work, ignored the excited clamor of the students.

1. The woman rests her knitting.
   The woman is in the photograph.
   She rests it on a table.
   The table is beside her.
   The table is small.
   The table is round. (,)
2. She looks dignified.
   She is wearing a dress and a shawl.
   The dress is simple.
   It is dark. (,)
   The shawl is white.
   The shawl is fringed. (,)
3. Her head is erect and her eyes peer ahead.
   Her head is covered by a white turban.
   Her eyes are behind wire spectacles.
   The spectacles are round. (,)
   The eyes are dark.
   They are penetrating. (,)
   They peer into space.
4. Nothing in the photo suggests that this woman is the hero.
   The photo is ordinary-looking.
   The hero is famous.
   The hero is American.
   The hero was called Sojourner Truth.
5. The woman inherited a mysticism.
   The woman was born about 1797.
   The birth was in upstate New York.
   The woman called herself Sojourner Truth. (ING)
   The mysticism was deep.
   The mysticism was from her mother.
6. She left New York City.
   It was one day in 1843.
   She carried only a small bag, twenty-five cents, and her new name: Sojourner Truth. (ING)
   It was a bag of clothes.
7. The woman lectured everywhere.
   She walked from one town to another. (ING)
   The woman was six foot tall.

Hyphens are inserted into phrases such as *six foot tall* when they become modifiers: *the six-foot-tall* man.

She lectured on women's rights.
She lectured on emancipation.

8. She used her eloquence and mind to debate some of the nation's leaders.
She was standing tall and erect.
She was on the speaker's platform.
Her eloquence was forceful.
Her eloquence was spellbinding.
Her mind was quick.
Her mind was incisive.
The leaders were most powerful.

9. She had a meeting.
It was during the Civil War.
It was with President Lincoln.
It was at the White House.

10. She proved that even one woman alone can affect the course of American history.
She integrated the streetcars. (ING)
The streetcars were in Washington.
She demanded the right to vote. (ING)
The vote was in a Presidential election.
She was speaking forcefully everywhere. (AND)

Review Exercise B

Although the following sentences contain no signals, by using the combining techniques you have studied, you can write each set as one sentence. (Some sets can be combined in more than one way.) Combine each set and write the finished sentences in paragraph form on a sheet of paper.

1. A group set out to climb the mountain.
They were filled with determination.
The group was composed entirely of women.
The mountain was the tenth-highest in the world.

2. The women were not intimidated by the face of the mountain.
There were nine women.
They were skilled in mountain climbing.
The face was stern.
The face was craggy.
The mountain was dangerous.
The mountain was called Annapurna.

3. A biochemist was the leader of the expedition.
The biochemist was from the University of California.
She was named Arlene Blum.
The expedition was historic.
The expedition was to the mountain's peak.

4. The women moved up walls.
   They were burdened with ropes and heavy packs.
   The walls were slippery.
   The walls were treacherous.
   These were walls of solid ice.

5. They carved footholds.
   They faced the possibility of death.
   This possibility was at any moment.
   The footholds were tiny.
   They were in the walls.
   The walls were of slick ice.

6. Avalanches slowed their progress.
   The avalanches threatened their safety.
   The avalanches were sudden.
   The avalanches were roaring.
   Their progress was careful.
   Their progress was painstaking.

7. The women waited out snowstorms.
   They huddled close together.
   They did this for warmth.
   The snowstorms were blinding.
   The snowstorms were howling.
   The snowstorms were of great fury.

8. Irene Miller and Vera Komarkova reached the summit.
   They reached it on October 15.
   This was after two months of climbing.
   Irene was forty-two years old.
   Vera was thirty-five years old.
   The summit was breathtaking.

9. The two women planted a banner.
   They were elated by success.
   They were tired.
   They were bruised.
   The banner stated, "A woman's place is at the top."
   They planted it on the summit.

10. Teams had tried to reach the top; the women were the fifth team to achieve that goal.
    This was in the past.
    Fourteen teams had tried.
    It was the top of the treacherous Annapurna.
    The women were hardy.
    The women were courageous.
    They were led by Mrs. Blum.

Writing Exercise A

If you look in the reference section of your high school or public library, you may find a volume titled *The Dictionary of American Biography.* This volume contains short biographies, or life stories, of noted Americans, giving details about an individual's birth, residence, and accomplishments. It explains why the individual is considered an outstanding American. Suppose that seventy years from now you were listed as a noted American in this reference book. What would your outstanding accomplishments be? Would you be listed for setting several world records in diving or skiing or for winning an Olympic gold medal? Would your achievements be in medicine or astronomy? Perhaps you will be remembered as an outstanding parent or as the writer of a best-selling book on friendship. Write an entry about yourself, seeing yourself as you would like the writers of this reference book to see you seventy years from now. You may make your entry a humorous one if you like; perhaps you set a world record for spitting watermelon seeds or starred in an Academy Award horror film. If possible, look at a short biography in one of your library reference books before you begin.

As you write your entry, use some of the sentence-combining skills you have studied in this unit.

Inserting Adjective Clauses

Inserting an *adjective clause* that modifies (or describes) a noun or pronoun in the base sentence is another way to add specific information to a sentence. An *adjective clause* is a group of words that has a subject and verb and that acts as an adjective. The clause contains a relative pronoun that sometimes acts as the subject of the clause.

Adjective clauses are discussed on pages 528–529 of "Using Grammar."

Base Sentence:	Mrs. Jefferson was elected to the city council last week.
Insert:	Mrs. Jefferson lost her sight a year ago. (WHO)
Combined:	Mrs. Jefferson, *who lost her sight a year ago,* was elected to the city council last week.

The combined sentence was formed by inserting the information about Mrs. Jefferson's loss of sight into the base sentence. Notice that the words *Mrs. Jefferson* are removed from the sentence to be inserted and replaced by the relative pronoun *who.* In the combined sentence the word *who* attaches the adjective clause to the words *Mrs. Jefferson.*

Adjective clauses often begin with one of the following words.

who, whom, that	relate to people
whose	relates to possessives (*its, her, his, their*)
when	relates to a time
where	relates to a place
which, that	relate to things
why	relates to a reason

When sentences are combined with adjective clauses, the signal tells which word takes the place of a noun or pronoun in the insert sentence and helps to *relate* the inserted information (the clause) to the base sentence. In the following examples notice that the relative pronoun is clearly attached to the word or words it modifies.

Base Sentence:	A young boy went on to become an Olympic swimmer.
Insert:	Lifeguards once rescued him from a riptide. (WHOM)
Combined:	A young boy *whom lifeguards once rescued from a riptide* went on to become an Olympic swimmer.
Base Sentence:	Mrs. Deitz donated a motorcycle from her shop to the boosters' raffle.
Insert:	Her son is on our football team. (WHOSE)
Combined:	Mrs. Deitz, *whose son is on our football team,* donated a motorcycle from her shop to the boosters' raffle.
Base Sentence:	She gave us directions to the restaurant.
Insert:	We are to meet for lunch at the restaurant tomorrow. (WHERE)
Combined:	She gave us directions to the restaurant *where we are to meet for lunch tomorrow.*

Clauses that are essential to a sentence's meaning are not set off by commas. In the following examples the clauses are necessary to understand the entire sentence.

Base Sentence:	Those drivers are a menace.
Insert:	The drivers change lanes without signaling. (WHO)
Combined:	Those drivers *who change lanes without signaling* are a menace.
Base Sentence:	She called him at the precise moment.
Insert:	He needed cheering up the most at the precise moment. (WHEN)
Combined:	She called him at the precise moment *when he needed cheering up the most.*

When an adjective clause can be omitted from a sentence without changing the meaning, set off the clause with a comma or paired commas. The commas indicate that the clause *is not essential.*

Base Sentence:	Mount St. Helens erupted in May of 1980.
Insert:	Mount St. Helens is located in Washington. (WHICH)
Combined:	Mount St. Helens**,** *which is located in Washington***,** erupted in May of 1980.

Exercise 5

Combine the following sets of sentences by inserting adjective clauses into the base sentences (the first sentence in each set). Be certain to use commas when the inserted clauses contain *nonessential* information. Signals for the clauses to use are provided for you. Study the examples before you write your sentences on a sheet of paper.

Examples

a. The committee chose club members to investigate the disappearance of the files.
The members were extremely trustworthy. (WHO)

a. The committee chose club members who were extremely trustworthy to investigate the disappearance of the files.

b. "Get-rich-quick" schemes are common in times of economic recession.
They rarely pay off. (WHICH)

b. "Get-rich-quick" schemes, which rarely pay off, are common in times of economic recession.

1. I admire creative people.
They are able to amuse themselves with crafts and other hobbies. (WHO)
2. Whenever we drive to the mountains, we play word games to pass the time.
The mountains are over eighty miles north of here. (WHICH)
3. The youth had either left town or carefully hidden himself somewhere.
The police wanted him for questioning. (WHOM)
4. Doctors are called pediatricians.
Their patients are babies and children. (WHOSE)
5. Erika bought the new convertible.
She had wanted it for a long time. (THAT)
6. Jesse reads a great deal and has an excellent vocabulary.
He is my next-door neighbor. (WHO)
7. When I arrived home from vacation, I was unable to find the place.
I had hidden my car keys in the place. (WHERE)
8. It is incredible that people still drive large luxury cars in this age.
In this age we are concerned with excessive fuel consumption. (WHEN)
9. The speaker presented several reasons.
For those reasons we should oppose the proposition. (WHY)
10. The photographs don't do the city justice.
I took them on my trip to Paris last summer. (THAT)

Inserting Appositives

Sometimes, as the following example shows, a sentence containing several adjective clauses may sound awkward or wordy.

Monopoly, *which is a notoriously long-lasting game,* was once played by two people in a bathtub for thirty-one hours, *which is a record noted in the* Modern-Day Almanac, *which is a reputable source.*

The preceding sentence can be improved by using *appositives* instead of adjective clauses.

> Monopoly, *a notoriously long-lasting game*, was once played by two people in a bathtub for thirty-one hours, *a record noted in the* Modern-Day Almanac, *a reputable source.*

Appositives are discussed on pages 514–515 of "Using Grammar."

An *appositive* is a word or group of words that means the same as a noun or pronoun in the sentence. In the following examples the words *the smallest planet in our solar system* have the same meaning as the word *Mercury*.

Base Sentence:	Mercury is the planet closest to the sun.
Insert:	It is the smallest planet in our solar system.
Combined:	Mercury, *the smallest planet in our solar system*, is the planet closest to the sun.

For greater variety the appositive can often be shifted to the beginning of the sentence, preceding the noun it modifies.

Base Sentence:	Croquet is rapidly experiencing a revival among youth today.
Insert:	It was a lawn game. It was popular in the early 1900s.
Combined:	Croquet, *a lawn game popular in the early 1900s*, is rapidly experiencing a revival among youth today.
or	
	A lawn game popular in the early 1900s, croquet is rapidly experiencing a revival among youth today.

Appositives are usually set off by commas because they provide additional information that is not essential for an understanding of the sentence's meaning.

Exercise 6

After studying the examples, combine each of the following sets of sentences by inserting the underlined words as an appositive. As you write the combined sentence on a sheet of paper, try shifting some appositives to the beginning of the sentence for variety.

Examples

a. Samuel Mudd died without clearing his name.
He was the doctor who treated John Wilkes Booth.
He was President Lincoln's assassin.

a. Samuel Mudd, the doctor who treated John Wilkes Booth, President Lincoln's assassin, died without clearing his name.

b. Dr. Schmidt teaches us how to keep our bodies alive and healthy.
She is an expert in social ecology.

b. An expert in social ecology, Dr. Schmidt teaches us how to keep our bodies alive and healthy.

1. The document is stored in the Library of Congress.
The document is a landmark in judicial history.

2. Our drama department is producing *Ten Little Indians.*
   It is a mystery by Agatha Christie.
3. Miguel sold his first book to a publisher.
   Miguel is a free-lance writer of children's stories.
4. The main course was prepared in a microwave oven.
   The main course was turkey tetrazzini.
5. Applause filled the theater as she read the name of the winner.
   The winner was a newcomer in the motion picture industry.
6. The music was a perfect accompaniment to the Renaissance wedding.
   The music was a harp and a mandolin.
7. Portuguese is the language of Brazil and Portugal.
   It is a Romance language.
8. Our vacation was the perfect ending to a wonderful summer.
   Our vacation was a week at my aunt's farm.
9. Vancouver is surrounded by waterways and spectacular mountains.
   It is a city closely tied both culturally and economically to the United States.
10. Reading and writing are taught to students throughout the world today.
    They were once skills belonging only to the clergy.

Exercise 7

The following sets of sentences lack underlining clues but can be combined by inserting appositives. After you study the examples, write a combined sentence on a sheet of paper for each of the sets. Remember that some appositives can be shifted to the beginning of the sentence.

Examples

a. "Mr. Ed" was patterned after "Francis."
   "Mr. Ed" was a talking horse in a popular television show.
   "Francis" was a talking mule in several old movies.

a. "Mr. Ed," a talking horse in a popular television show, was patterned after "Francis," a talking mule in several old movies.

b. Ida B. Wells helped organize the NAACP in 1909.
   She was a lifetime crusader against racial discrimination.

b. A lifetime crusader against racial discrimination, Ida B. Wells helped organize the NAACP in 1909.

1. The gift was thoroughly appreciated by the happy newlyweds.
   It was a brightly wrapped set of monogrammed towels.
   They were a young couple who had met in college.
2. Tornadoes have been known to circulate 500 mph winds.
   They are violently whirling columns of air.
   500 mph winds are a force capable of cutting a mile-wide path of destruction through cities and towns.

3. Dr. Daniel Hale Williams performed the first successful heart operation in 1893.
He was the founder of the first hospital for black Americans.

4. Coretta King has made important contributions to the cause of civil rights.
Coretta King is the widow of Martin Luther King, Jr.

5. Filled with hydrogen, the *Hindenburg* tragically exploded one hundred feet above its landing site.
Hydrogen is a highly flammable gas.
The *Hindenburg* was a German dirigible that had safely crossed the Atlantic.
The landing site was a crowded New Jersey airfield in 1937.

6. The Bee Gees popularized disco-rock in the late seventies.
The Bee Gees were a soft-rock group who first rose to fame in the early sixties.

7. Beverly Rivera is attending the university to obtain a degree in psychology.
She is a retired postal clerk.
Psychology is a field she always wanted to study.

8. Ms. Gianettia is well-known for her support of our athletic programs.
She is our assistant principal in charge of curriculum.

9. Vivien Leigh won a second Oscar for her performance as Blanche in *A Streetcar Named Desire.*
She was the Academy Award winning actress who played Scarlett in *Gone with the Wind.*
A Streetcar Named Desire was a 1952 movie that also starred Marlon Brando.

10. Charlie McCarthy was willed to the Smithsonian Institution by Edgar Bergen.
Charlie McCarthy was a loquacious wooden dummy.
Edgar Bergen was a famous ventriloquist.
The Smithsonian Institution is a national museum located in Washington, D.C.

Inserting Absolute Phrases

You can also enrich your sentences by inserting *absolute phrases.* An *absolute phrase* is related in meaning to the sentence in which it is inserted but does not modify a specific word in the sentence. The following examples show how absolute phrases are inserted into a base sentence.

Notice that the helping verbs *(was, were, is)* are omitted in the combined sentence.

Base Sentence:	The woman stood wearily in the doorway.
Insert:	*The children* were *asleep in their beds.*
Insert:	*The task of moving* was *finished.*
Combined:	*The children asleep in their beds, the task of moving finished,* the woman stood wearily in the doorway.

For variety, absolute phrases can also be inserted at the ending of the sentence:

Base Sentence:	The nurse pushed the last stretcher down the corridor.
Insert:	*The crisis* was *past.*
Insert:	*The halls* were *now dark and silent.* (AND)
Combined:	The nurse pushed the last stretcher down the corridor, *the crisis past and the halls now dark and silent.*

Absolute phrases are always separated from the rest of the sentence by a comma or commas.

Exercise 8

Study the following examples carefully and then combine each set of sentences by inserting absolute phrases. The underlining signal indicates which words will be inserted into each base sentence. When you write your sentences on a sheet of paper, put the absolute phrase at the beginning of some sentences for variety. Remember that commas separate an absolute phrase from the rest of the sentence.

Examples

a. Cilla enjoyed the colorful performance.
The dancers were twirling rapidly.
The sound of guitars was filling the air.

a. The dancers twirling rapidly, the sound of guitars filling the air, Cilla enjoyed the colorful performance.

b. They had to travel slowly and carefully.
The enemy was getting closer every hour.
Their trail was hidden in the riverbed.

b. The enemy getting closer every hour, they had to travel slowly and carefully, their trail hidden in the riverbed.

1. The carnival was a loud, colorful sight.
Balloons were flying overhead.
Firecrackers were exploding sharply.
Crowds of people in wild costumes were romping in the streets. (AND)
2. The hurricane unleashed its power on the coastline.
Winds were overturning cars.
Waves were crushing boats against their docks.
3. The scientist continued his experiments late into the night.
The research deadline was approaching quickly.
4. The old mule trudged wearily up the dirt road.
The cart was sagging from the weight of the gold.
5. The harsh ocean waves roared furiously behind.
Gusts of wind were carrying papers into the air.
Their force was blowing sand into our eyes. (AND)

6. Ray's hands were clutching the newspaper tightly.
His eyes were glued to the article in the upper right-hand corner.
7. They shopped carefully for a new car.
The money was already in the bank.
8. She put her hands on his shoulders with the tenderness of a mother's touch.
His face was contorted with pain.
Memories of the loss were still fresh in his mind.
9. Paula turned her attention to caring for the garden..
The effects of the heavy rain were past.
The day was sunny and clear. (AND)
10. She greeted us in her familiar, cheerful voice.
The previous day's disagreement was forgotten.

Review Exercise C

This exercise is a paragraph practice in which you are to use adjective clauses, appositives, and absolute phrases to combine each set of sentences. Follow the signals and combine the sentences in the order they appear. On a separate sheet of paper, write out the combined sentences as a paragraph.

1. Dr. Jane Wright is best known for her cancer research.
She is the first black woman to serve as associate dean of a medical school.
Her cancer research has brought her national and international acclaim. (WHICH)
2. She believes cancer may be caused by viruses.
She is a brilliant, dedicated researcher.
The viruses can be attacked with a combination of powerful drugs. (WHICH)
3. Her research in chemotherapy involves working in the laboratory.
Chemotherapy is the treatment of cancer with drugs.
She observes the effect of new drugs on cancer cells in test tubes. (WHERE)
4. However, in 1960 Dr. Wright left her research to take an unusual and worthwhile trip.
The trip was a medical safari.
The safari was sponsored by the African Research Foundation.
5. The foundation hoped to provide important medical essentials in remote areas.
Its leadership was working closely with local African governments.
Such medical care was badly needed. (WHERE)
6. The twelve members included a photographer, interpreters, a driver, and a cook.
The members participated in the medical safari. (WHO)
The cook prepared all the food. (WHO)

7. The mobile medical unit brought care to people.
The unit was a complete hospital.
It was equipped with X-ray and lab facilities.
The people could not reach a hospital or doctor. (WHO)

8. The medical unit treated 341 patients during a single week.
The four doctors were working constantly.
They were in Kenya. (WHEN)

9. Children were given important food supplements, and patients immediately received the medicine.
The children were severely undernourished. (WHO)
The patients' illnesses were diagnosed on the spot. (WHOSE)
They needed the medicine in order to recover. (WHICH)

10. Dr. Wright was convinced the medical safari should be a regular project.
She is a caring, sensitive physician.
The safari provided excellent care at a low cost. (WHICH)

Review Exercise D

The following sets of sentences do not contain signals but can be combined using adjective clauses, appositives, and absolute phrases. Decide which sentence in each set will be the base and then insert the other sentences to form a single sentence. On a separate sheet of paper, write the combined sentences in paragraph form.

1. The world's first Ferris wheel was created especially for the Columbian Exposition of 1893.
It was also the largest one ever built.
The exposition was a celebration honoring the 400th anniversary of Columbus' discovery of America.

2. George Ferris designed the unique ride.
He was a bridge builder.
He lived in Pittsburgh.
The ride would carry over 1200 people in thirty-six cars.

3. Ferris persisted and raised the money.
Fair officials were scoffing at his idea.
He needed the money to start his own company.

4. The pieces were shipped to the Chicago lake front.
Several companies were building the huge parts at different locations.
The lake front was where the wheel was to be assembled.

5. In March 1893 the axle arrived in Chicago from Pittsburgh.
The axle was a forty-five-foot-long piece of steel.
The piece of steel would turn the Ferris wheel.
Pittsburgh was where it had been built.

6. On June 9 the wheel got its first test; workers watched anxiously as the wheel revolved perfectly.

The test was a trial run without the cars attached.
The workers were located at strategic spots.
These were spots where they could see signs of trouble.

7. The Ferris wheel shone at night with the brilliance from thousands of the new incandescent lamps.
Visitors were flocking to it.
The wheel was now one of the exposition's most popular attractions.
These were the lamps which Thomas Edison invented.

8. The wheel was finally reassembled at a Chicago amusement park.
The wheel had been dismantled.
The wheel had been stored in railroad cars for a year.
It remained in the park until 1904.

9. The giant wheel was transported to St. Louis for another fair.
A buyer was purchasing it at auction in 1904 for $1,800.
This was a fraction of its original cost.
The fair was the Louisiana Purchase Exposition.

10. The wheel remained in St. Louis.
Transportation costs were soaring too high.
The wheel was now a gigantic eyesore.
In St. Louis it was sold to a wrecking company.
The company dismantled it in 1906, using 200 pounds of dynamite.

Writing Exercise B

At the end of every year, the portrait of an individual who has had a great effect on the world appears on the cover of *Time* magazine, and that person is designated Man or Woman of the Year. This honor is kept a secret, and readers enjoy wondering who will be chosen each year. In December many readers even send letters to the magazine nominating someone for this honor. Review the past year, thinking about the important events and the personalities who shaped them. What person do you feel had the greatest impact on the world or perhaps just on your own life?

In note form, list your reasons for believing this person should be Man or Woman of the Year. Support your ideas with specific details and use the library if you need further information. Then write a well-organized letter to the editor explaining whom you would nominate for this honor and developing your opinion with supporting detail.

Use some of the sentence-combining techniques you have learned to make the sentences in your letter interesting and varied.

Inserting Noun Clauses

Changing a sentence to a *noun clause* and inserting it into a base sentence is also an effective way to add sentence variety. A *noun clause* is a group of words that contains a subject and verb and that functions as a noun in the base sentence. The (WHO), (WHAT), (WHEN), (WHERE), (WHY), and

(HOW) signals in this lesson are used to insert noun clauses into sentences.

In the following examples the signal SOMETHING in the base sentence is *replaced* by all or part of the sentence following it.

Noun clauses are discussed on pages 532–533 of "Using Grammar."

Base: Dan Whitewater assumed SOMETHING.
Insert: His house was insured against natural disasters.
Combined: Dan Whitewater assumed *his house was insured against natural disasters.*

Base: We discussed SOMETHING.
Insert: We could build our float for the parade. (WHERE)
Combined: We discussed *where we could build our float for the parade.*

Base: My brother still doesn't understand SOMETHING.
Insert: Mom beat him in the bowling tournament. (HOW)
Combined: My brother still doesn't understand *how Mom beat him in the bowling tournament.*

Base: The Ortiz family never discovered SOMEONE.
Insert: Someone left a plant on their doorstep. (WHO)
Combined: The Ortiz family never discovered *who left a plant on their doorstep.*

The signals SOMEONE, SOMEHOW, and SOMEWHERE work in the same way as the signal SOMETHING.

Base: SOMETHING and SOMETHING were two problems that still perplexed the girls on the cross-country team.
Insert: They could purchase new uniforms. (HOW)
They could practice. (WHERE)
Combined: *How they could purchase new uniforms* and *where they could practice* were two problems that still perplexed the girls on the cross-country team.

Signals such as (IT . . . THAT), (IT . . . HOW), or (THE FACT THAT) are also often used to join the inserted clause with the base. In the following examples notice how these signals are used.

Base: The scientists excitedly announced SOMETHING.
Insert: A cure for the strange disease had been discovered. (THE FACT THAT)
Combined: The scientists excitedly announced *the fact that a cure for the strange disease had been discovered.*

Base: SOMETHING has come to our attention.
Insert: Ann has accepted a scholarship to the Wisconsin Technical Institute. (IT . . . THAT)
Combined: It has come to our attention *that Ann has accepted a scholarship to the Wisconsin Technical Institute.*

Exercise 9

On a separate sheet of paper, combine each of the following sets of sentences into a single sentence by inserting noun clauses into the base sentence (the first one in each set). The first ten sentences contain signals; the last five sentences are unsignaled, and you must decide how to insert noun clauses. Study the examples before you begin.

Examples

a. SOMETHING is beyond my comprehension.
These problems can be solved in so short a time. (HOW)
a. How these problems can be solved in so short a time is beyond my comprehension.

b. Mr. Herrera told him SOMETHING.
The tulip bulbs should be planted sometime. (WHEN)
b. Mr. Herrera told him when the tulip bulbs should be planted.

Eliminate *(of)* in the base sentence. It is included only to help understand the meaning of the base sentence.

1. In her first address to the student body as principal, Ms. Thomas assured the students (of) SOMETHING.
She would be as visible and accessible as possible. (THAT)
2. SOMETHING is the reason we must acquit him.
We have a reasonable doubt as to his guilt. (THE FACT THAT)
3. SOMETHING made me suspect SOMETHING.
Rosa hadn't written to me in many months. (THE FACT THAT)
Her health was failing. (THAT)
4. SOMETHING never occurred to Othello.
Iago could be a lying villain. (IT . . . THAT)
5. The whole city is talking about SOMEONE.
Someone will replace Mrs. Johnson as mayor. (WHO)
6. SOMETHING is an important part of the research.
You concluded something from your experiment. (WHAT)
7. SOMETHING amazes me.
So many people are ignorant of their rights and responsibilities as citizens. (IT . . . THAT)
8. SOMETHING isn't necessary.
You enclose a cover letter with your application. (IT . . . THAT)
9. I've always wanted to live SOMEWHERE.
The weather is mild all year long. (WHERE)
10. Would you please show me SOMETHING?
This camera differs from the one I've been using. (HOW)
11. Can you be so sure (of) SOMETHING?
Gold will drop in value soon.
12. All the entrants in the fifty-kilometer bicycle race were told SOMETHING.
They must complete seven laps of the course.
13. SOMETHING doesn't necessarily mean SOMETHING.
The applicant is older.
He or she will be better or worse at the job.
14. SOMETHING did not affect Flora's success as a real estate agent.
She was confined to a wheelchair.
15. The experiment Mrs. Espinoza ran for our class showed SOMETHING.
Magnets attract metal.

Possessives and a New Use of (ING)

The signal (POS) in this section indicates that two sentences can be combined by changing a noun to the *possessive* (the form of the noun that indicates ownership or relationship). The following sentences are combined by changing the nouns *Marie, children,* and *trees* to their possessive forms: *Marie's, children's, trees'.* Notice that the possessive is formed with an apostrophe (') or an *apostrophe* and the letter *s* ('s).

Base: The dog is a collie.
Insert: Marie owns the dog. (POS)
Combined: *Marie*'s dog is a collie.

Base: The museum in Indianapolis has a display of antique toys.
Insert: The toys belonged to children. (POS)
Combined: The museum in Indianapolis has a display of antique children's toys.

For more information about forming possessives, see pages 342–345.

Base: The leaves were turning gold and brown.
Insert: The leaves were on the trees. (POS)
Combined: The *trees'* leaves were turning gold and brown.

Pronouns used in these combinations have the following possessive forms.

PRONOUN	POSSESSIVE PRONOUN
I, me	my
we, us	our
you	your
he, him	his
she	her
they, them	their
it	its

Notice how possessive pronouns are used in the following examples:

Base: The wet jackets lay on the floor in a heap.
Insert: We owned the jackets. (POS)
Combined: *Our* wet jackets lay on the floor in a heap.

Base: After they washed and waxed it, the old car looked like a new model.
Insert: The car belonged to them. (POS)
Combined: After they washed and waxed it, *their* old car looked like a new model.

Possessives are often combined with the (ING) signal to convert a verb into a noun called a *gerund.* For example, in the sentence "The shouting in the hall interrupted our studying," the subject of the sentence is the gerund *shouting,* a noun formed by adding *-ing* to the verb *shout.* The direct object is the gerund *studying,* a noun formed by adding *-ing* to the verb *study.* In the following examples the (POS) signal and the (ING) signal are used together to replace SOMETHING in the base sentence.

Gerunds are discussed on pages 475–476 of "Using Grammar."

Base:	SOMETHING frightened me.
Insert:	Sean yelled. (POS + ING)
Combined:	*Sean's yelling* frightened me.
Base:	Elaine can listen to SOMETHING every day without getting bored.
Insert:	Barbra Streisand sings. (POS + ING)
Combined:	Elaine can listen to *Barbra Streisand's singing* every day without getting bored.
Base:	According to the coach SOMETHING is uncertain.
Insert:	We will receive the award. (POS + ING)
Combined:	According to the coach *our receiving the award* is uncertain.

Exercise 10

On a separate sheet of paper, combine each of the following sets of sentences into one sentence. The signals for inserting possessives and gerunds are given in the first five sentences; the last five sentences lack signals but can also be combined with possessives and gerunds. Study the examples before you begin.

Examples

a. SOMETHING made Sheila aware that he was choking.
Kevin gasped for breath. (POS + ING)

a. Kevin's gasping for breath made Sheila aware that he was choking.

b. SOMETHING disturbed the baby-sitter.
The child played with paint.

b. The child's playing with paint disturbed the baby-sitter.

1. SOMETHING surprised Mr. Alvarez.
The plants bloomed early in the spring. (POS + ING)
2. The coach encouraged SOMETHING.
They practiced good sportsmanship during scrimmages and league games. (POS + ING)
3. The audience applauded SOMETHING.
The students danced and sang in the production. (POS + ING)
4. It's inconceivable that SOMETHING would cause them to lose their jobs.
The men refused to work in the condemned building. (POS + ING)
5. SOMETHING will prevent SOMETHING.
I limp. (POS + ING)
I will ride in the race Sunday. (POS + ING)
6. SOMETHING shows how they appreciate SOMETHING.
The class laughs.
Ross jokes around.
7. SOMETHING makes SOMETHING believable.
The book cites numerous examples.
It predicts earthquakes.

8. SOMETHING interrupted SOMETHING.
   The telephone rang.
   I typed.
9. SOMETHING helped him to lose twenty pounds.
   Carlos dieted and exercised all summer.
10. Your parents will understand SOMETHING.
   You do not want to become a doctor.

Inserting Infinitives and Objects

An *infinitive phrase*, a phrase composed of the word *to* plus a *verb*, can also be used to insert one sentence into a base sentence. The (TO + VERB) combination may appear at the beginning, middle, or end of a sentence, as the following examples show.

Infinitive phrases are discussed on pages 512–513 of "Using Grammar."

Base:	Kuni needs SOMETHING.
Insert:	Kuni studies her lessons more thoroughly. (TO + VERB)
Combined:	Kuni needs *to study her lessons more thoroughly.*
Base:	SOMETHING is what our grandfather taught us.
Insert:	We treat older people with respect. (TO + VERB)
Combined:	*To treat older people with respect* is what our grandfather taught us.
Base:	Are you willing (to do) SOMETHING?
Insert:	You work overtime. (TO + VERB)
Combined:	Are you willing *to work overtime?*
Base:	SOMETHING is what Jerry likes to do during his leisure time.
Insert:	He goes down to the pier (to do) SOMETHING.
Insert:	He watches the people fishing and the boats.
Combined:	*To go down to the pier to watch the people fishing and the boats* is what Jerry likes to do during his leisure time.

Notice that in some cases the verb changes form when it is combined with the base sentence in an infinitive phrase: *goes/to go, improved/to improve.* Remember that *is, are, was,* and *were* are formed from the infinitive *to be.*

Exercise 11

After studying the examples, combine each of the following sets of sentences into a single sentence by following the (TO + VERB) signal. In the first five sentences the signals are given; in the last five sentences no signals are given, and you must decide how to combine the sentences by inserting infinitives.

Examples

a. The posters warned us SOMETHING.
   We are aware of the importance of fire prevention in the home. (TO + VERB)

a. The posters warned us to be aware of the importance of fire prevention in the home.

b. SOMETHING is her ambition in life.
She becomes an astronaut for NASA. (TO + VERB)

b. To become an astronaut for NASA is her ambition in life.

1. The brochure encouraged employers (to do) SOMETHING.
They hire the disabled. (TO + VERB)
2. Kit considered his boss SOMETHING.
His boss was the most honest and most intelligent person he had ever met. (TO + VERB)
3. The instructions told us (to do) SOMETHING and SOMETHING.
We read the advertisement. (TO + VERB)
We find the hidden persuasive devices. (TO + VERB)
4. SOMETHING and SOMETHING are the goals of Zen.
One attains enlightenment by intuition. (TO + VERB)
One achieves discipline through meditation. (TO + VERB)
5. SOMETHING requires that the partners have the ability (to do) SOMETHING.
The partners win at bridge. (TO + VERB)
The partners communicate successfully during the bidding about the cards in their hands. (TO + VERB)
6. SOMETHING and SOMETHING would be a harrowing experience.
One loses one's bearings in a crowded, foreign city.
One is unable to speak the language.
7. My parents gave me the self-assurance (to do) SOMETHING.
I try new experiences.
8. Do you prefer SOMETHING or SOMETHING during the summer?
You vacation out in the woods.
You relax at home.
9. SOMETHING is SOMETHING.
One neglects one's pet.
One is completely insensitive to the needs of animals.
10. Our coach is thrilled (to do) SOMETHING and then (to do) SOMETHING.
She gives us all the training and technique she can offer.
She sees it pay off in our winning first place.

Using the Colon, the Dash, and Parentheses

The *colon*, the *dash*, and *parentheses* can also be used to insert one or more sentences into a base sentence. However, each of these punctuation marks has a special, limited function. Writers must avoid using these marks incorrectly or relying on them too heavily. The new signals for these combinations are (COLON), (DASH), (PAIRED DASHES), and (PARENS).

For more information about the colon, dash, and parentheses, see the chapter "Punctuation."

In the following examples notice that the *colon* follows the base sentence and introduces a specific listing of something already mentioned. Notice that words repeated in the insert sentence can be dropped in the combined sentences.

Base: We had to look for the following objects on the treasure hunt.
Insert: The objects were an apple core, a hairpin, a stick of sugarless gum, and a ball of yellow yarn. (COLON)
Combined: We had to look for the following objects on the treasure hunt**:** *an apple core, a hairpin, a stick of sugarless gum, and a ball of yellow yarn.*

Base: His suitcase was stuffed with small gifts for the children.
Insert: The gifts were a harmonica for Eric, a card game for Amy, and a box of watercolors for Beth.
Combined: His suitcase was stuffed with small gifts for the children**:** *a harmonica for Eric, a card game for Amy, and a box of watercolors for Beth.*

The *dash* can be used to insert a specific listing of items *before* the base sentence that refers to them.

Base: These were the things she enjoyed while living on the farm.
Insert: She enjoyed caring for the livestock, working in the open fields, and working outside. (DASH)
Combined: *Caring for the livestock, working in the open fields, and working outside—these were the things she enjoyed while living on the farm.*

A *dash* or *paired dashes* can also be used to insert a sudden change of thought into a base sentence. The punctuation separates the interruption from the rest of the sentence.

Base: Last week we raked together all the leaves in our yard.
Insert: No, it was two weeks ago. (PAIRED DASHES)
Combined: Last week—*no, it was two weeks ago*—we raked together all the leaves in our yard.

Writers use parentheses to insert added information when they do not want to draw attention away from the base sentence.

A sentence within a sentence need not begin with a capital letter.

Base: Mrs. Beaker helped us start the stalled car.
Insert: Wouldn't you know she had jumper cables? (PARENS)
Combined: Mrs. Beaker (*wouldn't you know she had jumper cables?*) helped us start the stalled car.

Base: We visited Mrs. Hernandez and watched her work on a large metal sculpture.
Insert: She is my neighbor. (PARENS)
Combined: We visited Mrs. Hernandez (*my neighbor*) and watched her work on a large metal sculpture.

Exercise 12

On a sheet of paper, combine each of the following sentence sets into a single sentence by following the signal. Study the example before you begin.

Example

a. Marshall sent the gift to his aunt while she was in the hospital.
The gift was a thrilling mystery novel. (PARENS)

a. Marshall sent the gift (a thrilling mystery novel) to his aunt while she was in the hospital.

1. Each of these days was stormy last week.
The days were Monday, Tuesday, Thursday, and Saturday. (DASH)
2. Luisa played the role of Dr. Watson in the grade school play.
Luisa is my little sister. (PARENS)
3. There were two reasons I couldn't do my homework.
I lost my notebook and I had the flu. (COLON)
4. These are what I like best about school.
Geometry, music, and sports are what I like best. (DASH)
5. Geometry involves thinking problems through step by step.
Geometry is a course I love. (PARENS)
6. Our research papers are due on November 25.
They are due during class, not after. (PAIRED DASHES)
7. I especially enjoyed some of the acts put on by the students.
The acts were Lou's African dance, Marty's knife-throwing act, and Bart's talking dog. (COLON)
8. Your book report must include the following things.
The things are the title of the book, a description of the setting, and your opinion of the main character. (COLON)
9. Two teenage boys stopped when the accident occurred and helped direct traffic.
Maybe they were older. (PARENS)
10. You will need all of the following equipment for this experiment.
The equipment is two pieces of copper wire, a Bunsen burner, a magnet, and a large beaker. (COLON)

Review Exercise E

Each of the following sets of sentences can be combined by using the signals to create sentences containing noun clauses, gerunds, and infinitives. On a separate sheet of paper, write the combined sentences in the order they appear so that they form a paragraph.

1. *Renaissance* is the term used (to do) SOMETHING.
It identifies the revival of learning after the Middle Ages. (TO + VERB)
2. (To do) SOMETHING is impossible.
Precise dates can be assigned to the Renaissance, which lasted from the fourteenth to the sixteenth centuries. (TO + VERB)

3. However, historians do know SOMETHING.
The Renaissance began SOMEWHERE. (THAT)
European trade routes met in Italy. (WHERE)
4. They also know SOMETHING.
SOMETHING spurred the spread of this revival. (THAT)
William Caxton invented the printing press. (POS + ING)
5. Scholars and students no longer had (to do) SOMETHING.
They copied books slowly and painstakingly by hand. (TO + VERB)
6. Instead, the new press allowed scholars and the general public (to do) SOMETHING.
They have their own copies of new and old books. (TO + VERB)
7. SOMETHING also promoted this rebirth in the arts and education.
Universities expanded and new ones were formed. (THE FACT THAT)
8. Students and teachers at the universities were involved in SOMETHING.
They rediscovered the value of long-neglected Greek and Roman philosophy, art, and architecture. (ING)
9. Because they believed SOMETHING, these Renaissance scholars were called *humanists.*
People had the ability (to do) SOMETHING. (THAT)
They could improve their condition. (TO + VERB)
10. SOMETHING marked the transition from the Middle Ages to modern times.
The humanists learned in art, architecture, and science. (POS + ING)

Review Exercise F

Use the signals to combine each of the following sets into a single sentence. On a sheet of paper, write each of the combined sentences in the order it appears to form a paragraph.

1. The Renaissance was marked by outstanding achievements and discoveries in many areas.
The areas included art, music, science, and literature. (COLON)
2. These were the accomplishments of one man, Michelangelo Buonarroti.
The accomplishments were the designs for the Laurentian Library, the painting of the Sistine Chapel ceiling, and the sculpture *David.* (DASH)
3. Michelangelo's frescoes in the Sistine Chapel are based on religious themes.
The frescoes were completed in four years. (PARENS)
The themes were the creation of the world, Adam and Eve, and the Last Judgment. (COLON)
4. Leonardo da Vinci was another versatile artist of the Renaissance.
He was also Italian. (PARENS)
5. All of these were areas in which Leonardo excelled.
The areas were painting, sculpture, music, and engineering. (DASH)

6. These familiar masterpieces by Leonardo show his use of chiaroscuro. The masterpieces are *The Mona Lisa*, *The Last Supper*, and *St. John, the Baptist.* (COLON)
7. This important concept referred to SOMETHING.
   The concept was chiaroscuro. (PARENS)
   Leonardo opposed light against dark in his paintings. (POS + ING)
8. SOMETHING proves Leonardo da Vinci was equally talented as an engineer and inventor.
   He designed such items as a machine gun and an adjustable monkey wrench. (POS + ING)
9. The accomplishments of other Italian scientists also explain SOMETHING.
   Italy was considered the center of the Renaissance. (WHY)
10. In 1543 Copernicus found SOMETHING and published this knowledge.
    The sun, not the earth, is the center of our solar system. (THAT)
11. Later, Galileo Galilei became the first man (to do) SOMETHING.
    He studied the heavens with a telescope. (TO + VERB)
12. SOMETHING was also an important Renaissance achievement.
    Explorers sailed into unknown areas (to do) SOMETHING. (POS + ING)
    They discovered new continents and trade routes. (TO + VERB)
13. These voyages were all accomplished during the Renaissance.
    The voyages were Columbus' trip to America, Vasco da Gama's exploration of the West African coast, and Magellan's trips to South America and the East Indies. (DASH)
14. SOMETHING also marks the Renaissance as a great literary period.
    Shakespeare wrote all his famous tragedies and comedies then. (THE FACT THAT)
15. SOMETHING makes one realize SOMETHING.
    Someone studies the Renaissance closely. (TO + VERB)
    This was a time period in which much was accomplished. (THAT)

Review Exercise G

This paragraph exercise is a review of many of the sentence-combining skills you have studied. Combine each of the following sets of sentences into a single sentence by following the signals. On a separate sheet of paper, write the combined sentences in the order they appear, to form the finished paragraph.

1. Benjamin Banneker was a scientist.
   His ancestors were natives of Africa. (WHOSE)
   He was a <u>talented</u> scientist.

He was a versatile scientist. (,)
He was a scientist in Colonial America.

2. He attended school.
He was born in 1731.
He was born in Maryland.
He was fifteen. (UNTIL)

3. He built the first clock.
He was still a very young man. (WHEN)
The clock was made entirely in America.
He used parts and only a few tools. (ING)
The parts were from a small watch.

4. About the same time, George Endicott lent the boy books.
George Endicott was the neighbor of Benjamin. (POS)
The boy was curious.
The boy was extremely intelligent. (,)
The books were on mathematics and science.

5. Endicott planned SOMETHING.
He would explain the books to Benjamin. (TO + VERB)
He was surprised by SOMETHING. (BUT)
Benjamin was not at all confused by the books. (THE FACT THAT)

6. Benjamin had completely understood the books.
He found several errors. (NOT ONLY . . . BUT ALSO)
The writers had made the errors. (THAT)

7. Endicott lent the young boy other books.
Endicott was astounded.
Endicott was impressed. (AND)
The books introduced him to astronomy.

8. Banneker began SOMETHING.
A blanket was wrapped around his shoulders.
He spent whole nights outside. (TO + VERB)
He was under the pear tree.
He studied the revolutions of the planets. (ING)

9. Banneker lived a simple life.
This was as an adult.
Banneker was a bachelor.
The life was on a small farm.
The farm was located ten miles outside Baltimore.

10. These were all tasks he did for himself.
The tasks were cooking, cleaning, and washing his clothes. (DASH)
He preferred SOMETHING. (ING)
He lived in solitude. (TO + VERB)

11. He liked SOMETHING.
He studied all night. (AFTER)
He slept in the mornings. (TO + VERB)

During the afternoon he read and wrote letters to famous mathematicians. (;)
The mathematicians lived all over the world. (WHO)

12. Banneker issued his own almanac.
He was drawing on SOMETHING.
He knew something about science and astronomy. (WHAT)
He issued the almanac in 1791.

13. SOMETHING and SOMETHING made writing an almanac difficult.
The writer had to understand the moon, stars, and tides. (THE FACT THAT)
These elements affected the weather. (HOW)
The almanac was very accurate. (HOWEVER)
Banneker produced the almanac. (THAT)

14. In the same year Banneker was appointed to the commission.
The year was 1791. (PARENS)
The commission was national.
The commission would survey a piece of land. (THAT)
The land later became Washington, D.C. (THAT)
Washington, D.C., is our nation's capital.

15. Banneker established an important role for himself.
He was an unpretentious man. (ALTHOUGH)
He had little interest in honors or prestige. (WHO)
The role was in SOMETHING.
We built our nation. (ING)

Writing Exercise C

The following list contains specific details for a paragraph on the subject of blue whales. After reading the details, restrict the subject to a topic, organize the details, and write a paragraph on the restricted topic. As you do, use some of the sentence-combining skills you have learned to make your writing interesting and varied. It is not necessary to use all the details in your paragraph.

Largest animal in the world
Not a fish
A mammal
Length can be up to ninety feet
Weight can be 125 tons
Moves to warmer waters to breed
Usually found in polar seas
Rarely seen in tropical waters
Feeds on krill—animals that are like shrimp
Strains the krill from water
Uses plates of baleen to do this
Baleen plates fringe each side of whale's mouth.
The plates are made of horny material.
Plates are triangular.

The blue whale has baleen plates but no teeth.
When enough krill are caught in mouth, whale dives and swallows
Stomach holds two tons of food.
Whale is insulated by thick layers of fat or blubber
Can't smell
Can't see well
Relies on sense of hearing and touch
Research suggests that whales communicate by sound.
A solitary animal
Not found in schools
Schools are groups of whales.
Blue whale may become extinct
Too many were killed by whalers.

Writing Exercise D

Choose one or more of the following topics for writing. As you write, concentrate on using the sentence-combining skills you have studied to add interest and variety to your sentences.

1. Because of the decline in students' skills, some school districts have considered extending the school year and limiting summer vacation to the month of August. Board members in these districts argue that a longer school year will allow students to improve their basic skills and prepare more adequately for a job or college. Write about the advantages and disadvantages of this idea, stating your opinion on the issue.

2. A few years ago a young Chicago teenager faced a difficult decision. Born in Russia, he immigrated to the United States with his family. However, shortly after the move his parents decided to return to their homeland. The boy did not wish to leave America and the freedom he enjoyed here, but he was too young to go against his parents' decision. Against his parents' wishes, he filed a legal suit asking the United States to allow him to stay. If you were the judge who heard the case, what would you have done in the same situation? Write about what you would do, explaining the reasons for your decision.

3. Many teenagers acquire a part-time job as soon as they turn sixteen. Although it is wonderful to take home their first paycheck, some teens find that working affects their life in many ways they did not consider when they started job hunting. Write about the advantages and disadvantages of working during the school year. Consider how a job affects a student's free time, relationships with friends and family, and studies. Or discuss what a student should consider in looking for a job: transportation, uniforms, insurance on the job, and so on.

4. From the photograph on page 301, select a person who appears interesting to you. Now imagine what that person's background, interests,

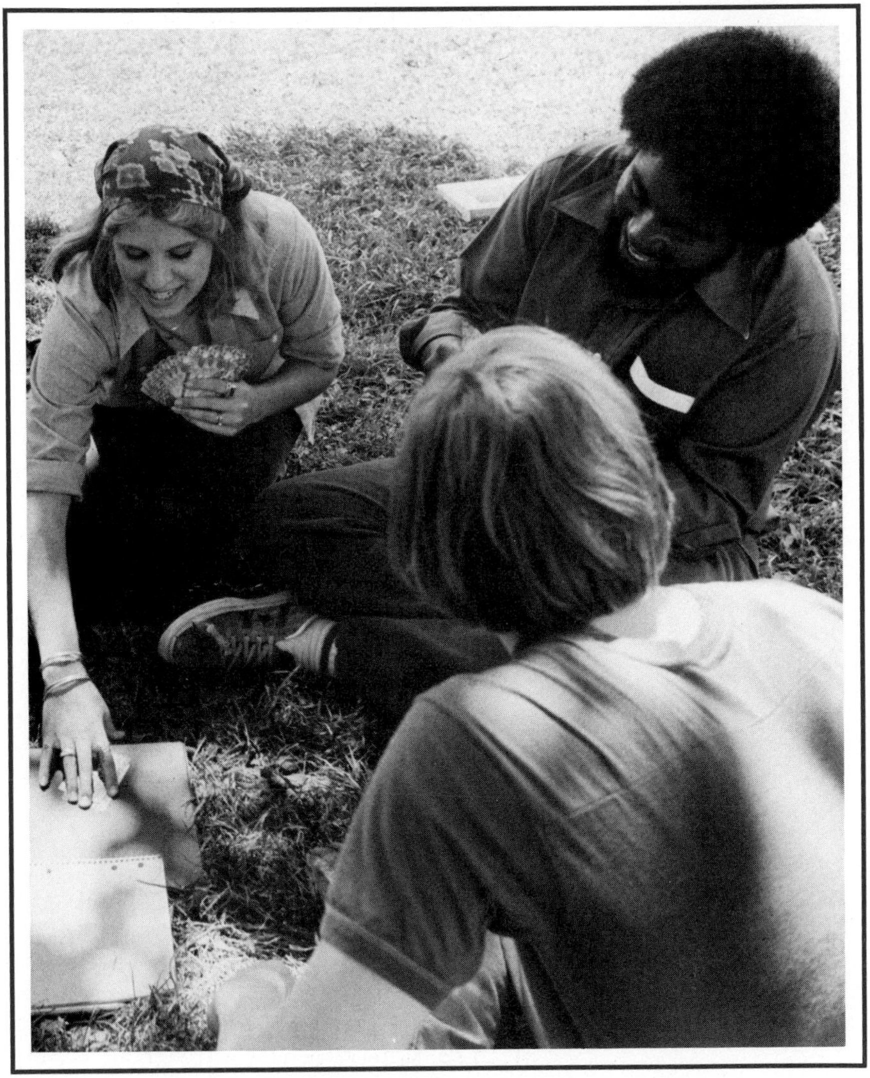

and homelife are like. Where does he or she work? What does he or she do for recreation? Is the person someone you would like to have as a friend? Write a description of the person you have selected, giving him or her a fictional history as though you had been acquainted for years.

5. In your community, there is a one-acre empty lot that has never had a house or other structure built on it. Over the years some people have dumped trash in the lot, and it is overgrown with weeds. You and a group of your friends have contacted the owner of the lot and asked for permission to clear out the trash and weeds. The owner has reacted

positively to this suggestion and has indicated that if you do complete the clean-up, you and your friends might be granted permission to use the lot—providing that the owner approves of the purpose for which you want to use it. Think about what you would like to do with that one-acre lot. Then write a proposal to the owner, stating what you would use the lot for and how you would go about achieving your goal. Be specific about what materials you would need and how you would maintain the lot.

PART

5 Language

14 The History of Language

Indo-European Beginnings

You can often tell that people are related by comparing their physical characteristics. Perhaps you have inherited your mother's hair color or your father's jaw. In the same way, when you observe close connections between the spelling and pronunciation of words, you know that the words are probably members of the same language family. For example, the English word *night* is related to the German *nacht;* the English word *sun* is kin to the Spanish word *sol.* Noting such similarities as these, language scholars have been able to trace the origins of English and several other languages back to their roots: all were born from a single language spoken by a group of people,

The language called *Indo-European* can be considered the grandparent of the English language.

When the Indo-Europeans began to form smaller groups and migrate to other parts of the world, they took with them their common language; however, over the centuries each separate group developed variations in vocabulary and pronunciation. New words were added as the experiences of the different groups changed, and gradually new languages grew out of the Indo-European ancestral language.

Germanic, which resulted from the Indo-Europeans' migration north and west out of central Europe, was one of these languages. It, in turn, eventually gave birth to English and to the linguistic brothers and sisters of English—Norwegian, Swedish, Danish, German, and Dutch.

The other offspring of Indo-European came from the movements to other geographical regions: Hellenic in Greece and its adjacent islands, Albanian and Balto-Slavic in the North and East, Italic on the Italian peninsula,

Armenian and Indo-Iranian from the Iranian Plateau to the Ganges, and Celtic in western Europe. These older languages eventually evolved into the modern languages of Greek, Russian, Polish, Czech, Italian, Spanish, French, Portuguese, Lithuanian, Armenian, Persian, Hindi, Welsh, and Gaelic—all cousins to English.

Language Activity 1

To review information on finding word derivations in the dictionary, turn to page 210.

Each of the following English words is derived from an Indo-European base word. Use a dictionary to find the original Indo-European form of the word. (The dictionary abbreviation for Indo-European is *IE.*) Then number a separate sheet of paper 1–10 and write out each word with its Indo-European base word.

Example

a. night — *a. night–nekwt*

1. acre
2. wheel
3. son
4. bright
5. thunder
6. daughter
7. bear
8. wind
9. father
10. gold

The Old English Period

English can trace its beginnings as a separate language to the year A.D. 449, when three groups of Germanic warriors conquered another Indo-European people, the *Celts.* At that time the Celts had occupied the area now known as England for more than 1,500 years.

These Germanic warriors, the Angles, Saxons, and Jutes, left their home in northern Europe to help the Celts repel an attack by an invading army. Within a century and a half, however, these three groups controlled almost all the Celts' territory themselves, pushing their hosts into what is now Wales, Ireland, and Scotland and christening their new home "Angle-land."

These three Germanic groups settled in different parts of England, and since they each spoke different forms (or dialects) of the same language, the country was soon divided into separate dialect areas. Because none of the *Anglo-Saxons,* as they came to be called, could read or write when they arrived in England, there is no way of knowing exactly what these dialects were like; however, something is known about the lives of these early Anglo-Saxons. Late in the sixth century, when Christian missionaries to England introduced the Roman alphabet and the practice of writing, the tales of great battles and brave deeds that had been passed along orally were written down, thus preserving a vivid picture of Anglo-Saxon life and values.

Such stories show that battle was a major part of Anglo-Saxon existence, for they contain hundreds of similar words for nouns such as *war, warrior, shield,* and *sword,* as well as countless verbs such as *afflict (ofsettan), oppress* *(onsettan), dispose (tósettan), put down (unsettan), resist (wiθ*settan), and *repel (wθdrifan).* The Anglo-Saxon vocabulary also tells some of the personal qualities the early people admired—intelligence, kindness, affection, pride, strength, and greatness of soul—as well as some they condemned—cowardice, folly, and greed. Words like *geférascipe (companionship)* and *giestlīθnes (hospitality)* suggest that the Anglo-Saxons were a social people who emphasized graciousness to their guests.

Had it not been for the missionaries, modern people might never have learned what these early English were like, for without writing, the old stories would eventually have been forgotten. Moreover, the missionaries also directly influenced the English language by adding more than 200 words to the English vocabulary. Among the most obvious contributions to vocabulary were words that represented the ideas, objects, and persons associated with the Catholic Church. Since the Anglo-Saxons worshiped many gods, they had no words for Christian concepts and therefore had to borrow many words from Latin, the language of the Church, to express these new ideas. Some of these borrowed words are still in use today—words such as *abbot, altar, discipline, hymn, mass, nun, priest, psalm,* and *temple.*

The missionaries also influenced Anglo-Saxon life in other ways, introducing concepts and words unrelated to the Church. They established schools, for example, and contributed words such as *grammatical, verse, master, history, title,* and even *school* itself. From their understanding of medicine came such words as *fever, cancer,* and *paralysis.* Even words for everyday items, such as *cap, sock, mat, chest, pear, cucumber,* and *ginger*, have their origins in the Latin used by the early Christian missionaries.

Interestingly, almost all the Latin words borrowed during this period are still in use, while only about 15 per cent of the approximately 50,000 purely Anglo-Saxon words have survived to the present. Among these Old English survivors, however, are many words commonly used today, words such as *a, and, be, child, drink, eat, for, good, have, in, it, live, man, of, sleep, that, the, to, we, wife, will,* and *you.*

Language Activity 2

Read the following translation of an excerpt from *Beowulf,* one of the oldest existing complete pieces of Anglo-Saxon literature. Then write a paragraph telling what Anglo-Saxon values it suggests.

The Building of Heorot[1]

Then Hrothgar, taking the throne, led
The Danes to such glory that comrades and kinsmen
Swore by his sword, and young men swelled
His armies, and he thought of greatness and resolved

---

[1]From *Beowulf,* translated by Burton Raffel. Copyright © 1963 by Burton Raffel. Reprinted by arrangement with The New American Library, Inc., New York, New York.

To build a hall that would hold his mighty
Band and reach higher toward heaven than anything
That had ever been known to the sons of men.
And in that hall he'd divide the spoils
Of their victories, to old and young what they'd earned
In battle, but leaving the common pastures
Untouched, and taking no lives. The work
Was ordered, the timbers tied and shaped
By the hosts that Hrothgar ruled. It was quickly
Ready, that most beautiful of dwellings, built
As he'd wanted, and then he whose word was obeyed
All over the earth named it Heorot.
His boast come true he commanded a banquet,
Opened out his treasure-full hands.

The Middle English Period

The traditional ending of the Old English Period is set as A.D. 1066, when William the Conqueror invaded England. William, Duke of Normandy, landed his Norman army in England, attacked and killed the English king in the Battle of Hastings, and forced the Anglo-Saxons to crown him king, a conquest that had far-reaching effects on English culture. Self-rule for England was threatened with extinction, and a number of policies established by the conquerors nearly destroyed the English language.

One of these policies was that the important governmental positions in England and all the great estates had to be given to the Norman French. As a result, for more than twenty years, French was the only language used by the powerful ruling class in England. Similarly, Normans were given all the important positions in the church, in the law courts, in the army and navy, and in the schools, so that French became the primary language in these areas as well. In fact, French might have replaced English altogether as the national language had two events not occurred that helped increase the importance of the Anglo-Saxon native tongue.

The first of these events was the Black Death, a terrible plague thought to have been introduced into England by crusaders returning from the East.

The plague began in southwest England in the summer of 1348 and by the end of the following year had killed around one third of the populace. The lower classes were more susceptible to the disease because of their living and working conditions, and in some places entire estates and villages were wiped out. The serious labor shortage caused by the plague served to increase the importance of workers, which in turn increased the importance of their language.

The second event was a prolonged and bitter struggle between France and England over the control of Scotland.

This military conflict, now known as the *Hundred Years War*, lasted from 1337 to 1453. During this period French became the language of the enemy for the first time since the Norman Invasion, and speaking English became an act of patriotism. Even after English was reestablished as the national language, however, the French influence continued to be felt. Thousands of French words had been introduced during the first 300 years of Norman rule, and most of these remained as part of the word-stock of English. The majority of these French loanwords reflect the new roles that Normans adopted when they settled in England. From Norman roles in politics and affairs of state came words such as *allegiance*, *government*, *majesty*, *mayor*, *noble*, *peasant*, *reign*, *tax*, *treason*, *treasurer*, and *treaty*. From Norman involvement in the Church, in the courts, and in the military came such words as *baptism*, *confession*, *prayer*, *religion*, *sacrifice*, and *savior; attorney*, *crime*, *felony*, *innocent*, *jury*, *justice*, *libel*, and *verdict; army*, *enemy*, *navy*, *peace*, *siege*, *soldier*, and *spy*. Other words reflect the French influence on fashion, food, entertainment, recreation, art, education, and medicine.

French was not the only language to influence English during this period, however; Latin continued to contribute hundreds of words related to law, learning, religion, science, and other concerns, including *client*, *conflict*, *desk*, *equator*, *infect*, *library*, *orbit* and *sanctuary*.

A final influence on vocabulary at this time was England's extensive trade with Holland, Flanders, and northern Germany. Words such as *deck*, *dock*, *easel*, *etching*, *freighter*, *landscape*, and *lighter* made their way into English from the languages of these countries.

Language Activity 3

Each of the words in the following list comes into Modern English from Latin by way of Old English. Number a separate sheet of paper 1–10 and make three columns with the headings MODERN ENGLISH, OLD ENGLISH, and LATIN. Copy the words listed below in the MODERN ENGLISH column on your paper. Then use a dictionary to find the OLD ENGLISH and LATIN derivations of these words and fill in the remaining two columns.

Example

MODERN ENGLISH	OLD ENGLISH	LATIN
a. sweet	*a. swot*	*a. suadere*

MODERN ENGLISH

1. lentil	6. chalice
2. cook	7. noon
3. candle	8. relic
4. plant	9. purple
5. oyster	10. martyr

Language Activity 4

The following passage is from Sir Thomas Malory's romance *Morte D'Arthur*, the only long prose work in Middle English that is still widely read. The passage describes King Arthur's reaction to his treacherous knight, Sir Mordred, after a bloody battle between their two armies. Although many words may look strange to you, you can probably guess the meanings of most of them. On a separate sheet of paper, write your own translation of the passage.[1]

Example

a. Than kynge Arthur loked aboute
a. Then King Arthur looked about

Than kynge Arthur loked aboute and was ware where stood sir Mordred leanyng uppon hys swerde amonge a grete hepe of dede men.

'Now gyff me my speare,' seyde kynge Arthur unto sir Lucan, 'for yondir I have aspyed be traytours that all thys woo hath wrought.' 'Sir, latte hym be,' seyde sir Lucan, 'for he ys unhappy. And yf ye passe this unhappy day, ye shall be ryzt well revenged. And, good lorde, remembre ye of your ny3tes dreme and what the spyryte of sir Gawayne tolde you tony3t, and yet god of hys grete goodnes hath preserved you hyddirto. And for goddes sake, my lorde, leve of thys; for, blyssed be god, ye have won the fyle. For yet we ben here three on lyve, and with sir Mordred ys nat one on lyve. And therefore if ye leve of now, thys wycked day of desteny ys paste.'

The Modern English Period

Languages are living things, continuously growing and changing. As English passed through the stages now called Old English and Middle English, the language acquired its basic form and character. Throughout the early Modern English Period, dating roughly from 1500 to 1650, English acquired polish and refinement of expression. A number of events during that time combined to mold English into the language you know today.

One of the most important events was the introduction of printing into England by William Caxton in 1477. William Caxton was not only the first English printer, but he was also the first to print books in the English language. Many of the books he printed were his own translations from Latin, French, and Dutch. The printing press had a tremendous impact on society. It made books available on a wider scale than was ever thought possible, and it affirmed the importance of the English language by offering English translations of classic texts and original English works. The printing press also helped to promote uniformity of language: the necessities of communicating to a wide audience influenced the standardizing of the many different dialects of English throughout the country. A good number of the rules now governing English, in fact, were first set down in the grammar books, language-teaching manuals, spellers, and dictionaries printed during that period.

The printing press worked with two other major influences of the time to expand the word-stock of English.

[1]From *The Morte D'Arthur* as it appears in *Medieval English* by Rolf Kaiser, Berlin, 1961.

The first of these influences was the Renaissance, which added thousands of loanwords to the English language.

The *Renaissance*, a word meaning "rebirth," is a term used to describe the rich cultural growth of western civilization as it moved from medieval to modern times. The Renaissance was characterized by a revival of interest in the culture of ancient Greece and Rome. In England Caxton's press made mass printing of English translations of classic literature possible. The greatest writers of that period—Shakespeare, Spenser, and Milton—all took interest in adding new words to English from foreign languages, from their Anglo-Saxon heritage, or from their own imagination. It is estimated that during the Renaissance 10,000 foreign loanwords were added to the English language, and with the influence of the printing press, these words passed into the common vocabulary.

Most of these loanwords came directly from Greek and Latin, but many entered through Latin's descendants, French and Italian (the languages used by a number of Renaissance scholars). Latin, for example, added words in current use such as *appendix, arena, circus, fungus,* and *toga;* French, *bourgeois, machine, pilot, pioneer, promenade,* and *vogue;* Italian, *balcony, cameo, gondola, parapet,* and *stucco;* Greek, *catastrophe, cosmos, criterion, encyclopedia, jurisprudence* and *pathos.*

The other major influence on the expansion of English was England's increasing contact with other parts of the world.

As new lands were explored and trade with other countries increased, English acquired still more new words, most describing objects, life, and activities previously unknown within England's shores. Dutch, Arabic, Spanish, and the languages of India were the main contributors during this early period. From them English gained such words as *spool, furlough, tattoo, easel,* and *knapsack* (Dutch); *harem, sash, cotton, algebra, mattress,* and *almanac* (Arabic); *corral, renegade, mosquito, iguana,* and *anchovy* (Spanish); and *cashmere, yoga, bandana, dungaree, cheetah,* and *guru* (Indian).

The English language is still growing and changing in response to the demands of a rapidly changing world. The effects of the printing press continue to be felt: books, magazines, newspapers, fliers, and signs all acquaint you with words you may not have known before and affect the way you use them. Radio and television bring you the spoken word from across the nation and around the world, familiarizing you with different experiences and ways of life and giving you a vocabulary to deal with them. Also, today's explorations into outer space, into ocean life, and into the regions of the human mind help to create a new vocabulary, enriching your language as words extend your knowledge.

Language Activity 5

The following twenty words were drawn from classical mythology, which was rediscovered by Europeans during the Renaissance and translated into English. Write a short report on the definition of one of these words, including information on the mythological character who inspired it.

1. Tantalize
2. Atlas
3. Iris
4. Cereal
5. Volcano
6. Panic
7. Aurora borealis
8. Amazon
9. Titanic
10. Protean
11. Odyssey
12. Martial
13. Vestal
14. Jovial
15. Mercurial
16. Achilles' heel
17. Plutonium
18. Calliope
19. Herculean
20. Furious

The Varieties of English

The English spoken in America today varies a great deal as you move from one geographical region to another, one cultural group to another, one job to another, and even one social situation to another.

The major variations within a language are called *dialects.*

No one dialect is superior to the others; all meet the communication needs of their speakers in various situations. To communicate clearly with others you will find it helpful to understand how their dialects may differ from your own.

Geographical Varieties

When you plan to go out with your friend Mary, do you pronounce her name *Māry*, with a long vowel sound, or *Măry*, with a short vowel sound? Do you tell her that you will pick her up at *a quarter of seven, a quarter to seven*, or *a quarter till seven?* After the movie will you stop off for a *soda*, some *pop*, or a *tonic?* These variations are differences in dialect. Language scholars studying differences in grammar, pronunciation, and vocabulary among speakers of American English have isolated three major speech regions in the United States—Northern, Midland, and Southern—which may be broken down still further into more specialized dialect communities.

Spoken English varies from one dialect to another. Scholars have noted, for example, that the name *Mary* is pronounced like *merry* in the North Midland dialects but like *may-ry* in the Southern; that Northerners say *a quarter of* while Southerners say *a quarter to;* and that carbonated drinks are often called *tonics* in the New England area but *pop* in the South.

Depending upon where you live, you may say that you had *hot cakes, pancakes, flapjacks*, or *griddlecakes* for breakfast; that you had a *mighty nice, right nice*, or *very nice* lunch or dinner at noon; and that you enjoyed *roasting ears, sweet corn*, or *corn on the cob* with your dinner or supper in the evening.

You may drop the *r* sound in words such as *car* and *park*, pronouncing them as *cah* and *pahk;* or insert an *r* sound in words such as *water* and *wash*, pronouncing them as *warter* and *warsh;* or you may change a *k* sound to a *t* sound in a word such as *ask*, pronouncing it *ast*.

These differences, which help to make English as varied and interesting as the people who compose the country itself, are not as great as they used to be. Many people today no longer live all their lives in only one part of the country, and television brings other dialects into areas that once were quite isolated. The result is that the language is becoming more uniform. Still, some differences continue to exist, and so long as they do, geographic dialects need to be understood and appreciated for what they are: important indicators of the richness and diversity of the American tongue.

Writers who want to give a regional flavor to their works often use characters who speak in geographical dialects. The writers represent these dialects by word choice and spelling. As you read the following passages showing two different regional dialects, notice the characteristics of grammar, spelling, and vocabulary that make each dialect distinct.

THE MIDWEST

I promised the Wife that if anybody ast me what kind of a time did I have at Palm Beach I'd say I had a swell time. And if they ast me who did we meet I'd tell 'em everybody that was worth meetin'. And if they ast me didn't the trip cost a lot I'd say Yes; but it was worth the money. I promised her I wouldn't spill none o' the real details. But if you can't break a promise you made to your own wife, what kind of a promise can you break? Answer me that, Edgar.

I'm not one o' these kind o' people that'd keep a joke to themself just because the joke was on them. But they's plenty of our friends that I wouldn't have 'em hear about it for the world. I wouldn't tell you, only I know you're not the village gossip and won't crack it to anybody. Not even to your own Missus, see? I don't trust no women.[1]

—from "Gullible's Travels" by Ring Lardner

THE SOUTH

Watt Tussie was one man that I didn't get around. He didn't look right outten his eyes and I was afraid of him. I think Uncle George was afraid of him too. He didn't belong to either clan of Tussies. He just heard about the big house where all the Tussies were a-comin, so he brought his family to jine the rest in peace, rest, and comfortable livin. Grandpa figured for hours to find out if he was any kin to Watt Tussie and he finally figured he was a son of his second cousin, Trueman Tussie. Watt Tussie wore brogan shoes laced with groundhog-hide strings.[2]

—from *Taps for Private Tussie* by Jesse Stuart

---

[1]From "Gullible's Travels" in *Gullible's Travels* by Ring Lardner. Copyright 1917, 1925 by Charles Scribner's Sons; renewal copyright 1953 by Ellis Lardner. Reprinted by permission of The University of Chicago Press.

[2]Excerpt from *Taps for Private Tussie* by Jesse Stuart. Copyright © by the Jesse Stuart Foundation. Reprinted by permission of the Foundation and its agents, Raines & Raines.

Language Activity 6

In your reading you have probably come across other examples of dialect usage. Find a paragraph that illustrates dialect writing by a writer other than Ring Lardner or Jesse Stuart. Bring this passage to class and be prepared to discuss its dialect features.

Language Activity 7

Perhaps you know of someone who has moved to your area from another part of the country, perhaps someone from your school, community, or even a member of your extended family. Write three or four questions to ask this person about his or her part of the country and write down or record the answers. Listen carefully to the response, noting features of geographical dialect that differ from your own. Then prepare a brief class report on the features of that person's dialect, taking both vocabulary and pronunciation into consideration. If possible, record the interview on tape so you can play back a portion to your class.

Black English

A *cultural dialect* is a dialect spoken by a group of people who share a common culture.

Black English is a cultural dialect spoken by many black people throughout the United States. Scholars believe that Black English resulted from the blending of the sounds and structures of English with those of other languages. When blacks from different African villages were captured and brought to slave trade centers during the seventeenth century, they quickly discovered the need for a common language to communicate with each other. Since English was the primary language spoken by their captors, they learned to speak English but a form that was strongly influenced by the pronunciation, grammar, and vocabulary of their native tongues. These early influences on Black English are still recognizable in the dialect spoken today.

In West African languages, for example, there are no pairs of consonants in words, and the *r* and *th* sounds are completely missing. These characteristics are reflected in such Black English pronunciations as *axe* for *ask*, *lass* for *last*, *show* for *sure*, *wif* for *with*, and *dis* for *this*. West African languages also have few long vowels or two-part vowels (called *diphthongs*), a fact that accounts for Black English pronunciations such as *rat* for *right* and *tahm* for *time*.

The influence of African languages also explains some of the grammatical differences between Black English and Standard English. In Standard English, for example, an *-s* ending is regularly added to third-person singular verbs in the present tense, as in the sentences "She *works* there" or "He *takes* the train." West African verbs, however, have no such special ending, a feature that may have influenced modern speakers of Black English who use such constructions as, "She *work* there" and "He *take* the train."

Many West African languages also lack an equivalent of the verb *to be,* so forms of this verb are often omitted in Black English sentences, such as, "He home today" or "That man my friend." In Black English, though, *be* itself is used when the speaker wants to indicate a recurring or habitual action, as in, "She be working every day" or "I be here all the time."

Black English has naturally adopted some of the grammatical practices of Standard English. For example, while West African languages have the same noun form for both singular and plural, Black English often follows the Standard English practice of adding an *-s* to show the plural, as in *street, streets.* In such Black English phrases as *five cent* and *two bushel,* however, the dialect once more suggests its African roots. Here numerical words such as *five* and *two* show the plural, so the noun form remains the same.

Language scholars have recognized these African influences on pronunciation and grammar for some time but are only now exploring their effects on the vocabulary of Black English. Among the more interesting discoveries is that many slang expressions popularized through Black English may actually be traced to the black languages of Africa. Some that seem to have been borrowed directly include *bug,* meaning "to bother, annoy," which is from the Mandingo word *baga,* meaning "to offend, annoy, harm," and the Wolof word *bugal,* meaning "to annoy, worry." *Dig,* which means, among other things, "to understand," comes from the Wolof term *deg,* meaning "to understand." *Hep,* or as it is now commonly spelled, *hip,* meaning "aware of what is happening," comes from the Wolof *hepi, hipi,* meaning the same thing.

Not all black Americans, of course, use Black English, and among those who do, many also speak Standard English. Like other cultural and geographical dialects, it is heard less frequently today than in the earlier periods of America's history, when people tended to remain isolated from each other. Nonetheless, Black English remains a part of the rich heritage of this country.

Language Activity 8

The following poem by Angela Jackson captures many of the sounds of Black English. (It is dedicated to another poet, Carolyn Rodgers.) Read the poem and make a list of its Black English features.[1]

carolyn.
singer of sass and blues. has come again.
the skinny knock-kneed little mama of "paper soul"
the pain-struck girl of "songs of a black bird"
has been transformed.
she is all grown up now. boldly beautiful
"blues gettin up" has got up and went. carolyn taken us

[1]Poem by Angela Jackson from the book *How I Got Ovah* by Carolyn Rodgers. Copyright © 1975 by Angela Jackson. Reprinted by permission of Doubleday & Company, Inc.

some where.
listen at her sanctified soul.
make u testify to truth.

her name is sister. she is yours.
everytime you look at her u see somebody u know.
she remind u of the church.
her eye is seeing holy. she remind u of the people on the corner
 her words be leaning on the buildings there.
she you sister. she everywhere.
carolyn can do the happy in the aisles of yo mind.
she so country and street and proper too.
she africa and greenville. monroe and pinebluff. chicagonewyorkphilly
l.a. boston batonrouge neworleans atlanta macon and alligator too.
carolyn say "the blues got class." she the blues and something else
everything too.
carolyn is a poet. a downhome choir in herself.
she a witness. will glorify u.
 will embarrass the ugly.
tell u bout yoself.
she a witness. humming her people
 to the promise/d land.

—*Angela Jackson*

Cajun English

One of the most interesting cultural groups in the United States today is the *Cajuns*. Unlike other nonnative Americans, most Cajuns have remained for the most part in the geographical area they first settled in—the rural areas of southern Louisiana's bayou country. Living closely as a group and in relative isolation from outside influences, the Cajuns have retained both their language and their culture.

Originally from the northern coast of France, the *Acadians*, as they were then called, came to the New World in 1604, settling first in the Canadian provinces of Nova Scotia and New Brunswick. When the English governor of Nova Scotia ordered their farms seized and burned in 1755, the Cajuns made their way south, eventually resettling in Louisiana. There they set up their own separate communities and began to raise cattle, to fish the swampy bayous, to trap muskrats and other small animals, and to grow small crops of sugar cane, cotton, corn, and sweet potatoes. In the twentieth century, life in these communities continues for modern Cajuns much as it did for their ancestors.

Until recently the Cajun language was entirely oral. The first book written in Cajun was not published until 1976, and the first grammar book on the language did not appear until 1977. Because it was not written down for so long, the Cajun language has never developed a standard form. Essentially a variation of French, it also has borrowed words from English, Spanish, German, Black English, and native American languages.

Foreign language influences on Cajun become apparent in a Cajun dialect sentence such as, "I buil' a house, me." Here the dropping of the final *d* sound in *build* may suggest a Black English influence, while the final *me* echoes the French practice of putting *moi (me)* in this position for emphasis. The French influence may also be seen in such usages as *gambleur* for *gambler, l'office de doctor* for *doctor's office,* and *la maison de show* for *movie theater.*

Some French words are so strongly entrenched in the Cajun language that they continue to be used even when their former meaning has been lost. *Amarrer,* for example, is a French verb meaning "to moor" a boat; the Cajuns now use the same verb to mean "to knot one's shoelace." Similarly, they use *viver de bord,* meaning "to come about" with a sailboat, in the same sense of "to turn around" an automobile on a street.

The application of nautical terms to nonnautical situations has been characteristic of Cajun language for some time. The early Acadians were seafarers, not farmers, and when they first journeyed to Louisiana from Nova Scotia, they spoke of "setting sail" on land, "navigating" the prairies, and "mooring" their horses.

No doubt many years will pass before the Cajun culture adopts Standard English as its first language or as a companion language to Cajun French. At present there are still large numbers of Cajun Americans living in isolated areas who know no English at all. As it is, the Cajun language and its English dialect remain as unique as the people who speak it.

Language Activity 9

In the following excerpt from George Washington Cable's *Old Creole Days,* set in southern Louisiana, the speaker's words are transcribed in a written form of the Cajun dialect. As you read, look for dialect features that differ from Edited Standard English. With your teacher and classmates discuss how these features of Cajun dialect differ from those of your own dialect.[1]

> "*Je dis,*" said St.-Ange, in response, "I thing you is juz right. I believe, me, strong-strong in the improvidence, yes. You know my papa he hown a sugah-plantation, you know. 'Jules, me son,' he say one time to me, 'I goin' to make one baril sugah to fedge the moze high price in New Orleans.' Well, he take his bez baril sugah—I nevah see a so careful man like me papa always to make a so beautiful sugah *et sirop.* 'Jules, go at Father Pierre an' ged this lill pitcher fill with holy-water, an' tell him sen' his tin bucket, and I will make it fill with *quitte.*' I ged the holy-water; my papa sprinkle it over the baril, an' make one cross on the 'ead of the baril."

---

[1]From *Old Creole Days* by George Washington Cable (New York: Charles Scribner's Sons, 1879). Reprinted by permission of Charles Scribner's Sons.

Vocational Varieties

If you were told to "cut your lead," "try out for the lead," or "check the lead," what would you do? In each instruction the key word is *lead*, but the meaning of the word varies according to the situation where it is used. A journalist will respond to the first command by shortening the opening, or *lead*, of a story; an actor will react to the second command by auditioning for the main, or *lead*, role; and an electrician will follow the third command by examining the main, or *lead*, electrical conductor.

Most occupations develop their own terminology. Collectively these special words and phrases are called *jargon*.

Most jargon probably arose from a need to communicate specialized information quickly. It requires far less time, for example, to tell a baseball player to "steal third" than to say, "Run to third base when none of the opposing players are looking." Jargon can also reduce confusion on the job. A chef will have no problem deciding how small to cut the vegetables for a dish if the recipe calls for them to be *minced*. A writer will understand that a story needs a humorous surprise in its final paragraph if the editor calls for a *kicker* there.

Jargon can be an efficient and colorful method of communication—so long as it is understandable to those who hear or read it. Unfortunately, however, jargon is often used unnecessarily, so that meaning is obscured rather than clarified. Some people, for example, needlessly rely on jargon to express very simple ideas, thinking that such language will be more impressive. Instead of short, direct statements such as "Think before you act," these speakers prefer longer, indirect constructions filled with semitechnical terms: "Input on relevant data is imperative before operational procedures conducive toward objectification of the desired outcome can be programmed for implementation."

Language Activity 10

The fields and occupations in the following list all have their own jargon. Select two that interest you and with which you are familiar and then make a list of five words and phrases that might be considered jargon in that field or occupation. Also, write the definitions for the words and phrases. For help in identifying jargon used in these areas, look through newspapers and magazines for articles about them.

Example

a. Television

a. Dolly—a platform where a camera is mounted
Pan—to move a camera to achieve a panoramic effect
Peasant—audience member who waves to a camera
Track—to follow closely with a camera
Cut—to stop photographing

1.	Music	6.	Law
2.	Business	7.	Medicine
3.	Sports	8.	Education
4.	Science	9.	Sociology
5.	Economics	10.	Agriculture

Social Varieties of Dialect

Speaking and writing, like other kinds of human behavior, change according to circumstance.

For example, when you write a letter applying for a job or write a letter to the editor to be published in the newspaper, you are communicating with a general audience that you hope to influence in some way. At such times you will use what is called *formal English.*

Formal English observes the requirements of Standard English: (1) accurate spelling, punctuation, and grammar; (2) clearly constructed sentences; and (3) a serious tone. It avoids slang and contractions such as *don't, they're,* and *isn't.* When you use formal English, you are, in effect, dressing up your language—being certain that it is neat, clean, and suitable to the occasion.

On the other hand, when you write to a close friend or relative, you are more likely to use *informal English.* Using informal English is like slipping into your favorite pair of jeans and T-shirt; it is comfortable language. More personal than formal English, informal English accepts contractions, slang, dialect words, and conversational tags such as *well.* Its sentences are loosely constructed and sometimes incomplete, just as they are in informal speaking situations. Informal English even allows some usages that may not be considered acceptable in Standard English, such as *It's me, Like I said,* and *Who did you see?*

Language Activity 11

Imagine that you are visiting a friend out of town when you run out of money. Write three letters asking for a short-term loan: (1) to a good friend at home, (2) to your parents, (3) to your local bank. As you write, pay attention to the formality or informality of your language. Be prepared to discuss the differences among your letters in class.

Avoiding Clichés

One of your most difficult tasks as a language user may be finding fresh, clear ways to express your observations and feelings. Since other people around you see the same scenes, share many of the same problems, and feel many of the same emotions, you may feel it almost impossible to find new ways to talk or write about these things. Consider, for example, the following examples.

Bitter end	Green with envy
Broad daylight	Last but not least
Clean break	Last straw
Crack of dawn	Ripe old age
Crying shame	Sink or swim
Crystal clear	Sneaking suspicion
Few and far between	Sunny smile
First and foremost	Whole new ball game

Expressions such as the preceding ones are called *clichés*, and although they are familiar and easy to use, reliance on them deadens your language. Clichés suggest to your reader or listener that you do not have anything new to say and that there is little reason to pay attention to your words.

To be an effective user of language, you must experiment with words, looking for new combinations to express your own unique perceptions of the world around you.

Language Activity 12

Individually or as a class project, compile a listing of clichés you have read and heard. Consider using this list to make a dictionary of clichés or writing a short story in which you incorporate many of the clichés.

Edited Standard English

While American dialect added an interesting color and richness to the language, it also created some problems. For example, in the early 1900s a major mail-order catalogue described one catalogue item as a *coal hod,* a *coal bucket, coal pail,* and *coal scuttle,* so that every potential customer, regardless of his or her regional dialect, would be reached. The need for a standard form for written English became apparent as businesses, newspapers, magazines, and literature developed. Such a form, called *Standard English,* developed to meet these needs.

In the United States today, Standard English is often referred to as the "language of the marketplace" because it is the English most accepted in business, industry, and commerce. As the English most often used by television and radio commentators, it has reached into every part of the United States, including previously isolated areas. For some Americans, perhaps those who speak a regional dialect or Black English, Standard English is a second dialect. They may speak in an Appalachian dialect or in Black English at home and among friends and then switch to Standard English in school and on the job.

In the "Using Grammar" part of this textbook, you will learn the written features of Standard English: subject-verb agreement, pronoun reference, and so on. Since in writing you have the opportunity to proofread, making changes that bring your writing into conformity with Standard English, the written form of Standard English is referred to by the authors of this textbook as "Edited Standard English."

15 How Language Means

The Meaning of Language

The term *language* refers in general to any method of communication.

For example, you have probably heard of body language, the language of art and music, and the sign language used by people who cannot hear or speak. Such means of communication are called *languages*, but what they can convey is limited in comparison with a spoken language.

While you can convey an attitude through bodily gestures, such as the raising of an eyebrow or the waving of a hand, body language alone is not able to express complex ideas. Similarly, you can convey a feeling or a general idea through music and art, but without words of explanation people may not always understand what you intend. Sign language comes closer to being a complete language, for it can communicate detailed information, ideas, and feelings, but sign language has this completeness because it is based on spoken language. The finger and hand positions of sign language represent combinations of sounds in *spoken language*, the most widely used type of communication.

Most often the word *language* refers to a specific set of sounds.

All true languages are sets of voiced sounds that have essentially the same meaning for the people who make and listen to them. *Written language* is a set of symbols that stands for the sounds of spoken language. Although spoken communication probably dates back to earliest times, the first written forms of language developed only 10,000 years or so ago.

There are many theories to explain why written forms of language finally evolved. Probably written records became a practical necessity for certain cultures, or perhaps people came to feel a need to leave accounts of what they said and believed and did. Possibly they wanted to preserve their culture and their history for later generations.

Whatever the reasons for their origin, the first written forms of communication were pictures representing ideas. Primitive people made the following records in the form of pictures that tell a story.

If you fill in the missing words, you can translate the story: "Home—(I) leave—(to go on a journey in a) canoe—(to be gone for) ten (days).—(I arrive on an) island (on which live) two families—(and there I meet a) friend.—We go together in my canoe—to (another) island—(where) we hunt with bows and arrows.—(We kill a) sea lion.—(We start our) return (journey—and) my friend returns in the canoe with me.—(After) ten (days—I arrive) home."[1]

While such picture stories met some of the need for communication, they were obviously limited in the amount of detail they could record. It was probably the need for increased, detailed communication that led to the development of an alphabet system. Alphabet systems contain characters that stand for, or *symbolize,* the sounds that make up languages. In this way an alphabet system allows the entire language to be recorded.

The symbols of the alphabet vary from language to language, as the sounds of the languages themselves vary. Not all alphabet systems represent individual sounds. The system used by Japanese and Chinese, for example, contains characters that stand for whole words. These characters are called *ideograms* because they express entire ideas rather than sets of sounds.

The alphabet of individual sounds and the alphabet of ideograms are both effective systems of representing spoken language. Writing does not

---

[1]From *The Twenty-Six Letters,* Revised edition by Oscar Ogg (T. Y. Crowell). Copyright 1948, © 1961, 1971 by Harper & Row, Publishers, Inc. Reprinted by permission of the Publisher.

determine how a culture uses language but rather shows how the language is used by the culture. When, for example, a society changes the ways it communicates orally, its written language reflects these changes. For this reason the written form of a language provides much valuable information about developments within a society and is a useful tool for the study of the language itself.

Language Activity 1
Compose a simple picture story similar to the one on page 321. If your teacher requests you to do so, exchange your paper with one of your classmates and write a translation of each other's story. Be prepared to discuss the details you could not learn from the pictures themselves.

Human Language and Animal Communication

All living creatures, human or otherwise, are born with the ability to communicate. Bees, for example, use a complicated kind of dance to signal the direction and distance of a honey source. Wolves vary their cries to let each other know when changes occur during a hunt, and whales and dolphins have highly complex communication systems compared by some scientists to human language.

None of these animals, however, actually possesses language in the human sense. Many differences exist between animal communication systems and those of people. Unlike human beings, animals seem to be born with fully developed communication systems. Human beings, on the other hand, have to be taught to understand language. At birth an infant can make some sounds, but it takes a child some time to learn the specific sounds that make up its language and to associate these sounds with meanings.

Once this association process begins, however, human beings can continue to learn new words all their lives. They can also learn entirely different sound and meaning associations by studying other languages. In contrast, many scientists believe that animals are limited to the communication signals they have at birth. If they encounter new kinds of places, creatures, or obstacles, the scientists believe, they cannot learn new signals to communicate these experiences.

As far as scientists know now, animals' signals are also limited to the expression of immediate concerns. A bee cannot tell the rest of the hive where it will look for honey tomorrow, any more than a wolf can describe to the pack the prey that got away yesterday. Only human language can deal fully with the past and the future, as well as the present.

Language Activity 2
Select one of the following subjects or a similar one of your own and prepare a report for class about the animal's communication system. Use the *Readers' Guide to Periodical Literature* for current information on your subject.

If you do not remember how to use the *Readers' Guide*, review pages 205–208.

1. Bees
2. Dolphins
3. Ants
4. Wolves
5. Chimpanzees
6. Birds
7. Rabbits
8. Cats
9. Dogs
10. Horses

Language Is Symbolic

Language can be described as a set of sounds that humans make to communicate with each other.

The characters in different alphabets stand for (or symbolize) the various sounds that people make. Furthermore, the sounds themselves are also symbolic. This means that the sounds in a language stand for things, ideas, and feelings. For example, when you say the word *shoe*, you use a combination of sounds to refer to a kind of footwear. The *word* is not a shoe itself, however, any more than a picture of a shoe in a magazine is a real shoe. The word is simply the symbol that this society has agreed will stand for *shoe*. The footwear could as easily be called a *glip* if everyone would accept that symbol instead.

Language also helps symbolize, or reflect, the person who uses it. Just as your room at home probably suggests a great deal about you, your tastes, and interests, in a similar way what you say and how you say it may tell others a great deal about you also. Your usual subjects of conversation reflect both what is important to you and what you have experienced. The way you talk about these subjects, your choice of words and how you use them, also influences the impression that you make on other people.

By examining an individual's use of language, you can learn a great deal about that person. By studying the language of a group of people, you can discover much about the ways of life of entire cultures. It is possible to know through vocabulary where the people of an ancient culture lived, by the sea or inland, in a warm climate or a cold one, how they survived, and what their way of life was like. Studies of the long-dead Indo-European language, for example, have revealed that its people lived in a temperate zone in northern or central Europe, in an area without a seacoast. Its vocabulary contains no words for *ocean* or for plants and animals native to Asia or the region by the Mediterranean. The vocabulary of different languages also reflects the nature of the people who speak them. A group of people living in the Philippines, for example, has no words to express the idea of war, and the absence of such words indicates their peace-loving nature.

Because language can reveal so much, scholars rely heavily on its study to learn about cultures that no longer exist. Scholars of the future no doubt will use written records of our own language to help determine what life was like in the twentieth century.

Language Activity 3

Most people understand that words act as symbols, but many times they still confuse the symbol with the thing for which it stands. Read the following excerpt from *A Portrait of the Artist as a Young Man* by James Joyce and prepare for a class discussion on how Joyce illustrates this confusion. The speaker is the young hero of the book, Stephen Dedalus.[1]

> It was very big to think about everything and everywhere. Only God could do that. He tried to think what a big thought that must be but he could only think of God. God was God's name just as his name was Stephen. *Dieu* was the French for God and that was God's name too; and when anyone prayed to God and said *Dieu* then God knew at once that it was a French person that was praying. But though there were different names for God in all the different languages in the world and God understood what all the people who prayed said in their different languages still God remained always the same God and God's real name was God.

Language Activity 4

Imagine that in the year 2999 a scholar decides to study the culture of twentieth-century America. Write a short paper explaining five key words that you think would give the scholar important information about your culture.

Language Activity 5

In the novel *Nineteen Eighty-Four* writer George Orwell creates a futuristic society in which Big Brother (the government) controls all human activity. One of the ways it maintains its control is by inventing a language, Newspeak, that eliminates words that stand for ideas the government does not support. In the Appendix to his novel, Orwell explains how Newspeak operated.[2]

> The word *free* still existed in Newspeak, but it could only be used in such statements as "This dog is free from lice" or "This field is free from weeds." It could not be used in its old sense of "politically free" or "intellectually free," since political and intellectual freedom no longer existed even as concepts, and were therefore of necessity nameless. Quite apart from the suppression of definitely heretical words, reduction of vocabulary was regarded as an end in itself, and no word that could be dispensed with was allowed to survive. Newspeak was designed not to extend but to *diminish* the range of thought, and this purpose was indirectly assisted by cutting the choice of words down to a minimum.

Heretical refers to an opinion that is opposed to official or established views.

Write a paragraph on one of the following questions.

---

[1]From *A Portrait of the Artist as a Young Man* by James Joyce. Copyright 1916 by B. W. Huebsch; 1944 by Nora Joyce. Copyright © 1964 by the Estate of James Joyce. Reprinted by permission of Viking Penguin Inc., The Society of Authors as the literary representative of the Estate of James Joyce, the Executors of the James Joyce Estate, and Jonathan Cape Ltd.

[2]From *Nineteen Eighty-Four* by George Orwell. Reprinted by permission of Harcourt Brace Jovanovich, Inc. A. M. Heath & Company Ltd., the estate of the late George Orwell, and Martin Secker & Warburg Ltd.

1. Aside from *free*, what other words do you think Newspeak eliminated?
2. Do you agree that the concept of freedom, for example, could not exist if there were no words to stand for it?
3. What do you think would be the effect on society in general of diminishing the vocabulary?

The Uses of Language

All language can be thought of as an end. The language user's ends may be personal or social, private or public. Sometimes, you use language simply to express yourself—you neither need nor want an audience for your words. You use language this way when you write in a journal or diary, sing when you are alone, or talk to yourself. Your purpose at such times may be to work out a problem, record your day's events, give voice to a feeling, or merely play with words.

People often devote at least part of each day to such private use of language, although most of the time they put their words to a more social, public use—to communicate with others. The most obvious use of language in public is to send and receive information. You may ask your friends about their after-school plans, explain how to work a math problem, or agree with a suggestion made by your teacher. In each case you are using language for an informational purpose.

You also often use language to persuade. Whenever you try to convince others to share your point of view, to do something, or to believe in something that you do, you are using language persuasively. Entertainment is another use of language. If you like to act in plays or tell jokes, write stories, poems, or songs, this function of language is probably very important to you.

Still another important function of language is to make verbal contact with others, to acknowledge their existence, and to signal the importance of your relationship with them. Even remarks such as "Good to see you!" and "Nice day, isn't it?" illustrate this use of language, as do the other instances of small talk you engage in with people every day.

Language Activity 6

The following is an excerpt from *Hannah Senesh: Her Life and Diary.* The entry was written in 1940, when the writer was about sixteen years old. Write a paragraph describing Hannah Senesh's purpose in using language in this entry, giving examples from the passage that support your description.[1]

> There are so many things I don't understand, least of all myself. I would like to know who and what I really am, but I can only ask the questions, not

---

[1]From *Hannah Senesh: Her Life and Diary* by Hannah Senesh. Copyright © by Hakibbutz Publishing House Ltd.; English edition copyright © 1971 by Nigel Marsh. Reprinted by permission of Schocken Books, Inc., and Vallentine, Mitchell & Company Ltd., London.

answer them. Either I have changed a lot, or the world around me has changed. Or have the eyes with which I see myself changed?

I feel uncertain, undecided, positive and negative at one and the same time. I'm attracted and repelled, I feel selfish and cooperative, and above all, I feel so superficial that I'm ashamed to admit it even to myself. Perhaps I feel this way only compared to Miryam because she knows her direction, and her judgment is more positive than mine. She can penetrate more deeply to the heart of things. Or is it because she is two years older than I? I'm already making excuses for myself, afraid to face facts. I say it's being optimistic to see the good side of everything. This is an easy attitude, but it doesn't lead very far.

My behavior toward others is so unnatural, so distant. Boys? I am really searching for someone, but I don't want second best. I'm kind, perhaps from habit—until I'm bored with being kind. I'm capricious, fickle, supercilious; perhaps I'm rough. Is this my nature? I want to believe it is not. But then why . . . ?

Supercilious means "characterized by pride or scorn."

Today I listened to music. Sound after sound melts into harmony, each in itself but a delicate touch, empty, colorless, pointless, but all together—music. One tone soft, one loud, staccato or long, resonant, vibrant. What am I? How do the many tones within me sound all together? Are they harmonious?

Language as a Changing System

All languages have their own systems for making sounds and for putting these sounds together into intelligible words and sentences. In the English system the meaning of sounds put together to form a sentence is largely determined by word order. For example, the sentence "The bit dog man the" communicates little to a speaker of English because the words are not put together in the usual way. Once the words are rearranged into the English system's natural word order, though, the meaning becomes clear: "The dog bit the man."

Not all language systems use word order to convey meaning. In Latin, for example, word order is not so important; meaning is conveyed through inflections, or changes in the form of words. It makes little difference in Latin if a sentence reads "Nero interfecit Agrippinam" or "Agrippinam interfecit Nero." In either sentence the meaning remains the same: "Nero killed Agrippina." The word endings indicate who is performing the action and who is receiving it. In English, word reversal of "The dog bit the man" could produce the sentence "The man bit the dog." This confusion does not arise with the Latin system.

No one knows for certain why language systems developed so differently. Scholars do know that in its earliest form English operated much like Latin, with a complicated set of word endings to show relationships. Over time, however, English speakers and writers dropped most of these endings, and the language evolved into its present form.

Changes are still occurring in English, for no language system is governed by rules that are fixed forever. Every language reflects the usage of its speakers and writers, and when enough people change the way they pronounce or spell a word, punctuate a sentence, or interpret a word's meaning, these changes become part of the language. Such changes do not make any language system better or worse than another. All languages are equal in the sense that they meet the needs of the people who use them.

Language Activity 7

Using an introductory textbook for another language, find at least one difference between that language system and your own. On a separate sheet of paper, write down what you find and be prepared to report on it for a class discussion. Look for differences in sentence structure, punctuation, grammar, or capitalization.

Example

I found that in the Spanish language system the word order is different from English word order. In English the adjective usually goes in front of the word it describes, as in "the pretty child." In Spanish the adjective goes after the word it describes, "la niña bonita," which in English would read, "the child pretty."

Language Is Concrete and Abstract

One way people express their perceptions of the world is through art. An artist makes an observation and then represents this observation visually with color, line, and form. Language may also be used to express perceptions, its words working in much the same way as the visual images of art.

Some artists choose to make almost exact representations of what they see. The result is a concrete visual image of the subject as it appears to the eye, almost like a photograph.

Like art, language also has concrete forms: words that refer specifically to details in the physical world. The names of plants, animals, objects, people and places are all examples of concrete language. When you hear the words *lily* instead of *plant, deer* instead of *animal, basketball* instead of *object, Eleanor of Aquitaine* instead of *person*, or *Times Square* instead of *place*, you are receiving concrete information.

Language also has levels of abstraction, enabling people to talk about ideas as well as about concrete details of daily life. When you talk in abstractions, you speak about things that are not *physically* present. A beautiful sunset, for example, is concrete; the ideas of beauty in general (anything beautiful—a person, painting, bicycle) are abstract.

Language Activity 8

Read the following poem by Marianne Moore titled "Silence." This poet is noted for combining abstractions with concrete physical details. Prepare for a class discussion on how the concrete words and the abstract words work together to communicate the poet's ideas.

Silence[1]

My father used to say,
"Superior people never make long visits,
have to show Longfellow's grave
or the glass flowers at Harvard.
Self-reliant like the cat—
that takes its prey to privacy,
the mouse's limp tail hanging like a shoelace from its mouth—
they sometimes enjoy solitude,
and can be robbed of speech
by speech which has delighted them.
The deepest feeling always shows itself in silence;
not in silence, but restraint."
Nor was he insincere in saying, "Make my house your inn."
Inns are not residences.

—*Marianne Moore*

---

[1]"Silence" from *Collected Poems* by Marianne Moore. Copyright 1935 by Marianne Moore; renewed 1963 by Marianne Moore and T. S. Eliot. Reprinted by permission of Macmillan Publishing Company, Inc., and Faber and Faber, Ltd.

PART

6 Using Grammar

16 Parts of Speech

Classifying English Words

The words in any English sentence can be classified according to their part of speech. There are eight parts of speech in English: *nouns, pronouns, verbs, adjectives, adverbs, prepositions, conjunctions,* and *interjections.* You probably already know that each of these can perform specific functions in a sentence and that many have features that distinguish them from other parts of speech.

In this chapter each part of speech is treated in two sections—an Understanding section and a Using section. In the Understanding sections, you will review the definition of each part of speech, its features (if any), and its special types or categories. In the Using sections, you will learn how to use each part of speech correctly in speaking and writing according to the accepted practices of Edited Standard English.

Understanding Nouns

Nouns name things. They name the objects you see around you—perhaps a chair, a window, or a tree. Your own name is a noun. Nouns also name some things that you cannot see, such as thoughts or ideas. You can learn to recognize nouns in three ways: by learning the definition of a noun, by studying the classes of nouns, and by learning the features that distinguish a noun from other parts of speech. In the following sections you will study and practice each of these ways to identify nouns.

Defining a Noun

A *noun* is usually defined as a word that names a person, a place, a thing, or an idea.

Lisa reads constantly.	[name of a person]
Death Valley is extremely hot and dry.	[name of a place]
The old *car* stalled again.	[name of a thing]
Honesty is important.	[name of an idea]

Exercise 1

Write out the following sentences, underlining each noun. Above each noun write whether it names a person, a place, a thing, or an idea.

Examples

a. Miss Lo grew up in China.

person *place*

a. Miss Lo grew up in China.

b. Martin Luther King, Jr., made many fine speeches about freedom.

person *thing* *idea*

b. Martin Luther King, Jr., made many fine speeches about freedom.

1. Luis can play trumpet and trombone.
2. Babylon was famous for its fabulous hanging gardens.
3. Ann saw several young cobras at the zoo in Oklahoma City.
4. Too much power may corrupt a person.
5. France gave the United States a statue symbolizing liberty.
6. Chief Joseph wanted freedom and peace for his people.
7. Anne Bradstreet was one of the first important poets in America.
8. Some scientists believe a huge serpent lives in Loch Ness, a lake in Scotland.
9. The law should provide justice and safety for all citizens.
10. Jimmy Carter grew up in Georgia on a farm where peanuts were the main crop.

Classifying Nouns

Two large classes of nouns are *proper nouns* and *common nouns.*

Proper nouns name specific persons, places, things, or ideas. All other nouns are called *common nouns.*

Genuine Risk won that race.

The noun *Genuine Risk* is proper because it names a specific horse.

A great *horse* won that race.

The noun *horse* is common because it is not a specific name.

Proper nouns are capitalized; common nouns are not.

Old Baldy loomed ahead of us.	[proper noun]
The *mountain* loomed ahead of us.	[common noun]
We visited *Utah.*	[proper noun]
We visited *the state.*	[common noun]
Marie Curie was from *Poland.*	[proper nouns]
The *scientist* was from another *country.*	[common nouns]

Many proper nouns, and some common nouns, are *compound nouns* because they are made up of more than one word.

Compound proper nouns have two or more capitalized words:

San Diego Freeway	[one thing]
Dodge City	[one place]
Mary McLeod Bethune	[one person]

Compound common nouns may be spelled as one word, as two separate words, or as a hyphenated word.

One Word:	baseball, silverware, classroom
Two Words:	tennis court, health club, police station
Hyphenated Word:	jack-in-the-box, son-in-law, self-confidence

Note: Consult your dictionary for the correct spelling of compound nouns.

In addition to being classified as proper or common, nouns may also be classified as *concrete* or *abstract.* A *concrete noun* names something that can be perceived through the senses (objects such as a house or the Lincoln Memorial). An *abstract noun* names a quality, a thought, or an idea (such as freedom or talent). The noun *house,* for example, is both common and concrete; *Julian Bond* is a proper noun and a concrete noun. The noun *friendship* is a common noun and an abstract noun.

Nouns that stand for a group are called *collective nouns.* Some collective nouns are *jury, group,* and *class.*

Exercise 2

Write out the following sentences, underlining common nouns once and proper nouns twice. Write *A* above each abstract noun.

Example

a. Robin Williams, who played Mork from Ork, also starred in the role of Popeye.

a. Robin Williams, who played Mork from Ork, also starred in the role of Popeye. (A above "role")

1. Daisy Bates of Little Rock, Arkansas, courageously saved her daughter-in-law.
2. The beautiful Ponca State Park is located in Nebraska on the Missouri River.
3. The S. S. *Titanic* met a tragic fate in the Atlantic Ocean.

4. In cartoons Mickey Mouse, created by Walt Disney, gave many children pleasure.
5. A famous member of the Harlem Globe Trotters was the player named Meadowlark Lemon.
6. Casey Jones, engineer of the Cannonball Express, worked for the Illinois Central Railroad.
7. Jim Henson, a puppeteer, created many popular characters, including Kermit the Frog, Miss Piggy, Fozzie Bear, and Professor Strangepork.
8. A successful modern dancer, José Limon was best known for his role as Othello in the ballet *The Moor's Pavane.*
9. The American spacecraft *Apollo 11* lifted off for the moon in the late sixties, with the astronauts Michael Collins, Neil Armstrong, and Edwin Aldrin aboard.
10. The name *America* was first used in 1507 when Martin Waldseemüller prepared a map showing the new continent with the name.

Finding a Noun by Its Features

Nouns have certain features that set them off from other parts of speech. Four features can help you identify nouns. Most nouns have at least one of these features; many have all four.

1. Nouns often follow determiners.

The most common determiners are the words *a, an,* and *the,* which are also called *articles.* Some other common determiners are *any, each, many, one (two, three . . .), some, that, these, this,* and *those.*

a girl	*four* cats
an automobile	*many* friends
the bird	*some* cities

2. Nouns may be either singular or plural.

Many nouns have both a *singular* and a *plural* form. The plural form names more than one person, place, thing, or idea. Some nouns have the same form for both the singular and plural.

SINGULAR	PLURAL
one baby	two bab**ies**
one deer	five deer
one finger	two finger**s**
one fox	several fox**es**
one house	many hous**es**

3. Nouns may show ownership or relationship.

Both singular and plural nouns have *possessive forms* that show ownership or relationship. The possessive forms are made by the addition of an apostrophe (') and *-s* or by just an apostrophe.

The horse that Felicia owns is a palomino. *Felicia*'s horse is a palomino.	[ownership]
The leg of the horse was broken. The *horse*'s leg was broken.	[relationship]

4. Nouns may be formed with a suffix such as *-ation*, *-ism*, *-ment*, *-ness*, or *-ance*.

A *noun suffix* is an ending that makes a word a noun. *Strange* becomes the noun *strangeness* when the suffix *-ness* is added. These suffixes are clues that the words are nouns.

attend + ance	=	attendance
capital + ism	=	capitalism
consider + ation	=	consideration
fond + ness	=	fondness
retire + ment	=	retirement

Most proper nouns do not exhibit as many noun features as common nouns do. Proper nouns, for instance, seldom take a plural form: there are few reasons to speak of *seven Albert Einsteins* or *two Australias*. Often proper nouns do not take a determiner—you seldom hear of *the Italy* or *the Jackie Robinson*. There are a few cases, however, where proper nouns do follow determiners: *the United States*, *the Rocky Mountains*, and *the Virgin Mary*. Nevertheless, proper nouns do exhibit one important characteristic of nouns; they can be made possessive: *United States'* resources, the *Rocky Mountains'* beauty, the *Virgin Mary's* statue.

Exercise 3

Using what you have learned about the features of a noun, identify the nouns in the following sentences. Write out the sentences, underlining each noun. (Your teacher may ask you to explain how you identified the nouns.)

Example

a. The students were disturbed by the sound of the car's stuck horn.

a. The students were disturbed by the sound of the car's stuck horn.

1. Many farmers and ranchers consider the coyote a pest and a danger.
2. There are several mistaken beliefs about this animal, which native Americans called "the smartest creature on earth."
3. The most widespread misconception about coyotes is that they prey on cattle and sheep.
4. The truth is that scientists have never documented a single case of coyotes killing either cattle or sheep.

5. Coyotes may feed on an animal that has died from other causes.
6. Experiments show that the coyote prefers meat that has not been freshly killed and would rather feast on an old carcass.
7. Despite these facts many people believe that coyotes are responsible for the killing of many lambs each year.
8. The lamb is one of the most helpless animals in existence and catches many diseases and ailments.
9. Sheep and lambs have a high mortality rate, and most coyotes apparently feed on animals killed by nature.
10. Nevertheless, traps and poisoned baits are set, killing thousands of coyotes each year (as well as destroying other wild animals—including many members of endangered species, such as the golden eagle).

Mastery Exercise A

The following paragraph about Niagara Falls contains twenty-one nouns, and the first three of them are underlined for you. Using what you have learned in the previous sections, list the remaining nineteen nouns on a sheet of paper. If the noun is concrete, write *C* beside it; if the noun is abstract, write *A*. Be prepared to explain how you identified each noun.

> Both the Canadians and Americans experimented with the violent power of the great falls. Three large British ships, used in the war of 1812 and stationed at Lake Erie, were condemned, and it was decided to send them over the falls to see the amount of destruction that resulted. The first boat was torn apart by the rapids before going over, and the second filled with water before it reached the falls, but the third "took the leap gallantly and retained her form till lost in the cloud of mist below." Only a fragment of it was later found.[1]

Mastery Exercise B

From a newspaper, magazine, or book select a passage about as long as that in Mastery Exercise A. Using what you have learned in the previous sections, identify the nouns in your excerpt and list them on a sheet of paper. Beside each noun write the classes to which it belongs: *concrete* or *abstract*, *compound*, *common* or *proper*, or *collective*.

Using Nouns

Forming the Regular Plurals of Nouns

The plurals of most nouns are formed by the addition of either the suffix *-s* or *-es* to the singular form. Plurals formed in this way are called *regular plurals*.

Form the regular plurals of most nouns by adding the suffix *-s*.

---

[1]From *Summertime: Photos of Americans at Play 1850–1900* by Floyd and Marion Rinhart. Copyright (c) 1978 by Floyd and Marion Rinhart. Reprinted by permission of Clarkson N. Potter, Inc., a division of Crown Publishers, Inc.

SINGULAR	PLURAL
one dog	two dog**s**
one animal	several animal**s**
one school	many school**s**

Form the regular plurals of nouns ending in *s, sh, ch, x,* or *z* by adding the suffix *-es.*

SINGULAR	PLURAL
one bus	several bus**es**
one wish	two wish**es**
one match	many match**es**
one box	ten box**es**
one buzz	a few buzz**es**

Form the plurals of nouns ending in *o* preceded by a vowel by adding the suffix *-s.* Form the plurals of most nouns ending in *o* preceded by a consonant by adding the suffix *-es.*

SINGULAR	PLURAL
one radio	three radio**s**
one patio	many patio**s**
one hero	several hero**es**
one potato	two potato**es**

Exception: The plurals of most nouns that end in *o* and that have to do with music take only the suffix *-s:* banjo*s*, solo*s*, piano*s*.
Note: The preceding rules apply also to proper names: the Cole*s*, the Jones*es*, the Moralese*s*.

Exercise 1

All the nouns in the following sentences are regular nouns and appear in *italics.* Write out the sentences and change each singular noun to its plural form by adding either *-s* or *-es*. Underline each noun you make plural.

Examples

a. The *church* and *synagogue* offered to help the *victim* of the *flood.*
a. The churches *and* synagogues *offered to help the* victims *of the* floods.
b. The *boy* trimmed the *bush* and the *shrub* and then swept the *sidewalk* and *porch.*
b. The boys *trimmed the* bushes *and the* shrubs *and then swept the* sidewalks *and* porches.

1. Only the *echo* from the *canyon* answered the barking *fox.*
2. The *bunch* of wild *grass* tied with *ribbon* decorated the *table.*
3. The strange, drooping *moss* and the *screech* of the *owl* made the *camper* nervous.
4. The *ax* and *torch* were found near the *arch* of the *fortress.*

5. The *clash* and *crash* of the *thunderbolt* shook the *birch* and *pine*.
6. The *buzz* from the power *line* ruined the *transmission* of the *radio*.
7. He had to pay *tax* on the antique *glass*, the gold *box*, and the jeweled *brooch*.
8. We had to fill in the *scratch* on the *piano* with *wax* and *polish*.
9. The *guard* inspected the *catch* on the *door* and the *latch* on the *window* during the *recess*.
10. The *fizz* and *hiss* of the *chemical* seem sinister to the *student* in the *class*.

Forming the Irregular Plurals of Nouns

Many *irregular plurals* are formed by a spelling change plus the suffixes *-s* or *-es*.

Form the plurals of most nouns that end in *y* preceded by a consonant by changing the *y* to *i* and adding the suffix *-es*.

SINGULAR	PLURAL
one battery	four batter**ies**
one celebrity	a dozen celebrit**ies**
one enemy	many enem**ies**

Form the plurals of nouns that end in **y** preceded by a vowel by adding the suffix *-s*.

SINGULAR	PLURAL
one buoy	two buoy**s**
one day	seven day**s**
one donkey	a billion donkey**s**

Exceptions: Proper nouns ending in *y* become plural simply by adding the suffix *-s: Kennedy, Kennedys; July, Julys; Langtry, Langtrys; Foy, Foys.*

Form the plural of some nouns ending in *f* or *fe* by changing the *f* or *fe* to *v* and adding the suffix *-es*.

SINGULAR	PLURAL	SINGULAR	PLURAL
calf	cal**ves**	self	sel**ves**
elf	el**ves**	sheaf	shea**ves**
half	hal**ves**	shelf	shel**ves**
knife	kni**ves**	thief	thie**ves**
life	li**ves**	wife	wi**ves**
loaf	loa**ves**	wolf	wol**ves**

Note: Not all words ending in *f* or *fe* form their plurals as the preceding words do. Some form their plurals with the addition of the suffix *-s* only:

SINGULAR	PLURAL
roof	roof**s**
dwarf	dwarf**s**
chief	chief**s**
belief	belief**s**
safe	safe**s**

If you are not certain how to form the plural of any noun, check your dictionary.

Exercise 2

Write out the following sentences, changing each of the nouns in *italics* to its plural form. Underline each noun you make plural.

Example

a. On *Friday* the *company* will give higher *salary* to their *staff*.

a. On Fridays *the* companies *will give higher* salaries *to their* staffs.

1. The family *crest* must have belonged to *McHaney* or *Kelly*.
2. The *cry* of the *monkey* startled the *calf* at the *zoo*.
3. The *sky* looked overcast, so the *thief* stole the *donkey* for the *journey*.
4. The *library* will be closed for the *party* and then for the *holiday*.
5. Our *family* climbed up on the *roof* to survey the *country* where the great *victory* took place.
6. What *key* should the *melody* be played in when the rhapsody is performed?
7. *Kennedy* became important in making government *policy* and establishing *priority*.
8. The *life* of the *fly* puzzled the *authority* in the *laboratory*.
9. Put the *knife* on the *shelf* away from the *baby*.
10. The *belief* about the *galaxy* presented *mystery* for the *university* to solve.

Form some irregular plurals by changing a vowel sound.

SINGULAR	PLURAL
mouse	m**i**ce
foot	f**ee**t
goose	g**ee**se
louse	l**i**ce
man	m**e**n
tooth	t**ee**th
woman	wom**e**n

Some words have the same form for both the singular and plural. Many nouns naming animals belong to this group, as well as some nouns naming nationalities.

Rosa caught a nice *trout.*
Rosa caught eight nice *trout.*

The following words also have the same form for singular and plural.

antelope	deer	moose	series
bream	elk	pike	species
carp	grouse	Portuguese	swine
Chinese	Japanese	salmon	trousers
cod	means	scissors	Vietnamese

Another group of irregular plurals fits no pattern. This group includes those nouns that have been adopted from foreign languages and whose plurals have retained their foreign endings. Some of the most common of these follow. Check other such plurals in your dictionary.

SINGULAR	PLURAL	SINGULAR	PLURAL
analysis	analys**es**	datum	dat**a**
axis	ax**es**	hypothesis	hypothes**es**
basis	bas**es**	larva	larv**ae**
crisis	cris**es**	medium	medi**a**
criterion	criter**ia**	phenomenon	phenomen**a**

Nouns that end in *-en* also form irregular plurals. The most common of these are *child, children; ox, oxen;* and *brother, brethren.* The word *brethren* is now rarely used except when speaking about religious matters. In most cases the regular plural *brothers* is used.

Exercise 3

Write out the following sentences, putting each noun appearing in *italics* into its correct plural form. Underline each noun you make plural.

Example

a. The *foot* of the *goose* will be webbed like the *foot* of the *duck.*
a. The feet *of the* geese *will be webbed like the* feet *of the* ducks.

1. The *woman* wondered how the *man* would face the *crisis.*
2. The *child* saw the *trout, catfish,* and *carp* swimming in the *pool.*
3. The *analysis* indicated the *louse* on the *swine* carried the *germ.*
4. Don't put your *foot* down wrong, or you may squash the tiny *mouse* or step on the *larva.*
5. The *woman* raised the *moose* and the *goose* to show at the exhibit.
6. The *phenomenon* of the habits of the *salmon* fascinated the *Japanese.*
7. The *tooth* of the *mouse* will be damaged by chewing on the *roof.*
8. The *child* decided not to buy any *coat* made from the skin of *deer.*
9. The stampeding *antelope* ran into our *clothes* and got tangled up in John's *trousers.*
10. The *datum* on the *larva* of the *grasshopper* became the *basis* of the new *hypothesis.*

Forming the Plurals of Compound Nouns

If a compound noun is written as one word, form the plural by adding *-s* or *-es*.

SINGULAR	PLURAL
one racehorse	some racehorse**s**
one spoonful	seven spoonful**s**
one wristwatch	three wristwatch**es**

Exception: The plural of *passerby* is *passersby*.

When compound nouns are written as separate words or are hyphenated, form the plural by making the most important word in the compound plural.

SINGULAR	PLURAL
sister-in-law	sister**s**-in-law
Congressional Medal of Honor	Congressional Medal**s** of Honor
vice president	vice president**s**
self-image	self-image**s**

Sometimes, it is difficult to tell which is the most important word in a compound noun *(fourteen-year-old, fourteen-year-olds)*. When in doubt, check your dictionary to find the plural form.

Exercise 4

Write out the following sentences, making each of the *italicized* nouns plural. Underline each of the plural nouns that you form.

Examples

a. Coretta's *brother-in-law* are both *police officer.*
a. Coretta's brothers-in-law *are both* police officers.
b. Julia Child put four *cupful* of stuffing in the duck.
b. Julia Child put four cupfuls *of stuffing in the duck.*

1. We put away our *hockey stick* and poured several *cupful* of cocoa.
2. Judy has two *sister-in-law* and three *stepbrother*.
3. The *ex-President* spoke to the radical *left-winger*.
4. I put several *handful* of *mothball* in the trunk.
5. Where are the *baseball*, the *tennis ball*, and the *scoreboard*?
6. The *attorney-general* from three states have collected *boxful* of complaints about that scheme.
7. My *daughter-in-law* supervised three *playground*.
8. The *seven-year-old* ran for the *merry-go-round* near the *campground*.
9. The two *girlfriend* had *snapshot* taken for their *yearbook*.
10. The earthquake caused waves in the *swimming pool*, but no *skyscraper* shook.

Review Exercise A

Each of the following sentences contains at least one noun that must be made plural. Write out the sentences with the correct plural forms, using a dictionary if necessary. Underline the nouns you make plural.

Examples

a. Some Pennsylvania-Dutch designs are supposed to offer protection from hex.

a. Some Pennsylvania-Dutch designs are supposed to offer protection from hexes.

b. Oils and acrylics are two medium the art class uses.

b. Oils and acrylics are two media the art class uses.

1. John found a mouse with four baby in his pack.
2. Dee Brown wrote about the many hero of the American frontier.
3. The girls' swimming team won all its match last year.
4. Daggers and dirks are two knife.
5. The community college is offering several judo class.
6. Observers reported many strange phenomenon in the arctic skies.
7. Both concerto called for two piano.
8. U Thant was one of the U.N.'s secretary-general.
9. Yes, you should pack the clothes in those box.
10. Several radio are on sale at Thompson's.
11. Swimming is a popular sport among woman.
12. The paintings were not genuine but only clever copy.
13. There were several good volley during the two tennis match.
14. The scientists were puzzled by the conflicting datum from the computers.
15. Jack puts in two spoonful of vinegar when he makes chili.
16. During the long bus trip Rosa read several mystery by Josephine Tey.
17. How many mother-in-law did King Solomon have?
18. The two sergeant-at-arms counted the votes.
19. The Smithsonian Institution displays the many inaugural dress of the President's wife.
20. The two witness told conflicting story.
21. This flashlight takes four battery.
22. Those wriggling creatures in that water tank are the larva of mosquito.
23. Both safe are guaranteed burglarproof!
24. Are those bush poisonous?
25. If you hear seven buzz of your front doorbell, it's Daniel!

The Possessive Form of Nouns

Nouns can be made *possessive*, to show ownership or relationship, as the following examples show.

*Emilio***'s** car is in better condition than *Fred***'s** car.
*The women***'s** club discussed the Equal Rights Amendment.
My *parents*' eyes are brown.

Possessive forms are indicated by an apostrophe (') and the letter *-s* or by an apostrophe only.

1. If a noun is singular, add an apostrophe and the letter *-s* to form the possessive.

SINGULAR NOUN	POSSESSIVE FORM
We saw the *queen*.	We saw the *queen's* palace.
The *bus* annoyed us.	The *bus's* fumes annoyed us.
The *berry* fell.	The *berry's* juice stained the rug.

2. If a noun is a plural and does not end in *-s*, add an apostrophe and the letter *-s* to form the possessive.

PLURAL NOUN	POSSESSIVE FORM
The *children* were loud.	The *children's* party was loud.
The *geese* awoke us.	The *geese's* honking awoke us.

3. If a noun is a plural and ends in *-s*, add only an apostrophe to form the possessive.

PLURAL NOUN	POSSESSIVE FORM
We have two *dogs*.	The *dogs'* flea collars need to be changed.
There are six old *cups*.	The *cups'* handles were missing.

For more about possessives, see pages 595–596, which discuss the use of the apostrophe.

Exercise 5

Please write out the following sentences, using the correct possessive form for each *italicized* noun. Underline the possessives you form.

Examples

a. *Mort* old football injury sometimes bothers him.
a. Mort's *old football injury sometimes bothers him.*

b. The *men* locker room was flooded.
b. The men's *locker room was flooded.*

1. The *book* ending surprised everyone.
2. Our *school* emblem is the panther.
3. The *pharaohs* tombs were pyramids filled with treasures.
4. The *oxen* endurance compensated for the slowness of their pace.

5. Two of *China* contributions to our culture are gunpowder and macaroni.
6. Many *poets* graves are located in Westminster Abbey.
7. The *Peasants* Revolt in the fourteenth century helped end serfdom in England.
8. Billie Jean King proved that *women* tennis is as exciting as *men*.
9. The *knives* rusted blades were another indication of the *climate* dampness.
10. *King Solomon* mines were reputed to be fabulously rich.
11. *Hannibal* elephants, used for war, were the ancient equivalent of *today* tanks.
12. The best-selling mystery novels in the world are *Agatha Christie*.
13. That *bush* leaves are only edible for a short time in the spring.
14. The French *fries* aroma drifted from the *school* cafeteria.
15. Two of the *century* finest women singers are Mahalia Jackson and Beverly Sills.
16. My *family* roots are difficult to trace.
17. Some *families* histories are long and well-documented.
18. The *guitar* string was broken, and the *piano* keyboard needed mending.
19. The *Navahos* silverwork is exceptionally fine.
20. Several of the *treaties* clauses were unfair.

Writing Exercise A

Each of the following sentences is wordy because groups of words are used where one possessive noun would do. Rewrite each sentence, using the possessive form of the noun but be careful not to change the meaning of the sentence. Underline the possessive nouns you form.

Examples

a. One bike that belongs to Jim is broken.

a. One of Jim's bikes is broken.

b. The fumes of the buses were overwhelming.

b. The buses' fumes were overwhelming.

1. The leafy branches of the trees offered welcome shade.
2. The seven sisters of Joan were visiting for the summer.
3. The sputtering and coughing of the motor didn't sound good!
4. Where did Rosie put the sweater of Alicia?
5. Schools will close tomorrow for the birthday of Martin Luther King, Jr.
6. Astronauts triumphantly stepped onto the surface belonging to the moon.

7. Advertisers know the potential benefit in reaching the vast audience belonging to television.
8. On Saturdays shoppers crowd the sidewalks of Van Ness.
9. That showcase will exhibit the projects of all the classes.
10. It's pleasant to sit in the backyard of the Marshes.

Review Exercise B

The following sentences contain singular nouns that need to be made plural and possessive nouns that need an apostrophe and in some cases a final *-s*. Write out the sentences correctly, underlining the nouns you change.

Example

a. My sister Lisa has all of Stevie Wonder record.
a. My sister Lisa has all of Stevie Wonder's records.

1. Sixteen mouse came running out of the woodwork and attacked my cat Morris.
2. One of the first woman to get a major political partys nomination for governor was Congresswoman Ella Grasso.
3. In 1888, 600,000 Brazilian slave were freed by Princess-Regent Isabelles declaration.
4. The two half of the nation were united by the Union Pacific Railroads tracks.
5. The four naturalists report focused on seven deers life.
6. Many industry need to cut back on the factories pollution of the air and water.
7. Pilot Bessie Colemans ability as a stunt pilot attracted the worlds attention.
8. In 1948 Alice Coachmans Olympic gold medal was for the womens high jump.
9. Two of the mens hero are Ralph Nader and Julian Bond.
10. Abigail Adams urged President John Adams expansion of females political power.

In Item 11 the singular form of the name is *Ynes Mexica*. In Item 12 the singular is *Mr. Simodo*.

11. Over 200 species of plant were discovered through Ynes Mexicas work in Mexico and South America.
12. Mr. Simodos painting are his familys most prized possessions.
13. Charles Eastman book, *Indian Boyhood*, is most interesting.
14. At camp Sarah saw two bear, five wolf, and nine deer.
15. Both of Sherry Smiths brother live near Rick Montezs family.
16. Crazy Horses many victory were due to his military genius.
17. The two spy smuggled out the messages by placing them in loaf of bread.

18. Seven angry goose chased me as if their life depended on humiliating me.
19. Don't handle those grouse, as they may have louse.
20. Radio station KJJJ plays melody for easy listening and features two singers albums each day.
21. Several country signed the two treaty concerning the whales safety in the Atlantic.
22. Fred and Luis were furious because their boss at Tudburys Department Store said they had to dress up as elf during the stores Christmas party.
23. Several woman have swum the English Channel, but Gertrude Ederles success was exceptionally exciting.
24. Are you familiar with Langston Hughes screenplay for the movie *Way Down South?*
25. Harris book discusses all the famous mummy, werewolf, and zombie, as well as Frankensteins monster.

In Item 23 the singular form of the name is *Gertrude Ederle.*

Capitalizing Proper Nouns

A noun can be either common or proper. A *proper noun* names a specific person, place, or thing and is always capitalized.

Capitalize the names and titles of specific people, places and things.

COMMON NOUN	PROPER NOUN
my friend	Lavinia Paters
our town	Detroit
a doll	Miss Muffett

Note: Capitalize words showing family relationships or titles only when they are part of a name or when they are used instead of a name.

COMMON NOUN	PROPER NOUN
my aunt	Aunt Iris
my grandfather	Did you call, Grandfather?
the professor	Professor Jane Washington
the doctor	Dr. J. Cohen, M.D.

Capitalize all important words in the name of a specific building, landmark, or institution. (Unimportant words are the articles *a*, *an*, and *the*, as well as prepositions and conjunctions with fewer than five letters.)

COMMON NOUN	PROPER NOUN
this building	the Museum of Modern Art
the monument	the Statue of Liberty
your school	the University of Wisconsin

Capitalize nouns that name specific regions of the country but not nouns that merely indicate direction.

Marin County is *north* of San Francisco.	[direction]
Cotton is not generally grown in the *North*.	[region]

Capitalize the first and last words and all important words in the title of a book, poem, story, song, movie, television series, or the name of a newspaper, magazine, or work of art.

COMMON NOUNS	PROPER NOUNS
book	*The Daughter of Time*
poem	"Taught Me Purple"
story	"The Interlopers"
song	"When I'm Sixty-Four"
movie	*Death on the Nile*
television show	"Coal: Solution or Pollution? [episode]
	All in the Family [series]
newspaper	*The New York Times*
	the *Los Angeles Times*
magazine	*New West* magazine
art	"The Bathers"

Note: The titles of longer works, such as novels, magazines, newspapers, movies, and television series, are *italicized* in print and underlined in handwriting. The titles of shorter works are enclosed in quotation marks. *The* is not capitalized unless it is part of a name, as in *The New York Times.*

Capitalize the names of nationalities, races, and religions.

COMMON NOUN	PROPER NOUN
a religion	Buddhism
a people	Hopi
the ancient ruler	the Egyptian pharaoh

Capitalize the name of a team, an organization, a government agency, or a business.

COMMON NOUN	PROPER NOUN
a team	the Los Angeles Dodgers
an organization	the Elks
an agency	the Central Intelligence Agency
a business	Peter Pan Cleaners

Capitalize nouns that name school courses when they are followed by a numeral or name a specific course. The names of language courses are capitalized. (Nouns followed by a letter or number are generally capitalized.)

Gretchen does well in science and especially enjoyed *Science 300*.
Ricardo signed up for algebra, band, geography, and *Spanish*.
I think that *Geometry II* is in *Room 444*.

Exercise 6

The following sentences contain both proper and common nouns. Write out each sentence, capitalizing the proper nouns. Underline the nouns you capitalize.

Example

a. The man sitting next to my uncle is dr. ling, who teaches biology at a college in the west.

a. The man sitting next to my uncle is Dr. Ling, who teaches biology at a college in the West.

1. My father's two favorite comedians were uncle miltie and moms mabley.
2. After the long winter mother said she wished we could move to the southwest.
3. "You can tell that to the judge," said sergeant pearson firmly.
4. Carlotta signed up for tennis, french, and history 400 for the summer session.
5. After church reverend murphy told my father that he'd known grandfather lopez.
6. Mr. agung comes from indonesia, which is south of asia.
7. The south's most able and respected general was general robert e. lee.
8. The native americans of the midwest were more nomadic than those of the southwest.
9. Kim can't take latin because she has physics 100 at that hour.
10. One of my aunt's law teachers was judge crater.

Writing Exercise B

Each of the following sentences is vague and general because only common nouns are used. Write out each of the sentences, rewording them and adding proper nouns. (Be certain to capitalize the proper nouns.) Underline the proper nouns you use.

Example

a. My friend took a course with that teacher.

a. Bertha Bayard took American Literature 404 with Ms. Ramirez.

1. My sister will go to that city for the holiday.
2. The grocery is next to the record store on that street.
3. Our doctor teaches at that university and works at that hospital.
4. The short story by that writer is my aunt's favorite.
5. We drive past the high school on that road on our way to the supermarket.
6. There's a picture of the mayor of that town on the front page of the newspaper.
7. Two theaters will show that movie one day next week.
8. My sister and her friend stayed at a big hotel in that foreign city one month last summer.

9. My teacher, my guidance counselor, and the principal recommend that I apply to that college.
10. My friend's photographs taken in those two states appeared one month in three different magazines.

Review Exercise C

Write out the following sentences, capitalizing and underlining the proper nouns. Be certain to capitalize all the important words in a proper noun made up of more than one word.

Example

a. Singer gladys knight attended archer high school, which is in the south, and studied music, english, and journalism.

a. Singer <u>Gladys Knight</u> attended <u>Archer High School</u>, which is in the <u>South</u>, and studied music, <u>English</u>, and journalism.

1. An italian, marco polo, was one of the first europeans to visit the east.
2. One of teresa's ponies won a prize at the missouri state fair.
3. High school students were once required to take greek, latin, botany, and algebra.
4. Have you ever been to cripple creek, colorado, dad?
5. This morning jessica court dissected a frog in biology, and this afternoon she dissected a sonnet in english.
6. These robberies just south of town are obviously the work of those bumbling thieves fingers filch and his two brothers-in-law bob burglar and rob robbery.
7. Robert's car is old, but linda's car should be in the ford antique auto museum.
8. Our next-door neighbor joe jones asked to borrow two cupfuls of money at income tax time.
9. The following classes will be taught by ms. washington: speech 100, drama 200, english literature 1, and american literature 1.
10. My aunt, flora thomas, lives south of here, near the brooklyn bridge.
11. Willa cather's book *my ántonia* is miss cartwright's favorite.
12. The speaker was master sergeant ruth chock of the u.s. national guard.
13. The poachers on charlie's land were caught with several foxes' pelts and three alaskan timber wolves' skins.
14. This morning jorge realized with horror that his homework was probably under several truckloads of garbage at the morton city landfill.
15. My uncle, dr. p. parks, called the san francisco fire department to get his cat, maggie, out of a tree.
16. In greek mythology the gods and goddesses lived on mount olympus.

17. My aunt irene had several boston terriers, an irish wolfhound, a st. bernard, and a golden retriever.
18. Wasn't dorothy sayers' book the *unpleasantness at the bellona club* shown on PBS's *masterpiece theater?*
19. One of the reasons the north was victorious over the south in the civil war was that the north had more industry.
20. David eisenhower's grandfather was both general eisenhower and president eisenhower; his father-in-law is former president richard nixon.
21. One of texas' most eloquent representatives was barbara jordan, who made a stirring speech at the 1976 democratic national convention.
22. In 1588 the spanish armada was defeated by sir francis drake and the english navy on the north sea.
23. Two of the most colorful personalities to capture america's attention during the nineteenth century were lola montez and lily langtry.
24. althea gibson's victories in tennis include winning both the singles and doubles championships at wimbledon, england.
25. When my uncle victor retired, the mayor gave him a swiss watch; lieutenant ree gave him a new fishing rod; and my aunt gave him a house in south dakota.

Writing Exercise C

Write at least a paragraph on one of the following suggested topics, being as specific as possible by using proper nouns. Form plural or possessive nouns as necessary.

1. Focus on all the nouns in the photograph on page 350. Think about when and where the photograph was taken and what the people are doing. Now write a paragraph or two about the photograph in the form of a newspaper article or a journal entry.
2. You have recently won a trip to anywhere you choose in the United States! Where will you go? What states will you visit? Which cities? What natural and architectural landmarks will you see? How will you travel (car, boat, plane, or bicycle)? Will you go alone? Relate the adventures of your trip.
3. You have just come up with a wonderful invention. What is it? How does it work? Does it save time? Energy? Write an article describing your invention and its merits, so that you can sell your idea to a manufacturer.

Understanding Pronouns

Because they take the place of nouns, pronouns save a speaker or writer from having to use a sentence such as the following one.

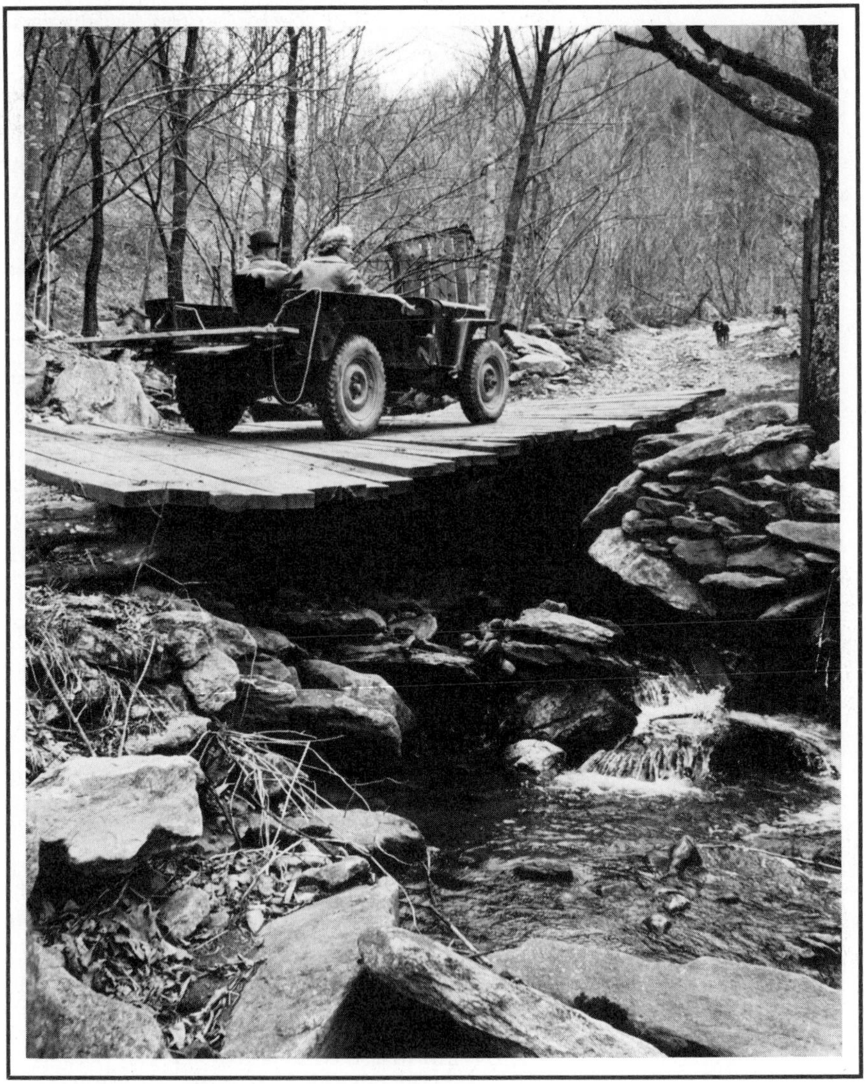

The teacher told the students that the students could leave early if the students' work was finished.

In the following sections you will learn to identify pronouns through their definition, their classification, and the features that distinguish them from other parts of speech.

Defining a Pronoun

A *pronoun* is usually defined as a word that takes the place of one or more nouns or other pronouns.

Marcia heard the news, but *she* didn't believe *it*.

The word (or words) to which a pronoun refers is called the *antecedent.* Antecedents usually come before the pronoun.

> Jenny thought the room was dull, and *she* decided to paint *it.*

A pronoun may refer to more than one antecedent:

> Professional players Ron Breuer, Marvin Delph, and Sidney Moncrief played on the same college team. *They* were called "The Three Basketeers."

In the preceding sentence the pronoun *they* has three antecedents: *Ron Breuer, Marvin Delph,* and *Sidney Moncrief.*

Sometimes, an antecedent follows its pronoun.

> When she found her ring, *Eileen* cried with happiness.
>
> Before their final exam *Connie* and *Duane* studied every night.
>
> Since they had grown up in Ecuador, the *children* had never seen snow.

The antecedent of a pronoun may also appear in a preceding sentence.

> *The Garners* couldn't open the *suitcase.* They had locked it and forgotten the key!

Sometimes, a pronoun replaces a word group that functions as a noun.

> *Tanaka's first novel,* which has just won an award, will be made into a movie.

A single pronoun can be used in place of an entire sentence.

> *The ladder will not collapse.* I'm sure of that!

Exercise 1

Write out the following sentences, underlining each pronoun. Then draw an arrow from the pronoun to its antecedent.

a. The statue was so badly broken that it couldn't be repaired.

a. The statue was so badly broken that it couldn't be repaired.

b. Last night's weather forecast, which predicted rain, was wrong.

b. Last night's weather forecast, which predicted rain, was wrong.

1. The car can't be driven. It has a dead battery.
2. Foxes and coyotes are extremely intelligent, but they are hard to tame.
3. Jim didn't do his chemistry assignment because he didn't understand it.
4. Lunch looked very strange today. It smelled even stranger.
5. Cheeses and meats are important foods because they are high in protein.
6. Käthe Kollwitz was a German artist who was famous for her print-making.

7. Juanita likes math because it is easy for her.
8. Because the Sioux and Cheyenne were great horse riders, they have been called "the best cavalry the world has ever seen."
9. Here today, gone tomorrow. That certainly is true!
10. Kim and Maury began writing a movie script, but they lost their patience and never finished it.

Grouping Pronouns by Classes

The following sections cover five classifications, or kinds, of *pronouns: personal, demonstrative, interrogative, relative,* and *indefinite.* Learning these classes will help you to identify pronouns and, in turn, to use them correctly in speaking and writing.

Personal Pronouns

Personal pronouns have different forms to show whether the speaker or writer refers to himself or herself, to the person or people being addressed, or to a third person or persons. Personal pronouns may be either singular or plural:

	SINGULAR	PLURAL
First Person:	I, me	we, us
Second Person:	you	you
Third Person:	he, she, him, her, it	they, them

When speakers and writers refer to themselves, they use *first-person pronouns.*

SINGULAR	PLURAL
I drive carefully	*We* drive carefully.
The movie bored *me*.	The movie bored *us*.

When speakers and writers refer to the person or persons being addressed, they use the *second person.* Notice that the pronoun *you* is both singular and plural.

You drive carefully.	*You* are all careful drivers.
The movie bored *you*.	The movie bored both of *you*.

When the speakers and writers refer neither to themselves nor to their audience, but to a third party, they use *third-person pronouns.*

SINGULAR	PLURAL
He / *She* / *It* drives carefully.	*They* drive carefully.

SINGULAR		PLURAL
The movie bored	*him* / *her.* / *it.*	The movie bored *them.*

Sometimes, personal pronouns combine with *-self* or *-selves* to make the *reflexive* forms of personal pronouns.

I woke *myself* up.
Give *yourself* a present!
He *himself* wrote that play.

	SINGULAR	PLURAL
First Person:	myself	ourselves
Second Person:	yourself	yourselves
Third Person:	himself / herself / itself	themselves

Note: The forms *hisself* and *theirselves* are not a part of Edited Standard English.

Reflexive pronouns have two uses. The first use is to refer back to the subject of the sentence and to repeat its meaning.

I woke *myself* up.
You can see for *yourself.*
Jim didn't hurt *himself* when he fell.
Evita made *herself* a purse.
This cellophane tape keeps sticking to *itself.*
The American colonies wanted to govern *themselves*.

Reflexive pronouns may also be used to add emphasis to a statement. When they do so, they are often called *intensive pronouns.* Intensive pronouns may immediately follow the noun or pronoun they intensify, or they may be moved to the end of the sentence.

The governor *himself* presented the award.
The governor presented this award *himself.*
I made this *myself.*

Exercise 2

Write out the following sentences and underline the personal pronouns. Write *1* above pronouns in the first person, *2* above pronouns in the second person, and *3* above pronouns in the third person.

Examples

a. Marcia taught her little brother how to fish.

3

a. Marcia taught her little brother how to fish.

b. The buzzer warned us of the end of the hour.

1

b. The buzzer warned <u>*us*</u> *of the end of the hour.*

1. We do not know much about the mysterious ruins at Stonehenge, England.
2. Have you seen Stonehenge? It is constructed of huge stone blocks and was probably built in 2200 B.C.
3. Stonehenge must have been built by primitive people, yet how did they move such great stones?
4. We visited the great pillars, and I wandered about the strange monument.
5. That man is an expert. Ask him to explain the mystery to us.
6. The circles of crude pillars with large slabs on top of them amazed me!
7. The Romans were in early Britain; perhaps they built Stonehenge by themselves.
8. Ms. Sybil Leek told us that she thinks ancient druid magicians were the builders. Should we believe her?
9. Professor G. S. Hawkins announced a startling fact. He discovered the stones were arranged so that certain stars appeared above them.
10. The unknown builders created a giant calendar of stone at Stonehenge. They may have used it for an observatory as well.

The Possessive Form of Personal Pronouns

Personal pronouns, like nouns, have possessive forms to show ownership or relationship.

	SINGULAR	PLURAL
First Person:	my, mine	our, ours
Second Person:	your, yours	your, yours
Third Person:	his her, hers its	their, theirs

Several possessive pronouns—*my, our, your, her,* and *their*—are always followed by a noun:

My sister and *your* sister wear *their* hair in the same style.
Our daughter must make up *her* own mind.

Some possessive pronouns can be used alone: *mine, ours, yours, hers,* and *theirs.*

That car is *mine*; the blue car is *yours*; and the green car is *theirs.*
Hers is the white house; *ours* is the red.

The possessive pronouns *his* and *its* can be used before a noun or alone.

Carlos enjoys using *his* camera. He likes *its* gadgets.
That camera is *his*. This case is *its*.

Note: Possessive pronouns *do not* have an apostrophe and an *s*.

Exercise 3

Write out the following sentences and underline each possessive pronoun.

Example

a. It's no wonder the cat is complaining; its bowl is empty.
a. It's no wonder the cat is complaining; its bowl is empty.

1. Marie Rothschild did not graduate from college because her family did not believe in higher education for women.
2. Her father was a scientist, and his specialty was insects—particularly the flea.
3. Marie, too, decided to study the flea and its habits.
4. Hers was important research. Two universities bestowed their highest honors on Marie.
5. By making movies of fleas, she analyzed their jumping power.
6. Theirs is great. If our jumping ability were compared with a flea's, ours would be much less.
7. My legs couldn't jump over a tall building 30,000 times. Could yours?
8. Your wildest guess would probably fall short of a flea's takeoff speed.
9. Its acceleration is twenty times greater than that of a moon rocket reentering earth's atmosphere. That beats mine!
10. Marie Rothschild also was an early protester of poison insecticides and their dangerous side effects. She certainly has my admiration.

Review Exercise A

Write out each of the following sentences, underlining the personal pronouns and their reflexive and possessive forms. Then draw an arrow from each pronoun to its antecedent.

Examples

a. Wherever she goes, Laura always carries her compass with her.
a. Wherever she goes, Laura always carries her compass with her.

b. Pedro, if you want to be sure of your answers, you should solve the problems yourself.
b. Pedro, if you want to be sure of your answers, you should solve the problems yourself.

1. Marcia, have you seen the giant cow towering above its surroundings in Janesville, Wisconsin?
2. Because they dig in the city, Kim and his friends call themselves "urban archeologists."
3. A city has much history hidden beneath its surface; often old buildings have been demolished and their contents buried.
4. Sally said, "Remember that John and his brother are my cousins."
5. Eleanor, Steve, and Karen said they grabbed their belongings and ran from the house as soon as it started to burn.
6. Since Loretta had forgotten her sweater, she asked Julio for his.
7. If the beige suitcase is yours, Margo, is the green suitcase yours also?
8. The airlines advertised, "Other companies might offer lower rates, but their service is not as good as ours."
9. Julio declared, "I photograph my subjects as I see them, not necessarily as they see themselves."
10. Jane loves her work, but hers is a thankless job.
11. When Bob calls, John will tell him that his package has arrived.
12. After they had gotten estimates from contractors, the Orlandos decided to build their house themselves.
13. If Lowell and Connie visit us this summer, my sister and I will teach them to roller skate while they are here!
14. When he was in the navy, Joel spent most of his time in San Diego.
15. Don't forget your key, Maria, because that door locks by itself when it closes.
16. Because it stings when applied to a cut, iodine is not Kiyo's first choice for an antiseptic; she wants a soothing salve on her cut!
17. Raoul, don't feed them if you want those kittens to stop hanging around your door.
18. Jennifer's dog hides its toys under her bed, so she hears it all night gnawing on a rubber bone.
19. Anita promised herself that she would earn enough money to buy a car, and she reached her goal. Now a new car is hers.
20. Hernando, Michael, and Rachel spent their vacations rafting on the Colorado River. They had trouble negotiating its rapids, but theirs was an exciting trip.

Demonstrative Pronouns

The small group known as *demonstrative pronouns* consists of only four words: *this, that, these,* and *those.* Demonstrative pronouns point out specific persons, places, things, or ideas.

> *This* is my sister.
> *That* costs too much.

Like the personal pronouns, the demonstrative pronouns have singular and plural forms. The words *this* and *that* point out singular nouns; the words *these* and *those* point out plural nouns.

> *This* is my favorite song. Jules bought *that.*
> I'm taking *those.*

Sometimes, a demonstrative pronoun has no antecedent, that is, no noun to which it refers. Its antecedent is understood.

> *This* (girl) is my sister.
> *That* (coat) costs too much for me to buy.
> *These* (wrenches) are the new tools for shop class.
> *Those* (facts) are amazing.

Note: When *this, that, these,* and *those* are used in front of nouns, they are modifiers, not pronouns.

> *This* book is a good one. [adjective]
> *These* animals are ocelots. [adjective]

Exercise 4

Write out each of the following sentences, underlining all demonstrative pronouns. (Be certain that the words you underline are demonstrative pronouns rather than noun modifiers.) If the words *this, that, these,* or *those* are used to modify a noun, circle both the word and the noun it modifies.

Examples

a. That was the biggest upset of our football season.
a. That was the biggest upset of our football season.
b. What is that watermelon doing in your locker?
b. What is that watermelon doing in your locker?

1. These are the arrowheads my sister found last summer.
2. Would you put this in your glove compartment, please?
3. I've never understood these forms.
4. I usually hate fish, but this is delicious.
5. Look, that is something crawling up your sleeve.
6. Watch out for that thing crawling up your sleeve.

7. That was the most embarrassing moment of my life.
8. We took those pictures at canoe camp last summer.
9. I'll take three of these, two of those, and this.
10. After seeing those films, I made up my mind about that.

Interrogative Pronouns

Interrogative pronouns are used in asking questions. The interrogative pronouns, *who, whom, whose, which,* and *what,* appear in place of unnamed people, places, or things.

> *Who* was the "Man in the Iron Mask"?
> *Whom* have you decided to nominate?
> *Whose* is the orange car?
> *Which* of these do you want?
> *What* will we do this Friday night?

Sometimes, a word such as *by, to, with, from, on,* or *for* may come before the interrogative pronoun.

> To *whom* should I give this note?
> For *which* of them is it?
> On *what* do you base your opinion?

Notice that in the preceding examples each interrogative pronoun stands for an unnamed person, place, or thing. None of the pronouns modifies a noun; rather, each takes the place of a noun in the question. If the words *which, what,* or *whose* are used in front of a noun, they are used as adjectives, not as interrogative pronouns.

Which do you like best?	[interrogative pronoun]
Which jeans do you like best?	[modifier]

Exercise 5

Write out each of the following sentences, underlining all interrogative pronouns. When the word *which, what,* or *whose* is used to modify a noun, circle both the word and the noun modified.

Examples

a. Who won the 1979 World Series?

a. Who won the 1979 World Series?

b. Which woman is Dr. Ling?

b. Which woman is Dr. Ling?

1. To whom do you refer?
2. Which is the article we're supposed to read?
3. Which hound chased what?

4. What made that terrible noise?
5. On what floor is Mr. Ortega's office?
6. Of whom does that girl remind you?
7. Who is the speaker at the assembly?
8. What right do they have to ask that?
9. Whose is the house on the hill?
10. What plane will they be taking?

Relative Pronouns

The *relative pronoun* introduces a group of words that modifies a noun or pronoun in the sentence. The relative pronoun is *related* to that noun or pronoun, which is its *antecedent.*

These are the slides *that* we made in biology lab.

In the preceding sentence the word *that* is a relative pronoun and refers to the antecedent *slides.* The relative pronoun connects *slides* to another group of words: *we made in biology lab.* This group of words has a subject, *we,* and a verb that tells what the subject did, *made.* A group of words that has a subject and a verb that tells what the subject is or does is called a *clause.* A clause introduced by a relative pronoun is called a *subordinate clause.* A more accurate definition of a relative pronoun is a pronoun that refers to an antecedent and connects or relates it to a subordinate clause.

For more information about subordinate clauses, see pages 524–540.

The following words are called *relative pronouns* when they are used to introduce a group of words that modify a noun or pronoun.

which	who	whose
that	whom	what

This book is by Ann Beattie, *who* wrote *Chilly Scenes of Winter.*
There is a film version of *Chilly Scenes of Winter, which* Ann Beattie wrote.
The book *that* Ann Beattie wrote was made into a movie.
We met Ann Beattie, *whose* second novel was well received.
Ann Beattie, *whom* you met last week, lives in Connecticut.

Note: Many of these words can act as modifiers, interrogative pronouns, or demonstrative pronouns, depending on their use in a sentence.

Which do you like?	[interrogative pronoun]
Which tractor do you like?	[modifier]
I'll buy the blue shirt, *which* is on sale.	[relative pronoun]
That is Max's cat.	[demonstrative pronoun]
That cat is Max's.	[modifier]
The cat *that* has black stripes is Max's.	[relative pronoun]

Exercise 6

The following sentences contain relative pronouns, each with a clear antecedent. Write out the sentences and circle the relative pronoun in each sentence. Underline the antecedent.

Examples

a. The tire that blew out was the right front one.

a. The tire (that) blew out was the right front one.

b. Those Navaho rugs, which are very old, are beautiful.

b. Those Navaho rugs, (which) are very old, are beautiful.

1. Americans did well at the 1964 Olympics, which were held in Tokyo.
2. Billy Mills, who is part Sioux, won the 10,000-meter run.
3. Six black Americans who competed in track events won gold medals.
4. The sport that the Japanese excelled in was judo.
5. American Al Oerter, whose discus throw won the gold medal, was a three-time winner of that title.
6. Luck wasn't with the Russian basketball players, whom the Americans defeated in a close contest.
7. Russian skater Lidia Skoblikova, however, won four gold medals for speed-skating, which is a demanding event.
8. The Olympic Games that the modern world knows are different from the ancient Greek games.
9. The early games, which are a part of recorded history, included chariot racing.
10. According to legend, Hercules, who is a mythical Greek hero, established the stadium at Olympia in 1222 B.C.

Indefinite Pronouns

Indefinite pronouns do not refer to specific persons or things. Often they do not have antecedents.

Each has its advantages.
Doesn't *something* look suspicious here?
Somebody wants to see you.

Some indefinite pronouns are always singular in meaning.

anybody	everybody	nobody
anyone	everyone	no one
anything	everything	one
each	much	somebody
either	neither	someone

Some indefinite pronouns are always plural in meaning.

both	few	many	others	several

A few indefinite pronouns may be either singular or plural, depending on how they are used in a sentence.

all	any	most	none	some

Some was spilled.	[singular]
Some were oak trees.	[plural]
All the money is lost.	[singular]
All the seats are taken.	[plural]

If a word is used in front of a noun, it is a modifier, not a pronoun.

Each of the apples is ripe.	[indefinite pronoun]
Each apple is ripe.	[modifier]

Exercise 7

Write out the following sentences, underlining the indefinite pronouns in each. Write *S* above the pronoun if it is singular or *P* if it is plural. (Some sentences have more than one indefinite pronoun, and some have indefinite pronouns used as modifiers.)

Examples

a. Each of the players is given a number.

S
a. Each of the players is given a number.

b. Some of the players were disqualified.

P
b. Some of the players were disqualified.

1. Someone in the class is going to the speech contest.
2. One of my hobbies is stamp collecting.
3. Something in the engine or the transmission is broken.
4. Both of the sheep were in the pasture.
5. Both twins promised to come, but neither is here.
6. Everybody says that nothing works.
7. Each of us was glad that some food was left.
8. The ones in the hall are mine; either is all right for you to use.
9. Each seed in the experiment has sprouted, so others are going to be planted.
10. Neither of these pairs of jeans fits, so each pair is going to have to be returned.

Finding a Pronoun by Its Features

Three features distinguish pronouns from other parts of speech.

1. A pronoun may be singular or plural.

Personal (including reflexive and possessive), demonstrative, and indefinite pronouns have singular or plural meanings.

	SINGULAR	PLURAL
Personal:	I, you, he, she, it, me, him, her	we, you, they, us, them
(Reflexive):	myself, yourself, himself, herself, itself	ourselves, yourselves, themselves
(Possessive):	my, mine, your, yours, his, her, hers, its	our, ours, your, yours, their, theirs
Demonstrative:	this, that	these, those
Indefinite:	anybody, everybody, each, nobody, one, someone, either	others, few, both, several, many

For more about pronoun-verb agreement, see pages 401–402.

Singular pronouns take the singular form of the verb; plural pronouns take the plural form of the verb.

She <u>*sings*</u> in the choir. *They* <u>*sing*</u> in the choir.

Notice that interrogative and relative pronouns do not have different forms for the singular and plural.

Which is yours?
Which are yours?

I want the dog *that* has brown spots.
I want the dogs *that* have brown spots.

2. Pronouns may change form to show their function in a sentence.

Personal pronouns have both subject forms and object forms.

SUBJECT FORMS	OBJECT FORMS
I, we	me, us
you	you
he, she, it, they	him, her, it, them

3. Pronouns may show gender.

Personal (including reflexive and possessive) pronouns may be masculine, feminine, or neuter.

Masculine:	he, him, his, himself
Feminine:	she, her, hers, herself
Neuter:	it, its, itself

Some pronouns can be either masculine or feminine, depending on the speaker or the person referred to:

> I, me, myself, you, yourself.

Some pronouns refer to groups of both men and women, depending on the meaning of the sentence:

> we, us, they, them, you, ourselves, themselves, yourselves

Exercise 8

Write out the following sentences, underlining each pronoun. Be prepared to explain the features by which you identified each one.

Examples

a. My grandfather knew a man who wrote one poem every day.

a. My grandfather knew a man who wrote one poem every day.

b. Don't you want that for your birthday?

b. Don't you want that for your birthday?

1. Our friend sent us her graduation picture.
2. If she gives me her address, I'll send her a card.
3. My sister told him a funny story about that.
4. That chair needs one of its legs mended.
5. Loretta's brother made that guitar himself.
6. His dog doesn't know its head from its tail.
7. Wrap this package and give it to me, please.
8. Which is the essay that you wrote, Rosa?
9. During her vacation Lindsey visited her aunt and uncle at their farm.
10. They left our tour group and wandered off by themselves to watch the fire burn itself out.

Review Exercise B

Each of the following quotations contains one or more pronouns. Number your paper 1–10 and list the pronouns that you find in each quotation; next to each pronoun write the classification to which it belongs.

Example

a. Photographs, which cannot themselves explain anything, are inexhaustible invitations to deductions, speculation, and fantasy.

—Susan Sontag

a. which—relative
themselves—personal (reflexive)
anything—indefinite

1. The Vice Presidency is sort of like the last cooky on the plate. Everybody insists he won't take it, but somebody always does. —*Bill Vaughan*
2. Slang is a language that rolls up its sleeves, spits on its hands and goes to work. —*Carl Sandburg*
3. I know only two tunes: one of them is "Yankee Doodle," and the other isn't. —*Ulysses S. Grant*
4. The man who has no inner life is the slave of his surroundings. —*Henri Frédéric Amiel*
5. Everybody is a genius at least once a year; a real genius has his original ideas closer together. —*G. C. Lichtenberg*
6. I don't know who my grandfather was; I am much more concerned to know what his grandson will be. —*Abraham Lincoln*
7. Nothing is terrible except fear itself. —*Francis Bacon*
8. To speak ill of others is a dishonest way of praising ourselves. —*Will and Ariel Durant*
9. Where I was born and where and how I have lived is unimportant. It is what I have done with where I have been that should be of interest. —*Georgia O'Keeffe*
10. And I, to whom so great a vision was given in my youth,—you see me now a pitiful old man who has done nothing, for the nation's hoop is broken and scattered. —*Black Elk*

Mastery Exercise A

On a sheet of paper, list the pronouns in the following paragraphs. Next to each pronoun write the classification to which it belongs. (Your teacher may ask you to explain how you identified each one.)

> The bicycle had what is called the "wabbles," and had them very badly. In order to keep my position, a good many things were required of me, and in every instance the thing required was against nature. Against nature, but not against the *laws* of nature. . . . whatever the needed thing might be, my nature, habit, and breeding moved me to attempt it in one way, while some immutable and unsuspected law of physics required that it be done in just the other way. I perceived by this how radically and grotesquely wrong had been the lifelong education of my body and members. They were steeped in ignorance; they knew nothing—nothing which it could profit them to know. For instance, if I found myself falling to the right, I put the tiller hard down the other way, by a quite natural impulse, and so violated a law, and kept on going down. The law required the opposite thing—the big wheel must be turned in the direction in which you are falling. It is hard to believe this, when you are told it.
>
> —*From "Taming the Bicycle" by Mark Twain*

> None of them knew the color of the sky. Their eyes glanced level, and were fastened upon the waves that swept toward them. These waves were of the hue of slate, save for the tops, which were of foaming white, and all of the men

knew the colors of the sea. The horizon narrowed and widened, and dipped and rose, and at all times its edge was jagged with waves that seemed thrust up in points like rocks.

Many a man ought to have a bathtub larger than the boat which here rode upon the sea. . . .

—From "The Open Boat" by Stephen Crane

The study of words is not merely something that has to do with literature. Words are your tools of thought. You can't even think at all without them. Try it. If you are planning to go downtown this afternoon you will find that you are saying to yourself: "I think I will go downtown this afternoon." You can't make such a simple decision as this without using words. . . .

Your words are all that we, your friends, have to know and judge you by. You have no other medium for telling us your thoughts—for convincing us, persuading us, giving us orders.[1]

—From Thirty Days to a More Powerful Vocabulary
by Wilfred Funk and Norman Lewis

Mastery Exercise B

From a magazine, newspaper, or book select several paragraphs about the length of those in Mastery Exercise A. Using what you have learned in the previous sections, identify the pronouns in your paragraphs and list them on a sheet of paper. Beside each pronoun write the classification to which it belongs.

Using Pronouns

Many of the problems in using pronouns arise in making pronouns agree with their antecedents and in using the various forms of personal pronouns. In the following sections you will practice using pronouns in a way that conforms to Edited Standard English. The writing exercises in those sections will give you practice using pronouns to make your writing more effective.

Agreement of Pronouns and Antecedents

In Edited Standard English pronouns must agree with their antecedents.

A pronoun must agree with its antecedent in number.

When an antecedent is singular, use a singular pronoun to refer to it.

The *dog* wagged *its* tail.

Ms. Yamoto read *her* summation to the jury.

When an antecedent is plural, use a plural pronoun to refer to it.

[1]From *Thirty Days to a More Powerful Vocabulary* by Wilfred Funk and Norman Lewis. Reprinted by permission of Harper & Row, Publishers, Inc.

Six *dogs* threw back *their* heads and howled at the moon.

We called *our* parents yesterday.

When an antecedent is followed by a prepositional phrase, be certain the pronoun agrees with the antecedent and not the object of the preposition.

The *winner* of both trophies read *his* speech.

The *contestants* on the game show changed *their* answers.

Exercise 1

Write out the following sentences, choosing the correct pronouns from those in parentheses. Underline the pronoun you select.

Example

a. The dogs in the pack threw (itself, themselves) across the ice, pulling the sled behind.

a. The dogs in the pack threw themselves across the ice, pulling the sled behind.

1. The gallery with the beautiful painting was destroyed when (its, their) roof collapsed.
2. Drivers who fail to study for the drivers examination only harm (itself, themselves).
3. Dr. Sanchez, who worked long hours in the emergency wards of both city hospitals, knew (her, their) patient would receive good care at Central Community.
4. The boughs of the old, gnarled apple tree on the Hudson farm sagged, pulling down (its, their) heavy load of fruit.
5. The small kittens sitting by the warm stove in our neighbors' kitchen purred and licked (itself, themselves) contentedly.
6. The senator outlined the state legislature's plans for a new conservation program in (his, its) interview with the press.
7. Pulling (their, his) cloak tight for warmth, Benjamin Banneker spent long nights outside studying the stars.
8. The wind howled at the small crowds huddled together on the city's street corners and stretched (its, their) icy tentacles toward (them, it).
9. Do all the countries that belong to the United Nations guarantee (its, their) citizens freedom of speech?
10. We cousins, who thought Grandmother to be very serious and strict, laughed (herself, ourselves) sick at (her, their) stories about our parents' antics as children.

Some indefinite pronouns are always singular, and some are always plural. Others, such as *all, any, some, most,* and *none,* may be either singular or plural, depending on their use in a sentence.

When an indefinite pronoun is the antecedent of another pronoun, the second pronoun should agree in number with its antecedent.

A complete list of singular and plural indefinite pronouns is on pages 360–361.

Each of the boys likes *his* hamburgers rare and juicy.

Several of the girls finished *their* projects ahead of time.

One of the women had on *her* coat; the *others* looked as if *they* needed *theirs*.

All of the cherries were ripe, so we picked *them*. [plural meaning]

All of the milk was sour, so we threw *it* out. [singular meaning]

Three situations regarding antecedents and pronouns demand special care on the writer's part.

1. Use a plural pronoun when two or more antecedents are joined by *and.*

   A sister and brother may sometimes have *their* differences.

   My friends and I caught *our* limit of catfish.

2. Use a singular pronoun when two or more singular antecedents are joined by *or* or *nor.*

   Deanna *or* Stacey must have forgotten *her* books when *she* left.

   Neither Don *nor* Malcolm likes *his* part-time job.

   Use a plural pronoun when two or more plural antecedents are joined by *or* or *nor.*

   Either skunks *or* chipmunks let *their* presence be strongly known.

   Neither oaks *nor* maples keep *their* leaves in winter.

3. When singular and plural antecedents are joined by *or* or *nor*, the pronoun agrees with the nearer antecedent.

   Neither Cassie *nor* her cousins could eat the pizza *they* made.

   Either the Jackson twins *or* Steven will lend you *his* camping equipment.

Exercise 2

Write out the following sentences, inserting the correct pronouns from the choices in parentheses. Underline the pronoun you select.

Example

a. Some of the girls in the musical have already learned all (their, her) lines, and one of the girls has mastered (her, their) dance routine.

a. Some of the girls in the musical have already learned all <u>their</u> lines, and one of the girls has mastered <u>her</u> dance routine.

1. Some of his shirts were in bad condition, so Manuel carefully washed and mended (them, it).
2. Either Mrs. Ortego or her sons will be happy to show you (her, their) backyard and garden.
3. Several of the rosebushes had been sorely neglected, so we pruned (them, it) and put on fertilizer.

4. I left a dish of dried apricots here last night; did you find (them, it)?
5. The man and woman who run the veterinary clinic in Sandwich have (their, her) own ambulance for emergency pet care.
6. Several of the children in the class had finished (its, their) finger paintings, but others hadn't begun (it, theirs).
7. After the game neither the coaches nor the players could locate (his, their) bus.
8. Either one of the neighbors' boys or my little brother left (his, their) jacket on the porch.
9. Since all the old furniture was still in good condition, we decided to use (it, them) in the family room.
10. In all the commotion neither my aunt nor my parents could find (their, her) coats and other belongings after the family reunion.

Agreement of Pronouns and Antecedents in Gender

A pronoun must agree in gender with its antecedent.

Singular antecedents create few problems. When a singular antecedent is masculine, use the masculine pronouns *he, his,* or *him* to refer to it. When a singular antecedent is feminine, use the pronouns *she, her,* or *hers.* When the antecedent is neuter, use *it* or *its* to refer to the antecedent.

Hernando took *his* children to *his* office yesterday.

Did you hear Eileen read *her* report to the committee?

One of the dogs has ticks in *its* fur.

Sometimes, however, an antecedent is a singular indefinite pronoun that can refer to either a male, a female, or a mixed group. Traditionally the masculine pronoun has been used when the gender of the antecedent is unclear.

Each of the students will have *his* picture taken.

More recently, however, many speakers and writers have begun to use *his or her* in this situation or to recast the sentence so that the antecedent is plural.

Each of the students will have *his or her* picture taken.

The students will have *their* pictures taken.

Exercise 3

Write out each of the following sentences, choosing the correct pronoun from those given in parentheses. Underline the pronoun that you select.

Examples

a. Either Cecily Tyson or Leslie Uggams started (her, their) career as a singer, not as an actress.

a. Either Cecily Tyson or Leslie Uggams started her career as a singer, not as an actress.

b. Anyone who has frequent headaches should have (his or her, their) eyes checked.

b. Anyone who has frequent headaches should have his or her eyes checked.

1. Neither of the others gave any reason for (his or her, their) lateness.
2. All the speakers must have gotten (his or her, their) jokes from the world's oldest joke book.
3. Jennifer or her sisters must decide for (themselves, herself) how much (they, she) will spend.
4. Either the members of the finance committee or the president will give (his or her, their) views first.
5. Lois or her brothers might hurt (himself, herself, themselves) if (he, she, they) trip over that wire.
6. One of the women wanted (her, their) money back, but the others were satisfied with (her, their) purchases.
7. Both Lana and Kathy wanted (her, their) own way.
8. One of the members of the boys' choir lost (their, his) place, and suddenly everyone was off key.
9. Either the Washington sisters or Martha will bring (her, their) projector.
10. Some of the club members wanted to plan (his, their) picnic (himself, themselves).

Using Subject Pronouns

The *subject forms* of the personal pronouns (sometimes called the *nominative case*) are as follows:

SINGULAR	PLURAL
I	we
you	you
he, she, it	they

1. Use the subject form whenever the pronoun is the subject of a verb.

I hope the party starts soon.
We know that *she* will arrive shortly.
Ken and *she* knew the answer.

When a pronoun is part of a compound subject, use the subject form.

Nicole and *I* went to the movies.
Linda and *he* are bringing records to the party.

If you are uncertain which form of the pronoun to use in a compound construction, use the form you would use if the pronoun were by itself.

Note: When using a personal pronoun to refer to yourself, always place the pronoun that refers to you last.

Bob and *I* completed the project.

2. Use the subject form whenever the pronoun follows a form of the verb *be* and identifies or renames the subject of the sentence.

The winner of the art contest was *she*.
The speaker will be *he*.
It is *I*.

Note: The expression *It's me* is acceptable in informal spoken English. In formal situations and in Edited Standard English, however, use the subject form when the pronoun is a subject complement.

It's *I*.
It is *we* who complained.
Julio answered the phone, "This is *he*."

3. When a pronoun is simply used with a noun that is the subject of the sentence or with a noun that follows a form of *be* and identifies or renames the subject, use the subject form of the pronoun.

An asterisk (*) denotes a sentence with a feature that is not part of ESE.

We tenants complained to the landlord.
*Us tenants complained to the landlord.

It was *we* women whom you saw.
*It was us women whom you saw.

Exercise 4

Write out the following sentences, choosing the correct form of the pronoun from the choices given in parentheses. Underline the pronoun you select.

Examples

a. It was (they, them) who played that trick.
a. It was they who played that trick.

b. Maria and (she, her) recently moved to Iowa.
b. Maria and she recently moved to Iowa.

1. (We, Us) students collected cans for the recycling drive.
2. Kathy and (she, her) bought identical dresses for the party.
3. I thought I saw Michael, but it wasn't (he, him).
4. Freddy and (she, her) made all the furniture in their house.
5. The judges for the photo contest are Luis, (she, her), and (I, me).
6. It was (we, us) sophomores who won the tournament.
7. (He and I, I and he) joined the museum.
8. The president of the committee will be either (she or I, her or I).
9. (Them and us, Them and we, They and we) are concerned about the energy crisis.

10. (You and me, You and I) saw Marcia, or at least, I think it was (she, her).

Using Object Pronouns

The *object form* of the personal pronoun is called the *objective case.*

SINGULAR	PLURAL
me	us
you	you
him, her, it	them

1. Use the object form of the personal pronoun when the pronoun is the direct object of the verb.

   The class elected *her*.
   Don't call *me*! I'll call *you*.

2. Use an object form of the personal pronoun when the pronoun is the indirect object of the verb.

   The salesperson gave *them* a free sample.
   Are you going to give *me* an excuse for not calling?

3. Use an object form of a personal pronoun when the pronoun is the object of a preposition.

   The tiny dog was barking at *us*.
   There are few secrets between *him* and *me*.

4. Use an object form of the personal pronoun when the pronoun is the subject, object, or predicate pronoun of an infinitive. The infinitive form of the verb begins with the word *to: to pray, to call.* Infinitive phrases have subjects, objects, or complements.

For more on infinitive phrases, see pages 512–513.

The lifeguard told *us* to stop splashing.	[subject of the infinitive]
Does she want Irene to wake *her*?	[object of the infinitive]
Ken wants the star to be *him*.	[predicate pronoun]

When a pronoun is part of a compound object, use the *object form.*

An asterisk (*) denotes a sentence with a feature that is not part of ESE.

*Nobody told my *parents* and *I* the news.
Nobody told my *parents* and *me* the news.

*I saw *you* and *he*.
I saw *you* and *him*.

When a pronoun is joined with a noun that is the object, use the object form of the pronoun.

*Few people understand *we* geniuses.
Few people understand *us* geniuses.

*Several of *we* sophomores recounted the votes.
Several of *us* sophomores recounted the votes.

Exercise 5

Write out each of the following sentences, choosing the correct pronouns from those given in parentheses. Underline the pronouns you select.

Examples

a. Are you going with Pat and (he, him)?

a. Are you going with Pat and him?

b. I hope they invite (we, us) seniors.

b. I hope they invite us seniors.

1. The Joneses asked (she, her) to baby-sit.
2. That book was a present from (they, them) to (us, we).
3. Don't scare (he and I, him and me, he and me) with your stories!
4. The teacher gave too much work to (we, us) overworked students.
5. Nobody likes (him and her, he and she) to sing.
6. Between (you and I, you and me) I think this movie is terrible.
7. Both of her sisters want to be (she, her).
8. The party won't be the same without Theresa and (him, he).
9. If you want (we, us) to be there, call (he or I, him or me).
10. Did anyone give (we, us) drivers a reason to take (they, them)?

Review Exercise A

Write out each of the following sentences, correcting any problems in pronoun usage. Underline the corrected pronouns. (Some sentences contain more than one error.)

Examples

a. Some members of the audience shouted its disapproval of the villain of the play.

a. Some members of the audience shouted their disapproval of the villain of the play.

b. Ms. Washington gave the best report topic to Cloris and I.

b. Ms. Washington gave the best report topic to Cloris and me.

1. Each of the writers explained their philosophy to the audience.
2. To whom should Tanya and me speak about the problem?
3. Either Dan or Pete has forgotten it is their turn to feed the dogs.
4. Not one of the radio stations had the story on their news.
5. Neither the cat nor the dogs liked wearing its new flea collars.
6. One of the women on the magazine staff prided themselves for the award-winning spring issue.
7. Mark and me were late because we had car trouble this morning.

8. All bookworms are grateful to Andrew Carnegie and he.
9. The exchange student shyly asked Lilly and I about some slang terms he had heard.
10. Please tell we amateur poets who wrote this poem.
11. The captains are Marcia and he, and the alternates are you and me.
12. One of the radios you lent my brother and I has something wrong with their volume control.
13. Neither an orange nor those grapes are enough in itself to be a good lunch.
14. Please ask that woman if it is she whose dog had their picture in *Time* magazine.
15. Reporters for the newspaper staff this semester will be Coretta, him, and me.
16. Us English students love grammar and all of their interesting rules.
17. Nobody in their right mind would want to be bitten by a vampire bat.
18. Our neighbors and us spent the weekend with Tomi and he at Tomi's cabin by the lake.
19. Is it him who knows the officers of the science fiction club?
20. Flo, will you and her explain your answer to Rick and I?
21. Pat and me will give these forms to she to fill out.
22. Either an oriole or a mockingbird was singing their song near Beth and I.
23. Both Peg and Mary wondered how she did on her chemistry test.
24. Besides you and I, Jeff has allowed only she to drive his car.
25. If you were me, would you tell Terry and she about the problem?

Writing Exercise A

The following sentences contain many repetitions of the same nouns. Rewrite each sentence and replace the overused nouns with the appropriate personal, possessive, or reflexive pronouns, being certain not to change the meaning of the original sentence.

Examples

a. Confucius was famous for Confucius' wisdom and for Confucius' pithy sayings.

a. Confucius was famous for his wisdom and for his pithy sayings.

b. Pandora promised Pandora that Pandora would not look in the box Pandora had been forbidden to open.

b. Pandora promised herself that she would not look in the box she had been forbidden to open.

1. When the kitten saw the kitten in the mirror, the kitten arched the kitten's back and spat.

2. Larry voted for Larry in the class elections, but Larry told Carmen that Larry had voted for Carmen.
3. The ancient Greeks were the greatest thinkers of the Greeks' time, and the Greeks were also fine artists and warriors.
4. Scientists quickly learned that the Eskimos' equipment was superior to the scientists' for dealing with the arctic winter and the winter's dangers.
5. The sulfur was sending the sulfur's evil smell all around the volcano, and the tourists were all holding the tourists' noses.
6. Walt is taking Spanish because Spanish will help Walt when Walt visits Mexico next summer with Walt's family.
7. Coretta surprised Coretta; Coretta never thought Coretta would be that brave.
8. Pete went over to Renee's house so that Pete and Renee could practice Pete and Renee's duet for the concert.
9. Halley's comet, which will return near the earth in 1986, is composed of ice and cosmic dust; the comet's head is larger than Mars, and the comet's tail is 37 million miles long.
10. One Egyptian pharaoh loved the cherries of Lebanon so much that the pharaoh had homing pigeons make 400-mile flights to bring the cherries to the pharaoh.

Using *Who* and *Whom*

The relative and interrogative pronouns *who* and *whom* are sometimes a source of confusion. Although the word *whom* is being used less and less in recent years, in formal writing the distinction between *who* and *whom* should be recognized.

Who is the subject form and should be used when the pronoun serves a subject function. *Whom* is the object form of the pronoun and should be used for direct and indirect objects and objects of the preposition. *Who* and *whom* are interrogative pronouns when they are used to ask a question.

Who goes there?	[subject of sentence]
The winner is *who*?	[predicate nominative]
Whom did they elect?	[direct object]
Whom did they tell that story?	[indirect object]
To *whom* shall I give this check?	[object of the preposition]

Who and *whom* are relative pronouns when they introduce a subordinate clause. To choose the proper form decide how the pronoun functions within the clause.

For a full discussion of subordinate clauses, see pages 524–540.

I need to know *who* wrote *My Ántonia.*	[subject of clause]
I saw the teacher *who* is replacing Miss Hughes.	[subject of clause]
She was the one *whom* I asked.	[direct object of the verb *asked* in the clause]

The object form *whom* is also used as the subject of the infinitive.

We wondered *whom* to see about the problem.
Nobody knew *whom* to blame.

Exercise 6

Write out the following sentences, filling in the blanks with either *who* or *whom*. Underline the pronoun that you supply.

Example

a. _______ shall I say is calling?

a. Who shall I say is calling?

1. For _______ did she buy that funny valentine?
2. _______ is going to the game by bus?
3. _______ at the party danced the most?
4. The winner was _______ ?
5. The man on the corner is the one _______ has the used car for sale.
6. You will take the place of _______ in the contest?
7. Mr. Jones told us with _______ to talk about our problem.
8. I want to have the teacher _______ gives the least homework.
9. He is the friend _______ I most admire.
10. _______ did the judges select as the winner?

Incomplete Constructions

In an incomplete construction, use the same form of the pronoun that you would use if the sentence were completed.

An *incomplete construction* is a sentence with part left for the reader to complete.

Penny received more votes than I.	[*than I did*]
Did James run faster than she?	[*than she did*]

In the preceding sentences the pronouns are in the subject form. If the pronoun functions as the subject of a missing verb, use the subject form of the pronoun. When the pronoun functions as an object, use the object form.

Did she call you more often than me? [*than she called me*—object]

Choose your pronouns carefully when you write incomplete constructions because the meaning of an incomplete construction sometimes can be ambiguous. If you use a subject form of the pronoun, the sentence will have one meaning. If you use the object form, the sentence will mean something entirely different.

Subject:	Did she call you more often than I?	[*than I called you*]
Object:	Did she call you more often than me?	[*than she called me*]

Using Possessive Pronouns

Personal pronouns have a completely different form to show possession (see pages 354–355). Interrogative and relative pronouns show possession with the form *whose.*

Whose car is that blue one?
I saw a woman *whose* hair was green.

The indefinite pronouns that can be made possessive form their possessives as nouns do, by adding an apostrophe and an *-s: everyone's, everybody's, somebody's, anybody's, anyone's, one's.*

The main problem presented by the possessive pronouns is that of spelling. Notice that the indefinite possessive pronoun is the *only one* that uses an apostrophe.

The following words are contractions and not possessive pronouns.

it's [*it is*], you're [*you are*], they're [*they are*], who's [*who is*]

Do not use an apostrophe with a possessive pronoun other than the indefinite pronoun.

everyone's idea	its power
somebody's dream	your house
anybody's guess	their hometown
one's hopes	whose hat

Exercise 7

Write out each of the following sentences and choose the correct pronoun form from the pair given in parentheses. Underline the pronouns that you select.

Example

a. Our cat caught (its, it's) tail in the door.
a. Our cat caught <u>its</u> tail in the door.

1. The other team scored more points than (we, us).
2. My sister asked if you would bring (your, you're) guitar.
3. (Who's, Whose) going to find out (who's, whose) books these are?
4. No one in this class has studied longer than (she, her).
5. I don't know whether (their, they're) ready or not.
6. (Everyones, Everyone's) idea of a good time is not the same as (yours, you'res).
7. (Their, They're) car has a flat tire on (its, it's) left side.
8. For whom was (your, you're) letter of complaint intended?
9. The hamster has chewed (its, it's) way out of (its, it's) cage.
10. Who would dare insult (your, you're) cousin, (whose, who's) seven feet tall!

Avoiding Unnecessary Pronouns

An asterisk (*) indicates a sentence with a feature that is not a part of ESE.

Do not use a pronoun following a noun to form a double subject. When you write and speak, you should avoid these unnecessary pronouns.

*My friend she just bought a new car.
My friend just bought a new car.

*José he won a Merit Scholarship.
José won a Merit Scholarship.

Avoiding Shifts in Pronouns

When writing, do not shift needlessly from one person to another, for such shifting can cause confusion, as the following examples show.

*I hate eating in a restaurant where you sit in the dark, struggling to find your spaghetti by the dim light of one small candle.
[Needless shift from first person to second person]

I hate eating in a restaurant where *I* sit in the dark, struggling to find *my* spaghetti by the dim light of one small candle.

An asterisk (*) indicates a sentence with a feature that is not a part of ESE.

*One's grades usually correspond to your study habits.
[Needless shift from third person to second person]

One's grades usually correspond to *one's* study habits.

or

Your grades usually correspond to *your* study habits.

Now look at the following paragraph:

It seems as if students are always being criticized. If **you** are quiet and mind **your** own business, commentators say **you** are apathetic and uninvolved. If the students do become involved and politically active, then **they** are called rebels and troublemakers. **They** are called names if **they** don't take a stand on every issue and if **they** do. **We** simply can't win.

The previous paragraph uses person inconsistently; the students are referred to as *you*, as *they*, and as *we*. The following example shows the paragraph rewritten in third person. Notice how much easier it is to understand.

It seems as if students are always being criticized. If they are quiet and mind their own business, commentators say they are apathetic and uninvolved. If the students do become involved and politically active, then they are called rebels and troublemakers. They are called names if they don't take a stand on every issue and if they do. They simply can't win.

Writing Exercise B

Each of the following sentences contains an unnecessary shift in pronoun usage. Rewrite each sentence, correcting the use of pronouns. Underline the pronoun you have substituted for the incorrectly used pronoun. (In some cases you may have to change a verb as well as the pronoun.)

Example

a. A person doesn't know how much he or she can accomplish until you try.

a. A person doesn't know how much he or she can accomplish until he or she tries.

1. If those people went to the party, I'm sure you enjoyed yourselves.
2. Whenever a person buys a used car, you may be buying trouble.
3. If you snore in class, a student can expect an angry teacher.
4. Somebody thinks it's easy to find a parking place, until you look for one.
5. I hate movies where you have to wait in line.
6. Dog owners can make their pets obey if you follow a few simple rules.
7. When one hasn't had enough sleep, you can expect your brain and body to react sluggishly.
8. Any person who dares to sample Jo Ann's chili will get the surprise of your life.
9. When you start a diet, a person learns what suffering is.
10. When people are in love, you may do silly things sometimes.

Using Antecedents Clearly

When you write or speak, be certain that the antecedents of all your pronouns are clear, so that readers and listeners will have no trouble understanding to whom or what any pronoun refers. You should avoid ambiguous, general, and indefinite pronoun references.

1. Reword sentences in which the antecedent of the pronoun is ambiguous.

   If an antecedent is *ambiguous*, it has two or more meanings.

Ambiguous:	Maria and Sally drove her car. [Whose car?]
Clear:	Maria and Sally drove Sally's car.
Ambiguous:	Don called Phil after he had taken his final exam. [Who took the exam?]
Clear:	Don called Phil after Phil had taken his final exam.

2. Reword sentences in which the pronouns *which, this, that,* or *it* refer to vague ideas.

General:	The extreme heat put a strain on the city's power. People ran their air conditioners and fans to maximum capacity. Overuse caused shorts. *This* led to fires. [What, exactly, caused the fires?]
Clear:	The extreme heat strained the city's power supply because people used air conditioners and fans to maximum capacity. This overuse of electrical equipment led to shorts and subsequently to fires.

General: Our band won first place in the state contest and was selected to march at the Orange Bowl, *which* makes us very proud. [*Which* refers to no particular word or idea but is used to sum up several ideas.]

Clear: Our band won first place in the state contest and was selected to march at the Orange Bowl, honors that make us very proud.

3. Do not use *you* or *they* without clear antecedents. Avoid using *you* or *they* with unknown antecedents; instead, try to name clear and specific antecedents.

Indefinite: *You* sometimes feel lost in a large high school. *They* have so many students that *they* don't learn *your* name until the semester is half over.

Clear: A *student* sometimes feels lost in a large high school, where *teachers* have many *students*. A teacher may not learn a *pupil's* name until the semester is half over.

Writing Exercise C

Each of the following sentences or passages contains a pronoun that does not clearly refer to an antecedent. Make revisions that will remedy the faulty references.

Examples

a. Larry reminded Mick that he needed to call home.

a. Larry reminded Mick to call home.

b. Their new car has power steering and power brakes, automatic windows, air conditioning, and a tape deck, which make it expensive.

b. Their new car has power steering and power brakes, automatic windows, air conditioning, and a tape deck. These features make it expensive.

1. The Martins asked the Washingtons if they could drive them to the airport.
2. The lab smelled of rotten eggs, chlorine gas, and alcohol, which gave me a headache.
3. When you go to college, they make you work hard.
4. My mother dislikes that company because they are so pushy about selling you their product.
5. This morning I got a shock from the toaster, tripped over the cat, spilled orange juice on my homework, and brushed my teeth with hair cream by mistake. It made me want to go back to bed and stay there.
6. Linda told Marcia that her brother was waiting for her.

7. When you swim at the city pool, they don't put up with any nonsense in the water.
8. The Blazers and the Bucks were tied in the third quarter, but they finally won by two points.
9. The silverware was dirty, the food was overcooked, and the waitress was rude. That made me angry.
10. When Dawkins and the other player both leaped for the ball, a foul was called on him.

Review Exercise B

Rewrite each of the following sentences so that the pronoun refers clearly to its antecedent. Also, correct any other pronoun problems. (There may be more than one way to correct any one sentence.)

Examples

a. Carla informed Marcie that she would receive the science prize.

a. Carla informed Marcie that Marcie would receive the science prize.

b. Don't hitchhike or accept rides with people you don't know; it could be dangerous.

b. Don't hitchhike or accept rides with people you don't know; such practices could be dangerous.

1. Jack reminded Malcolm that he needed to get gas.
2. My sister she went through my drawers, took my best pen, borrowed half my notebook paper, and spilled milk on my homework, which made me mad.
3. When a customer enters that jewelry store, he or she will notice how snobbish they seem.
4. Lydia told Carmen she could ride with her cousin.
5. You should never stare fixedly at a baboon or grin at one; it seems like an act of aggression and may trigger an attack.
6. When a person joins the army, they put you through they're rigorous physical training.
7. I ate too much popcorn at the fair and then rode the roller coaster; it made me feel queasy.
8. Lisa asked Karen if she knew who's barbecue was on for Saturday.
9. Campers should check for ticks because they can give you several nasty diseases.
10. I dislike going to sales because they push and shove you to get at the bargains.
11. The Millers told the O'Haras about the prowler in their neighborhood.
12. I tripped in the cafeteria and spilled milk on the principal and a plate of spaghetti on the vice-principal. Nobody laughed at it though.

13. The radiator in study hall is noisy, the chairs are uncomfortable, and the temperature is always stifling, which makes it difficult to concentrate.
14. Carlos told Nick that he owed him a dollar.
15. The athletic department at the university is excellent; they always have championship teams.
16. If a person picks up a stinkbug, you learn very quickly why it has such a name.
17. Margie was even in the race with the other girl until she tripped.
18. My Great Dane accidentally sat on a mouse; it let out a surprised shriek.
19. The tides they are strong at that beach, and there is no lifeguard.
20. The food exploded in it's dish in the oven; it was completely ruined.
21. Margie bet Pam that she would get a perfect score on the biology test.
22. The local newspaper is terrible; they have typographical errors in every edition.
23. The children watched the workers until they had to leave.
24. Mike lifts weights, jumps rope, jogs, and swims; it keeps him in top shape.
25. The customer at that restaurant gets an unpleasant surprise when you look at the bill.

Writing Exercise D

Using one of the following suggested topics, write at least a paragraph, concentrating on using pronouns for variety and clarity. Use care in making pronouns agree with their antecedents, in using subject and object forms of pronouns, and in using clear pronoun reference.

1. Describe how someone or something taught you a lesson, such as how to appreciate something, avoid something, or do something. Be certain that your account includes someone other than yourself and that your pronoun references are clear.
2. Suppose you were living many centuries into the future. What would life be like? Write at least a paragraph describing some aspect of your future daily life, perhaps a meal. What would you eat? How would the food be prepared? Another possibility is to describe your home. What does it look like? With what appliances is it filled?
3. You have been asked to invent a new game or sport, either an outdoor sport, like baseball, or a board game. Describe the game you invent. What is its goal? How does someone win? How many players are involved? How do people play it?
4. Describe your favorite movie. Write at least a paragraph explaining its plot and describing the important characters. Include any other information about the film that you think might interest people.

Understanding Verbs

Every complete sentence must have at least one verb. Used effectively, verbs can communicate the emotion, thought, or action that is the essence of a good sentence. In the following sections you will begin your study of verbs by learning to recognize them through their definition, the classes into which they can be grouped, and the features that distinguish them from other parts of speech.

Defining a Verb

A *verb* is usually defined as a word that expresses action or a state of being.

Superman *leaps* over the building.	[action]
Jennifer Gaston *worked* for the Peace Corps.	[action]
A caterpillar *becomes* a butterfly or moth.	[being]
Tina *is* intelligent.	[being]

Exercise 1

Write out the following sentences, underlining the verb in each.

Examples

a. Jackie won the school's science prize.

a. Jackie <u>won</u> the school's science prize.

b. The city is famous for its antipollution laws.

b. The city <u>is</u> famous for its antipollution laws.

c. Workers examined the new communications satellite carefully before its launching.

c. Workers <u>examined</u> the new communications satellite carefully before its launching.

1. KoKo the gorilla is a most unusual animal.
2. She talks in sign language.
3. KoKo's trainer is animal researcher Francine Patterson.
4. Ms. Patterson trained KoKo for six years.
5. In those years the gorilla mastered about 375 words.
6. She communicates with her trainer and others by American Sign Language.
7. Her IQ is only slightly below that of a human child.
8. She identifies pictures in books by name.
9. She answers Ms. Patterson's questions with obvious intelligence.
10. Oddly enough, KoKo discovered two unfortunate byproducts of language on her own—the lie and the insult.

Grouping Verbs by Classes

Verbs function either as *action verbs* or *linking verbs.* In addition, if a verb is part of a verb phrase, it is either a *main verb* or a *helping verb.*

1. *Action Verbs*

An *action verb* shows either physical or mental action.

The hungry baby *shrieked* relentlessly.	[physical action]
Cars *screeched* to a halt at the light.	[physical action]
Romma *thought* of a plan.	[mental action]
The skiers *hoped* for snow.	[mental action]

2. *Linking Verbs*

See pages 492–496 for a full discussion of predicate nouns and adjectives.

A *linking verb* links the subject of the sentence with a noun, a pronoun, or an adjective in the predicate.

Boris *is* a dancer. [*Is* links the subject *Boris* with *dancer.*]
Lemons *taste* sour! [*Taste* links the subject *lemons* with *sour.*]

The most commonly used linking verbs include forms of the verb *to be: am, are, is, was, were, been,* and *being.* The following list gives some other commonly used linking verbs.

appear	look	sound
become	remain	stay
feel	seem	taste
grow	smell	turn

Notice that many of the verbs in the preceding list may be either action or linking verbs. Look at the way a verb is used in a sentence to decide whether or not it shows action.

Action:	Jan *tasted* the sour milk.
Linking:	The milk *tasted* sour.
Action:	Please *turn* the page, Lisa.
Linking:	Lisa *turned* gray with horror.

In general, if you can substitute the verb *became* or *was* in its place, a verb is a linking verb.

The milk *tasted* sour. [*The milk* was *sour.*]
Lisa *turned* gray with horror. [*Lisa* became *gray with horror.*]

3. *Main Verbs and Helping Verbs*

A verb may be either a single verb or part of a verb phrase. (A *verb phrase* contains two or more verbs that act as a single verb.) The last verb of a verb phrase is the *main verb.* The other verbs in the verb phrase are called *helping verbs* because they *help* the main verb express action or state of being. In the following sentences the helping verbs are underlined once, and the main verbs are underlined twice.

Mark will stay until Saturday.

Jack has seen many movies.

I should have walked to school.

Helping verbs include the forms of *be* as well as some other frequently used words:

is	be	can	would	might
am	been	could	have	must
was	do	will	has	
were	does	shall	had	
are	did	should	may	

Sometimes, a main verb is separated from the helping verb by words such as *always*, *usually*, *never*, *not*, and so on. These words are not part of the verb phrase.

I will (always) remember Mama.

Jack has (never) been afraid of heights.

You should (not) have driven so long.

Did you (ever) see this play?

Exercise 2

Write out each of the following sentences, underlining each verb. If a sentence contains a verb phrase, underline all the verbs in the phrase once and the main verb twice. Write *A* over every main verb that is an action verb. Write *L* over every main verb that is a linking verb.

Examples

a. Has anyone seen *The Empire Strikes Back?*

A

a. Has anyone seen The Empire Strikes Back?

b. I have never been so proud!

L

b. I have never been so proud!

1. The fire has been raging all night.
2. Elaine has been a singer for years.
3. The television has never broken before.
4. Who will bring the potato salad to the picnic?
5. Do you feel faint?
6. You must feel this velvet fabric.
7. The dog was growling ferociously.
8. Have you been skiing this winter?
9. I will think of you every day!
10. We must not forget the key.

Finding a Verb by Its Features

Verbs have one or more of the following features.

1. A verb has *tense.* It shows events happening in time.

I *study* today.
I *studied* yesterday.
I *will study* tomorrow.

There are six verb tenses—three *simple* and three *perfect tenses*: *simple present*, *simple past*, *simple future*, *present perfect*, *past perfect*, and *future perfect*.

I *smile* every day.	[present]	simple tenses
I *smiled* yesterday.	[past]	
I *will smile* tomorrow.	[future]	
I *have smiled* often.	[present perfect]	perfect tenses
You knew I *had smiled* yesterday.	[past perfect]	
By Sunday I *will have smiled* seven times.	[future perfect]	

The *principal parts* of a verb are used with helping verbs to form the different tenses. Every verb has three principal parts: the *present*, the *past*, and the *past participle.*

PRESENT	PAST	PAST PARTICIPLE
sing	sang	(has) sung
try	tried	(has) tried
laugh	laughed	(has) laughed
see	saw	(has) seen

See pages 388–398 for a full discussion of the verb tenses and how they are used.

2. Verbs have a form that ends in *-ing*.

The *-ing* form of the verb, used with a form of the helping verb *be*, forms the *progressive form* of various tenses.

She *is reading*.	[present progressive]
She *was reading*.	[past progressive]
She *will be reading*.	[future progressive]

3. A verb agrees with its subject in number.

I *jog*.	He *jogs*.
You *study*.	She *studies*.

Almost all verbs in the present tense have a final *-s* added when their subject is in the third-person singular.

Exercise 3

Write out the following sentences, underlining each verb or verb phrase. Your teacher may ask you to explain whether you used the traditional definition or the description of verb features to identify the verbs.

Examples

a. Juanita Hall won many acting awards.

a. Juanita Hall won many acting awards.

b. Their new car will be an economy model.

b. Their new car will be an economy model.

1. The group recorded its first demonstration tape in a garage.
2. Terry will pursue a career in veterinary science.
3. The Phoenician alphabet is the ancestor of our own.
4. The strange hills in northeastern Nebraska were formed by glaciers in the last ice age.
5. The famous Hope Diamond supposedly carries a curse.
6. Our class was discussing the possibility of life on other planets.
7. Detroit produced many popular singers.
8. My sister will buy a typewriter with her birthday money.
9. According to legend Romulus was the first king of Rome.
10. Dracula was created by the writer Bram Stoker.

Review Exercise A

Write out the following sentences, underlining each verb or verb phrase. Write *A* over each action verb, *L* over each linking verb, and *H* over each helping verb.

Examples

a. Susan has not tasted the soup, which smells delicious.

H A L

a. Susan has not tasted the soup, which smells delicious.

b. Joanne will be studying for her exams all next week.

H H A

b. Joanne will be studying for her exams all next week.

1. The little boy laughs whenever he sees a clown.
2. Roberta may never sing again.
3. By the end of the summer, we will have traveled through fourteen states.
4. Hasn't Ann seemed sad lately?
5. Juan, please taste this sauce and add some salt if necessary.
6. The cat has been sleeping in the same spot all day.
7. Elliot, you must not speak so loudly because the baby is sleeping.
8. The icy water felt wonderful.
9. Wendy feels certain that we should not leave so late.
10. The phone has been ringing all evening.
11. That water looks calm, but it is really quite treacherous.
12. I have never been so embarrassed in my life!

13. Next week we will look at a new apartment.
14. John was a lawyer before he changed careers.
15. The Clarksons have traded their old car for a newer one.
16. That door has always locked by itself.
17. That bright light on the horizon could possibly be a ship.
18. The electric company is constantly raising its prices.
19. Does Eleanora ever sing professionally?
20. Why did the alarm ring so early?

Mastery Exercise A

As you read the following paragraphs about treasure hunters, identify the verbs and verb phrases. (Note: In the phrase *treasure-hunting, hunting* should not be counted as a verb. Other verb forms you have not yet studied are enclosed in brackets. Do not include these forms.) List the verbs and verb phrases in this selection on a sheet of paper in the order in which they appear.

Example

a. Gold can be repeatedly melted and remelted without [damaging] the material itself in any way.

a. can be melted; remelted

Archaeologists and historians deplore the whole [treasure-hunting] business. They contend that treasure hunters destroy much of the historical value of any find in their grab for the gold. Some of the larger [treasure-hunting] companies have tried [to make] their peace with the archaeologists and combine [treasure-hunting] with science. This venture has not been entirely successful. Most marine archaeologists and historians are still calling for a complete ban on [treasure-hunting] activities off the U.S. coast. Such a ban would doubtless be a boon to archaeology and history but a loss to romance and adventure.

In recent years much of the popular attention has been focused on [sunken] treasures. But, to my mind at least, there is nothing that quite matches the allure of [buried] treasure. Perhaps that is a notion that grew out of [reading] Robert Louis Stevenson's classic, *Treasure Island.* [Buried] treasures are not nearly as common in fact as they have been in fiction. But there have been some real [buried] treasures, and hints and rumors of many, many more.

The notorious Blackbeard the pirate reportedly stashed much of his [ill-gotten] gains on Amelia Island, some thirty miles north of Jacksonville, Florida. You can still buy "treasure maps" [showing] where Blackbeard was supposed [to have buried] the treasure. Why don't the people [selling] the maps dig up the treasure themselves? Simple; the maps are fake. No one has yet found Blackbeard's treasure.[1]

---

[1]From *Gold: The Fascinating Story of the Noble Metal Through the Ages* by Daniel Cohen. Copyright (c) 1976 by Daniel Cohen. Reprinted by permission of the publisher, M. Evans and Company, Inc., New York, N.Y. 10017, the author, and Henry Morrison Inc., his agents.

Using Verbs

The emphasis in the following sections changes from understanding to *using* verbs: using verb tenses correctly, solving problems in verb agreement, choosing between easily confused verbs, and writing effectively with verbs. As you work through the sections, use the preceding Understanding Verbs sections for any help you may need in recognizing verbs.

Using Verb Tenses

The *tense* of a verb indicates the time of the action or state of being. The three simple tenses are *present, past,* and *future.*

1. *Verbs in the Present Tense*

Use the present form of the verb to express *present tense.* In the present tense add *-s* or *-es* to the verb that is used with singular nouns or with *he, she,* or *it.* No ending is added when the verb is used with plural nouns or with the words *I, you, we,* or *they.*

He She It Clair	*leaves* tomorrow.	I You We They Clair's sisters	*leave* tomorrow.

Verbs in the present tense can describe two different kinds of action: an action happening right now (in the present) or an action that is habitual (happens repeatedly).

A fly *crawls* up the window. [happening now]
A fly *spreads* germs. [habitual action]

2. *Verbs in the Past Tense*

See pages 564–569 for spelling rules.

Actions that happened in the past are described by verbs in the *past tense.* Form the past tense of most verbs by adding the endings *-d* or *-ed.* (The same ending is used whether the verb's subject is singular or plural.)

Rosa Bonheur *painted* in a style different from that of Renaissance artists.
A wagon train *carried* the settlers out west.
Thousands of wagon trains *carried* settlers out west.

Note: Some verbs—such as *carry*—undergo spelling changes when the *-ed* ending is added.

Many verbs, however, use forms other than *-d* or *-ed* to mark the past tense. Such verbs are called *irregular,* and their endings must be memorized, though you know many of them already.

Lena Horne *sang* on Broadway and in the movies.
A great white shark *swam* beneath our boat.

Use of the past participle is explained on pages 392–394.

The following list is of commonly used verbs that have irregular past tense forms.

PRESENT	PAST	PAST PARTICIPLE
become	became	become
begin	began	begun
blow	blew	blown
break	broke	broken
bring	brought	brought
build	built	built
burst	burst	burst
buy	bought	bought
choose	chose	chosen
come	came	come
dive	dived or dove	dived
do	did	done
draw	drew	drawn
drink	drank	drunk
drive	drove	driven
eat	ate	eaten
fall	fell	fallen
fly	flew	flown
freeze	froze	frozen
give	gave	given
go	went	gone
grow	grew	grown
keep	kept	kept
know	knew	known
lay	laid	laid
lead	led	led
leave	left	left
lie	lay	lain
meet	met	met
ride	rode	ridden
ring	rang	rung
rise	rose	risen
run	ran	run
say	said	said
see	saw	seen
shake	shook	shaken
shrink	shrank	shrunk
sing	sang	sung
sink	sank	sunk
slay	slew or slayed	slain
sleep	slept	slept
speak	spoke	spoken
spend	spent	spent

spring	sprang	sprung
stand	stood	stood
steal	stole	stolen
swear	swore	sworn
swim	swam	swum
take	took	taken
teach	taught	taught
think	thought	thought
throw	threw	thrown
wake	woke or waked	waked
wear	wore	worn
write	wrote	written

Exercise 1

Write out the following sentences, changing the present tense verbs to verbs in the simple past tense. Underline the verbs you change.

Examples

a. When the rain falls, my shirt and socks shrink.

a. When the rain fell, my shirt and socks shrank.

b. My little sister blows up a balloon until it breaks.

b. My little sister blew up a balloon until it broke.

1. We freeze our peaches so they keep well.
2. Television series from the new fall season come and go.
3. The angry golfer frequently takes his club and throws it down.
4. Students choose the project that they do.
5. Robin Hood, the English outlaw, steals from the rich and gives to the poor.
6. None of us ride with him because of the way he drives.
7. The lifeguard throws off her sunglasses and swims to the rescue.
8. My father says his government job brings him money, but the government taxes take it right back.
9. Bob throws his money away, but Caroline spends hers carefully.
10. He thinks before he speaks, and he always chooses his words carefully.

Exercise 2

Write out the following sentences and choose the correct form of each verb from the choices given in parentheses. Underline each verb you select.

Example

a. Jane _______ several articles on extrasensory perception. (written, wrote)

a. Jane wrote several articles on extrasensory perception.

1. Eddie's car ________ gasoline on the trip. (drunk, drank)
2. Our dog barked insanely when it ________ the letter carrier. (saw, seen)
3. A raccoon ________ into our garbage cans last night. (gone, went)
4. The President of the United States ________ at a local political rally. (spoke, spoken)
5. Lucky Lady ________ her best mile ever. (run, ran)
6. The school record ________ unchallenged for several years. (stand, stood)
7. Suddenly the lion pounced, and the zebras ________ away. (sprung, sprang)
8. In violation of the law, the bus driver ________ all night. (driven, drove)
9. Remembering that good things often come in small packages, I ________ the smaller one. (chosen, chose)
10. At the break of day, the sun ________ slowly over the hill. (rose, rise)

3. *Verbs in the Future Tense*

The *future tense* is composed of the helping verb *will* or *shall* and a main verb.

The main verb does not change its ending in any way.

> The Science Fiction Convention *will meet* in London.
> Your restaurant *will* never *succeed*.

The future tense expresses an action that will take place in the future.

> The comet *will reappear* in forty years.

The future tense is sometimes used to make predictions.

> Arkansas *will defeat* Texas by a wide margin.

The difference between *shall* and *will* is growing less distinct all the time, and few speakers now differentiate between the two. One use of *shall*, however, is to imply that the future action *must* be performed because of specific circumstances.

> This criminal *shall* be confined for ten to fifteen years.
> You *shall* be very sorry for that.

In formal English the words *I* and *we* take *shall* instead of *will* for a helping verb.

> General MacArthur said, "I *shall* return."
> We *shall* work out this problem.

Exercise 3

Write out the following sentences, supplying the future tense form of each verb that is shown in parentheses. Use *shall* with the words *I* and *we;* elsewhere use *will.* Underline the verb phrases you form.

Examples

a. Many scientists hope that solar power ______ our energy needs. (answer)
a. Many scientists hope that solar power will answer our energy needs.

b. We ______ a better mousetrap. (build)
b. We shall build a better mousetrap.

1. The weather forecaster on the evening news predicts it ______ cool and sunny. (be)
2. Inflation probably ______ to grow worse. (continue)
3. Perhaps someday scientists ______ a cure for cancer. (discover)
4. Maya Angelou ______ at the convention. (speak)
5. Before the end of the century, it is possible that Americans ______ on Mars. (walk)
6. I ______ 10,000 erasers for misbehaving in class. (clean)
7. Ecologists hope that the whooping crane and other endangered species ______. (survive)
8. We always ______ for a cure for the common cold. (hope)
9. The school ______ some hearty turkey hash just before Thanksgiving vacation. (serve)
10. "We ______ again," chuckled the villain, curling the infamous mustache. (meet)

Verbs in the Perfect Tenses

The three perfect tenses are the *present perfect*, the *past perfect*, and the *future perfect*. The perfect tenses are composed of a main verb preceded by a helping verb that is a form of *have (have, has, had).*

1. *Present Perfect Tense*

The *present perfect tense* is composed of the helping verbs *have* or *has* and the past participle of a verb. The present perfect tense usually describes an action begun in the past that may continue to the present. It is frequently used to describe an ongoing action.

Mike *has worked* at the drive-in for six months.
My sisters *have taken* up golf.

In the preceding examples the working at the drive-in and the playing of golf started in the past and continue in the present.

Another use of the perfect tense is to describe an action that is already completed.

He *has taken* the test already.
The stores *have announced* when the sales will begin.

2. *Past Perfect Tense*

The *past perfect tense* is formed with the helping verb *had* and the past participle of a verb. The past perfect tense usually describes an action that took place in the past before another action.

> I *had been* sixteen for a month before I took my drivers exam.
> Maria tried to get the library book, but someone *had checked* it out.

In both of the preceding sentences the past perfect tense describes an action that took place before another did.

3. *Future Perfect Tense*

The *future perfect tense* is composed of the helping verbs *will have* or *shall have* with the past participle of the verb. The future perfect tense describes a future action that will be completed before another future action.

> By September I *shall have lost* fourteen pounds.
> After this graduation Joanne *will have earned* two degrees.

Exercise 4

For each of the following sentences, decide whether the verb in parentheses should be placed in the sentence in the present perfect or past perfect tense. Write out the sentences, supplying the present perfect or past perfect form of the verb. Underline the verb phrases you form.

Examples

a. The radio station ______ the story before it checked the facts. (broadcast)

a. The radio station had broadcast the story before it checked the facts.

b. My grandmother ______ New York every year for the last eighteen years. (visit)

b. My grandmother has visited New York every year for the last eighteen years.

1. Julius Caesar went to the Forum, although the soothsayer ______ against going. (warned)
2. The United States ______ a member of the United Nations from the beginning. (be)
3. Maria ran back to the bus, but her purse ______. (disappear)
4. Liz and Jeff ______ debate again this year. (take)
5. I ______ this movie five times already! (see)
6. Fortunately, just before the accident, the hospital staff ______ its emergency procedures. (rehearsed)
7. Mr. Sung said he ______ our term papers over the weekend. (grade)
8. Lisa ______ in every basketball game this season. (play)

9. The fire ______ because of an overloaded circuit. (start)
10. The mayor ______ us repeatedly to solve the problem, but so far he's done nothing. (promise)

Exercise 5

On a separate sheet of paper, write out each of the following sentences, supplying the correct future perfect form for the verb in parentheses. Underline the verb phrase you insert in the blank.

Example

a. When I finish *Huck Finn*, I ______ four books in one month. (read)
a. When I finish Huck Finn, *I shall have read four books in one month.*

1. By the end of this week, I ______ forty pages in my journal. (write)
2. The coach ______ our game strategy by the time we report for practice on Thursday. (decide)
3. Because this bus is so late, my family ______ dinner when I arrive home. (finish)
4. We ______ a great opportunity if we don't attend the ballet while this professional troupe is in town. (miss)
5. You needn't worry that the train ______ the station by the time we purchase our tickets. (left)
6. Knowing my grandmother as I do, I bet that she ______ several exciting excursions for us. (arrange)
7. After August 1, you ______ an entire year of music training, won't you? (complete)
8. By the time this letter arrives, you ______ already ______ the sweater. (receive)
9. You ______ every aspect of automobile maintenance when you complete this course, Anita. (study)
10. The weather ______ much colder by Thanksgiving, so we will need warm clothes for hiking. (turn)

Using the Progressive Forms of Verbs

The *progressive forms* of verbs express ongoing action. These verb phrases are composed of a form of the helping verb *be* and a main verb ending in *-ing*. Each of the six tenses has a progressive form.

PRESENT TENSE, PROGRESSIVE FORM

SINGULAR	PLURAL
I am learning.	We / You / They } are learning.
You are learning.	
He / She / It } is learning.	

PAST TENSE, PROGRESSIVE FORM

SINGULAR		PLURAL	
I was learning.		We	
You were learning.		You	were learning.
He		They	
She	was learning.		
It			

FUTURE TENSE, PROGRESSIVE FORM

SINGULAR		PLURAL	
I shall be learning.		We shall be learning.	
You		You	will be learning.
He		They	
She	will be learning.		
It			

PRESENT PERFECT TENSE, PROGRESSIVE FORM

SINGULAR		PLURAL	
I	have been learning.	We	
You		You	have been learning.
He		They	
She	has been learning.		
It			

PAST PERFECT TENSE, PROGRESSIVE FORM

SINGULAR		PLURAL	
I		We	
You		You	had been learning.
He	had been learning.	They	
She			
It			

FUTURE PERFECT TENSE, PROGRESSIVE FORM

SINGULAR		PLURAL	
I shall have been learning.		We shall have been learning.	
You		You	will have been learning.
He		They	
She	will have been learning.		
It			

Exercise 6

Write out the following sentences, changing the *italicized* verbs to their progressive forms. Do not change the tense of the verb. Underline the verb phrases you form.

Examples

a. Odetta *sings* at the Newport Folk Festival.
a. Odetta is singing at the Newport Folk Festival.

b. The Blazers *have played* the Milwaukee Bucks for several years.
b. The Blazers have been playing the Milwaukee Bucks for several years.

1. Our team seemed full of spirit as they *played* the last few minutes.
2. As Luis and Laura finished, it *began* to rain.
3. At that time the authorities *should have taken* drastic measures.
4. The principal *will ask* to see you in her office tomorrow.
5. When they finally found the answer, scientists *had tried* for years to unlock the secret.
6. Some scientists *predict* a new ice age.
7. The Cornhuskers *led* Alabama seven to six.
8. Leslie Uggams and Ben Vereen *played* those roles in *Roots.*
9. The electronics store *will have* a sale on speakers.
10. By next month the class *will have prepared* for the dance for six months.

Review Exercise A

Write out the following sentences, supplying the tense and form of the verb that is shown in parentheses. Underline the verbs or verb phrases that you supply.

Examples

a. Sandy and Carol ________ on a fifty-mile canoe trip next summer. (*go*, future tense)

a. Sandy and Carol will go on a fifty-mile canoe trip next summer.

b. The criminal ________ behind a perfect set of fingerprints. (*leave*, past perfect tense)

b. The criminal had left behind a perfect set of fingerprints.

1. My mother ________ a night course in law at the university. (*take*, present tense, progressive form)
2. Tennis player Evonne Goolagong Cawley ________ from Australia. (*come*, past tense)
3. By the time he was twenty-five, Alexander the Great ________ the entire Persian Empire. (*conquer*, past perfect tense)
4. After Jennifer visits Utah, she ________ in the Great Salt Lake. (*swim*, future perfect tense)
5. Mr. Washington ________ us several bushels of homework in geometry. (*assign*, present perfect tense)
6. We ________ a film about volcanoes in geography class. (*see*, past tense)
7. Muhammad Ali ________ life back to the declining sport of boxing. (*bring*, past tense)
8. Our quarterback ________ his foot in the same place he ________ it last year. (*break*, present perfect tense) (*break*, past tense)
9. Al ________ his tires on those rocky back roads. (*wear*, past perfect tense)

10. By the end of the fourteenth century, plague ______ a million English lives. (*take*, past perfect tense)
11. When the bell ______, I ______ only half my lunch. (*ring*, past tense) (*eat*, past perfect tense)
12. Miguel ______ a plan of the house he ______ someday. (*draw*, past tense) (*build*, future tense)
13. Kim ______ in a helicopter, but he never ______ one. (*ride*, present perfect tense) (*fly*, present perfect tense)
14. The plant ______ so huge that we ______ it out. (*grow*, past perfect tense) (*throw*, past tense)
15. Beowulf ______ into the monster's lair, and there he ______ the beast. (*swim*, past tense) (*slay*, past tense)
16. The witness ______ the oath that he ______ to be truthful. (*forget*, past tense, progressive form) (*swear*, past perfect tense)
17. You ______ the words you ______ today, you cad. (*regret*, future tense) (*speak*, present perfect tense)
18. My locker ______ with things because I always ______ never to throw anything away. (*bulge*, present tense, progressive form) (*strive*, present perfect tense)
19. The temperature ______, so maybe the cold spell ______. (*rise*, present perfect tense) (*break*, present tense, progressive form)
20. The deadline ______ and ______, and we have completely forgotten it. (*come*, present perfect tense) (*go*, present perfect tense)
21. My allowance ______ to nothing; my money ______ away. (*shrink*, present perfect tense) (*fly*, present perfect tense)
22. Martha ______ up 500 balloons for the prom, and she ______ nicely. (*blow*, past tense) (*recuperate*, present tense, progressive form)
23. Lou Brock ______ the day we ______ the Cardinals. (*play*, past tense, progressive form) (*see*, past tense)
24. Marcus ______ in study hall and ______ so loudly that he ______ himself up. (*sleep*, past tense) (*snore*, past tense, progressive form) (*wake*, past tense)
25. Miss Fisbee ______ the same slides to the meeting that she ______ last year. (*bring*, present tense, progressive form) (*bring*, past tense)

Writing Exercise A

Write an original sentence for each of the following verbs, using the tense indicated. Underline the verbs and verb phrases you form.

Examples

a. *ring*—past tense

a. The salesperson <u>rang</u> the doorbell persistently.

b. *write*—present tense, progressive form
b. *John is writing an article about sharks.*

1. *go*—past perfect tense
2. *come*—present perfect tense
3. *swim*—future perfect tense
4. *teach*—past tense, progressive form
5. *run*—future tense
6. *know*—past tense
7. *choose*—past perfect tense
8. *keep*—present perfect tense
9. *weave*—past tense
10. *ride*—future perfect tense
11. *give*—present tense, progressive form
12. *take*—past perfect tense
13. *freeze*—future tense
14. *build*—past tense
15. *bring*—present perfect tense
16. *sing*—past perfect tense, progressive form
17. *break*—present perfect tense
18. *buy*—future tense, progressive form
19. *do*—past tense
20. *eat*—future perfect tense
21. *fly*—present tense, progressive form
22. *see*—future perfect tense
23. *dive*—past perfect tense, progressive form
24. *spend*—future tense
25. *shrink*—past tense

Solving Problems in Verb Agreement

One hallmark of verbs is that they have tense; another is that a verb *agrees* with its subject.

A verb must agree with its subject in number. If a subject is singular, use the singular form of the verb; if the subject is plural, use the plural form of the verb.

Except for the verb *be*, the only tense forms of a verb that change to show agreement are those in the present tense. In the present tense, verbs take the ending *-s* or *-es* if their subjects are either singular nouns or the pronouns *he, she,* or *it.* Plural nouns and the pronouns *I, you, we,* and *they* take the verb form without the *-s* or *-es* ending.

The car *races*.

He / She / It } *races*. [Singular nouns and these pronouns take the *-s* or *-es* ending in the present tense.]

The eight cars race.

I / You / They / We } race. [Plural nouns and these pronouns do not take the *-s* or *-es* ending in the present tense.]

Unlike other verbs, the verb *be* has three forms for the present tense. The extra form is for the pronoun *I*, and it is the verb *am*. The verb *am* is used only with *I*, whether it is used as a main verb or as a helping verb.

I *am* tired.
I *am dissecting* a frog in biology.

She *is* Korean.
She *is getting* a drivers license.

They *are* vegetarians.
They *are filming* the news story.

Other verbs have only one form in the past tense. The verb *be*, used by itself or as a helping verb, has two forms in the past tense: *was* and *were*. The form *was* is used with singular nouns and the pronouns *I*, *he*, *she*, and *it*. The form *were* is used with plural nouns and with the pronouns *we*, *you*, and *they*.

I *was* sick. — I *was sneezing* violently.
It *was* cold outside. — It *was snowing* hard.

You *were* healthy. — You *were doing* pushups.
They *were* termites. — They *were destroying* our garage.

Exercise 7

Write out the following sentences, supplying the correct form of *be* from the forms given in parentheses. Underline the form of *be* you select.

Example

a. We (was, were) studying grammar.

a. We were studying grammar.

1. I (am, is) taking the bus downtown.
2. They (was, were) playing ball in the empty lot.
3. It looks as though the Tigers (are, is) going to lose this game.
4. We have been too busy; we (is, are) exhausted.
5. These pumpkins that we (was, were) going to make into jack-o'-lanterns (are, is) rotten.

6. Summer has ended now that the trees (is, are) turning colors.
7. Hardly any vegetable (are, is) blue, except for ripe eggplants, which almost (is, are).
8. You (wasn't, weren't) at home when they (were, was).
9. We (was, were) wondering if we (was, were) ever going to understand this lesson.
10. If you (are, is) late, I (am, is) going to leave without you.

Finding the True Subject to Determine Agreement

Sometimes, the true subject of a sentence and the verb may be separated by other words. If a phrase comes between the subject and the verb, do not be tempted to make the verb agree with the noun closest to the verb. Find the true subject.

*A bowl of *apples* were on the table.	[incorrect agreement]
A bowl of apples was on the table.	[correct agreement]

In the preceding sentences the agreement error is easy to make because the plural noun *apples* comes between the verb and its singular true subject, *bowl*. In the following example several nouns separate the true subject (*S*) and its verb (*V*):

The goal (*S*) of the other first *explorers*, *fur trappers*, and *traders* was (*V*) different from the missionaries' goals.

Another problem in agreement arises when the true subject of the sentence comes *after* the verb. Often questions reverse the usual order of subject and verb.

There is (*V*) no reason (*S*) to stop the experiments.

Why are (*V*) lemons (*S*) sour?

Exercise 8

In the following sentences the verbs or verb phrases do not agree with their true subjects. Write out each sentence, changing each verb to its correct form. Underline the true subject once and the verb or verb phrase twice.

Examples

a. One of the joys of vacations are sleeping late.
a. One of the joys of vacations is sleeping late.
b. What is the history assignments I missed?
b. What are the history assignments I missed?

1. One of the members were sick.
2. Why has the armadillos become so numerous when other animals grow scarcer?
3. Every single member of all the choirs have food poisoning.
4. There is early morning speed-reading classes every day.
5. The problem that faced the settlers, the miners, the traders, and the merchants were overwhelming.
6. Why is the power company's workers in the building today?
7. The salaries of the coach and the English teacher is not equal.
8. The line for both movie theaters are around the corner.
9. Where are the set of golf clubs that you want to sell?
10. The magazine for enlisted people and veterans print true-life adventure stories.

Agreement with Indefinite Pronouns

When an indefinite pronoun is the subject of a sentence, its verb must agree with it in number. Some indefinite pronouns are singular in meaning; other indefinite pronouns are always plural; and a few can be either singular or plural, depending on their meaning in a particular sentence.

The following indefinite pronouns are always singular and take a singular verb.

For more information about indefinite pronouns, see pages 360–361.

anybody	everybody	no one
anyone	everyone	one
each	neither	somebody
either	nobody	someone

Everybody is invited to the grand opening of the new museum.

Each of the thousands of insects works for the good of the colony.

Neither of the twins likes to dress alike.

One of those records is good for dancing.

The indefinite pronouns *both*, *many*, *several*, *few*, and *others* are always plural and take the plural form of the verb.

Both of the children are geniuses.

Many of those restaurants require ties.

Are several of those paintings original oils?

The pronouns *all*, *any*, *most*, *some*, and *none* may be either singular or plural. If the pronoun refers to one person or thing, it is singular and takes a singular verb. If it refers to more than one, it is plural.

None of the house has been painted yet. [singular meaning]

None of the chairs have been painted yet. [plural meaning]

Most of the guests have left. [plural meaning]
Most of the dress is stained. [singular meaning]

Notice that the noun that comes between the indefinite pronoun (the subject) and the verb gives a clue as to whether the indefinite pronoun is singular or plural in meaning.

Exercise 9

Write out the following sentences, choosing the correct verb from those in parentheses. Underline the subject once and the verb or verb phrase that agrees with it twice.

Examples

a. Each of the girls on the drill team (furnish, furnishes) her own uniform.
a. Each of the girls on the drill team furnishes her own uniform.

b. Neither of those shows (interest, interests) him very much.
b. Neither of those shows interests him very much.

1. Each of us (pay, pays) for some part of the trip.
2. We checked the windows, and none (was, were) damaged.
3. One of these dogs (has, have) tangled with a skunk recently.
4. Either Vicki Carr or Stevie Wonder (is, are) appearing on that show tonight.
5. We asked Mary and Sam to the party, but neither (is, are) able to come.
6. Not one of the students in the sophomore class (has, have) type AB blood.
7. Both of those objects (is, are) hovering over the lake!
8. I've tried on every gym suit, and each (is, are) too big for me.
9. Nobody ever (remember, remembers) how to spell Ms. Yrkoeufski's name.
10. None of these books (is, are) overdue at the library.

Subject-Verb Agreement with Compound Subjects

Two or more subjects joined by the word *and* always take the plural form of the verb.

Jack *and* Jill are waiting.
The students *and* the professor have spoken at the conference.
Red, yellow, *and* blue are the primary colors.

Note: Some subjects that seem to be plural are actually singular. For instance, *chicken and dumplings* is considered as *one* dish, not *two;* you use a singular form of the verb.

Chicken and dumplings is our family's favorite meal.

The names of businesses and brands usually take the singular form of the verb.

Washington, Gomez, and Ling is the best law firm in town.

Bright and Early is a new alarm clock that plays "the Star-Spangled Banner" and shakes your bed.

When a compound noun names something considered as a single unit, use a singular verb.
Two or more singular subjects joined by *or* or *nor* take the singular form of the verb.

Mark or Kevin has drawn this cartoon.

Either biology lab or algebra class is canceled today.

Unfortunately, neither rain, sleet, nor snow stops the post office from delivering bills.

Two or more plural subjects joined by *or* or *nor* take the plural form of the verb.

Either frogs *or* toads live by that pond.

Neither roses *nor* peonies bloom in winter.

When a singular subject and a plural subject are joined by *or* or *nor*, the verb agrees with the subject nearer to it.

Either Lisa *or* the Ortega sisters are going to the game with us.

Neither chives *nor* garlic is needed in this recipe.

Either the dog *or* the cats are going to have to stay outside.

Exercise 10

Write out the following sentences, choosing the correct verb from the pair of words in parentheses. Underline the subject once and the verb or verb phrase twice.

Examples

a. Rags and Riches (is, are) the most unusual clothing store in town.
a. Rags and Riches is the most unusual clothing store in town.

b. Maurice and Kim (was, were) excused from school early today.
b. Maurice and Kim were excused from school early today.

1. Rings and Things (is, are) the name of the new jewelry store.
2. First National Savings and Loan (is, are) where I keep my money.
3. Neither cereal nor eggs (appeal, appeals) to me.
4. The bank and the bakery (buy, buys) ads in the student paper.
5. Atchison, Topeka, and Santa Fe (was, were) stops along a famous western railroad.

6. Either Abbott or Costello (ask, asks), "Who's on First?"
7. Both station wagons and the pickup truck (has, have) flat tires.
8. Kelly or her sisters (is, are) baby-sitting for us.
9. The teacher and the students (send, sends) their letters of complaint to the "Growls and Howls" department of the school paper.
10. Records or a song book (is, are) the best gift for Raoul.

Collective Nouns and Agreement Problems

Words like *team*, *group*, *committee*, and *audience* are called *collective nouns* because they name a collection of individuals acting together as a unit. If a collective noun refers to a group working as a unit, it takes the singular form of the verb. If the noun refers to the individual members of the group, it takes the verb's plural form.

> The audience is leaving. [The audience is regarded as a unit.]
>
> The audience were cheering as if their lives depended on it. [meaning the people in the audience]
>
> The committee is announcing its decision today. [The committee is regarded as a unit.]
>
> The committee are having disagreements on that subject. [meaning the members of the committee]

Note: Most collective nouns form their plurals as other nouns do—with the suffix *-s*.

> The team is practicing.
>
> Both teams are practicing.

Plural collective nouns, of course, always take the plural form of the verb.

Exercise 11

Each of the following sentences contains a collective noun used as a subject. Decide which of the verbs in parentheses is most appropriate to the meaning of each sentence and then rewrite the sentence with the verb you have selected. Underline the main verb or verb phrase in the sentence.

Examples

a. The band (is, are) marching in the town's centennial parade.

a. The band is marching in the town's centennial parade.

b. The band (buy, buys) all of their own uniforms.

b. The band buy all of their own uniforms.

1. A crowd (was, were) gathered around the display of electric trains.
2. The crowd (was, were) waving their signs and placards angrily.

3. The flock (graze, grazes) peacefully on the green hillside.
4. The flock (run, runs) off in twenty different directions.
5. The orchestra (was, were) taking out their instruments and tuning up.
6. The orchestra (give, gives) its first concert tomorrow night.
7. The public (demand, demands) honesty from its elected officials.
8. The public (has, have) argued about many concerns.
9. The swarm (was, were) buzzing around the hollow tree trunk.
10. The swarm (was, were) buzzing wildly as they tried to protect their queen and their honey stores.

Review Exercise B

Write out the following sentences, underlining the simple subject once and the verb or verb phrase twice. If there is an error in agreement, correct the verb.

Examples

a. Clarissa have already spent her paycheck.
a. Clarissa has already spent her paycheck.
b. One of those bags of peanuts are mine.
b. One of those bags of peanuts is mine.

1. A grove of trees are in the center of the picture.
2. In what cabinet is the sugar and flour?
3. One of the dogs bark all the time.
4. Our neighbors and my oldest sister is going to Mexico for the holidays.
5. Our team were badly behind at the half.
6. The best explanation for these occurrences are cosmic rays.
7. Biscuits and gravy are a favorite Southern breakfast dish.
8. The directions for solving this problem doesn't make any sense.
9. Mary and Eddie is out of school with strep throat.
10. Marcia play flute in the city orchestra's winter concert.
11. *Sanford and Son* were very popular with television viewers.
12. Where is my scarf and gloves?
13. The neighbors' dog or their cats has been digging in my garden.
14. A plate of ham and eggs sound good to me right now.
15. How does the birds know the way south in the winter?
16. These two paintings and that print is the work of Frederic Remington.
17. The ferret, the weasel, and the polecat is sometimes seen for sale in pet stores.
18. A team of experts have been appointed to investigate the reports.

19. One of the players object to the new rule; the others support it.
20. A pound of cashew nuts are very high in calories.
21. Some of the milk have spilled, but most of it is still in the pitcher.
22. Neither Lisa nor Jody are studying hard for the math exam.
23. Spurs, branding irons, and a silver saddle decorates one of the new restaurants; a painting of fruits and vegetables decorate the other.
24. The cafeteria doesn't provide enough variety, and many of the people who eat there is bored.
25. A portion of the peas were set aside to be frozen.

Some More Agreement Situations

1. Don't *and* Doesn't

Some speakers and writers have difficulty handling the words *don't* and *doesn't* in Edited Standard English. Both *don't* and *doesn't* are *contractions;* that is, they are shortened forms for the phrases *do not* and *does not.*

Don't is the contraction of *do not.* Use *don't* with plural subjects and the pronouns *I, you, we,* and *they.*

Many people don't like anchovies. [plural subject]
You don't like anchovies.

Doesn't is the contraction of *does not.* Use *doesn't* with singular nouns and the pronouns *he, she,* and *it.*

The cat doesn't like riding in the car. [singular noun]
He doesn't exercise enough.
It really doesn't matter anymore.

2. *Nouns That Are Plural in Form*

Use the singular form of the verb for nouns that are plural in form but have a singular meaning.

athletics	genetics	news
civics	mathematics	physics
economics	mumps	politics

Politics is one subject I never discuss!
Mumps is a painful disease.

3. *Nouns That Have No Singular Form*

Use a plural form of the verb with nouns that have no singular form.

pliers	shears	trousers	pants
scissors	jeans	slacks	suspenders

Western jeans are expensive in Europe.

Are those scissors sharp?

Note: If the word *pair* precedes the noun, use a singular form of the verb.

That pair of scissors is not sharp.

4. *Titles and Names of Countries*

Use the singular form of the verb for titles or works of art or for the names of countries.

The Netherlands is known for its tulips.

Ahmal and the Night Visitors is a popular opera at Christmas.

Short Stories has fifty tales by contemporary writers.

5. *Amounts*

Use a singular form of the verb for words and phrases that express time and amounts (money, fractions, weight, and volume).

Two miles is more than two kilometers.

Three quarters of my garden has been eaten by animals.

Five dollars isn't enough for both of us to see that movie.

When these amounts are thought of individually and not as a unit, the plural form of the verb may be used.

These last miles are taking forever to drive.

Years go by quickly as you get older.

6. *Predicate Nominative*

When the subject and the predicate nominative (a noun or pronoun in the predicate that means the same as the subject) are different in number, use a verb that agrees in number with the subject.

My job includes typing and mailing the bills.

The woods and the meadow are part of my property.

7. Every *and* Many a

When the words *every* or *many a* precede the subject, use the singular form of the verb.

Many a farmer bemoans this drought.

Every dog, cat, and hamster in the house is hungry.

Exercise 12

Write out the following sentences, choosing the form of the verb in parentheses that agrees with the subject. Underline the form you choose.

Examples

a. She (don't, doesn't) play tennis.
a. She doesn't play tennis.

b. Every leaf and flower (is, are) in bloom.
b. Every leaf and flower is in bloom.

1. The United States (have, has) great variety in its terrain.
2. More money and shorter hours (is, are) the union's demand.
3. Dinner and the movies (cost, costs) ten dollars.
4. Twenty dollars (is, are) the necessary deposit to reserve a room.
5. Either political science or civics (is, are) John's favorite course.
6. Two thirds of the seats (is, are) empty every night.
7. *Anna and the King of Siam* (is, are) the story on which the play *The King and I* was based.
8. Many a sailor (has, have) dreamed of sailing around the world.
9. The years (doesn't, don't) go quickly enough when you're young.
10. Those pants (is, are) too short!

Verbs Often Confused

lie/lay

The words *lie* and *lay* are easy to confuse if you do not remember their principal parts.

PRESENT	PAST	PAST PARTICIPLE
lie	lay	(has, have, had) lain
lay	laid	(has, have, had) laid

The verb *lie* means "to rest in" or "to get into" a horizontal position.

I *lie* on the beach. [I *rest in a horizontal position.*]
I *lay* on the beach.
I *have lain* on the beach.

The verb *lay* means "to place something," or "to put it somewhere." When using the verb *lay*, state the object that is being put or placed.

We *lay* the mail on the counter. [I *place* the *mail.*]
We *laid* the mail on the counter.
We *have laid* the mail on the counter.

rise/raise

The verb *rise* means "to go up" or "to get up." The verb *raise* means "to move something upward." When using the verb *raise*, tell the object that is being moved upward.

Raise is a regular verb, but *rise* is an irregular verb. Notice the principal parts:

PRESENT	PAST	PAST PARTICIPLE
rise	rose	(has, have, had) risen
raise	raised	(has, have, had) raised

The temperature *rises* every afternoon.
The temperature *rose* ten degrees yesterday afternoon.
The temperature *has risen* twenty degrees since this morning.

Julio *raises* the flag on holidays.
Julio *raised* the flag yesterday.
Julio *has raised* the flag again.

sit/set

The verb *sit* means "to be seated." The verb *set* means "to place something" or "to put it somewhere." When you use the verb *set*, always tell what object is being placed.

The cat *sits* on the porch. [The cat *is seated.*]

I *set* the dishes on the table. [I *placed* the *dishes.*]

The verbs *sit* and *set* each have different principal parts.

PRESENT	PAST	PAST PARTICIPLE
sit	sat	(has, have, had) sat
set	set	(has, have, had) set

Miriam *sits* at the first desk.
Miriam *sat* at the first desk.
Miriam *has sat* at the first desk.

He *sets* the radio on the night stand.
He *set* the radio on the night stand.
He *has set* the radio on the night stand.

Exercise 13

Write out each of the following sentences and supply the correct form of the verb from the pair of words given in parentheses. Underline the verbs you choose.

Examples

a. I hate to _______ over the wheel on a bus trip. (sit, set)

a. I hate to sit over the wheel on a bus trip.

b. Prices _______ sharply last month. (rose, raised)

b. Prices rose sharply last month.

1. My brother has dirty socks _______ all over his room. (lying, laying)
2. I had just _______ down the groceries when I heard the phone ring. (sat, set)
3. Yesterday I _______ new tiles in the kitchen. (lay, laid)
4. The camper had _______ down on an anthill. (lain, laid)

5. The market has ______ the price of meat. (raised, risen)
6. Yesterday Wanda ______ under the apple tree, reading all afternoon. (lay, laid)
7. ______ down your books and ______ down and have some cocoa. (Sit, Set) (sit, set)
8. Ralph ______ serious questions about the state of the economy. (rose, raised)
9. Marcia ______ at the counter and ______ her packages beside her. (set, sat) (set, sat)
10. The price of gold ______ and then dropped again. (raised, rose)

Review Exercise C

Write out the following sentences, completing each by choosing the correct form of the verb given in parentheses. Underline your choice.

Examples

a. Bernice has (lain, laid) in that chair all day, reading a mystery.

a. Bernice has lain in that chair all day, reading a mystery.

b. Ms. Washington (don't, doesn't) approve of sloppy writing or speaking habits.

b. Ms. Washington doesn't approve of sloppy writing or speaking habits.

1. The Mesozoic Era—or the Reptile Age, as it is often called—(was, were) the years when dinosaurs ruled the world.
2. Many a dinosaur (was, were) in existence then.
3. One type of dinosaur (was, were) the water-dwellers, such as the brontosaurus.
4. The United States (has, have) some rich stores of dinosaur bones.
5. A complete dinosaur skeleton was found (lying, laying) in Wyoming.
6. Five years (was, were) spent reassembling the bones of this giant dinosaur.
7. Every leg bone, vertebra, and rib (was, were) put into its proper place.
8. Many a scientist (was, were) busy (setting, sitting) the bones in place.
9. (Doesn't, Don't) the reason for the disappearance of the great dinosaurs puzzle you?
10. The extinction of the dinosaurs has (raised, risen) many questions among scientists.
11. I'm sure that millions of dollars (has, have) been spent trying to solve the riddle of the dinosaurs.
12. I (sat, set) up most of last night reading about tyrannosaurus, the fiercest of the dinosaurs.

13. After having (lain, laid) the book down, I tried to go to sleep, but I just (lay, laid) there envisioning dinosaurs.
14. I dreamed of huge beasts (raising, rising) their heads out of swamps, and I (sat, set) up with a start.
15. (Is, Are) ten dollars enough to buy that book?
16. *Lost Creatures* (has, have) wonderful drawings of prehistoric creatures on every page.
17. News about new scientific discoveries (is, are) always exciting; politics certainly (interests, interest) me less than science does.
18. Please (sit, set) that book over there where the other books about dinosaurs are (lying, laying).
19. (Do, Does) changes in climate explain why dinosaurs disappeared?
20. Those suspenders (have, has) dinosaurs on them! A pair of those suspenders certainly (raises, raise, rises, rise) my spirits!
21. (Do, Does) you ever wonder if scientists have assembled the dinosaur bones they have found (laying, lying) around in the right arrangement?
22. The scientists' problems (includes, include) finding the bones, identifying them, and arranging them in the proper order.
23. Three quarters of my day (is, are) spent thinking about prehistoric times.
24. I imagine that many a dinosaur (set, sat) its foot down in my backyard.
25. *Daydreams and Dinosaurs* (is, are) the title of my autobiography.

Using the Active and Passive Voices

Verbs may be in either the *active* or the *passive voice.* When the subject performs the action expressed by the verb, the verb is in the *active voice.* The object of the verb receives the action.

> Carolyn washed and waxed the car. [The subject, *Carolyn,* performs the action of washing and waxing; the object, *car,* receives that action.]
>
> The dog buried the bone. [The subject, *dog,* performs the action of burying; the object that receives that action is *bone.*]

Now consider the following examples.

> The car was washed and waxed by Carolyn.
> The bone was buried by the dog.

In the preceding examples the subject receives the action expressed by the verb. When the verb expresses action received by the subject, the verb is in the *passive voice.* Notice that the one who performs the action is expressed in a prepositional phrase *(by Carolyn, by the dog).*

A verb in the passive voice is composed of a form of the helping verb *be* with the past participle.

Passive: Michael *is adored* by his children.
Active: His children *adore* Michael.

Passive: Those cabins *were built* of logs.
Active: People *built* those cabins out of logs.

For a complete discussion of the active and passive voices, see pages 550–551 in the section on sentences.

One use of the passive voice in writing is for variety. Also, if the performer of an action is unknown or unimportant, the passive voice may express a statement better than the active voice can. You must be careful, however, because overusing the passive voice can make writing static, and sentences written in the passive voice sound awkward sometimes.

Exercise 14

Write out each of the following sentences. If a sentence is in the active voice, rewrite it in the passive; if it is in the passive voice, rewrite the sentence in the active voice.

Example

a. Marilyn was stung by a bee.
a. A bee stung Marilyn.

1. The huge elm tree was struck by lightning.
2. Rick slammed the baseball out of the park.
3. Joel and Marge planned a party for Luiz.
4. The idea was first thought of by Diane.
5. The fire was started by two careless campers.
6. Flames consumed the forest.
7. The camera was invented by a Frenchman in 1839.
8. Carrie raised some questions about the new budget.
9. The eclipse will be observed by both amateur and professional astronomers.
10. The judge found the defendant guilty of the crime.

Consistency of Tenses

One common flaw in writing occurs when the writer, for no apparent reason, changes verb tenses. The following passage illustrates the difficulty of following writing that shifts from tense to tense.

An asterisk(*) indicates writing with a feature that is not part of Edited Standard English.

**The Divine Comedy* by Dante begins when the narrator is lost in a dark wood. The time was just before Easter. As he tried to find his way through the forest, his path was barred by a leopard, a lion, and a wolf. He gives himself up for lost, when suddenly a white figure appeared. It is the spirit of the Roman poet Virgil, who was sent to help the narrator by the Blessed Virgin and by Beatrice. (Beatrice, the woman the narrator loved, was in heaven.) Virgil takes the narrator on a tour of Purgatory and the nine circles of Hell. Then Virgil led him to Heaven.

Reading such a passage is like being caught in a time machine that has short-circuited. The reader is thrown from the present to the past and then is jolted back to the present, only to be transported to the past again.

Notice how much more smoothly the passage reads when the tenses do not shift about:

> *The Divine Comedy* by Dante begins when the narrator is lost in a dark wood. The time is just before Easter. As he tries to find his way through the forest, his path is barred by a leopard, a lion, and a wolf. He gives himself up for lost, when suddenly a white figure appears. It is the spirit of the Roman poet Virgil. He has been sent to help the narrator by the Blessed Virgin and by Beatrice. (Beatrice, the woman the narrator loves, is in Heaven.) Virgil takes the narrator on a tour of Purgatory and the nine circles of Hell. Then Virgil leads him to Heaven.

The preceding passage has been rewritten in the present tense. When the present tense is used, as it is above, to describe events that actually took place in the past, it is called the *narrative present*. The narrative present has several uses: to summarize the events of a story, play, or novel; or to describe the events in a process, as in the following examples.

1. Moss *grows* on the northern side of trees because this side of a tree *is* generally moister. The southern side of a tree *is* that which usually *gets* the most sunshine and *is* therefore drier and warmer. Mosses *prefer* the cooler, damper side.

2. When we *inhale*, the air sacs in the lungs *fill* with air. Oxygen molecules from the air pass through the capillary walls and into the blood, where they *combine* with hemoglobin of the red blood cells. At the same time, the blood stream *sends* molecules of carbon dioxide back into the air sacs, and these molecules *leave* the system when we *exhale*.

Sometimes, the narrative present is used to tell entire short stories or novels. It is also commonly used in telling jokes or anecdotes.

Exercise 15

The following passages are written in a mixture of present and past tense. Rewrite each passage according to the tense indicated in parentheses after it. Underline the verbs whose tense you change.

Example

a. Two turtles go into a restaurant and order sodas. It suddenly begins to rain. One turtle said to the other, "You better go home and get our umbrella." "Okay," replied the second turtle, "but don't drink my soda while I'm gone."

   Three months passed. The first turtle muttered, "I guess he isn't coming back. I'll drink his soda." From outside came the voice of the second turtle: "If you drink my soda, I won't go home and get the umbrella."

a. *Two turtles go into a restaurant and order sodas. It suddenly begins to rain. One turtle says to the other, "You better go home and get our umbrella." "Okay," replies the second turtle, "but don't drink my soda while I'm gone."*

Three months pass. The first turtle mutters, "I guess he isn't coming back. I'll drink his soda." From outside comes the voice of the second turtle: "If you drink my soda, I won't go home and get the umbrella."

1. *Don Quixote* is the story of an old Spanish gentleman who reads so many romances that they affect his mind. He decided to become a knight, although knights no longer existed except in the books he read. He mounts a bony old horse he called his steed, placed a basin on his head for a helmet, and rode out to right the wrongs of the world. (Change to present tense.)
2. Raindrops form from the tiny droplets in clouds. Water vapor condensed on these droplets and made them larger, or else several droplets stuck together. If the temperature of the air through which the raindrops fell is freezing, the drops turn into sleet. In summer strong air currents sometimes blew the drops upward into freezing air. The frozen droplets fall, collect a layer of water droplets in the cloud, and freeze. When the droplets became too heavy for the air currents to hold up, they fell to earth as hail. (Change to present tense.)
3. In the 1890s Carry Nation became famous for her war against liquor. She knew the suffering alcohol could cause and decided to put saloons out of business. In a typical protest she enters a saloon carrying a hatchet. She is accompanied by her followers, who sing hymns. She swings her hatchet and splinters bars, tables, and bottles. Although she is frequently arrested for disturbing the peace, she does not end her crusade. Neither jails nor jeers can stop her. She carries on her crusade for years, until age and failing health force her to retire. She died in 1911. (Change to past tense.)

Review Exercise D

Write out each of the following sentences, choosing the correct verb form from the pair given in parentheses. Underline the verb you choose.

Examples

a. The rain (began, begun) to fall gently at first and then increased in force.

a. *The rain began to fall gently at first and then increased in force.*

b. I accidentally (threw, throwed) away the dead plant that was part of my sister's science project.

b. *I accidentally threw away the dead plant that was part of my sister's science project.*

1. It seemed as if the wind (blew, blowed) all night long.
2. Marcie (swam, swum) to the pier to take a rest.
3. Who was the person who (brang, brought) the king snake to biology class?
4. Just then the bell (rang, rung), and we (knew, known) we were late.
5. Just when the pitcher turned away, Laura (stealed, stole) third base.
6. When the balloon (busted, burst), the cat leaped away in fright.
7. When I washed my new jeans, they (shrank, shrunk).
8. We used to have some gerbils, but they all have (run, ran) away.
9. The lake had not (frozen, froze) completely, so we could not skate in safety.
10. He did it, even though he (saw, seen) it was wrong.
11. The senator who had not yet (spoke, spoken) finally (raised, rose) her hand to be recognized.
12. The old sofa had not completely (wore, worn) out, so we still (sat, set) on it comfortably.
13. As the cat approached the feeder, the birds all (flied, flew) away.
14. The horse had been (rode, ridden) too hard, so it just (lay, laid) down.
15. The sun had (rose, risen), and long shadows fluttered in the fields of grain.
16. During the night the pipe connected to the kitchen sink (sprang, sprung) a leak.
17. We visited a laboratory where penicillin cultures were (growed, grown).
18. He had (dived, dove) into the icy water and quickly (rose, raised) to the surface.
19. I had (wrote, written) down my homework assignment, but then I couldn't find my notebook.
20. The tomatoes were so heavy they had (broke, broken) off the vines.
21. I (drove, driven) all night but fortunately had (laid, lain) down for a nap before beginning the trip.
22. The jury was (swore, sworn) in, and the trial began.
23. Shirley offered us some dinner, but we had already (ate, eaten).
24. If we had (knew, known) about the sale, we could have saved almost seventy-five dollars.
25. We could see that Margo had been (shaken, shook) by her near-accident.

Review Exercise E

Write out each of the following paragraphs, supplying the proper form of each verb in parentheses. Underline the verbs you supply.

Example

a. The common house mouse is a social animal who likes to live in groups. Its breeding season (be) from spring to fall, and each pair of mice possibly (raise) up to ten litters a year. In cold climates or cold seasons, mice (seek) shelter in buildings. A house rarely (have) just one mouse; a building usually (have) several. Mice (be) destructive. Once in the house, they (eat) food, cloth, and other goods. They are (know) to carry parasites and germs. The pest originally (come) from Asia, but it now (be) found all over North and South America.

a. The common house mouse is a social animal who likes to live in groups. Its breeding season is from spring to fall, and each pair of mice possibly raises up to ten litters a year. In cold climates or cold seasons, mice seek shelter in buildings. A house rarely has just one mouse; a building usually has several. Mice are destructive. Once in the house, they eat food, cloth, and other goods. They are known to carry parasites and germs. The pest originally came from Asia, but it now is found all over North and South America.

1. During the Civil War many women (be) spies and scouts. The greatest of these heroes (be) Harriet Tubman, a former slave. By the time her career ended, she (make) nineteen trips into the South and (lead) many runaway slaves to freedom. Tubman (work) unpaid as a nurse during the early years of the war and (treat) both black and white soldiers. She also (spy), since she could travel easily through the South. Having (see) how slaves might escape, she (gather) information and (show) the fugitives an escape route. Tubman (take) part in army raids, sometimes serving as a military leader, sometimes as a guide. For these brave acts and others, she (earn) the title "General Tubman."

2. I was taking an evening stroll by the edge of the golf course with my dog Mo. It (be) a warm and pleasant evening, but strangely quiet and misty. I (see) that Mo and I (be) alone this evening. No neighbors (be) out stretching their legs after dinner. As the sky (grow) darker, we (begin) to start back home. Suddenly, as we passed a small pond, I heard a strange noise and stopped. Mo perked up his ears and (growl). Bubbles (rise) swiftly to the surface of the pond. I (think) it (be) a muskrat or large snapping turtle, but then the bubbles become huge and boiling, and I realized something enormous must be under the water—but what? Suddenly something long and black (burst) upward from the water! Sleek, wet, and striped with yellow, it (stand) almost six feet tall. For a moment I (think) a sea serpent was surfacing, but then I realized the truth—it was only a thrifty skin diver in a wet suit, who was collecting golf balls from the bottom of the pond.

3. The body uses copper to form red blood cells and hair pigment. Copper (be) found in muscle fibers, nerve coverings, and enzymes that help build tissues. Humans (require) only a small amount of copper, so deficiencies in copper (be) rare. Similarly, an overdose of copper (be) equally rare, since the body (tend) to discard unneeded quantities. Liver and shellfish

(be) foods rich in copper; nuts, raisins, brewer's yeast, and cereals also (be) good sources of copper.

Writing Exercise B

Write at least a paragraph on one of the following choices, being as specific as possible with your choice of verbs. Check to be certain that your tenses are consistent, that your verb forms are correct, and that all of your verbs agree with their subjects.

1. What action do you see taking place in the photograph on page 419? Write a paragraph describing the action that has just taken place and that is about to happen. Make your verbs as vivid as possible.
2. Describe a process to a friend, perhaps how to cook, repair, or build something. Write out the process so your friend could complete it by following your instructions.
3. Describe a sporting event. It could be the final inning of an exciting baseball game, the deciding game of a tennis match, or the end of the last quarter of a football game. Who does what? Describe the actions that might take place.
4. Suppose you overhear two people having an argument. Write their dialogue, trying to capture each person's emotions. Did anyone yell, shout, stammer, or howl? The argument could be about any subject you choose.

Understanding Adjectives

Adjectives, which describe or modify nouns, add detail to writing to make it more descriptive and more interesting. Notice, for example, how much more vivid the second sentence below is than the first one.

> Cows rested near the barn in the meadow.
>
> Large brown-and-white spotted cows rested near the old, weathered barn in the lush green meadow.

In the following sections you will learn to identify adjectives in three ways: by their definition, by their division into classes, and by the features that distinguish them from the other parts of speech.

Defining Adjectives

An *adjective* is usually defined as a word that modifies a noun or pronoun.

Adjectives answer certain questions about nouns or pronouns:

What Kind?	*new* car, *old* car, *speedy* car, *inexpensive* car
Which One?	*this* car, *that* car, *those* cars
What Quantity?	*three* cars, *few* cars, *all* cars, *several* cars
How Much or How Many?	*limited* quantity

Adjectives are often placed near the words they modify, but sometimes other words may separate the adjective from the word it modifies:

The book was *funny*.

The bus is usually *late* during the rush hour.

We became a little *anxious* about the odd noises.

Exercise 1

Write out each of the following sentences, underlining all adjectives. Draw an arrow from each adjective to the word it modifies. (Do not include the words *a*, *an*, or *the*.)

Examples

a. This book is a new collection of ghost stories by famous writers.

a. This book is a new collection of ghost stories by famous writers.

b. Every customer who ate a cheese sandwich at that restaurant got a terrible stomachache.

b. Every customer who ate a cheese sandwich at that restaurant got a terrible stomachache.

1. Several cardinals come each morning to the bird feeder.
2. Our three dogs made a large hole under the wire fence and then had a digging contest in the tulip garden.
3. A large bolt of lightning struck the oak tree in the backyard last night.
4. Many people are nervous about several reports of unidentified flying objects in the night sky.
5. Many people believe that goats eat tin cans, but the goats really nibble only the can labels.
6. In Greek mythology the golden apple was really the common apricot.
7. Hungry porcupines do much damage to young trees in American forests.
8. The largest bell in the world is a Russian one that weighs 180 tons.
9. The fuzz on a tennis ball gives the ball a slower flight and a trickier bounce.
10. Both of our neighbors were in car accidents, but neither one was hurt, since both drivers wore safety belts.

Grouping Adjectives by Classes

Some adjectives, such as *pretty*, *hungry*, *old*, and *new*, do not belong to a special class. Other adjectives, however, can be grouped into one of five categories.

1. *Articles*

The most frequently used group of adjectives is the one called *articles—the*, *a*, and *an*.

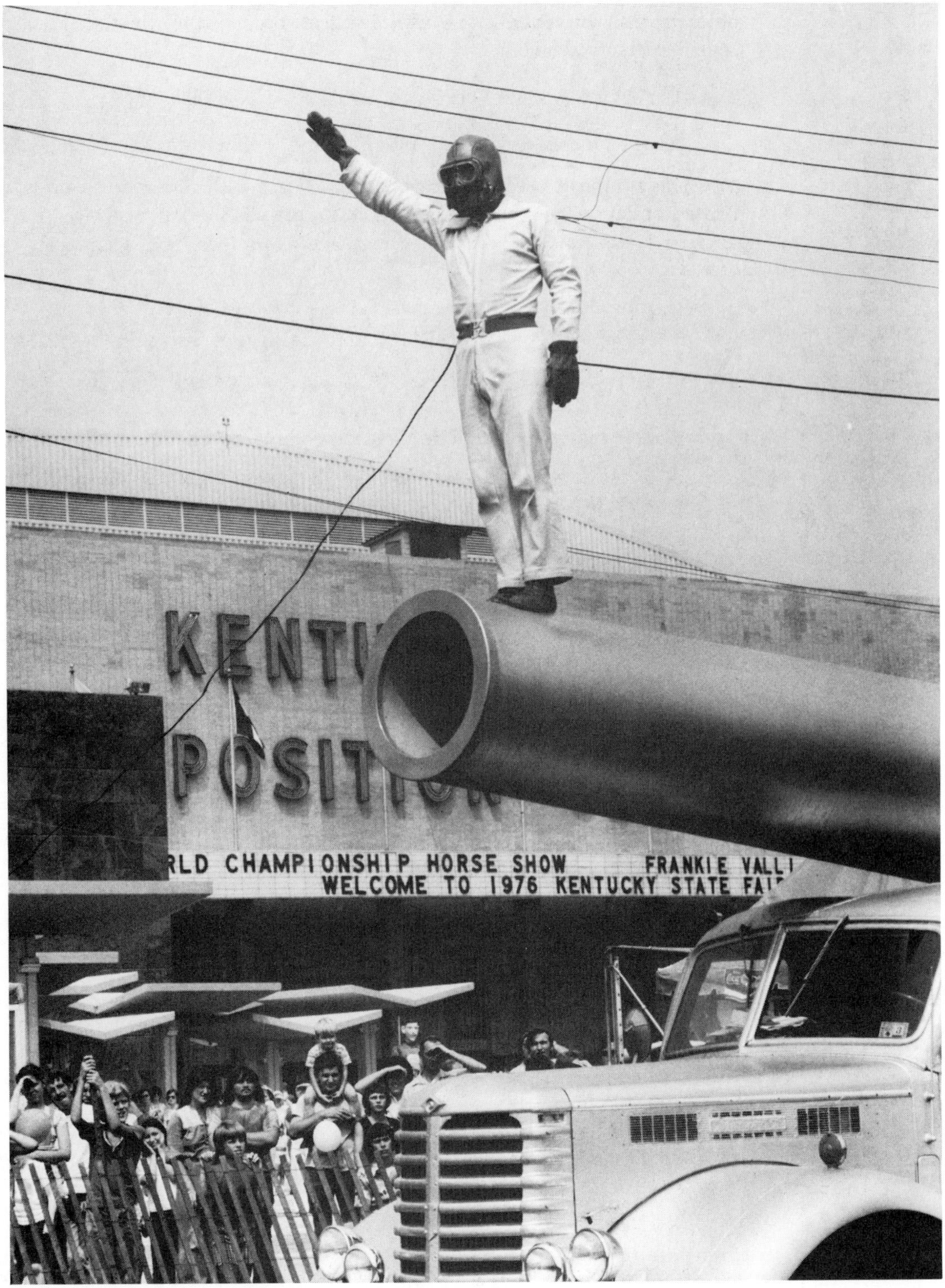
KENTU
POSITIO
RLD CHAMPIONSHIP HORSE SHOW
FRANKIE VALLI
WELCOME TO 1976 KENTUCKY STATE FAI

The is called a *definite article* because it refers to a definite person or object. *A* and *an* are called *indefinite articles* because they do not indicate a specific person or object.

We saw *the* movie last night.	[specific movie]
Should we go out and get *a* sandwich?	[no particular sandwich]
This recipe calls for *an* orange.	[no particular orange]

The word *a* is used before words that begin with consonant sounds; *an* is used before words that begin with vowel sounds.

an apple	*a* grape
an hour	*a* minute
an Airedale	*a* beagle
an empty glass	*a* full glass

2. *Proper Adjectives*

Proper adjectives are formed from proper nouns and from nouns that are capitalized.

PROPER NOUN	PROPER ADJECTIVE
America	*American* wheat
East	*Eastern* climate
Boston	*Bostonian* accent
Africa	*African* continent
Japan	*Japanese* pottery

3. *Pronouns That Work as Adjectives*

Some words can act as either pronouns or as adjectives in a sentence.

PRONOUN	ADJECTIVE
That is right.	*That* answer is right.
We need *more*.	We need *more* lumber.
Please hold *these*.	Please hold *these* eggs.

The word is used as a pronoun if it stands alone and replaces a noun or other pronoun within the sentence. The word is an adjective if it modifies a noun or pronoun but does not replace one.

The following words may be used as both pronouns and adjectives.

all	either	much	some	those
another	few	neither	such	what
any	many	one	that	which
both	more	other	these	
each	most	several	this	

4. *Nouns That Work as Adjectives*

Nouns are frequently used as adjectives to describe or clarify another noun or a pronoun.

Where is the *gasoline* pump?

A *winter* coat must be warm.

Have a *cheese* sandwich for lunch.

My *ice* skates are too small.

That *cement* mixer is huge!

When a word that is normally a noun does the work of an adjective in a sentence or phrase, it is considered an adjective.

Note: A possessive noun is considered a noun, not an adjective. The sentence "John's book has been lost" contains no adjectives.

5. *Predicate Adjectives*

A complete list of linking verbs is on page 383.

An adjective that follows a linking verb and modifies the subject of the sentence is a *predicate adjective.*

Alaska is *cold* in the winter.

Janine seems *worried* about her sister.

Carla felt *proud* after winning her tennis match.

Exercise 2

Write out the following sentences, underlining the adjectives. Where appropriate, label the adjectives *A* for *article*, *P* for *proper adjective*, *PA* for *predicate adjective*, *N* for *noun used as adjective*, and *PR* for *pronoun used as adjective.* (Remember that some adjectives do not fall into any of these categories.)

Examples

a. Two early leaders in the suffrage movement were sisters.

A N

a. Two early leaders in the suffrage movement were sisters.

b. They believed all American women should have the right to vote.

PR P A

b. They believed all American women should have the right to vote.

1. These two women, Victoria Woodhull and Tennessee Clafin, were extraordinary.
2. When they were young, the girls traveled with a family medicine show.
3. In their teens they met an American financier, who offered them some excellent advice about the stock market.
4. These women became the first female brokers on Wall Street and also started a controversial newspaper.
5. In 1871 the two sisters appeared before a congressional committee to ask for equal rights for all women.
6. Victoria's stirring speech made her a popular figure in the suffrage movement.

7. She even organized her own political party and ran as a Presidential candidate.
8. On election day, however, both sisters were in jail because of an unfortunate incident.
9. They had published an angry article about a famous preacher, and shocked officials imprisoned them.
10. This setback did not stop the spunky sisters; they emerged from jail and continued to be strong, influential women.

Finding an Adjective by Its Features

Three features may distinguish adjectives from other parts of speech.

1. Adjectives may change form to show comparison.

There are three degrees of comparison: *positive, comparative,* and *superlative.* The "regular" form of an adjective, which simply describes a quality, is the *positive degree.* The *comparative degree* is used to compare two persons or things; the *superlative* compares three or more persons or things.

Positive:	This music is *loud.*
Comparative:	This band's music is *louder* than that band's.
Superlative:	This music is the *loudest* I have ever heard.

Most one-syllable adjectives and some two-syllable adjectives add *-er* to form the comparative degree. Adjectives of more than two syllables and some two-syllable adjectives form the comparative with the word *more.*

POSITIVE	COMPARATIVE	POSITIVE	COMPARATIVE
happy	*happier*	difficult	*more* difficult
light	*lighter*	even	*more* even
loose	*looser*	expensive	*more* expensive
tan	*tanner*	harmful	*more* harmful

Similarly, most one-syllable adjectives and some two-syllable adjectives form their superlatives by adding *-est.* Some two-syllable adjectives and all adjectives of more than two syllables form their superlative degree with *most.*

POSITIVE	SUPERLATIVE	POSITIVE	SUPERLATIVE
happy	*happiest*	difficult	*most* difficult
light	*lightest*	even	*most* even
loose	*loosest*	expensive	*most* expensive
tan	*tannest*	harmful	*most* harmful

The words *less* and *least* are used before all adjectives to show less of a quality.

POSITIVE	COMPARATIVE	SUPERLATIVE
dangerous	*less* dangerous	*least* dangerous
interesting	*less* interesting	*least* interesting
silly	*less* silly	*least* silly

See page 427 for a discussion of irregular adjectives.

Some adjectives form the comparative and superlative forms in an irregular way.

Exercise 3

The following passage contains ten **boldface** adjectives. Number your paper 1–10 and write down each adjective. State whether it is in its comparative or superlative form.

Example

a. My love for you, my sugarplum, is **higher** than the **highest** mountain, **deeper** than the **deepest** ocean, **more enduring** than stone or steel.

a. *1. higher—comparative*
2. highest—superlative
3. deeper—comparative
4. deepest—superlative
5. more enduring—comparative

Perhaps the **largest** natural explosion in recent times was the eruption of Krakatoa, an island off Indonesia, in 1883. When Krakatoa exploded with a force twenty-six times **greater** than an H-bomb, smoke and clouds turned a huge area **darker** than the **most starless** night. The fiery explosion created an even **more terrible** disaster: one of the **largest** tidal waves in memory. The **biggest** waves sank boats and destroyed villages. The **most conservative** estimate of deaths was 36,417. The explosion has been called "the **loudest** noise in history." In comparison with Krakatoa, other volcanic eruptions have been **less devastating**.

2. Adjectives may follow intensifiers.

A small group of words called *intensifiers* sometimes work with adjectives. (An *intensifier* is a word such as *very*, *quite*, *rather*, *really*, *too*, and *fairly*.) Intensifiers modify other modifiers (such as adjectives) by telling "to what extent."

I was *very* hungry.	A *fairly* large dog guarded the house.
I was *quite* hungry.	A *really* large dog guarded the house.
I was *rather* hungry.	A *somewhat* large dog guarded the house.

3. Adjectives may have suffixes.

Some adjectives have suffixes that distinguish them from other kinds of words. Recognizing these suffixes as a feature of adjectives can help you identify them. The following list shows the most common adjective suffixes.

NOUN	+	SUFFIX	=	ADJECTIVE
rain		-y		*rainy*
friend		-less		*friendless*
fear		-ful		*fearful*
danger		-ous		*dangerous*
honor		-able		*honorable*
child		-ish		*childish*
child		-like		*childlike*
nation		-al		*national*
awe		-some		*awesome*

VERB	+	SUFFIX	=	ADJECTIVE
help		-ful		*helpful*
consider		-ate		*considerate*
manage		-able		*manageable*
thank		-less		*thankless*
act		-ive		*active*

Some words require slight spelling changes. Check a dictionary for help with spelling.

Exercise 4

Write out the following sentences, underlining all adjectives. Label intensifiers *I* and circle the suffixes of adjectives formed with suffixes.

Example

a. Mike thinks skydiving is quite glorious, but I think it's dangerous and somewhat crazy.

a. Mike thinks skydiving is (I) quite glori(ous), but I think it's danger(ous) and (I) somewhat crazy.

1. The speedy service at that restaurant makes it a very dependable place for a quick lunch.
2. We saw a really funny play about a forgetful professor who invented a comical vegetable like a grunion.
3. A somewhat rusty car with a mysterious license plate was found along the coastal road.
4. Scrooge was quite selfish until a frightful experience made him generous and cheerful.
5. My Irish setter was pretty, courageous, intelligent, and very destructive to shoes and other chewable items.
6. A really sleepy driver should pull off the road and take a brief rest.
7. I am returning this product because it is defective and too expensive and has an awful odor.
8. The extremely cool mountain air smelled tangy and wonderful.
9. In this terrifying novel a virtuous young girl is held prisoner by a devilish sorcerer who, by using a magical potion, wants to turn her into a vampire.

10. My very talented brother has a rather large collection of extremely life-like sculptures.

Review Exercise A

Write out the following paragraphs and underline at least sixty adjectives, including articles. (The first two appear in **boldface** for you.) When you have finished, be prepared to explain how you identified each adjective. Does it fit the definition of an adjective? Does it fit into one of the large classes of adjectives? Does it have any of the distinguishing features of an adjective?

> **One** night we turned on **the** evening news and learned that some teenagers had just taken a record-breaking ride on a Ferris wheel—for no apparent reason. Well, these dauntless riders did, in fact, have a logical motive. They were seeking a place for themselves in the *Guinness Book of World Records* by completing the longest ride on a Ferris wheel! The drive to break an established record has spurred many people on to superhuman feats. The big question, it seems to me, is this: who thinks of these outlandish stunts?
>
> A quick flip through the amazing *Book of Records* is always a humorous experience. If, for instance, we thought we could spin more plates at the same time than other people, we, too, might see our names on the printed page. But we would have to beat the masterful spinning of Holley Gray who, while he appeared on British television, spun the greatest number of plates at one time and won the championship title.
>
> The strange records that people have attained are endless. One man walked fifteen miles while he balanced a milk bottle on his head! Another secured a world record by simply balancing on one leg for thirteen hours. Perhaps other acrobats could maintain a longer balance—well, good luck to them.

Mastery Exercise A

In the following description of a bookstore from Ernest Hemingway's novel *A Moveable Feast*, there are more than forty adjectives, with the first three appearing in **boldface** for you. Read the selection carefully, using what you have learned to identify the adjectives. Then list at least forty of them on a sheet of paper. (Do not include articles.)[1]

> In **those** days there was **no** money to buy books. I borrowed books from **the** rental library of Shakespeare and Company, which was the library and bookstore of Sylvia Beach at 12 rue de l'Odéon. On a cold windswept street, this was a warm, cheerful place with a big stove in winter, tables and shelves of books, new books in the window, and photographs on the wall of famous writers both dead and living. The photographs all looked like snapshots and even the dead writers looked as though they had really been alive. Sylvia had a lively, sharply sculptured face, brown eyes that were as alive as a small animal's and as gay as a young girl's, and wavy brown hair that was brushed back from her fine forehead and cut thick below her ears and at the line of the collar of the brown velvet jacket she wore. She had pretty legs and she was kind,

---

[1]From "Shakespeare & Company" in *A Moveable Feast* by Ernest Hemingway. Copyright © 1964 by Ernest Hemingway, Ltd. (New York: Charles Scribner's Sons, 1964). Reprinted by permission of Charles Scribner's Sons, the Executors of the Ernest Hemingway Estate, and Jonathan Cape Ltd.

cheerful and interested, and loved to make jokes and gossip. No one that I ever knew was nicer to me.

I was very shy when I first went into the bookshop and I did not have enough money on me to join the rental library. She told me I could pay the deposit any time I had the money and made me out a card and said I could take as many books as I wished.

There was no reason for her to trust me. She did not know me and the address I had given her, 74 rue Cardinal Lemoine, could not have been a poorer one. But she was delightful and charming and welcoming and behind her, as high as the wall and stretching out into the back room which gave onto the inner court of the building, were shelves and shelves of the wealth of the library.

Hint: Count *stretching* as an adjective.

Mastery Exercise B

Find several paragraphs in a book or newspaper or magazine that describe some place or someone. Then on a sheet of paper, list the adjectives that you find. Next rewrite the paragraphs, leaving out all adjectives. What information is omitted with the adjectives? How has the "sense" of the selection changed?

Using Adjectives

Throughout the following sections you will be be asked to put your knowledge of adjectives to use in these ways: selecting the proper comparative and superlative forms of adjectives, using clear and logical comparisons, and writing effectively with adjectives. For any help you may need in recognizing adjectives and their different forms, refer to the preceding Understanding Adjectives sections.

Using the Comparative and Superlative Forms

Studying the following four points about the comparative and superlative forms of adjectives will help you to use these forms correctly.

1. Remember that the comparative and superlative forms are each used for a specific purpose.

   Use the comparative form to compare two persons or things.

   This watch is *better* than my old one.
   Their team is *more experienced* than ours.
   A cheetah is *faster* than a greyhound.

   Use the superlative form to compare more than two persons or things.

   This watch is the *best* one manufactured in the United States.
   Their team is the *most experienced* in the Big Ten.
   The cheetah is the *fastest* of all mammals.

Most short adjectives, those of one or two syllables, form their comparatives and superlatives with *-er* and *-est*.

low—*lower*—*lowest*	high—*higher*—*highest*
sleepy—*sleepier*—*sleepiest*	happy—*happier*—*happiest*

2. Some adjectives require spelling changes before adding the *-er* and *-est* suffixes.

If the positive degree ends in the letter *y*, change the *y* to *i* before adding *-er* or *-est*.

POSITIVE	COMPARATIVE	SUPERLATIVE
silly	*sillier*	*silliest*
lively	*livelier*	*liveliest*
spicy	*spicier*	*spiciest*

If the positive degree ends in the letter *e*, drop the *e* before adding *-er* or *-est*.

POSITIVE	COMPARATIVE	SUPERLATIVE
fine	*finer*	*finest*
pale	*paler*	*palest*
true	*truer*	*truest*

If the positive degree ends in a single consonant preceded by a single vowel, double the final consonant before adding *-er* or *-est*.

POSITIVE	COMPARATIVE	SUPERLATIVE
thin	*thinner*	*thinnest*
hot	*hotter*	*hottest*
fat	*fatter*	*fattest*

3. Some adjectives are irregular.

Some adjectives do not form their degrees of comparison with *-er* and *-est* or *more* and *most* and *less* and *least*. These adjectives change form completely for the comparative and superlative degrees:

POSITIVE	COMPARATIVE	SUPERLATIVE
good	*better*	*best*
bad, ill	*worse*	*worst*
far	*farther*	*farthest*
many, much	*more*	*most*
little	*less* or *lesser*	*least*

Your cold is *worse* than mine, but Sam's is *worst* of all.
This location is *better* than that one.
This job requires *more* time than the other one.

Exercise 1

Write out the following sentences, supplying the correct form of the adjective in parentheses. Underline the adjective you supply.

Examples

a. Today is ______ than yesterday. (sunny)
a. Today is sunnier than yesterday.

b. That is the ______ road in the state. (wide)
b. That is the widest road in the state.

1. Mario is the ______ person I have ever known. (brave)
2. The record store has many classical albums but ______ popular records. (many)
3. I thought the movie *Horse Feathers* was ______ than *Duck Soup.* (funny)
4. The tornado did its ______ damage in an unpopulated area. (bad)
5. I have only a little money, but Denise has even ______ than I do. (little)
6. That is the ______ orange I have ever eaten! (juicy)
7. The water in the Caribbean seems ______ than the water in the north Atlantic. (blue)
8. *Jaws* was much ______ than *Jaws II!* (scary)
9. No one was ______ than I was when the game was canceled. (sad)
10. Is Chinese food usually ______ than Mexican food? (spicy)
11. Indian food is often the ______ of all. (spicy)
12. The distance between my house and the market is far, but the ride to the movies is even ______. (far)
13. Copper pots are more efficient because copper is a ______ conductor of heat than iron is. (good)
14. Was last summer's hurricane ______ than the storm of '62? People say that the one in 1962 was the ______ of all. (bad)
15. Michelle's puppy is ______ than my five-year-old dog! (big)
16. I felt ill last night, and I feel ______ this morning. (ill)
17. Dale seemed a little worried, but Julie showed ______ concern. (little)
18. That was the ______ movie I have ever seen—even ______ than the one I saw last night. (dull)
19. Which was the ______ of all the ancient reptiles? (large)
20. My friend at camp was the ______ cook I ever met, but I really wasn't much ______ than he. (bad) (good)

4. When using the comparative or superlative form of adjectives, avoid double comparisons.

An asterisk (*) denotes a feature that is not part of Edited Standard English.

Do not add *-er* or *-est* to irregular forms.

*This snowstorm was worser than the last one.
This snowstorm was *worse* than the last one.
*That was the bestest movie I've ever seen.
That was the *best* movie I've ever seen.

Similarly, do not add *more* or *most* to irregular forms or to adjectives that use *-er* or *-est* to form the comparative and superlative.

*This pen is more better than the old one.
This pen is *better* than the old one.
*It seems more colder than it is.
It seems *colder* than it is.

Using Comparative and Superlative Forms Clearly

Comparisons should be stated clearly and in logical form. The following guidelines will help you to use comparisons clearly and logically.

1. The reader must understand clearly what things are being compared.

*The blossoms of the lilac are more colorful than many bushes.

In the preceding statement blossoms are being compared to bushes, not to other blossoms. The sentence should be revised:

The blossoms of the lilac are more colorful than the blossoms of many bushes.

Similarly, the following sentence does not clearly state what two things are being compared.

*The President's job is far more demanding than most people.

The sentence should be revised for greater clarity and precision:

The President's job is far more demanding than that of most people.

2. Use the words *other* or *else* when comparing a person or thing with the rest of the group to which it belongs.

*Oklahoma City covers a larger area than any city in the United States.

The preceding sentence is not logically sound because Oklahoma City is a city in the United States; the sentence, therefore, implies that Oklahoma City covers a larger area than it does itself. Such illogical comparisons can usually be corrected by the addition of the word *other* or *else*.

Oklahoma City covers a larger area than any *other* city in the United States.

Exercise 2

The following sentences either have double comparisons or have comparisons that are not clearly or logically stated. Rewrite the sentences, revising each sentence to correct the double comparisons and the unclear or illogical comparisons.

Examples

a. A bulldog's disposition is actually much more agreeable than a terrier.

a. A bulldog's disposition is actually much more agreeable than a terrier's disposition.

b. Jupiter is larger than any planet in our solar system.
b. Jupiter is larger than any other planet in our solar system.

1. The hazards of skiing are greater than mountain climbing.
2. Lincoln was taller than any American President.
3. The pitcher was more fatigued than anyone on the team.
4. Mixing this sauce by hand is more better than mixing it with a blender.
5. The hamster was more fonder of bananas than it was of any food.
6. Oregon is more concerned about ecology than any state.
7. This dog is smarter than any dog we've ever had.
8. Audie Murphy received more decorations than any soldier in World War II.
9. Queen Victoria had a longer reign than any British monarch.
10. The durability of steel is greater than aluminum.

Review Exercise A

Some of the following sentences contain adjectives that are incorrect or that are part of an unclear or illogical statement. Revise and improve these sentences. If a sentence is correct, write *C* beside its number.

Examples

a. The day was more hotter than we had expected.
a. The day was hotter than we had expected.

b. The intelligence of the dolphin is greater than that of the shark.
b. C

1. Our chances in this game now look gooder than they did at the half.
2. Clarence is the tallest of the two boys.
3. Clarence is the tallest of the three boys.
4. I never felt more embarrasseder in my life.
5. The taste of sugar is far sweeter than honey.
6. Shelly is a higher scorer than anyone on her bowling team.
7. Emily Brontë may have been the more talented of the three gifted Brontë sisters.
8. That movie has to be absolutely the most worst movie ever made.
9. Which of the two moons of Mars is more larger?
10. After two hours of horseback riding, I didn't know which part of my body was sorer.
11. Writing a short story is harder than a poem.
12. The last skit in the show was the funniest of them all.
13. Which of those three cities has the lesser air pollution?
14. Not only did he not apologize, but also he didn't seem the leastest bit sorry.

15. This small, battered coin is valuabler than that large gold one.
16. Many people have one foot that is slightly larger than the other.
17. The salary of the supervisor is higher than the cook.
18. Our tire went flat, but what was more bad, our spare was flat, too.
19. Chuck has the deeper voice of anyone in choir.
20. Chuck has the deeper voice of the two soloists.

Writing with Adjectives

A sentence such as the following one makes a statement but certainly not a very striking statement.

A house stood on the hill.

Adjectives can be used to impart important details to a bare and lifeless sentence.

A *sinister, old* house stood on the *barren* hill.
A *small, white* house stood on the *grassy* hill.
A *tumbledown little* house stood on the *rocky* hill.

To be effective, adjectives should add clear and exact detail to the nouns they modify. Some adjectives, however, are used so often and so automatically that they have lost their force. These overworked adjectives fall into three main groups.

1. *Vague, All-Purpose Adjectives*

Certain adjectives are so general that they offer readers and listeners little that is specific or truly descriptive.

This book is *good.*
The weather was *nice.*
The homework assignment was *bad.*

Such statements would be clearer and more meaningful if they did not rely on tired, all-purpose adjectives to convey their message.

This book is *fast-moving, suspenseful,* and *well plotted.*
The weather was *brisk, sunny,* and *cold.*
The homework assignment was *long, tedious,* and *confusing.*

2. *Too-Popular Adjectives*

Certain adjectives have become so popular that they are overused, and their effectiveness has dwindled. The field of advertising has helped overwork a large group of words, such as *fabulous, fantastic, spectacular, sensational, terrific, incredible,* and *spellbinding.* Overuse has drawn these words away from their original meanings, and many are now merely fancy, overused synonyms for the words *good* or *bad* or *interesting.* Something *fabulous,* for instance, is something from myth or fable, or something astounding. A fire-breathing dragon may be fabulous; the Taj Mahal may be fabulous, but hamburgers and T-shirts are not fabulous, no matter how admirable they may be.

Similarly, there are adjectives that become so popular that they dominate many speakers' conversations for a few months or years and then disappear. A few years later these adjectives, usually favorite slang terms, sound dated and silly. The following list of adjectives from past decades illustrates them.

1920s:	He's a *bully* fellow.	She's a *grand* girl.
1930s:	He's a *square* fellow.	She's an *all-right* girl.
1940s:	He's a *reet* fellow.	She's a *zooly* girl.
1950s:	He's a *cool* fellow.	She's a *neat* girl.
1960s:	He's an *outasite* fellow.	She's a *tough* girl.
1970s:	He's a *bad* fellow.	She's a *mean* girl.

3. *Clichés*

Some phrases, originally fresh and accurate, were so fresh and accurate that they were used repeatedly. As a result, their freshness staled and their originality withered until they became trite, hackneyed phrases, or *clichés*. Many clichés involve adjectives linked with nouns in a combination you have heard or read many times. If such a tired and expected adjective should creep into your writing, try to replace it with one that is not so overworked.

Clichés:	The *majestic* mountains rose to *dizzying* heights.
Clichés:	This soap will give you a *dazzling* wash with *lightning* speed.
Clichés:	The *fiery* redness of the setting sun was a *breathtaking* sight.

Sometimes, an adjective that has become a cliché in a phrase can be replaced by another adjective. Other times, however, it is better to recast the sentence and use different parts of speech to express the descriptive details.

Cliché:	The *kingly* lion snored in its cage.
Improved:	The lion slept in its cage like an old monarch, lost in his dreams and snores.
Improved:	Even as the lion snored in its cage, it seemed regal.

Exercise 3

Each of the following ten sentences relies on a vague and overused adjective. Rewrite the sentences, replacing each of the *italicized* adjectives with two or three more specific, vivid ones. You may need to make other slight changes in the sentence.

Examples

a. The soup was *awful.*
a. The soup was cold, lumpy, and greasy.

b. Our coach is *nice.*
b. Our coach is fair and patient.

1. The movie was *good.*
2. The storm was *bad.*
3. Those shoes are *nice.*
4. My dog is *great.*
5. My car is *awful.*
6. You look *fine.*
7. The sandwiches were *delicious.*
8. The night was *beautiful.*
9. The hike was *unpleasant.*
10. The play was *terrible.*

Exercise 4

The following description relies on some imprecise and overworked adjectives. Rewrite the paragraph so it is more vivid and specific. You may want to replace the **boldface** adjectives with other adjectives, or you may want to recast the sentences to gain more detail.

Example

a. I bought a **fantastic** new backpack and a **groovy** sleeping bag.

a. I bought a lightweight, well-balanced backpack and a warm sleeping bag with down filling.

We went to a **fabulous** party and had a **nice** time. The food was **fantastic: terrific** pizza, **delicious** punch, **good** dessert, and **neat** fortune cookies with **funny** sayings inside them. We listened to some **sensational** records and heard some **great** songs.

Exercise 5

The following paragraph is vague and boring because it contains so many clichés. Rewrite the paragraph, replacing each **boldface** adjective with a better one or recasting the sentences to add better detail. You may need to make other slight changes in the paragraph.

Example

a. I approached the **gloomy** house with **trembling** steps and a **pounding** heart.

a. With unsteady steps and a heart that thudded crazily in my chest, I approached the dark, sad house.

Nature offers us many **beautiful** sights. There are **snow-capped** mountains and **vast** deserts, **boundless** seas and **babbling** brooks. There are **mighty** oaks, **lofty** pines, and **waving** wheat fields. There are **fluffy** clouds, **gorgeous** sunsets, and **twinkling** stars.

Writing Exercise A

Choose one of the following suggested topics and write two or three paragraphs about it. Concentrate on using specific adjectives to make your descriptions vivid and interesting. Use care when forming comparatives and superlatives.

1. Write a description of a place you know well or a place you have visited in your imagination. Make the description detailed, vivid, and convincing so that your readers should have no difficulty visualizing the scene from your writing.
2. The two photographs on pages 434 and 435 show the same spot, but the photographs were taken many years apart. How do the scenes compare? Write one or two descriptive paragraphs comparing and contrasting the two views.
3. Think of a good friend or someone else whom you like very much. How would you describe that person? Write a description that accurately and vividly describes him or her.
4. Write a paragraph or two comparing and contrasting two subjects, such as sports, cities, comedians, concerts, or houses where you have lived. Make your comparisons as detailed as possible.

Understanding Adverbs

Adverbs, like adjectives, are words that modify. By adding details to your writing, they make it more specific and interesting. You can recognize adverbs through their definition, their division into classes, and the features that separate them from other parts of speech.

Defining Adverbs

An *adverb* is usually defined as a word that modifies a verb, an adjective, or another adverb.

Modifying a Verb:	Marissa left *early* so she could practice *longer.*
	The doves cooed *mournfully.*
Modifying an Adjective:	The fog was *unusually* thick.
	Duane is an *exceptionally* talented singer.
Modifying an Adverb:	He behaved *very* cleverly.
	Almost miraculously, the accident was avoided.

Adverbs supply details of time, place, and manner by answering the questions *how? how often? when? where?* and *to what extent?*

How:	The sun glared *mercilessly*.
How Often:	Do tulips bloom *annually*?
When:	Sherry will arrive *tomorrow*.
Where:	The cat strolled *outside*.
To What Extent:	The fan ran *too* noisily.

Exercise 1

Write out the following sentences, underlining each adverb. Then draw an arrow from each adverb to the word it modifies. (Be prepared to tell if the adverb modifies a verb, an adjective, or another adverb. You should also be able to tell what question the adverb answers.)

Examples

a. The documents were completely destroyed in the fire.

a. The documents were completely destroyed in the fire.

b. The landlord is here now.

b. The landlord is here now.

1. The mothers very proudly discussed their children.
2. The sweater that Cassie bought yesterday is dark blue.
3. The scientists excitedly discussed a completely new transportation system.
4. The two sisters seldom see each other, but they write often and frequently talk on the phone.
5. The very active baby completely destroyed her new toy.
6. The politician earnestly promised a vastly improved tax structure.
7. Was the sun terribly strong yesterday?
8. Denise decisively returned her opponent's serve.
9. I nearly forgot to pack my light beige shoes.
10. The irate customer quickly turned and walked angrily out of the store.

Grouping Adverbs by Classes

Not all adverbs easily fall into classes or groups. Adverbs such as *sometimes*, *suddenly*, *eagerly*, *quickly*, and *happily* conform to the definition of an adverb but cannot be grouped into a special class. There are, however, four special kinds of adverbs. Recognizing these four classes will help you identify the words as adverbs.

1. *Interrogative Adverbs*

Adverbs used to ask questions are called *interrogative adverbs.*

Where is the ball game being played?
When will you call?
How do you winterize a car?
Why don't planets twinkle as stars do?

The interrogative adverbs are *where, when, how, why*, and the less common *whence* and *whither*. These adverbs may be used in asking direct questions: *Where are the pliers?* They may also be used to introduce indirect questions within a sentence: *I don't know where the pliers are.* They are also used alone from time to time: *Jerry wanted to fix his radio, but he didn't know how.*

2. *Affirmative and Negative Adverbs*

A small group of adverbs is called the *affirmative and negative adverbs.* The only affirmative adverb, the word *yes*, frequently occurs as an independent element in a sentence.

> *Yes*, I saw that movie.

The most common negative adverbs are the words *no* and *not*.

> *No*, we will *not* go.
> That plant is *not* ragweed.

The word *not* often appears as the contraction *n't (will not = won't).* Sometimes, you must add the helping verb *do* when using the word *not*.

> Jane wants a puppy.
> Jane does *not* want a puppy.

Note: *No* is used more often as an adjective than as an adverb. To distinguish the adverb *no* from the adjective *no*, look at the word that is modified. Adverbs modify verbs, adjectives, and other adverbs. Adjectives modify nouns and pronouns.

No, I did not hear that.	[adverb]
I will wait *no* longer.	[adverb]
That is *no* reason to cry.	[adjective]
No citizen should neglect the duty of voting.	[adjective]

3. *Intensifiers*

Intensifiers (adverbs that answer the question *to what extent?)* can modify both adjectives and adverbs. Intensifiers always come directly in front of the word they modify. Some common intensifiers are *very, too, completely, quite, rather, somewhat, unusually, extremely, totally*, and *so*.

I am *totally* confused! Our house is *rather* small.	[modifying adjectives]
Juan drove *extremely* carefully. Kim amazed everyone by singing *so* beautifully.	[modifying adverbs]

An asterisk (*) denotes a feature that is not a part of Edited Standard English.

Note: Unlike other adverbs, intensifiers can modify adverbs and adjectives but not always verbs. The following statement, for instance, is incomplete.

> *We fought very!

4. *Nouns Used as Adverbs*

Sometimes, nouns—especially those naming a time or place—are used as adverbs. Some pronouns may also act as adverbs.

We went *home.*

We went *yesterday.*

We can't go *either.*

Exercise 2

Each of the following quotations contains one or more adverbs. Write out the quotations, underlining all adverbs. If an adverb belongs to a special class, indicate the class beneath the quotation.

Example

a. You can always tell a real friend: when you've made a fool of yourself, he does not make you feel you've done a permanent job.

a. *You can always tell a real friend: when you've made a fool of yourself, he does not make you feel you've done a permanent job.*
not = negative

1. When I want to understand what is happening today or try to decide what will happen tomorrow, I look back.
—Oliver Wendell Holmes, Jr.

2. A little credulity helps one on through life very smoothly.
—Elizabeth Cleghorn Gaskell

3. I won't think about it today. I'll think about it tomorrow when I can stand it. —Margaret Mitchell

4. Tomorrow we again embark upon the boundless sea. —Horace

5. No great man is ever born too soon or too late. —Norman Douglas

6. Then they will realize that we Indians know the One true God, and that we pray to Him continually. —Black Elk

7. How do I love thee? Let me count the ways.
—Elizabeth Barrett Browning

8. Old soldiers never die;
They only fade away! —British Army song

9. People often grudge others what they cannot enjoy themselves.
—Aesop

10. We often despise what is most useful to us. —Aesop

Finding an Adverb by Its Features

The following two features help to distinguish adverbs from other parts of speech.

1. Adverbs may change form to show degrees of comparison.

Most one-syllable adverbs add *-er* for the comparative form and *-est* for the superlative form.

POSITIVE	COMPARATIVE	SUPERLATIVE
early	*earlier*	*earliest*
fast	*faster*	*fastest*
hard	*harder*	*hardest*
late	*later*	*latest*
long	*longer*	*longest*
near	*nearer*	*nearest*
quick	*quicker*	*quickest*
slow	*slower*	*slowest*
soon	*sooner*	*soonest*

Most adverbs, however, show degrees of comparison by adding *more* and *most* or *less* and *least.*

POSITIVE	COMPARATIVE	SUPERLATIVE
rudely	*more* rudely	*most* rudely
proudly	*more* proudly	*most* proudly
desperately	*more* desperately	*most* desperately
economically	*less* economically	*least* economically
likely	*less* likely	*least* likely
popularly	*less* popularly	*least* popularly

2. Adverbs may be formed with suffixes.

Many adverbs end in the suffix *-ly*. Such adverbs are frequently formed by adding *-ly* to an adjective.

neat—*neatly*	impatient—*impatiently*
happy—*happily*	courageous—*courageously*

Other adverb suffixes are *-ward*, *-ways*, and *-wise.*

Exercise 3

Write out the following sentences, underlining the adverbs. Then draw an arrow from each adverb to the word it modifies. (Be prepared to explain how you identified each adverb.)

Example

a. Is it fairly common that storms arise so quickly?

a. Is it fairly common that storms arise so quickly?

1. Why do some women recall their dreams more easily than others?
2. Yesterday I worked so hard that I fell asleep instantly.
3. That bus leaves earlier than the train, but the train arrives sooner.
4. I frequently transfer my day's worries into my dreams, so I toss constantly all night.
5. Our air conditioner works best when the humidity is low; when the humidity is high, the air conditioner works only moderately well.
6. Janice plays tennis better than I do, but she doesn't mind playing with me.
7. Clarissa, who has a fairly even disposition, became extremely angry when the salesperson treated her so rudely.
8. Kevin studied the most diligently of everyone else in the class, so he confidently entered the exam room and finished the test more quickly than I did.
9. Moose are rarely seen in New York State, but yesterday a large moose marched assuredly across the New York Thruway.
10. Yes, that remark is certainly true. Diane absolutely travels the most often of anyone in the family.

Review Exercise A

Write out the following sentences, underlining all adverbs. Then draw an arrow from each adverb to the word or words it modifies.

Examples

a. Recently astronomers have discovered some extremely puzzling phenomena.

a. Recently astronomers have discovered some extremely puzzling phenomena.

b. Even today, we are not certain about the nature of these discoveries.

b. Even today, we are not certain about the nature of these discoveries.

1. Neutron stars are rather large stars that have apparently collapsed.
2. These collapsed stars are incredibly dense and quite small.
3. Neutron stars, sometimes called *white dwarf stars*, can rotate very rapidly.
4. A swiftly spinning neutron star regularly emits bursts of radiation.
5. Such stars, constantly sending out radioactive signals, are now called *pulsars*.
6. Only very small stars could rotate so rapidly and not fly apart.
7. More mysterious than the pulsars are the newly discovered "black holes."
8. A black hole is still smaller and even denser than a neutron star.

9. Scientists presently believe black holes are the result of the collapse of really large stars.
10. Einstein predicted black holes years ago, but they have only recently been detected.
11. Most simply, the large star is so compressed that its gravity becomes exceptionally strong.
12. So great is the pull of gravity that light cannot escape it.
13. The star simply seems to disappear forever.
14. Still, scientists believe the star exists, now permanently invisible.
15. Its gravity may be one of the most powerfully strong forces in the universe.
16. Absolutely invisible, but unbelievably powerful, the black hole is a scientific puzzle.
17. What would happen to an object drawn directly inside a black hole's force?
18. Scientists certainly won't learn the answer quickly.
19. We will never be able actually to see inside a black hole.
20. When will we ever know what happens to something once caught in its force?

Mastery Exercise A

In the following paragraphs from Richard Connell's story "The Most Dangerous Game," there are more than twenty adverbs. (The first two are underlined for you.) Using what you have learned in the previous sections, identify at least twenty adverbs and list them on a sheet of paper in the order in which they appear.[1]

> He lifted the knocker, and it creaked up stiffly, as if it had never before been used. He let it fall, and it startled him with its booming loudness. He thought he heard steps within; the door remained closed. Again Rainsford lifted the heavy knocker, and let it fall. The door opened then, opened as suddenly as if it were on a spring, and Rainsford stood blinking in the river of glaring gold light that poured out. The first thing Rainsford's eyes discerned was the largest man Rainsford had ever seen—a gigantic creature, solidly made and black-bearded to the waist. In his hand the man held a long-barreled revolver, and he was pointing it straight at Rainsford's heart.
>
> Out of the snarl of beard two small eyes regarded Rainsford.
>
> "Don't be alarmed," said Rainsford, with a smile which he hoped was disarming. "I'm no robber. I fell off a yacht. My name is Sanger Rainsford of New York City."

---

[1]From "The Most Dangerous Game" by Richard Connell. Copyright 1924 by Richard Connell; copyright renewed 1952 by Louise Fox Connell. Reprinted by permission of Brandt & Brandt Literary Agents Inc.

The menacing look in his eyes did not change. The revolver pointed as rigidly as if the giant were a statue. He gave no sign that he understood Rainsford's words, or that he had even heard them. He was dressed in uniform, a black uniform trimmed with gray astrakhan.

"I'm Sanger Rainsford of New York," Rainsford began again. "I fell off a yacht. I am hungry."

The man's only answer was to raise with his thumb the hammer of his revolver. Then Rainsford saw the man's free hand go to his forehead in a military salute, and he saw him click his heels together and stand at attention. Another man was coming down the broad marble steps, an erect, slender man in evening clothes. He advanced to Rainsford and held out his hand.

In a cultivated voice marked by a slight accent that gave it added precision and deliberateness, he said: "It is a very great pleasure and honor to welcome Mr. Sanger Rainsford, the celebrated hunter, to my home."

Automatically Rainsford shook the man's hand.

"I've read your book about hunting snow leopards in Tibet, you see," explained the man. "I am General Zaroff."

Rainsford's first impression was that the man was singularly handsome; his second was that there was an original, almost bizarre quality about the general's face. He was a tall man past middle age, for his hair was a vivid white; but his thick eyebrows and pointed military mustache were as black as the night from which Rainsford had come.

Mastery Exercise B

From a magazine, book, or newspaper, select several paragraphs and list all the adverbs you find in them. Then choose five sentences from the selection and rewrite them omitting all the adverbs. How do the meaning and feeling conveyed by the sentences change?

Using Adverbs

In the following sections you will practice using the different forms of adverbs, learn to distinguish between easily confused adjectives and adverbs, and learn to avoid double negatives. As you work through the sections, refer back to Understanding Adverbs for any help you may need in identifying adverbs.

Using the Comparative and Superlative Forms

Form the comparative and superlative degrees of some one-syllable adverbs by adding *-er* and *-est: soon, sooner, soonest.*

Form the comparative and superlative degrees of adverbs ending in *-ly* by adding *more* and *most* or *less* and *least.*

POSITIVE	COMPARATIVE	SUPERLATIVE
swiftly	*more* swiftly	*most* swiftly
fortunately	*more* fortunately	*most* fortunately

POSITIVE	COMPARATIVE	SUPERLATIVE
swiftly	*less* swiftly	*least* swiftly
fortunately	*less* fortunately	*least* fortunately

Form the comparatives and superlatives of some adverbs in an irregular fashion.

POSITIVE	COMPARATIVE	SUPERLATIVE
badly/ill	*worse*	*worst*
far	*farther/further*	*farthest/furthest*
little	*less*	*least*
much	*more*	*most*
well	*better*	*best*

The comparative degree of the adverb is used when comparing two things.

A hawk can see *better* than an owl.
Trains use fuel *more efficiently* than trucks.
Sara swims *less often* than last year.

The superlative degree is used when comparing more than two.

The batter who hits *most consistently* of anyone else on the team is Gomez.
Of the four choir members the one who sings *best* will be given the solo.

When using the comparative and superlative forms of adverbs, you should avoid the following errors.

An asterisk (*) denotes a feature that is not a part of Edited Standard English.

1. Do not add *-er* or *-est* to irregular forms.

*This engine acts worser than it did yesterday.
This engine acts *worse* than it did yesterday.
*He ran lastest in the race.
He ran *last* in the race.

2. Similarly, do not add *more* or *most* to adverbs that use *-er* or *-est* in their comparative and superlative forms. Avoid this double comparison.

*They arrived more sooner than we had expected.
They arrived *sooner* than we had expected.
*Roberto scored most earliest in the game.
Roberto scored *earliest* in the game.

Exercise 1

Write out the following sentences, supplying the correct forms of the adverbs indicated in parentheses. Underline the adverbs you supply.

Example

a. I don't exercise much; I should try to do so ________. (often)

a. I don't exercise much; I should try to do so more often.

1. The team wasn't playing well at the start of the new season, but they're doing ________ now. (well)
2. I came late, and Ralph came later still, but Gina came ________ of all. (late)
3. The horse behaved somewhat badly this morning, and unfortunately it is acting even ________ now. (badly)
4. This band sounded terrible last week, but surprisingly it's playing a bit ________ this time. (well)
5. Of all the sports, Kim enjoys basketball ________. (little)
6. The rabbit jumped ________ than the cat did. (high)
7. The snow was high everywhere but drifted ________ of all against the garage door. (deeply)
8. The fans cheered ________ when Sugar Ray Leonard stepped into the ring than they had cheered earlier. (loudly)
9. The information that arrives ________ of all is the information we will have to use. (soon)
10. Malcolm can run the mile race ________ than Scott. (fast)

Choosing Between Adjectives and Adverbs

Most adjectives and adverbs offer little difficulty to speakers and writers. Three pairs of words, however, create some confusion: *bad* and *badly*, *good* and *well*, and *slow* and *slowly*.

The following rule will help you distinguish in general whether an adjective or an adverb should be used.

Use an adverb to modify a verb, an adjective, or another adverb; use an adjective to modify a noun or pronoun. (Remember that a word following a linking verb and modifying the subject of a sentence must be an adjective.)

The man looked *slyly* at the money.
[adverb following an action verb, telling in what manner the man looked]

The man looked *sly*.
[adjective following a linking verb, describing the subject *man*]

bad/badly

Bad, an adjective, is often used after linking verbs (such as *be, become, seem, feel*, and *taste). Badly*, in Edited Standard English, is always an adverb that is used to modify action verbs, adjectives, or other adverbs.

I had a *bad* headache.	[adjective]
My head was aching *badly*.	[adverb]
This apple is *bad*.	[adjective]
The apples had rotted *badly*.	[adverb]

good/well

Good, an adjective, is not used to modify a verb.

He makes *good* soup.

These tacos taste *good*!

Well can be used as either an adjective or an adverb. *Well* can follow a linking verb and can be used as an adjective to express three different meanings:

1. *Well* can be used as an adjective meaning "in good health."

   The sick chicken is now *well*.

   Linda feels *well* again.

2. *Well* can be used as an adjective meaning "in a good or satisfactory state."

   It is *well* that we've had such good weather.

3. *Well* can be used as an adjective meaning "nicely dressed or groomed."

   You look *well* in that color.

   Joe looks *well* with his mustache.

The adverb *well* means "satisfactorily" or "in a pleasing or capable manner." When it modifies an action verb, *well* tells how an action was performed.

The team played *well* in the tournament.

Tina does *well* in math.

slow/slowly

Slow is an adjective used to modify nouns and pronouns.

The train is *slow* tonight.

A *slow* walk is relaxing.

Slowly, an adverb, is used to modify an action verb, an adjective, and other adverbs.

Juan speaks *slowly* when he wants to make his point.

The *slowly* rising tide became rough.

Note the comparative forms of *slow* and *slowly:*

POSITIVE	COMPARATIVE	SUPERLATIVE
slow	*slower*	*slowest*
slowly	*more* slowly	*most* slowly

Note: The word *slow* is sometimes used as an adverb following the verbs *drive* or *go*, as on traffic signs.

Exercise 2

Write out the following sentences, selecting the correct word from the words in parentheses. Underline the word you choose.

Examples

a. The team played (good, well).

a. The team played well.

b. Elm trees are (good, well) for shade, and fortunately they don't grow too (slow, slowly).

b. Elm trees are good for shade, and fortunately they don't grow too slowly.

1. The car was working (good, well) when we left, but after about an hour the engine began to knock (bad, badly).
2. Jennie is (good, well) at science, and her sister does (good, well) in art.
3. Larry didn't go to practice because his knee hurt (bad, badly).
4. I thought I knew how to take pictures (good, well), but all my snapshots were (bad, badly).
5. The time went so (slow, slowly) that I couldn't concentrate very (good, well).
6. Although this work season is (slow, slowly), we all are feeling (good, well).
7. The milk still tasted (good, well), but the homemade ice cream didn't freeze (good, well) enough.
8. Soon the patient was (good, well) enough to walk (slow, slowly) through the halls.
9. The bloodhounds were able to smell (good, well), and they immediately knew that the air didn't smell (good, well).
10. The acting in the play was rather (bad, badly), but the musical numbers were done (good, well).

Avoiding Double Negatives

When two negative words are used where only one is necessary, the construction is called a *double negative.* Double negatives are not a feature of Edited Standard English.

An asterisk (*) denotes a feature that is not a part of Edited Standard English.

*I didn't do nothing.
I *didn't* do anything. [or] I did *nothing*.
*I don't have none.
I *don't* have any. [or] I have *none*.

Do not use the adverb *not* with any of the following words to make a single negative statement.

hardly, scarcely, no, nothing, none, *and in some cases* but *and* only

*I don't hardly ever go to the movies.
I *hardly ever* go to the movies.
I *don't usually* go to the movies.

Avoid double negatives when using the words *only* and *but* in a negative way, meaning "no more than."

*I don't have but three dollars.
I have *but* three dollars.
*I *don't* have *only* three dollars.
I have *only* three dollars.

Using Adverbs Clearly and Logically

Comparisons involving adverbs, like those involving adjectives, should be stated clearly and logically. It should be clear to the reader exactly what things are being compared.

I like lizards better than my brother. [unclear]

This statement is not clear since it could mean two things:

I like lizards better than my brother does.
or
I like lizards better than I like my brother.

Such a sentence should be revised.

Consider another example:

I've known Laura longer than Carla.	[unclear]
I've known Laura longer than Carla has.	[clear]
I've known Laura longer than I've known Carla.	[clear]

Include the word *else* or *other* when comparing one thing in a group to the other members of the group.

Sarah Bernhardt acted more brilliantly than any actress of her time. [illogical]

The preceding statement is not logical. Since Sarah Bernhardt was an actress of her time, the statement therefore asserts that she acted better than herself—which is illogical. Such statements can usually be revised by adding the word *other* or *else.*

Sarah Bernhardt acted more brilliantly than any other actress of her time.

Exercise 3

The following sentences use adverbs in such a way that the sentences they are a part of are unclear or illogical, or they contain double negatives. Write out the sentences, revising them so that they conform to Edited Standard English.

Examples

a. I hate fried liver more than my sister.

a. I hate fried liver more than my sister does.

b. Man-o'-War could run faster than any racehorse of his day.

b. Man-o'-War could run faster than any other racehorse of his day.

1. I take care of my sister more often than my brother.
2. Forty-nine-year-old "George" the gander lived longer than any goose in history.
3. I don't have no need to study English.
4. She doesn't have hardly any of her allowance left.
5. I talked to Jerry longer than Luis.
6. Elaine studies harder than anybody in her class.
7. I don't have only enough money to see one movie.
8. Birds eat more insects than frogs.
9. It was a beautiful Saturday night, but they didn't have nothing to do.
10. I like spinach better than you.

Review Exercise A

Some of the following sentences contain adverbs used inappropriately. Rewrite these sentences to eliminate the error. If a sentence is correct, write *C* beside the sentence number on your paper.

Examples

a. We had to hike more farther than we thought.

a. We had to hike farther than we thought.

b. The planet that shines more brightly of all in the evening is Venus.

b. The planet that shines most brightly of all in the evening is Venus.

1. Which of the two stores is more nearer?
2. Of all the buses, that one is the slower.
3. I played more badly today than I did yesterday.
4. I never thought that no other cookout could be as bad as our first one.
5. The dog eats more slow than the cat.
6. Which of the two skaters practices most often?
7. The new school bells ring more loud than the old ones.
8. I think that of all recording stars, Ray Charles sings most well.
9. Which of the twins studies most?
10. The cat moved slow to the fireplace, curled up, and fell asleep.
11. Jan's essay was the best written of the two.
12. It seemed that Max didn't never feel good.
13. Gina never pitched more well in no game than she did in our last one.

14. Can't you speak slower?
15. One of the twin cities is slightly larger than the other.
16. Of all brass instruments, the French horn is more difficult to play.
17. It was hard to tell which was coldest, my hands or my feet.
18. I can't hardly decide if Spanish or French is easiest to learn.
19. The horse stumbled and near fell down.
20. Carol noticed the slow leaking faucet.

Writing with Adverbs

Adverbs can come to the writer's aid in several ways. They help make the description of a person, a place, or an event more exact and vivid. Adverbs can also help writers organize their material because, used carefully, they clearly show time and space relationships. Adverbs can also clarify the relationships between ideas, as you can see from the following passage in which the **boldface** adverbs emphasize the connection between statements.

> **Supposedly**, threatened species of whales were protected by the regulations of the International Whaling Commission. What **actually** happened was that regulations were **not** strict **enough. Consequently**, almost 40,000 whales were hunted and killed in 1971. Unless the commission tightens its regulations, many endangered species of whales will **subsequently** become extinct. Laws are **now** tighter, but violation of them is **still** frequent. **Indeed**, several countries have **not** complied with the regulations. The whales are **also** threatened by "pirate whalers." The threatened whales will **obviously** become extinct if such groups are allowed to continue.

Some adverbs that show the relationship between ideas appear in the following list.

accordingly	differently	originally
actually	first (second, third)	previously
also	indeed	primarily
besides	initially	similarly
comparatively	mainly	subsequently
consequently	obviously	supposedly

Writing Exercise A

Rewrite the following paragraph, adding adverbs to enrich the description by providing details of time, place, and manner. The adverbs you choose might also clarify the time and spatial relationships between the objects and events. (Feel free to add any adjectives you might like, as well.)

> We drove along a road and came to a house. Near the house was a pond. There were some geese and ducks by the pond. The house seemed empty, though we did see a dog and two cats. We paused. A woman appeared near the house and frightened us. We looked again, and she was gone. We looked,

and all the animals had disappeared. We shut our eyes and when we opened them were surprised to see that the house was still there. We started the car and drove away.

Writing Exercise B

Using adverbs to provide details of time, place, and manner and to clarify relationships, write two or three paragraphs on one of the following suggested topics. Use care in forming the comparative and superlative degrees.

1. Write an account that vividly describes the action of an event you have witnessed or one that you create from your imagination—perhaps a sports event, an unusual street occurrence, an accident, or a natural disaster (such as a tornado or a hurricane).
2. Write an account of how to do something, listing the events in the order they should be performed. You may choose any subject you like: how to make a pizza, how to change a tire, how to stand on your head, or how to survive being marooned on an island. Use adverbs to help the reader keep track of the order in which events should occur or actions should be performed.
3. Write an account of how to get somewhere. You may give directions on how to get to your house, to a lake, or to an imaginary place (such as a secret room concealed in a mansion). Use adverbs to keep your reader clearly oriented so that he or she could easily follow the directions.
4. Take a stand on some issue and explain your reasons for feeling as you do. Support your opinion as fully as possible, trying to use some of the adverbs listed on page 449 to link your statements together and to make the progression of your argument clear.

Understanding Prepositions

Prepositions help words work together in a sentence by showing relationships between the words. Learning the definitions of prepositions and recognizing the way they work in a sentence are two ways to begin your study of this part of speech.

Defining a Preposition

A *preposition* is usually defined as a word that shows a relationship between a noun or pronoun and another word or words in the sentence.

Notice, in the following examples, how the preposition shows different relationships.

The bird flew *into* the tree.
The bird flew *near* the tree.
The bird flew *over* the tree.
The bird flew *under* the tree.

In each of the preceding sentences, the preposition shows the relationship between the noun *tree* and the verb *flew* by indicating where the bird flew in relation to the tree: *into* it, *near* it, *over* it, or *under* it.

Since a preposition connects words, it never appears alone; instead, it is always part of a prepositional phrase.

A *prepositional phrase* consists of the preposition *(P)*, its object *(O)*, and any modifiers *(M)* the object may have.

In the following examples the prepositional phrases are *italicized* and the parts labeled.

P O
The story was *beyond belief.*

P M M O
We ran *out the back door.*

P M M O
The monster's mouth was filled *with long, gleaming fangs.*

Sometimes, a preposition has a compound object, as in the following prepositional phrases.

P O O
The library will remain closed *during the winter and spring.*

P O O O
We wrote a letter *to Joel, Barry, and Corinne.*

Sometimes, as well, the object of a preposition is a group of words:

P O
I will vote *for whichever candidate has the best tax proposal.*

In the following list are the most common one-word prepositions.

about	beside	into	throughout
above	besides	like	till
across	between	near	to
after	beyond	of	toward
against	but [*meaning* except]	off	under
along	by	on	underneath
amid	concerning	onto	until
among	down	out	unto
around	during	outside	up
at	except	over	upon
before	for	past	with
behind	from	since	within
below	in	through	without
beneath	inside		

Compound prepositions are those consisting of more than one word.

according to	by way of	on account of
along with	in addition to	out of
aside from	in front of	prior to
because of	in spite of	together with
by means of	instead of	with respect to

Exercise 1

Write out the following sentences, underlining all prepositional phrases. Then write *P* above the preposition and *O* above the objects. (Remember that a preposition can have more than one object.)

Example

a. The view from the mountaintop was awesome.

P O

a. The view from the mountaintop was awesome.

1. A popular tune by a famous country-and-western singer boomed over the loudspeakers in the Nashville bus station.
2. A large knapsack of green khaki lay on the floor beside a weary youth.
3. Dressed in blue jeans and plaid shirt, the youth sat on an orange plastic chair in the waiting room.
4. Across from him a patient father amused his small daughter with whimsical stories about the advertisements in a magazine.
5. Crowds gathered in neat lines by the ticket counter, where a smiling young man in a blue uniform worked steadily.
6. The loudspeaker crackled with static as the delay of the bus from Atlanta was announced.
7. Amid the confusion caused by the heavy holiday traffic, an angry woman argued with the ticket agent about her missing luggage.
8. Tired of the magazine and her father's stories, the young child climbed on his lap and closed her eyes.
9. An attractive woman burdened with a briefcase and several packages wrapped in bright paper looked around the waiting room.
10. Spying the man with the sleeping child in his arms, the woman raised her arms in greeting and moved toward them.

Some words in the list on page 451 can also be used as other parts of speech.

The cat is *outside.*	[adverb]
The player ran *outside* the foul line.	[preposition]

If a word is used as a preposition, it must have an object. To determine if a word is an adverb or a part of a prepositional phrase, determine its use in the sentence. An adverb modifies a verb, an adjective, or another adverb. A preposition introduces a prepositional phrase that links its object to another word or words in the sentence.

Note: When *to* is followed by the plain form of a verb, it is considered part of an infinitive and is not considered a preposition: *to* dance, *to* play, *to* sing (infinitives).

Exercise 2

Write out the following passage, underlining the prepositional phrases. Then label the prepositions *P* and the objects *O*. (Be certain that a word is actually being used as a preposition and not as an adverb or as some other part of speech.)

Example

a. Muhammad Ali was sent to Africa on a mission by President Carter.

P O P O P O

a. Muhammad Ali was sent to Africa on a mission by President Carter.

(The following passage by Tom Brown, Jr., is a true story of a younger man trained in woodlore by an old Apache. The narrator has just met Rick, the old man's grandson, and the boys immediately have become friends.)[1]

> After we had talked through half the afternoon, Rick took me home to meet his grandfather, a man who would be my teacher and guide for the next nine years. Stalking Wolf had come to New Jersey to be near his son, who lived there. I was in awe of him from the beginning. He was of medium height and lean, the grandson of a medicine man, and a tracker and hunter for his Apache band. To Rick and me he was the Spirit of the Woods.

Mastery Exercise A

In the following paragraphs from Dorothy Johnson's "Scars of Honor," there are more than twenty-five prepositional phrases, with the first one underlined. Using what you have learned in the preceding sections, identify at least twenty-five prepositional phrases, listing them on a sheet of paper.[2]

> Charles Lockjaw died last summer on the reservation. He was very old—a hundred years, he had claimed. He still wore his hair in braids, as only the older men do in his tribe, and the braids were thin and white. His fierce old face was like a withered apple. He was bent and frail and trembling, and his voice was like a wailing of the wind across the prairie grass.
>
> Old Charley died in his sleep in the canvas-covered tepee where he lived in warm weather. In the winter he was crowded with the younger ones among his descendants in a two-room log cabin, but in summer they pitched the tepee. Sometimes they left him alone there, and sometimes his great-grandchildren scrambled in with him like a bunch of puppies.
>
> His death was no surprise to anyone. What startled the Indian agent and some of Charley's own people, and the white ranchers when they heard about it, was the fact that some of the young men of the tribe sacrificed a horse on

---

[1]From *The Tracker: The Story of Tom Brown, Jr.* as told to William Jon Watkins, as it appears in the *Reader's Digest*, November 1978. Copyright © 1978 by Tom Brown, Jr. and William Jon Watkins. Reprinted by permission of Prentice-Hall, Inc. and *Reader's Digest*.

[2]From "Scars of Honor" by Dorothy M. Johnson. Copyright 1950; renewed © 1977 by Dorothy M. Johnson. First published in Argosy. Reprinted by permission of McIntosh and Otis, Inc.

his grave. Charley wasn't buried on holy ground; he never went near the mission. He was buried in a grove of cottonwoods down by the creek that is named for a dead chief. His lame great-grandson, Joe Walking Wolf, and three other young Indians took this horse out there and shot it. It was a fine sorrel gelding, only seven years old, broke fairly gentle and nothing wrong with it. Young Joe had been offered eighty dollars for that horse. [*underscore added*]

Mastery Exercise B

From a science textbook or library book, select a passage containing at least ten prepositional phrases. List the phrases on your paper in the order in which they appear in the selection. Decide whether or not the same information could have been conveyed in any other way, perhaps by a single-word adjective or by an adverb.

Using Prepositions

In the following sections you will practice using prepositions in a way that conforms to Edited Standard English. You will also practice varying the placement of prepositional phrases to give your writing clarity and variety.

Commonly Confused Prepositions

The following guidelines will help you to use prepositions in a way that conforms to Edited Standard English.

accept/except

Accept is a verb meaning "to receive or take possession of something."

> I *accept* this award with my usual great humility.

Except is a preposition meaning "with the exception of" or "not including."

> Everyone voted on the issue *except* Ms. Jefferson.

among/between

Use *between* when referring to two people or things.

> There are profound differences *between* the United States and the Soviet Union.
> We need to keep this a secret *between* you and me.

Use *among* when referring to more than two people or things.

> Competition *among* the players grew intense.
> Keep this a secret *among* the three of us.

Use *between* when referring to the individual relationships between two items, even if the items are part of a larger group.

Weeds grew *between* the rows of corn.
The distance *between* the stars is great.

beside/besides

Beside means "being next to."

I was walking down the street with my dog *beside* me.

Besides means "in addition to" or "moreover."

Besides turkey, there were also ham and chicken on the table.

in/into

In means "already inside."

The pearls are *in* the safe.

Into is used to indicate the act of entering or being put inside.

We went *into* the kitchen to investigate the strange noise.

past/passed

Past can be used as an adjective, an adverb, or a preposition.

We talked over *past* times.	[adjective modifying *times*]
Did you see Harold when he drove *past*?	[adverb modifying *drove*]
The truck roared *past* us, honking loudly.	[preposition]

The word *past*, however, should not be used as a verb. The verb that it sounds like is correctly written *passed*.

One of the linemen *passed* the ball to Mean Joe Green.

Exercise 1

Write out the following sentences, choosing the correct word from the choices in parentheses. Underline the word you select.

Example

a. The skiing competition will be most fierce (between, among) Germany and the U.S.S.R.

a. The skiing competition will be most fierce between Germany and the U.S.S.R.

1. I like all winter sports (accept, except) ice-skating.
2. We ran (in, into) the kitchen to check the stove.
3. No one liked the movie (accept, except) Henry.
4. Carrie continued studying well (past, passed) midnight.

5. No one (beside, besides) Carol was late.
6. Please put the small table (beside, besides) the sofa.
7. Those moles seem to live (in, into) our garden.
8. Are there any similarities (between, among) the Spanish and Portuguese languages?
9. Have you lived anywhere else (beside, besides) California?
10. There were constant arguments (between, among) the six delegates.

Problems in Using Prepositions

The following list will help you avoid some common problems in using prepositions. Sometimes, people use unnecessary prepositions or use one preposition when another is correct according to Edited Standard English.

An asterisk (*) denotes a sentence with a feature that is not part of Edited Standard English.

about Use either *about* or *at* with expressions of time, but not both.

*We will arrive at about 9 o'clock.
We will arrive *at* 9 o'clock.
We will arrive *about* 9 o'clock.

at Do not use *at* with *where.*

*Do you know where the movie is at?
Do you know *where* the movie is?

by Do not use *by* to mean "with."

*That movie is all right by us.
That movie is all right *with* us.

of Do not use *of* instead of the helping verb *have.*

*We could of won if we'd played better.
We could *have* won if we'd played better.

off Use just the preposition *off,* not *off of.*

*The cat fell off of the bed.
The cat fell *off* the bed.

on Do not use the word *on* with the verb *blame.* Use *blame* by itself.

*Who blamed it on me?
Who *blamed* me for it?

to Do not use *to* as a replacement for *at.*

*I'll call when I arrive to the bus station.
I'll call when I arrive *at* the bus station.

Do not use *to* when it is unnecessary.

*Where are you going to?
Where are you going?

than Do not use the preposition *than* with the word *different*. Use *from* instead.

> *Your essay is different than mine.
> Your essay is *different from* mine.

with Do not use *with* when it is unnecessary.

> *We visited with Ms. Sanders.
> We visited Ms. Sanders.
> *We continued with our journey.
> We continued our journey.
> *The students were issued with library passes.
> The students were issued library passes.

Exercise 2

Write out each of the following sentences, changing prepositions to conform to Edited Standard English. (It might be necessary to reword a sentence slightly.) Underline any changes you make.

Example

a. If you want to live in Boston for the summer, it's all right by me.
a. If you want to live in Boston for the summer, it's all right <u>with</u> me.

1. Does anyone know where the fireworks are at?
2. I was so hungry I could of eaten a whole box of crackers.
3. All of the employees were issued with discount coupons.
4. If the flowerpots fell off of the balcony, don't blame it on me.
5. Downhill skiing is quite different than cross-country skiing.
6. The play should begin at about 8:30.
7. Please save us a seat when you arrive to the concert.
8. In what way is rayon different than nylon?
9. I can't remember where I put the keys at.
10. If I had a schedule, I would of known where the train was going to.
11. When you got besides their guard, you should have past the ball to Lisa.
12. I shouldn't of excepted the invitation without asking my parents.
13. I ran in the kitchen and found the cat into the bowl of tuna salad.
14. The three delegates argued hotly between themselves.
15. After the storm past over, we continued our hike.
16. Rickie's stock car pulled up besides the lead car, then past it.
17. I should of studied longer, but I stopped at about 9 o'clock.
18. It is all right by Sheila if you want to meet with Julian Bond in person.
19. I couldn't of been mistaken; the witnesses saw someone jump off of the roof!

20. I jumped in the pool, and then I realized I was into water deeper than I had expected.

Writing with Prepositions

Prepositional phrases can function as adjectives to modify a noun or pronoun.

The spy *in the trenchcoat* approached. [adjective]

Prepositional phrases can also function as adverbs, to modify verbs, adjectives, or other adverbs.

The spy approached *with caution.* [modifying verb]
His heart was full *of apprehension.* [modifying adjective]
He walked down *through the long alley.* [modifying adverb]

Prepositional phrases should be placed so they clearly modify the appropriate word. The following newspaper advertisement shows the results of a poorly placed prepositional phrase.

Lost—Wristwatch by a lady with a cracked face.

The placement of a prepositional phrase can affect the meaning of a sentence.

The professor spoke to the students from Sweden.
The professor from Sweden spoke to the students.

If a prepositional phrase is used as an adjective, it is usually placed next to the noun or pronoun it modifies.

The woman *from France* took a boat *from Australia.*
With few errors, the paper was judged the best in class.

If a prepositional phrase is used as an adverb, it can sometimes be moved within a sentence without changing the meaning.

We will leave *in the morning.*
In the morning we will leave.

If a sentence contains more than one verb, be certain the prepositional phrase modifies the correct verb.

The car that we rented broke down *during the afternoon.*
[*During the afternoon* tells when the car broke down.]
The car that we rented *during the afternoon* broke down.
[*During the afternoon* modifies *rented,* telling when the car was rented.]

Writing Exercise A

Some of the following sentences are unclear because the prepositional phrase is not well placed. Revise these sentences so that their meaning is clear. If a sentence is clear, write *C* after that number on your paper.

Example

a. The lion growled ferociously at the children in the cage.
a. The lion in the cage growled ferociously at the children.

1. I bought a dress after parking the car in the new boutique.
2. We walked over the ocean for several miles to watch the sun set.
3. The dog loves to sleep on the blanket with a bushy tail.
4. The cat hid after chasing the visitor under the couch.
5. Have you ever noticed the bird that nests in the tree with red wings?
6. The high winds during the hurricane damaged the house.
7. My friend with automatic transmission just bought a new car.
8. Because she suffered an injury, Noele could no longer play tennis on her wrist.
9. The children with spots enjoyed watching the cows.
10. After school Elyse and Juan worked on their science project.

Review Exercise A

Each of the following sentences contains one or more prepositions that are not used according to Edited Standard English. Revise the sentences to correspond with standard usage.

Example

a. We should of followed the directions more closely.
a. We should have followed the directions more closely.

1. I would of enjoyed my skiing trip more if I hadn't had to travel so far among the mountain and my cabin.
2. I'd except the award gladly, but I'd be happier if some one else won beside me.
3. Our newspaper reporter visited with the woman just named mayor.
4. Between you, Steve, and me, we can come up with only five dollars for gas.
5. When the principal sent for us, we were afraid we were into trouble.
6. Igor, we shall continue with the experiment and create a monster different than the last one.
7. We past the accident at about 7 o'clock.
8. All the science students accept Ann were issued with new microscopes, which were quite different than the old ones.
9. I should of eaten something beside toast for breakfast.
10. If you had decided first where you were going to, you could of planned your trip better.

Writing Exercise B

The following list contains proverbs, or familiar sayings, you have probably heard many times. Use one or more of these sayings as a topic for writing and do one of the following assignments: (a) use an incident to explain how the proverb has or has not been true in your life, (b) use several examples to prove that the proverb is or is not good advice, or (c) write about the contradictory advice in two or more proverbs. In your writing pay special attention to using prepositions in a way that conforms to Edited Standard English and to placing prepositional phrases so that your meaning is clear.

1. If at first you don't succeed, try, try again.
2. Don't beat your head against a stone wall.
3. Too many cooks spoil the broth.
4. You are never too old to learn.
5. Two heads are better than one.
6. Absence makes the heart grow fonder.
7. You can't teach an old dog new tricks.
8. Out of sight, out of mind.
9. Don't cry over spilled milk.
10. People who live in glass houses shouldn't throw stones.

Understanding Conjunctions

Like prepositions, conjunctions help to show the relationship between words or groups of words in a sentence. You can identify conjunctions by learning their definition and the classes into which they can be grouped.

Defining a Conjunction

A *conjunction* is usually defined as a word that connects other words or groups of words.

Conjunctions can connect words:

Do you prefer <u>apples</u> *or* <u>pears</u>?

The apples were <u>old</u> *but* <u>good</u>.

Julio <u>picked</u> *and* <u>ate</u> some apples.

That sheep dog is <u>large</u> *yet* <u>gentle</u>.

Conjunctions can connect phrases:

The car backed <u>out the driveway</u> *and* <u>into the street</u>.

Conjunctions can also connect sentences and clauses:

I like cats, *but* they make me sneeze.
We can't go to the movies *until* the dishes are done.

Exercise 1

Write out the following sentences, underlining all conjunctions. (Your teacher may ask you to explain what words or group of words each conjunction connects.)

Examples

a. Is it quicker to walk through the woods or around the lake?
a. Is it quicker to walk through the woods or around the lake?

b. I like mangoes, but I have never tasted a papaya.
b. I like mangoes, but I have never tasted a papaya.

1. The plot of the story was confusing yet exciting.
2. Juanita walks to work every day, for she enjoys the exercise.
3. Neither Pluto nor Jupiter is visible without a telescope.
4. Sam and I would like to visit Japan and China next year.
5. King Tut's tomb was an exceptional find, for few Egyptian tombs have survived without being plundered for their treasure.
6. Avocados are tasty but fattening!
7. The architect I. M. Pei is working on buildings in both America and China.
8. Kim will not swim in the ocean, nor will she swim in a pool.
9. I have searched the house and the car, but I still can't find my keys and my glasses.
10. Lake Tahoe is on the border of two states, so a visitor there can stay either in California or in Nevada.

Classifying Conjunctions

There are three kinds of conjunctions: *coordinating conjunctions*, *subordinating conjunctions*, and *correlative conjunctions*.

1. *Coordinating Conjunctions*

Coordinating conjunctions join elements of equal rank, such as two nouns (or a noun and a pronoun), two verbs, two phrases, or two independent clauses. The most common coordinating conjunctions are *and*, *but*, *or*, *nor*, *for*, and *yet*.

Ken bought a bicycle *and* roller skates.
Does the baby walk *or* talk yet?
The scissors are in the drawer *or* on the desk.
Karen visited Madrid, *but* she didn't go to Barcelona.
Jenny speaks Spanish well, *for* she lived in Mexico last year.

Exercise 2

On a sheet of paper, copy the following passage about Manhattan, underlining the ten coordinating conjunctions. The first one is done for you.

> Images of confinement certainly haunt me in Manhattan but the first thing that always strikes me, when I land once more on the island, is its fearful and mysterious beauty. Other cities have built higher now, or sprawl more boisterously over their landscapes, but there is still nothing like the looming thicket of the Manhattan skyscrapers, jumbled and overbearing. Le Corbusier hated this ill-disciplined spectacle, and conceived his own Radiant City, an antiseptic hybrid of art and ideology, in direct antithesis to it. His ideas, though, mostly bounced off this vast mass of vanity. Tempered though it has been from time to time by zoning law and social trend, Manhattan remains a mammoth mess, a stupendous clashing of light and dark and illusory perspective, splotched here and there by wastelands of slum or demolition, wanly patterned by the grid of its street system, but essentially, whatever the improvers do to it, whatever economy decrees or architectural fashion advises, the supreme monument to that elemental human instinct, Free-For-All.[1]

Le Corbusier was a famous and influential French architect who helped design the United Nations headquarters in New York.

2. *Subordinating Conjunctions*

The *subordinating conjunction* joins unequal elements in a sentence.

The following list contains some of the most common subordinating conjunctions.

after	as much as	before	since	till	whenever
although	as soon as	if	so that	unless	where
as if	as though	in order that	than	whatever	wherever
as long as	because	provided	though	when	while

The subordinating conjunction may link a word or phrase to a main clause.

A *clause* is a group of words with a subject and a verb.

> *When* angry, count ten before you speak, *if* very angry, an hundred.
> —Thomas Jefferson

The most common use of the subordinating conjunction, however, is to join two clauses.

> We got our allowance *after* we raked the yard and washed the car.
> I always listen to the radio *while* I am driving.
> *Because* he likes to cook, Len opened a restaurant.

A clause begun by a subordinating conjunction is always a dependent clause and cannot stand alone. It must be joined to an independent clause.

For a discussion of independent and subordinate clauses, see pages 525–527.

Exercise 3

Write out the following sentences, underlining the subordinating conjunctions you find.

---

[1]From *Destinations: Essays from Rolling Stone* by Jan Morris. © 1980 by Rolling Stone Press and Jan Morris. Reprinted by permission of Oxford University Press, Inc. (This credit was omitted from the first printing of this book.)

Example

a. Carlos didn't show his anger although he felt it boiling inside him.

a. Carlos didn't show his anger although he felt it boiling inside him.

1. We wanted to go camping somewhere where there wouldn't be a lot of other people.
2. On our last camping trip it seemed as if half the city had come out to camp with us.
3. Wherever we stepped, there was litter or another camper or someone's equipment.
4. When night came, we discovered that the people next to us had brought their portable television set.
5. It's hard to enjoy the wilderness while a rerun of *Gilligan's Island* is blaring in the background.
6. As soon as I got to sleep, I was awakened by someone screaming about a bear.
7. A neighboring camper was in a pine tree yelling because a bear had tried to get in his sleeping bag.
8. After we investigated the situation, we discovered the "bear" was only another camper's large poodle.
9. We then had to call the fire department, since the man wouldn't come down from the tree.
10. Next time we won't set up camp unless we are really in the wilderness.

Exercise 4

The following paragraphs contain fifteen conjunctions. List them in order on your paper and tell if the conjunction is coordinating or subordinating. (Not all of the sentences contain conjunctions.)[1]

Example

a. We wanted to go downtown and do some shopping because the stores were having some good clearance sales.

a. and—coordinating conjunction; because—subordinating conjunction

Norman Rockwell painted with a passion for the visual truth and, almost invariably, worked from live models. Long before brush touched canvas, he arranged the props, the scenery, the lighting, and acted out precisely the expression he wanted from his human models. With animals he showed Olympian patience. How do you pose a chicken?

"You pick up the chicken and rock him back and forth a few times," Rockwell wrote in his autobiography. "When you set him down, he will stand

Olympian refers to the Greek gods of Mount Olympus and means "exalted or majestic."

[1]From *Norman Rockwell: My Adventures as an Illustrator* by Norman Rockwell. © 1979 by The Curtis Publishing Company. Reprinted with permission of The Saturday Evening Post Company.

just as you've placed him for four or five minutes. Of course, you have to run behind the easel quickly to do much painting before the chicken moves.

"If you want to paint the chicken full face, the procedure is even more complicated because the eyes of a chicken are on the sides of his head and when he looks at you he turns his head. I finally got a long stick, and after I'd set the chicken down and gone behind my easel, I'd rap the wall at one side of the chicken and he'd turn his head toward me to look at the wall. It's very strenuous painting a chicken."

3. *Correlative Conjunctions*

Correlative conjunctions are used only in pairs.

both . . . and	not only . . . but also	as . . . as
either . . . or	whether . . . or	as . . . so
neither . . . nor		so . . . as

Neither Katy *nor* Kim knew which bus to take.
We don't know *whether* we should sell the car *or* get the motor repaired.
As the plane rolled over, *so* did my stomach.

Exercise 5

Write out the following sentences, underlining the correlative conjunctions that you find.

Example

a. Fred not only broke his collarbone but also his wrist and thumb.
a. Fred not only broke his collarbone but also his wrist and thumb.

1. Send either a check or money order for your purchase.
2. The streets were not only icy but also winding.
3. John can play both flute and saxophone.
4. Do you know whether Stan's Inn or Harry's Hotel has any vacancy?
5. We don't know whether our dog was lost or stolen.
6. As a magnet draws iron filings, so a picnic seems to draw ants.
7. Helen has not only a parrot but also two cockatiels and a toucan.
8. Either we need a new television set or a better antenna.
9. Either Linda or Karen will call us when Sheila and Pam arrive.
10. People should visit the dentist regularly, whether they want to or not.

Review Exercise A

Write out the following sayings, underlining all the conjunctions. Beneath each sentence write each conjunction and the class to which it belongs: coordinating, subordinating, or correlative. (Some sentences have more than one conjunction.)

Example

a. When the cat's away, the mice will play.

a. When the cat's away, the mice will play.
when—subordinating

1. I cannot be your friend and your flatterer, too.
2. When two play, one must lose.
3. There is nothing either good or bad but thinking makes it so.
4. As the twig is bent, so is the tree inclined.
5. While there's life, there's hope.
6. Don't count your chickens before they're hatched.
7. None are so blind as those who refuse to see.
8. If you have a bad name, you are half-hanged.
9. The thread will break where it is weakest.
10. Lock the stable door before the horse is stolen.
11. Nobody does as much work today as he is going to do tomorrow.
12. As the worker is good or bad, so the work is.
13. When we are out of sympathy with the young, our work in the world is over.
14. People who eat until they are sick must fast until they are well.
15. As a moth gnaws at a garment, so does envy consume those who are envious.
16. If you fear to suffer, you will suffer from fear.
17. People without hope need no enemies because they have defeated themselves.
18. Sheep flock together, but eagles fly alone.
19. A lie can go around the world while the truth is getting its britches on.
20. Though malice may dim truth, it cannot put it out.

Mastery Exercise A

In the following passage about blue-jeans from Jean Libman's essay "The Pants Worn Round the World," there are twenty-two conjunctions. List them on a sheet of paper in the order they appear. (Correlative conjunctions are counted as one conjunction each.)

Example

a. As Yale law professor Charles Reich has said, jeans "express freedom and wholeness of self," and isn't that what everyone craves these days?

a. as—subordinating conjunction; and—coordinating conjunction; and—coordinating conjunction

The world is in the grip of a blue-jeans frenzy. Once the no-nonsense work pants of farmers, lumberjacks and miners—and few others—jeans now strut, stride, stroll and slouch everywhere, on the job and off. They are at home in palaces (Princess Anne of England wore them when she had her hair done on her wedding day) and at parties (author Norman Mailer and actor Marlon Brando have appeared in them at black-tie affairs).

Why the "jeaning" of the world? "A fashion is easier to follow if it is both chic and cheap," explains one manufacturer. And jeans are undeniably fashionable and affordable, as well as sturdy and comfortable. You can dress down in $2 recycled jeans from Goodwill—or dress up in a $200 sky-blue jean suit.

By the 1950s, jeans had become the staple play-garb of children, and teenagers began battling parents and high-school administrators for the right to wear jeans to classes. In the course of this struggle, jeans themselves became a symbol of defiance against authority or oppression, whether parental or political, real or imagined.

But a funny thing happened on the way to the barricades. Fashion discovered blue jeans. Suddenly, stores blossomed with jeans, not only for blue-collar workers and rebellious youth but for family members of all ages and all income levels.[1]

Mastery Exercise B

From a magazine, newspaper or book, select a passage several paragraphs in length. Using what you have learned in the previous sections, identify the conjunctions and list them on a sheet of paper. Beside each conjunction write the class to which it belongs.

Using Conjunctions

In the following sections you will learn how to use conjunctions in a way that conforms to Edited Standard English. As you work through the following sections, use the preceding Understanding Conjunctions sections for any help you may need in identifying conjunctions.

Choosing the Right Conjunction

Conjunctions not only combine elements such as words, phrases, and clauses, but they also show relationships, as you can see in the following examples.

Marcia will go, *and* Anne will go, too.
Marcia will go, *but* Anne cannot.

Either Anne will go *or* Marcia will.
Neither Anne *nor* Marcia will go.

Anne went *because* Marcia could not.
Anne went *although* Marcia could not.

[1]From "The Pants Worn Round the World" by Jean Libman from *Reader's Digest*, August 1974. Reprinted by permission of *Reader's Digest*.

To use conjunctions effectively, you must be conscious of the differences among their meanings. Some writers tend to use *and* as an all-purpose conjunction.

For more work with using conjunctions to combine sentences, see Part 4, "Sentence Combining."

> I really wanted to go to the game, *and* there were no tickets left, *and* I stayed home.

Such a stringy sentence does not give the reader clear signals about the meanings between the statements. A good revision incorporates conjunctions that express the relationships more precisely:

> I really wanted to go to the game, *but* there were no tickets left; *so* I stayed home.

Sometimes, changing a weak conjunction means you have to change other parts of the sentence as well, perhaps even the order of clauses.

> I wanted to see better, *and* I stood up.
> I stood up *because* I wanted to see better.
> *Because* I wanted to see better, I stood up.

Writing Exercise A

Revise the following sentences by replacing the vague conjunctions with ones that state the intended meaning more precisely. In some sentences you may have to change more than just the conjunction to make the sentence clear and tight. Remember to use commas where necessary.

Examples

a. One of Dinah's sister is quite tall, and the other is shorter than average.
a. One of Dinah's sisters is quite tall, but the other is shorter than average.

b. The dog was lonely, and it began to howl mournfully.
b. The dog was lonely, so it began to howl mournfully.

or

Because the dog was lonely, it began to howl mournfully.

1. The other team was favored to win, and we beat them.
2. We are putting a new floor in our attic, and we will have more storage space.
3. I would jingle the car keys, and the dog would always know that we were going for a ride.
4. Margo doesn't like physical exercise, and she signed up for tennis anyway.
5. Arlo wants to strengthen his shoulder muscles, and he is working with weights.
6. Most packaged food products contain sugar, and people get more sugar than they realize.

7. I spilled pepper on my sleeve, and I began sneezing.
8. I finished my homework, and David was just beginning.
9. We always shop at that store, and it has excellent bargains.
10. This brand is cheaper, and it's a better product than many higher-priced items.

Troublesome Conjunctions

The following information will help you avoid common problems in using conjunctions.

An asterisk (*) denotes a sentence with a feature that is not part of Edited Standard English.

as *As* is not used to mean "that" or "whether."

> *I don't know as I should tell you what she said.
> I don't know *that* I should tell you what she said.
> or
> I don't know *whether* I should tell you what she said.

as to whether This construction uses more words than necessary to express its meaning. The word *whether* alone will suffice.

> *The President would not say as to whether he would veto the bill.
> The President would not say *whether* he would veto the bill.

but what The construction *but what* is frequently heard in conversations but is not a feature of Edited Standard English.

> *I don't know but what the store overcharged us.
> I think *perhaps* the store overcharged us.
> I think *that* the store overcharged us.

either . . . or, neither . . . nor The word *either* used as part of a correlative construction needs to be followed by the word *or*. The word *neither* is followed by the word *nor*.

> *Either snow nor rain will make us cancel the trip.
> *Either* snow *or* rain will make us cancel the trip.
> *Neither* snow *nor* rain will make us cancel the trip.

except *Except* should not be used as a conjunction. The conjunction *unless* should be substituted for it.

> *I can't go except I get an advance on my allowance.
> I can't go *unless* I get an advance on my allowance.

like *Like* should not be used as a conjunction. The subordinating conjunctions *as* or *as if* should be used when a subordinate clause is to be used to make a comparison.

For the definition of *subordinate clause*, see page 525.

*The movie monster looked like it was made of clay.
The movie monster looked as *if* it were made of clay.

try and Avoid using *try and.* Use the more accurate expression *try to.*

*I will try and study harder.
I will *try to* study harder.

where *Where* should not be substituted for the conjunction *that* in writing.

*I see where gasoline prices are going up again.
I see *that* gasoline prices are going up again.

while The conjunction *while* means "at the same time as"; it should not be substituted for *although* or *though.*

*While Shirley MacLaine began her career as a dancer, her greatest success was as an actress.

Although [or *Though*] Shirley MacLaine began her career as a dancer, her greatest success was as an actress.

Writing Exercise B

Each of the following sentences contains a conjunction (or a word used as a conjunction) that is not a feature of Edited Standard English. Revise the sentence so that the inexact or wordy conjunction is eliminated.

Examples

a. While Bill Cosby was a dropout in his youth, he later received a doctor's degree in education.
a. Although Bill Cosby was a dropout in his youth, he later received a doctor's degree in education.

b. Your health will benefit if you consume neither large amounts of sugar or excessive quantities of starch.
b. Your health will benefit if you consume neither large amounts of sugar nor excessive quantities of starch.

1. I don't know as I'd be brave enough to ride that wild horse.
2. Kelly read where scientists may soon find a cure for the common cold.
3. My room always looks like a tornado has just passed through it.
4. I can't yet say as to whether we can go with you Friday night.
5. I see where the movie we have wanted to see is now playing.
6. Will you try and remember to pay me the money you owe me?
7. A student can't go to the library except the teacher writes a pass.
8. I don't know but what the Dodgers will win the pennant this year.
9. Neither poodles or schnauzers shed much, so they make tidy pets.
10. I'll try and find a fishing rod to give you.

Writing Exercise C

Rewrite each of the following sets of sentences as one sentence, using conjunctions that will help the reader understand the relationships between ideas. Underline the conjunctions you add.

Examples

a. Sarah and Cara Washington are twins. Lisa and Luisa Perez are not.

a. Sarah and Cara Washington are twins, but Lisa and Luisa Perez are not.

b. I go for walks. My cat always follows me.

b. Whenever I go for walks, my cat always follows me.

1. The dog looked like an English setter. It was really only a handsome mutt.
2. I practiced playing my bagpipes. The neighbors complained I was giving them headaches.
3. Pedro made the honor roll. Lisa made the honor roll. Kim made the honor roll.
4. I need a car. I could get a job at Delivery Service Company.
5. I cooked the potatoes. My brother set the table.
6. I can go to the movies. My homework must be done first.
7. I don't like to drive on the freeway. I have to do it every day to get to work.
8. The dog tried to tunnel out of its pen. It caught its collar on the bottom of the fence. It couldn't escape after all.
9. I was walking down the street. I saw a motorcycle accident.
10. The temperature dropped. A storm was coming. We hurriedly gathered our swimming things. We went home.

Writing Exercise D

Write one or two well-developed paragraphs on one of the following subjects. Use conjunctions that help make your paragraphs coherent and clear.

1. Do you think there is life on other planets? Why or why not? If the answer is yes, what sort of life forms do you think exist? Are they like or unlike humans? If unlike, how are they different?
2. Select one or two products you use daily, perhaps a convenience item such as plastic food wrap or adhesive tape. Do you think these products are necessary? What ecological problems might they cause? Could you live without them? Write one or two paragraphs stating your ideas.
3. Imagine that you have been chosen the host of a new television talk show. What guests would you have? If you would prefer to focus your show around a specific topic, what might it be? Why? Discuss your show.

4. Almost everyone has a favorite singer (or group of singers or musicians). State your favorite singers, why you like them, and why you prefer them to other singers or groups.

Understanding Interjections

An *interjection* is usually defined as a word that expresses strong or sudden emotion. The interjection can also show milder emotion, such as surprise.

Interjections are not grammatically related to the rest of the sentence; they serve as independent elements to show feeling or to summon attention.

Various parts of speech may be used as interjections.

Rats!	[noun]
Help!	[verb]
Great!	[adjective]
Never!	[adverb]
In a pig's eye!	[prepositional phrase]

Other words are never used as anything other than interjections: *Oh! Gee! Gosh! Ah! Alas! Hark! Oops! Eek! Wow! Jumping Jiminy!*

Exercise 1

Write out the following sentences, underlining each interjection.

Examples

a. Alas! We've ruined another meal.

a. <u>Alas!</u> We've ruined another meal.

b. Furiously she replied, "Never!"

b. Furiously she replied, "<u>Never!</u>"

1. Stop! You're about to sit on a scorpion!
2. When one United States general was asked to surrender, he sent back a one-word reply: "Nuts!"
3. This boa constrictor could not possibly hurt me—help!
4. Good grief, the dog has eaten my sandwich.
5. Hark! The herald angels sing!
6. Ouch! That switch gave me a shock!
7. Come on! You know you can win.
8. Aha! I've caught you in the act, Mr. Snodberry!
9. And now I will juggle not four, but five, of these raw eggs simultaneously—oops!
10. Warning! These grounds are patrolled by attack dogs.

Using Interjections

An interjection expressing strong emotion is usually set off by an exclamation point.

> Ugh**!** There's a fly in my soup!
> The weather forecaster predicted enough snow to close the schools. Hooray**!**

An interjection that expresses a relatively mild emotion is usually set off by a comma.

> Oh**,** I don't know about that.
> Uh-oh**,** I forgot to mail that letter.

The punctuation that you use with an interjection indicates the amount of emotion you want to convey. Notice that if an interjection is followed by an exclamation point, the next word is capitalized because it really begins a new sentence. If the interjection is followed by a comma, the next word merely continues the sentence and is not capitalized.

> Ugh**!** *That* food looks disgusting.
> Oh**,** *that* food doesn't look very appetizing.
> "Aha**!**" Pete exclaimed. "*We've* found the solution."
> "Well**,**" Pete said, "*we're* still working on the problem."

Exercise 1

Write out the following sentences, underlining the interjections. Place an exclamation point after interjections you think show strong emotion. Place a comma after those that you think are milder interjections. Capitalize words that need it. Circle the punctuation you insert and underline the words you capitalize.

Example

a. Help get me out of here.

a. Help(!) Get me out of here.

1. Well we could go to the movies tomorrow.
2. Watch out that highway is a dangerous road to drive.
3. Oops I have forgotten Megan's address as well as her phone number.
4. Oh no Julia has locked the keys in the car.
5. Great I'd love to hike through that national park.
6. Never no one else besides me can ever drive my car.
7. Oh the cat will get itself down from that tree.
8. Whew I thought this heat wave would never break.
9. Hey you're not supposed to be on that property.
10. Thank goodness this long, tiring day is over.

Writing with Interjections

Interjections are more common in prose, drama, and fiction than in essays, school papers, articles, and similar expository prose. Unless very strong emotion is being expressed, interjections often seem out of place. Too many interjections in an essay or article may make the writer sound too angry, hysterical, or pushy. Notice how the interjections in the following piece make it seem silly and overemotional.

Is the Dog a Person's Best Friend?

Is a dog a person's best friend? Ha! Dogs are dirty. Ick! They get fleas and disgusting ticks—yech! Oh, yeah, dogs are supposed to be friendly and loving. Phooey, a dog is friendly and loving because it knows people will feed it and pet it if it acts that way. Dogs grovel and wag and slurp in your face. Repulsive! Would a sane person own a dog? Never!

Writing Exercise A

Choose one of the following suggested topics and write a short dialogue about it. Use interjections to add emotion where appropriate, but be careful about overusing them. Check pages 597–600 for rules about using quotation marks and other punctuation marks with dialogue.

1. You and your family have just moved into a new house or an apartment, and a neighbor tells you that it is supposedly haunted. How do you feel? Write a dialogue between yourself and someone else (perhaps a friend to whom you are talking on the phone) describing this first night in your "haunted" house.
2. You have just discovered how to turn any common material into gold! How do you do it? How excited are you? Do you have any plans? Write a conversation in which you explain your discovery to a friend.
3. You come home one day to find that your dog has learned to speak. What does it say? How do people react? Write the dialogue between you and your dog.

Understanding Verbals

Verbal phrases are discussed on pages 508–514.

Although not classified as a part of speech, verbals function almost like a ninth part of speech. In the next sections you will begin a study of verbals by learning to recognize them and their functions in a sentence.

Defining a Verbal

A *verbal* is usually defined as a word that is formed from a verb but used in a sentence as an adjective, an adverb, or a noun. There are three kinds of verbals: the *participle*, the *gerund*, and the *infinitive*.

1. *Participles*

A *participle* is usually defined as a word formed from a verb that is used as an adjective.

> We heard the *howling* wind.
>
> We listened to the *screaming* gulls and *pounding* waves.
>
> The *fluttering* leaves warned us of an *approaching* storm.

Each of the *italicized* words functions as an adjective, but each is formed from a verb. These words, formed by adding *-ing* to the present form of the verb, are called *present participles.*

Remember that the *-ing* form of the verb can also be used with one or more helping verbs to form a verb phrase. Only when the *-ing* verb form modifies a noun or pronoun in the sentence is it a participle.

The wind *was howling.*	[verb phrase]
The *howling* wind rattled the windows.	[participle]
Howling mightily, the wind rattled the windows.	[participle]

Past participles, which are the past participle form of the verb, describe a completed action.

> *Shattered* glass covered the floor.
>
> The *rusted* lock was useless.
>
> We can never replace the *destroyed* documents.
>
> The *broken* limb lay in the backyard.

Like the present participle, the past participle has a double nature. If it has a helping verb, it is part of the verb phrase of the sentence. If it modifies a noun or pronoun, it serves as an adjective. Since participles have this double nature, it is important to see exactly how they are used in a sentence: as part of a verb phrase or as a participle that functions as an adjective.

Our basement *had been flooded* by the storm.	[verb phrase]
Our *flooded* basement was full of carp.	[participle]
Marilyn *had broken* the swimming record.	[verb phrase]
The *broken* jar leaked honey.	[participle]

When a participle performs as an adjective, it may appear before the word it modifies or after it.

> The *galloping* horse raced across the canyon floor.
>
> The horse, *galloping* across the canyon floor, left its pursuers far behind.
>
> The *forgotten* treasure lay in the cave for years.
>
> The treasure, *forgotten,* lay in the cave for years.

Exercise 1

Write out the following sentences, underlining the participles used as adjectives. Then draw an arrow from each participle to the word it modifies.

Examples

a. The cheering crowd gave the players new courage.

a. The cheering crowd gave the players new courage.

b. The tornado, veering and twisting, swept across the fields.

b. The tornado, veering and twisting, swept across the fields.

1. The cackling hens were scratching in the barnyard dust.
2. Tired and distracted, the driver was jolted by the flashing lights.
3. Marcia, excited about her vacation, was going downtown to buy some new skiing equipment.
4. The freshly fallen snow twinkled in the rays of the setting sun.
5. The traveling musicians had hoped to leave on the early bus, but they played an encore for the cheering audience.
6. The glowing campfire embers and the rustling pines were making Pat feel drowsy.
7. The smoke rising from the outdated chimneys was clouding the early morning air.
8. The trained accountants balanced the confusing books quickly.
9. Wandering aimlessly, Mack was unnerved by the milling crowds and rushing traffic.
10. The creeping tortoise was gaining ground slowly with its plodding pace.

2. *Gerunds*

Gerunds are usually defined as words ending in *-ing* that are formed from verbs and that function as nouns.

You need sturdy, well-fitting shoes for *hiking*.
Dreaming is a mysterious process.
Many people dread *dieting*.
Boiling will purify that water.

Gerunds can be used in all the ways that nouns are used.

Yodeling isn't hard to learn.	[gerund as subject]
Are we born with the fear of *falling*?	[gerund as object of a preposition]
Gary's hobby is *cooking*.	[gerund as predicate nominative]
Mary hates *ironing*.	[gerund as direct object]
She gives *spelling* a lot of attention.	[gerund as indirect object]

Gerunds always do the work of nouns. Be careful not to confuse gerunds with participles performing a different function: working as adjectives or as parts of a verb phrase.

Writing is one of humanity's greatest inventions.	[gerund]
Marcia is *writing* a report on dolphins.	[part of verb phrase]
I need some extra *writing* paper.	[participle as adjective]

Exercise 2

Write out the following sentences, underlining all gerunds.

Examples

a. Jogging is good for circulation.

a. <u>Jogging</u> is good for circulation.

b. We were startled by the sound of coughing.

b. We were startled by the sound of <u>coughing.</u>

1. Exercising is necessary for physical fitness.
2. Running is becoming popular for overall exercise.
3. Another good activity is swimming.
4. I'm noticing that many people enjoy backpacking.
5. Sailing and snorkeling are two popular water sports.
6. Landlubbers may prefer biking or horseback riding.
7. The daring may like spelunking, or cave exploring.
8. Handball offers lots of running and lunging and is an exhausting sport.
9. The Lunts are opening a gym with equipment for exercising.
10. Sweating and panting are good for you—within reasonable limits.

3. *Infinitives*

An *infinitive* is a verb form preceded by the word *to*: *to have, to look, to lower.*

Working in a sentence, an *infinitive* is defined as a form of the verb, usually preceded by the word *to*, that is used as a noun, an adjective, or an adverb.

We like *to bowl.*	[infinitive used as a noun—direct object]
We need a place *to stay.*	[infinitive used as an adjective, modifying the noun *place*]
It's too late *to register.*	[infinitive used as an adverb, modifying the adjective *late*]

When functioning as nouns, infinitives are commonly used in positions where nouns occur; that is, they are used as subjects, direct objects, and predicate nominatives, as well as other kinds of complements.

To succeed will be very hard.	[subject]
We need *to win*.	[direct object]
Our plan is *to cooperate*.	[predicate nominative]

Do not confuse the *to* in an infinitive with the preposition *to*, which is always followed by a noun or pronoun.

INFINITIVES (*to* followed by verb)	PREPOSITIONAL PHRASES (*to* followed by noun or pronoun)
I love *to dream*.	We walked *to church*. (P: *to*, OP: *church*)
I like *to feel* warm.	Please give these books *to them*. (P: *to*, OP: *them*)
Are you able *to see* clearly?	Can we wear jeans *to school?* (P: *to*, OP: *school*)

Exercise 3

The following sentences all contain infinitives. Write out the sentences and underline each infinitive. Beneath the sentence tell whether the infinitive is used as a noun, an adjective, or an adverb.

Examples

a. Carrie has always liked to swim.

a. Carrie has always liked <u>to swim.</u>
to swim—noun

b. I have an important letter to answer.

b. I have an important letter <u>to answer.</u>
to answer—adjective

1. Luisa hopes to finish.
2. Melissa left to phone.
3. That target is hard to hit.
4. The person to see is the guidance counselor.
5. My only goal is to pass.
6. To leave would seem impolite.
7. I still have all these raffle tickets to sell.
8. We came too late to apply.
9. The algebra problems were easy to solve.
10. The perfect Saturday morning project is to sleep.

Review Exercise A

Write out the following sentences, underlining the verbals in each. Beneath each sentence identify the verbals as *present participle, past participle, gerund,* or *infinitive.*

Examples

a. The first great Central American culture to arise was the Olmec civilization.

a. The first great Central American culture to arise was the Olmec civilization.
to arise—infinitive

b. The shriveled grass and falling leaves told us that summer was almost over.

b. The shriveled grass and falling leaves told us that summer was almost over.
shriveled—past participle
falling—present participle

1. Chinese is an interesting language, but it is difficult to learn.
2. The damaged roofs and fallen trees indicated the tornado's path.
3. The dogs, growling and barking, frightened the prowler away.
4. Skiing is an enjoyable sport, but the equipment is too expensive for me.
5. The lock, rusted and crumbling, broke easily.
6. The siren was only a warning, not a signal of immediate danger.
7. Through the frosted glass we could see the snow sparkling in the moonlight.
8. Hiking, camping, and canoeing are Pete's favorite activities.
9. The sleeping student suddenly awoke, yawning and blushing.
10. The old barn, weathered and sagging, was painted by several artists.

Mastery Exercise A

Write out the following sentences, underlining the verbals. Beneath each sentence identify the verbal as *present participle, past participle, gerund,* or *infinitive.* Also, tell how the verbal is used in the sentence: as a *noun,* an *adjective,* or an *adverb.*

Examples

a. The ice made the roads difficult to travel.

a. The ice made the roads difficult to travel.
to travel—infinitive—adverb

b. The blazing lights and scattered confetti helped to create the carnival's frantic atmosphere.

b. The blazing lights and scattered confetti helped to create the carnival's frantic atmosphere.
blazing—present participle—adjective
scattered—past participle—adjective
to create—infinitive—noun

1. A prefabricated log cabin is easy to build.
2. The black, staring windows and gaping door gave the house an eerie look.
3. Tired and aching, the players limped from the field.
4. Writing should be precise, not vague and general.
5. Knitting and crocheting are Alison's favorite hobbies.
6. We intend to continue, and we intend to succeed.
7. The story was pleasant to read but difficult to understand.
8. Smoking and sputtering, the old truck came to a screeching halt.
9. Swimming comes naturally to my sister, who enjoys surfing, snorkeling, and skin diving.
10. The burning sand and scalding light made us regret our trip to the beach.
11. The neighbors jog, and they also perform demanding workouts at the gym.
12. The books, stacked and numbered, were ready for the new library.
13. Using the clay pot Alice gave him, David has learned to cook excellent casseroles.
14. Working together, Manuel's family plans to remodel their new house by Thanksgiving.
15. Checking your home once each year for fire hazards is a good way to avoid a needless disaster.
16. Housed in the old city hall, the small museum plans to expand in the spring.
17. Reading mystery novels on the bus in the morning keeps Mrs. Ortega from getting bored.
18. After studying at the university, she plans to work as a legal aide in the city.
19. Standing outside the door of the workroom, I heard the humming, screeching sounds of the machines used by the printing company.
20. Cheating, lying, and mistreating others are things my father has taught us never to do.

Using Verbals

In your own writing you have probably used verbals—participles, gerunds, and infinitives—even before you were able to define them. Sometimes, however, it is helpful to understand how a structure works. As you practice writing with verbals in the following section, use the preceding Understanding Verbals section for any help you may need in recognizing verbals and their functions in sentences.

Writing with Verbals

Verbals help make writing concise by providing a realm of words that have the vitality of verbs but that can do more than verbs alone, as you can see from the following pairs of examples. In the second example in each pair, a verbal has been used to combine and condense ideas into a compact and vivid sentence.

The horse neighed. The horse stood at the gate. The *neighing* horse stood at the gate.	[participle]
The lawn mower broke. The lawn mower sat in the yard. The *broken* lawn mower sat in the yard.	[participle]
My brother bowls. This is his favorite sport. My brother's favorite sport is *bowling*.	[gerund]
Many people diet. They find it difficult. Many people find it difficult *to diet*.	[infinitive]

Writing Exercise A

Combine each of the following sets of sentences into one sentence by making the *italicized* word into a verbal. (The words in parentheses tell you what kind of verbal to form.) Underline the verbal you form.

Examples

a. The wind swung the shutter back and forth. The shutter *creaked*. (present participle)

a. The wind swung the creaking shutter back and forth.

b. George *stares*. His sister told him this was impolite. (infinitive)

b. George's sister told him it was impolite to stare.

1. The flower *wilts*. The flower drooped in its vase. (present participle)
2. Treasure can be *discovered*. It is difficult. (infinitive)
3. The glass *shattered*. The glass flew through the air. (past participle)
4. Maria Tallchief *danced*. It was her profession. (gerund)
5. Everyone *errs*. It is easy. (infinitive)
6. The wolf sat on the canyon rim. The wolf *howled*. (present participle)
7. The jeans *tore*. The jeans could not be mended. (past participle)
8. You must *plan* a good trip. A good trip demands this. (gerund)
9. The cat *slept*. The mice did not disturb the cat. (present participle)
10. The water pipe *froze*. The water pipes burst from the pressure. (past participle)

Using Participles as Modifiers

Participles may precede or follow the word they modify.

The *leaping* frog eluded the heron. [present participles]
The frog, *leaping*, eluded the heron.

The *polished* table looked like new. [past participles]
The table, *polished*, looked like new.

Notice how a participle following the word it modifies is set off by punctuation.

The fans, *screaming*, jumped to their feet.

Note: A participle that precedes the word it modifies may sometimes be set off with punctuation.

More than one participle may be used to modify a word.

The dog, *running* and *panting*, couldn't catch the rabbit.
The rug, *stained* and *muddied*, was sent to the cleaners.
A *freezing*, *blasting* wind drove us back inside the cabin.
The *torn*, *dog-eared* book was barely legible.

Notice that when two participles precede the word they modify, they can be separated by commas. Two participles following a modifier are usually joined by *and*.

Writing Exercise B

Choose one of the following three topics as the basis for one or two well-developed paragraphs. As you write, concentrate on making your description more vivid by using participles and by varying the position of participles in your sentences.

1. Imagine that you are an astronaut and that your spacecraft has been pulled into a black hole. What do you see, hear, and feel?
2. Imagine that you have just won an Oscar! Why have you won it? How do you react? What is your acceptance speech?
3. Describe what it is like to change classes in your school, giving concrete details of the movements, sounds, people, and objects. Try to make your description vivid enough to show someone who has never experienced changing classes exactly what it is like.

17 Basic Sentence Structure

Understanding Sentences

A *sentence* is usually defined as a group of words that expresses a complete thought.

A group of words that does not express a complete thought is called a *sentence fragment.*

Sentence Fragment:	on the weekend or on Monday the striped cat on the chair Maria and her aunt
Complete Sentence:	We will leave either on the weekend or on Monday. The striped cat on the chair hasn't moved for hours! When will Maria and her aunt arrive?

Exercise 1

Number your paper 1–10. If one of the following groups of words does not express a complete thought, write *SF* next to its number. If a group of words is a sentence, write out the sentence. Begin each sentence with a capital letter and place the appropriate punctuation at its end.

Examples

a. beyond any chance of recovery

a. SF

b. movie production has stopped because the actors are on strike

b. Movie production has stopped because the actors are on strike.

1. with a song in my heart
2. an earsplitting concert Saturday night

3. julio's new car gets very good mileage
4. she wrote the book in nine months, and it's a best seller
5. the plot is exciting, and the characters fairly interesting
6. never in a million years
7. because the library and the school
8. which of the two records would you rather have
9. a double-record set of new songs
10. a large glacier is moving south into some shipping lanes

Kinds of Sentences

Sentences may be divided into four main types, each type serving a different purpose: *declarative, interrogative, imperative,* and *exclamatory.*

1. The *declarative sentence* makes a statement and ends with a period.

   The only poisonous lizard in the United States is the Gila monster.

2. An *interrogative sentence* asks a question and ends with a question mark.

   Are there any poisonous lizards in the United States?

3. An *imperative sentence* gives an order or makes a request. Mildly imperative sentences usually end with a period; strongly imperative sentences may end with an exclamation point.

   Name a poisonous lizard native to the United States.
   Remove that lizard now!

4. An *exclamatory sentence* expresses surprise or strong feeling and ends with an exclamation point.

   A Gila monster is chasing me!

Exercise 2
Write out each of the following sentences, adding the appropriate end mark. Beside each sentence identify it as *declarative, interrogative, imperative,* or *exclamatory.*

Examples
a. Do not fold, spindle, or mutilate.
a. Do not fold, spindle, or mutilate. (imperative)
b. Rosita is the best singer in the choir.
b. Rosita is the best singer in the choir. (declarative)

1. Can you explain what a quasar is
2. Never put bananas in the refrigerator
3. The world's largest medical center is in Chicago, Illinois

4. Waiter, there's a fly in my soup
5. Does everyone always dream in color
6. The Faversham Oyster Fish Company has been in existence for over 800 years
7. Don't leave your keys in your car
8. Good grief, all the rats are loose in the biology room
9. Please tell me what time the movie is over
10. Shangri-La is a mythical kingdom where no one grows old

The Structure of a Sentence

In order to express a complete thought, a sentence must have two parts: a *subject* and a *predicate.* The *subject* of the sentence is the person, place, thing, or idea that the sentence is about. The *predicate* says something about the subject.

SUBJECT	PREDICATE
My dog	has fleas.
Odetta	is a famous folk singer.
The letter on the desk	came this afternoon.
All the food in the store	was ruined by the flood.

The Subject

A *subject* may be only one word, or it may be several. All the words composing the subject are called the *complete subject.* The main word or words in the complete subject are called the *simple subject.*

The only person for this job is Susette.
Complete Subject: *The only person for this job*
Simple Subject: *person*

Mrs. Yuan's daughters run the China Flower Restaurant.
Complete Subject: *Mrs. Yuan's daughters*
Simple Subject: *daughters*

Joslyn Art Museum in Omaha has a fine collection of native American art.
Complete Subject: *Joslyn Art Museum in Omaha*
Simple Subject: *Joslyn Art Museum*

Exercise 3

Write out the following sentences. Underline each complete subject once and each simple subject twice.

Example

a. The program after the news will be a special on nuclear plants.

a. The program after the news will be a special on nuclear plants.

1. The tallest animal in the world is the giraffe.
2. The world's heaviest creature is probably the blue whale.
3. A length of up to 140 feet makes the sea-dwelling ribbon worm the longest animal.
4. The largest brain in the animal kingdom belongs to the sperm whale.
5. The world's largest eggs are laid by the whale shark.
6. The eyes of the giant squid are larger than long-playing records.
7. The record for long-distance land speed belongs to the antelope.
8. The fastest of all swimming birds is the genoo penguin.
9. The living reptile of greatest size is the saltwater crocodile.
10. The longest-living mammal in the world is the human.

Compound Subjects

A *compound subject* consists of two or more simple subjects that are joined by a coordinating conjunction and that have the same verb.

Compound simple subjects are *italicized* in the following sentences.

Books and *magazines* are available in the library.

Complete Subject:	Books and magazines
Compound Simple Subjects:	Books magazines

Marian Anderson, *Beverly Sills*, and *Leontyne Price* are great singers.

Complete Subject:	Marian Anderson, Beverly Sills, and Leontyne Price
Compound Simple Subjects:	Marian Anderson Beverly Sills Leontyne Price

Compound subjects, like one-word simple subjects, may take modifiers.

The *Ambassador* from Ghana and the British *manufacturer* agreed.

Compound Simple Subjects:	Ambassador manufacturer

An old, dilapidated *barn* and a *shed* with no roof were on the property.

Compound Simple Subjects:	barn shed

Understood Subjects

The imperative sentence, which gives an order or makes a request, is different from other sentences: it does not name the subject. The subject is always *You*, meaning the person being addressed. Subjects of this kind are called *understood subjects.*

Lend me five dollars, please.
Understood Subject: *You* [*You* lend me five dollars, please.]

Call me about the assignment.
Understood Subject: *You* [*You* call me about the assignment.]

Look at that strange storm cloud.
Understood Subject: *You* [*You* look at that strange storm cloud.]

Even if the sentence names the person who is addressed, the true subject is still the understood *You.*

Hand me that wrench, Nicky.
Subject: *you* [understood]

Officer, please give me some directions.
Subject: *you* [understood]

Exercise 4

Write out the following sentences, underlining the complete subject of each. If the sentence has a compound subject, circle each of the simple subjects. If the sentence has an understood subject, write *You (understood)* beneath it.

Examples

a. Maria and Kim have the leads in the one-act play.

a. Maria and Kim have the leads in the one-act play.

b. Dad, lend me the car keys, please.

b. Dad, lend me the car keys, please.
Subject: You (understood)

1. Report this to the authorities at once.
2. Shirley Chisholm and Gloria Steinem appeared on the talk show.
3. The checkered shirt and the jeans with the patch are mine.
4. Wait for the dial tone.
5. *Liberty*, *Fraternity*, and *Equality* were the watchwords of the French Revolution.
6. The priest from St. Anne's and the new rabbi play golf together.
7. Mankowitz or Washington will substitute for the injured player.
8. Dr. Frankenstein, show us your experiment.
9. Our metal fence and our television antenna were struck by lightning.
10. Don't forget to take your tickets.

Subjects in Inverted Order

The subject usually is placed in the first part of the sentence, with the predicate following. Sometimes, however, this order is reversed: the predicate precedes the subject.

When the predicate comes before its subject, the sentence is in *inverted order.*

Questions are frequently in inverted order.

Which candidate do you like best?

To find the simple subject of a question, rephrase the question to make it a statement.

You do like which candidate best?
Simple Subject: you
Verb: do like

Questions are not the only sentences that use inverted order. Sentences that begin with prepositional phrases often use inverted order, also. To find the simple subject of such a sentence, find the word whose action or state of being is described by the verb.

Deep in the marsh grows the rare blue mushroom.
Verb: grows
Who or what grows? the mushroom

Note: A simple subject is *never* part of a prepositional phrase. Sometimes, a simple subject is modified by a prepositional phrase, but do not mistake part of the phrase for the subject.

One of the players was disqualified.

One of our calves wins ribbons at the fair.

Expletives

When the words *here* and *there* introduce a verb that precedes its subject, they are called *expletives.*

There *is* (V) no *homework* (S) in Spanish today.

Here *comes* (V) the news *bulletin* (S).

The words *here* and *there* are never used as subjects of a sentence. When they begin a sentence, it is usually a sign that the verb will come before the subject.

There *go* (V) our *chances* (S) for the championship.

Here *stands* (V) a famous *landmark* (S).

Exercise 5

Write out the following sentences, underlining each simple subject.

Examples

a. Across the desert crept the tiny caravan.

a. Across the desert crept the tiny caravan. (underlined: caravan)

b. Are any tickets available yet?

b. Are any tickets available yet? (underlined: tickets)

1. Out of the Old West comes the Long Ranger.
2. Here is the bus to Prairie Grove.
3. Where is my library book about heart transplants?
4. There are many stories about that old house.
5. Will you give me some change for a phone call?
6. Under the fence and across the courtyard slithered the cobra.
7. What will we have for breakfast tomorrow?
8. There are several methods for putting out fires.
9. In the Kingdom of Camelot lived a magician.
10. Do you have some good hiking boots?

The Predicate

The *predicate* of the sentence says something about the subject. Every predicate must contain a *verb* or a *verb phrase.* (A *verb phrase* is two or more verbs working as a unit.) Sometimes, a predicate consists of the verb only.

SUBJECT	PREDICATE
The traffic	slowed.
The dogs	had barked.
The papers	must have been lost.

All the words that compose the predicate are called the *complete predicate.* The verb or verb phrase is called the *simple predicate.*

Mike practices on his tuba every day.

Complete Predicate: practices on his tuba every day
Simple Predicate: practices

His sister has always played in marching bands.

Strange lights often are seen down in the swamp.

The adverbs *always* and *often* are not part of the simple predicate.

Exercise 6

Write out the following sentences. Then underline each complete predicate once and each simple predicate twice.

Examples

a. The rain fell in torrents.
a. The rain fell in torrents.

b. Phillis Wheatley was an early American poet.
b. Phillis Wheatley was an early American poet.

1. More people speak Chinese than any other language.
2. Chinese is also the oldest spoken language.
3. English ranks as the second dominant language in the world.

4. Hindustani is spoken by the third-largest group of people.
5. Written language originated first in Mesopotamia.
6. The Cherokees invented the first written native American language in North America.
7. The most recent new language has developed in the last hundred years.
8. This language is called New Guinea Pidgin English.
9. Over 3,000 different languages now exist in the world.
10. Of these languages English contains the largest number of words.

Compound Verbs

A *compound verb* has two or more verbs or verb phrases that share the same subject.

> The buffalo (S) *snorted* (V) and *charged* (V).
>
> We (S) *have worked* (V) very hard and *deserve* (V) a reward.
>
> The backpacker (S) *took* (V) the wrong trail, *forgot* (V) the camping equipment, and then *stepped* (V) on a snake.

Exercise 7

Each of the following sentences contains a compound verb. Write out each sentence, underlining the simple subject once and the verb phrase or verbs that make up the compound verb twice.

Examples

a. The broadcast begins at 9 o'clock and ends at noon.
a. The broadcast begins at 9 o'clock and ends at noon.

b. This wonderful invention slices, dices, and mashes vegetables.
b. This wonderful invention slices, dices, and mashes vegetables.

1. The mystery of the ship *Mary Celeste* has puzzled and intrigued people for years.
2. In 1872 the crew of the ship *Dei Gratia* saw the *Mary Celeste* and noticed its strange movements.
3. A sailor rowed over and boarded the small ship.
4. He searched the ship and discovered no crew or passengers.
5. The ship showed little damage and offered few clues.
6. Food still was on the table and seemed fresh.
7. An unfinished letter was found but offered no explanation.
8. The ship's windows were covered and battened with boards.
9. Perhaps pirates had boarded and kidnaped the crew.
10. Many people have studied but never solved this strange case.

Review Exercise A

Write out each of the following sentences, underlining each complete subject once and each complete predicate twice. Then beneath each sentence write the simple subject and the simple predicate.

Example

a. Only one of the fields was damaged by the hail.

a. Only one of the fields was damaged by the hail.
Simple subject—one
Simple predicate—was damaged

1. The packet of letters had suddenly disappeared.
2. Both of the girls are here now.
3. Under the cushion of the couch was my class ring.
4. A few of the cattle were lost in the last blizzard.
5. Half a quart of milk is needed for this recipe.
6. Six of the houses were damaged in the earthquake.
7. Can you show me how to solve this problem?
8. Much of our time was wasted there.
9. Both the new movies have had good reviews.
10. Are two of those mine?
11. Have you seen my shoes and socks?
12. The dog has eaten the plant and the newspaper.
13. At the beginning of the school year, everyone has new notebooks.
14. Maggie will write and perform those songs.
15. We don't have enough towels for the beach.
16. Has anyone fed the cats?
17. All the laundry is clean and folded.
18. Do you have any good radio stations in this town?
19. During the night a storm knocked over that tree.
20. Where should I park the car?

Sentence Patterns

Billions of English sentences have been written and spoken, but most sentences follow six patterns:

1. *S–V* (Subject–Verb)
2. *S–LV–PA* (Subject–Linking Verb–Predicate Adjective)
3. *S–LV–PN* (Subject–Linking Verb–Predicate Nominative)

4. *S–V–DO* (Subject–Verb–Direct Object)
5. *S–V–IO–DO* (Subject–Verb–Indirect Object–Direct Object)
6. *S–V–DO–OC* (Subject–Verb–Direct Object–Object Complement)

In the following sections you will learn to recognize the different sentence patterns and the components that make up each of them.

S–V Sentence Pattern

The simplest sentence pattern in English consists of a subject *(S)* and a verb *(V)*.

S	*V*
Joe	slept.
She	finished.
This	works.

Few sentences are as brief as the preceding ones, but many are still basically this simple pattern. The subject may have some kind of modification, and the verb may be a verb phrase, but the pattern remains the same. When a pattern has modifiers added to it, it has been *expanded*. Just as the subject may have modifiers, so may the verb, as the following examples show.

Joe	is sleeping	*very soundly.*	[adverbs added]
She	has finished	*now.*	[adverb added]
This	will work	*in an emergency.*	[prepositional phrase added]
Laura	writes	*for the paper.*	[prepositional phrase added]
I	*often* wrote	*to my cousin.*	[adverb and prepositional phrase added]

In addition to modification, a sentence may have compound subjects or predicates while retaining the basic sentence pattern.

S V V
Joe woke and yawned.
S S V
Laura and she finished.
S S V V
Laura and she paint and write.

Both modifiers and compounds may be used to expand the basic *S–V* pattern.

S V V
Joe woke slowly and yawned with pleasure.
S S V
Laura and she quickly finished.
S S V V
Laura and she always paint in the evening and sometimes write.

Exercise 8

Write out the following sentences, underlining the subjects once and the verbs or verb phrases twice. Then label your answers *S* for subject, and *V* for verb.

Examples

a. The bells were ringing loudly.

S V

a. The bells were ringing loudly.

b. He and his friend left here in a big hurry.

S S V

b. He and his friend left here in a big hurry.

1. Janice surfs in the summer.
2. Somewhere the sun is shining brightly.
3. The man and the boys with the cameras stood aside.
4. The alarm will flash and beep in case of emergency.
5. Mr. Scoggins golfs and fishes for recreation.
6. The hounds were baying excitedly at the raccoon.
7. Our climb to the top was stopped by the snowstorm.
8. The choir and the soloist will be performing in both programs.
9. A yellow-bellied sapsucker was singing by my window.
10. The two horror movies will be showing at the drive-in until Saturday.

Complements

In sentences that follow the *S–V* pattern, the subject and verb are able to express a complete thought. Sentences that follow the other patterns, however, need yet another element to express a complete thought: a *complement.*

A *complement* is a word or a group of words that completes the statement begun by the subject and verb.

The shot was nearly *foul.*
The bruise felt *painful.*
That woman will be *mayor.*

There are three different kinds of complements: *subject complements, objects*, and *object complements.*

Subject Complements

A *subject complement* is a noun, a pronoun, or an adjective that gives information about the subject.

Rats are extremely *destructive.*
Rats are *rodents.*

The adjective *destructive* above describes the subject *rats.* In the second sentence the noun *rodents* identifies *rats* as a specific sort of animal.

A subject complement must follow a linking verb.

For a complete list of linking verbs, see page 383.

The most common linking verb is *be*. Other common linking verbs are *become, feel, look, remain, seem, smell, sound, stay, taste,* and *turn*.

The bread is *stale*.

The subject *bread* is linked to its complement *stale*.

These paintings were *masterpieces*.

The subject *paintings* is linked to its complement *masterpieces*.

Predicate Adjectives

There are two kinds of subject complements. The first is the *predicate adjective*, which describes or modifies the subject.

The knight was *loyal*.
The lemonade was *sour*.
The two hall monitors were *angry*.

Predicate adjectives modify the subject, and they can be further modified themselves.

Helen of Troy was very *beautiful*. [adverb modifying predicate adjective]

She was *famous* for her beauty. [prepositional phrase modifying predicate adjective]

Predicate adjectives, in addition to taking modifiers, can also be *compound*. That is, two or more predicate adjectives can describe the subject.

The band uniforms are *green* and *white*.
The popcorn tasted *burnt* and *stale*.
The new coach was *tall*, *bearded*, and *bald*.

Exercise 9

Write out the following sentences and underline the predicate adjectives. Then draw an arrow from each predicate adjective to the simple subject it modifies.

Examples

a. The house seemed strangely quiet.
a. The house seemed strangely quiet.
b. The air was full of angry hornets.
b. The air was full of angry hornets.

1. The hike was exhilarating.
2. The air smelled fresh and clean in the mountains.
3. The chipmunks looked fat and sassy.

4. The trail became steeper in the afternoon.
5. Our packs seemed much heavier then.
6. The weather turned hot and clear.
7. Our lunch tasted good in the open air.
8. Before sunset the sky grew cloudy again.
9. The evening breeze was gentle but crisp.
10. Our legs were heavy with fatigue.

Predicate Nominatives

The second kind of subject complement is the *predicate nominative*, which is a noun or pronoun joined to the subject by a linking verb. Rather than describing the subject as the predicate adjective does, the predicate nominative *identifies* or *renames* the subject.

The new vice president is *Sheila.*
You are the lucky *winner.*
The winners were *Ken* and *she.*

Note: If the predicate nominative is a pronoun, remember to use the subject form.

The winner is *she.*

Like predicate adjectives, predicate nominatives can be compound. Two or more of them may be used to identify the subject.

Ethel Waters was a *singer* and fine *actress.*

Exercise 10

Write out the following sentences and underline each predicate nominative.

Example

a. The mysterious stranger in black was I.
a. The mysterious stranger in black was I.

1. The Phoenicians were great traders and sailors of the ancient world.
2. Their greatest cities were Tyre, Sidon, and Byblos.
3. People influenced by the Phoenicians are you, most other Americans, and I.
4. Our heritage from them is their written alphabet.
5. Two more of their inventions are purple dye and false teeth!
6. Great inventors, merchants, and navigators were they.
7. The Phoenicians were also expert workers and artists with glass.
8. The Phoenicians may have been the first navigators around Africa and the early discoverers of America.

9. The first planners of a Suez Canal may have been the Egyptians or they.
10. Lucky heirs of their foresight are we of the modern world.

Sentence Patterns with Subject Complements: *S—LV—PA, S—LV—PN*

Abbreviations for sentence patterns with subject complements are *S–LV–PA* (Subject–Linking Verb–Predicate Adjective) and *S–LV–PN* (Subject–Linking Verb–Predicate Nominative).

Modifiers can be added to this pattern without changing the basic sentence pattern.

SUBJECT	LINKING VERB (LV)	PREDICATE ADJECTIVE (PA)
The *roses*	*are*	deep *red* with long stems.
The *ducklings*	*look*	comically *fuzzy* with their yellow down.

SUBJECT	LINKING VERB	PREDICATE NOMINATIVE
Wild *roses*	*are* not	very large *flowers.*
Good old *Mickey*	*is*	the new *captain* of the team.

Sentences that follow these two patterns can be expanded by compounds.

S LV PN PN
Kevin is an Explorer *scout* and *member* of the band.

S LV PA PA PA
The accident *victims were pale, shaken,* but *unhurt.*

S LV PN PN
Two famous Western *women were Calamity Jane* and *Belle Starr.*

S LV PA PA
The *solution* to the problem *is plain* and *simple.*

Exercise 11

Write out the following sentences and underline the subject, the verb or verb phrase, and the predicate adjective or predicate nominative. Above each basic sentence part, write the appropriate abbreviation.

Examples

a. Diana Ross is a singer and a fine actress.

S LV PN PN
a. Diana Ross is a singer and a fine actress.

b. The litmus paper turned pink in the solution.

S LV PA
b. The litmus paper turned pink in the solution.

1. Two widely known columnists are Abigail Van Buren and Ann Landers.
2. Their advice columns are extremely popular.

3. Their answers to letters are witty and wise.
4. Actually the two women are identical twin sisters.
5. "Ann Landers' " real name is Esther Lederer.
6. "Dear Abby" is really Pauline Phillips.
7. The birthplace of the twins is Sioux City, Iowa.
8. In 1955 Esther became "Ann Landers" of newspaper fame.
9. Pauline became "Dear Abby" just six months later.
10. One hundred million readers are their devoted audience.

Direct Objects

The *direct object*, another kind of complement, completes the statement begun by the subject and verb.

A *direct object* is a word or a group of words that appears in the predicate and receives the action expressed by the verb.

Direct objects are used only after *action verbs*.

S *V* *DO*
My dog chases *wasps.*

The direct object *wasps* completes the statement begun by the subject and verb. Because the verb describes an action that is performed upon something, *chases* is an action verb. The noun or pronoun upon which the action is performed is the direct object of the verb.

The direct object is a noun or pronoun answering the question *what?* or *whom?* about the subject and verb.

William G. Sill composed *symphonies.*
[William G. Sill composed *what? Symphonies* is the direct object.]

Like other complements, direct objects can be expanded and modified.

Joanne chased the *dog* with the red collar.
[prepositional phrase modifying the direct object *dog*]

Have you read the new *book* about the astronauts?
[prepositional phrase modifying the direct object *book*]

When the direct object is a pronoun, be certain that the pronoun is in the object form.

I called *him* last night.
We never saw *them* again.

Transitive and Intransitive Verbs

Not all action verbs can take direct objects. Those that do are called *transitive verbs* because they transmit their action to the direct object. Certain action verbs, such as *sleep* and *go,* seldom take direct objects. Action verbs that do not take direct objects are called *intransitive verbs. Intransitive* means "not transitive, not transmitting action to an object."

We *bought* a car.	[transitive]
The snow *fell.*	[intransitive]

Many verbs can be used in different ways. The following sentences show the same verb as a linking verb, a transitive verb, and an intransitive verb.

The chili *smelled* spicy.	[linking verb]
We *smelled* the different perfumes.	[transitive verb]
Those rotten eggs certainly *smelled.*	[intransitive verb]

Since verbs have this versatility, they require special attention when you are analyzing or writing sentences. You must determine exactly how the verb is being used to understand if it is linking, transitive, or intransitive.

Sentence Patterns with Direct Objects: *S–V–DO*

The pattern of a sentence containing a direct object is Subject–Verb–Direct Object (*S–V–DO*).

SUBJECT	VERB	DIRECT OBJECT
Elephants	like	peanuts.
We	rode	mopeds.
Pam	plays	tennis.

Like other patterns, this one may be expanded by adding modifiers.

SUBJECT	VERB	DIRECT OBJECT
Hungry *elephants*	always *like*	*peanuts* in the shell.
After supper *we*	sometimes *ride*	our twin *mopeds.*
The athletic *Pam*	faithfully *plays*	*tennis* every afternoon.

Direct objects, like other elements in a sentence pattern, can be made compound. A verb may take two or more direct objects.

SUBJECT	VERB	DIRECT OBJECT		DIRECT OBJECT
Elephants	like	peanuts	and	carrots.
Elephants	dislike	mice	and	nose colds.

Exercise 12

Write out the following sentences and underline each simple subject, verb or verb phrase, and direct object. Then write the appropriate label over each of these parts of the *S–V–DO* sentence pattern.

Examples

a. The doctor wrote a prescription for the cough medicine.

S V DO

a. The doctor wrote a prescription for the cough medicine.

b. Marcia uses no chemicals or sprays on her garden.

S V DO DO
b. Marcia uses no chemicals or sprays on her garden.

1. Native Americans gave many words to the English vocabulary.
2. They also provided names for many places.
3. Nebraska and the Dakotas take their names from native American words.
4. Similarly, Black English introduced many words and phrases into the English language.
5. It originated *jazz*, *yam*, and *galoot*.
6. The Portuguese donated *savvy* and *palaver* to English.
7. Chinese immigrants invented *look-see* and *Johnny-come-lately*.
8. Spanish speakers added *cafeteria*, *adobe*, and *chili* to the American vocabulary.
9. Jewish immigrants provided *schmaltzy* and *schlep*.
10. All these contributions add vitality and diversity to American English.

Review Exercise B

Write out each of the following sentences and underline the key words in its sentence pattern. Above these words write the appropriate abbreviations.

Examples

a. Sea otters swim off the coast of California.

S V
a. Sea otters swim off the coast of California.

b. The trees were white with frost.

S LV PA
b. The trees were white with frost.

c. The phoenix hatched its egg in a strange way.

S V DO
c. The phoenix hatched its egg in a strange way.

1. Mythology is a fascinating subject.
2. Many peculiar animals exist in mythology.
3. The unicorn is a horse with one horn in the center of its forehead.
4. It has cloven hooves and a beard.
5. The griffin is the oldest creature in legend.
6. It has the head and wings of an eagle.
7. The griffin's body and tail resemble a lion's hindquarters.
8. The kraken lived in the depths of the sea.
9. The monstrous kraken, fortunately, usually slept.
10. It could attack and destroy its prey with ease.

11. The Gorgons were women with snakes for hair.
12. Their appearance was terrible indeed.
13. They turned living humans into stone.
14. Another ancient mythological beast is the dragon.
15. Dragons are huge, scaly, and serpentine, with great claws and teeth.
16. Dragons love gold, treasure, and meadows in which to frolic.
17. The Harpies were disgusting creatures with horrible reputations.
18. They had the heads of women and the bodies of vultures.
19. They were always hungry and greedy and wicked.
20. They also smelled extremely foul.

Sentence Patterns with Indirect Objects: *S–V–IO–DO*

An *indirect object* is a noun or pronoun in the predicate that comes before the direct object and tells *to whom* or *for whom.*

SUBJECT	VERB	INDIRECT OBJECT	DIRECT OBJECT
The *plumber*	*sent*	*us*	the *bill.*
My *sister*	*mailed*	*me*	a *postcard.*
Marcia	*presented*	*him*	the *award.*
My *aunt*	*will give*	*you*	a *cat.*
Herb	*baked*	*us*	some *bread.*
Charlotte	*sang*	the *children*	a *ballad.*

The abbreviation for this type of sentence pattern is *S–V–IO–DO*. In order for a sentence to have an indirect object, there must also be a direct object.

Indirect objects can be changed into prepositional phrases by moving them to the end of the sentence and adding *to* or *for* in front of them.

That nice man sold *me* the Brooklyn Bridge. [indirect object]
That nice man sold the Brooklyn Bridge *to me*. [prepositional phrase]

If the preposition *to* or *for* appears before the noun or pronoun, the group of words is a prepositional phrase. An indirect object is never part of a prepositional phrase. An indirect object is a noun or pronoun following the verb and occupying the appropriate position in this sentence pattern:

SUBJECT	VERB	INDIRECT OBJECT	DIRECT OBJECT
Spiders	*give*	*me*	the *shivers.*

Expanding Indirect Objects

Indirect objects, like nouns and pronouns in other sentence positions, can be modified. Two common modifiers are the adjective and the prepositional phrase.

S *V* *IO* *DO*
The *ad offered people* with computer experience good *jobs*.

S V IO DO
Juan gave the new *student* in school a *smile.*

Like other complements, indirect objects can be compound. A verb may take two or more indirect objects.

S V IO IO DO
I showed *Marcia* and *Freddie* the assignment.

When a pronoun functions as an indirect object, it must be in its object form, just as it must when it is a direct object.

Sherry promised *Terry* and *me* a ride home. [not *Terry and I*]
We gave *him* and *her* matching T-shirts. [not *he and she*]

Exercise 13

Write out each of the following sentences, underlining the key words in its sentence pattern. Above these words write the appropriate abbreviations.

Examples

a. The old explorer gave the tall man with a map a puzzled stare.

S V IO DO
a. The old explorer gave the tall man with a map a puzzled stare.

b. The saleswoman showed Pat and me the selection of records.

S V IO IO DO
b. The saleswoman showed Pat and me the selection of records.

1. Carrie mailed her cousin from Tennessee a bar mitzvah present.
2. The zoo attendant showed Pam and me the baby cobras.
3. The manager told the woman with the complaint the store policy.
4. The rescuers cooked Jan and me some soup.
5. Mr. Diaz presented the child a savings bank.
6. That problem gave the others and me a hard time.
7. Lisa made the orphaned lamb a bed by the stove.
8. George sent his two sisters in the navy funny postcards.
9. The detective told the butler and her the strange story.
10. The government gave every soldier with a good record a pay increase.

Sentence Patterns with Object Complements: S–V–DO–OC

An *object complement* is a noun or an adjective in the predicate that identifies or explains the direct object.

The sentence pattern using the object complement is abbreviated *S–V–DO–OC.* This sixth sentence pattern closely resembles the pattern *S–V–IO–DO*. The similarity, as well as the difference, is shown in the following examples.

S V IO DO
I showed Ralph a turkey.
S V DO OC
I called Ralph a turkey.

The nouns in the predicate of the first sentence above are the indirect object and the direct object. They refer to two different things, *Ralph* and the *turkey*. The nouns in the predicate of the second sentence are the direct object and the *object complement*. They both refer to the same person.

Just as a limited number of verbs take indirect objects, so only a few take object complements. The following examples show some of these verbs at work.

SUBJECT	VERB	DIRECT OBJECT	OBJECT COMPLEMENT
We	*elected*	*Luisa*	*vice president.*
They	*named*	the *horse*	*Shadow.*
The *judge*	*pronounced*	*him*	a free *man.*
They	*considered*	*you*	a *hero.*
The *Queen*	*made*	*him*	a *knight.*
We	*thought*	the *play*	a *mistake.*

Occasionally an adjective serves as an object complement.

SUBJECT	VERB	DIRECT OBJECT	OBJECT COMPLEMENT
We	*thought*	the *meal*	*terrible.*
The *judge*	*pronounced*	*them*	*guilty.*
We	*believed*	the *answer*	*right.*
She	*found*	the *play*	*boring.*
They	*considered*	the *incident*	*forgotten.*
The *umpire*	*called*	the *ball*	*foul.*

Like other sentence elements, object complements can be compounded and modified.

S V DO OC OC
We found her *pleasant* and most *cooperative.*
S V DO OC
They elected you *leader* of the club.
S V DO OC
We found the room very *messy.*
S V DO OC OC
The veterinarian pronounced my puppy *dead* and *gone.*

Exercise 14

Write out each of the following sentences, underlining each of the key parts in its sentence pattern. Then write the appropriate abbreviation above each of these parts.

Examples

a. Cassy believes jogging healthful.

S V DO OC
a. Cassy believes jogging healthful.

b. Scientists declare smoking a waste of money and a threat to health.

S V DO OC OC

b. Scientists declare smoking a waste of money and a threat to health.

1. The referee declared the play illegal.
2. The doctor pronounced the patient completely cured.
3. We named the puppy with the spots Patch.
4. Marcus considers flying saucers a complete hoax.
5. A man in the crowd called the astronaut a hero.
6. Rita found Mexican food exceptionally delicious.
7. Aunt Petunia named me heir of her entire fortune.
8. Irv considers houseflies the lowest form of life in the universe.
9. The President appointed Mrs. Black an ambassador to Africa.
10. The Master of Ceremonies crowned her the new Miss Tangerine.

Review Exercise C

Write out each of the following sentences, underlining the key parts in its sentence pattern. Then write the appropriate abbreviation above each of the parts.

Examples

a. Janet sent her old classmates a note last week.

S V IO DO

a. Janet sent her old classmates a note last week.

b. They crowned me queen of the Rhubarb Festival.

S V DO OC

b. They crowned me queen of the Rhubarb Festival.

1. The city council and the mayor gave the park a new name.
2. The voters considered Mrs. Diaz the best candidate.
3. I love roast turkey with all the trimmings.
4. We elected Kim, Jackson, and Pat the new class officers.
5. The police officer presented the embarrassed speeder a ticket.
6. The librarian sent me a list of my overdue books.
7. That dinner gave a terrible stomachache to my sister.
8. The judge thought the watermelon pickles the best at the fair.
9. My cousin collects old envelopes with unusual postmarks.
10. I firmly believe my client innocent of this crime.
11. The magazine awarded Ardis the top prize in the short story contest.
12. Joe sent his sister at camp some powerful poison ivy medicine.
13. Joan wants a watch with a silver band and a big book of mystery stories.
14. Evelyn mailed her friend a copy of the newspaper article.

15. My tuba playing nearly drives our dog insane.
16. Ralph considers astrology a bunch of nonsense.
17. The assistant mayor of Little Rock presented Miss Angelou the key to the city.
18. Red Cloud sent a terse message about the treaty to the general.
19. Far below we could see the winding rivers and tiny, doll-like houses.
20. I called my new invention an automatic homework machine.

Summary of Sentence Patterns

A sentence needs a subject and a predicate to state a complete thought. One sentence pattern consists of a subject and a verb or verb phrase: *S–V*.

S V
Snow melts.
S V
Babies cry.
S V
Elephants remember.

Modifiers and compounds can be used to expand a sentence pattern.

S S V
Several *students* and *teachers attended.*
S V
The quick brown *fox ran* away.
S V
The *heap* of leaves *burned* quickly.
S V
She replied with a smile.

Some predicates require more than a verb or verb phrase to state a complete thought. They must also have *complements*, a word or group of words that completes the meaning of the sentence. Subject complements may be either *predicate adjectives* or *predicate nominatives*. These patterns are *S–LV–PA* and *S–LV–PN*.

S LV PA
That smells delicious.
S LV PA
The *dogs looked strange* in their sweaters.
S LV PN
Toads are amphibians.
S LV PN
A *sonnet is* a lyrical *poem* with fourteen lines.

The fourth sentence pattern has a different kind of complement, the direct object: *S–V–DO*.

S V DO
The *mice ate* the *crackers*.

S V DO
Shirley wanted some new *boots* with low tops.

The fifth sentence pattern consists of both a direct object and an indirect object: *S–V–IO–DO.*

S V IO DO
The *store sent* the wrong *person* the *bill.*
S V IO DO
The *school presented* the top *student* a large *prize.*

The sixth sentence pattern consists of both a direct object and an object complement: *S–V–DO–OC.*

S V DO OC
They elected her secretary.
S V DO OC
The *neighbors consider* the *man snobbish.*
S V DO OC
The *mechanic pronounced* my old *car dead.*

Review Exercise D

Write out each of the following sentences, underlining the key parts of its sentence structure. Then write the appropriate labels above these parts. Finally beneath each sentence write the sequence of abbreviations that shows its sentence pattern.

Examples

a. The old tree fell down with a thunderous crash.

S V
a. The old tree fell down with a thunderous crash.
Sentence pattern: S–V

b. The horse looked strong and full of spirit.

S LV PA PA
b. The horse looked strong and full of spirit.
Sentence pattern: S–LV–PA

1. Many superstitions exist.
2. Owls are tremendously wise.
3. A vampire must sleep in a coffin.
4. Snakes are slimy and moist.
5. Bats fly into your hair.
6. Midnight is a haunted hour.
7. A horse chestnut brings you good luck.
8. All bats have made Dracula their master.
9. A crow always flies straight.
10. Lightning never strikes twice in the same place.

11. All animals kneel on Christmas Eve.
12. Redheads are quick of temper.
13. Opals cause you terrible misfortune of some kind.
14. A toad or frog gives you warts.
15. A four-leaf clover is lucky in the extreme.
16. A black cat is a bad omen at any time.
17. The sound of thunder will sour fresh milk.
18. Dragons consider all gold their personal property.
19. Leprechauns and ghostly horses live in Ireland.
20. Tea leaves will tell your fortune to you.

Mastery Exercise A

Write out each of the following sentences, underlining and labeling each of the basic sentence parts. Then after each sentence write its sentence pattern.

Examples

a. The typewriter is a useful invention.

S LV PN

a. The typewriter is a useful invention. S–LV–PN

b. The first typewriter could type only five words in a minute.

S V DO

b. The first typewriter could type only five words in a minute. S–V–DO

1. The earliest typewriters had one big disadvantage.
2. Typists could not see the typewritten words on the paper in the typewriter.
3. Without doubt these typewriters gave typists some problems.
4. In 1874 Christopher Sholes invented a better typewriter.
5. His typewriter might seem strange to us today.
6. It could type only capital letters.
7. During the next few years people gave the typewriter improvements.
8. In the 1880s typists could see typewritten words without removing the paper from the typewriter.
9. Typists declared the typewriter a success!
10. There began a new era for typists.

18 The Phrase

Understanding Phrases

A *phrase* is a group of words that does not contain both a subject and a predicate and that works to perform a single function in a sentence.

In the following sections you will learn about four types of phrases: *verb phrases*, *prepositional phrases*, *verbal phrases*, and *appositive phrases.*

Verb Phrases

A *verb phrase* is a group of words composed of a main verb and one or more helping verbs that together act as the main verb in a sentence.

Kelly *must have been wondering* about us.
Kelly *will wonder* about us.
Kelly *is* always *wondering* about us.

Each of the groups of *italicized* words in the preceding sentences is a verb phrase. Standing by themselves, they contain no word that could be a subject. They work as a single verb might work, acting as the main verb of a sentence: Kelly *wondered* about us.

Prepositional Phrases

Just as verb phrases do the work of a single verb, so prepositional phrases do the work of an adjective or adverb. A prepositional phrase that modifies a noun or pronoun is called an *adjective phrase.*

The people *from Japan* toured our city.

Some *of us* couldn't see the stage well.

The words *from Japan* and *of us* are prepositional phrases modifying the noun *people* and the pronoun *some.*

A prepositional phrase that modifies a verb, an adverb, or an adjective is called an *adverb phrase.*

The package should arrive *before this weekend.*

The prepositional phrase *before this weekend* modifies the verb phrase *should arrive,* telling when the package will arrive.

Prepositional phrases are almost always used as adjective or adverbial phrases.

We read the article *about the arctic expedition.*
[adjective phrase modifying the noun *article*]

The alligator slithered *into the swamp.*
[adverb phrase modifying the verb *slithered*]

Those *with passes* may go to the library.
[adjective phrase modifying the pronoun *those*]

My fingers were numb *with cold.*
[adverb phrase modifying the adjective *numb*]

Exercise 1

Write out the following sentences, underlining each verb phrase and prepositional phrase. Then label each verb phrase *VP*, each prepositional phrase that acts as an adjective *ADJ*, and each prepositional phrase that acts as an adverb *ADV*.

Example

a. The submarine has disappeared beneath the sea's surface.

a. The submarine has disappeared (VP) beneath the sea's surface (ADV).

1. They had survived the worst hurricane in history.
2. Jane might be practicing in the band room.
3. The Mississippi River is called "The Father of Waters."
4. Joan of Arc certainly must be one of history's most remarkable women.
5. Our quarterback must have been hurt by the tackle.
6. My homework is finished on time.
7. The ruler of the Norse gods was called Odin.
8. Crows and ravens are considered very intelligent by scientists.
9. The new students at school were taking a tour of the library.
10. The bottom of the boat was thick with barnacles.

Verbal Phrases

Verbals are words formed from verbs that function as nouns, adjectives, or adverbs. Verbals can take modifiers, just as nouns, adjectives, and adverbs can. Verbals also take complements, since they are formed from verbs.

A verbal with its modifiers and complements is called a *verbal phrase* and can be used as a single noun, adjective, or adverb is used. In the following sections you will study three kinds of verbal phrases: the *participle*, the *gerund*, and the *infinitive*.

Participial Phrases

A *participle* is a verb form used as an adjective.

We watched the *smoldering* pile of leaves.	[present participle]
The young woman, *sobbing*, withdrew.	[present participle]
The *reduced* price caught our attention.	[past participle]
The house, *gutted* by fire, was torn down.	[past participle]

A *present participle* is formed by adding *-ing* to the present verb form. A *past participle* is formed from the past form of the verb. (Past participles usually end in *-ed*, *-d*, *-t*, *-en*, or *-n*.)

Like regular adjectives, participles can be modified by single-word adverbs and by prepositional phrases that function as adverbs.

A *participial phrase* is a participle plus its modifiers and complements.

Juanita, *arriving early*, noticed something strange.
[present participle modified by an adverb]

Juanita, *arriving with the keys*, noticed something strange.
[present participle modified by a prepositional phrase]

The lawn mower, *ruined completely*, was sold for scrap.
[past participle modified by an adverb]

The lawn mower, *ruined by misuse*, was sold for scrap.
[past participle modified by a prepositional phrase]

Juanita, *arriving early with the keys*, noticed something strange.
[present participle modified by both an adverb and a prepositional phrase]

The lawn mower, *completely ruined by misuse*, was sold for scrap.
[past participle modified by both an adverb and a prepositional phrase]

Since participles are formed from verbs, they can also take complements. The complement may be any of the several kinds of complements but most commonly is a direct object.

The man *teaching the class* (DO: class) is Fred Washington.

The kangaroo, *taking the carrot* (DO: carrot), accidentally bit me.

DO

Into the office came a tall woman *carrying a briefcase.*

In each of the preceding sentences, the participle takes a direct object as its complement.

Notice, too, that participial phrases may come before or after the noun or pronoun they modify.

Excited about the award, Ms. Bard gave a short speech.

Ms. Bard, *excited about the award*, gave a short speech.

Busily writing a letter, Ken didn't hear the telephone.

Ken, *busily writing a letter*, didn't hear the telephone.

Exercise 2

Write out the following sentences, underlining the participial phrases. Then draw an arrow from each participle to the noun or pronoun that it modifies.

Examples

a. The lawyer winning that case was Mrs. Zabinski.

a. The lawyer winning that case was Mrs. Zabinski.

b. Floating lazily in the shallows, the huge bass ignored my bait.

b. Floating lazily in the shallows, the huge bass ignored my bait.

1. The window broken by my baseball was an expensive one.
2. The teacher giving the fewest homework assignments gets a prize.
3. Wounded by the porcupine quills, the dog had to be taken to the vet.
4. A special safety film will be shown to the students taking drivers education.
5. Feeling embarrassed by the attention, Elena nodded shyly to the audience.
6. The canal-like constructions seen on the surface of Mars are really natural formations.
7. My sister has read every book written by James Baldwin.
8. Scanning the sky for a sign of clouds, the hikers plodded on.
9. Miss Redwing, hearing the results of the election, smiled broadly.
10. The principal, presenting our class the trophy, looked a bit dubious.

Gerund Phrases

A *gerund* is a verb form ending in *-ing* that acts as a noun.

You need sturdy, well-fitting shoes for *hiking.*
Dreaming is a mysterious process.
Many people dread *dieting.*
Boiling will purify that water.

A *gerund phrase* consists of a gerund and its modifiers and complements.

Gerunds can be modified by adjectives, adverbs, and prepositional phrases.

Whistling loudly is the parrot's only trick.
[gerund modified by adverb]

Whistling in the dark helps keep up your courage.
[gerund modified by prepositional phrase]

Loud whistling at strangers is rude, crude, and vulgar.
[gerund modified by adjective and prepositional phrase]

Gerunds can also take complements.

Whistling the national anthem is difficult.
[gerund taking a complement—the direct object *national anthem*]

Like a single gerund, gerund phrases may be used in all the ways that nouns can.

The constant dripping of the faucet is most distracting.
[gerund phrase as subject]

My most unusual experience was *falling into a vat of mayonnaise.*
[gerund phrase as predicate nominative]

We heard *the low grumbling of the thunder.*
[gerund phrase as direct object]

They saved themselves by *keeping active during the blizzard.*
[gerund phrase as object of a preposition]

Exercise 3

Write out the following sentences, underlining each gerund phrase. Then beneath each sentence identify the function of the gerund phrase. (Be prepared to identify the parts of the phrase.)

Examples

a. Doing difficult crossword puzzles is Ann's favorite pastime.

a. Doing difficult crossword puzzles is Ann's favorite pastime.
Doing difficult crossword puzzles—subject

b. We were kept awake last night by the yowling of cats in the alley.

b. We were kept awake last night by the yowling of cats in the alley.
the yowling of cats in the alley—object of preposition

1. Western civilization has a long history of disliking certain animals.
2. Hating all snakes seems natural to some people.
3. These people dislike the snake's crawling and sinister hissing.
4. Chinese thinking on snakes is altogether different.
5. The snake is revered for having great intelligence and beauty.
6. Calling a woman a snake is a compliment in China.

7. Another western tradition is hating wolves intensely.
8. Killing livestock, children, and travelers are supposedly the wolf's favorite activities.
9. Actually wolves are renowned for their quick thinking and remarkably deep feeling for one another.
10. Being wolfish can also mean being intelligent, loyal, and generous to your fellows.

Review Exercise A

Write out each of the following sentences and underline each verbal phrase. Below each sentence indicate the type of verbal phrase it contains and tell how the verbal phrase is used in the sentence. Watch out for participles that are part of a verb phrase.

Examples

a. The solution favored by the mayor was not adopted.

a. The solution favored by the mayor was not adopted.
participial phrase used as adjective to modify solution.

b. Great-grandmother remembers riding a mule to school.

b. Great-grandmother remembers riding a mule to school.
gerund phrase used as direct object

1. Many mysteries, still unexplained by science, exist.
2. "The Baghdad Battery," discovered in the ruins of a 2,000-year-old village, is one of these.
3. Workers excavating the ruins came across the strange object.
4. Studying archeology was a hobby of a German, William Koenig.
5. Living in Iraq, Koenig heard about the peculiar find.
6. Koenig, seeing the artifact, was extremely puzzled.
7. It was an earthenware vase sealed with a copper lid.
8. The lid was lined with asphaltum and had a copper cylinder piercing through into the jar.
9. An iron rod running through the copper pipe had signs of corrosion.
10. Calling it a battery seemed impossible but inevitable.
11. An American engineer, hearing of the find, made a model.
12. The model, filled with an electrolyte, produced electric current.
13. Learning more about the battery became Koenig's goal.
14. He learned of several similar devices stored in a Berlin museum.
15. The museum was storing three more vases containing the metal rods and asphaltum.
16. These devices, also discovered near Baghdad, were even more complex.
17. Koenig, studying the puzzle, could only find one solution.

18. Working with gold and other metals flourished in early Baghdad.
19. Modern metalworkers use electroplating for gold coatings.
20. Perhaps ancient gold-plating was done with the "batteries."
21. Plating gold to another surface can be done by modern, relatively simple electric machines.
22. The Near East, having a long history of scientific discoveries, may have created the battery.
23. Metalworking in modern Baghdad employs primitive electric cells.
24. Perhaps this technique, closely guarded, has been handed down for twenty centuries.
25. Discovering electricity may not have been Ben Franklin's feat after all.

Infinitive Phrases

An *infinitive* is a verb form preceded by the word *to.*

In sentences infinitives are verb forms, usually preceded by the word *to*, that function as nouns, adjectives, or adverbs.

An *infinitive phrase* is an infinitive plus its modifiers and complements.

Jan likes *to walk slowly.*
[infinitive phrase = infinitive + adverb]

Jan likes *to walk slowly along the beach.*
[infinitive phrase = infinitive + adverb + prepositional phrase]

Jan likes *to walk her horse slowly along the beach.*
[infinitive phrase = infinitive + direct object + adverb + prepositional phrase]

When used as nouns, infinitive phrases can perform most of the functions that a noun can perform: subject, direct object, predicate nominative, and object of a preposition.

To lie to the voters is wrong.
[infinitive phrase used as subject]

We need *to buy a present for our cousin.*
[infinitive phrase used as direct object]

Sharon's greatest ambition is *to climb Mount Everest.*
[infinitive phrase used as predicate nominative]

Infinitive phrases are often used as adjectives and adverbs.

Infinitive phrases used as adjectives act like single-word modifiers to modify nouns or pronouns.

We need a place *to stay right now.*

That dinner was something *to remember for a long while.*

Infinitive phrases used as adverbs act like single-word modifiers to modify verbs, adjectives, and other adverbs.

Todd has registered *to vote in the next election.*
[infinitive phrase modifying a verb]

It's too late *to register for this class.*
[infinitive phrase modifying an adjective]

We are driving too slowly *to arrive on time.*
[infinitive phrase modifying an adverb]

Exercise 4

Write out the following sentences and underline each infinitive phrase. Beneath each sentence write how the infinitive phrase is used: as a noun, an adjective, or an adverb. If it is used as a noun, tell how it is used: subject, direct object, predicate nominative, or object of a preposition.

Examples

a. Several foolish people have attempted to go over Niagara Falls in a barrel.

a. Several foolish people have attempted to go over Niagara Falls in a barrel.
infinitive phrase used as a noun (direct object)

b. The mechanic left to get a new part.

b. The mechanic left to get a new part.
infinitive phrase used as an adverb to modify left

1. To eat crackers in bed is a crumby experience.
2. Lori exercised to build up her endurance for the hike.
3. Here is a magazine to read until your appointment.
4. I have always wanted to own an antique convertible.
5. To dream of missing a final exam is supposedly very common.
6. We were pleased to see our relatives from El Paso.
7. It is hard to peel onions without shedding some tears.
8. J.B. is expected to make the all-American team.
9. LeRoy decided to ask for a raise in his allowance.
10. This is the soap to make your dingy wash dazzling once again.

Review Exercise B

Write out the following sentences, underlining the verbal phrase in each. Then below each sentence write the kind of verbal phrase it contains: participial, gerund, or infinitive. Also, tell the function of the phrase: adjective, adverb, subject, direct object, predicate nominative, or object of a preposition.

Examples

a. To do that would be wrong.

a. To do that would be wrong.
infinitive phrase used as subject

b. The girl carrying the French horn is Stacey.

b. The girl carrying the French horn is Stacey.
participial phrase used as adjective to modify girl

1. The first publisher to print valentines was Esther Howland.
2. Gertrude Rainey was famous for her singing of the blues.
3. Dusting the living room and den is Pat's job.
4. We went to see the Pointer Sisters' concert.
5. The name written on the envelope was indecipherable.
6. The old dog growled lazily at the cat strolling through the yard.
7. The dates printed in yesterday's paper were wrong.
8. Writer Maya Angelou originally wanted to be a dancer.
9. Last night I dreamed about a little lizard wearing a space suit.
10. Katy's hobby is collecting old jazz records.
11. The world's largest pizza was one measuring forty feet in diameter.
12. That old bench, weathered by wind and rain, won't hold much weight.
13. We are never too busy to watch a *Star Trek* rerun.
14. Bounding into a thicket, the rabbit escaped the dogs.
15. The player was penalized for stepping over the free-throw line.
16. Pete enjoys writing comic skits about school.
17. I leaped back to avoid the spattering grease.
18. The best book to read on that subject is Alex Haley's *Roots.*
19. We were glad to get off the hot, crowded subway car.
20. The group performing at the Civic Center is Earth, Wind, and Fire.

Appositive Phrases

An *appositive* is a noun or pronoun that follows or precedes another noun or pronoun to identify or clarify it.

Ms. Jefferson, the *lawyer*, appealed the case.

The winner, *Secretariat*, was a great horse.

A *scavenger*, the buzzard serves as one of nature's sanitation workers.

Like other nouns and pronouns, appositives can be modified by adjectives and adjective phrases to form *appositive phrases.*

My aunt, *a lieutenant in the WAF's*, is stationed in Puerto Rico.
[The prepositional phrase *in the WAF's* modifies the appositive *lieutenant.*]

Cheops' pyramid, *the largest Egyptian pyramid*, is 147 meters high.
[The adjectives *the*, *largest*, and *Egyptian* modify the appositive *pyramid.*]

Exercise 5

Write out the following sentences, underlining each appositive phrase. Then draw an arrow from it to the noun or pronoun it modifies. (Be prepared to identify the modifiers and complements in the phrases.)

Example

a. I ordered a healthburger, a sandwich of peanut butter and bean sprouts.

a. I ordered a healthburger, a sandwich of peanut butter and bean sprouts.

1. Language, humanity's greatest invention, exists in many forms.
2. Eyak, an Alaskan Indian language, is spoken only by two elderly sisters.
3. There are several equally rare languages, tongues with only a handful of surviving speakers.
4. The Chippewas, native Americans of Minnesota, had one of the most complex languages in the world.
5. English has the most irregular verbs, at least 194 of the troublesome critters.
6. The simplest verb system belongs to Esperanto, an invention of modern times.
7. An idea that never developed, Esperanto is artificial.
8. It was designed to be a universal language, one simple and easy to learn.
9. Swahili, an African language, has no irregular verbs.
10. Dr. Harold Williams, a language whiz, could communicate in fifty-two different languages, a modern record.

Mastery Exercise A

In the following selection from Stephen Crane's *The Red Badge of Courage*, there are many phrases of the types you have studied in the previous sections: verb, prepositional, participial, gerund, and infinitive. On a sheet of paper, list at least thirty phrases in order in which they appear. Beside each phrase identify its type. (When prepositional phrases appear as modifiers in other phrases, do not count them as separate phrases. For example, in the sentence, *Walking down the long corridor, we saw tangled cobwebs*, list *walking down the long corridor* as a participial phrase.) The first two phrases in the selection are underlined for you; do not include them in your list.

> The lieutenant sprang forward bawling. The youth saw his features wrathfully red, and saw him make a dab with his sword. His one thought of the incident was that the lieutenant was a peculiar creature to feel interested in such matters upon this occasion.
>
> He ran like a blind man. Two or three times he fell down. Once he knocked his shoulder so heavily against a tree that he went headlong.
>
> Since he had turned his back upon the fight, his fears had been wondrously magnified. Death about to thrust him between the shoulder blades was far more dreadful than death about to smite him between the eyes. When he thought of it later, he conceived the impression that it is better to view the appalling than to be merely within hearing. The noises of the battle were like stone; he believed himself liable to be crushed.

As he ran on he mingled with others. He dimly saw men on his right and on his left, and he heard footsteps behind him. He thought that all the regiment was fleeing, pursued by these ominous crashes.

In his flight the sound of these following footsteps gave him his one meager relief. He felt vaguely that death must make a first choice of the men who were nearest; the initial morsels for the dragons would be then those who were following him. So he displayed the zeal of an insane sprinter in his purpose to keep them in the rear. There was a race.

Mastery Exercise B

From a magazine, book, or newspaper you have read, select a passage about the length of that in Mastery Exercise A. Then on a sheet of paper, write out the first twenty phrases in the selection, including verb, prepositional, participial, gerund, and infinitive phrases. Next to each phrase identify its type and function in the sentence. Finally rewrite the passage, replacing each phrase with a single-word verb or modifier. How does this change affect the piece of writing?

Using Phrases

In the following sections you will study and practice using phrases in your own writing. You will learn how to use commas with phrases, how to place phrases in sentences to avoid ambiguity, and how to use nouns and pronouns as modifiers of gerunds. In addition, you will learn some special uses of infinitive phrases. As you work on using phrases in your writing, refer back to the sections in Understanding Phrases for any help you may need in identifying the different kinds of phrases.

Using Commas with Participial Phrases

A participial phrase used at the beginning of a sentence is called an *introductory participial phrase* and is always set off by a comma.

Driving through the pouring rain, we could barely see the road ahead.
Signed and witnessed, the document was official.
Tired and aching from practice, the players limped away.

For a review of present and past participles, see page 474.

Sometimes, a participial phrase appears within a sentence. If the phrase is necessary to the meaning of the sentence, it is called an *essential phrase* and is *not* set off by commas.

All students *having passes* are excused from school.
[If the participial phrase *having passes* is removed, the meaning changes to *All students are excused from school.*]

The person *sitting by Cindy* is the new exchange student.
[The phrase *sitting by Cindy* is essential because it identifies the person.]

Essential participial phrases usually identify someone or something; they point out *which one* is being discussed.

A phrase that merely adds description or extra information but does not identify anything or anyone is *nonessential.* Set off nonessential participial phrases from the rest of the sentence with commas.

> The center, *dribbling down the court*, suddenly tripped.
> [nonessential phrase, set off by commas]
>
> The player *dribbling down the court* is our center.
> [essential phrase, not set off]
>
> The towels, *soaked by the sea*, were wadded into our beach bags.
> [nonessential phrase, set off by commas]
>
> The towels *hanging on the line* were pulled down by the dog.
> [essential phrase, not set off]

One way to determine whether a phrase is essential or nonessential is to ask yourself if the participial phrase identifies the word it modifies, or if it only adds extra description. Another way is to say the sentence aloud. If the phrase is essential, it should flow, without pause, into the rest of the sentence. A speaker usually pauses slightly before and after a nonessential phrase.

Exercise 6

Write out each of the following sentences, underlining each participial phrase. If the phrase is nonessential, add the appropriate commas. If the phrase is essential and needs no punctuation, write *essential phrase, no punctuation needed* beneath the sentence. Circle the commas you insert.

Examples

a. The crowd cheering and stamping drowned out the announcer.
a. The crowd, cheering and stamping, drowned out the announcer.

b. The contestant selected as most talented was the juggler.
b. The contestant selected as most talented was the juggler.
essential phrase, no punctuation needed

1. The person elected secretary will be in charge of publicity, too.
2. Hearing the new evidence the lawyer shook her head in disbelief.
3. A lone windmill creaking mournfully overlooked the deserted farm.
4. The band members exhausted by marching practice were all ready for a break.
5. The shorts given to me for gym class are five sizes too big.
6. First published in 1936 the novel is still a best seller.
7. The woman wearing the silk dress is Miss Ling.
8. The four books picked by Kevin were detective novels.
9. The bacon burned to a crisp filled the air with smoke.
10. The player breaking Babe Ruth's record for home runs is Hank Aaron.

Placing Participial Phrases

Participial phrases must be carefully placed in a sentence, or they will seem to modify a different word than the writer intended, with confusing or unintentionally humorous results. Introductory participial phrases demand particular attention: they must always modify the noun or pronoun following them. If they do not, their effect may be misleading or ridiculous.

Scratching fleas and hanging by its tail, the photographer watched the monkey.
Covered with butter, I served the pancakes.

As you can see, the preceding sentences have misplaced participial phrases. The sentences must be revised so that the participial phrases clearly modify the correct word.

Scratching fleas and hanging by its tail, the monkey was watched by the photographer.
The pancakes, covered with butter, were served by me.

Another common problem in placing participial phrases occurs when the writer forgets to put *any* word within the sentence that the phrase modifies. A participial phrase *must* modify some word within the sentence.

Waving and shouting, the rescue plane came near.
Tired from the long hike, even a meal of beans sounded tempting.

Participial phrases such as those in the preceding examples are called *dangling participles*, since they dangle from the sentence and are not attached to any word or words they can modify. To eliminate a dangling participle, rewrite the sentence so that the participle has a word it logically modifies.

Waving and shouting, the stranded sailors saw the plane come near.
Tired from the long hike, Patty thought even a meal of beans sounded tempting.

Exercise 7

Write out the following sentences and provide the proper punctuation. If the participial phrase does not clearly modify a proper word, revise and rewrite the sentence so that it does. Underline the participial phrase and circle any commas you insert.

Example

a. Spurring her horse Carla raced after the other riders.
a. Spurring her horse, Carla raced after the other riders.

1. Freshly washed and folded the sheets were stacked in the hospital linen closet.
2. Possessing great agility the animal outwitted its enemy.
3. Jody watched a comet sitting in his backyard.
4. Waiting for ticket sales to begin the night grew colder.

5. The students will meet in that room selling yearbooks.
6. The teakettle whistling shrilly filled the room with steam.
7. Jack puzzled by the metric measurements in the cookbook put too much salt in the casserole.
8. Suspended over the rooftops we saw the full moon.
9. Not knowing any of the answers the test was graded zero.
10. I drowsily watched the countryside riding in the bus.

Using the Possessive Form Before a Gerund

A noun or pronoun preceding a gerund is in the possessive form.

The boat's tossing made us a bit seasick.

The gerund phrase *The boat's tossing* is the subject of the sentence. The possessive form *boat's* is used because it modifies the gerund *tossing*, telling which tossing: *the tossing of the boat.*

For a review of noun and pronoun possessives, see pages 342–344 and 354–356.

His saying that was not very wise.

The gerund phrase *His saying that* is the subject of the sentence. The possessive form *His* is used because the pronoun *His* modifies the gerund *saying.*

Exercise 8

Write out the following sentences, supplying the correct form of the noun or pronoun in parentheses. Underline the word you supply.

Examples

a. For many years scientists puzzled over the ______ twinkling. (firefly)

a. For many years scientists puzzled over the firefly's twinkling.

b. The ______ starting and dying indicated a problem with the gas line. (engine)

b. The engine's starting and dying indicated a problem with the gas line.

1. ______ pitching was a legend in its time. (Satchel Paige)
2. ______ hurling for the National Negro League set records. (He)
3. An ______ best playing is usually over in a few short years. (athlete)
4. Part of Paige's legend is ______ enduring so long as a major athlete. (he)
5. Athletes are, unfortunately, noted for ______ early fading. (they)
6. ______ playing professionally past the age of forty or so is unusual. (They)

7. This phenomenal _______ playing was still good when he was fifty-nine. (man)
8. Paige was equally famous for _______ witty sayings. (he)
9. Of course, _______ achieving 300 shutouts had already made him a baseball immortal. (he)
10. He advised against a _______ carrying on in society, eating fried foods, and running at all. (person)

The Infinitive Without *To*

The infinitive is usually the word *to* plus the present form of a verb, such as *to love, to praise,* or *to go.* Occasionally, however, the word *to* is dropped from the infinitive or infinitive phrase.

We didn't hear the bell *ring.*

The word *ring* is a shortened form of the infinitive *to ring.* The infinitive often drops the word *to* when it is used with certain verbs, such as *dare, feel, hear, help, know, let, make, need, please, see,* and *watch.*

We felt the line *(to) jerk.*
The fire fighters made the crowd *(to) move* back.
We helped Luisa *(to) pack* her suitcase.

The Infinitive as an Independent Element

Sometimes, phrases are *independent elements* in a sentence. An independent element is not a basic part of a sentence; it is not subject, object, verb, or modifier. It is connected to the sentence by idea but not by structure; that is, it has no grammatical connection with any part of the sentence but rather adds an extra thought, a tacked-on comment. Infinitive phrases are frequently used as independent elements. Independent elements, like modifying nonessential phrases, should be set off by commas.

To put it bluntly, this meat loaf tastes like burnt rubber.
The test, *to tell the truth,* was not altogether fair.
I failed, *to be perfectly frank.*

Each of the preceding *italicized* phrases is an infinitive phrase used as an independent element, and each is set off by punctuation. Notice the importance of the comma in the third sentence. Without the comma, *to be perfectly frank* becomes the direct object, and the sentence has an altogether different meaning.

Exercise 9

Write out each of the following sentences, underlining the infinitive phrase. Beneath the sentence identify the infinitive phrase as an independent element or as an infinitive with the *to* omitted. If the infinitive phrase is an independent element, supply the comma that it needs. Circle the commas you insert.

Examples

a. To be honest I can't tell you that.

a. To be honest, I can't tell you that.
independent element

b. No one dared go out in the blizzard.

b. No one dared go out in the blizzard.
infinitive with to omitted

1. Someone let the boat drift away from the shore.
2. To be perfectly clear on this point I am not a crook.
3. We heard the motor sputter its death gasp.
4. Jana saw the coach signal from the sidelines.
5. To make a long story short I got the job.
6. We helped index the new books in the library.
7. To get to the main point I need a raise.
8. The mayor to put it briefly as possible was simply wrong about the whole issue.
9. We watched the girls' tennis teams practice.
10. Mr. Whitewater makes all his dogs behave very well.

Review Exercise C

Write out each of the following sentences, correcting any errors that have been made in using phrases. Underline the corrected phrase. Circle any commas you insert and underline any words you make possessive.

Examples

a. Quivering with pain the dog allowed the vet to remove the porcupine needles from its nose.

a. Quivering with pain, the dog allowed the vet to remove the porcupine needles from its nose.

b. I saw a rattlesnake riding my motorcycle.

b. Riding my motorcycle, I saw a rattlesnake.

c. The teacher was irritated by the students whispering.

c. The teacher was irritated by the students' whispering.

1. My socks covered with cockleburs were itching and cutting me.
2. Him barging into the meeting like that was extremely rude.
3. Anne gave her Saint Bernard a bath no easy task.
4. Walking to school in the rain the bus passed without stopping.
5. To make a long story short we caught the thief.

6. The blue jays shrieking and divebombing attacked the bloodthirsty weasel.
7. Roberto getting the scholarship didn't surprise anyone.
8. Infested with fleas our garage had to be sprayed by the exterminator.
9. To get back to the main point I need help on my physics project.
10. The principal commended Miss Teeter student teaching.
11. The dog a Doberman pinscher helps guard the warehouse.
12. *Gulliver's Travels* a satire makes fun of human failings.
13. The fire crew dug trenches to stop the blaze spreading farther.
14. We saw several fish standing on the dock.
15. Whirling its propeller furiously the takeoff was completed.
16. We were all surprised by him saying that.
17. A speech was given by Richard Kim the exchange student from Korea.
18. Finished with dinner we cleared the table.
19. The rocks worn by centuries of rain and wind had peculiar shapes.
20. The California condor an endangered species may soon become extinct.

Writing Exercise A

Using a variety of phrases to add variety to your sentence structure, write one or two well-developed paragraphs on one of the following suggested topics. Use care in punctuating and placing the phrases you use.

1. Because of the increasing number of traffic accidents involving teenage drivers, some state legislatures have discussed passing a law that would not permit anyone under twenty-one to drive. Take a stand for or against such a law and discuss the advantages or disadvantages of such proposed legislation.
2. Recently a major newspaper sponsored a contest asking readers to send in their nominations for the Worst Television Program of the Year. Readers were asked to write a short essay about the program they nominated. Decide what program you would vote the worst of the year and explain the reasons for your choice.
3. Teenagers who vandalize their schools by writing on the walls, littering the halls, or destroying equipment waste thousands of tax dollars each year. In your writing discuss why you think some students become involved in vandalism and what could be done to combat the practice.
4. In the photograph on page 523 a young woman is riding in a convertible as part of a parade. She has obviously been crowned queen of whatever festivities are going on. Describe the parade from her point of view or discuss your feelings about beauty contests in general. Do such contests focus too much attention on physical appearance alone? Should these contests be banned?

VFW QUEEN
4033 - MISS AMERICANISM

19 The Clause

Understanding Clauses

The clause, a group of words that has its own subject and verb, is a basic structure in the English language. In the following sections you will begin your study of clauses by learning to identify two kinds: independent and subordinate. You will also study three types of subordinate clauses: adjective, adverb, and noun.

Defining a Clause

A *clause* is usually defined as a group of related words having both a subject and a verb.

To determine whether a group of words is a clause or a phrase, ask if the group of words contains *both* a subject and a verb. If both a subject and verb are present, the group of words is a clause.

Clause:	I left *as soon as the movie was over.* [The subject is *movie;* the verb is *was over.*]
Phrase:	I left *after the movie.* [*After the movie* is a prepositional phrase.]
Clause:	Ms. Washington stayed home *because she had the flu.* [*She* is the subject; *had the flu* is the predicate.]
Phrase:	Ms. Washington stayed home *because of illness.* [*Because of illness* is a prepositional phrase.]

Independent and Subordinate Clauses

There are two kinds of clauses: those that can stand alone and those that cannot.

A clause that can stand alone is called an *independent clause* because it can express a complete thought by itself. Every sentence must contain an independent clause.

The team ran out onto the court.
The fans cheered wildly.

For more about joining independent clauses see pages 255–260.

Each of the preceding sentences is really an independent clause, standing by itself. Independent clauses can be joined together by the coordinating conjunctions *and, but, or, nor, for, so,* and *yet.* When two independent clauses are joined into one sentence, the result is called a *compound sentence.*

The team ran onto the court, and the fans cheered wildly.
The team ran onto the court, so the fans cheered wildly.
The team left the court, but the fans still cheered wildly.

Now look at the following example:

Marcia is a good athlete although she is small.

The independent clause in the preceding sentence is *Marcia is a good athlete.* This clause can stand alone. The second clause, however, could not be a sentence, since it does not express a complete thought.

Sentences that do not conform to Edited Standard English are marked with an asterisk (*).

*Although she is small.

A clause that does not express a complete thought is called a *subordinate clause.* It must be joined to an independent clause to form a part of a sentence.

A subordinate clause may come either before an independent clause or after it:

INDEPENDENT CLAUSE	SUBORDINATE CLAUSE
I liked the book	because it was exciting.
We stood in line an hour	before the tickets went on sale.
I vacuumed the rug	while my sister raked the leaves.

SUBORDINATE CLAUSE	INDEPENDENT CLAUSE
When the package didn't arrive,	we were puzzled.
After the pearls were recovered,	the detective claimed a large reward.
If you want to be on time,	you need to hurry.

A subordinate clause may also appear in the middle of an independent clause. In the following sentences the subordinate clauses are *italicized*.

The dog *that bit me* was a poodle.
The person *who sells the most* wins a prize.
The place *where we shop* is Smith's Emporium.

Exercise 1

Write out the following sentences, underlining each independent clause once and each subordinate clause twice. Above the subject of each clause write *S*; above the verb or verb phrase write *V*. (Some sentences contain two independent clauses; some contain an independent clause and a subordinate clause.)

Examples

a. We saw the house where Laura Ingalls Wilder lived.

S V S V

a. We saw the house where Laura Ingalls Wilder lived.

b. We have a car, but it is being repaired.

S V S V

b. We have a car, but it is being repaired.

1. Pat likes being a camp counselor although the pay is low.
2. Whenever Terry is near a rose, she sneezes violently.
3. Muhammad Ali's victory looked doubtful, but he won the fight.
4. Rita will drive if we help pay for the gas.
5. Owls look wise, yet they are not exceptionally intelligent.
6. I had better get to the library because I have a report due on Monday.
7. I want to visit Loch Ness, where the fabulous monster is supposed to be.
8. My sister saw the King Tut exhibit when it was on tour.
9. We couldn't leave for the party until Fred found his shoes.
10. Delores won the acting award, and everyone applauded.

The subject of a subordinate clause may be either a noun or a pronoun. In addition to such pronouns as *he, she,* and *it,* many subordinate clauses use another kind of pronoun for a subject (*S*): words such as *who, whose, whoever, what, which,* and *that.*

S

We saw the movie *that was filmed in Antarctica.*

S

The lawyer examined the evidence, *which seemed most crucial.*

S

A "Trekkie" is a fan *who is devoted to* Star Trek.

S

Mark mistakenly threw away the pumpkin *that was to become the jack-o'-lantern.*

One peculiarity of the subordinate clause is that it may sometimes begin with a pronoun that is not the subject (*S*), but the direct object (*DO*), as the following sentences illustrate.

DO S V
We listened to the new records *that Liz got.*

DO S V
Mother Teresa is a person *whom many people admire.*

DO S V
These must be the keys *that Nickie lost.*

Exercise 2

Write out the following sentences, underlining each subordinate clause. Then label the subject of the subordinate clause *S*, the verb or verb phrase *V*, and the direct object (if there is one) *DO*.

For a review of the direct object, see pages 496–501.

Examples

a. When people diet, they should still eat balanced meals.

S V
a. When people diet, they should still eat balanced meals.

b. This is the model of the medieval castle that we made for history class.

DO S V
b. This is the model of the medieval castle that we made for history class.

1. There are few people who are more versatile than Pearl Bailey.
2. When she began her career, she was a dancer in New York.
3. Later, she became known as a jazz singer who also had a way with comedy.
4. She added acting to her list of accomplishments when she appeared on Broadway in 1946.
5. After she scored a huge success on Broadway, she appeared in a number of films.
6. She appeared on television, which she added to her list of successes.
7. When the all-black performance of *Hello, Dolly* was produced, she received excellent reviews for her starring role.
8. In 1975 she received an honor that she has treasured.
9. She was one of the people who were appointed as U.S. delegates to the United Nations.
10. In 1977 she was given an honorary degree by Georgetown University because she has made so many contributions to society.

Three Types of Subordinate Clauses

A subordinate clause can act as an adjective, an adverb, or a noun. Although the clause is longer than a single-word part of speech and frequently longer than a phrase, it functions exactly as a single-word adjective, adverb, or noun would.

Adjective Clauses

A subordinate clause that modifies a noun or pronoun is called an *adjective clause.*

This is the watch *that I got for my birthday.*

The subordinate clause *that I got for my birthday* modifies the noun *watch.* It answers the question *Which?*

The *italicized* part of each of the following sentences is an adjective clause. An arrow has been drawn from the first word of the adjective clause to the noun or pronoun that is modified.

The people at the party *who saw the UFO* were interviewed by the Air Force. [Notice that the adjective clause does not always come directly after the word it modifies.]

At the party John wore a tie *that lit up.*

The state *where the largest scout camp is located* is New Mexico.

Brown recluse spiders, *which are highly poisonous,* like secluded, quiet places.

For more information about relative pronouns, see pages 359–360.

Most adjective clauses begin with a relative pronoun. *Relative pronouns* are the words *who, whom, which, that,* and *those.* These pronouns are closely related to the word they modify because they restate that word.

I caught the mouse *that got into our pantry.*

We met an astronaut *who had walked on the moon.*

A *pronoun* is a word that takes the place of a noun or another pronoun. The noun or the pronoun that the pronoun stands in place of is called the pronoun's *antecedent.* In the preceding sentences the antecedents are *mouse* and *astronaut.*

Within the adjective clause itself, the relative pronoun may serve as a subject or an object.

There are a few fish *that* (S) *can travel* (V) *on land.*

We read an article *that* (DO) *a famous scientist* (S) *wrote* (V).

Exercise 3

Write out the following sentences, underlining each adjective clause and circling each relative pronoun. Then draw an arrow from the relative pronoun to its antecedent. Below each sentence write whether the relative pronoun is the subject of the adjective clause or the direct object.

Examples

a. My favorite sweat shirt is one that is several sizes too large.

a. My favorite sweat shirt is one (that) is several sizes too large.
that = subject of the adjective clause

b. Ms. Washington announced the members whom she had picked for the stage crew.

b. Ms. Washington announced the members whom she had picked for the stage crew.
whom = direct object of the adjective clause

1. Empress Maria Theresa of Austria was a remarkable woman, who saved her country from bankruptcy and revolution.
2. Abigail Adams sent the American forces coded information on the British in the letters that she wrote to her husband.
3. Cleopatra was the famous queen whom both Julius Caesar and Mark Antony loved.
4. The Sahara Desert, which is nearly as large as the United States, has less than an inch of rainfall each year.
5. There may be thousands of planets in our galaxy that could support life.
6. The states that are most often struck by tornadoes are in the South and Midwest.
7. The term *boulder* means "a stone that is larger than ten inches in diameter."
8. People who want to see falling stars should watch the sky between midnight and dawn.
9. The state where the wind blows most constantly is Oklahoma.
10. The highest peak that is in North America is Mount McKinley.

Adverb Clauses

A subordinate clause that modifies a verb, an adjective, or an adverb is an *adverb clause.*

The hogs ate *as if they wanted to set a record for greediness.*

The subordinate clause in the preceding sentence functions as an adverb clause, modifying the word *ate,* and answers the question *How?*

The *italicized* part in each of the following sentences is an adverb clause, modifying the verb of the main clause.

Before the tornado struck, the air grew still and oppressive.
[*When* did the air grow still and oppressive?]

We went skin diving *where there were no sharks.*
[*Where* did the skin diving take place?]

We didn't take that apartment *because the manager didn't allow pets.*
[*Why* wasn't the apartment taken?]

Akira went to the party *although he had to leave early.*
[*Under what conditions* did Akira go to the party?]

Adverb clauses can also modify adjectives or adverbs.

This pizza is spicier *than you like.*
[modifies the adjective *spicier*]

The team played harder *than they ever had before.*
[modifies the adverb *harder*]

The first word in an adverb clause is usually a *subordinating conjunction*, which joins the adverb clause to a word or words in the main clause. Subordinating conjunctions perform two functions: they *link* the adverb clause to the main clause of the sentence, and they show the *relationship* between the two clauses.

Penny went to Howard University *because her brother went there.*

The adverb clause *because her brother went there* modifies the verb *went.* The subordinating conjunction *because* joins the adverb clause to the main clause and also shows the relationship between the two clauses. In this instance the adverb clause states the cause of something; it tells why.

For further information on subordinating conjunctions, see pages 462–464.

The following words are commonly used as subordinating conjunctions. Some consist of more than one word. These compound subordinating conjunctions function as a unit, working in exactly the same way as one-word subordinating conjunctions.

after	even though	though
although	if	until
as far as	in order that	when
as if	provided that	whenever
as long as	since	where
as though	so that	wherever
because	than	whether
before	that	while

Exercise 4

Write out the following sentences, underlining the adverb clauses and circling the subordinating conjunctions. Below each sentence identify the word that is modified by the clause and tell its part of speech.

Examples

a. After my brother saw the Harlem Globetrotters, he became their biggest fan.

a. After my brother saw the Harlem Globetrotters, he became their biggest fan.
The adverb clause modifies the verb became.

b. The wallaby is smaller than its relative, the kangaroo, is.

b. The wallaby is smaller than its relative, the kangaroo, is.
The adverb clause modifies the adjective smaller.

1. Biologist Rachel Carson wrote about environmental problems before most other people were aware of them.
2. When people read her books, they became concerned about ecology.
3. Pollution was more widespread than they had suspected.
4. Some of this pollution was so dangerous that people were frightened.
5. Ms. Carson was certain that the pollution must be stopped.
6. She fought against many chemical pesticides, since their poisons can pass through the whole food chain.
7. Although the poisons are meant for insects, they can contaminate plants and other animals.
8. Poultry and animals could eat contaminated grains, so that the poisons could end up on our dinner tables.
9. The disadvantages of these pesticides might be greater than any advantages they might have.
10. Because Ms. Carson campaigned long and hard, legislation against dangerous chemical pesticides was passed.

Elliptical Adverb Clauses

Sometimes, an adverb clause appears incomplete; it may lack a subject, a predicate, or both. These "incomplete" structures are still considered adverb clauses, however, because the missing parts are understood.

> You have a better chance *than I.*
> [You have a better chance *than I do:* verb understood.]

> *When riding in a car,* you should always wear a seat belt.
> [*When you are riding in a car,* you should always wear a seat belt: subject and helping verb understood]

Clauses whose missing parts are filled in by the reader are called *elliptical adverb clauses. Elliptical* means "a part has been omitted."

> Younger people require larger quantities of food *than elderly people.*
> [elliptical adverb clause: *than elderly people require*]

> I never saw a wild deer *before moving here.*
> [elliptical adverb clause: *before I moved here*]

Some elliptical clauses, such as *before moving here,* resemble participial phrases (see pages 508–509). An elliptical adverb clause is *always* introduced by a subordinating conjunction; a participial phrase is not.

I never saw a deer before moving here.	[elliptical adverb clause]
Moving here, I finally saw a deer.	[participial phrase]

Exercise 5

The following sentences contain adverb clauses, some of which are elliptical. Write out each sentence, underlining each adverb clause. Below the sentence identify the subject and verb of the adverb clause. If the clause is elliptical, supply the understood parts beneath the sentence.

Examples

a. When visiting the South Pole, people are often startled by the beautiful auroras.

a. When visiting the South Pole, people are often startled by the beautiful auroras.
subject: people
verb: are visiting

b. My sister wanted to work a year before she went to college.

b. My sister wanted to work a year before she went to college.
subject: she
verb: went

1. If the Platte River were any more shallow, it wouldn't be there.
2. When early explorers named it, they named it aptly.
3. The word *Platte* is appropriate because it means "flat."
4. When first seen, the Platte looks "a mile wide and an inch deep."
5. In some places it seems no deeper than a puddle.
6. When hot weather rolls around, much of the Platte goes dry.
7. It will be full of sandbars as far as you can see.
8. When the pioneers moved westward, many followed the Platte River.
9. This was not surprising because one of the world's great natural roads ran beside the river.
10. It was a natural highway better than many constructed roads.

Noun Clauses

When a subordinate clause functions as a noun in a sentence, it is called a *noun clause.*

A noun clause can perform any function that an ordinary noun can: it can serve as subject, direct object, indirect object, predicate noun, appositive, or object of a preposition.

Whoever donates to the fund gets an inscribed plaque.
[noun clause as subject]

The mechanic didn't know *what the problem was.*
[noun clause as direct object]

Grandfather will give *whatever is robbing the henhouse* a load of buckshot.
[noun clause as indirect object]

I wouldn't want to guess about *what will happen.*
[noun clause as object of the preposition *about*]

The executive's problem was *that she hated to fire anyone.*
[noun clause as predicate noun]

The biggest trophy goes to the champion team, *whoever wins the conference title.*
[noun clause as appositive]

Words That Introduce Noun Clauses

Noun clauses usually begin with one of the following words: *who, whom, whomsoever, whomever, what, whatever, that, which, when, how, where, wherever,* or *whether.* Sometimes, the introductory word serves merely as a conjunction to join the noun clause to the main clause of the sentence. Other times, however, the introductory word may function as the subject, direct object, or modifier within the noun clause itself.

I knew *that she called.*
[*She* is the subject of the noun clause; *that* serves only to join the clause to the rest of the sentence.]

I know *how we can accomplish the task.*
[*We* is the subject of the noun clause; *how* is an adverb modifying *can accomplish.*]

When the conjunction serves only to join the noun clause to the remainder of the sentence, it can usually be dropped without changing the sentence's meaning.

We knew *that we should leave early.*
We knew *we should leave early.*

Exercise 6

Write out the following sentences, underlining each noun clause and circling the word that introduces the clause. If the introductory word can be dropped without changing the meaning of the sentence, draw an X through it. Beneath each sentence tell how the noun clause functions within the sentence.

Examples

a. We could order whatever we wanted at the restaurant.
a. We could order whatever we wanted at the restaurant.
direct object.

b. I believe that the guilty person is Colonel Mustard.
b. I believe that the guilty person is Colonel Mustard.
direct object

1. The director thought that the play was moving too slowly.
2. How the squirrels got into our attic is a mystery.
3. The old prospector claimed that there were large uranium deposits in the mountains.
4. The customers demanded that the store return their money.
5. I know who put the salt in the sugar bowl.
6. What I want for my birthday is a pair of chinchillas.
7. Miss Shimura is who can help you.

8. Give these old magazines to whoever wants them.
9. I think that I have eaten too much guacamole.
10. California is where most American movies are made.

Mastery Exercise A

Write out the following sentences, underlining the subordinate clauses. Beneath each sentence write whether the subordinate clause is an adjective, an adverb, or a noun clause. If it is an adjective or an adverb clause, draw an arrow from the clause to the word or words it modifies. If it is a noun clause, write its function beneath the sentence.

Examples

a. Early arctic explorers quickly discovered that their scientifically designed equipment was inadequate.

a. *Early arctic explorers quickly discovered <u>that their scientifically designed equipment was inadequate.</u>*
noun clause, direct object

b. The clothing and tools that the Eskimos had designed were superior in many cases.

b. *The clothing and tools <u>that the Eskimos had designed</u> were superior in many cases.*
adjective clause

1. One of the most gifted writers who ever lived was William Shakespeare.
2. Although his works are famous throughout the world, we know relatively little about his life.
3. We know that he was born in April 1564 in the English town of Stratford-on-Avon.
4. Although we have much information on other writers of the time, we know little about Shakespeare's youth, habits, personality, or education.
5. We do not even know what his religion was.
6. What we do know is that he created some of the greatest characters in literature.
7. He presents these characters in situations that are dramatic and revealing.
8. The character Othello, for instance, shows how jealousy can destroy a noble mind.
9. Hamlet is an appealing, bright, young man who is trapped in an impossible situation.
10. Romeo and Juliet dramatize the sort of passionate love that can be destructive.
11. The play *King Lear* presents characters who are representatives of the best and worst of humanity.

12. Shakespeare is often praised because he portrayed realistic and spirited women.
13. His best heroines are women who speak their minds and are not passive.
14. His Cleopatra is a woman who is unforgettable.
15. There is Cordelia, who is honest, loving, and brave.
16. Portia, who is a character in *The Merchant of Venice,* is quick-witted and spunky.
17. Few writers could invent villains that are nastier than Shakespeare's.
18. Iago is one of the most despicable characters that ever walked a stage.
19. What he wants to do is destroy the brave Othello.
20. He employs a plan that is a masterpiece of coldblooded cunning.
21. King Lear's two eldest daughters are women who seem monstrous.
22. What distinguishes them is their absolute selfishness and cruelty.
23. When Shakespeare turned his hand to comedy, he was also unsurpassed.
24. Falstaff is a fat, cowardly soldier, whose high jinks are still amusing.
25. Kate, who is the spunky star of *The Taming of the Shrew,* is a comic masterpiece.

Using Clauses

In the following sections you will practice punctuating clauses and using clauses to vary sentence structure in your writing. As you work through the exercises in the next sections, refer to Understanding Clauses for any help you might need in recognizing the different kinds of clauses and their functions in a sentence.

Punctuating Adjective Clauses

An *essential adjective clause* adds information that is necessary to the meaning of a sentence.

The physics teacher will give an *A* to every student *who gets an* A *on the final.*

The adjective clause in the preceding example is *who gets an* A *on the final.* It is an essential clause since the meaning of the sentence would change radically if the clause were dropped:

The physics teacher will give an *A* to every student.

Do not use commas with an essential adjective clause.

Sometimes, however, the adjective clause only adds extra information, information that does not change the basic meaning of the sentence.

Riko**,** *who is a good student***,** received an *A* in physics.

The adjective clause in the preceding sentence, *who is a good student,* is *nonessential* because the basic meaning of the sentence would remain the same if the clause were dropped:

> Riko received an *A* in physics.

A speaker generally pauses before and after a nonessential clause. Read the following sentences aloud, and you will see how the pauses set the nonessential clauses off a bit from the rest of the sentence.

> My car, *which is eleven years old,* probably won't last much longer.
> In Hawaii we saw Mrs. Diaz, *who was visiting her daughter.*
> We visited the city of St. Joseph, Missouri, *where the pony express started.*

Exercise 1

Write out the following sentences, using commas to set off any nonessential clause from the rest of its sentence. Underline the adjective clauses and circle the commas you insert.

Examples

a. Dianne Feinstein who is a Democrat was elected mayor of San Francisco.

a. Dianne Feinstein, who is a Democrat, was elected mayor of San Francisco.

b. The first person who developed a pure white marigold received an enormous cash prize.

b. The first person who developed a pure white marigold received an enormous cash prize.

1. The Wright brothers were not the first persons who flew by mechanical means.
2. In 1380 J. B. Dante who was an Italian mathematician built a set of artificial wings.
3. He made several flights over a local lake that were quite successful.
4. Later, he had an accident that caused the left wing to break.
5. His subsequent fall which broke his leg ended his flying career.
6. In 1678 Besnier who was a French locksmith perfected a glider.
7. He did not take many chances on his first test flight which was off a chair.
8. He later made a flight that took him over a neighbor's roof.
9. Besnier who was not a daredevil sold his glider to a traveling acrobat.
10. The acrobat used the glider in demonstrations that made him the hit of county fairs.

Punctuating Adverb Clauses

An introductory adverb clause is *always* followed by a comma.

When I ate, my dog kept looking at me soulfully.

If the introductory clause were not set off, the reader might run the two clauses together and get a jolt:

When I ate my dog / kept looking at me soulfully.

The comma prevents momentary confusion.

Most adverb clauses are not set off by a comma when they appear at the end of a sentence. However, a comma is often used before adverb clauses that begin with *though* and *although* and before *as* and *since* when they mean "because."

Jenny didn't do well on the test, *although* she had studied very hard.

We didn't remove the storm windows, *as* we thought the cold weather would continue.

Raoul withdrew from the contest, *since* he found he was ineligible.

Exercise 2

Write out the following sentences, adding commas wherever they are necessary. Underline the adverb clauses and circle the commas you insert.

Examples

a. When the school band gave its holiday concert the band director put a large bow on her baton.

a. When the school band gave its holiday concert, the band director put a large bow on her baton.

b. We shouldn't swim there if there isn't a lifeguard.

b. We shouldn't swim there if there isn't a lifeguard.

1. When Europeans first came to South America the Incas had a great civilization.
2. They had developed an irrigation system better than any developed in Europe.
3. They were also better engineers than the Europeans were.
4. When the Inca empire was at its height it had highly skilled surgeons and dentists.
5. We owe much of our modern diet to the Incas since they were the first to cultivate the potato and several other vegetables.
6. Although native Americans supposedly never discovered the wheel there are indications that the Incas may have used wheels.
7. The Incas built towers so that they could observe the sun's movements.
8. They may have had a calendar though this is not certain.

9. Certain statues and structures look as though they might have been decorated with symbols for days and months.
10. Many of the Incas' fine statues and beautiful goldwork remain although much was looted or destroyed by the Europeans.

Review Exercise A

Write out each of the following sentences, underlining each adjective clause and circling the noun or pronoun that it modifies. Add commas where necessary to set off a nonessential clause from the rest of the sentence. Circle the commas you insert.

Examples

a. The Supremes who were three high school girls from Detroit became one of America's top singing groups.

a. The Supremes, who were three high school girls from Detroit, became one of America's top singing groups.

b. The American animal that is most dangerous is the buffalo.

b. The American animal that is most dangerous is the buffalo.

1. The nineteenth-century American who went West by covered wagon was a hardy soul.
2. These westward treks which were long and arduous were often made by groups of people.
3. A large group that traveled together formed a "wagon train."
4. Roads that were rugged or nonexistent often made the trip uncomfortable.
5. Oxen which were slow but extremely hardy made the best work animals.
6. The jolting ride was one that shook the pioneer's teeth and bones.
7. Enterprising pioneer women learned to use the jolting which marked every mile of the journey.
8. Those who owned cows would milk them in the morning.
9. They hung buckets of cream on the wagons which jiggled and jolted all day long.
10. By evening the cream that had been in the bucket had turned to fresh butter.
11. Some pioneers tried taking all their household goods which included pianos, organs, and heavy trunks.
12. These people who started out with high hopes often left their family treasures to rot on the prairie.
13. Loads had to be kept light on a journey that took so long.
14. Many a young bride who had grown up protected and pampered found herself trying to cook outdoors in a pouring rain.

15. The parasols that they had once carried for looks now became important cooking tools.
16. The parasol which had been designed to protect complexions from the sun now protected biscuits from washing away in the rain.
17. Hoop skirts which were popular in the cities were awkward on the prairie.
18. Those who wanted to remain in fashion had to weight their skirts with iron bars.
19. There were few women who were vain enough to bother.
20. Tempers could easily fray on these journeys which were often several months long.

Review Exercise B

Write out the following sentences and add all necessary punctuation. Underline each adverb clause and circle the commas you insert. (Remember that adverb clauses may be elliptical clauses.)

Examples

a. It takes more facial muscles to frown than it does to smile.

a. It takes more facial muscles to frown than it does to smile.

b. When the mail carrier arrives my dog barks wildly.

b. When the mail carrier arrives, my dog barks wildly.

1. Winds are caused when air temperatures differ.
2. The sun heats some portions of the earth more than it heats others.
3. When the earth's surface is warmed the heat is conducted into the air.
4. Warm air is lighter than cool air.
5. It is warmer because its molecules are moving more rapidly.
6. The rapidly moving molecules spread farther apart than cold air molecules.
7. Because the molecules are less dense the warm air exerts lower pressure.
8. Wherever one of these low pressure centers exists colder, heavier air flows toward it.
9. The winds blow because differences in temperature and pressure cause the air to move.
10. You can predict coming weather if you carefully observe the wind.
11. If the wind is high a change will probably be speedy.
12. In our climate northern winds are usually colder than southern winds.
13. When a wind blows over a large body of water it picks up water vapor.
14. This vapor may grow so dense that it forms rain-bearing clouds.
15. Clear weather usually occurs if the winds have been blowing over dry land.

16. Whenever winds blow regularly over the same route they are called prevailing winds.
17. These prevailing winds affect weather because they carry large masses of air with them.
18. The prevailing winds are regular although the air they carry may be hot, cold, wet, or dry.
19. When a large quantity of warm air does not move it is called a warm air mass.
20. Similarly, a cold air mass occurs when cool air stays still.

Writing Exercise A

Using adjective, adverb, and noun clauses to vary your sentence structure and to show relationships between ideas, write one or two well-developed paragraphs on one of the following suggested topics. Use care in punctuating adjective and adverb clauses.

1. Assume that a distant relative leaves you $500 in a will but asks that you use the money to help someone other than yourself—a club, a charitable organization, or an individual. Explain how you would use the money and your reasons for using it in that way.
2. Some high schools have developed programs that help students who have just moved learn about the school, become acquainted with its activities and make new friends. Explain the new-student program at your school or write about a program your school could develop for new students.
3. *To be eccentric* means "to be unconventional or out of the ordinary." Write about someone you admire because he or she is eccentric in some way.
4. A person who has been convicted of a felony in the United States is not allowed to vote. Should a person who has committed a serious crime lose this privilege? In your writing state why you agree or disagree with this policy.

20 The Sentence

Using Sentences

In this chapter you will learn to use sentences effectively in your writing. As a first step you will learn the four basic sentence types. This knowledge will help you to vary your sentence structure, an important part of effective writing.

Four Sentence Structures

There are two kinds of clauses: *independent* and *subordinate.* Every sentence must contain at least one independent clause, and some sentences contain more than one or contain subordinate clauses as well. Sentences can be classified according to the types of clauses they contain. Every sentence belongs to one of four basic sentence types: *simple, compound, complex,* or *compound-complex.*

1. *Simple Sentences*

A *simple sentence* contains only one independent clause and no subordinate clauses.

S *V*
Fish swim.

The subject and verb in a simple sentence may have complements and modifying words and phrases.

S V DO
The brightly colored fish at the aquarium fill the tanks.

A simple sentence may contain a compound subject, a compound verb, or both a compound subject and verb. It remains a simple sentence, however; the compound elements are part of only one independent clause.

S S S V V
Kathy, Julio, and Kim made the posters and distributed them.

2. *Compound Sentences*

A *compound sentence* contains more than one independent clause but no subordinate clause.

INDEPENDENT CLAUSE		INDEPENDENT CLAUSE
The sky was cloudy,	and	a chilly drizzle was falling.

The independent clauses may have compound subjects and verbs, but they must be two (or more) independent clauses.

S S V S V
Cows and zebras are herbivorous; they eat vegetable matter.

3. *Complex Sentences*

A *complex sentence* contains only one independent clause, but it can have several subordinate clauses.

SUBORDINATE	INDEPENDENT	SUBORDINATE
After Troy fell,	Aeneas fled with his father,	who had to be carried.

4. *Compound-Complex Sentences*

A *compound-complex sentence* contains more than one independent clause and at least one subordinate clause.

SUBORDINATE	INDEPENDENT		INDEPENDENT
After they ate,	Carol went home,	and	Anne went to work.

Exercise 1

Write out the following sentences, underlining each independent clause once and each subordinate clause twice. Below each sentence identify the sentence as *simple*, *compound*, *complex*, or *compound-complex*.

Examples

a. When water freezes, it expands.

a. When water freezes, it expands.
complex sentence

b. The Rocky Mountains were called "The Shining Mountains" by native Americans.

b. The Rocky Mountains were called "The Shining Mountains" by native Americans.
simple sentence

1. The roller skate was invented in Belgium in the eighteenth century.
2. The four-wheeled roller skate, as we know it, did not appear until almost a century later.
3. The first roller rink opened in Rhode Island in 1866, and rinks appeared in Europe soon afterward.
4. When the Grand Hall Olympia Rink opened in London, it was the world's largest rink, but it operated for only four years.
5. The largest modern rink, which is located in Illinois, is the Fireside Roll-Arena.
6. Roller hockey was invented in 1870, and now there is an international Roller Hockey Association that sponsors world championship competitions.
7. Britain took the first world championship, but Portugal, which has won eleven championships, is the most frequent victor.
8. Skates can be speedy; the world's official record is almost twenty-six miles an hour.
9. This record was set in Italy, where a number of speeding records have been made.
10. A Canadian who was a glutton for punishment skated from New York to California, which is a trip of 3,100 miles.

Review Exercise A

Write out each of the following sentences and beneath each one list and label the independent clauses and the subordinate clauses. Then underline the simple subject or subjects of each clause once and the verb or verbs twice. Finally identify the sentence structure as *simple, compound, complex,* or *compound-complex.*

Example

a. My brother is now playing the bagpipes, which doesn't make our neighbors too happy.

a. My brother is now playing the bagpipes, which doesn't make our neighbors too happy.
My brother is now playing the bagpipes—independent clause
which doesn't make our neighbors too happy—dependent clause
complex sentence

1. The world's largest geyser is Waimangu, which is in New Zealand.
2. This geyser resembles a volcano erupting.
3. Waimangu is a relatively young geyser; it was formed in 1886.
4. The geyser was created when a great volcanic eruption altered much of the island.
5. The American geyser Old Faithful erupts regularly and with the same force each time.

6. The eruptions of Waimangu are both irregular and dangerous.
7. The geyser sometimes explodes unexpectedly; when this happens, steam and boiling mud are flung into the air.
8. Although the eruptions are always spectacular, the geyser is more active at certain times than it is at others.
9. At its peak performance, it flings stones, mud, and water to a height of 1,500 feet.
10. An unexpected eruption that killed three people resulted in the geyser's basin being railed as a safety precaution.
11. Visitors traveling through the region will see a mysterious and alien landscape.
12. Ponds boil and craters seethe like witches' cooking pots.
13. One particularly dangerous area is named The Inferno, meaning "hell."
14. The rocks are stained yellow with sulfur, and the earth is hot to touch.
15. Poking a stick into the ground causes a spurt of steam or boiling water to rise.
16. Since the lakes are often steaming and sulfurous, a foul smell hangs in the air, and large mudholes burble while puffs of steam rise and drift.
17. Although there are ghastly and unearthly sights, there is beauty in the area as well; strangely colored lakes make the spectator feel as if he or she is in some sort of wonderland.
18. Although you can take scores of snapshots, you can never capture the strange magnificence of this exotic world.
19. Naturally heated pools of clear water are good for swimming.
20. The major lake, Rotomahana, seems to be a slab of turquoise; in addition, it has green islands full of ferns and vines.

Avoiding Run-On Sentences

When two or more sentences are joined together with a comma or with no punctuation at all, the resulting group of words is called a *run-on sentence.*

Run-On: Go down to the end of this block, then look to the left.
Correct: Go down to the end of this block**.** Then look to the left.

Run-On: Davey is a good pitcher his sister is a good fielder.
Correct: Davey is a good pitcher**;** his sister is a good fielder.

Run-on sentences may be corrected by separating the sentences completely or by joining them with appropriate punctuation or wording.

1. You may separate the sentences with end punctuation.

Run-On: Today is Julian Bond's birthday, mine is tomorrow.
Correct: Today is Julian Bond's birthday**.** Mine is tomorrow.

2. You may use a semicolon to separate closely related sentences.

Run-On:	Robin can't go on the canoe trip he has a broken arm.
Correct:	Robin can't go on the canoe trip; he has a broken arm.

You may also use a semicolon and a conjunctive adverb to join the two sentences. The adverb, which is always followed by a comma, shows the relationship of one of the sentences to the other.

Run-On:	I can no longer work full time, maintain the household, and still serve on four committees, I resign.
Correct:	I can no longer work full time, maintain the household, and still serve on four committees; *therefore*, I resign.

3. You may use a comma followed by a coordinating conjunction to combine the two sentences.

Run-On:	Art is building a burglar alarm system his sister is helping him.
Correct:	Art is building a burglar alarm system, *and* his sister is helping him.

4. You may change one of the sentences into a subordinate clause.

Run-On:	Sophia Sanchez has been appointed to the mayor's special task force, she is director of the Community Health Agency.
Correct:	Sophia Sanchez, *who is director of the Community Health Agency*, has been appointed to the mayor's special task force.
Run-On:	Max Goldenberg suggested that the tenants buy the apartment house from the owner, that is exactly what happened.
Correct:	Max Goldenberg suggested that the tenants buy the apartment house from the owner, *which is exactly what happened.*

Exercise 2

Using any of the methods in the previous section, correct each of the following run-on sentences. Write out the corrected sentences.

Example

a. Nancy Lieberman is first-round draft pick of the Dallas Diamonds, she played a game with the Celtics.

a. Nancy Lieberman, who is first-round draft pick of the Dallas Diamonds, played a game with the Celtics.

1. On his sixty-fifth birthday, Jack LaLanne towed sixty-five rowboats for a mile, they were loaded with 6,500 pounds of wood pulp.
2. A strep throat outbreak has spread among 900 inmates at the county jail, the jail has been quarantined since last weekend.
3. Jerome Robbins is a choreographer for the New York City Ballet, he has also choreographed Broadway musicals, such as *Fiddler on the Roof.*
4. The trucking industry has been deregulated one bus company has lowered its fares by 10 per cent.

5. Strokes are caused by blockages or breaks in blood vessels supplying the brain, during a stroke a part of the brain is destroyed because of a lack of blood.
6. Fleer Corporation of Philadelphia claims that it invented bubble gum, it is suing Topps Chewing Gum Company for monopolizing the rights to photos of major league baseball players for bubble gum cards.
7. Cities in the North report that they are losing industries, more and more industries are moving to the Sunbelt states.
8. The administration has endorsed a settlement between the federal government and the Passamaquoddy, Penobscot, and Malecites more than 12.5 million acres of land in Maine are in dispute.
9. Volcanic ash has covered the Boeing training field in Moses Lake, Washington, Boeing is temporarily moving its training operation to Montana.
10. In a journal called *Signs of Spring*, Laurel Lee writes about her life-and-death battle with Hodgkins's disease, she is a divorced mother of three young children.

Avoiding Sentence Fragments

Run-on sentences are too much for a single sentence. Fragments, on the other hand, are not enough to make up a sentence. Remember the three requirements for a complete sentences:

1. A sentence expresses a complete thought.
2. A sentence has a subject.
3. A sentence has a verb.

In a sentence fragment, one of more of these requirements is missing.

Sentences that do not conform to Edited Standard English are marked with an asterisk (*).

Incomplete Thought:	*Because it is so hot.
Sentence:	Because it is so hot, few people entered the marathon.
No Subject:	*Hurried into the river.
Sentence:	A mother duck and thirteen ducklings hurried into the river.
No Verb:	*The Beaux Arts Trio appearing in a Beethoven concert.
Sentence:	The Beaux Arts Trio are appearing in a Beethoven concert.

1. *Phrases as Fragments*

A phrase does not have both a subject and a predicate, nor does it express a complete thought. When a prepositional phrase, infinitive phrase, participial phrase, or gerund phrase is written as a sentence, it is a sentence fragment.

See pages 506–523 for a review of phrases.

Fragment:	*In the stacks of the university library.
Sentence:	Teresa spent three days working in the stacks of the university library.

Fragment: *Hank waiting for the Staten Island ferry.
Sentence: Hank, waiting for the Staten Island ferry, met an old neighbor from Decatur, Georgia.

Fragment: *Singing in the rain.
Sentence: Singing in the rain can lead to pneumonia.

2. *Clauses as Fragments*

See pages 524–540 for a discussion of subordinate clauses.

A *subordinate clause* contains both a subject and a verb but does not express a complete thought. Subordinate clauses must be attached to an independent clause; they cannot stand alone.

Fragment: *Before the bus leaves for Sea World.
Sentence: Before the bus leaves for Sea World, be sure to check the return schedule.

Fragment: *Because he gives her too much work.
Sentence: Alice is angry with Frank because he gives her too much work.

3. *Appositives as Fragments*

For a review of appositives, see pages 514–515.

An *appositive* is a word or group of words that identifies a noun or pronoun. An appositive cannot be punctuated as a sentence because it does not express a complete thought.

Fragment: *A delicious dish of cheese-stuffed pasta in tomato sauce.
Sentence: Al's mother made manicotti, a delicious dish of cheese-stuffed pasta in tomato sauce.

Exercise 3

Revise the following sentences, correcting all sentence fragments. (There may be several ways to correct any one fragment.)

Examples

a. Marika had to throw the lobster back. Because it was too little.
a. Marika had to throw the lobster back because it was too little.

b. Ira Gershwin wrote the lyrics to "They Can't Take That Away from Me." Which is from the movie *Shall We Dance?* with Fred Astaire and Ginger Rogers.
b. Ira Gershwin wrote the lyrics to "They Can't Take That Away from Me," which is from the movie Shall We Dance? *with Fred Astaire and Ginger Rogers.*

1. In order to finish before the deadline. We will have to work late every night.
2. Jeremy is working at a used car lot on South Street. Washing and waxing the cars.
3. Because two of the students are still missing. We cannot leave yet.
4. We bought a nylon tent. With twenty-six books of stamps saved from the supermarket.

5. She brewed a fragrant pot of tea. A blend of mountain teas, oranges, and spices.
6. The Ammers found many changes in their life style. After moving to Boston from San Francisco.
7. Tracy sketched the sleeping male mandrill. A baboon with blue and scarlet markings on its face.
8. Although it is well past midnight. None of the children show any signs of being sleepy.
9. Have you read *The Invisible Man?* Ralph Ellison's only published novel.
10. More than a hundred and fifty people applied for the job. Creating unbelievable chaos in the normally quiet office.

Review Exercise B

Revise each of the following, correcting errors in sentence fragments and run-ons.

1. Albacore is an important game fish in the Atlantic and Pacific Oceans, it is found in waters of 60- to 66-degrees Fahrenheit.
2. Child-resistant containers have significantly reduced accidental poisoning deaths, for example, deaths from lye products for children under five have decreased 50 per cent.
3. The highest navigable lake is 2½-mile-high Lake Titicaca. Known as the Lake of the Clouds.
4. Selenium was discovered by the Swedish scientist Jöns Berzelius, it is used in photocopy machines and TV cameras.
5. Benjamin Hook urges every black citizen to register and vote, by becoming a political force, he believes, blacks can influence national and local elected leaders.
6. A new kind of nuclear weapon has been developed. Which is deadly to humans but does much less damage to buildings and property than H-bombs.
7. You can nod and say "Howdy" to a stranger on the trail according to *The Cowboy Catalogue* don't wave because raising a hand can cause a horse to bolt.
8. Graphologists say that a far-forward slant indicates an outgoing, warm personality, a very large capital *I* shows a writer with a high opinion of himself or herself.
9. *Walden Two* is a novel about a utopian community. Written by B. F. Skinner, the leading behaviorist psychologist.
10. It is a good idea to throw a jacket or other object in its path. When being chased by a bull.
11. Americans suffering from acne spend almost $200 million a year for doctors, they spend at least $125 million for medicine.

12. The state with the greatest percentage of shoreline as its boundary is Hawaii. Which is made up of eight islands.
13. Pope John Paul II visited Brazil. Where he urged enthusiastic audiences to embrace traditional values and secure the family.
14. An important index to the nation's economy is the Gross National Product (GNP), it is the total output of goods and services.
15. In 1886 in Haymarket Square in Chicago. A crowd of labor unionists and police clashed in the Haymarket Riot.
16. The word *bachelor* comes originally from two Latin words that mean "dairy farm." *Bacca*, cow, and *-arium*, place.
17. In geometry a decahedron is a solid figure having ten surfaces, a hendecahedron has eleven surfaces.
18. Several years ago a syndicated columnist asked her readers if they would have children if they had to do it all over again more than 70 per cent said no.
19. Bees build honeycomb, rows of hexagonal cells from wax, it is used for storing honey, pollen, and eggs.
20. The most famous of the mythical gorgons is Medusa. Whose glance could turn a human to stone.

Writing Effective Sentences

By now you have probably discovered that it is not always easy to say what you mean clearly and smoothly. A sentence may be grammatically correct and still not effective. This section will give you some suggestions on improving your writing style.

Diction

When students are serious about trying to improve their writing, they sometimes try to use difficult words and write in long, involved sentences. Such writing, they think, sounds "more educated." However, the aim of all your writing should be to express your ideas as clearly and as simply as possible. Look at the following sentences, for example.

Poor: By elevating the window, she was able to observe that the atmospheric conditions had undergone a change and that there was precipitation of a rather heavy nature.

Better: By raising the window, she saw that the weather had changed and that it was raining heavily.

Diction means "word choice." Whenever you write, you must think about your audience and purpose, for these considerations affect your choice of words. You can see that a letter to a friend, for example, would have more informal language than a term paper in English. Even when you write a formal paper, however, keep in mind that your goal is always to say what you mean in the clearest—which usually means the simplest—way possible. In this sense, *simple* does not mean writing a series of short, choppy sentences that sound like the writing of a third-grader. *Simple* does mean using a vocabulary that accomplishes your purpose without forcing the reader to resort to an unabridged dictionary or to a technical book. *Simple* also means that your sentences sound smooth and are reasonable in length.

Poor: During our sojourn at your celebration, our level of pleasure rose to extremely high degrees.
Better: We enjoyed ourselves immensely at your party.
Poor: The bovine creature catapulted over the lunar solar body.
Better: The cow jumped over the moon.

Conciseness

Another writing trap is wordiness. Writers sometimes go on and on, repeating themselves endlessly. The following two guidelines will help you improve your writing:

1. Get to the point.
2. Do not waste words.

Being concise does not mean that your writing needs to sound like a telegram. It does mean, however, that you should always proofread your first draft to eliminate wordiness, stalling, and unnecessary repetition. Do not be afraid to come right out and say what you mean.

Poor: It has come to my attention that certain correspondences pertaining to the romantic relationship between my parents in the days before their marriage are located in a cardboard receptacle on the topmost storage shelf in the closet near the front door of the apartment.
Better: I found my parents' old love letters in a box on the top shelf of the front closet.

Poor: In the event that nobody would communicate with her about an excursion for the Fourth of July, Suzanne had several alternate plans in mind for ways in which she might occupy herself on that day.
Better: In case no one called her with plans for the Fourth of July, Suzanne had several things in mind that she could do.

Weak Constructions

Action verbs may be written in either the active voice or the passive voice.

For a review of the active and passive voices, see pages 411–412.

Active: The right fielder *caught* the line drive.
Passive: The line drive *was caught* by the right fielder.

Whenever possible, use the active voice instead of the passive voice. The active voice is stronger and more effective.

Weaker: At the graduation ceremony, tickets were taken and programs were handed out by eleventh-graders.

Stronger: At the graduation ceremony, eleventh-graders took the tickets and handed out the programs.

Sentences that begin with "There is . . ." and "There are . . ." are also a weak construction that should be avoided whenever it is possible to rephrase the sentence.

Weaker: There are three reasons why everyone objected to the new rule.
Stronger: Everyone objected to the new rule for three reasons.

Weaker: There is not enough time for the performers to attend the party before the play.
Stronger: The performers do not have enough time to attend the party before the play.

Exercise 4

Revise the following sentences to improve diction, conciseness, and weak constructions. Write out the revised sentences.

Example

a. The consensus of opinion among the elected delegates by a show of hands was to adjourn the proceedings until the next day.
a. The delegates voted to adjourn the meeting until the next day.

1. There are few people who realize how lucky they are to enjoy good health until disease strikes them.
2. The variegated hues of the hibiscus graced the foliage adjacent to the fence.
3. There was something that needed to be discussed, but neither of them wanted to be the first to bring it up.
4. Invitations to the young artists' preview were sent by the gallery owner to members of the press.
5. In the event that you do not find me or any of the members of my family in our abode, please attempt to reach me by telephone.
6. Three reasons for requesting zoning variances were given by the young lawyer representing the developer.
7. The books were packed by Gwen and taken to the Veterans' Hospital.
8. There is a certain kind of tool, which must be sharp, that is necessary for anyone who is trying to cut a linoleum block.
9. The names of the three winners are announced by the disc jockey at noon every Saturday.
10. It is the job of one full-time county employee to give water and to give fertilizer to every potted plant in the offices of the county government.

Writing Exercise A

In trying to convince someone to do something, you need to present your arguments clearly and effectively. Choose one of the following situations and write a rough draft of what you would say to persuade the other person. If you wish, you can also write what the other person says and your responses to that. When you have finished your rough draft, proofread it carefully, being certain that your sentences are complete and effective. Then write a final copy. (Make up any details that you need to write an effective appeal.)

1. You are a student trying to convince a store owner to hire you for a part-time job even though you have had no experience.
2. You are a son or daughter trying to convince a parent or guardian to reinstate your driving privileges even though you have been in a minor accident.
3. You are an employee trying to convince your boss that you deserve a raise.
4. You are a customer trying to convince a store manager that you deserve a refund for defective merchandise even though you no longer have the receipt.
5. You are a student trying to convince the assistant principal to let you skip lunch and rearrange your schedule so that you can leave school every day at 1 o'clock.

PART

7 Mechanics

21 Spelling

Spelling Correctly

Many writers think the ability to spell correctly is a mysterious gift, but nothing is further from the truth. The key to successful spelling involves proofreading carefully, correcting individual spelling errors, and learning the basic spelling rules.

1. Proofread carefully.

Even the very best writers make some mistakes, but good writers check their work carefully. Proofreading for spelling errors will be easier if you start at the bottom of the page. Use a ruler to mark the line you are proofreading. As you move up the page, read backwards, from right to left, and look at each word separately. If you are not certain that a word is spelled correctly, circle it lightly in pencil and check its spelling.

2. Use your dictionary as a spelling aid.

When you are uncertain about how a word is spelled, do not guess. Once you are familiar with the dictionary, it takes only a moment to check a word's spelling. If a word does not appear as you have written it, try alternative spellings.

3. Keep a record of your spelling errors.

Many students record the words they have misspelled on a special page in their notebooks. Divide the page into three columns. In the first column write the correct spelling of the word and underline the letter or letters that are causing you to misspell it. In the second column write the word again, but this time divide it into syllables and show the accent. In the third column write down any information that will help you learn the word. For example, you may misspell the word because you pronounce it incorrectly. Noting this fact beside the word will help you remember that correct pronunciation is the key to spelling this word correctly.

Examples

library	li′brar·y	Pronounce the *r* in the second syllable.
science	sci′ence	An exception to the *ie* rule.

Another good idea is to write the correct spelling of your problem words on cards. To study the words take a card and look closely at the letters and their order. Then turn the card over and write the word on a piece of paper. Check what you have written with the spelling on the card and keep practicing until you have mastered each problem word.

4. Learn the basic spelling rules.

Students sometimes discover that many of their spelling errors occur because they do not understand the basic spelling rules. For example, they may frequently misspell words containing *ie* or *ei* combinations. Learning the rules for these words will help eliminate errors with many words. Even though there are some exceptions to the rules, mastering them saves time and worry.

5. Use the *see-say-write* method.

For difficult words that follow a rule, use the *see-say-write* method. Most good spellers see a word in their mind before they spell it. Try to develop this habit, perhaps picturing the word written on a mental blackboard. Then say the word to yourself but be certain you pronounce it correctly. Finally write the word and compare your spelling with the correct one. With practice this technique will become automatic.

Troublesome Words

The words in the following sections can be especially troublesome. Two words may be pronounced the same but spelled in different ways. The words *here* and *hear*, for example, sound the same but are not spelled alike. Other words, such as *quite* and *quiet*, look similar and have some identical letters but have different meanings. The next sections will deal with words that create spelling problems when they are confused. Learn to distinguish between these words and practice using them correctly.

1. **accept** — Ali **accept**ed the photography assignment from *Ebony* magazine. [*Accept* is a verb meaning "to receive with consent."]
2. **except** — **Except** for a lunch break, the teens worked all day on the neighborhood cleanup project. [*Except* is a preposition meaning "with the exclusion of."]

3. **advice** — Many customers at the lumberyard seek Nan's **advice** about grades of wood. [*Advice* is a noun.]

4. **advise** — As a member of the National Youth Administration, Mary Bethune **advise**d President Roosevelt about issues relating to youth. [*Advise* is a verb.]

5. **affect** — The severe snowstorm **affect**ed the bus schedule and caused minor delays throughout the city. [*Affect* is a verb.]

6. **effect** — Anita's recent hearing loss had no **effect** on her successful career as a florist. [The noun *effect* is a consequence or result.]
We could not **effect** a change in their attitudes. [The verb *effect* means "to accomplish."]

7. **aisle** — Because he had to leave early, Mario chose a seat on the **aisle**. [An *aisle* is a passageway.]

8. **isle** — Can you help me locate the **Isle** of Wight on this map? [An *isle* is a small island.]

9. **allowed** — My father never **allowed** us to eat between meals. [*Allow* is a verb meaning "to permit."]

10. **aloud** — The unruly child talked **aloud** during Ms. Howard's report. [*Aloud* is an adverb meaning "with sound."]

11. **altogether** — Since the estimate was **altogether** too expensive, the Medley family remodeled the bathroom by themselves. [*Altogether* means "entirely."]

12. **all together** — When the parts were finally **all together,** the result was very impressive. [*All together* means "all in one place."]

13. **capital** — Alfredo's speech raised some interesting questions about **capital** punishment.
With great determination but little **capital,** Mary Bethune founded the school that became Bethune College. Springfield is the **capital** city of Illinois. [*Capital* has several meanings, but it is not the building in which a legislature meets.]

14. **capitol** — On what street in Springfield is the **Capitol** located? [*Capitol* is the building in which a legislature meets.]

Exercise 1

Write out the following sentences, choosing the correct word from the pair given in parentheses. Use the preceding sentences to aid you. Underline the word you choose.

Example

a. The recycling center is open every day _______ Sundays and holidays. (accept, except)

a. The recycling center is open every day except Sundays and holidays.

1. Dr. Theodore Lawless conducted research that had a significant _______ on the treatment of leprosy. (affect, effect)

2. Last week Miss Washington _______ our class to visit her art supply store. (allowed, aloud)
3. After we washed the walls, the apartment seemed _______ different. (all together, altogether)
4. Shouldn't this proper noun be written with a _______ letter? (capital, capitol)
5. When they were _______ in the gym, the girls discussed the strategy for Thursday's game. (altogether, all together)
6. In his youth Arthur Mitchell walked sixty-five miles to _______ an office job with Booker T. Washington. (accept, except)
7. The small fire caused needless injury because the _______ were filled with boxes that hindered fire fighters. (aisles, isles)
8. _______ for a little rust, which can be scrubbed off, these pots and pans are in excellent condition. (accept, except)
9. Marian Anderson's concert in front of the Lincoln Memorial deeply _______ the crowd that gathered to hear her. (affected, effected)
10. Palm trees and exotic plants bordered the beaches of the tropical _______. (aisle, isle)
11. W. E. B. Du Bois _______ his students to gain a liberal education and to learn about the arts. (adviced, advised)
12. I followed my grandfather's _______ about the sauce, and the spaghetti turned out perfectly. (advice, advise)
13. This summer Jenny is working as a senate page in the state _______. (capital, capitol)
14. Mrs. Nobura's article suggests that the government's antipollution laws are _______ too liberal. (all together, altogether)
15. If you repeat these theorems _______, you will remember them better. (allowed, aloud)

15.	**clothes**	Luis packed sturdy **clothes** and a warm jacket for his little brother's camping trip. [*Clothes* refers to wearing apparel.]
16.	**cloths**	Painters use drop **cloths** to protect floors while they are painting. [*Cloths* are pieces of fabric.]
17.	**des′ert**	The artist Georgia O'Keeffe has lived in the New Mexico **desert** for many years. [A *dés·ert* is a dry, sandy region.]
18.	**de·sert′**	The child would not **desert** the sick puppy even for a moment. [*De·sért* is a verb meaning "abandon."]
19.	**dessert**	For **dessert** Mr. Okimi served tiny slivers of fresh cantaloupe. [*Dessert* is the final course of a meal.]
20.	**dyeing**	**Dyeing** the Easter eggs in onionskins made them a rich, deep brown. [*Dyeing* involves changing the color of an object.]

21. **dying** Dr. Elizabeth Kübler-Ross has done important research on death and **dying**. [*Dying* is the process of losing life.]

22. **formally** At today's press conference Margarita Suarez will **formally** announce her candidacy for the state legislature. [*Formally* means "according to conventions, or properly."]

23. **formerly** **Formerly,** scientists considered the atom the smallest particle of matter. [*Formerly* means "previously, in the past."]

24. **hole** According to some astronomers a black **hole** is created when a massive star collapses into itself. [A *hole* is an opening.]

25. **whole** Every other week, my mother deposits her **whole** check in our savings account. [*Whole* means "complete or entire in itself."]

26. **knew** I **knew** you'd enjoy this biography of Willie Mays, so I bought it at the rummage sale. [*Knew* is past tense of the verb *to know.*]

27. **new** Dolores is the **new** dispatcher at the police department. [*New* means "recent, not old."]

28. **lead** Walt Goldenberg, who is an electrician, will **lead** a workshop on the repair of small appliances. [The verb *lead* means "to go first."]

29. **led** The green stripes on the floor of the corridor **led** us straight to the eye clinic. [*Led* is the past tense of *lead.*]

30. **lead** Drawing or sketching requires a pencil with a soft **lead.** [*Lead* is a metal.]

31. **later** Richmond Barthe first produced paintings; **later**, by chance, he discovered his great talent for sculpture. [*Later* means "more recently."]

32. **latter** Mary read through magazines and a book on landscaping but found the **latter** more helpful because of its detailed explanations. [The *latter* is the second of two.]

33. **loose** Our instructor suggested we wear **loose** clothing when we practice yoga exercises at home. [*Loose* means "not securely attached, not tight."]

34. **lose** Because she did not want to **lose** the interest on her savings, Hiromi planned her withdrawals carefully. [*Lose* means "to suffer loss."]

Exercise 2

Write out the following sentences and supply the correct word from the pairs given in parentheses. Use the preceding sentences to guide you. Underline the word you choose.

Example

a. Because of his first-aid training, Julio _______ exactly what to do when Chris burned his hand. (new, knew)

a. Because of his first-aid training, Julio knew exactly what to do when Chris burned his hand.

1. The _______ tree was covered with small, sweet-smelling blossoms. (hole, whole)
2. In France _______ is often a selection of cheeses and fruit. (desert, dessert)
3. We will need some clean _______ to use when we wash the windows. (clothes, cloths)
4. _______ the kitchen curtains to match the _______ wallpaper was a good solution and cost very little. (Dyeing, Dying) (knew, new)
5. Alex Haley, _______ known only as a journalist, is now most noted for his book *Roots*. (formally, formerly)
6. Dad's begonias seemed to be _______ until he moved them to a shadier spot. (dyeing, dying)
7. Evenings in the _______ are always quite chilly, so be sure to bring some warm _______. (desert, dessert) (clothes, cloths)
8. Tulip bulbs should be planted in a _______ about eight inches deep. (hole, whole)
9. Each party's candidate is _______ nominated at a national convention. (formally, formerly)
10. Soon after he learned to play the trumpet, Louis Armstrong _______ that he wanted to be a musician. (knew, new)
11. Until she retired and moved out of state, Miss Osaka _______ the city's youth orchestra. (lead, led)
12. Ralph Bunche was a college professor, a university president, and _______ a mediator for the United Nations. (later, latter)
13. Pottery finished with a _______ glaze should not be used for cooking or eating. (lead, led)
14. As a youth Edward Ellington was talented both in art and music, but he chose to pursue a career in the _______. (later, latter)
15. If we repair the _______ lid on this chest, it will be an excellent place to store records. (loose, lose)

35.	**passed**	This African tale has been **passed** down through all the generations of our family. [*Passed* is a form of the verb *to pass*.]
36.	**past**	Jim spent the **past** summer with his father in Connecticut. [*Past* means "ended, bygone or beyond."]

37. **peace**	I enjoy the **peace** of the city just before dawn. [*Peace* is a state of security and quiet calm.]
38. **piece**	Marinating this **piece** of meat will make it more tender. [A *piece* is a part of something.]
39. **plain**	My grandmother helped me sew a **plain** corduroy cover for this bed. The Angus cattle grazed contentedly on the **plain**. [The adjective *plain* means "clear" or "simple." The noun *plain* refers to a flat area of land.]
40. **plane**	We used a **plane** to smooth the edge of the wood. Ms. Chin teaches calculus and **plane** geometry. We could not see our apartment building from the **plane**. [The word *plane* may refer to a tool, a flat surface, or an airplane.]
41. **principal**	The **principal** discussed the school cleanup campaign with members of the student council. Carelessness was the **principal** cause of the fire. [The noun *principal* refers to the head of a school; the adjective *principal* means "main or most important."]
42. **principle**	Martin Luther King, Jr. was devoted to the **principle** of nonviolent reform. [A *principle* is a basic truth, standard, or rule of behavior.]
43. **quiet**	After Mr. Marshall put the children to bed, the house seemed very **quiet**. [*Quiet* means "silent, still."]
44. **quite**	My friend is **quite** relaxed about discussing her disability with new acquaintances. [*Quite* means "to a great extent."]
45. **shone**	Susan polished the kitchen floor until it **shone**. [*Shone* is a form of the verb *to shine.*]
46. **shown**	The animated film that our class helped produce will be **shown** next week. [*Shown* is a form of the verb *to show.*]
47. **their**	Jellyroll Morton, King Oliver, and Kid Ory are remembered for **their** contributions to the development of American jazz. [*Their* is the possessive form of the pronoun *they*.]
48. **there**	We expected the bus to be late, but **there** was no delay. [*There* is used to begin a sentence or to indicate a location.]
49. **they're**	**They're** doing a report on solar energy for science class. [*They're* is a contraction of *they are.*]

Exercise 3

Write out the following sentences and choose the correct word from the pairs given in parentheses. Use the definitions and explanations you have just read to help you. Underline the word you choose.

Example

a. To ______ the impatient children Dad told them several stories and taught them a word game. (quiet, quite)

a. To quiet the impatient children Dad told them several stories and taught them a word game.

1. Through its vivid imagery this poem suggests that ______ is a state of mind. (peace, piece)
2. The door closed tightly after she used a ______ to shave off a tiny ______ of wood from its bottom edge. (plain, plane) (peace, piece)
3. Pride ______ in Mr. Lee's eyes as he talked of his wife's success in journalism. (shone, shown)
4. My uncle's decisions seem always to be based on the ______ of consideration for others. (principal, principle)
5. The plants Nick raised from seed added life to the room and made it seem less ______ . (plain, plane)
6. In the ______ the book exchange at the youth center has been ______ successful. (passed, past) (quiet, quite)
7. ______ grandfather helped them refinish this antique dresser. (Their, There, They're)
8. ______ is no reason to drive to the post office, since it's only a short walk. (Their, There, They're)
9. Now that she has retired, my neighbor's ______ interests are canoeing and camping. (principal, principle)
10. Since the cafeteria is not very ______ , ______ studying in the biology room. (quiet, quite) (their, there, they're)
11. In the last moments of the city marathon, my brother ______ the other runners one by one. (passed, past)
12. Before you plant the geranium, put these small ______ of rock in the bottom of the pot. (peaces, pieces)
13. This book on finances has ______ me several ways to improve the family budget. (shone, shown)
14. Mrs. McMahon taught art until she became the assistant ______ at the high school. (principal, principle)
15. In 1950, Ralph Bunche received the Nobel ______ Prize for his efforts as a United Nations mediator. (Peace, Piece)

50.	**threw**	My grandfather **threw** a fast pitch that caught the batter unaware. [*Threw* is a form of the verb *to throw*.]
51.	**through**	**Through** the doors of this school pass some of the city's finest students. [The preposition *through* means "from one side to another."]
52.	**waist**	To avoid injuring your back, bend at your knees, not at your **waist**. [The *waist* is the middle part of the body.]

53. **waste** — Rather than **waste** the leftover meat, Dad cooked a good casserole.
Great care must be taken to dispose of nuclear **waste** safely. [The verb *waste* means "to squander." The noun *waste* refers to refuse or unused material.]

54. **weak** — Because I skipped breakfast, I felt **weak** and tired all morning. [The adjective *weak* means "feeble, not strong."]

55. **week** — Our neighbor, who just turned sixty, will graduate from Middleton College next **week**. [A *week* is seven days.]

56. **weather** — Even in poor **weather**, Cecilia and Tom run two miles every morning. [*Weather* refers to the climate outdoors.]

57. **whether** — We don't know **whether** Anita is still working at the foundry or is on her way home. [*Whether* is a conjunction expressing doubt.]

58. **who's** — **Who's** the new receptionist in your aunt's real estate office? [*Who's* is a contraction of *who is* or *who has.*]

59. **whose** — She is the biologist **whose** research proved most accurate. [*Whose* is the possessive form of *who.*]

60. **your** — What does **your** job at the processing plant involve, Mrs. Ortega? [*Your* is the possessive form of *you.*]

61. **you're** — I see **you're** reading Robert Frost's poetry. [*You're* is a contraction of *you are.*]

Exercise 4

Write out the following sentences and choose the correct word from the pairs given in parentheses. Use the explanations and definitions you have just read to help you. Underline the word you choose.

Example

a. This skirt is a little tight at the ______ , but I'm sure I can alter it. (waste, waist)

a. This skirt is a little tight at the <u>waist</u>, but I'm sure I can alter it.

1. Rosa ______ several handfuls of sand on the campfire to be sure it was completely out. (threw, through)
2. Adding ______ stripping around doors and windows is one way to cut the ______ of energy. (weather, whether) (waist, waste)
3. We don't know ______ the new energy legislation will be passed by the state legislature. (weather, whether)
4. Please don't use ______ ladder again until we fix this ______ rung. (your, you're) (weak, week)
5. ______ replacing Thomas as the team's business manager? (Who's, Whose)
6. Bill, ______ sister is already at West Point, will start his studies ______ next fall. (who's, whose) (there, their)

7. _______ careful analysis of the contractors' estimates for the new school, Mrs. Michaels uncovered several ways the school board could save money. (Threw, Through)
8. In his speech here last _______, the Reverend Jesse Jackson emphasized the need for education and discouraged students from dropping out of school. (week, weak)
9. Repairing the torn elastic in the _______ of _______ pants wasn't difficult. (waist, waste) (your, you're)
10. Since he lived in Chicago, _______ sure to find information about Nelson Algren at the Chicago Public Library. (your, you're)

Review Exercise A

In each of the following sentences, select the correct word from the pair given in parentheses. Write out each of the sentences and underline the word you choose.

Example

a. Ann Petry's book about Harriet Tubman made the _______ come alive for our class. (passed, past)

a. Ann Petry's book about Harriet Tubman made the past come alive for our class.

1. _______, my grandfather taught second grade, but he has a _______ job as supervisor of the day-care center. (Formally, Formerly) (knew, new)
2. In the Soviet Union writers who criticize the government are sometimes not _______ to publish _______ work. (allowed, aloud) (their, there, they're)
3. _______ the efforts of John Hope, the colleges of Atlanta University were unified into a strong educational system. (Threw, Through)
4. Ms. Amoto translates both Russian and Spanish but prefers to translate the _______. (later, latter)
5. _______ for proofreading the final draft, I have finished my short story. (Accept, Except)
6. Could I have a small _______ of melon for _______? (peace, piece) (desert, dessert)
7. W. E. B. Du Bois _______ students to gain a liberal education rather than just vocational training. (adviced, advised)
8. The batik process involves knotting and _______ fabric to create an artistic pattern. (dyeing, dying)
9. _______ great-aunt has _______ us everything we need to know to reupholster the couch. (Your, You're) (shone, shown)
10. As a safety precaution the manager tacked down the _______ rug in the _______ of the theater. (loose, lose) (aisle, isle)

11. Nuclear _______ are usually stored in containers lined with _______. (waists, wastes) (lead, led)
12. Ted tried mending the _______ in his jacket with a small _______ of _______ fabric. (whole, hole) (peace, piece) (plain, plane)
13. Although she started with very little _______, Mrs. Cortez has made her hardware business _______ successful. (capital, capitol) (quiet, quite)
14. _______, Dr. Ernest Just produced two books and over sixty important scientific papers. (All together, Altogether)
15. Ms. Wong's exhibit shows that she has mastered the _______ of photography. (principals, principles)
16. _______ planning to raise a garden this summer on one of the small plots the city rents to people. (Their, There, They're)
17. _______ that she was called "Moses," I _______ little about Harriet Tubman when I started the report. (Except, Accept) (knew, new)
18. _______ essay as a _______ is good, but why don't you improve the introduction? (Your, You're) (hole, whole)
19. According to the newspaper the volcano's eruption will _______ our _______ for several years. (affect, effect) (weather, whether)
20. Our _______ should _______ the student council's proposal for a bicycle safety clinic. (principal, principle) (accept, except)

Learning Spelling Rules

The following spelling rules cover the spelling of hundreds of words. If you master these rules, you will avoid some of the most common spelling mistakes, but remember that there are some exceptions to these rules. Once you know each rule, work on learning the few words that are exceptions.

1. If a word is spelled with an *ie* or *ei* combination that sounds like the long *e* in *feet*, write *ie* except after the letter *c*.

   ie sounded as long *e*: belief, thief, yield, retrieve
   ei after *c*: conceive, ceiling, receipt
   Exceptions: neither, either, leisure, sheik, seize

2. If a word is spelled with an *ie* or *ei* combination and is not pronounced with an *e*, write *ei*, especially when the sound is a long *a*, as in *weigh*.

   ei sounded as long *a*: weight, reign, eight
   ei not sounded as long *e*: heir, foreign, sleight
   Exceptions: mischief, friend, handkerchief, science

3. Words with a syllable that is pronounced like the word *seed* are spelled in one of the following three ways.

1	*2*	*3*
supersede	exceed	accede
	proceed	concede
	succeed	intercede
		precede
		recede
		secede

Supersede is unique; it is the only word in English with a *-sede* ending. Notice that only three words *(exceed, proceed* and *succeed)* are written with a *-ceed* ending. However, because these three words are used so often, you should concentrate on learning the correct ending for this threesome. All the other words with a *seed* sound have a *-cede* ending.

Exercise 5

Write out each of the following sentences and add the correct *ei* or *ie* combination or ending for the *-seed* sound that is missing. Underline the complete word. Your teacher may ask you to explain which rule you used to decide the correct spelling.

Example

a. Although she lost her sight in an accident, our n__ghbor continued to study and completed her degree in computer programming.

a. *Although she lost her sight in an accident, our neighbor continued to study and completed her degree in computer programming. (Neighbor* has a long *a* sound.)

1. In the course of her research about her family, Amy discovered that her great-grandfather was a Blackfoot ch__f.
2. Who ate the last p__ce of the homemade bread I made?
3. During his l__sure time Eduardo works as a volunteer at the children's hospital.
4. On his job as a welder, Mr. Jones must wear a metal safety sh__ld.
5. We should __ther close the windows or turn off the air conditioner.
6. Inspecting d__sel engines is one aspect of her job Rosaria really enjoys.
7. Karim gained valuable exper__nce from his br__f summer job for a gardener.
8. The w__ght of the baby beluga whale at the county zoo now ex__s 300 pounds.
9. After the drum and bugle corps demonstration, the parade pro__ed down Michigan Avenue to the park.
10. Thurgood Marshall suc__ed in winning over thirty of the civil rights cases he tried before the Supreme Court.

11. I can't inter___ for you; you must earn the job on your own merits.
12. My aunt won't con___ that Uncle Ramon is a better cook than she is.
13. The positive response to our n___ghborhood clothing drive far ex___ed our expectations.
14. Dan says his re_____ing hairline makes him feel truly an adult.
15. Concerns about the fertilizer plant's effect on the local environment super_____ed consideration of the jobs it would bring to the community.

4. If a prefix is added to a root word, the spelling of the root word does not change.

PREFIX	+	ROOT	
il	+	legible	George had trouble typing the report because his employer's handwriting is almost *illegible*.
un	+	certain	If you are *uncertain* about the safety of the wiring in your new house, have an electrician check it.
re	+	commend	I *recommend* Mrs. Sakudo; she is an excellent accountant.

5. If a root word ends in an *e*, drop the *e* before adding a suffix that begins with a vowel.

ROOT WORD	+	SUFFIX	
care	+	ing	Ricardo is a responsible and *caring* first-grade teacher.
believe	+	able	*Maud Martha* is an interesting and *believable* novel about a young girl growing up in Chicago.
please	+	ant	Jenni's grandfather took her on a *pleasant* canoe trip down the Fox River.

If the suffix begins with a consonant, do not drop the final *e* from the root word.

ROOT WORD	+	SUFFIX	
care	+	less	Proofreading will help you eliminate *careless* errors.
hope	+	ful	She is *hopeful* that their relationship will last.

Exercise 6

Write out each of the following sentences. For each blank, insert the correctly spelled combination of the root word and suffix given in parentheses. Underline the new word.

Example

a. Maria is especially _______ when she uses the radial arm saw. (care + ful)

a. Maria is especially careful when she uses the radial arm saw.

1. Mrs. Garcia showed us how to eliminate the _______ on our stereo system. (interfere + ence)
2. Ali read the _______ _______s for the new toaster before he used it. (safe + ty) (regulate + ion)
3. Dr. Ernest Just, a Harvard University professor, was an early _______ of cell structure. (investigate + or)
4. Mrs. Hopkins is the _______ bus driver in our school district. (nice + est)
5. As a child, Duke Ellington often composed skillful musical _______s from his piano lessons. (arrange + ment)
6. My grandfather skillfully mended the rip in the tent _______. (line + ing)
7. To save money Mrs. Lowery repaired the garbage _______ herself. (dispose + al)
8. James Weldon Johnson's _______ prepared him to teach, but he achieved fame as a _______. (educate + ion) (write + er)
9. Ralph Bunche attended the University of California on an _______ scholarship but worked as a janitor in order to pay his other expenses. (athlete + ic)
10. On her first job as a journalist, Ann Petry wrote _______s for a Harlem newspaper. (advertise + ment)

6. If a root word ends with a *y* preceded by a consonant, change the *y* to *i* before adding a suffix that begins with a letter other than *i*.

ROOT WORD	+	SUFFIX	
worry	+	ed	The whole neighborhood *worried* until it was learned that none of the large maple trees would be cut down when the street was widened.
hasty	+	ly	If you shop *hastily*, you will not shop wisely.

Note: Words that end in a *y* preceded by a vowel usually do not change their spelling when a suffix is added.

joyful (joy + ful) coyest (coy + est) boyhood (boy + hood)

If the suffix begins with an *i*, do not drop the final *y*.

ROOT WORD	+	SUFFIX	
worry	+	ing	*Worrying* is not a solution to the problem.
study	+	ing	As a carpenter's apprentice, Felicia combines *studying* and working.

Exercise 7

Write out the following sentences. In each blank, insert the correctly spelled combination of the root word and suffix given in parentheses. Be sure to underline the word you form.

Example

a. The cold, ______ wind blew in our faces as we walked to school. (pity + less)

a. The cold, pitiless wind blew in our faces as we walked to school.

1. Mrs. Kim ______ about her horticulture exam, but she did very well on it. (worry + ed)
2. Although he didn't catch any fish, Dad ______ the ones Mom caught. (fry + ed)
3. My great-aunt is always at her ______ when she starts one of her remodeling projects. (merry + est)
4. ______ my brother does all the family laundry, but this week he's out of town. (Ordinary + ly)
5. Wayne, the ______ pinochle player I know, is teaching me to read the Braille on his deck of cards. (lively + est)
6. JoAnne is the most ______ and ______ student in the new nursing class at the hospital. (rely + able) (industry + ous)
7. Lou talked ______ about the committee's plans for the African Folk Arts Festival. (happy + ly)
8. The ______ of the politician's speech did not impress the audience, who wanted clear answers for their questions. (wordy + ness)
9. Role-playing scenes from the book made our small group discussions much ______. (easy + er)
10. The President believes the nation's ______ on a limited supply of energy will lead to serious problems. (depend + ence)

7. Double the final consonant before a suffix beginning with a vowel when both of the following conditions exist: (a) the word has one syllable, or the accent is on the last syllable, and (b) the word ends in a single consonant preceded by a single vowel.

ROOT WORD	+	SUFFIX	
plan	+	ing	*Planning* the truck's route is part of Mr. Smith's job. [one-syllable word]
for·get′	+	ing	*Forgetting* to feed the cat was a thoughtless mistake. [accent is on the second syllable]

If both of these conditions are not met, the final consonant is not doubled before a suffix.

cook	+	ed	Jane *cooked* a Mexican meal for us last week. [a single consonant preceded by a double vowel.]
con·fer′	+	ence	Margarita thought the *conference* on soil conservation was valuable. [The accent shifts to the first syllable when a suffix is added.]

Exercise 8

Write the correct words for the following root-and-suffix combinations. Your teacher may ask you to explain why you did or did not double the final consonant. Use a dictionary to check the accent in words of more than one syllable.

Examples

a. hit + er — *a. hitter (one-syllable word)*

b. dif·fer + ence — *b. difference (accent on the first syllable)*

1. shop + er
2. con·trol + ed
3. hop + ed
4. soak + ing
5. plan + ed
6. re·fer + al
7. de·vel·op + ed
8. re·mit + ance
9. con·fer + ed
10. shov·el + ed

Noun Plurals

Forming noun plurals causes spelling problems for some students. For information and exercises about noun plurals, see the section Using Nouns on pages 335–341.

Mastery Exercise A

The following sentences contain many of the words you have studied in this chapter. Write out each sentence and correct the spelling of any misspelled word. Underline the words you correct.

Example

a. In thier sereis of six tennis matches, my grandfather beat Dad soundly.

a. In <u>their</u> <u>series</u> of six tennis matches, my grandfather beat Dad soundly.

1. Officer Wilson said she new the rober had triped the alarm in the dark building.
2. As the whether got hoter, we tryed harder to stay cool.
3. With no encouragment but much determineation, Jan Matzeliger spent ten years inventing a machine to improve shoe manufactureing.

4. The inhalator that Garret A. Morgan designed in the early twentyth century allowed rescue workers to save people traped in mines.
5. G. W. Carver worryed that the South's relyance on only one crop, cotton, would led to disaster.
6. Carver's continueous research showed farmers that the soybean and peanut could be profittable crops.
7. Although Carver was less fameous as a painter, his paintings were exhibitted at the Columbian Exposition in 1893.
8. Carver's acheivements were so valueable that he was asked to make an appearrance before Congress.
9. Puting insulateion under the cieling might reduce you're heating expenses.
10. Senator Nancy Chen is one of the President's advicors on foriegn affairs.
11. Mrs. Varga's investigateion will probablely led to several changes in the city's traffic plan.
12. They're uneasyness about rideing in a small plain was unfounded.
13. Howard spent nearly a weak shoping for the sillyest presents he could find for his freind.
14. Keepping a journal will give you a collection of createive ideas for you're compositions.
15. Do you know weather the biding at the auction was heavyer this morning?

Mastery Exercise B

Thirty words that you have studied are misspelled in the following paragraphs from a student's report. Write the correct spelling for each word on a sheet of paper numbered 1–30.

As a teenager in Connecticut, Ann Petry thought of her writeing only as an amuseing hobby for her liesure time, since she planed to attend college and become a pharmacist. She studyed at the University of Connecticut and graduateed in 1934. Then she worked for a breif time in her family's drugstore, but gradually writing became her principle interest.

In 1938 she marryed George Petry and moved to New York City. Their she excepted a job with a Harlem newspaper to gain some expereince as a reporter. In the begining Ann simplely wrote ads and sold advertiseing copy. She also was involved in organizeing a nieghborhood recreational program for poor children.

In 1943 she succeded in haveing one of her stories published in *Phylon*. Latter three of her stories appearred in the magazine *Crisis*, and an important editor adviced her to write a novel. Mrs. Petry adaptted some of the short peaces she had writen about the greifs, joys, and troubles of her knew friends on 116th Street in Harlem. She new if she put these altogether, they might work as a small book. Within two years Mrs. Petry had finished *The Street*, her first novel. The book's popularity exceded all her hopes.

22 Punctuation

The Uses of Punctuation

In general, punctuation works in four ways: to separate, to link, to enclose, and to show omission.

1. *To separate*

   Use a mark of punctuation that separates when you want to keep certain ideas or elements in your writing from running together. For example, a period (.) separates one sentence from another. A comma (,) separates items within a sentence.

   > Tom campaigned vigorously, stirred enthusiasm, and won. In fact, he won in a landslide.

2. *To link*

   A linking mark of punctuation joins ideas or words together. For example, a hyphen (–) joins parts of compound words.

   > Mary is my sister–in–law.

3. *To enclose*

   Quotation marks (" "), for example, are usually used in pairs to enclose a speaker's exact words.

   > "I'll cook some chili," Sam announced.

   Note that quotation marks have a dual role. They enclose a direct quotation and, at the same time, separate the speaker's words from the rest of the sentence.

4. *To show omission*

An apostrophe (') always shows that a letter or letters have been omitted from a word, as in the contraction *didn't.*

Jackie didn't call. [Jackie *did not* call.]

Exercise 1

Write out each of the following sentences. Beneath each sentence indicate whether the **boldface** mark or marks of punctuation separate, link, enclose, or show omission.

Example

a. Let's go to the antique show. It opens tomorrow.
a. apostrophe—shows omission; period—separates

1. Early American patchwork quilts followed certain patterns. One pattern is called "courthouse steps."
2. "That quilt is in flawless condition," the man argued.
3. We bought a couch, a rug, and two lamps.
4. I hope my grandmother hasn't thrown out her oak rocking chair.
5. Where's my coat? I left it here, but now I can't find it.
6. The Shakers were very inventive. Did you know they invented the clothespin?
7. "I can't imagine that old table is valuable," Louise laughed.
8. Linda bought some fabric, quickly cut out panels, and made curtains for her kitchen.
9. Wouldn't you love a big, soft, comfortable sofa?
10. My sister-in-law keeps her books in an old library cabinet. Those cabinets aren't made anymore.

The Period

The *period* is used as an end mark to separate sentences or as a mark that shows the omission of letters in abbreviations.

A *declarative sentence* makes a statement.

1. Place a period after a declarative sentence.

It has started to rain.
We wondered when the rain would stop.

An *imperative sentence* makes a command.

2. Place a period after a mildly imperative sentence.

Please wait in line.
Call me tomorrow.

3. Generally, use a period to show that letters have been omitted from some abbreviations.

Dr.	doctor
A.M.	*ante meridiem* [before noon]
P.M.	*post meridiem* [after noon]
Sr.	senior
Mr.	mister
Sgt.	sergeant
Chas.	Charles

Use a period with some abbreviations (such as *Ms.* and *Mrs.*) that cannot be spelled out.

Note: Do not use a period following the abbreviations for metric units *(5 cc, 20 kg, 100 ml)*, two-letter postal abbreviations for states in addresses *(NJ—New Jersey, CA—California, TX—Texas)*, and for most governmental agencies *(NATO, NASA, TVA)*. In addition, some large corporations have abbreviated their names without using periods, and some other common abbreviations are also written without periods: *CBS, TWA, YWCA, AM, FM, mph, TV.*

Exercise 2

Write out the following sentences, placing periods where necessary. Remember to capitalize the first word in each sentence. Circle the periods you insert.

Examples

a. Mr. Burton is a disc jockey on AM radio he never plays disco music.

a. Mr. Burton is a disc jockey on AM radio⊙ He never plays disco music.

b. Call Jack Wallace, Jr, to see if his party starts at 7 P M.

b. Call Jack Wallace, Jr⊙, to see if his party starts at 7 P⊙M.

1. Dr Walters has a TV in her office in town you can watch it while awaiting your appointment.
2. Mrs Lytton has a job interview tomorrow at Computerage, Inc in Dayton she's applying for a job as a division supervisor.
3. Pour 100 ml of liquid onto the piece of stone according to our professor, Dr A Morton, the stone will turn blue.
4. Carl's uncle works for the FBI he is stationed in St Louis.
5. While in Egypt, Sgt B Lyons visited the Pyramid of Cheops it was built earlier than 2000 B C and is still standing!
6. That toaster is guaranteed for two years send the warranty card to the following address:
   Electrik Ease, Inc
   Product Div
   1500 Genl Robt E Lee Pl
   Atlanta, GA 30336

7. All the recipes in Ms Greene's cookbook have been converted to the metric system instead of saying, "Add 1 oz," the recipe now reads, "Add 28 gr of chocolate."
8. At 10 A M tomorrow "The Humor Hour" will feature the works of S J Perelman and Mark Twain the program's station is 1050 on the AM dial.
9. John Jordan, Jr, used to be in the CIA now he works for IBM.
10. Prof Wm Marks invited us to a lunch and lecture at St Joseph's College his lecture is titled "Life in the American Home in A D 2000," but he may change his topic.

The Question Mark

A question, or an *interrogative sentence,* ends with a question mark that separates it from the sentence that follows.

> Who brought the coleslaw? It's delicious.
> Why didn't you wear a raincoat? It's pouring!

Note: When a question is part of a declarative sentence, it is an *indirect question* and is followed by a period.

> Who broke the statue? [question]
> Eddie wondered who had broken the statue. [indirect question]

The Exclamation Point

An exclamation point indicates strong feeling.

1. Place an exclamation point after a strongly imperative sentence.

> Close the windows! There are bees outside.
> Stop chasing that dog immediately! It's only a puppy.

Remember that a mild imperative can end with a period. An exclamation point shows stronger feeling.

> Please wait for the bell.
> Run quickly!

2. Place an exclamation point after an exclamation.

> Help! I'm falling!
> How happy we are that you'll stay! We love company.
> Watch out! The sidewalk is slippery.

Exercise 3

Write out the following sentences, placing a question mark, an exclamation point, or a period where necessary. Circle the punctuation marks you insert.

Examples

a. Where are the scissors You used them yesterday

a. Where are the scissors? You used them yesterday.

b. Watch out That dog bites

b. Watch out! That dog bites.

1. Hurry Bring some water
2. Why hasn't the package arrived yet When did you mail it
3. Hush There are deer right outside the door
4. Please be seated The show is about to begin
5. Congratulations When was the baby born
6. Mike asked if he had to wear a tie
7. Drive carefully, please Do you know the quickest route
8. Would you like dessert now, or would you rather wait until later
9. Ouch Who left pins on the floor
10. Diane wondered who had ordered the beautiful flowers Was it Allen

---

The Comma

The comma separates words, phrases, or clauses within sentences.

1. Use a comma to separate words or word groups in a series.

We have a dog, three cats, and a parrot.

Our family has lived at the beach, on a farm, and in Boston.

The producers knew they had a hit when the play went smoothly, when the audience cheered, and when the reviewers gave rave notices.

Note: When the last two items in a series are joined by a coordinating conjunction (such as *and* or *or*), a comma precedes the conjunction. When *all* the items in a series are joined by a coordinating conjunction, do not use commas.

For breakfast we had orange juice, bacon and eggs, and toast. [Notice that when items commonly go together—such as *bacon and eggs*—they can be paired as one item.]

After breakfast we took a walk and visited friends and then shopped.

After breakfast we took a walk, visited friends, and then shopped.

2. When two or more adjectives precede a noun, use a comma to separate the adjectives.

A narrow, winding, overgrown path twisted up to the house.

Two small, furry puppies barked incessantly.

Note: Do not use a comma between the last adjective and the noun that follows it. In some instances you should not use a comma between adjectives.

Do not use a comma unless the conjunction *and* makes sense in its place.

Ann cherished her gold wedding ring.
[You would not say "gold *and* wedding ring."]

Larry couldn't part with his faded, worn-out dungarees.

Larry couldn't part with his faded *and* worn-out dungarees.
[The *and* makes sense; therefore, use a comma.]

Exercise 4

Write out each of the following sentences, inserting commas where necessary. Circle the commas you insert.

Examples

a. Sara is allergic to milk eggs and butter.
a. Sara is allergic to milk(,) eggs(,) and butter.

b. Dark threatening clouds rolled by.
b. Dark(,) threatening clouds rolled by.

1. The antique wooden box was filled with old coins rare stamps and valuable jewelry.
2. Eager energetic tourists climbed the staircase in the castle's tower walked to the narrow window and peered out.
3. Mix together the flour water eggs and sugar.
4. The room was filled with lilacs and roses and daffodils; flowers were in pitchers in vases and in baskets.
5. The play's director the star and the producer waited anxiously paced the floor and rushed for the reviews in the morning paper.
6. Every morning Wendy does sit-ups jumps rope and walks on her hands; she has an effective efficient exercise program.
7. My three biggest fears are being trapped in an elevator being chased by a bear and being caught in a fire.
8. Would you rather drive across the country camp in Canada or sail on a freighter on your long summer vacation?
9. Five restaurants two boutiques a pharmacy a hardware store a card shop and a supermarket have rented space at the new mall and expect a busy successful year.
10. Having lived in his house for forty years, the tired lonely man packed his possessions swept the floor and left.

3. Use a comma to separate independent clauses that are joined by the coordinating conjunctions *and, but, or, nor, for, so,* or *yet.*

I locked the car, *but* I foolishly left the windows open.

The car thief had an easy job, *for* the windows were open.

My car was robbed, *and* it was my own fault.

Now I always check my car doors and windows, *so* I don't make the same mistake twice.

Note: In placing commas, watch out for compound verbs. Be certain that the sentence actually has two independent clauses.

Exercise 5

Write out the following sentences, placing commas where necessary. Circle the commas you insert.

Example

a. We were exhausted for we had been driving all day.

a. We were exhausted(,) for we had been driving all day.

1. Herman told a story that was hard to believe but he promised it was true.
2. One day Herman's friend Bert left his office and he absent-mindedly got into the wrong car.
3. Bert started the car and drove off for his key fit in the ignition.
4. The car's rightful owner (Paul) realized his car was missing so he called the police and reported it stolen.
5. Bert soon returned to his office and calmly went back to work for he had no idea that he had driven the wrong car.
6. Paul left work and expected to walk home yet he saw his car parked where he had left it.
7. Paul thought, "Either I've gone crazy and lost my mind or someone has played a trick on me!"
8. Paul was glad to have his car back so he got in and drove off.
9. Paul was immediately arrested for driving a stolen car for he had reported the "theft" to the police.
10. Now Paul never parks on the street near his office nor does Bert ever enter a car without checking the license!

4. Use a comma to separate introductory adverb clauses, introductory participial phrases, and long or successive introductory prepositional phrases from the rest of the sentence.

INTRODUCTORY ADVERB CLAUSES

Before the featured movie began, the audience saw three short films.

When the movie ended, half the audience was asleep.

INTRODUCTORY PARTICIPIAL PHRASES

Exercising every day, Marge lost five pounds easily.

Filled with a sense of adventure, Juan traveled all over the world.

LONG OR SUCCESSIVE INTRODUCTORY PREPOSITIONAL PHRASES

Late in the afternoon on a beautiful spring day, we packed a picnic basket and drove into the country.

In the shop on the corner of Madison Avenue and Sixty-Fifth Street, beautiful winter clothes are on sale.

Note: Short introductory prepositional phrases usually are not followed by a comma unless the comma is needed to make the meaning clear.

After the movie we went to dinner.
[no comma]

In the room above, the baby cried for hours.
[Use a comma so the sentence is not misread "above the baby."]

5. Use a comma to separate some short introductory elements from the rest of the sentence.

Use a comma following mild interjections and the words *yes, no, well, why, still,* and *now* when they introduce a sentence.

No, I'm not leaving.

Heavens, it's cold outside.

Yes, I do want some dessert.

Note: When these words are used as adverbs, they should not be followed by a comma.

Now it's getting dark. [no comma]

Use a comma after the noun of direct address when it appears at the beginning of a sentence.

Julio, when is the soccer match?

Ms. Lauder, I'll finish the assignment by Friday.

Note: A noun of direct address at the end of a sentence is preceded by a comma.

When would you like an appointment, Mr. Clarke?

Introductory transitional expressions such as *however, accordingly, thus, consequently, yet, hence, therefore,* and *besides* are followed by a comma.

Consequently, all shops will be open late on Fridays.

However, the restaurant will close at six o'clock.

Note: A transitional expression at the end of a sentence is preceded by a comma.

I prefer to shop early in the day, however.

In general, place a comma after any introductory expression that would be followed by a pause if you were speaking.

6. Use a comma to separate contrasting words, phrases, and clauses introduced by the word *not.*

   The fund needs money, not good intentions.

   That magazine is published weekly, not monthly.

Exercise 6

Write out the following sentences, placing commas where necessary. Circle the commas you insert.

Example

a. After eating a huge meal Carla stretched out on the sofa and took a nap.

a. After eating a huge meal(,) Carla stretched out on the sofa and took a nap.

1. When America held its Bicentennial celebration cities and towns featured many anniversary events.
2. On the Fourth of July in 1976 thousands of ships sailed around Manhattan.
3. Having set sail from Newport, Rhode Island many old sailing vessels made their way down the East Coast.
4. Yes the Bicentennial generated much patriotic spirit.
5. In Lexington and Concord near Boston people enacted colonial events.
6. Excited by the boats and fireworks huge crowds of people flocked to the water.
7. That boat is really an old ship not a modern replica.
8. Well many people did make money selling Bicentennial souvenirs.
9. Frances I saw you dressed as Betsy Ross in the parade.
10. Still many children had live history lessons during the anniversary celebration.

Review Exercise A

Write out the following sentences, placing periods, exclamation points, question marks, and commas where they belong. Circle the punctuation marks you insert.

Examples

a. Mrs Nunzio Mr Lathrop and Dr Martin spoke at the graduation

a. Mrs(.) Nunzio(,) Mr(.) Lathrop(,) and Dr(.) Martin spoke at the graduation(.)

b. Quick Martha where is the doctor's phone number

b. Quick(!) Martha(,) where is the doctor's phone number(?)

1. Wow My sister just got a job for Rocket Records, Inc and she'll send me free records
2. Dr Collier please send my medical insurance form to my home not to my office at TWA
3. Fill in the forms enclose a coupon and mail everything to this address:
   Capt Clark's Safari Contest
   1435 Mt Hood Dr
   Portland, OR 99305
4. Nevertheless my frayed worn blue sweater is still my favorite of all my sweaters
5. When Prof J Adams announced that class would end at 2 P M everyone applauded
6. Watch out That old creaky chair is shaky and it looks as if it's about to break
7. Although people usually use parsley only for decoration it is rich in vitamin C and tasty
8. John Molinari, Sr, lives in an enormous old-fashioned Victorian house; however he has knocked down walls put in new windows and decorated the house with modern furnishings
9. After a childhood marked by illness Wilma Rudolph went on to become a great athlete; in fact she won Olympic medals
10. Ms March the members of NOW are continuing the fight for women's rights which was begun a century ago by Susan B Anthony Lucy Stone and Elizabeth Cady Stanton
11. Yes I do like herbal teas My favorites are chamomile alfalfa and mint
12. In the middle of the garden in Greenwood Park someone has planted a tree in memory of Sgt L T Taylor
13. Rev March would be able to attend a dinner next week in honor of Dr Burton L Winkler
14. If you want to arrive in Dallas by late afternoon you can take a TWA flight that leaves here at 1 P M
15. A well-informed personable representative from NASA spoke to reporters from NBC ABC and CBS After giving a general outline of the agency's future plans the representative announced the schedule for launching new space probes
16. Ms Tanner airline regulations once allowed each passenger to carry twenty kg of luggage; however the number of pieces of luggage is what matters not the weight
17. In the evening I either listen to FM radio read or watch TV
18. Yes I'm familiar with several books by Dr Seuss Don't your children love them
19. Although we eat turkey at Thanksgiving the first settlers probably ate goose In those early days of the country wild turkeys weren't too tasty

20. Dr Thames knew his rusty dented car wouldn't make it through another winter; thus he went to Best Buy Motors, Inc looked at their selection and bought a new car

When words, phrases, and clauses appear within—or interrupt—the sentence, place a comma both before and after the expression. Paired commas enclose these words, phrases, or clauses and separate them from the rest of the sentence in which they appear.

7. Use paired commas with nouns of direct address when they interrupt the flow of a sentence.

   When, Karen, will the job be finished?

8. Use paired commas with transitional expressions that interrupt the flow of the sentence.

   People left, however, when it began to rain.

Note: Be certain that a phrase is really used as an interrupter.

We'll leave, I hope, before sunrise.	[interrupter]
I hope that we'll leave before sunrise.	[no commas]

9. Use paired commas with contrasting expressions when they interrupt the sentence.

   I like to watch ice hockey, not field hockey, on TV.

Exercise 7

Write out the following sentences, using paired commas where necessary. Circle the commas you insert.

Examples

a. Did you know that Tallahassee not Miami is the capital of Florida?

a. Did you know that Tallahassee, not Miami, is the capital of Florida?

b. The market carries plums only in the summer; strawberries on the other hand are usually available all year.

b. The market carries plums only in the summer; strawberries, on the other hand, are usually available all year.

1. How do you know Ms. Farmer that the store will be open Monday night?
2. A steady diet of balanced meals not a crash diet is the best way to stay thin and healthy.
3. The university's work-study program is based on the theory that on-the-job experience not just classroom training is important.
4. It's unpleasant I imagine to have cats if you're allergic to them.
5. Cantonese food is not spicy; Szechwan food on the other hand is hot.
6. Will the strike be over Mayor by the beginning of next term?

7. Riding a bicycle in fact is good exercise.
8. I have heard Luis that you play tennis well; the tennis camp I think is looking for an instructor.
9. Vacations in my opinion are important for people who work hard.
10. An almanac not an encyclopedia is the best place to find weather predictions.

10. Use paired commas to enclose nonessential phrases and nonessential clauses and to separate them from the rest of the sentence.

Nonessential phrases and *clauses* are those that could be omitted without changing the meaning of a sentence. They are not essential to the main thought conveyed by a sentence.

> The Tyler house, *which is on the corner of Market Street*, is a historical landmark. [nonessential adjective clause]
>
> Barbara Ling, *running the fund-raising campaign*, raised money for the flood victims. [nonessential participial phrase]

In the preceding sentences the phrase and clause set off by commas are not necessary to the meaning of the sentences. Essential phrases and clauses, on the other hand, are necessary to the meaning of a sentence and are not set off by commas.

> The house *that is on the corner of Market Street* is a historical landmark. [The adjective clause *that is on the corner of Market Street* identifies the house and is essential to the meaning of the sentence.]
>
> The woman *running the fund-raising campaign* raised money for the flood victims. [essential participial phrase]

Note: When a nonessential phrase or clause appears at the end of a sentence, use only one comma preceding it.

> My first cat was Tabby, who was gray with black stripes.

11. Use paired commas to enclose nonessential appositives and nonessential appositive phrases that interrupt a sentence.

When an appositive merely explains the meaning of the noun or pronoun to which it refers—and the appositive could be removed without changing the meaning of the sentence—it is nonessential and should be set off by paired commas.

> Dr. Marcus, my dentist, is always busy.
>
> Georgia O'Keeffe, an American painter, has lived in New Mexico for many years.

When an appositive distinguishes the noun or pronoun it explains from other people or things, it is essential and is not set off by commas.

> My cousin Frank and I are good friends. [*Frank* identifies the cousin.]
>
> The movie *Hair* was an adaptation of a Broadway play. [*Hair* identifies the movie.]

Note: When a nonessential appositive appears at the beginning or end of a sentence, one of the paired commas is omitted.

> *A dedicated teacher*, Lynn Evans teaches night courses and summer sessions.
>
> We spent every summer at "Hillside Acres," *our farm in Pennsylvania.*

Exercise 8

Write out the following sentences, placing commas where necessary. Circle the commas you insert.

Examples

a. Frank Townsend my closest friend lives in Burbank.

a. Frank Townsend(,) my closest friend(,) lives in Burbank.

b. The British Museum which is in London houses the original Magna Carta.

b. The British Museum(,) which is in London(,) houses the original Magna Carta.

1. Reruns of *The Mary Tyler Moore Show* which ran on Saturday nights for many years are still shown on daytime TV.
2. Chicago which is located on the shores of Lake Michigan is exceptionally windy in winter.
3. A student who has studied in Paris said that the courses at the Sorbonne which is in Paris are challenging.
4. My friend Lola was in *A Chorus Line* a successful Broadway play.
5. Dr. Alonzo Cruz head of the veterinary hospital complained that his dog won't eat any food that comes from a dog-food can!
6. An avid skier Tommy Ling heads for the slopes every weekend that is cold and snowy.
7. Burnett Sullivan living in Mexico sends a letter every week to his friend who lives in Tucson.
8. Marcella King who has a newborn baby works on her novel when her child naps.
9. My oldest sister Denise has invited me to spend my vacation at her ranch which is in New Mexico.
10. Before we sign the final papers for the house that we want to buy, we must consult our lawyer who will make certain everything is in order.

Commas are also used to separate a variety of items that may occur within a sentence. These conventional uses of the comma do not follow the rule of placing a comma where a pause would occur in speech. Rather, custom and tradition dictate the placement of these commas.

12. Use a comma to separate parts of geographical names and of dates. When dates and geographical names occur within a sentence, use a comma to separate the entire name or date from the rest of the sentence.

We lived in Tucson, Arizona, when I was a child.

Mail your entry card by January 15, 1984, to Big Bargain Sweepstakes, 1375 Los Altimiros Drive, Los Angeles, California 91603.

The Carters were married on Monday, April 12, 1975, in London, England.

Note: In addresses a comma is not used between the street number and the street name, nor between a state and the ZIP code. In dates a comma is not used between the name of the month and the date. A comma is not necessary when only a month and year are given in a date *(October 14, 1947,* but *October 1947).*

13. Use a comma to separate a person's name from a degree, title, or affiliation that follows it.

Louisa Maya, Ph.D.

Jack Jackson, Sr.

Joel Walters, RAF

Note: When used in a sentence, the degree or title is also followed by a comma.

Professor Julia Lewis, Ph.D., was named head of the history department.

Exercise 9

Write out the following sentences, placing commas where they belong. Circle the commas you insert.

Example

a. The movie was filmed on location in Paris France and in Venice Italy.

a. The movie was filmed on location in Paris, France, and in Venice, Italy.

1. Although Columbus Day really falls on Wednesday October 12 people celebrate it on Monday October 10.
2. Amy Weng Ph.D. had announced the opening of her office on Monday September 22 1984 at 1033 Park Avenue Plainfield New Jersey.
3. I was born on August 20 1950; it was a Tuesday that year.
4. Joel Parks Sr. and Wendy Miller were married in October 1980; in fact, they were married on October 29 1980.
5. Kendra Slywyn M.D. went to college in San Diego California and to medical school in Chicago Illinois.
6. Last month's snowstorm was the worst to hit Philadelphia Pennsylvania since the blizzard of February 1948.
7. Please send your cards to Emma Peel M.D. 121 Carpenter Street South Orange New Jersey 07079.

8. On January 31 1978 we were in Paris France and about to leave for Vienna Austria.
9. Although Martha was born in Atlanta Georgia, she grew up in Seattle Washington.
10. Did you send the letter to 101 West 78th Street New York New York 10024 or to 101 East 78th Street New York New York 10021?

Review Exercise B

Write out the following sentences, placing commas where necessary. Circle the commas you insert.

Example

a. How long Senator will it be before the day-care program for which we have lobbied so long goes into effect?

a. How long(,) Senator(,) will it be before the day-care program(,) for which we have lobbied so long(,) goes into effect?

1. Olana a beautiful house on the Hudson River was built by Frederick Church who was an American painter.
2. Joanna Perez who married my uncle had a baby girl on Tuesday January 4.
3. Solar heating which can be highly effective is of interest to people who are looking for new sources of energy.
4. Martin Cohen M.D. a doctor in Coral Gables Florida collects cobra venom which is useful in treating some medical ailments.
5. A local doctor Julio Martinez has become interested in acupuncture which has been used in China for centuries.
6. There is an enormous arch visible from the air in St. Louis Missouri. It was built I believe by the architect Eero Saarinen.
7. The Indianapolis 500 which is held in Indianapolis Indiana each year is the most famous auto race in the United States.
8. The ancient Egyptians not the Aztecs wrote on papyrus which grew along the banks of the Nile.
9. On March 12 1978 David's older brother Nick opened a photography gallery at 3137 Larchmont Road East Lansing Michigan 48823.
10. I suggest Mr. Curtis that you take the bus not drive your car.
11. The Royale Bakery in fact is not far from my office; the bakery which is very good moved to its new location in May 1979.
12. I think that Marcy's house which was built by Frank Lloyd Wright is spectacular; its location on the other hand is not convenient.
13. Yes the wedding is at the bride's home at 756 November Trail Weston Connecticut; the reception however is at the Punch Lounge.

14. The pin that you lost Martha wasn't valuable; I don't have another one like it however.
15. The books at the auction are interesting; one book for instance is autographed by Charles Dickens who is one of my favorite writers.
16. Lacrosse which is played in many schools today is an old sport; early settlers in America learned the sport I believe from the native Americans who were playing it here.
17. Doctor should I come back for a checkup in June 1984, or can I wait until September? I already have an appointment I believe for September 15 1984.
18. My favorite aunt who teaches at the university studied film with the woman who directed *Girlfriends* which was a successful movie.
19. Botulism which is caused by a deadly bacillus grows in canned goods that aren't prepared at the right temperature. Large companies as a matter of fact take many precautions against botulism.
20. Camphor Diane will protect your clothing from moths; however Mrs. Minton who used to own a cleaning shop advises using plain soap which has no strong smell.

The Semicolon

The *semicolon*, a stronger mark of punctuation than the comma, signals a more definite break in thought—a longer pause. In fact, you might think of the semicolon as a "weak period." There are four main uses for the semicolon.

1. Use a semicolon to separate closely related independent clauses that are not joined by a coordinating conjunction.

   One of the twins has traveled all over the world; the other rarely leaves home.

   August is the busiest month at the beach; it's easier to find a place to stay in July.

2. Use a semicolon between independent clauses when the second clause begins with a transitional expression such as *therefore, however, besides, in fact*, or *for example.*

   This was Sue's first trip to Wyoming; *in fact*, it was her first trip west of the Mississippi.

   Everyone had already seen the local movie; *therefore*, we decided to go bowling.

3. Use a semicolon to separate items in a series when one or more of the items contains commas.

   The judges for the dog show were Dr. Martin Hall, a veterinarian; Mary Stewart, a trainer; and Dr. Alma Lopez, a researcher.

   Drivers examinations will be given on Monday, June 12; Monday, June 19; and Wednesday, June 21.

4. Use a semicolon between independent clauses when commas appear within the clauses.

We had wanted to drive from Colorado to Arizona; but since a blizzard made driving hazardous, we decided to fly.

Having studied all week, Linda entered the exam confidently; she still found the test challenging, however.

Exercise 10

Write out the following sentences, using semicolons where necessary. Circle the semicolons you insert.

Example

a. Jogging is good exercise however, runners should be careful about overexertion.

a. Jogging is good exercise(;) however, runners should be careful about overexertion.

1. José loved to cook in fact, he planned to open a restaurant.
2. Local artists contributed work to the benefit the show was a great success.
3. The international menu included couscous, a dish from North Africa, Peking duck, a Chinese delicacy, and borsch, a Russian beet soup.
4. The actors' contracts will be up in June nevertheless, they will star in the show next year.
5. Large dogs effectively scare most intruders however, big dogs need a lot of space.
6. Before Jack entered the Boston Marathon, he ran every day as a result, he was able to run the distance in good time.
7. After receiving her Ph.D., Joanne hoped to teach but she had trouble finding a job.
8. Alan Alda starred in last week's episode of *M*A*S*H* he also wrote and directed it.
9. The collection of French paintings will travel to museums in Philadelphia, Pennsylvania Atlanta, Georgia Dallas, Texas and Phoenix, Arizona.
10. National parks are crowded with tourists in the summer visitors must therefore make reservations in advance.

The Colon

When a *colon* separates elements within a sentence, it calls attention to the word, phrase, or list that follows it.

1. Use a colon to separate a list of items from an introductory statement,

which often contains the words *as follows, the following, these,* or a number.

Be sure to pack *the following* items**:** a toothbrush, a pair of slippers, a robe, and a towel.

These are the main ingredients in the salad**:** cabbage, bean sprouts, water chestnuts, and snow peas.

The hotel offers *four* types of accommodations**:** room with bath, suite, private villa, and cabin.

Note: The introductory statement preceding a colon should be a complete sentence. Do not use a colon between a verb and its direct object or after a preposition.

An asterisk (*) denotes a sentence with a feature that is not part of Edited Standard English.

*For the hike you should pack: walking shoes, insect repellent, and a hat.

For the hike you should pack the following items**:** walking shoes, insect repellent, and a hat.

2. Use a colon to separate an introductory statement from an explanation, an appositive, or a quotation.

His adventures had earned him an apt nickname**:** "Fearless Herman."

Heed these words of advice**:** "Look before you leap."

The colon should also be used in three conventional situations. These uses have grown from custom and tradition.

3. Use a colon to separate a salutation from the body of a business letter.

Dear Lois Nathan**:** Dear Dr. Navarro**:**

4. Use a colon to separate hour and minutes in expressions of time.

12**:**15 P.M. 7**:**30 this evening

5. Use a colon to separate chapter numbers from verse numbers in references from the Bible.

Job 4**:**9 John 5**:**15

Exercise 11

Write out the following sentences, placing colons where necessary. Circle the colons you insert.

Examples

a. The concert begins at 8 30 P.M.

a. The concert begins at 8(:)30 P.M.

b. When I saw the Missouri, I understood its nickname "Big Muddy."

b. When I saw the Missouri, I understood its nickname(:) "Big Muddy."

1. Sitting at the typewriter, John wrote these words "Now is the time for all good men to come to the aid of their party."
2. The YWCA offers three courses in physical fitness yoga, calisthenics, and dance exercise.
3. Have you ever read any of these classic mysteries *The Moonstone*, *The Murder of Roger Ackroyd*, or *Five Red Herrings?*
4. Everyone knows Louis Armstrong's nickname "Satchmo."
5. Rev. Thomas referred us to these readings John 13 1, Job 12 3, and Proverbs 12 5.
6. Which of these proverbs makes more sense "Out of sight, out of mind" or "Absence makes the heart grow fonder"?
7. Both of these old movies start at 6 15 tonight *The Lady Vanishes* and *Laura.*
8. Bob always gives the same advice "Look wise and seem mysterious."
9. There's only one word to describe a Midwestern winter freezing.
10. Which of the following presents would you prefer a book, some records, a wallet, or a calculator?

The Dash

The *dash* is similar in use to the colon. However, you might think of the dash as pointing backward, since it calls attention to the word or word group that precedes it.

1. Use a dash to separate an introductory series or thought from the explanation that follows.

   Making the swimming team—that was my main goal.
   Decorations in red and black—these colors gave the party a Chinese flavor.

2. Use a dash to separate a sudden change in thought.

   I could daydream all day about the beach—oh, the phone is ringing.
   First we'll have dinner and then go out—I wonder what I'll cook.

3. Use a dash to show omission of words in dialogue. The dash shows a break in a person's speech.

   "What is—?" Susan began.

When the elements separated by a dash occur within a sentence, use dashes in pairs to enclose the word or group of words and to separate them from the rest of the sentence.

4. Use paired dashes to enclose a phrase or clause that shows a sudden break in thought or a sharp change in tone.

Bert finished the exam—can you believe it?—in two hours.
We have all dreamed—now admit it—of being famous stars.

5. Use paired dashes to enclose appositive phrases that require a stronger pause than that for commas. Use paired dashes for parenthetical phrases containing commas.

People hurried indoors when the northeaster—a severe storm with heavy wind and rain—swept over the island.

Tim's dogs—a spaniel and a terrier—barked loudly.

Some science courses—biology, for example—require laboratory as well as classroom time.

Two companies—Langor, Inc., and Smith, Jones, and Wells—have merged.

Exercise 12

Write out the following sentences, using dashes where necessary. Circle the dashes you insert.

Example

a. Roast beef sandwiches yes, they're my favorite.

a. Roast beef sandwiches⊖yes, they're my favorite.

1. Just run the distance that was the thought in my mind during the marathon.
2. Grandma Moses you won't believe this first began to paint when she was over seventy years old!
3. "You never let me," Jackie began.
4. The ski slope a steep, bumpy hill was not for beginners.
5. "Devil's Face" they didn't give the mountain that name without good reason.
6. Patience that's the main requisite for birdwatching.
7. Joanie said that Bob wherever he is would bring some cassettes.
8. Has anyone ever heard Sarah she just cut a record sing old blues songs?
9. Visitors to Notre Dame a beautiful cathedral in Paris, France are always overwhelmed by its stained-glass windows.
10. I love the beach so much that I could spend a month make that two months just living by the ocean.

Parentheses

Used to enclose elements that interrupt a sentence, *parentheses* show a stronger break than do commas or dashes. In fact, words in parentheses are set aside from the rest of the sentence. Parentheses enclose items that are really additional information.

A few foods (oranges and apricots) are rich in potassium.

Mrs. King's plant shop (exotic plants) opens next week.

Mozart (1756–1791) was a child prodigy.

Exercise 13

Write out the following sentences, using parentheses where necessary. Circle the parentheses you insert.

Examples

a. French and Spanish both Romance languages have words that are similar.

a. French and Spanish (both Romance languages) have words that are similar.

b. Would you like a glass of H_2O water?

b. Would you like a glass of H_2O (water)?

Notice that the punctuation mark appears outside the parentheses at the end of a sentence.

1. Mercury the planet nearest to the sun is too hot to sustain life as we know it.
2. The school is on Summer Street the street near the library and is convenient to public transportation.
3. In order to learn calligraphy the art of beautiful handwriting, you must have patience.
4. Dorothea Lange 1895–1965 was an American photographer who documented the life of migrant farmers during the Depression.
5. The members of NATO North Atlantic Treaty Organization signed a new trade agreement last week.
6. Add two cups of brown sauce see directions for brown sauce on page 234 to the vegetables.
7. Wall Street the home of the New York Stock Exchange took its name from a defense wall that had been erected there in 1653.
8. Tokyo the capital of Japan has a very low crime rate.
9. The bazaar was filled with decorative items made of brass an alloy of copper and zinc.
10. Having decided that her wardrobe was dull, Janice bought purple shoes and a magenta a reddish-purplish hue skirt.

Review Exercise C

Write out the following sentences, using colons, semicolons, dashes, and parentheses where necessary. In some instances you could correctly use more than one mark of punctuation, depending on the meaning you want to convey. Circle the punctuation marks you insert.

Example

a. The San Diego Zoo one of the best in the country has established a breeding colony for koala bears they're becoming extinct.

a. *The San Diego Zoo—one of the best in the country—has established a breeding colony for koala bears (they're becoming extinct).*

1. The speakers at the career seminar include Ms. Nancy Juarez, Chief of Nurses at Montgomery Hospital Eileen Nash, a marketing expert at Douglass Products, Inc., Paul Swain, owner of Fairprice Market and Leonard Fisch, professor of English at Caler State.
2. The Art Students League offers the following courses Figure Drawing 1, Still Life 302, and Advanced Watercolor Techniques a difficult course.
3. When school was over, Alicia like everyone else applied for a summer job at the bakery but she had applied too late.
4. Pablo Picasso 1881–1973 was a dominant influence on twentieth-century art many other artists imitated his work.
5. These are my plans for the summer working for two months as a clerk, taking a typing course at night, and taking a two-week vacation that's the best plan.
6. Martina got the highest mark she said she hardly studied on the biology exam.
7. They're predicting rain let's go fishing anyway.
8. The oldest restaurant in town Lawler and Travis is renovating its main dining room however the owners say they will not raise their prices.
9. These are the contest rules no essay can be longer than 500 words all entries must be postmarked no later than 12 00 P.M., Saturday, July 29 all entries must be original.
10. Of course I know Jane in fact, she's my best friend.
11. When Phillip saw the letter that began "Dear Occupant," he knew it was junk mail yet he opened it anyway.
12. I spent last weekend with my grandmother she's eighty-three years old in Baltimore we laughed all weekend.
13. My bracelet I'm not sure where I put it was made in the 1930s I love it.
14. Marta has named her chili appropriately "Five-Alarm Fire."
15. The bus it was supposed to have been an express made seven stops New York, Newark, New Brunswick, Trenton the longest wait, Philadelphia, Wilmington, and Baltimore.
16. Since Joan expected cold weather, she packed a warm hat, a bulky sweater, woolen socks, scarves, and mittens unfortunately, she couldn't close her suitcase.
17. For years Fred's restaurant had served the best desserts in town he deserved his title "The King of Cake."

18. John Dickson Carr the mystery writer also wrote stories under another name Carter Dickson.

19. The water near the Caribbean island of Bonaire the water is always warm there is filled with exotic fish and beautiful coral it's a popular area for snorkeling.

20. The Parthenon built between 447 B.C. and 432 B.C. has been standing for many centuries now, however, the air pollution in Athens is damaging the marble.

The Hyphen

The *hyphen* is used to link the parts of some compound words. It also links the part of a word begun on one line with the part finished on the next. Although some general rules govern the use of the hyphen, make it a habit to consult a dictionary if you are unsure about how to hyphenate any given word.

1. Use a hyphen to link the parts of compound nouns that begin with the prefixes *ex-*, *self-*, *all-*, and *great-* or that end with the suffix *-elect.*

ex-president	great-grandfather
self-image	president-elect
all-star	

2. Use a hyphen to link the parts of compound nouns that include a prepositional phrase.

man-of-war	son-in-law

Many compound nouns are not hyphenated. Some are written as two separate words *(tennis court);* others are written as a single word *(baseball).*

3. Use a hyphen to link prefixes with proper nouns or adjectives.

mid-January	pre-Columbian
anti-American	un-American

4. In general, use a hyphen to link the parts of a compound adjective when it precedes the noun.

short-term lease	thought-provoking idea
two-ton truck	300-page book

Note: Do not use a hyphen if the adjective follows the noun. *(The idea was thought provoking.)*

5. Use a hyphen to link parts of a fraction used as an adjective.

one-half fare	two-thirds full

Note: You may omit the hyphen when the fraction is used as a noun. *(One fifth of the seats were taken.)*

6. Use a hyphen to link the parts of a compound number between twenty-one and ninety-nine.

   twenty-five dollars — thirty-nine steps

7. Use a hyphen when a word is divided at the end of a line.

   After a long search we found the missing con-
   tainer of coins.

   Judy had cleaned the room and must have misplaced the box.

Note: Place a hyphen only between syllables; one-syllable words cannot be hyphenated. A word should not be hyphenated if doing so would leave just one letter on either line. A word that already contains a hyphen should be divided only at the hyphen.

An asterisk (*) denotes a sentence with a feature that is not part of Edited Standard English.

*I beg you not to le-
ave. — [The word *leave* should not be hyphenated.]

*I am sad whenever you go a-
way. — [The word *away* should not be hyphenated.]

*The audience was a pro-Ran-
ger group. — [The term *pro-Ranger* should be divided only at its hyphen.]

Do not hyphenate abbreviations at the end of a line.

*The movie begins at 8 P.-
M. — [Do not hyphenate P.M.]

Exercise 14

Write out each of the following sentences, using hyphens where necessary. Circle the hyphens you insert.

Example

a. The baby always takes a mid afternoon nap.

a. The baby always takes a mid⊖afternoon nap.

1. My brother in law doesn't like to swim in the ocean; he is afraid of being stung by a man of war.
2. We always heard the same words of advice from our great grandmother: "Self respect is most important."
3. Jim's grandmother is a self reliant woman; she lives in the Midwest for one half of the year and travels south in mid December for the winter.
4. An ear splitting explosion tore through the just finished building.

5. The ex President's speech stirred a lot of pro American feeling; heart warming applause filled the room.
6. Since almost two thirds of the class had previously taken a course in pre Columbian art, the professor skipped some of the basic material.
7. Melissa's down to earth attitude calmed everyone during the crisis.
8. The artists of the post Impressionist era are now much admired; in the 1890s, however, the members of that just formed group were not well respected artists.
9. Charles raced off on his ten speed bike and finished his paper route in record breaking time.
10. Gloria's well worn jeans were paint stained and patched, so she discarded them with a halfhearted toss.

The Apostrophe

The *apostrophe* is used to show the omission of letters or numbers, to form the plural of letters or numbers, and to form possessive nouns.

1. Use an apostrophe to show that a letter or letters have been omitted from contractions.

can**'**t	cannot
isn**'**t	is not
I**'**ll	I will
o**'**clock	of the clock

2. Use an apostrophe to show that the first two numbers have been omitted from a year.

'80 **'**76

3. Use an apostrophe to form the plural of letters, numbers, and words.

He**'**s in his late 20**'**s.

There are four *i***'**s in *Mississippi.*

Do not use so many *and***'**s and *but***'**s when you speak.

Note: No apostrophe is needed when making centuries and decades plural.

What will the 1980s be like?
Photography was invented during the 1800s.

4. Add an apostrophe and an *s* to make a singular noun possessive.

Bill	Bill**'***s* car
house	house**'***s* yard

5. To show possession add an apostrophe and an *s* to a plural noun that does not end in *s*.

women	women'*s*
children	children'*s*

6. When a plural noun ends in *s*, add only an apostrophe to show possession.

dogs	dogs'
windows	windows'

For a more complete look at the possessive forms of nouns and pronouns, see pages 342–344 and 354–355.

Note: The possessive forms of personal pronouns do not have apostrophes. By using an apostrophe with a personal pronoun, you are showing omission, not possession.

its	[possession]
it's	[contraction of *it is*]
whose	[possession]
who's	[contraction for *who is*]

Exercise 15

Write out the following sentences, using apostrophes where needed. Circle the apostrophes you insert.

Example

a. I cant believe hes in his 40s.

a. I can't believe he's in his 40's.

1. I can always recognize Mrs. Martins handwriting by the way in which she dots her *is*.
2. People dont believe were nearing the end of the 1900s; the 90s will be quite a decade!
3. Marshas car is fast, but it cant be as fast as Mikes.
4. Its amazing that the Smiths dog can wag its tail so quickly.
5. How many *ns* are in Jennifers name?
6. Carlos grandfather—whos in his 90s—cant walk quickly, yet his mind is as quick as yours or mine.
7. Havent you heard the expression "Mind your *ps* and *qs*"? Whats its meaning?
8. When Juanita was in her 20s, she thought people in their 40s were old; now shes older and has changed her mind.
9. Theyve promised to be home by the childrens curfew, which is 12 oclock.
10. The Winklers car is from the 1950s; its in great condition.

Quotation Marks

Quotation marks, which usually occur in pairs, enclose a word or group of words and separate them from the rest of the sentence.

Use quotation marks to enclose a speaker's or writer's exact words.

"I'll be a Yankee fan forever," Julie asserted.

The hitchhiker's sign read, "Denver or Dubuque."

"Why does it always rain," Nicole asked, "on my birthday?"

Notice that in the last example sentence the direct quotation is interrupted by the words *Nicole asked.* The second part of the quotation does not begin with a capital letter because it is not a new sentence. Use a capital letter to begin each new quotation and each new sentence within a quotation.

For more information on the use of capital letters and quotation marks, see page 604.

Note: Use quotation marks only to enclose a speaker's exact words. Do not use quotation marks in an indirect quotation.

"Where's the party?" Jim asked.	[direct quotation]
Jim asked where the party was.	[indirect quotation]

A direct quotation is often separated from the rest of the sentence by commas. In some instances a question mark or an exclamation point is used with quotation marks. The following rules will tell you how to place marks of punctuation used with quotation marks.

1. Place commas and periods inside closing quotation marks.

   "I hope the movie ends soon," whispered Jake.

   Julio replied, "It will be over in five minutes."

2. Place colons and semicolons outside closing quotation marks.

   Lewis calls his cat "The Craziest Feline in Georgia"; however, he's never seen my cat.

   Two reasons explain why the class voted Janice "Most Likely to Succeed": she's smart and she works hard.

3. Place question marks and exclamation points inside the closing quotation marks if just the quotation is a question or an exclamation. If the whole sentence is a question or an exclamation, place the marks outside.

   Jean asked, "Where's my coat?"

   Do you want to read a story called "A Year in the Rain"?

   Jack could only utter, "Watch out!"

   "Sit down!" Judy yelled.

4. Use quotation marks to enclose the titles of short stories, essays, short poems, songs, television programs, magazine articles, and parts of a book.

Have you ever read Hawthorne's story "The Ambitious Guest"?

Joan Didion's essay "The White Album" is an interesting piece on the 1960s.

The Bee Gees' hit song "Saturday Night Fever" has sold millions of copies.

An article entitled "Early American Weather Vanes" (from *Antiques* magazine) supplied much of the information for Chapter 12, "Folk Art," in our book on American art.

5. Use quotation marks to enclose nicknames and slang expressions.

Benny Goodman was called "The King of Swing."

In the 1950s "pad" and "groovy" were popular expressions among the "beat generation."

Exercise 16

Write out the following sentences, using quotation marks where needed. Circle the quotation marks you insert.

Example

a. Linda Ronstadt's hit songs, such as Heat Wave and Blue Bayou, have earned her this title: Superstar.

a. Linda Ronstadt's hit songs, such as "Heat Wave" and "Blue Bayou," have earned her this title: Superstar.

1. Many people were horrified when Elvis Presley first appeared on television and sang Jailhouse Rock.
2. Who will win the New Hampshire primary? Neil asked.
3. Pedro said that the weirdest movie he had ever seen was based on Shirley Jackson's *The Haunting of Hill House*; he shivered just remembering when Julie Harris said, Whose hand was I holding?
4. Did you know that dogs and cats can't see colors? Mitzi asked. Then she added, Even so, I know my dog's favorite color is red!
5. The following stores have been listed as Best Bets: Benjamin Buzz Burn's Discount Center and The Bargain Hunter.
6. Denise wrote the article Household Hints, which appeared in *Living* magazine; the first hint reads, Use club soda to remove stains from clothes or carpeting.
7. I have a friend, Lena said, who is a fabulous tennis player. She has won every state tournament this year.
8. Three famous monarchs of Russia were Peter I, known as The Great; Catherine II, also known as The Great; and Nicholas II, who was the last Russian czar.
9. Did you ever see the painting by Monet, Penny asked, that hangs in the Metropolitan Museum of Art?
10. Was Lon Chaney called The Man of a Thousand Faces? I just read about him in the essay Horror Greats.

Single Quotation Marks Use single quotation marks to enclose a direct quotation that occurs inside another quotation. Use single quotation marks to enclose titles normally enclosed in double quotation marks when these titles occur within a direct quotation.

> Meg queried, "Who said, 'To be or not to be'?"
>
> Ivan complained, "I just listened to Bob Dylan's song 'Positively Fourth Street' and didn't understand the words."

Writing Dialogue When you write the words said by two or more people having a conversation, you write *dialogue*. The exact words of the speakers are enclosed in quotation marks. Usually the speakers are identified by "words of saying"—*Janet said, cried Tom, Lisbeth wondered, asked Janet.* These "words of saying" are not enclosed in quotation marks and are often separated from the quoted material by commas.

> "I am studying medicine," Lisa stated proudly.
>
> Lee cheered, "We're going to win!"
>
> "Please bring my sweater," José said, "and my scarf."

1. If a question mark or an exclamation point occurs where one of these separating commas should be used, omit the comma and use the question mark or exclamation point to separate the quoted material.

   > "Don't be late!" Bill warned.

2. When writing dialogue, begin a new paragraph whenever the speaker changes.

   > "I think the city's budget for snow removal is too large," Jessica argued. "The money could be better used in other ways."
   >
   > "You're mistaken," John countered. "If the city is unprepared for a big storm, a heavy snow would cripple it. Look what happened during the winter of '79!"
   >
   > Victoria was unconvinced. "Well, I just disagree."

3. Sometimes, a direct quotation runs for more than one paragraph. When this happens, use quotation marks at the beginning of the quotation, at the beginning of each subsequent paragraph, and at the end of the entire quotation. (Notice that this is one situation in which quotation marks are not used in pairs.)

   > Kim began, "People just use too much energy. Fuel has now become an expensive and increasingly less available item, and we must adjust our life styles.
   >
   > "At one time the fuel supply seemed endless. All of us surrounded ourselves with more and more energy-using devices: big cars, electric gadgets for

the home, electric heaters, and so on. Now electricity is too expensive, and the supply is dwindling.

"The problem is not insurmountable. Americans will simply have to slow down their life style. Soon we might all be bicycling to work, wearing thermal clothes in winter, and eating by candlelight."

Review Exercise D

Write out the following sentences, using hyphens, apostrophes, quotation marks, and single quotation marks where necessary. Circle the punctuation marks you insert.

1. Won't the President elect campaign with his brother in law Pamela asked.
2. In Hoboken theres a diner that advertises late night snacks for road weary travelers.
3. Professor Bank has been giving the same half baked lecture since the 30s, Mitchell complained.
4. Ive read a bizarre short story called The Landlady, Martinas mother said. Its an extremely odd tale, she continued.
5. Dogs respond to a whistles high pitched tone; its a highly effective way of summoning them.
6. New Yorks buses and subways charge one half fare on Sundays; the special fares are in effect from 12 oclock Saturday until mid Sunday.
7. Will you accept a part time job if a full time position isnt available queried Mrs. Lundoff.
8. After the advertising company had launched its hard sell campaign, its clients sales skyrocketed Bert exclaimed.
9. Heres the reason for the so called Gold Fever: the all powerful dollar weakened, gold prices soared, and people with get rich quick hopes bought and sold gold.
10. Janice asked, Havent you heard Leroy—nicknamed Satchel—Paiges advice on staying young? He said, Dont look back. Something might be gaining on you!
11. Noahs a jack of all trades when it comes to sports, Lisa said. She added, Hes just been named to the all star team in baseball.
12. Ive just finished reading Chapter 12, Award Winning Recipes from Hollywoods Stars, in my mother in laws cookbook, Lois said. Some of the dishes sound mouthwatering.
13. Americas national anthem, The Star Spangled Banner, is difficult to sing; its tune is hard to carry.
14. Theres always a long line at the self service pumps at Morrisons Garage because gas is cheaper at those pumps; even Lucys great grandfather, whos eighty two years old, waits in line to serve himself.

15. Alicias short story about dieting, Confessions of an Ex Heavyweight, seems to be a long term project, remarked Karen, because shes been working on it for three quarters of a year.

16. The Andersons house, which is on Floridas west coast, is called Gulf Gardens; its well landscaped gardens face the sea.

17. The psychiatrist suggested, You need to improve your self image. You might try reading the essay How to Feel More Confident by L. Barker; its full of confidence building hints.

18. Peters morning snack—eaten every day at 11 oclock—consists of freshly squeezed juice, two hard boiled eggs, well buttered toast, and half a grapefruit.

19. Dan exclaimed, Ive never seen anything as amazing as these stunts by the aviator Daredevil Dan: double loop spins, one after the other, in his two winged, hand painted plane. He will be the most famous aviator of the 1980s, he assured us.

20. During World War II the Germans secret messages were sent by the Enigma cipher machine Donald explained, but their once secret code was broken by the Allies.

Mastery Exercise A

Write out the following paragraphs, using punctuation where necessary. Circle the marks of punctuation you insert.

Without a shadow of a doubt the all American sport is baseball nicknamed The National Pastime. Its appeal the game originated in the US has now spread beyond our borders for example the Japanese have enthusiastically embraced the game.

Baseball was probably invented by Abner Doubleday 1819–1893 in 1839. During the rest of the 1800s the sport underwent changes and the addition of well defined rules. Its popularity was immediate and soldiers played baseball during the Civil War. In 1869 the first professional team the Cincinnati Red Stockings played big time baseball had its start.

Each year in mid October the World Series only footballs Super Bowl has the same popularity captures the attention of thousands of fans. According to the rules of the World Series the team that wins four games wins the title a seven game series fires excitement. High drama creating a tension filled stadium surrounds the deciding game. One team has won twenty one championships the Yankees. Who can forget the Yankees hard won victory over the Dodgers in 77

Baseball heroes are honored in the Baseball Hall of Fame in Cooperstown New York. Immortalized there are players such as Ty Cobb Stan the Man Musial Roberto Clemente and Hank Aaron.

Professional baseball is serious business on the other hand anyone can play the game. Its equipment requirements are few a bat a ball and a glove. Moreover you need some players and some space in which to play dont worry about having the regulation ninety feet apart bases. Then you are ready to play ball!

Mastery Exercise B

Write out the following dialogue, using punctuation where necessary. Circle the punctuation marks you insert.

Movies seem so simple John said when you watch them on the screen. I bet however that things dont always go smoothly behind the scenes!

Im sure youre right Paulette agreed. There must be Im sure problems among the cast who surely disagree now and then problems with the budget which I imagine is always too small and pressures about the deadline. Although the audience only sees the results I know problems must start with the casting. Werent there some well known problems with filming *Gone with the Wind* the film classic of the 30s

Yes I believe there were said John When they were choosing the stars the producer wanted Bette Davis I think Im right about this to play Scarlett O'Hara. She was under contract with another studio however so the producer had to find someone else.

Luis added Heres another example of a movie that had casting problems *Casablanca.* Did you know that the leading roles which were played by Ingrid Bergman and Humphrey Bogart were originally intended for other stars He continued Only Bogey not anyone else could have said these famous words Heres looking at you kid.

Were taking Mrs Ortegas film course which meets at 400 P M on Monday Wednesday and Friday Paulette offered. We thought wed film a short story for our final project and we were considering Willa Cathers The Sculptors Funeral however I hope we dont have too many problems! Because we have such a tight schedule the problems wont go on forever she continued. The film has to be finished for the final project which is due on Friday June 19 1984.

Good luck! Luis shouted and waved goodbye. Youll be busy!

23 Capitalization

Learning to Capitalize

The rules of capitalization that follow indicate the uses of capitals in Edited Standard English. By following these rules when you write, you increase the likelihood that your meaning will be readily understood. For example, consider the following sentences.

> Let's meet at the store on Elm Street at 6:30.
> Let's meet at The Store at 6:30.

In the first sentence above, *the store* means a shop on Elm Street; when capitalized, *The Store* refers to a specific shop, which is named "The Store." The meaning of the sentence changes when the words *the store* are capitalized.

Capitalization That Sets Off Groups of Words

An important use of capitalization is to set off groups of words.

1. Always capitalize the first word of a sentence.

A capital letter immediately signals a new sentence. By capitalizing the first word of each sentence, you separate that sentence from the one that precedes it.

An asterisk (*) denotes a sentence with a feature that is not a part of Edited Standard English.

> *The freeways are convenient. during rush hours, however, traffic creeps along these crowded highways.
>
> **T**he freeways are convenient. **D**uring rush hours, however, traffic creeps along these crowded highways.

2. Capitalize the first word of a direct quotation.

Capitalize the first word of a direct quotation, even if the quotation is a fragment.

> "**Y**ou're a fabulous swimmer," Jana exclaimed.
>
> "**I**t takes a lot of practice," Shelley said. Then she laughed and admitted, "**A**nd strong arms!"

Note: When a direct quotation is interrupted, capitalize the word that begins the quotation but not the one that begins the second part of the quotation.

> "**I**t takes a lot of practice," admitted Shelley, "and strong arms!"

Exercise 1

Write out each of the following sentences, inserting capital letters where necessary. Underline the words you capitalize.

Examples

a. many animals are now endangered species. their habitats have been destroyed.

a. Many animals are now endangered species. Their habitats have been destroyed.

b. "zoos are helping to preserve some species," Len explained. he added, "the zoos try to duplicate the animals' natural environment."

b. "Zoos are helping to preserve some species," Len explained. He added, "The zoos try to duplicate the animals' natural environment."

1. "have you ever played backgammon?" Luke asked.
2. "no, I haven't," Alicia replied, "but I'd like to learn."
3. backgammon is easier than chess. you can learn the basics much more quickly.
4. "i prefer backgammon because the games are quicker," Joan offered.
5. most checkerboards have a backgammon board on the back. have you noticed that?
6. "so that's what that board is," Paul remarked. "can you use the checkers to play?"
7. because it involves throwing dice, backgammon is half skill and half luck.
8. "you move pieces quickly around the board," Sheila explained, "and at the same time try to block your opponent's pieces."
9. "a good throw of the dice can help you out," Jill explained. "that," she added, "is where the luck comes in."
10. "watch out!" Amanda warned. "once you begin playing you can go on for hours."

3. Usually capitalize the first word in a complete line of poetry.

   (Capitalization in poetry sometimes varies with the poet's style.)

   Two ears and but a single tongue
   By nature's laws to us belong.
   The lesson she would teach is clear:
   Repeat but half of what you hear.

4. Capitalize the first word, the last word, and all other important words in the title of a work of art.

This rule applies to the titles of books, chapters, stories, magazines, poems, plays, movies, newspapers, musical works, paintings, sculptures, and television shows and series. Unimportant words are prepositions and conjunctions with fewer than five letters.

Breaking Away is a delightful movie about teenagers.
Anne of the Thousand Days is a movie about Anne Boleyn.
"**T**he **D**estructors" is a short story by Graham Greene.

Exercise 2

Write out the following sentences, capitalizing the titles according to the rules you have learned. Underline the words you capitalize. (Titles of books and other works of art that are *italicized* in print should be underlined in handwriting. Underline these titles twice when you capitalize them.)

Example

a. *star wars* and *the invasion of the body snatchers* are both science fiction movies.

a. Star Wars *and* The Invasion of the Body Snatchers *are both science fiction movies.*

1. The song "as time goes by" from the movie *casablanca* has become a classic.
2. The Broadway musical *west side story* is based on Shakespeare's *romeo and juliet.*
3. Ms. Harris would rather listen to any opera, like *the magic flute*, than listen to popular music, like the Beatles' song *when I'm sixty-four.*
4. Did you ever hear Judy Garland sing "somewhere over the rainbow" from *the wizard of oz?*
5. I love the "march of the tin soldiers" from *the nutcracker.*
6. The book *summertime*, which tells the history of many American resorts, talks about Atlantic City in Chapter 2, "by the sea."
7. The rights of apartment tenants are well explained in an article titled "how to get the most from your lease," which appeared in *new york* magazine.

8. Two of my favorite essays in Joan Didion's book *the white album* are "quiet days in malibu" and "in the islands."
9. Did you ever see the "chuckles the clown" episode on *the mary tyler moore show?*
10. The scenic Hudson Valley is captured in paintings such as Weir's *view of the highlands from west point* and Johnson's *off constitution island.*

Capitalization That Sets Off Single Words

Capital letters are used for proper nouns and proper adjectives. A *proper noun* is the name of a specific person, place, animal, or thing; a *proper adjective* is an adjective formed from a proper noun. The following rules are for capitalizing proper nouns.

5. Capitalize the names of specific people.

Jackie, **A**nita, and **R**aoul won prizes.
Pauline **C**ohen is my best friend.

6. Capitalize a title that precedes, or takes the place of, a person's name, as in direct address.

Judge Marks spoke to the witness.
When, **J**udge, will you speak to the witness?
Marcia wrote an interesting paper on **G**eneral Patton.

Note: Capitalize the words *President* and *Vice President* only when they precede a person's name or when they refer to the highest government offices.

President Kennedy was a charismatic figure.
The **P**resident will address the nation on Tuesday.
The vice president of the student council announced the committees.

7. Capitalize words that show family relationships when they precede a person's name or when they are used in place of someone's name.

Aunt Edith just opened an antique shop in Philadelphia.
Where did you put the scissors, **G**randfather?

Note: Do not capitalize words that show family relationships when they are preceded by a personal pronoun.

I would like you to meet my mother.

8. Capitalize the abbreviation for a person's name or title.

Dr. Jaffee is a good dentist.
Ms. Helbrun's brother is John Helbrun, **J**r., who runs the biggest department store in town.

Exercise 3

Write out the following sentences, using capital letters where necessary. Underline the words you capitalize.

Examples

a. Yesterday joanne collier invited my brother to a party.
a. Yesterday Joanne Collier invited my brother to a party.

b. When, doctor, do you expect the nurse to return?
b. When, Doctor, do you expect the nurse to return?

1. Students enjoyed professor yen's course even though he was the strictest professor at the university.
2. The senator, juan cortes, used to live next door to my aunt, mrs. nickels.
3. Martin mandez, jr., looks just like his father.
4. Would it be all right, mother, if joanna and I spent the weekend at aunt grace's?
5. My sister is doing research with dr. adams, who is a well-known heart specialist.
6. My grandfather wrote a letter to the president to complain about inflation; the vice president answered.
7. Irene's father, paul dodge, sr., said that judge wainscott is an extremely fair judge.
8. Did you hear, mother, that the president has asked our senator to join his cabinet? senator jakes has accepted.
9. My friend barbara has invited aunt alice to dinner.
10. The members chose miss peng and rev. johnson to represent them on the panel; the first meeting is at governor gray's office.

9. Capitalize the names of specific places.

We flew over the **G**rand **C**anyon in **A**rizona during our flight to **S**an **D**iego.
Is **L**ake **M**ead in **N**evada?
The corner of **H**ollywood and **V**ine is a famous **H**ollywood intersection.
The **A**mazon **R**iver flows through dense jungle in **B**razil.

Note: Capitalize the names of compass directions only if they refer to a specific region or are part of an address.

Three blocks north on Broadway is **W**est Forty-sixth Street.
Carmen is from the **S**outh and isn't used to cold, **N**orthern winters.
Ellen lives in a small town in the northwest corner of South Dakota.

10. Capitalize the names of buildings, institutions, monuments, businesses, and organizations (and the abbreviations of organizations).

New **Y**ork **U**niversity is one of several colleges located in New York City.
The **B**allet **F**olklorico from Mexico will appear next weekend in Philadelphia at the **A**cademy of **M**usic.
Carlos works for **IBM** in a new building near the campus of **C**ornell **U**niversity.

11. Capitalize the names of nationalities, religions, races, and languages. The proper adjectives formed from these nouns are also capitalized.

Two **F**rench students visited our school.
Our **M**oroccan guide spoke **E**nglish, **F**rench, and **A**rabic.
Many **A**mericans love **C**hinese food, especially when it's spicy!

12. Capitalize the abbreviations A.D., B.C., A.M., and P.M. Note that abbreviations for measurements (*kg, cm, oz., lb.*) are not capitalized.

The party starts at 9 **P.M.**
The Parthenon in Athens was built in 432 **B.C.**

13. Capitalize the names of stars, planets, and other heavenly bodies.

Did the Mariner spacecraft visit **M**ars or **J**upiter?

You can usually locate the constellation **O**rion by the three stars that make up its belt.

Note: The words *sun, moon,* and *earth* are not usually capitalized and never so when they follow the word *the.*

We should all be concerned with the ecology of earth.
How far is the earth from the sun?

Exercise 4

Write out the following sentences, using capitals where needed. Underline the words you capitalize.

Example

a. The touro synagogue in newport, rhode island, is the oldest synagogue in the united states.

a. The Touro Synagogue in Newport, Rhode Island, is the oldest synagogue in the United States.

1. Some parts of maine are located farther north than some areas of southern canada.
2. The meeting begins at 7:30 p.m. at the buddhist retreat situated on a hill overlooking the pacific ocean.
3. An enormous volcanic eruption occurred on the greek island of santorini in 1400 b.c. and completely destroyed the island.
4. Can you imagine being launched from cape kennedy one morning at 7 a.m. and then orbiting the earth in a spaceship?
5. The getty museum in los angeles is modeled after an ancient roman villa that was buried in ash after the eruption of vesuvius.
6. Did you know that leningrad, russia, is called "the venice of the north"?
7. The british museum in london has ancient greek statues that were taken from the parthenon in athens.
8. We joined a group called friends of the animals, which is a national organization to protect wildlife; the organization has an office in the east in washington, d.c.

9. At night in california's yosemite national park, the sky is so bright that constellations like the big dipper are clearly visible.
10. Many people living along the coast in southern france speak italian as well as french; some—especially near nice—speak a local dialect called nicoise.

14. Capitalize words referring to the deity, holy families, holy books of all religions, and religious terms. Capitalize personal pronouns when they refer to deities.

The story of the **J**ews' exodus from Egypt is in the **O**ld **T**estament.
Ramadan is an important holiday in the **M**oslem faith.
Gothic cathedrals were built higher and higher in an attempt to reach up to **G**od and heaven.

Note: Do not capitalize the word *god* when it refers to a god of ancient mythology; capitalize the names of specific gods because they are proper nouns.

Zeus and the other Greek gods lived on Mount Olympus.

Review Exercise A

Write out the following sentences, using capital letters where necessary. Underline the words you capitalize. Underline titles in *italics* twice.

Example

a. My mother's favorite old movie is *all about eve* starring bette davis.
a. *My mother's favorite old movie is* All About Eve *starring* Bette Davis.

1. The rivoli theater has just opened on west forty-sixth street in new york with a new production of *oklahoma!*
2. Kim wong submitted a report entitled "five ways to conserve energy" to the president of the student council. everyone applauded the report.
3. "Meet me at 7:15 p.m. in front of the national bank of dallas," Jackie said. "it's located on washington boulevard near the bowmont trading corporation."
4. Was king george III the king of england when george washington was president of our country?
5. "according to a report from the packman planetarium, venus will be highly visible on Friday night," luis said. "do you think, ms. alvarez, that we'll see it?"
6. Can you believe, mother, that swallowing goldfish was once a fad? Did you or aunt marissa ever swallow any when you were at chapman university?
7. "a book called *remarkable names of real people* claims there's a doctor whose name is dr. doctor!" exclaimed tom.

8. I understand, senator, that you went to school with uncle tim at midland high school and that you both then worked in the markham building on first avenue.
9. agatha christie's play *the mousetrap* has been playing in london since 1952. every night at 8 p.m. the theater—I think it's the royale theatre—is packed with an excited audience.
10. "my cat is fat," said miss starr, "because it eats all day long. my son joshua and I can't believe its appetite."
11. Marc rogers will play hamlet and read the famous line, "to be, or not to be," in the dellwood amateur theater company's production next week in gordon park.
12. "the new york blackout of 1965 inspired the movie *where were you when the lights went out?*" said raoul. "during the blackout I was trapped in the empire state building."
13. Mary l. salner got a job as a reporter for the *san francisco chronicle;* her first big story was called "citizens fight back against crime."
14. In 1974 a painting entitled *lady writing a letter with her maid* was stolen from the home of sir alfred beit in ireland.
15. "a man has died and left his restaurant to his cat," john exclaimed, "and now a cat owns fred's fish joint!"
16. When the show of king tut's treasures arrived at the los angeles county museum of art, record-breaking crowds lined wilshire boulevard waiting to see the treasures.
17. Then mrs. noble asked, "has the crime rate decreased, sergeant?" fortunately, sergeant parker assured her that it had.
18. "*wait until dark* is a terrifying movie," dr. lawrence said. "my niece and I saw it in france, dubbed in french with english subtitles."
19. The wallers' trip included a stop in denver, a trip through the grand canyon on the colorado river, a drive west to the california coast, and a rest in palm springs.
20. My mother, my father, and I live with aunt helen during the summer. her house is in northern michigan on the shores of lake worth, next door to father julian's church.

15. Capitalize the names of months, days of the week, holidays, and special events.

Thanksgiving is always the fourth **T**hursday in **N**ovember.
Many people watch the **R**ose **B**owl **G**ame on **N**ew **Y**ear's **D**ay.
The **W**imbledon tennis matches are held every **S**eptember in England.

Note: The names of seasons are not usually capitalized.

The first day of winter is December 21.

16. Capitalize the names of historical periods and events.

Leonardo da Vinci and Michelangelo were two leading artists of the **R**enaissance.

17. Capitalize the names of school subjects when they are formed from proper nouns, are followed by a number, or name a specific course.

Although there are several science courses open to sophomores, you cannot take **B**iology II unless you have completed **B**iology I.

If I take **L**atin and a course in **A**merican history, I won't have time to take **W**omen in **L**iterature. [Only the part of the name formed from the proper noun is capitalized, as in **A**merican history.]

Note: Nouns followed by a number or a letter are usually capitalized.

If you live in **E**lection **D**istrict **17**, you vote at the machine in **R**oom **24**.
Are there seats available on **F**light **405** to Chicago?

18. Capitalize the names of political parties (but not the word *party*). Capitalize the names of government departments, agencies, bureaus, and their abbreviations.

Has the **D**emocratic party ever held a convention in St. Louis, Missouri?
All milk products must maintain standards set by the **U**nited **S**tates **D**epartment of **A**griculture (USDA).

Exercise 5
Write out each of the following sentences, adding capital letters where necessary. Underline the words you capitalize.

Example
a. Dr. Franklin's course, history of art 101, meets in room 616 on thursday.
a. Dr. Franklin's course, <u>History of Art 101</u>, meets in <u>Room 616</u> on <u>Thursday</u>.

1. Professor Rashid, who teaches religious thought 401, is an expert on the koran and the teachings of muhammad.
2. The holidays of easter and passover are not always at exactly the same time, but both are always in the spring.
3. Much of the art that we studied in our greek art course was done during ancient greece's golden age of pericles.
4. Although memorial day falls on wednesday, it will be celebrated officially on monday, may 28.
5. All final exams in literature, french, and german will be given during the third week in june.
6. If it rains on monday, october 15, the world series will begin the next day.
7. Will the banks be closed on tuesday, november 7, which is election day?

8. There will be a valentine's day party on friday night in room 725 at the elks club.
9. Because of the delay of flight 201, I missed the family's rosh hashana celebration
10. Sometimes, we have a republican president but a democratic congress.

19. Capitalize the names of specific ships, trains, airplanes, and spacecraft.

Sailing in ***The Golden Hind***, Magellan was the first explorer to circumnavigate the earth.

Everyone was astonished when ***Sputnik 1*** was launched into orbit by the Soviets.

20. Capitalize brand names of specific products.

Our car is the dark blue **S**pritz.
Jellfast is only one brand of gelatin dessert.

21. Capitalize the first word and each noun in the salutation of a letter. Capitalize only the first word in a closing.

Dear **D**r. **S**charf:
My dear **G**randmother,
Yours truly,

22. Capitalize the pronoun *I* and the interjection *O*.

When should **I** call you?
My humble apologies, **O** wise one.

Note: Capitalize the interjection *oh* only when it is used at the beginning of a sentence.

Oh, I forgot my homework.
I was, oh, so weary of his idle chatter.

23. Capitalize the first word of each topic of an outline.

1. **P**opular house plants
   a. **P**lants needing sunlight
   b. **P**lants needing shade
2. **C**are of house plants
   a. **A**mount of water
   b. **S**pecial fertilizing

Exercise 6

Write out the following sentences, using capital letters where necessary. Underline the words you capitalized. Underline words in *italics* twice.

Example

a. Visitors to Long Beach, California, can see the *queen mary*, once a luxury liner.

a. Visitors to Long Beach, California, can see the Queen Mary, *once a luxury liner.*

1. In her outline Marilyn listed seven breeds under the heading "popular cats."
2. Although all nail polish is similar, i like chelsea nail paints best.
3. When i read the greeting, "dear fellow consumer," i thought "what, oh what, are they selling me now!"
4. The s.s. *france* was a luxury cruise ship renowned for its fine food.
5. Tell me, o friend, how i might thank you.
6. Do you think "fondly yours" is too informal a closing for a business letter?
7. Lenny's sporting company sells all brands of running shoes, including zorro.
8. The *mariner* spacecraft sent back beautiful pictures of Mars.
9. Yesterday i bought market basket bread, which is the store brand, and it was the cheapest of all.
10. The *concorde*—a very fast plane—flies from New York to Paris in four hours; i took it last week. oh it was fast!

SUMMARY OF THE CAPITALIZATION OF PROPER NOUNS

1. **Have** you studied dancing?		
2. Governor Jones said, "**Please** be seated, **Mayor**."	*but*	The governor and the mayor were seated.
3. I visited **Aunt** Clara.	*but*	I visited my aunt.
4. **Ms.** Harker and Carl Morton, **Jr.**, run the shop.		
5. It's sunny in **Acapulco, Mexico.**		
6. The air is dry in the **Southwest.**	*but*	We drove southwest until we reached the desert.
7. All **Catholic** masses are no longer said in **Latin.**		
8. Did you visit the **Fogg Museum** at **Harvard University**?		
9. The **Humane Society** endorsed the **Bark Dog Food Company.**		
10. The meeting was at 8 **P.M.**		
11. Have you ever seen **Mars**?	*but*	That's a picture of the earth taken from the moon.
12. The **Bible** tells of **God's** miracles.	*but*	Thor is a god in Norse mythology.
13. The **Senior Prom** is on **Memorial Day, Monday, May 31.**		
14. Heads rolled during the **French Revolution.**		
15. When did **World War II** end?		

16. **French I** and **History 42** meet in **Room 703.** *but* I take a history course in that room.
17. The **Bureau of Child Welfare** finds foster homes for children.
18. The **Republican** party supported the boycott.
19. **Maxwell** shoes are expensive.
20. The ***Orient Express*** was an opulent train.
21. **My** dear **Joseph,**
22. **With** fond regards,
23. Then **I** said, "Shine, shine, **O** glorious sun."
24. 1. **Trees** of summer
25. Who wrote ***Of Mice and Men***?

Review Exercise B

Write out the following sentences, using capital letters where necessary. Underline the words you capitalize. (Underline titles that appear in *italics* twice.)

Example

a. having found chapter 5 (which covered the middle ages) so boring, i could hardly face the next two chapters.

a. Having found Chapter 5 (which covered the Middle Ages) so boring, I could hardly face the next two chapters.

1. last saturday maurie and i ate mexican food at lobo's cantina, which is on the northeast corner of prince street and richmond avenue.
2. having taught us the fundamentals of sketching in her art class, ms. hendricks recommended that we take drawings by masters I. it meets on tuesday at 2 p.m.
3. all of the judges except judge mason agreed that the case should go to the united states supreme court.
4. i always buy gas at marty's self-service station because it has the cheapest gas in janesville.
5. looking at the temple of dendur in the metropolitan museum of art, my aunt exclaimed, "it's hard to believe that this ancient temple once sat on the banks of the nile in egypt."
6. senator clarkson said, "i'm a republican and will back my party's candidate for president in the november election."
7. during the historic landing of *apollo 11*, american astronauts left their lunar module, the *eagle*, and walked on the moon.

8. agatha christie's story *and then there were none* has become a classic mystery book.
9. "if you're concerned about the plight of the whales," allen said, "you can join greenpeace—a canadian organization concerned with their preservation."
10. a catholic priest, a protestant minister, and a jewish rabbi held a joint service for christmas and hanukkah; they led prayers to the lord and asked him for peace.
11. walker ling, jr., visited milwaukee for a national convention of the shoe manufacturers of america.
12. the charleton hotel has a new bible in every room.
13. if you travel south in morocco, you pass through the snow-covered atlas mountains and eventually reach the the sahara desert.
14. during the 1930s president roosevelt established the wpa, an agency that sponsored such projects as the building of the lincoln tunnel between new york and new jersey.
15. "imagine henry ford's amazement," lena said, "when he received a letter from the notorious criminal john dillinger." lena added, "dillinger wrote to say how much he enjoyed driving a ford!"
16. mercury, zeus, and apollo were some of the ancient gods i studied in my mythology course, mythology 153.
17. maggie's poem began, "noble lion, o most regal jungle beast."
18. our social studies assignment is to outline chapter 14, "agriculture and the economy of china." the first topic will be "major agricultural crops."
19. the story of cain and abel is in the old testament in genesis.
20. during the drought and dust storms of the 1930s, many farmers migrated west to california.

Mastery Exercise A

Some of the forty nouns and word groups that follow are common nouns; others are proper nouns. Make two headings on your paper—COMMON NOUNS and PROPER NOUNS—and list each noun under the appropriate heading. Insert capital letters where necessary.

Example

COMMON NOUNS	PROPER NOUNS
dog	*Rover*
avenue	*Fairmont Place*

1. new mexico
2. fifty states
3. teacher
4. high school
5. university of wisconsin
6. a playwright
7. president truman
8. elizabeth blackwell

9. carlos mendoza
10. highway
11. biltmore theater
12. san diego freeway
13. navaho
14. a holy book
15. governor ella grasso
16. new testament
17. play-right toy company
18. a senator
19. women's shoes
20. chestnut nursing home
21. a winding street
22. halloween
23. the space shuttle
24. a month
25. friday
26. boeing 747
27. unit 3
28. mrs. romano
29. a long chapter
30. hank aaron
31. hockey
32. carnegie hall
33. candlestick park
34. declaration of independence
35. lake tahoe
36. my uncle
37. u.s. department of defense
38. hilton hotel
39. a government agency
40. my brother

Mastery Exercise B

The following letter has more than fifty words or abbreviations that need capital letters. Write out the letter and use capitals where needed, underlining the words you capitalize.

dear aunt irene,

we're finally settled in our new house here in hollywood, but a lot of things have gone wrong. first of all, speed-o moving company, which shipped all our belongings from detroit, arrived a week late; we didn't get anything until last saturday. our street, sunshine terrace, is very quiet; but palm shopping mall is just around the corner, and the traffic from the christmas shoppers has been nonstop! our faithful car stopped running, so we had to buy a new one. although we can walk to the shops around the corner, john has had to rely on the rapid transit company to get to his job at casablanca records.

our neighbors are friendly. ms. teng, who is the principal at farley school, lives next door. her mother is visiting, and she has helped us get settled. i've also met some people from the park community center. they're having a party on new year's eve, and we're going.

well, now i have to run and pick david up at his tennis lesson at the starwood health club. then he and nancy are taking a spanish class at the ymca. tonight at 7:30 P.M. i have a meeting at the league of women voters. then i'll collapse!

give my love to uncle paul and my two favorite cousins.

your harried niece,

beverly

PART 8 Speaking/Listening

24 Building Speaking and Listening Skills

Preparing a Persuasive Speech

Persuasive speech is the use of the spoken word to influence others.

The speaker may want to influence someone to change a belief he or she holds, or the speaker's purpose may be to persuade the listener to behave in a different way. In this chapter you will learn how you, as a speaker, can use persuasive speech to influence others. You will also study how words are used to change the way you think.

Choosing Persuasive Topics

The purpose of persuasive speech is to convince others to think, feel, or behave in a certain way. In persuasive speech you express an opinion, hoping to persuade listeners to adopt it as their own.

Since an opinion is at the heart of every persuasive speech, there are only certain topics that can be called persuasive. To determine whether a topic fits into this category, consider the following suggestions.

A topic should be controversial. No persuasion occurs unless there are at least two or more opinions that can be expressed about a topic. Therefore, a topic must be controversial, or two-sided. There is nothing two-sided about statistics that say that the average American who lives to be sixty-five has spent the equivalent of nine full years of his or her life watching television. There is something controversial about the topic, though, when you express your opinion. If you say that Americans spend too much time viewing television, or that television viewing is harmful, or that children's television viewing time should be limited, then you have found the controversy in the topic.

A topic should arouse listeners' interest. You will never persuade listeners if you speak to controversies that do not concern or interest them. Your challenge as a speaker is to relate to your listeners' needs and interests. You must either choose a topic that is of immediate concern to the audience or show them why they should be concerned about the topic.

A topic should present a speaker's claim or belief about an idea. Your persuasive topic should clearly state to listeners that you have made a claim or accepted a belief about the way things should be done. That claim is usually one of three types: a claim concerning fact, value, or policy.

If you choose a *fact claim,* you try to persuade listeners to believe that something is or is not true, will or will not happen. Lawyers use this claim every time they try to convince a jury that someone is or is not guilty. You may use this claim when you argue that a certain college football team will win the national championship. Eventually people will know whether you are right or wrong.

A *value claim* arises when you, as a persuader, try to say that something is good or bad, right or wrong, desirable or undesirable. You may try to argue that English is a more important course than biology, that a certain person would make a good President, that America is the strongest military country in the world, or that students are brighter today than in previous generations. If you make a value claim, you cannot absolutely prove that your idea is correct, but you can try to prove your idea beyond a reasonable doubt.

The final claim is a *policy claim.* If you choose this type of topic, you will give reasons why an existing rule, law, or policy should be changed. If you say that government should outlaw strikes, you suggest a change that people should make. If you try to persuade your school administrators that all classes should be electives, you suggest a change in the way school is run. Policy claims, then, mean that something should be done differently from the way it is now done.

A topic should have information to support it. No opinion will carry much weight unless it can be supported with information. You may want to persuade your classmates that teenage marriages should be outlawed, but your opinion will only be as strong as the information you have to support it. If there is no objective information to support your opinion, your arguments will be weakened, so before you make a final topic selection, check your library to be certain you can find supporting information.

Activity 1

For a review of brainstorming, see pages 27–29.

As a class or small-group project, do some brainstorming about actual controversies that fall under the following headings: School, Local community, State, National, and International. For example, in your school there might be a controversy about open lunch policies, or in your state there might be a controversy concerning returnable bottles. On the blackboard put the five different headings and list as many topics as you can under each one. It does not make any difference if some of the topics seem farfetched, since your task is to discover as many ideas as possible. Have someone record the lists and save them for use as persuasive speech topics.

Activity 2

Either individually or as a group, brainstorm about controversies that come under one of the following headings. Share your ideas with the entire class and keep them for use as persuasive speech topics.

Business	Medicine	History
Politics	Books	The future
Life styles	Justice/Law	Public figures
Music	Environment	Teenagers
Sports	Education	Families
Science	Television/Films	Morals

Activity 3

Think of two topics that are fact claims, two that are value claims, and two that are policy claims. Share your ideas with your classmates.

Activity 4

Clip out three different editorials and three different letters-to-the-editor from any newspaper or magazine. Bring your clippings to class and discuss the different controversies expressed in this printed material. Would any of these ideas be good to use as persuasive speech topics?

Researching Your Topic

Since you want to make certain that listeners will accept your opinion, you now need to find information to support it. To strengthen your opinion you should research both sides of the controversy so that you know the pros and cons of the issue. Having a good defense requires research—the first step in preparing a persuasive speech.

Read a general article. Researching a topic means that you must first gain some background about it. The easiest way to do this is to read one or two general sources such as a newspaper or magazine article, a book chapter, a pamphlet, or an encyclopedia entry. These articles will suggest ideas that you need to explore as you prepare your opinion and its defense.

Ask questions. After gaining a general knowledge of the speech topic, a good persuader will think of every conceivable question that could be asked about it. Asking questions will give the speaker some direction as he or she searches for specific information. Research questions for a persuasive speech usually fall into four different categories: *background questions, problem questions, solution questions*, and *effect questions.*

1. *Background Questions*

You must understand what your topic is all about if you expect to be persuasive. Asking background questions such as the following ones will give you a basis for other questions you need to ask.

What words need to be precisely defined?
What exactly is the controversy concerning the topic?

When did the topic become controversial?
Who are the famous and not-so-famous people concerned with this topic?
What people are considered authorities on this topic?
If the topic deals with the way something works, how does that something function?
What people or groups make decisions concerning this topic?
What people does this topic most affect? Why?

2. *Problem Questions*

You develop an opinion because you see problems with what others believe about a subject. As you research your topic, ask questions that will help you to define those problems, such as the following ones.

What problems have occurred because of the other side's opinion?
What problems will occur if someone does not accept your opinion?
What causes these problems?
How harmful are these problems?
What are the effects of these problems?

3. *Solution Questions*

When you research problems, you should also research solutions or answers to those problems. Your opinion is your general answer, but you should be more specific. Again, the best way to get at specifics is to ask questions, such as the following ones.

What exactly would you like to have your listeners believe about your topic?
What exactly would you like to have your listeners do?
Does your answer solve all the problems in your opponent's position?
How does your answer solve the problems?
How will you put your answer to work?

4. *Effect Questions*

You will be more persuasive if you can tell a listener how your ideas will work and how they will benefit him or her. In other words you must know what good things will happen if people accept your opinion. Two questions will help you determine the effects of your ideas:

What will happen if people support your opinion?
How will people benefit from accepting your ideas?

Gathering information. Once you know what questions to ask, you can begin to find specific information to answer them. In a library you will find magazines, newspapers, books, pamphlets, filmstrips, tapes, phonograph records, and reference books that have information about your subject. You may also find that community people can be invaluable resources. Interviews with knowledgeable people can provide you with answers that you may not find in printed material.

Once you have gathered your sources, scan the material for answers. Look for arguments, reasons, explanations, examples, solutions, descriptions, statistics, definitions, or brief stories that writers use to explain their ideas on your topic. Do not neglect the sources that support the other side of your issue, however. Finding out what others say against your position can help you to strengthen that position when you write the speech.

You will use these details to support your arguments, so record them on note cards as speech reference material. The best way to record details is to put one fact on one note card. A subject heading that labels the detail can be written in the card's upper left-hand corner. The source of the material can be recorded at the bottom so that you can return to the source later if you need to.

List all arguments. Before you can actually write the speech, you need to know the arguments for and against your position. After reading through your notes, draw a line lengthwise down the middle of a piece of paper. On one side of the line, list all the statements or arguments that support your opinion. On the other side, list all the statements or arguments your opponents might use. You do not need to list actual facts, only those ideas that can be supported by the facts you have found. An example concerning a school open lunch policy (a policy in which students are free to leave school grounds for lunch) might look something like the following one.

PRO	CON
The school cafeteria can't handle all the students.	The school cafeteria can serve all the students if the lunch periods are lengthened slightly.
Local restaurants are within walking distance of the school.	Local restaurants want to cater only to business people.
Open lunch breaks up the day for the students.	A closed lunch period still gives students a break.
Students are responsible enough to handle the freedom.	Students aren't responsible enough to handle the freedom.

By listing all arguments, both pro and con, you will have a better idea of how to approach the writing of your speech.

Revise your opinion. Before sitting down to draft your speech, ask yourself if you still want to argue your original position. During your research you may find information that leads you to different conclusions. If this happens to you, speak only to issues that you can truly support. If the facts you have gathered convince you to do so, change your opinion and your speech topic. You may also find that your opinion is too broad to support adequately. Limiting your position or opinion only to the statement that you can actually defend is important. If you cannot prove all of your points, you will have trouble persuading your listeners that your opinion is correct.

Activity 5

First select a persuasive speech topic from a previous activity or use one you create for this activity. Next read at least two general articles about the topic. After reading the articles, try to answer the background, problem, solution, and effect questions found on pages 620–621. You may want to put each question and its answer on a separate note card for future use when you write the speech. Share these note cards with your teacher.

Activity 6

Using the topic you chose in Activity 5, find arguments, reasons, explanations, examples, solutions, descriptions, statistics, definitions, or brief stories that provide support for your opinion. Put each fact you find on separate note cards so that it looks something like the following one.

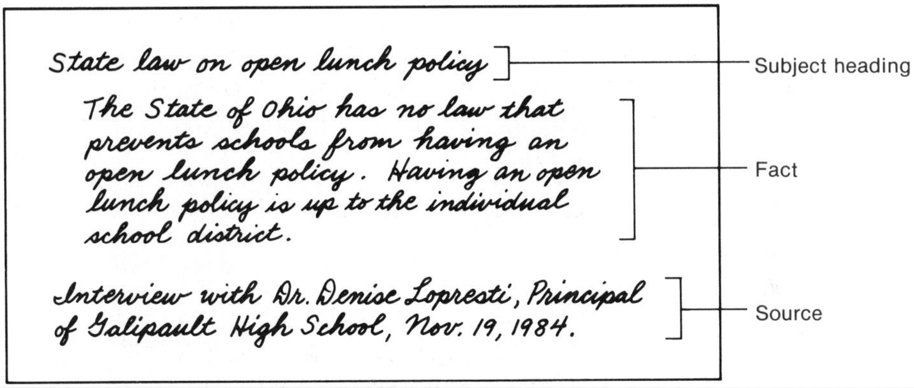

Be certain that you include a subject heading in the upper left-hand corner and the source of the material at the bottom.

Activity 7

On a sheet of paper, list the pro and con arguments concerning your persuasive speech topic. Write all pro arguments on one side of the paper and all con arguments on the other side. Share your list with others to see if they can suggest more arguments. After making your list, revise your opinion so that it says exactly what you want it to say.

Organizing the Persuasive Speech

Unless they have reasons, most people will not change their beliefs or actions. If you want to change someone's behavior, you must provide him or her with some reasons to do so. You must also organize those need-for-a-change arguments in a way that will cause your listeners to accept your ideas. The organization of a persuasive speech follows the same basic pattern you used to research your topic. This pattern deals with problems and solutions but also with some other steps that are needed when you actually give the speech. In all, there is a progression of six steps you should carry out when organizing your persuasive speech:

1. Establish listeners' interest.

You want listeners to pay attention to your speech so that you can persuade them to change their views. When you begin your speech, therefore, you must immediately get listeners interested and involved with your topic. You must catch their attention and tell them what you are going to do in the speech. The following examples illustrate some ways to accomplish these goals.

a. Reference to listeners—You can start your speech by appealing immediately to the needs and interests of your listeners.
b. Use of an illustration or example—If you are persuading people to become vegetarians, you can begin your speech with examples or stories about famous people who are vegetarians.
c. Quotation—Catch your listeners' attention by using and explaining a quotation relating to your subject.
d. Direct approach—Immediately telling your listeners what your subject is and what you plan to do can be effective. If your topic is interesting enough by itself and does not need any buildup, the direct approach can be used.
e. Statistics—A numerical fact is often a good way to establish interest in a topic, especially if it is unusual or controversial.
f. Use of a personal reference—Telling listeners something personal about yourself as it relates to your topic can heighten their interest in you and your speech.
g. Combination—Using more than one method may be necessary. Therefore, any combination of methods can be used.

If you were to attempt to persuade a school faculty to support your efforts to have open lunch, your introduction (using a combination method) might sound like the following one.

> Missy McCarthy, our student council president, says, "It is the one issue most important to this year's student body. It is also the only issue that all students support." You and I both know that she's talking about open lunch, and that's why I'm here today. As students we are asking that you also support our efforts to open up the lunch period. Some of you may already agree with us, but let me give all of you the reasons why we need to change the school's present policy of a closed lunch period.

2. Explain your topic's background.

After you have your listeners' attention, you need to switch gears for a few seconds from persuasive to informative speaking. Before you can give arguments for an opinion, you should be certain that your listeners are familiar with your topic. You may have to give them a brief history, explanation, or definition about the controversy.

3. Explain your arguments.

In this step you present your need-for-a-change arguments. You tell your listeners the reasons why they need to change their beliefs. To choose what arguments to use, review the research you have done. You have already uncovered problems that have occurred or will occur if your opinion is not accepted. Tell your listeners about these problems, letting them know that there is a definite need for change.

In this part of your speech, you can also share with your listeners those arguments that may not describe a problem but that still back your opinion. If students are responsible enough to handle an open lunch, use that as an argument. This argument does not describe a problem, but it still presents the listeners with a definite need for a change.

4. Describe your answer.

After you establish a need for change, you should next describe in detail what you want your listeners to believe or do. Give listeners the answers to the problems you raise. Show them how your arguments logically support your opinion or proposal. Be specific about how your solution works. Finally make certain that they understand exactly what your answers are. You cannot change opinions if listeners do not comprehend exactly what you want them to do.

5. Explain the benefits.

Listeners will not be totally convinced that you are right until you explain the benefits of your belief. Telling listeners what is to be gained by accepting your view is the next step in your speech. This step is crucial in persuasion, since most people will change beliefs more easily if they can expect to gain from such a change.

6. Redirect listeners' attention.

As you end the speech in this final step, you want to leave your listeners with a favorable impression, and you want them to agree with you. To secure their acceptance, you need to do two things in your concluding remarks. First, summarize your background statements, your arguments, and your benefits. Plant those ideas firmly in your listeners' minds by repeating the main ideas of each section. You do not want to go into detail, but you do want to say enough so that your listeners will remember your ideas.

Second, review your answer or opinion and suggest a listener response to it. Do not leave your listeners in doubt about what you want them to believe or do; instead, be firm and direct about the commitment you want them to make. End your speech on a definite note by focusing your listeners' final thoughts on your speech purpose—an acceptance of your opinion.

Reading a Persuasive Speech

In the following persuasive speech the speaker supports an open lunch policy. By speaking at a teachers' meeting, the speaker is trying to persuade the faculty to support this policy change. Notice how the speaker, even in a very short speech, still works through the six steps of organizing a persuasive speech.

Establish listeners' interest.

Missy McCarthy, our student council president, says "It is the one issue most important to this year's student body. It is also the only issue that all students support." You and I both know that she's talking about open lunch, and that's why I'm here today. As students we are asking that you also support our efforts to open up the lunch period. Some of you may already agree with us, but let me give all of you the reasons why we need to change the school's present policy of a closed lunch period.

Explain the topic's background.

First, though, let me explain some points about open lunch. We are asking only to be allowed to leave school during our lunch period, to have the option of eating someplace other than the school cafeteria. We're not talking about leaving school during study halls or during any other part of the day. All we would like to have is the same privilege we had as younger students when we used to walk home for lunch. We would also like to have the same privilege that students here at Galipault High had before 1969. For you see, until 1969 Galipault High had open lunch. It was during the 1969–1970 school year that the administration closed the lunch period. At the time some parents complained about the policy, and school officials responded to those complaints.

Explain your arguments.

Times have changed, however, and there is a real need to consider the open lunch option again. First of all, our school cafeteria no longer can feed all the students during the lunch hour. We have too many students, not enough room, not enough cooks, and not enough time to accommodate everyone. Some students stand in line for thirty-five to forty minutes before they are served. Even if the lunch period is lengthened, the long wait will not be cut down. Also, the school board has no money to hire more help or to add on room to the present cafeteria. Therefore, there's no relief in sight.

Our community, however, can serve student needs, as there are many restaurants within walking distance of the school. A survey shows that there are no fewer than ten restaurants within a quarter-mile radius of the school. Add that to the number of restaurants within driving distance, and students can easily eat somewhere and be back in time for their next class.

Another reason why you should support open lunch is that it breaks up the day for students. Students have a chance to get out for some fresh air and for a change of scenery. This change of pace and routine, as you well know, is necessary for morale and efficiency.

Finally the question of responsibility arises. Many adults say that we students can't handle this freedom. Some say that we would misuse the privilege. To be honest I can't guarantee that there won't be some students who will take advantage of an open lunch period, but I can guarantee that the majority of us won't. We know that open lunch is a privilege, and we're responsible enough to honor it as such. We realize that we won't have the choice of eating out if most of us misuse this freedom; therefore, we're going to abide by the rules. We're also going to put pressure on those who don't because we don't want them spoiling open lunch for the rest of us.

Describe your answer.

For these reasons we think that the plan we're asking you to support will best fit our school's needs. We think that all students should be given the open lunch option if they have a parent's written permission. Once they have permission, we think that they should sign a pledge card stating that they will abide by the school's rules while exercising the open lunch privilege. If any student breaks the pledge, the school can take away his or her open lunch privilege.

Explain the benefits.

This simple plan will work because it protects students, parents, and the school. It protects parents because students won't be allowed to leave without permission. It protects the student majority against those who might abuse this privilege because those who do so will have their open lunch option taken away from them. Finally it protects the school because both parents and students know what has to be done to keep open lunch working smoothly.

Redirect listeners' attention.

As you can see, there is a need to regain the open lunch option that Galipault students once had. There's a need because of cafeteria overcrowding, which can only be lessened by allowing students to use local restaurants. Open lunch is also needed to break up a student's day and to show everyone that Galipault students are responsible, capable people, who take pride in their school's image.

Because everyone is protected by our open lunch plan, we would like you to support it when we ask for the school board's approval. Without your help the school board may turn us down. With your help we can continue to make Galipault High one of the state's best schools.

Activity 8

Analyze the student speaker's open lunch speech by answering the following questions.

1. What method did the speaker use to establish the audience's interest?
2. What facts were used to explain the topic's background?
3. What arguments did the speaker use to support open lunch?
4. Were there any facts used to support the arguments?
5. What three specific things did the speaker describe when giving an answer?
6. How is the speaker's plan supposed to benefit people?
7. What ideas did the speaker summarize when the audience's attention was redirected?

Activity 9

Using the persuasive speech topic from a previous activity or one you select now, jot down the basic ideas you would use for the six parts of a persuasive speech. (You can fill in the details later.) An example of such a partial listing might look like the following.

ESTABLISH LISTENERS' INTEREST

1. *Use quotation by student council president to explain importance of the topic.*

2. *Ask for teachers' support of open lunch.*

EXPLAIN THE TOPIC'S BACKGROUND

1. *Explain to teachers what open lunch really means.*
2. *Tell them how Galipault students used to have this privilege.*

Delivering a Persuasive Speech

Listeners will pay as much attention to how a speech is delivered as to what is said in the speech. In fact, a speaker's delivery often determines an audience's interest and response to ideas in the first place. This is especially true in a persuasive speech because listeners will not change their beliefs unless a speaker motivates them to do so. That motivation comes from how listeners perceive the speaker. That perception, in turn, is primarily built on what listeners *see* during the speech.

How do you appear to your listeners? Before you give your persuasive speech, analyze your delivery. If you appear to be uncertain, nervous, untrustworthy, bored, incompetent, or insincere, your message will be unmotivating. Listeners will respond favorably if they perceive you as being honest, poised, confident, sincere, friendly, well-informed about the topic, interested and energetic about your ideas, good-natured, and genuinely concerned for their welfare.

How do you achieve a good appearance? Of course, you cannot be sincere, confident, poised, or friendly unless you really are that way. Most listeners will see through a speaker's attempts to "create an image." However, if you have selected a subject that you really care about, that you have researched well, and that you want to share with your listeners, you already have a basis for achieving a favorable impression. All you really need to do is check your delivery against the following questions and then practice the speech until you feel comfortable enough with what you want to say.

Do you speak loudly enough to be heard?
Do you articulate your words clearly?
Is your voice energetic and interesting to listen to?
Do you speak in a relaxed, conversational manner?
Do you use any *um*'s, *okay*'s, *you know*'s in your speech?
Are you speaking too quickly for people to hear you?
Do you stand with confidence before your listeners?
Are you gesturing enough to catch your listeners' attention?
Does your facial expression reflect what you are saying?
Do you develop eye contact with your listeners?

Activity 10

If you have worked through this chapter's activities, you have already chosen a topic, researched it, developed pro and con arguments, and organized your ideas by using the six-step method of persuasive speech making. For this activity write your speech and prepare to deliver it. Before writing, analyze your audience and choose your persuasive approaches based on that analysis.

Once you have the speech written, jot down the main ideas on note cards to use when giving the speech. Be certain that you do not write the whole speech on note cards, however, since you want to do more than read your speech. Finally practice delivering your speech in front of a mirror, in front of others, and (if possible) with a tape recorder. Check your delivery against the questions about speech delivery in the preceding section.

Listening to Persuasive Speaking

Although you spend a great deal of time trying to persuade others, you actually spend more time being a listener, or consumer, of other people's persuasive attempts. As a listener you must constantly decide whether or not to buy a persuader's bill of goods. Whether you vote for a particular candidate, buy a certain product, support a local cause, or have negative feelings about an idea often depends on your ability as a listening consumer.

Learning to listen well means learning to uncover the meaning in what you hear. This can be done if you practice and develop certain skills associated with listening.

Prepare yourself to listen. Before you hear the first word, work on developing certain attitudes that will help you to listen. You must, first of all, prepare yourself by deciding that you *want* to listen. Motivation begins not with the speaker but with the listener, since only you can decide whether or not you want to listen.

Once you mentally commit yourself to listen, you can then get yourself ready to listen. Get comfortable in your seat, concentrate on the speaker's message, and avoid letting your thoughts be distracted by events around you. Whenever your mind starts to wander, try looking at the speaker again and mentally repeat his or her words. Whatever you do, try to maintain your focus only on the speaker's message.

Use the thinking versus speaking time difference. On the average most people can think three times faster than they can speak. If a person speaks about 125 words per minute, a listener can think anywhere from 300 to 400 words per minute. Since a listener can think faster than a speaker can talk, the listener can put this extra time to use in two important ways.

First (as a listener), you can mentally review what has been said. By repeating ideas to yourself, you will have a better chance of remembering them. This summarizing will also help you to focus on the speech.

Second, you can mentally ask questions about the message. Asking questions that help you to analyze the structure and content of the speech and the speaker's delivery will also help you to improve your listening skills. You may ask questions such as the following ones.

1. What is the speaker's purpose?
2. How does that idea relate to the main purpose?
3. How many main ideas are there?
4. Why doesn't the speaker have any support for that point?

5. Does the speaker have any more examples to support that thought?
6. What's the speaker going to say next?
7. Is the speaker leaving anything out?
8. Is that explanation really clearly stated?
9. Why does the speaker avoid looking at the audience?
10. Why is the speaker getting so excited?
11. Why is the speaker using only emotional appeals?

Evaluate the persuasive techniques. When listening to persuasive messages, you need to take your speech analysis even one step further, since the questions you have already asked about the speech's content may not be enough. Since a persuasive speaker's intent is to change your beliefs or actions, you need to evaluate the truth, the reasonableness, and the believability of those techniques. Many times a speaker's appeals do not relate to you, no matter how much he or she tries to convince you otherwise. Many times, too, a speaker does not use fair and logical arguments to present the case. As a listener you will be the one harmed if you unquestioningly accept this speaker's ideas; therefore, your responsibility is to protect yourself by listening critically to the speaker's message. This can be done by learning to evaluate the two persuasive approaches discussed earlier in this chapter:

1. Evaluate the emotional appeals used.

In most situations a persuasive speaker will appeal to important biological, social, or personal needs. Many of these appeals are reasonable and just. However, as a listener, you are the one to determine your response to an emotional appeal.

A critical listener will pick out the emotional appeals and then will ask some questions to determine whether to accept or reject those appeals. When you listen, you might ask yourself questions like these: "What need is the speaker appealing to?" "Is it a need that I really have?" "Is it a strong need within me, or is it as strong as the persuader would have me believe?" "Will the speaker's idea, product, or service really fulfill that need, as the speaker claims?"

Advertisements are sometimes very good at convincing people that they have needs that they really do not have, or the advertisements convince people that a need they do have is stronger than it actually is. When people buy the products and find out that these products do not fulfill the emotional needs the advertisements said they would, it may be because the people were not critical listeners who asked questions.

2. Evaluate the thought appeals used.

Some ideas sound logical and sensible until they are examined more closely. A good listener realizes that a speaker who sounds like an authority may not be one. A good listener must weigh the evidence used and the ideas presented and then evaluate the truth in what a speaker says.

As a listener you will have to determine whether ideas are based on sound reasoning. A good way to prepare yourself for this task is to become familiar with the types of illogical arguments you hear daily. These arguments are discussed in the chapter "Persuasive Writing." Review them as a basis for the activities on listening to persuasive speeches.

Activity 11

Find or write a speech that is carefully organized around major ideas. Have someone tape-record the speech at a rate of no more than 125 words per minute. Tell the class how many major ideas are in the speech and then play the tape. While the tape is playing, have everyone mentally repeat the main ideas. As soon as the tape is finished, everyone should write down the main points. Then check to see how accurate everyone is. If a tape recorder is not available, have someone read the speeches.

Activity 12

Have someone read a well-organized speech to the entire class. Have that same person ring a bell five or six times during the speech. When the bell rings, class members should immediately write down the idea being expressed at exactly the moment the bell is rung. Check to see how well everyone concentrated on the message.

Glossary of Terms

Absolute phrase A phrase, usually consisting of a noun or pronoun and a participle, related in meaning to the sentence in which it is inserted but not modifying a specific word in the sentence

Abstract noun A noun that names a quality, thought, or idea

Action Any physical or mental thing that has happened or is happening

Action verb A verb that shows either physical or mental action

Active voice A verb feature used when the subject performs the action expressed by the verb

Adjective A word that modifies a noun or pronoun

Adjective clause A group of words with a subject and verb functioning as an adjective

Adjective phrase A prepositional phrase that modifies a noun or pronoun

Adverb A word that modifies a verb, an adjective, or another adverb

Adverb clause A subordinate clause that modifies a verb, an adjective, or an adverb

Adverb phrase A prepositional phrase that modifies a verb, an adverb, or an adjective

Affix One or more letters added to the front or back of a word to modify or to change its meaning or to change its part of speech

Alliteration Use of words in poetry that begin with the same sound

Almanac An annually published book of facts and figures on a wide range of subjects

Apostrophe Punctuation mark (') used to show the omission of letters or numbers, to form the plural of letters or numbers, and to form possessive nouns

Appositive A noun or pronoun that follows or precedes another noun or pronoun to identify or clarify it

Argumentation Persuasion through logical reasoning

Article One of the frequently used adjectives—*the*, *a*, or *an*

Assonance The repetition of vowel sounds in poetry to create a rhyme

Atlas A book of maps

Autobiography A writer's own account of his or her life

Bibliography An alphabetical listing of sources used in preparing a book, or of closely related sources

Biography An account of a person's life, written by another

Black English A cultural dialect spoken by many black people throughout the United States

Brainstorming A system in which participants allow ideas and possibilities to flow as freely as possible

Call number A group of numbers and letters placed on a book to indicate its location in the library

Card catalogue A cabinet containing, in alphabetical order, title, subject, and author cards

Clause A group of related words having both a subject and a verb

Cliché A trite, hackneyed phrase or expression

Close reading A type of reading to remember and understand major ideas and details

Clustering system A system to encourage a flow of ideas and to group ideas as they come

Coherent writing Writing in which the logical relationships between ideas are apparent

Collective noun A noun that stands for a class of items

Colon Punctuation mark (:) used to separate elements within a sentence to call attention to the word, phrase, or list that follows it

Comma Punctuation mark (,) used to separate words, phrases, or clauses within sentences

Common noun A noun that does not specify a particular person, place, thing, or idea

Comparative degree The form of an adjective or adverb that compares two persons or things

Complement A word or group of words that completes the statement begun by the subject and verb

Complex sentence A sentence that contains only one independent clause and at least one subordinate clause

Compound–complex sentence A sentence that contains more than one independent clause and at least one subordinate clause

Compound sentence A sentence that contains more than one independent clause but no subordinate clause

Concluding sentence Final sentence in a paragraph that restates the central idea in a new and interesting way or that sums up the information presented

Concrete noun A noun that names something that can be perceived through the senses

Conflict A struggle either within a person or between one person and some other person or force

Conjunction A word that connects other words or groups of words

Connector A word used to make effective connections between sentences

Connotative meaning The meaning of a word that includes the feelings associated with it

Consonance The repetition of consonant sounds in poetry to create a rhyme

Context The other words and sentences that surround a word

Context clues Hints about the meaning of a word supplied by surrounding words, phrases, and sentences

Coordinating conjunction A connector that joins two statements of equal importance by indicating a relationship between the two

Copyright Legal right of an author or publisher to publish, sell, and distribute a work

Creativity The ability to think in an original way

Cultural dialect A dialect spoken by a group of people who share a common culture

Dash Punctuation mark (—) used to call attention to the word or word group that precedes it

Declarative sentence A type of sentence that makes a statement and ends with a period

Deductive organization An organization of writing that begins with the main idea and then gives evidence or data for it

Definite article The adjective *the* that refers to a definite person or object

Demonstrative pronoun A pronoun that points out a specific person, place, thing, or idea

Denotative meaning The dictionary meaning of a word

Derivative word A word formed, or derived, from a shorter word

Description A word picture that helps the reader form a mental image of the subject

Dewey decimal number A number assigned to a nonfiction book filed under the Dewey decimal system

Dialect A major variation within a language

Dialogue Words said by two or more people having a conversation

Direct object A word or group of words that appears in the predicate and receives the action expressed by the verb

Double negative A construction when two negative words are used where only one is necessary

Elliptical adverb clause A clause whose missing parts are filled in by the reader

Encyclopedia A collection of articles on a wide variety of subjects, arranged alphabetically

Exact rhyme Repetition in poetry of almost identical sounds

Example A specific case that illustrates a general idea or statement

Exclamation point Punctuation mark (!) used to indicate strong feeling

Exclamatory sentence A type of sentence that expresses surprise or strong feeling and ends with an exclamation point

Exposition Writing to present factual information or to explain ideas and feelings

Fact Information that has been or can be proved true

Factual detail Detail used in objective description that does not include the writer's thoughts and feelings

Fiction Books in which events and people are from the writer's imagination

First-person pronoun A pronoun used when speakers and writers refer to themselves (*I*)

Footnote A short note at the bottom of a page or at the end of a chapter providing specific information about particular material in the text

Formal poetry Poetry that follows a standard form

Free verse Nonformal poetry that does not use all the formal elements of rhyme and regular meter and stanzas

Frontispiece An illustration that faces or immediately precedes the title page of a book

Future perfect tense A verb tense that describes a future action that will be completed before another future action

Future tense A verb tense that describes an action that will happen in the future

Gerund A word ending in *-ing* that is formed from a verb and that functions as a noun

Gerund phrase A verbal phrase consisting of a gerund and its modifiers and complements

Helping verb A verb that helps the main verb express action or state of being

Hyphen Punctuation mark (-) used to link the parts of some compound words or to link the part of a word begun on one line with the part finished on the next

Image A vivid, sensory detail

Imperative sentence A type of sentence that gives an order or makes a request

Incomplete construction A sentence with part left for the reader to complete

Indefinite article One of the adjectives *a* or *an* that does not refer to a specific person or object

Indefinite pronoun A pronoun that does not refer to a specific person or thing

Independent clause A clause that can stand alone because it can express a complete thought by itself

Index An alphabetical listing of topics covered in a book, with page numbers

Indirect object A noun or pronoun in the predicate that comes before the direct object and tells *to whom* or *for whom*

Inductive organization An organization of writing in which the main idea appears at the end of a passage or does not appear at all and must be interpreted

Infinitive A verb form preceded by the word *to*

Infinitive phrase An infinitive plus its modifiers and complements

Informal outline An outline that uses neither numerals nor letters; subheads are identified by indentions

Intensifier An adverb such as *very*, *quite*, *rather*, or *too* that answers the question *to what extent?*

Interjection A word that expresses strong or sudden emotion, or surprise

Interrogative adverb An adverb used to ask questions

Interrogative pronoun A pronoun used in asking a question

Interrogative sentence A type of sentence that asks a question and ends with a question mark

Intransitive verb A verb that does not take a direct object

Jargon Special words and phrases used within a specific occupation

Journal A series of personal writing pieces

Language A method of communication

Letter of adjustment Letter in which the writer is trying to convince a company or individual to replace damaged merchandise, refund money, or correct an error in billing

Letter of application A letter written to apply for a job

Letter of appreciation The business letter counterpart of a thank-you note

Letter of request Letter in which the writer is asking for something

Library of Congress system A method for classifying books using twenty-one categories designated by letters of the alphabet

Light reading A relaxed method of reading for pleasure

Linking verb A verb that links the subject of the sentence with a noun, a pronoun, or an adjective in the predicate

Logical fallacies Errors in reasoning

Logical organization An ordering of thoughts and ideas that makes sense

Main verb Usually the last verb of a verb phrase; the part of the verb phrase that is not a helping verb

Marginal note A note printed in the margin to the left or the right of the page's main text

Metaphor Figurative language that makes a connection between two different types of items

Meter A pattern in poetry of repeating rhythm

Modifier A word that describes another word

Nonfiction Books about real-life people and events

Noun A word that names a person, a place, a thing, or an idea

Noun clause A group of words that contain a subject and verb and that function as a noun

Object complement A noun or an adjective in the predicate that identifies or explains the direct object

Order letter Letter in which the writer is requesting that a company send merchandise

Paired connectors A set of connectors used to make a connection between two sentences of equal importance

Paraphrase To restate words in a different way without changing the meaning

Parentheses Punctuation mark ( ) used to enclose elements that interrupt a sentence

Participial phrase A participle plus its modifiers and complements

Participle A word formed from a verb that is used as an adjective

Passive voice A verb feature used when the verb expresses action received by the subject

Past perfect tense A verb tense that describes an action that took place in the past before another action

Past tense A verb tense that describes an action that happened in the past

Pentad A set of five questions for gathering information

Period A punctuation mark (.) used as an end mark to separate sentences or as a mark that shows the omission of letters in abbreviations

Personal detail Detail shaped by the writer's thoughts and feelings and used to describe the subject as it appears to the writer

Personal pronoun A pronoun that refers to the speaker or writer, to the person or people being addressed, or to a third person or people

Personal writing Writing that is about the writer's thoughts and feelings

Persuasive essay An essay that makes an argument

Persuasive speech Use of the spoken word to influence others

Persuasive writing Writing that tries to convince readers to think, believe, or act a certain way

Phrase A group of words that does not contain both a subject and a predicate and that works to perform a single function in a sentence

Phrase modifier A string of words with no subject and no verb that acts as an adjective or adverb

Plot A series of events, along with the motivations for them and the relationships between them

Plural A form that stands for more than one of something

Positive degree The regular form of an adjective or adverb that describes a quality

Possessive noun The form of a noun that indicates ownership or relationship

Predicate The part of a sentence that says something about the subject and contains a verb or verb phrase

Predicate adjective An adjective that follows a linking verb and modifies the subject of the sentence

Predicate nominative A noun or pronoun that identifies or renames the subject and is joined to it by a linking verb

Prefix A letter or letters added to the front of a word to change or modify its meaning

Preposition A word that shows a relationship between a noun or pronoun and another word or words in the sentence

Prepositional phrase A phrase that consists of a preposition, its object, and any modifiers the object may have

Present perfect tense A verb tense that describes an action begun in the past that may continue to the present

Present tense A verb tense that describes an action happening now or an action that is habitual or repeated

Progressive A form of a verb that expresses ongoing action

Pronoun A word that takes the place of one or more nouns or other pronouns

Proofreading Checking writing for errors in spelling, grammar, and mechanics

Proper adjective An adjective formed from a proper noun

Proper noun A noun that names a specific person, place, thing, or idea

Public journal A journal written for an audience that does not contain thoughts, feelings, or experiences the writer does not want to share

Question mark A punctuation mark (?) used as an end mark for an interrogative sentence

Quotation marks Punctuation marks (" ") used to enclose a word or group of words and separate them from the rest of the sentence

Readers' Guide to Periodical Literature An author and subject index to periodicals of general interest published in the United States.

Reason An explanation for an idea or opinion that answers the question *Why?*

Reference book Book containing specialized knowledge

Relative pronoun A pronoun that introduces an adjective clause and that has a function within the clause

Research paper Long, formal essay presenting specific information drawn from several sources

Revising Making changes in the content of the writing itself

Rough draft The first draft, or copy, of a composition

Run-on sentence A group of words that result when two or more sentences are joined together with a comma or with no punctuation at all

Scanning A fast type of reading in which one looks over written material very quickly to locate a specific piece of information

Second-person pronoun A pronoun used when speakers and writers refer to the person or persons being addressed

Semicolon Punctuation mark (;) used to signal a more definite break in thought

Sensory details Details of sight, sound, taste, smell, and touch

Sentence A group of words that expresses a complete thought

Sentence fragment A group of words that does not express a complete thought

Sentence outline An outline in which the headings are stated as complete sentences

Simile A comparison stated with *like, as,* or *than* and sometimes with verbs such as *seems* and *appears*

Simple sentence A sentence that contains only one independent clause and no subordinate clauses

Single quotation marks Punctuation marks (' ') used to enclose a direct quotation that occurs inside another quotation

Skimming A type of reading done quickly to get a general idea of content

Statistic A fact containing a number

Stressed Accented or spoken more loudly

Subject The part of a sentence that is the person, place, thing, or idea that the sentence is about

Subject complement A noun, pronoun, or adjective that follows a linking verb and that describes or explains the simple subject

Subordinate clause A clause that does not express a complete thought

Subordinating conjunction A word that links a lesser statement to a major statement by indicating the relationship between the two

Suffix One or more letters added to the end of a word that change its part of speech or its meaning

Superlative degree The form of an adjective or adverb that compares three or more persons or things

Synonyms Words with nearly the same meanings

Tense A verb feature that indicates the time of the action or state of being

Thesis statement A sentence that clearly states the thesis, or topic, of the composition

Third-person pronoun A pronoun used when speakers and writers refer neither to themselves nor to their audience, but to a third party

Topic outline An outline in which only words and phrases are used as headings

Topic sentence Sentence in a paragraph that introduces the central idea or topic that the rest of the paragraph develops

Transitive verb A verb that can transmit its action to the direct object

Verb A word that expresses action or a state of being

Verb phrase A group of words composed of a main verb and one or more helping verbs that together act as the main verb in a sentence

Verbal A word formed from a verb but used in a sentence as an adjective, an adverb, or a noun

Verbal phrase A verbal with its modifiers and complements used as a single noun, adjective, or adverb

Index of Authors and Titles

Index

Q

R

Skills Index

D
E
F
G
H
I
J

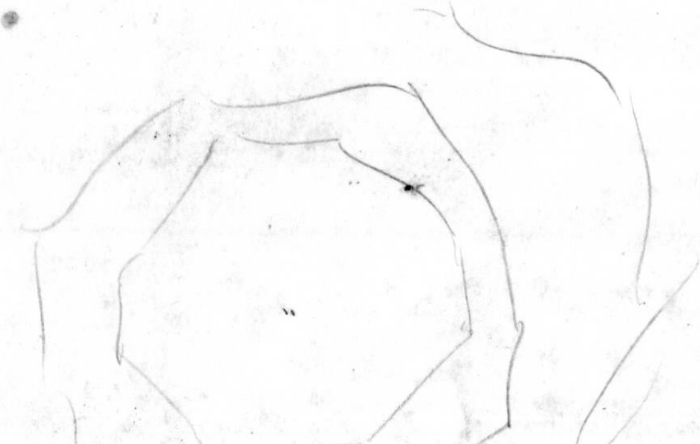